Conserving China's Northwest Frontier

Conserving China's Northwest Frontier

Nature, Culture, and Future

You-tien Hsing

OXFORD
UNIVERSITY PRESS

OXFORD
UNIVERSITY PRESS

Great Clarendon Street, Oxford, OX2 6DP,
United Kingdom

Oxford University Press is a department of the University of Oxford.
It furthers the University's objective of excellence in research, scholarship,
and education by publishing worldwide. Oxford is a registered trade mark of
Oxford University Press in the UK and in certain other countries

Published in the United States and the United Kingdom by Oxford University Press

British Library Cataloguing in Publication Data
Data available

Library of Congress Control Number: 2024949853

ISBN 9780198867173

DOI: 10.1093/9780191903908.001.0001

Printed and bound by
CPI Group (UK) Ltd, Croydon, CR0 4YY

For Tina

Preface

The radical transformation of China's northwest in recent decades holds the key to China's internal economic restructuring and global reach.[1] Yet the land-locked, resource-rich and ethnically diverse territory of 3.74 million (compared to India's 3.3 million) sq. km, 40% of China's total, remains largely opaque compared to China's prosperous eastern seaboard. Compared with China's other frontier regions like the northeast and southwest, publications on China's immense northwest are scant, and most of the works on the northwest are historical accounts of the imperial era.[2] The northwest seems to be most alive in its past. Not by coincidence, my first guides to China's northwest were archaeologists and historians who led me treading across the Silk Roads and visiting ancient ruins in various places of the northwest during the 2000s and 2010s. But on these journeys to the northwest's past, I was equally impressed by the future-making projects in the arid landscape.[3]

Quite a few future projects have been attempted in the northwest in recent decades. Most notably in the 2000s, the northwest spearheaded China's "Go West" projects under the then-Chinese Communist Party (CCP) leader Jiang, Zeming. Since the early 2010s, the northwest has been a key site of current leader Xi, Jinping's signature "Belt and Road Initiatives" (BRI).[4] Both "Go West" and BRI are loosely assembled sets of large-scale development programs. But the BRI has a significantly grander ambition of reaching far beyond China's national border through infrastructure and energy investment in Central Asia, Southwest Asia, and Africa. While the northwest once sat at the center of the Go West projects of national scope, it now serves as the launching pad of the BRI, emblematic of China's global ascent. In a region appearing to be stuck in the past, the future turns out to be overwhelmingly present in the northwest: I saw new mega-cities anticipating influxes of people and investment, new six-lane roads and highways projecting an ever-growing economy, and gigantic mining and industrial complexes juxtaposed against sprawling wind mills and solar farms, promising to power them all.

What is more intriguing is the diversity in the scope of the future projects in the northwest. In addition to the usual expansionist feat of infrastructure, energy, and urban development, I also saw conservation projects aiming to fix environmental crises and save cultural relics. Newly established ecological protection zones, heritage parks, and museums were sprouting up in every northwestern province I visited. In the age of soft power, the northwest's role in China seems to have expanded (but not shifted) from a resource frontier to a key player in China's rising developmental ethos of environmental and heritage conservationism.

The northwest's expanded role in China's conservationism can be explained by an alignment in space and time.

On the environmental front, northwest leaders take advantage of the region's timely fragility. The arid northwest has long been known for droughts, floods, and soil erosion, to name just a few. In policy and popular discourse throughout the 20th century, environmental fragility of the northwest has been used to explain the region's penury and "backwardness." The peripheral region received limited political attention until 2000, when a series of super sandstorms blew from the northwest to Beijing. It was also a moment when state leaders were preparing to take on the green agenda. The super sandstorms qualified as an environmental crisis, and an officially designated crisis could be used to demonstrate the state's capacity for crisis management. The northwest, with its nationally recognized ecological victimhood, made a ready candidate for policy loans and grants for watershed restoration, afforestation, and other conservation projects.

Among the various crisis management projects in the northwest, combating desertification has been most prominent. Desertification is a global concern. China's success in addressing the concern could serve as a model for other nations, and the success story could enhance China's soft power. According to the government report on the aforementioned BRI, four out of the six "Belt and Road Economic Corridors" in Asia, Europe, and Africa are facing severe desertification and are thus in need of Chinese know-how to fix the problem. Chinese know-how includes planting trees and drought-tolerant cash crops in the desert, installing solar panels and wind turbines, and mobilizing green finance. The goal of these endeavours is not just to fix the desert but also make the desert productive for the future. Domestically, rendering the crisis productive is consistent with CCP's political mandate which pairs environmental conservation with poverty alleviation. This pair makes a policy platform of what I call "productive conservation," which I will elaborate on in the Introduction, entitled "A Productive Crisis."

State investment is accompanied by state-endorsed green entrepreneurs, exemplified by an Inner Mongolia (IM)-based company, Elion Resource Group (detailed in Chapter 1). In 2015, Elion Resource Group was recognized by the United Nations Convention to Combat Desertification (UNCCD) for its achievement in "transforming over 11,000 sq. km of degraded land into productive land." Elion's Green Silk Road Equity Investment Fund was also commended by the UNCCD for advancing the environmental restoration project along the Silk Roads.[5] The green growth that Elion championed also made the cut to be a leading agenda item at the BRI summit in Beijing in 2019. Standing at the center of official narratives on environmental crisis, the northwest had now been rebranded to showcase China's soft power as a global model in mitigating desertification.

On the cultural heritage front, the northwest is fashionably old. Home to political capitals from over a dozen dynasties and kingdoms in China's imperial history and political centers of various steppe powers, including the Mongolian empire, the northwest is endowed with ample remnants of royal tombs, palaces, temples, settlements, walled cities, and border fortification structures, including the Great Wall (detailed in Chapter 10). Thanks to the arid climate and slower development compared to China's coastal region in the past half a century, many of these remnants have been better preserved. The northwest is also home to many of China's minority nationalities who, in popular and policy discourse, are often associated with the past. Such association further reinforces the imaginaries of the northwest as a place of antiquity.

Then came China's heritage boom in the early 2000s. Since then, the northwest has transformed from a place of the bygone era to a land revered for its rich heritage endowment. While antiquity was a dirty word under Mao's revolutionary morality, it now demonstrates China's civilizational longevity, vitality, and superiority. Like the ecological fragility that staged China's championship in mitigating environmental crises, the ancient ruins of the northwest support another pillar for China's expanding soft power. Closely linked with the global heritage boom since the late 20th century, China has been an active and successful contender in the global heritage race. In 2019, China took over the championship in the number of United Nations Educational, Scientific, and Cultural Organization (UNESCO) World Heritage Sites with its 55th inscription, after a two- decade-long race as an aspiring close second to Italy. The global heritage race is more than a nostalgic longing for the past. Rather, it draws inspiration from 19th century European modernist thinking that links conservation with cultural supremacy, social progress, and political identity, not to mention the contribution of heritage tourism to domestic economies. Riding on the worldwide boom of heritage modernity in the new millennium and the Chinese government's quest for global heritage championship, the northwest has been rising on China's map of cultural conservation.

Similar to China's desert-fixing enterprises that fortify the Chinese model of green futures, China's heritage championship underwrites the Chinese model of heritage modernity. The inscription of the ancient Silk Roads on the list of UNESCO World Heritage sites makes a good example. The 5,000-kilometers-long Silk Road extends from the metropolis of Xi'an in China's northwest to the Zhetysu region of Kazakhstan. With its heritagization know-how and key heritage sites in the northwest, China spearheaded a joint project with two Central Asian states, Kyrgyzstan and Kazakhstan, in a successful bid to inscribe "Silk Roads: The Routes Network of Chang'an-Tianshan Corridor" onto the World Heritage list in 2014.[6]

The northwest rises at a moment when China strives to be a global leader in green future and heritage modernity. But what do China's global aspirations mean locally in the northwest? For local government leaders, the northwest's timely fragility and fashionable antiquity has brought an unprecedented opportunity to catch up. The land-locked northwest has long lagged behind the coastal metropolises in the industrialization and urbanization races of post-Mao China, scoring the lowest GDP growth in the nation. The new development ethos paves new paths forward, and the new paths bring new funds for local leaders to push for conservation projects that can be politically and economically productive. Seeking to seize the moment with a "catching-up" mentality to turn crises into opportunity and antiquity into modernity, northwest government leaders proceed with conservation projects at an expedited pace and on a spectacular scale, often with drastic measures and uneven success.

Emerging from the arid northwest are future-oriented conservation projects and new ruins from the aborted future projects.[7]

Successful or not, these conservation-themed projects trigger contradictions and aspirations for grassroots actors in the northwest, including farmers, herders, agropastoralists, green entrepreneurs, minority students, rural officials, popular historians, and environmental nongovernmental organization (ENGO)s. These projects also draw an assortment of less expected actors, like photographers, villager-turned Han Chinese and Mongolian heritage guardians, and even Alibaba, China's e-commerce and fin-tech giant. In the arid and multiethnic frontier, these actors of vastly varying capacities and aspirations have embarked on diverse paths to the ecological and heritage futures across the northwest.

The ecological future of the northwest frontier has been animated through the state's productive conservation projects built on the hope of stretching nature's limits and consolidating the state's territorial reach. The heritage future was approached by the state via synchronizing the national and local memories and visions in the multiethnic frontier. But the processes of state policy implementation rarely follow the script and the results are often unintended. Looking from the ground up, the roads to the future are paved with contradictory visions, contested practices, and competing memories, subject to deviation, suspension and/or retreat. The complex ecologies, diverse livelihoods and peoples, intra-regional disparities, and geopolitical marginality of the northwest drylands have made its future outlooks unpredictable and its future outlets tentative. Projects of hope introduce anxiety and disillusionment just as much as they engender inspiration. On the ground, the future looks more like contentious processes of becoming.

Three Research Sites in China's Northwest

This book is drawn from my pilot studies in Shanxi, Shaanxi, Ningxia, and Inner Mongolia in 2010 and 2011, which were followed by intensive fieldwork in three research sites located in two regions: Inner Mongolia Autonomous Region (IMAR)[8] and Gansu Province between 2012 and 2019. I also conducted follow-up phone interviews between 2020 and 2022. I trace the state and non-state actors' aspirations, strategies, disillusionment, despair, and resilience on the ground in the age of conservationism in China's northwest. These grassroots stories of the northwest are contextualized within China's evolving national and global aspirations. Temporally, I lodge the contemporary dynamics of future-making in the northwest's tumultuous histories. There are many ways the past mingles with the present and the future. To better understand such entanglements, I use oral histories as well as archival and secondary materials to trace the geopolitical, ethnoterritorial, and environmental histories across different periods of time that span various lengths between the mid-18th century to the early 2020s. Stories of longer time spans cast more local actors, including the Mongol nobles, Han Chinese land and water barons, European missionaries, warlords, multiethnic bandits, rebels, and last but not least, the refugees of various plights during the turbulent 19th and 20th centuries: war, land appropriation, famine, and ethnic massacre. There is no shortage of drama in the northwest's ethnoterritorial, sociocultural, and environmental transformation. Yet, the quotidian details of everyday struggles and strategies on the ground are just as, if not more, vibrant and provocative.

Three research sites[9] anchor my stories (see Figure P.1).

Figure P.1 Three research sites
Source: Cartographer: Alan Pong.

The first site is Ejina Banner under the jurisdiction of Alxa League of western IMAR. Ejina is a predominantly pastoral banner located in the southern Gobi Desert at the westernmost end of IMAR, sharing a border with Mongolia. Mongols are the dominant ethnic minority in Ejina. My four visits to Ejina between 2012 and 2014, supplemented by fieldwork in Ordos and Bayannur Municipalities, Xilingol League, and Alxa Left Banner of Alxa League in IMAR between 2010 and 2014, builds Part I, "Pastoral Possibilities in Inner Mongolia's Gobi Desert" in two chapters. In Chapter 1, "A Miracle Shrub: Suosuo for Combating Desertification," I focus on suosuo, a tall shrub native to China's northwest that has animated green mobilization nationwide and drawn an unlikely assemblage of participants, including relocated herders, local officials, environmental NGOs, green entrepreneurs, urban consumers, and China's fin-tech and eCommerce giant, Alibaba, to plant suosuo in real and virtual deserts. In Chapter 2, "Mobility Under Restrictions: Ejina Herders Surviving Rangeland Conservation," I trace the survival strategies of herders who navigated the shifts from pastoral collectivism to decollectivization and onto the contemporary regime of ecological relocation and productive conservation (see Introduction). With varied capacities, these herders pursued different strategies that brought vastly different levels of success. Some have found new possibilities in rangeland conservation, but many others encountered mounting impossibilities. I then zoom in on a Mongol herding family and their relatives in Ejina who tried to survive ecological relocation and destocking policies by developing a new mode of mobility in the rapidly diversifying pastoral economy of western Inner Mongolia.

The second site is Minqin County of the Hexi Corridor of central Gansu Province. Minqin is an oasis sandwiched between two deserts, Badain Jaran and Tengger, and has a long history of irrigated farming since the early imperial era. Today, the residents of Minqin are predominantly Han Chinese. My fieldwork in Minqin between 2013 and 2016 anchors the stories of Part II, "Agricultural Futures of Gansu's Salty Soil" in two chapters: in Chapter 3, "Hope of the Hopeless: Recharging the Dried-up Qingtu Lake in Minqin," I use archival and secondary sources to recount Minqin's geopolitical and environmental histories that illustrate both path dependency and independency. By the late 20th century, Minqin had become a hopelessly depleted swamp with declining groundwater and salty and sandified soil, expected to be swallowed up by the two encroaching deserts. But, in the early 2000s, Minqin made an unexpected turn and rose to stardom in China's campaign of combating desertification. Its star status brought much hope, including interbasin water transfers, a disproportionate share of state funding, and unprecedented media attention. With the support and attention came intensified scrutiny from high-level authorities. Minqin's dramatic ascent exemplifies what it takes to make productive conservation work, and the limits of such green hope. In Chapter 4, "Opportunity in Scarcity: Building a National Model of Water Conservancy," I zoom in on water on the surface and underground in Minqin, and the prize and price of Minqin's stardom. I trace grassroots officials, farmers and entrepreneurs' strategies to implement, survive and thrive in Minqin's water conservancy regime under China's turn towards a neoliberal approach in resource management. In the programs designed to turn resource scarcity into opportunity, I find gaps between the lived and constructed scarcity and those between lived and constructed opportunity. The chapter concludes with the story of an "ecological refugee" family's survival strategies and their persistent aspirations across three generations to move up the social ladder and out of Minqin's salty soil.

Both pastoral Ejina and agricultural Minqin have recorded 40 to 100 mm of annual precipitation and over 2,600 mm annual evaporation rates in the past three decades. Considered to be China's epicenters of desertification, both places have been chosen by policy makers to demonstrate the state's capacity to mitigate environmental crises—one in a pastoral, the other in a farming environment. The binary association of Mongols with pastoralism and Han Chinese with farming in Parts I and II helps tell legible stories about complex places and times. Yet the binary structure also overlooks the dynamics of ethnoterritorial and livelihood mixes and shifts in the drylands. This is where the third site, Horqin Right Front (Horqin RF)[10] Banner comes in.

Horqin RF sits at the foothill of the Daxing'anling Mountains in eastern IMAR with a 400 to 600 mm annual precipitation rate. It is a place where the binary pairing of Mongols with herders and Han Chinese with farmers breaks down. The majority of the rural Mongols in Horqin RF are farmers or pastoagriculturalists, and they are part of the broader trend in which more than two-thirds of ethnic Mongols in rural IM today are farmers, pastoagriculturalists, or agropastoralists, not "pure" herders, as has been imagined in popular discourse.

Geographically, Horqin RF is located at the eastern end of IMAR's lengthy east-west span across China's northern frontier. It is part of China's northeast, not northwest. Yet Horqin RF is indispensable in my story about conservationism in the northwest. As mentioned earlier, the banner's ethnoterritorial and livelihood mixes and shifts complicate the otherwise clean-cut divisions between farming and herding and the fixed pairing between Han Farmers and Mongol herders.

Of equal importance is the methodological consideration to include Horqin RF. Horqin RF shows the generative and pedagogical power of place-driven ethnography. In the midst of my field research in Ejina and Minqin, which are framed by the pastoral-agricultural dichotomy, a chance encounter led me to four Mongol-majority farming villages in Horqin RF in 2017. During the trip I learned about the ethnoterritorial and livelihood mixes and shifts in the villages from the mid-20th century through the present moment. The visit was followed by in-person and online interviews until 2022. During the iterative process of writing and learning about the mixed livelihoods of Horqin RF, I stumbled into a much bigger geography and longer history than I had planned to study at the onset of this project. I found myself immersed in the tumultuous geopolitical, ethnoterritorial, and environmental histories across different subregions of the immense IM steppe since the 18th century.

I regrettably do not know the Mongolian language and am unable to consult Mongolian materials. Thus, I resort to gazetteers and other primary and secondary sources in Chinese. I also rely on about two dozen doctoral dissertations and monographs, and several master's theses on agrarian and ethnoterritorial transformation in eastern IM. Published between the 2000s and 2010s, these historical accounts are authored by three generations of multilingual Mongolian scholars who use Mongolian, Manchurian, Chinese, Japanese and/or Russian materials and oral histories to write in Chinese about their home banners and gachas.[11] This body of work is by no means a substitute for primary sources in Mongolian and other non-Chinese materials. But these local histories greatly help contextualize and extend my own ethnographic work and oral history collection in Horqin RF. For my fieldwork, I recruited translators for conversation with village elders. Given the fact that most younger generation Mongols in IM, especially eastern IM, speak Putonghua (the official Chinese language), I was able to communicate with them directly. (See Conclusion, Telling Place-Driven Stories: Methods, Analyses, and Theorization," for my reflections on ethnography.)

Prompted by the Mongol farmers in Horqin RF, this evolving book project now expands across three centuries of struggles and interactions between pastoral and agricultural actors and institutions in three subregions of the steppe in today's Inner

Mongolia Autonomous Region (IMAR). The generative power of Horqin RF spawns four chapters in Part III, "Agropastoral Entanglements of Inner Mongolia's Turbulent Steppes." In Chapter 5, "Mongols as China's Triple Minority: A Comparison with Tibetans and Uyghurs," I contextualize Horqin RF in IMAR and China's national ethnoterritorial map. With Mongols accounting for 17% to 18% and Han Chinese close to 80% of IMAR's total population today, Mongols are not only a minority at the national level, but also a minority at the regional and local levels, hence the title of the chapter. A triple minority means that Mongols are not just a numerical minority by population size, but also spatially dispersed and highly mixed with the dominant Chinese majority in the autonomous region that bears their name. To understand the making of IMAR's ethnoterritorial fragmentation, I recount the geopolitical compromise the Mongolian communist leaders made in the 1950s in their uncompromisable pursuits to unify the ancestral land of today's IMAR under CCP rule. To contextualize IMAR's distinctive ethnoterritorial history and structure, I compare IMAR with China's two other large autonomous regions: Tibet Autonomous Region (TAR) and Xinjiang Uyghur Autonomous Region (XUAR). While IMAR and TAR share a similar ethnoterritorial dilemma between unification of the ancestral lands and dilution of minority population in the territory that bears their names, the way such dilemmas play out in the two autonomous regions are starkly different.

IMAR's ethnoterritorial fragmentation, in addition to the geopolitical maneuvering outlined in Chapter 5, has much to do with its long history of cultivation expansion, which left lasting impacts on its conservation politics today. I trace IMAR's ethnoterritorial, environmental, and geopolitical history in the three subsequent chapters, each focusing on a subregion of IMAR at a critical historical juncture, led by the key local actors in cultivation expansion. Chapter 6, "Land Commodification: Emperors and Princes in Central IM in the 18th–19th Centuries," outlines the dynamics of land rights transfers from Mongol nobles to Han Chinese land merchants, which went hand in hand with land use conversion from grazing to cropping in Central IM, the first mover of large-scale cultivation expansion in the northern steppes. I also compare two places within Central IM to show the uneven geopolitical relationships between the Manchu Qing emperors and Mongolian manorial princes. The divergent relationships had, in turn, shaped the different paths of land commodification.

Chapter 7, "Hydro Turfdoms: Barons, Priests and Bandits in West IM in the 19th–20th Centuries," focuses on the expansion of irrigated farming in the Yellow River Loop Plain in west IM between the mid-19th and mid-20th centuries. Water, land, and guns afforded this story key ingredients, which is led by a pair of rivalrous non-state actors: one is the Han Chinese land-water barons, the other the Belgium Catholic missionaries. These two leading actors divided up the Yellow River Loop Plain and built fiercely guarded and highly autonomous turfs. They fit neither the Wittfogelian model of hydraulic empire under a centralized authority nor the Geertzian model of decentralized irrigation society. In the 19th century northwest frontier where the state's presence was thin, they were not quite the Chinese gentry that brokered between the state and peasantry either.[12] They are, instead, what I call hydro-turfdom builders, each with a distinctive brand of territorial entrepreneurship. Chapter 8, "Mongol Farmers: Massacre Refugees in East IM in the 20th–21st Centuries," starts with the intertwined resource and ethnic violence in Central IM in the first half of the 20th century that escalated to an atrocious massacre of Mongols. Tens of thousands of Mongol massacre refugees fled from central to eastern IM, and subsequently brought intensive cropping to the cold and hilly eastern terrains, where my third research site, Horqin RF, is located. In the second half of this chapter, my ethnographical materials and oral histories collected in Horqin RF, supported by secondary sources, permit me to tell more granular stories at multiple territorial scales at the banner, sub-banner, village, and household levels. Rooted in a history of repeated dispossession and desperate escapes from violence that had bred swelling hordes of refugees, rebels, and bandits in East IM since the early 20th century, I recount the ethnoterritorial and livelihood mixes and shifts of three sub-banner ecological zones and subzones in the hilly Horqin HR Banner. I then zoom in on two Mongolian families' shifting livelihood strategies, future aspirations, disappointments, desperation and resilience across four generations from the 1940s to the early 2020s, covering the eras of the Communist Revolution, collectivization, decollectivization, and conservationism of the current moment.

Territorial Dynamism

This multi-scalar expansion of the story at national, regional, and several local levels and the probing of geopolitical, ethnoterritorial, and environmental histories at different times and places in IM and Gansu, as presented in the summaries of Chapters 1 through 8 so far, is framed mainly by the concept of *territorial dynamism*. Territorial dynamism is my attempt to spatialize what historian Di Cosmo (1999) calls the "autonomous dynamics" in his analysis of the transformation of the Central Asian steppes over the past two millennia. Di Cosmo maintains that the steppes' transformation was generated from within, more so than a response to external stimuli.[13] Inspired by this concept, I ask the geographical question about the dynamics across the "within" and "without" at different spatial scales in China's northwest, and the ways of delineating the physical, sociocultural, and geopolitical boundaries that are often incoherent, elusive, and unstable.

In this book, I use territorial dynamism to explore the "autonomous dynamics" of the vast and varied northwest at different territorial scales. Territorial dynamism is a toolkit that includes the following analytical devices.

First, seeing place and territory as *processes*, not things. In my operational definition, a place is composed of three interconnected layers: the physical location and environment, the socio-organizational locale, and the discursively constructed sense of place. These three analytical layers—the physical, the social, and the discursive—are not segregated "components" like sticks that are bundled together to make a place, but rather interwoven processes that shape one another in an unbounded place.[14] These interwoven processes evolve over time. Place is, therefore, a nexus of time and space, and place renders and is rendered by processes. From place comes territory.[15] Territory is politicized place, the marriage of place and power. Like place, territory is also processes. Territorial processes concern the struggle to occupy and control, and to exclude and include access to place at physical, social, and discursive levels. Place builds the analytical foundation of this book. Yet few places are free of power dynamics. As such, most places can be seen as territories, including the best seat in front of the television in one's living room.

Second, identifying and connecting territorial processes *across multiple territorial scales.* The application of the term territory or territorial process is not limited by the state's sovereignty or empire's reach. Territorial processes transpire across multiple scales from the global to the regional, national, subnational, local, and anywhere in between.[16] More importantly, whichever territorial scale I choose as an analytical anchor for a particular place story, the story almost always stretches to the higher and/or lower territorial scales and often extends sideways for contextualization. Contextualization unveils the interconnections across multiple territorial scales.

Together, the previous two analytical devices enable what I call *territorialized social analysis*, the third tool I apply in this study. Territorializing social analysis refers to activating the role of territory that shapes social transformation. It differs from the usual "social-spatial analysis" that presumes the role of space as a passive container of social dynamics. Territorial processes of occupation, control, exclusion, and inclusion converge in place. These processes are not just shaped by, but also actively shape social transformation. Take the question of boundary—a key territorial concept—as an example. The boundary, be it a national border or a fence that encloses grazing land, is rarely absolute nor stable. But it is often assumed that once the boundaries are drawn on the map, marked on the ground, and protected by property rights regulations, boundaries are automatically and permanently established, and ambiguity is completely eliminated. Such a static view of the boundary as a motionless and timeless fixture (especially when the boundary markers are made of durable materials like mason or steel with a formidable presence like China's Great Wall or Trump's wall with Mexico) prevents us from seeing the politics that a boundary—a territorial *process*—engenders. Such processes go beyond the familiar disputes and conflicts over national borders. At a smaller territorial scale, for example, attempts to draw boundaries during the onset of decollectivization of rangeland in IM, as will be illustrated in Chapter 2, spurred antagonism between neighbors that lead to sabotage, disputes, negotiation, compromises, coping mechanisms, and counter strategies while the boundary-triggered territorial tensions persisted and intensified. In another example from Chapter 2, the high cost of fence-building has exposed cash-poor herders to trespassers and to faster degeneration of their grazing land which, in turn, contributed to widening the social gap among herding families. The boundary, in other words, sets in motion contentious processes of defending and defying territorial control and social change. Meanwhile, the physical fence and the act of fencing—their implications in social disparity as well as in the discursive framing of individualized land use rights in the era of decollectivization—shape one another in this territorial process. The seemingly conclusive act of building a fence to clarify a property line is endorsed by neoliberal economic and legal thinkers as being the most decisive step towards a productive property rights regime. Stories framed by this line of thinking often end the moment a boundary is drawn on the map. On the ground, however, it only marks the beginning of a territorialized story. Using the analytical tool of territorialized social analysis, attempts to build a fence activate the territorial processes of building, guarding, trespassing, and redrawing the boundary that shape the transformation of the pastoral society.

Together, the three analytical tools of seeing place and territory as processes, stretching across multi-scalar territories, and territorializing social analysis build the territorial dynamisms of the place in question. Territorial dynamism can be seen as a framing tool as well. Using this framework, I tell stories about the agentive territorial actors as well as the multi-scalar territorial processes and tensions that shape social transformation.

Territorial dynamism as a set of analytical tools braces my theoretical experiment. This theoretical experiment begins with the premise that being theoretical does not mean building a definitive theoretical truth. Rather, I see theorization as an exploratory process. Place-driven stories are endlessly fertile. The theorization process driven by autonomous places and agentive actors precludes a singular storyline. My theoretical concern in this book is, instead, to denormalize and denaturalize what is often perceived as a given, connect what appears separate, and disconnect or reconfigure presumed linkages, offer alternative and reflexive redescriptions, and render opaque events more intelligible.[17] Most of all, my aspiration concerns theorization *with* the concept of territory, instead of building a theory *of* or *about* territory. I will reflect on the methodological, analytical and theoretical implications of telling place-driven stories in the concluding chapter of this book. For now, let me introduce the last part of the book, conserving culture in China's northwest.

In Part IV, "Sociocultural Aspirations across the Great Wall," the stories turn from the territorial dynamism of conserving nature to that of conserving culture. For sure, culture and nature are inseparable.[18] And stories from the previous three parts on conserving nature entail plenty of cultural dynamics as well. But for clarity, I separate the stories about nature and culture into different parts, each told through distinctive analytical lenses: the chapters on conserving nature mainly concern the territorial struggle to access resources like land and water. The two chapters in Part IV on conserving culture are framed by the territorial dynamisms and contradictions in the production of identities and meanings. In these two chapters, I tell stories about intangible culture such as languages, and tangible culture such as monuments.

In Chapter 9, "Moving Up and Out: Mongol Students in China's College and Job Races," I begin with the bilingual school system in IMAR, a pillar in China's minority policies. While bilingual education in IMAR has continued to shrink in recent decades, Mongol students are also increasingly entrenched in China's hyper-competitive college race. Meanwhile, bilingual schooling has turned into a trilingual labyrinth of Mandarin, Mongolian, and English for the minority students who aspire to move up the social ladder and move out of the rural periphery of IMAR. I follow a Mongol farm girl's three-decade-long academic pursuit to maximize her chances in moving up and out via the hyper competitive middle school, high school, and college entrance exams. Her aspiration was not just to get into a high-ranking university, but also to obtain a stable white-collar, state-sector job in a metropolitan center outside of IMAR. As youth unemployment rates in IMAR and in China have shot up since the 2010s, the competition to enter prestigious universities that promise better urban jobs has fueled an anxiety economy, represented by China's US$180 to 300 billion-strong tutoring industry. The anxiety has also propelled the state to intensify its expectation and frustration management. The roots of the widely criticized linguistic "sinicization" of Mongolian youths, as it turns out, goes deeper than the question of preserving minority languages. Rather, the question is entrenched in a nationwide sociocultural milieu of hyper competition for a metropolitan future. As the Mongol students navigate the national institution of social mobility, this story does not develop an alternative modernity or a separate future for Mongols in China. Rather, it tells the tale about intertwined modernities across ethnic boundaries shaped by the highly uneven paths towards a shared future aspiration.

The Mongol farm girl who leads the story about the college race in Chapter 9 is none other than the daughter of one of the farming families in Horqin RF featured in Chapter 8 of Part III. Her story evinces the interwoven connection between nature and culture, and again, shows the generative power of place. In retrospect, all three places, Ejina, Minqin, and Horqin RF, have come to anchor this book out of chance encounters. As an outsider, I have little say in choosing an *ideal* research site that fits *my* research plans and answers *my* research questions. Instead, place selects me, and people in these places steer my inquiries. Place, in other words, drives and tells stories.[19]

Place tells place-specific stories. Place also tells shared stories. Chapter 10, "Popularizing the Monument: The Wild Great Walls," tells of such a shared story. During my visits to Ejina and Minqin, among other places in the northwest, I often came across ruins of border defence structures from the imperial eras in varied conditions. Some of them are stand-alone structures like beacon towers. Others are sections of walls of varied lengths and heights, made of rammed earth or even dried suosuo wood. Still others are trenches below ground level. Archeologists refer to them as remnants of the Great Wall, the emblematic monument of China's national identity. Local villagers see the battered ruins as dirt mounds that can be recycled to make fertilizer, or brick piles that can be reused to mend animal pens. In any event, these remnants look vastly different from the manicured Badaling section of the Great Wall near Beijing that I have visited. What is the Great Wall? And what does the Wall mean for Han Chinese and Mongols in the northwest today?

A Beijing-based archaeologist, to whom I brought my questions in 2017, sent me to Lao Zhang (meaning "Old Zhang") for answers. Lao Zhang is a Han Chinese peasant in his 50s living in the hilly eastern Hebei Province. He is among the first of 5,000 government-appointed Great Wall guardians at the grassroots level across China's 16 northern provinces that host the remnants of the reportedly 20,000 kilometer-long Great Wall in China's northern "Great Wall region" of 40,000 sq. km, about the size of Denmark.

Lao Zhang's home village sits at the foothill of a section of Great Wall ruins. The Wall ruins in the remote village have their very own, localized and personalized story to tell about the national monument. It also reveals the historical and territorial contradictions in Great Wall heritage conservation in China today. Lao Zhang's role as a peasant-turned guardian of the Great Wall brought him to national TV programs and newspapers to showcase the popular support for China's Great Wall Revivalism. In addition to the peasant-turned Great Wall guardians, other participants have also contributed to making the monumental Great Wall popular. These participants included popular historians who located the fragmentary wall relics on the map that is aligned with the nation's territorial order and unified the fragments under the umbrella term, "Great Wall." Urban-based artists and photographers have visualized the Wall as a symbol of national identity via wallscape photos and photographic reenactment. In addition, village entrepreneurs at the fringes of the Beijing metropolitan area would run the so-called "wild great wall" (*yechangcheng*) tourism ventures.

The urban and rural actors listed above are Han Chinese viewing from the south of the Wall. What about those located to the north of the Wall? The Great Wall has long been seen as a civilizational and territorial partition between the rival powers of Mongols of the pastoral north and Han Chinese of the agrarian south. Today, the Wall is monumentalized to symbolize the Chinese nation's multiethnic unity across the Wall. Could this territorial and historical contradiction be reconciled on the ground in IMAR, where more than one-third of the Wall remnants are located? The last actor in this chapter, the Mongol Camelback Heritage Patrol, leads the stories about IMAR officials' attempts to tread the line between Chinese and Mongolian nationalisms.

In this process of popular participation in monumentalizing the Great Wall, varied actors create different meanings through their diverse approaches to conserving the Great Wall. As a result, they give life to many "wild great walls." The Great Wall and the many wild great walls enable and derail one another under China's Great Wall Revivalism of the new millennium.

Such tension between enabling and derailing drives the stories not just in Chapter 10. This tension runs across temporal and territorial scales throughout this book. As state and non-state actors continue to aspire and strategize for their shared and disparate futures in the northwest, their actions enable and derail one another, and their stories infringe a conclusive ending. While the ending to the story remains elusive, the nuances and contingencies of the evolving tales promise to, as historian Maya Jasanoff puts it, "change the look of the big picture and reveal a different view."[20]

Notes

1. China's northwest region usually includes the autonomous regions of Xinjiang (Uyghur), Ningxia (Hui), and the western part of Inner Mongolia, as well as the provinces of Qinghai, Gansu, and Shaanxi.
2. Most of the book-length accounts on China's frontiers published in the past three decades in English have focused on the geopolitical and resource politics of the imperial and the Republican eras. Among these accounts, many focus on the western frontier, today's Xinjiang, as well as northeastern and southwestern frontiers. A selective list of the historical

accounts on China's northern, western and northeastern frontiers and its central Asian neighbors includes: Barfield, Thomas. 1989. *The Perilous Frontier: Nomadic Empires and China, 221 BC and AD 1757*. Cambridge, MA: Blackwell; Elliot, Mark. 2001. *The Manchu Way: The Eight Banners and Ethnic Identity in Late Imperial China*. Redwood City, CA: Stanford University Press; Di Cosmo, Nicola. 2002. *Ancient China and its Enemies: The Rise of Nomadic Power in East Asian History*. Cambridge: Cambridge University Press; Perdue, Peter. 2005. *China Marches West: The Qing Conquest of Central Eurasia*. Cambridge, MA: Harvard University Press; Millward, James. 2007. *Eurasian Crossroads: A History of Xinjiang*. New York: Columbia University Press; Kim, Kwangmin. 2016. *Borderland Capitalism: Turkestan Produce, Qing Silver, and the Birth of an Eastern Market*. Stanford University Press; Johnathan Schlesinger. 2017. *The World Trimmed with Fur: Wild Things, Pristine Places and the Natural Fringe of Qing Rule*. Redwood City, CA: Stanford University Press; Kinzley, Judd. 2018. *Natural Resources and the New Frontier: Constructing Modern China's Borderlands*. Chicago, IL: The University of Chicago Press; Wang, Liping. 2022. *The Imperial Creation of Ethnicity: Chinese Policies and the Ethnic Turn in Inner Mongolian Politics, 1900–1930*. Leiden, NETH.: Brill; Rossabi, Morris. 2011. *The Mongols and Global History*. New York: W. W. Norton & Company; and Wu, Shellen Xiao. 2023. *Birth of the Geopolitical Age: Global Frontiers and the Making of Modern China*. Redwood City, CA: Stanford University Press. There are also important Chinese publications on the imperial history of these regions, such as Xiao, Qiqing, 2007, *Neibeiguoer waizhongguo: mengyuanshiyanjiu (The northern perspective on China as an outsider in the south: Studies of the History of Mongol Yuan Dynasty)*. Beijing: Zhonghua Publisher. English publications on contemporary northwest regions, especially Inner Mongolia and Gansu, the focus on this book, are sparse. The few classics on today's Inner Mongolia and Mongolia include Bulag, Uradyn. 2002. *The Mongols at China's Edge: History and the Politics of National Unity*, Lanham: Rowman & Littlefield; and Bulag, Uradyn. 2010. *Collaborative Nationalism and the Politics of Friendship on China's Mongolian Frontier*. Lanham: Rowman & Littlefield; Liu, Xiaoyuan. 2003. *Frontier Passages: Ethnopolitics and the Rise of Chinese Communism, 1921–1945*. Redwood City, CA: Stanford University Press; and Liu, Xiaoyuan. 2006. *Reins of Liberation: An Entangled History of Mongolian Independence, Chinese Territoriality, and Great Power Hegemony, 1911–1950*. Redwood City, CA.: Stanford University Press. Beyond Mongolia, Matthew Erie (2016) wrote about the relationship between sharia and state law in Ningxia, an autonomous region in the northwest, where Muslim Hui are the dominant minority nationality. See Erie, Matthew. 2016. *China and Islam: The prophet, the Party and Law*. Cambridge: Cambridge University Press. However, these studies of 20th and 21st century Mongolia and Ningxia do not focus on the politics of conservation, the theme of this book.

3. I thank Daniel Cuong O'Neill of UC Berkeley East Asian Languages and Cultures for the discussion of future and futurity. See O'Neill, Cuong Daniel. 2019. "Rewilding futures: Japan's nuclear exclusion zone and post 3.11 eco-cinema." *Journal of Japanese and Korean Cinema*. 11 (1): 85–100. O'Neill, Cuong Daniel. 2023. "Ecomedia in the Wild: Camera Traps, Geiger Counters and Radioactive Boars," *Critical Inquiry*. 49 (3): 337–358. For an overview of the role of future in development studies, see Appadurai, Arjun. 2013. *The Future as Cultural Fact: Essays on the Global Condition*. London: Verso. Appadurai brings the studies of future beyond the fields of science and technology and calls future-making as a widespread "cultural fact." As an anthropologist, Appadurai also points out

that "the capacity to aspire" is an unevenly distributed social good in circumstances where the stakes for human survival are high. For reviews of the studies of future in different disciplines, also see Adelson, Leslie. 2013. "Futurity Now: An Introduction." *The Germanic Review* 88: 213–218; Braun, Bruce. 2015. "Futures: Imagining Socioecological Transformation: An Introduction." *Annals of the Association of American Geographers*, 105 (2): 239–243; and Suckert, Lisa. 2022. "Back to the future: sociological perspectives on expectations, aspirations and imagined futures." *European Journal of Sociology* 63 (3): 393–428.

4. For an analysis of the BRI and its social and environmental implications, see Rodenbiker, Jesse. 2023. "Green silk roads, partner state development, and environmental governance: Belt and road infrastructure on the Sino-East African frontier." *Critical Asian Studies* 55 (2): 169–192.
5. United Nations Convention to Combat Desertification's official website. [http://www2.unccd.int/2015-land-life-award-winners]. Accessed March 21, 2024. A more detailed and contextualized story about Elion can be found in Chapter 1 of this book.
6. https://whc.unesco.org/en/list/1442/. Accessed March 20, 2024.
7. Every time period has its own future projects, every remnant of the past bears future imaginary, and every ruin has the potential to generate new futures. The history of the future is as long as history itself. For studies of the history of future making and imagining, see, for example, Mullaney, Thomas. 2011. *Coming to Terms with the Nation: Ethnic Classification in Modern China*. Oakland, CA: University of California Press; and Masco, Joseph. 2006. *The Nuclear Borderlands: The Manhattan Project in Post-Cold War New Mexico*. Princeton, NJ: Princeton University Press.
8. China has five autonomous regions wherein minority populations concentrate. These autonomous regions are: Inner Mongolia Autonomous Region (AR), Xinjiang Uyghur AR, Tibet AR, Guangxi Zhuang AR, and Ningxia Hui AR. In China's contemporary territorial hierarchy, the autonomous region shares the same jurisdictional rank as the province.
9. In this book, I choose not to fictionalize the names of jurisdictions at the county (banner in IMAR) level. One of the reasons being that many of the archival materials and publications that I reference throughout the book contain their names already. However, I do fictionalize some of the township names when necessary, and I fictionalize all the names of the villages that appear in the text. I also note all the names that are fictionalized.
10. A banner in Inner Mongolia Autonomous Region (IMAR) ranks at the same jurisdictional level as a county in other parts of China.
11. Gacha is the word for village in IMAR.
12. Wittfogel, Karl. 1957. *Oriental Despotism: A Comparative Study of Total Power*. New Haven, CT: Yale University Press. Geertz, Clifford. 1980. Negara: The Theater State in Nineteenth Century Bali. Princeton. NJ: Princeton University Press; Chang, Chung-Li. 1955. The Chinese Gentry: Studies on Their Role in Nineteenth-Century Chinese Society. Seattle, WA: University of Washington Press; Esherick, Joseph and Mary Rankin eds. 1990. Chinese Local Elites and Patterns of Dominance. Oakland, CA: University of California Press.
13. Di Cosmo, Nicola. 1999. "State formation and periodization in Inner Asia history." *Journal of World History* 10 (1): 1–40.
14. For discussion of place, see for example, Agnew, John. 1987. *Place and Politics*. Boston, MA: Allen and Unwin; Massey, Doreen. 1994. *Space, Pace and Gender*, Minneapolis, MN:

University of Minnesota Press; Creswell, Tim. 2004. *Place: A Short Introduction*. Oxford: Blackwell; and Hsing, You-tien. 2010. *The Great Urban Transformation: Politics of Land and Property in China*. Oxford: Oxford University Press.

15. For discussion of territory, (de- and re-)territorialization, and territoriality, see, for example, Smith, Neil and Cindy Katz. 1993. "Grounding metaphor: towards a spatialized politics." In Keith, Michael and Steve Pile eds. *Place and the Politics of Identity*, pp. 66–81. New York: Routledge; Vandergeest, Peter, and Nancy Lee Peluso. 1995. "Territorialization and State Power in Thailand." *Theory and Society* 24 (3): 385–426; Delaney, David. 1998. *Race, Place and the Law 1836–1948*. Austin, TX: University of Texas Press; Brenner, Neil. 1999. "Beyond state centrism? Space, territory, and geographical scale in globalization studies." *Theory and Society* 28: 39–78; Delaney, David. 2005. *Territory: A Short Introduction*. Oxford: Blackwell; and Deleuze, Gilles and Felix Guattari. 1987. *A Thousand Plateaus: Capitalism and Schizophrenia*, tran. Brian Massumi. Minneapolis, MN: University of Minnesota Press.
16. For discussion of "civic territoriality" and territorial politics across different territorial scales in China's post-Mao urban transformation, see Hsing, You-tien. 2010. Ibid. pp. 14–19, 73–85, 181–224.
17. For a review of theorization as a process that does not have a resolute and final theoretical truth, see Barnes, Trevor (2001). "Retheorizing economic geography: From the quantitative revolution to the 'cultural turn.'" *Annals of Association of American Geographers* 91: 546–565. Although Barnes focused on economic geography, his discussion applies to a much broader inquiry about how we understand and how we understand our understanding. On the question of what makes a work theoretical, Barnes referenced, among others, Culler, Jonathan. 1982. *On Deconstruction: Theory and Criticism after Structuralism*. London: Routledge & Kegan Paul; and Culler, Jonathan. 1997. *Literary Theory: A Very Short Introduction*. Oxford: Oxford University Press.
18. For a review of nature/culture interconnections, see Watts, Michael. 2005. "Nature: Culture," in Johnston, Ron and Paul Cloke eds. *Spaces of Geographical Thought: Deconstructing Human Geographies' Binaries*, pp. 142–174. London: Sage.
19. Place also deselects me and drives me away from stories I had hoped to explore. When my access to fieldwork was denied, I had few choices but to abandon some of the most critical environmental dynamics in China's northwest today, such as mining. I have tried to visit several coal mining sites in Shaanxi and Inner Mongolia, but I failed to build sustainable research connections. As a result, this project does not claim to offer a comprehensive review of all the critical environmental issues in China's northwest today. See the "Conclusion" for my reflection on the ways in which the research plan-defying place shapes my ethnographical methods, analyses and theorization.
20. Jasanoff, Maya. 2005. *Edge of Empire: Lives, Culture and Conquest in the East, 1750–1850*. New York: Vintage Books. p. 8.

Acknowledgements

A lengthy book like this one accumulates a long list of people to be acknowledged. Relying heavily on fieldwork, this book also accumulates an even longer list of people who can only be acknowledged anonymously. I would like to first thank the farmers, herders, traders, entrepreneurs, local officials, NGO organizers, social and environmental activists, school teachers, journalists, writers, and scholars in China, who have guided me through this project but whose identities cannot be disclosed.

My intellectual home, the Department of Geography in the Social Sciences Division of UC Berkeley, has enabled and nourished this project with a stimulating intellectual environment and supportive institutional setup. I feel immensely proud and profoundly grateful to be a member of this community.

I am very grateful the following colleagues who have patiently read and insightfully commented on various chapters of the manuscript: Gillian Hart, I-tien Hsing, Jovan Lewis, John K. C. Liu, Daniel Cuong O'Neill, Peter Perdue, Nathan Sayre, Michael Watts, Xian Xue, and Wen-hsin Yeh. I am deeply indebted to Ken Pomeranz, who reviewed the entire manuscript, provided meticulous and incisive comments and helped me improve this project in fundamental ways.

I am also very grateful to the following colleagues across different fields who have lent their expertise and shaped this interdisciplinary project: Pheng Cheah, John Chiang, Kurt Cuffey, Shu-min Huang, Lynn Huntsinger, Kang Won Lee, Chih-shian Liou, Shao-hua Liu, Jie Liao, Feng Luo, Jianxiong Ma, Tim Oakes, Kevin O'Brien, Yuan Shen, Vivienne Shue, Helen Siu, Chung-min Tsai, Jian Wei, Emily Yeh, and Yimeng Zhang.

My gratitude extends to Alan Pong, who masterfully sorted through various base maps and data sets to create seven illuminating maps for this book, which say more than words could ever do. My former and current graduate students have energized this project. Max Woodworth and Jesse Rodenbiker have provided judicious feedback on multiple versions of the manuscript. Haibo Bao, Chris Christobal Chan, Xixi Jiang, Min Lee, Bingzhe Lu, Catherine Park, Ettore Santi, Cecilia Springer, Jenny Zhang, and Zhehang Zhang have assisted in data collection, editing, and, most of all, offering merciless comments on various chapters of the manuscript.

Other colleagues at Berkeley Geography have been indispensable to this project as well: Alicia Cowart and John Isom provided cartographical advice at the early stage. Josh Mandel and Danielle Molina manage my research grants efficiently and effectively. Ambrosia Shapiro holds up the community for us all. And Eron Budi–what can I say, Eron, my computer listens to no one else but you.

Librarians at Berkeley are my heroes. Among them, Albert Chung at Berkeley's East Asian Library has been most patient with my repeated requests for numerous book renewals. Jianye He, Librarian for Chinese Collections at the East Asian Library, performs magic in locating obscure sources across continents and eras, responds to my requests in a matter of minutes, and has been devoted to my project as if it were her own. Jianye, you are like a co-author of this book.

Alin Li and Xiaohui Lin have been my faithful partners in research ventures. They turned my impulses into action plans and my casual observations into meaningful questions. They have lifted me up from many trying moments during this eventful journey.

I am very grateful for Jade Dixon and Adam Swallow at Oxford University Press for their patience and support during the prolonged process of writing and editing this book. I am also grateful for Kanimozhi Ramamurthy at Integra for her efficient production management. At UC Berkeley, I am grateful for the research support provided by Pamela P. Fong and Family Distinguished Chair in China Studies Fund, Abigail Reynolds Hodgen Publication Fund, and the Center for Chinese Studies at the Institute of East Asian Studies.

Finally, my family. I must have done something unusually virtuous in my previous life to be born into the Hsings. My late parents, my siblings, and their families indulge me, not least by taking care of my daughter every summer and winter for many years to free me for fieldwork in China's northwest. I also felt greatly encouraged as they never seemed to be tired of the stories I have to tell. The profound sense of security they give me is beyond what I can express through words of love. My daughter, Tina, has grown up with this protracted project. As a teenager, she welcomed my return from numerous fieldwork trips with handmade gifts. Among them, one was a drawing of a sheep grazing under a tree; another was a ceramic baby camel wearing a knitted and beaded wreath around the neck. In the last few years of this 15-year-long project, she has grown to be my tireless sounding board and keen and first reader. This book is for Tina, my anchor and my wings.

Contents

List of Figures

Introduction

A Productive Crisis: Desertification in China's Northwest

This book covers the politics of conserving nature and culture. Parts I, II, and III are devoted to the politics of conserving nature; Part IV to that of conserving culture. The current Introduction serves to contextualize the first three Parts of the book. I will elaborate on the logic of conserving culture in the Introduction to Part IV, entitled "Sociocultural Aspirations across the Great Wall."

What does environmental conservation mean and how does it work in China and in China's northwest? In this Introduction, I contextualize China's conservation programs into three sections. In the first section I will place conservation within China's contemporary territorial governance. In the second section, I will zoom in on one of the key conservation-territorial questions, that is, the relocation of conservation refugees from protected zones to new settlements, with a focus on the arid lands of China's northwest. In the final section, I will trace the way the globally shared conceptualization of desertification has legitimized building new settlements for ecological refugees in the northwest's deserts. For the Chinese Communist Party (CCP) leadership, environmental crises should not deter development; quite the contrary, the crisis of desertification serves as an opportunity to advance development. The mitigation of the crisis contributes to expanding production, hence the title of this Introduction: A Productive Crisis.

Environmental conservation, paired with poverty alleviation, are integral parts of China's territorial governance agenda today. The pair builds a policy platform of productive conservation. The productive conservation programs are to facilitate the three political mandates of the CCP. Those mandates are, first and foremost,

Conserving China's Northwest Frontier. You-tien Hsing, Oxford University Press. © You-tien Hsing (2025).
DOI: 10.1093/9780191903908.003.0001

sustaining economic growth in the post-financial crisis era. Second, maintaining social stability, especially but not exclusively, in the ethnic minority regions. And third, elevating China's global standing in hard and soft power. These three mandates are central to the CCP's legitimacy in the new millennium.

Under these leading mandates, conservation concerns managing nature with strong administrative intervention and advanced technologies. The ideas of conservation and sustainable development serve the purpose of sustaining and improving productivity.

This logic of productive conservation in the new millennium does not stray far from Mao's project of mastering nature.[1] It just updates Mao's project at a time when the state boasts a much stronger financial and organizational capacity. During Mao's era and the early phase of market reforms, nature was made to be productive to meet human needs. The key word was "resource scarcity": with too many people and too little cultivable land, China needed to produce more food to feed the people and to extract more resources in order to accelerate development.

While the Malthusian concept of scarcity[2] never disappeared from the discourse on national food security in the 2000s, conservation narratives have expanded to incorporate the concept of environmental crises. Chinese leaders acknowledged the excessive resource extraction of earlier eras that had led to widespread environmental disasters, such as desertification, deforestation, groundwater depletion, soil erosion, and various types of pollution. The list of environmental crises is long and the economic and social costs high. The crises made the need to adopt advanced technologies and explore new measures to restore nature while sustaining productivity all the more urgent. Derivative of these crisis narratives, the new policy goal was to turn crises into opportunities, and to make solutions productive. The productivity gain, therefore, is not just a rudimentary Maoist cry to "demand food" from the forests and the lakes but also stems from cultivating economic opportunities in crisis-induced acts of conservation. If Mao's ideas were founded on unlimited nature, today's conservationism in China builds on unlimited hope.

In China today, productive conservation and territorial governance converge in conservation relocation programs. In the second section, I will examine the execution of relocation programs in the northwest and ask a critical yet rarely examined question: where were the massive number of conservation refugees in the northwest moved to? I will contextualize the northwest in China's national territorial development plans in the new millennium. The arid northwest is made to absorb multiplying responsibilities in national development. The expanding state mandates have led to escalating land use competition. In their search for places to settle millions of conservation refugees, local leaders found their answer in the desert. The new farming settlements in the desert came to be the ultimate site of productive conservation in the northwest.

But how were building new settlements and expanding cultivation in the desert justified and materialized in a time of conservation? In the final section, I will examine the popular perception that confuses deserts with desertification. Stemming from this confusion is the practice of massive afforestation campaigns to turn brown and barren deserts green. Widely supported afforestation programs made it possible to build new settlements and farms in the windy and sandy desert. Popularly perceived as being in a chronic state of crisis—and thus needing continual improvement—the desert presents the ultimate space for productive conservation.

From policymakers' perspectives, productivity can and should be gained from fixing the crisis of the desert. This aspiration has profoundly shaped the conservation landscape of China's northwest.

I Governing China through Conservation

China's environmental agenda has been perennially embedded in the productivity question, and both are fundamental to state legitimacy.[3] But the way these twin agendas are linked has varied over time.

Mao's quest for productivity focused on producing an agricultural surplus to accelerate industrialization. As historian Sigrid Schmalzer (2016)[4] has pointed out, the red revolution was deeply intertwined with the green revolution. For the newly established CCP regime in the midst of the Cold War, food sovereignty was a political mandate. China's population almost tripled between the 18th and 19th centuries, creating one of the world's highest population-to-land ratios, and, hence, extremely intensive farming.[5] By 1949, upon the establishment of the CCP regime, more than half of China's farmland and infrastructure was destroyed by a series of wars that took place on China's territory in the decades prior to 1949. Agricultural productivity and food sovereignty were imperative for the new regime to prevent another revolution, and for the CCP to accelerate its modern industrial projects.

Under such imperatives, rivers were dammed, lakes filled, and forests cleared to expand cultivation. In environmental historian Robert Marks' (2016)[6] view, these practices only achieved production gains via increased labor input and bringing more marginal land under cultivation; they did not achieve gains in productivity per unit of labor or land. Adopting Clifford Geertz's (1963)[7] argument derived from Indonesia, Philip Huang (1985)[8] called this China's agricultural involution. The exhausted soil, without sufficient technological inputs, hindered socialist China from attaining speedy industrialization as Mao had hoped. Meanwhile, China's environment deteriorated further. Judith Shapiro (2001)[9] traced this process in her book, *Mao's War Against Nature*. This war has only intensified since the market reforms of the 1980s, prompting ever louder criticisms.[10]

In the 2000s, the Chinese government started to take decisive actions to address the proliferating environmental issues. But this did not mark a shift in developmental discourse from production to conservation. Rather, it was a diversification of China's developmental discourses, that is, incorporating ideas of sustainability and fixing environmental crises into its ever-expanding party-state mandates and growth projects.

Now the question is how. How do Chinese leaders tackle the issue of growth in an era of environmental conservationism?

The CCP's political legitimacy in the new millennium, as mentioned earlier, is built on upholding economic growth, maintaining social stability, and elevating China's global standing. These agendas have grown increasingly tangible since 2012, when President Xi Jinping ascended to the CCP leadership. Under Xi, the role that conservation plays in advancing the CCP's three political mandates is made clear.

I.1 Poverty Alleviation

The most significant connection between the CCP's political mandates and conservation is the agenda of poverty alleviation. China's modern poverty alleviation programs began in the 1990s under relatively low profile. In 2015, Xi ramped up this agenda by several notches, rebranding it as "targeted poverty alleviation" and making it one of his legacy projects.

Politicizing poverty has a long history in China and beyond. Rural poverty gave the CCP its political identity during the revolutionary years.[11] Classifying peasants based on their poverty levels and organizing the starving people were where the Red Army found its answer to grassroots mobilization, which eventually helped the CCP win the civil war in 1949. Peasants' collectivized labor and land contributed greatly to the building of modern socialist China, and their decollectivized labor to post-Mao market reforms. Since the 2000s, the government has launched tax abolition and subsidy programs to "give back" to the peasants.[12]

To alleviate poverty, the three political mandates of sustainable growth, social stability, and global influence are framed in the following ways.

First, to sustain growth at a time of a global economic downturn, China's poverty alleviation program focused on creating income-generating opportunities for poor rural households. Measures include promoting agro- and eco-tourism, resource extraction, commodity crops (including medicinal herbs), as well as investing in infrastructure. Like most development programs, an increase in household cash income, including various forms of relocation and ecological compensation, is the measurement of project success.[13]

Second, poverty alleviation through income generation is widely perceived to be a remedy to treat social instability, especially in the minority regions. China's fifty-five ethnic minorities are concentrated in the interior half of China's territory. The minority question has been central to the CCP's continued nation-building project of a "unified plurality".[14] As many of the minority areas fall under the officially defined poverty line, poverty alleviation in minority regions is a key governing tool in maintaining China's territorial integrity. The most contentious regions of Xinjiang and Tibet have absorbed the lion's share of national poverty alleviation funds and state subsidies.[15] Local governments of other less contentious minority regions also place poverty alleviation high on their priority lists. In 2012, for example, the Party Secretary of Inner Mongolia Autonomous Region (IMAR) pledged RMB 1 billion yuan to combat poverty in counties where ethnic Mongolians are concentrated.[16] Gansu Province, home to the Muslim Hui and Dongxiang as well as Tibetan peoples, followed suit. In his public announcement in 2015, the Governor of Gansu Province explicitly linked poverty alleviation with social stability and ethnic minorities. The Governor was committed to channeling government funding to the minority counties in southern Gansu for conservation and poverty alleviation programs.[17]

Third, poverty alleviation contributes to advancing China's global standing in soft power beyond its economic influence. At the World Bank-International Monetary Fund (IMF) Annual Joint Meeting in October 2017, Jim Yong Kim, the president of the World Bank at the time, praised China's achievement of "lifting 800 million people out of poverty" since 1990, calling it "one of the great stories in human history." In Kim's telling, "... most of the progress from 40% of the world living in extreme poverty to now less than 10% happened in China." Kim concluded that "we're always looking for the lessons from that experience."[18] Kim's remarks, in which he cited China's leadership role in the global campaign of poverty eradication and praised the Chinese model, were widely circulated in Chinese media.[19]

I.2 Productive Conservation

Tasked with the political mandates of sustaining economic growth, maintaining social stability, and advancing China's global standing, poverty alleviation programs came to shape China's conservation practices in the 2010s. Environmental crises and the need for conservation serve as a toolkit for framing poverty: it identifies the cause of *and* provides the solution for poverty. Under this framework, the unproductive and degraded environment is the cause for rural poverty. Fixing the environment will enhance productivity and reduce poverty.

In 2011, China's highest policy-making body, the State Council, issued the "Outline for Development-Oriented Poverty Reduction for China's Rural Areas," which emphasized the importance of poverty alleviation in environmental conservation programs. The Ministry of Environmental Protection (MEP) also issued a Biodiversity Conservation Strategy and Action Plan that suggested the importance of improving people's living standards in the construction of an ecological civilization.

At the end of his first five-year term, President Xi gave a speech at the 19th CCP National Congress on October 18, 2017.[20] Over the course of his three-and-a-half hours long delivery, Xi ranked "construction of ecological civilization" at ninth place out of the 13 policy areas that he would hone to strengthen the Chinese brand of socialism. Most of Xi's talk about "constructing ecological civilization" reiterated his predecessor's, Hu Jintao, points on saving energy and reducing carbon dioxide emissions. However, Xi made explicit points about making conservation productive by putting environmental industries and green technologies at the top of his list. He emphasized that "lucid waters and lush mountains are invaluable assets like gold and silver" and "protecting the environment is the way to protect productivity; improving the environment is the way to advance productivity." That was not the first time Xi employed these expressions, which had been widely quoted since the mid-2010s. Xi's 2017 speech just reaffirmed local government leaders' interpretation of the new political wind under Xi: the environment should be restored and mobilized to sustain the economy and to improve people's income.[21]

In Maoist revolutionary logic, rural poverty was explained as a matter of distribution. The blame was placed on landlords' exploitation of the peasant class. Since 1949, the revolutionary logic has been replaced by a Malthusian connection between overpopulation, resource scarcity, and poverty. In the era of conservationism, the Malthusian logic is reinforced by a managerial twist that emphasizes peasants' inadequate environmental practices and the need for them to practice self-improvement. As many of the designated areas of poverty also overlap with minority jurisdictions, a causal connection is built between rural poverty, under-enlightened ethnic minorities, and unsustainable environmental practices, with the consequential environmental degradation.[22] This is a familiar logic that is also found in Central Asia under British colonial regime and Soviet rule,[23] among other times and places.

As the blame for poverty is individualized (poor people need self-improvement) and often racialized (minorities are in need of enlightenment), it is also localized. Under Mao, the unproductive environment was seen as a stage on which to demonstrate the superiority of socialism: *despite* the "deficient mountains and vicious waters" (*qiongshan eshui*) of a place, peasants who worked arduously under the CCP's guidance can overcome nature's deficiency and improve productivity for the nation's future. Now, the logic follows that it is *because of* the unproductive environment that peasants are poor. The place itself shares the blame with those who live there. According to the Development and Reform Commission, 95% of China's impoverished population can be found in environmentally vulnerable and degraded rural areas.[24] The environmental crisis of degradation and the socioeconomic crisis of poverty have hence converged.

The solution to the problem of location-induced poverty—the two-sided social and environmental crisis—is relocation: removing the poor from degraded and unproductive environments is the first step towards lifting them out of poverty.

In the northwest, the areas that are officially designated as "degraded" are marked as protection zones, where pastures are enclosed, grazing and cultivation are banned or reduced, and irrigation wells are sealed. Peasants and herders residing in the protected zones are relocated to new settlements, where new income-generating opportunities are promised.

II Conserving the Arid Northwest

By the early 2010s, protected areas (parks, game reserves, and wilderness areas) worldwide were estimated to count for 13% of Earth's terrestrial surface, which is larger than the area of South America.[25] The enclosure of rural lands, although imposed in the name of conservation, is highly contentious due to its detrimental impact on local livelihoods. What makes the act of land enclosure for conservation even more explosive is the removal of local residents from their homes in the protected areas.

Relocation is common practice in the global conservation paradigm. Drawing on cases from Africa, South America, South Asia, and the US, Mark Dowie (2009)[26] reported that the establishment of protected conservation areas, which began in the colonial era of the 19th century and proliferated in the 1990s, has displaced millions of native inhabitants worldwide and turned them into conservation refugees. Dowie corrected the popular misconception that confuses "conservation refugees" with "ecological refugees." He argues that conservation refugees' displacement is not necessarily caused by environmental degradation. Rather, it is eviction in the name of conservation. A growing body of literature also calls conservation-framed land grabbing and displacement "green grabbing."[27]

In China, *conservation* relocation and *ecological* relocation are often used interchangeably. China's Eleventh Five Year Plan (2006–10) included a plan of relocating residents of seriously eroded hillsides and degraded grassland. Given the causal connection between environmental degradation and rural poverty in policy discourse, conservation relocation is often justified as ecological relocation. Regardless of labels, the final goal is to improve the income levels and living conditions of the refugees. As a result, all environmentally branded relocations were indiscriminately referred to as "ecological relocation" (*shengtai yimin*) in the 2000s.

In the 2010s, as criticism towards ecological relocation grew and poverty alleviation discourse rose to prominence, China's "ecological relocation" programs were renamed "poverty alleviation through relocation" (*yidi fupin*). *Yidi fupin* was elaborated by the slogan "move away from the den of poverty, upgrade the low-income job, improve the decrepit villages and homes, and yank out the roots of poverty."[28]

According to the Chinese National Development and Reform Commission, between 2001 and 2015, 12 million people were relocated nationwide under poverty alleviation and conservation programs and as the result of natural disasters. Close to 7 million of whom were relocated in the five years between 2010 and 2015, a 137% increase from the preceding ten years.[29]

Massive-scale semi-voluntary and involuntary relocation are not new phenomena in China. Elizabeth Croll (1999)[30] estimated that between 1950 and 1989, 17.6 million people in China were resettled to make room for transportation and reservoir projects. Prior to market reforms, resettlement was implemented as a single event based on compensation with a one-time payment. Since the mid-1980s, resettlement policy was reconfigured as "developmental resettlement." Growing out of the World Bank-endorsed global paradigm of "sustainable development," as mentioned earlier, developmental resettlement was conceived as a longer-term process combining relocation compensation with economic development in the new location. The Three Gorges Dam project, which relocated 1 million people in the 1990s, is a textbook case for developmental resettlement. The promise was that life would be better off with resettlement.

Developmental resettlement was an attempt to turn the negative connotation of livelihood destruction into a positive promise of reconstruction, focusing on the opportunity to rebuild one's life in the new place, furnished with subsidized housing, schools, farmland, and job opportunities. To facilitate the construction of the Three Gorges Dam, the legacy project of the veteran CCP leader Jiang Zemin, local governments set up special offices to deal with the daunting task of persuading and negotiating with the dam refugees. Local officials were given additional training in universities that offered professional degrees on relocation administration, such as mobilization through education and persuasion to win the co-operation of relocatees; methods of allocating cash compensation as well as land and housing; and production development to create jobs and improve relocatees' income.

Other than mobilizing villagers to move out, the most trying task for local officials was to find resettlement sites for the dam refugees.[31] China already has one of the highest population-to-land ratios in the world. The Yangtze River basin, in which the dam was built, has one of the highest population densities in China. Where can one find land that is not yet occupied and farmed to settle the dam refugees? Local governments of the neighboring jurisdictions were extremely reluctant to accept refugees from the inundated areas. In order to induce compliance from officials in neighboring counties and provinces, the central government redrew jurisdictional boundaries, twisted arms, and offered favors. But most of the land that the local officials obtained to build new homes and farms for the refugees was located on steep hill slopes of high altitude, had poor soil quality, and lacked sufficient infrastructure and water supplies. In addition, the "dam migrants," as they were termed in official papers and media, experienced discrimination from residents of the host region, thus creating more social conflict. The Three Gorges Dam resettlement brought as much poverty and contention as development. Many refugees moved back while others launched protests, both of which seriously threatened social stability. As the regime of social stability maintenance rose in the 1990s and expanded in the 2000s, a publicized social protest could cost local leaders their jobs.[32]

Compared to the relocation programs of the Three Gorges Dam, some of the relocation programs in the northwest were of even greater scales. Also, many of the relocatees of the northwest were of minority nationalities. But these programs have received much less public attention.

An example can be found in Ningxia Hui Autonomous Region (NHAR from here on). Sandwiched between Gansu Province and IMAR, NHAR is where Hui Muslims are concentrated. Most of the conservation refugees in NHAR are from its southern mountains, a region known as Xihaigu, where Chinese Muslim Hui lived, farmed and kept stocks. Officially identified as one of the 14 National Priority Poverty Regions in China, Xihaigu occupies an enormous area of 43,000 sq. km, accounts for 65% of NHAR's landmass, and had more than 2.5 million inhabitants in the 1970s, which was about 41% of NHAR's total population at the time. According to policy papers, the mountainous Xihaigu has long suffered frequent droughts, soil erosion, and population exodus. While some emigration was organized by the government, others were self-initiated. Between the 1980s and 2000s, 660,000 people moved out. As part of the Twelfth Five Year Plan (2011–15), 350,000 more people were relocated to various resettlements in NHAR, some of which have over 40,000 people in one site. Altogether in the past three and a half decades, about 1 million people—mostly peasants—were relocated from Xihaigu under government programs.[33] In Gansu Province, between 2006 and 2020, no less than 1.6 million residents were relocated under poverty alleviation and conservation programs. Many were from Gansu's mountainous south, where Muslim Hui, Yugu, Dongxiang, and Tibetan minorities were concentrated.[34]

The execution of these relocation programs of the northwest was similar to that of the Three Gorges Dam programs in many ways: payment of relocation compensation in cash (now named "ecological compensation" as framed by the popular concept of "payment for ecosystem services," or, PES), the promise of housing and farmland provision, and new job opportunities at the new sites. Social conflicts created by underdelivered—and undelivered-promises after the relocation were also similar. Most of all, local officials of the northwest also faced the challenging task of identifying a resettlement site that could convincingly offer the relocatees a future better than where they were moved out of. Only that in the northwest's arid lands, the task was even more daunting and the options were even fewer.

Constraints in carrying out the mission impossible there were quite a few. Not least due to the contradictions between the popular perception of the northwest as an empty expanse eagerly awaiting development and the under-appreciated reality that the land of the northwest had already been overburdened.

I.1 Multitasking the Northwest

While national leaders strove to boost China's global status and expand the policy agenda, local governments' tasks mushroomed. Across China in the new millennium, local leaders had to sign multiple "responsibility contracts" with their superiors on various priority tasks. These wide-ranging responsibility contracts included environmental protection, elderly support, resettlement construction, combating desertification, and education of scientific knowledge, among others. Practiced at every level of the bureaucracy, the target-driven, quantifiable responsibility contract system was used for cadre performance evaluation and promotion.

The swelling responsibilities of local governments were spatially manifested in escalating land use competition in their jurisdictions. Under rising conservationism, "ecological land" was added to the long list of land use categories on par with urban and industrial zones. Ecological land is a land use category that is vaguely defined as "land reserved to maintain ecological balance, recovery and production." Like other land use categories, "ecological land" was identified in specific locations and required to occupy a minimum percentage in the total of the planned area, colored in green on the zoning maps.

But where to insert the green-coded ecological zone in a country that has one of the highest man-to-land ratios in the world? To make the task even more challenging, China has gone through unprecedented urban expansion and farmland loss since the late 20th century, and the agenda of national food security and farm land protection has been yet another priority item on local leaders' "responsibility contracts."[35]

The land use dilemma to accommodate the ballooning policy initiatives is particularly acute in the arid northwest.

China's northwest has two faces. One is its popular image as a place of poverty and environmental ills. The other face, much less recognized in popular discourse, is its role as one of China's primary breadbaskets. The agricultural geography of China's northwest is divided roughly into two types of farming: rain-fed, dryland farming and irrigated farming. While dryland farming is practiced in the immense arid hills, irrigated farming has long been the norm in the alluvial plains and oases.

As for its role as the breadbasket of China, thanks to the great rivers that run through the northwest, several subregions have been among China's primary producers of staple grains. The northern alluvial plain of Ningxia, through which the Yellow River traverses, has had wet rice paddies since the sixth century.[36] The Yellow River also has fed wheat fields of the Yellow River Loop (*hetao*) area of western Inner Mongolia (IM) (Chapter 7). In central Gansu, where four snow-fed interior rivers run from its southern mountains to northern lowlands, oases have formed along the Hexi Corridor and made the corridor an important wheat region throughout most of the imperial era through the present day (Chapters 3 and 4).

Beyond the river-fed farms in the flatland and oases, the hilly lands supported mixed livelihoods of pastoralism and dryland farming. During the Maoist era, irrigation in the flatland and oases was much expanded to create "artificial oases"; many hilly slopes and pastures were turned into terrace cropland; and hilltops were flattened to make rain-fed platform fields.

Environmental historian Robert Marks (2011)[37] has commented on China's long history of "upward and outward" cultivation expansion into ever more marginal lands. The northwest is an integral part to this history. And the northwest is even less suitable for massive expansion of irrigated farming than other regions.

The northwest's aridity, thin topsoil, soil salinity, and susceptibility to frequent natural calamities lead to low productivity in its arid and cold hills and its sunny and sandy lowlands. Low productivity in turn has created a pattern of sprawling farming in the northwest. Large areas of land are brought under cultivation to compensate for low yields. At a more granular level, growing conditions vary greatly, hence the varying state of cultivation from parcel to parcel in a given year or season. Some parcels are cultivated but not planted; some are planted but not irrigated or only occasionally irrigated, while others lie fallow or are abandoned for varying lengths of time due to soil or water exhaustion (often both). The ratio between the total area of "cultivated land" to "planted land" in any given location and time can be as large as 10:1, and sometimes even larger. The irregularity of water supplies and growing conditions, as well as greater exposure to natural calamities, such as droughts, floods, pests, hail, and wind, frequently lead to the abandonment of large areas of land that were once cultivated.[38] This mode of "planting widely and harvesting thinly" (*guangzhong boshou*) keeps pushing land reclamation up and out in the northwest.

Expansion of both irrigated farming in the lowlands and rain-fed farming in the hills and sandy lands continued during the socialist and the reform eras. The three major regions of irrigated farming—the Hexi Corridor of Gansu, the northern Ningxia plains, and the Yellow River Loop of western IM—are among China's primary breadbaskets. These fertile lands with access to irrigation have long been the destination of several waves of Han immigrants from south of the Great Wall since the late 19th century, and cultivation has continued to expand.

These irrigated farming areas are the centers of food production in the immense arid lands of the northwest. They are also the destination of government-organized and self-initiated migration that leads to cultivation expansion in these areas. Some of the most dramatic instances of cultivation expansion in recent memory took place in the late 1970s. In 1977, the Hexi Corridor was designated by China's economic planners as one of the 10 national "Production Bases of Commodity Grains,"[39] which formally legitimized farmland expansion within the Corridor. To accommodate the expanded farms, groundwater was extracted to supplement surface runoff. In the post-reform era, irrigated agriculture has continued to expand at the edge of existing farming areas into surrounding rangeland and gravel or sandy land, while more terraced farms have been built on the cold, dry hillsides. Between 1949 and 1992, cultivation in the Hexi Corridor surged from 363,000 to 900,000 hectares.[40] As land reclamation persisted upward and outward, the highlands and the edge of the oases experienced serious soil deterioration. But the deteriorated irrigated areas of the Hexi Corridor and the northern Ningxia plains have continued to serve as resettlement sites for conservation refugees from the cold, dry mountains. And the role of the northwest—especially its flatlands and oases—have become even more important in sustaining China's national growth project in the 2010s.

In 2010, as an attempt to manage increasing land use competition, China's State Council announced a national development plan called the "Core-Function Regional Development Plan" (CFRD Plan from here on). Prepared by the National Development and Reform Commission, China's highest authority for economic planning, the CFRD Plan was an attempt to resolve the problems of land use conversion from farm to nonfarm uses that threaten China's ecological and food security. It was also meant to enhance regional comparative advantages to ensure the nation's economic growth.[41] The CFRD Plan divided China's territory into four major functional regions, each assigned a "core function." Unsurprisingly, the northern coast around the Bohai Sea (including Beijing and Tianjin), the Lower Yangtze Delta led by Shanghai, and the Pearl River Delta of the southern coast (centering on Guangzhou, Shenzhen, and Hong Kong) were appointed as "Development Priority Regions." This particular designation allows these regions to attract more investment with few restrictions. Eighteen other metropolises of central and inland regions were deemed "Key Development Regions," which gave similar privileges, but on a smaller scale. The rest of China, which accounts for over 50% of the national territory, were named "Restricted Development" and "Zero-Development" regions.

According to the plan, the "core functions" of the Priority and Key Regions are urban and industrial development, with small shares of land allocated to (therefore bearing relatively lighter responsibility for) agriculture and environmental protection. The core function of Restricted Development Regions is agricultural production, with restrictions on urban and industrial development. The core function of the Zero-Development Regions, which includes all national nature reserves and parks, is to receive protection and provide ecological services in exchange for ecological compensation.[42]

Over half of the northwestern provinces' territory falls into the category of "Restricted Development," with a focus on agricultural production, especially on high-yielding and high-value varieties of cotton and wheat. To make it feasible for the revenue-poor northwest provinces to carry out such low revenue-yielding assignments, central transfers for agricultural investment—especially in hydraulic and sand-control infrastructures—have increased. Meanwhile, local governments are expected to procure matching funds and attract private capital to carry out the tasks.

Increased responsibility for agricultural production under the CFRD Plan in the age of conservation was not the only assignment that the northwest received. In 2011, the National Development and Reform Committee issued China's 12th Five-Year Energy Development Plan. In this Plan, all five National-Level Integrated Energy Bases (including both renewable and nonrenewable energy) are located in the northwest, the region endowed with solar, wind, and mineral resources.[43]

In short, urban expansion and farmland contraction in China's coastal east has generated increasing pressure on the arid northwest to step up its agricultural production. The resource-rich northwest is also expected to shoulder the country's energy demands. All these assignments are to be materialized with the land in the northwest. Increasing numbers of industrial farms, dams, mines, windbreak forests, solar power plants, and wind farms pop up in northwestern mountains, deserts, and pastures. China's northwest of the new millennium, not unlike the American west of the 19th century described by Frederick Jackson Turner (1893),[44] serves as the boundless frontier to accommodate the ceaseless expansion impulses that have spilled over from the eastern seaboard.

Using remote sensing data collected between 1987 and 2013, a group of geographers reported that while the total area of China's cultivated land remained relatively stable, the national aggregate data did not reflect the dramatic regional shift of China's agricultural production. Between 1987 and 2010, the increase in cultivation in the arid north compensated for the dramatically reduced cultivated land in the rapidly urbanizing south. Within the northern territory, the relatively more humid northeast had played a dominant role in agricultural expansion. But since 2010, the center of agricultural expansion in China's north has shifted from the relatively humid northeast to the arid west and northwest. A significant portion of the newly added cultivated land in the northwest is virgin land that was traditionally considered uncultivatable, such as highly salinized land, mobile sand dunes, and gravel gobi.[45]

As the demands on the northwest multiplied and land use competition heated up, the seemingly infinite frontier was now compressed. That was the condition in which local officials were tasked to find not just additional "ecological zones," but more critically, sites that promised a better future for the massive number of conservation relocatees. Because many of the relocatees were minority nationalities, local officials were also made responsible for an additional political mission of "avoiding harming the inter-ethnic solidarity" while carrying out the highly explosive programs of relocation.

The conservation crunch triggered new local contradictions. The increasing demands on land to accommodate ballooning mandates within each jurisdiction have greatly thwarted local leaders' capacity and willingness to share their precious land with conservation refugees from other jurisdictions. It did not help that the resettlements are frequently a source of social conflict. Refugees' protests over undelivered-promises have become one of the major causes of social instability in host jurisdictions. To counteract threats to social stability, governments of the host jurisdiction would often have to bear additional administrative and security expenses. The political costs have also increased. If conflicts escalated and were publicized, local leaders could lose their jobs. Under such circumstances, local officials chose to close their doors for cross-jurisdictional relocatees.

Jurisdictional territorialism has always been a part of the Chinese polity. In the case of the Three Gorges Dam, neighboring provinces and counties of the area inundated by the dam were under unprecedented pressure to facilitate this legacy project for the powerful CCP leader Jiang Zemin. Province and county officials were threatened with sticks and cajoled with carrots to accept dam refugees from other jurisdictions to their turfs and to allocate land, however marginal, to the refugees. But that was more of an exception than the norm.

For most relocation programs, due to neighboring jurisdictions' growing reluctance to accept conservation refugees, resettlement compounds were mostly built within the boundary of the refugees' home jurisdictions. The provincial-level relocation program managers tried to find resettlement sites within the provincial jurisdiction, and county-level relocation within the county jurisdiction. This way, negotiation complications with other provinces or counties would be minimized. However, pressure on land use within the jurisdiction, often already plagued by soil degradation, increased.

Where could local leaders find land within the boundary of the province or the county to accommodate the large number of conservation refugees? A closer look at the location of the resettlement sites offers some insight.

II.2 Tasking the Desert

State-owned farms are one important source of land for resettlements of conservation refugees in the northwest.

State farms, forests, and rangelands are a socialist legacy. These production units are also among the largest land owners in the rural northwest today. In my earlier studies of China's urban politics,[46] I used the term "Socialist Land Master" to characterize China's state land users (e.g., military units, state-owned enterprises, and government agencies) to whom large chunks of urban land under the planned economy were allocated. During the reform era, these state land users became de facto land owners and powerful developers in China's large cities.

State farms are the socialist land masters of the countryside. They were founded in the revolutionary years of the 1930s in CCP-occupied areas of the northwest. State farms followed the millennia-old practice of integrating frontier defence with cultivation to solve food supply problems.[47] After 1949, the state farms were consolidated into the paramilitary Production and Construction Corps in the western and northern borders in order to "station troops to reclaim land and defend the frontier" (*tunken xubian*).

The territorial significance of stationing the Production Corps in the frontier is evident. Among these establishments, Xinjiang Production and Construction Corps (XPCC) has been the most prominent and long lasting. The Production and Construction Corps in other northwestern provinces of Gansu, Ningxia, and IM were smaller, weaker, and shorter-lived. Long- or short-lived, the Production and Construction Corps in China's frontiers share two features: large land holdings and status as the socialist land masters of the countryside.

The next question is, what kind of land do these Production Corps hold? By the 1950s when the Production Corps were established, the fertile oases of the Hexi Corridor and the Yellow River-fed northern Ningxia Plain were already crowded with waves of war and famine refugees. The Production Corps resorted to appropriating villagers' land, which caused considerable conflict with both local Han Chinese and non-Han people.[48] Production Corps soldier-farmers also levelled the sand dunes at the edge of existing farmlands, attempting to turn them into farms. At the peak of the campaign to "demand food from the desert," Divisions and Battalions of the Production Corps competed to reclaim large areas of sandy and gravel land and built large irrigation works. Between 1949 and 1998, cultivation in the drylands increased by 626% in IM, 207% in Gansu, and 2,667% in Xinjiang.[49]

Beyond the official figures, however, "demanding food from the desert" is easier said than done. During the political turmoil that persisted from the late 1950s to the late 1970s, the Production Corps' farms in the desert, despite their immense size, were mostly a failure, both in terms of per unit productivity and overall production. None had managed to produce more than half the food their own members consumed. Dams and irrigation canals that were built in haste during the Great Leap Forward and Cultural Revolution ended up mostly unused.[50] Electric power was in short supply in the remote desert, insufficient to operate well-drilling machines for irrigation. On average, only 10% to 20% of the land that the state farms claimed to have reclaimed was cultivated, and only 2% to 3% of the cultivated land was planted and irrigated regularly.[51] The case of Bayin Maodao Production Corps is telling. Located in Wulan Buh Desert in central-western IM, the Production Corps channelled water from the Yellow River to irrigate a new farm, and proudly reported a reclamation of 7,800 hectares in the 1970s. By the 2000s, only 667 hectares were under cultivation, while the rest—91.5% of the total area—was abandoned. When land is reclaimed and quickly abandoned, the thin topsoil is destroyed, soil moisture is depleted, and the soil structure undergoes irreversible change. Abandoned and increasingly sandified soil turns semifixed sand dunes into mobile dunes, and leads to intensified sandification.[52] In short, however heroic the slogan of "demanding food from the desert" might have sounded in the Production Corps era, there was little the poorly equipped Production Corps in the northwest frontier could do to spawn miracles.

The fact that the soldier-farmers of the corps were mainly Sent-Down (*xia-fang*) youths from the cities during the 1950s and 1960s, with limited experience with farming or the arid climate (or both), did not help. The sent-down youth of the corps in IM have written about the toil of levelling sand dunes, digging through gravel ground and salt crust, planting seeds in saline soil, and carrying water over long distances. They also recount the debilitating hunger, freezing winters, and roasting summers in the desert. As many of these young soldier-farmers were from politically disgraced families in the city, joining the Production Corps—although in a punishing location, still a respectable state-sector unit—was an opportunity to redeem themselves socially and politically in the new China. It was also one of their few career options.[53]

The desert could not be conquered easily, or at least not without abundant investment and skilled labor. By the mid-1970s, the national Administration of Production Corps was dismantled and its managerial authority was transferred to provincial governments under the supervision of the Bureau of Agricultural Reclamation in Beijing. Production Corps became state farms, while their signature industrial farming and ownership of large tracts of land remained.

During the market reforms of the 1980s and 1990s, like state-owned enterprises (SOEs from here on) in other sectors, state farms went through waves of restructuring. While some farmland was subcontracted to its member households, large areas of industrial farms were turned into shareholding companies with the local government as the majority shareholder and decision-maker. The most resourceful state farms were listed on China's stock exchange, similar to SOEs in other sectors. What distinguished these agricultural SOEs and what has given them a competitive edge on the stock market is their massive land reserves, which have decisively sustained their share values. Ningxia Agricultural Reclamation Company (*Ningxia Nongken*), for example, had a recorded 214,400 hectares of land reserves in 1988, which is an expansion from the 33,000 hectares recorded in the 1950s.[54]

State farms, like other SOEs that enjoyed privileged access to land, capital, and political support, also share the responsibility of supporting government programs, including providing land for conservation resettlements. Many of the large resettlement projects in the northwest, therefore, came from the land-rich state farms that are now owned by the local government.

However, the land that was still available to build new settlements for conservation refugees was the least cultivatable land among the state farms. This land had been claimed by state farms in the 1950s and 1960s but remained uncultivated for decades or was abandoned due to poor planting conditions and water shortages. These lots were located at the tail end of, or disconnected altogether from, the farms' irrigation systems. As a result, by the 2010s, what the state farms could and would offer the refugees was mostly degraded land. A lot of work needed to be done to turn the land into habitable settlements and productive farms.

In the mid-reaches of the Shule River basin in the Hexi Corridor of Gansu, for example, the two state farms Huanghua and Yinma together have hosted 6,500 refugees from the minority regions of the southern Gansu mountains since the early 2000s.[55] The state farms contributed a total of 300,000 mu (20,000 hectares) of land to build the Shule Basin Developmental Relocation Program. About a quarter of the refugees were of Muslim Hui, Dongxiang, or Tibetan minority nationalities. To make the degraded land productive again for this high-profile resettlement project, central and provincial governments, together with international lenders, chipped in: they funded reservoir and irrigation channel construction and turned the new farming settlement into the largest irrigation district in Gansu Province.

Other mega resettlements went beyond the turf of state farms. These were built on land that was abandoned and/or unclaimed by the state farms. Hongsibu in central NHAR, for example, boasted the largest relocation settlement in China. Surrounded by three major deserts to its north, west, and east, Ningxia has had a complex and violent history of Muslim Hui striving for autonomy since the imperial era. Under the CCP, Ningxia championed the programs of relocating Hui people from its southern mountains to its northern plains. These efforts began in the 1980s and have continued into the new millennium, as mentioned earlier.

By the 2010s, however, agricultural expansion was saturated and soil quality deteriorated in the traditional migration destinations of the northern plains of Ningxia. The mega-scale flagship resettlements had to be built somewhere else. Planners found central Ningxia. The immense central Ningxia, which China's physical geographers call the "wind and sand" region, accounts for 45% of Ningxia's total land mass of 23,000 sq. km. The region is made of plateaus, hills and upland basins at an altitude of 1,200 to 2,000 meters. It is extremely dry without sufficient surface runoff as in the northern plains and records an annual precipitation rate of 200 to 300 mm and an evaporation rate of over 2,200 mm. It constitutes a high-altitude desert. The region is prone to calamities such as droughts, frost, hail, and dust storms. Under Mao's production drive between the 1950s and 1970s, this cold, arid, and hilly land was brought under cultivation, which resulted in severe soil erosion. Until the 1990s, central Ningxia was a region of abandoned cultivation and a source of out-migration.

But the regional leaders were not deterred. The land that local residents of central Ningxia left behind, though depleted, carried the advantages of greater accessibility and large land areas that could be turned into a new mega settlement. Emboldened by central government funding and their confidence in advanced hydraulic and farming technologies and motivated by the prospect of securing a place on China's map of productive conservation, leaders of Ningxia built the mega resettlement of Hongsibu in the heart of the arid and calamity-prone central Ningxia highlands.[56]

Between 1999 and 2015, 300,000 conservation refugees were settled in Hongsibu. 60% of the settlers were ethnic Hui from Xihaigu, a mountainous region in southern Ningxia mentioned earlier. Refugee-sending Xihaigu was well publicized for its poverty induced by environmental crises, which justified the massive relocation programs. On the other hand, the refugee-receiving site of Hongsibu in the central highlands was just as fragile and fraught with deteriorated soil.[57] But the poor environmental conditions of the resettlement area in Hongsibu were rarely mentioned in the media or policy papers. The sparsely populated arid hills of Hongsibu were instead portrayed as a land of hope. Meanwhile, to prevent conservation refugees from returning to Xihaigu, old dwellings were razed to the ground, power cables cut, and roads returning home destroyed with explosives.[58]

Indeed, Hongsibu can be seen as a place that has gone through unfathomable transformation. Mega hydraulic works were installed to pump water up from the Yellow River in the northern plain through 39 pumping stations that lifted water 300 meters uphill and through a 4,000 km-long network of canals. As a result, the government reported a successful reclamation of 700,000 mu (47,000 hectares) of land. A Ningxia-based journalist wrote extensively on the new Hongsibu as a place replete with "oases and high rises," while briefly quoting local folklore that depicted Hongsibu's recent past: "wind blew all year round from winter to spring, sand and gravel swirled; no birds in the sky."[59] With massive investment, a place that had been deemed to be beyond hope now promised transformative future development.

I will devote the next four chapters, in greater ethnographic and historical detail, to the changed lives and livelihoods in the refugee-sending and refugee-receiving places in the northwest. In this chapter, the key point is that land use competition in the northwest has left local governments with little choice but to build new resettlements on the least productive soil. To succeed, decisive government investment in large-scale irrigation systems would be critical. This may be seen as a worthy political investment to maintain social stability in the Muslim Hui-concentrated region.

But to ensure economic worthiness of the costly water projects, local officials also follow another set of cost-benefit analyses. Central Ningxia's barren plateaus store rich mineral reserves, and its coal reserves are said to account for 95% of Ningxia's total but have yet to be extracted.[60] The investment in much of the waterworks for the farming resettlements, therefore, can be diverted from farming to mining when the time comes. In fact, many of the dam projects in the upper reaches of the Yellow and Wuding Rivers in northwestern and northern China, which were originally built for agricultural irrigation, have been diverted to support coal and coal chemical industries.[61] Poverty alleviation-framed irrigation projects make for persuasive funding proposals to the central government. But what happened after the projects were built and how the water might be diverted for other nonfarm uses often faced less scrutiny. As such, social contestations grew.

In addition to the large-scale and high-density flagship resettlements, there are numerous smaller-scale, resettlements dispersed in townships and villages that host refugees from within the county proper. In many cases, various local government agencies used low-grade or un-registered "black" farmland and woodlands at their discretion for smaller settlements of a few hundred households. In other cases, local officials built resettlement compounds in the desert land of their jurisdiction at the undesirable distant edge of farming areas. Usually, these land tracts of poor quality were not distributed to individual households under decollectivization, and thus were still in the hands of the local government. Yet another source of land for building resettlements in villages and townships came from recycling policy-designated land from an earlier era under a different program. For example, previously designated "desertified land" that was put under protection, was now reborn as agricultural development zones attached to the new conservation resettlements. The same piece of land, in other words, could bear layers of identities from policies that could be contradictory to one another, as policy priorities shifted over time.

The two types of resettlement areas in the northwest—large/dense, and small/dispersed—create settlement and farm sprawls. Large or small, they share three common features:

First is their marginal location. The majority of recent resettlements were built on marginal land with the least fertile soil. The flagship project of Hongsibu was in a vast marginal plateau far from existing farming areas. The smaller resettlements were located at the edge of farming areas where most of the land tracts were once cultivated but have since been abandoned and left degraded or were too salty to farm.

Second, the dual purposes of conservation and poverty alleviation of the relocation program created parallel processes of intensive and extensive farming in the dryland. To make the ostensibly underutilized land productive, massive investments in irrigation expansion and other infrastructure is required, aided by cash crops and intensive use of land, water, fertilizers, pesticides and other inputs. Meanwhile, the pressure to find more land to build new farming resettlements pushed new land reclamation efforts into the desert. It is a simultaneous process of intensification of extraction and expansion in cultivation.

Last but not least, relocation is central to territorial governance. Relocation serves to consolidate the CCP's grassroots organizational structure. Each type of resettlement comes with its own mode of party organization: in new large-scale resettlements, new party branches are established; in settlements attached to state farms, existing party branches are expanded to manage the new arrivals; in the case of "comprehensive relocation," in which an entire village is relocated to a new settlement, its original party branch will move to the new location. The party secretary of Tianzhu County, a key refugee-exporting county in mountainous southern Gansu where ethnic Tibetans are concentrated, commented that the relocation has greatly facilitated the maintenance of social stability.[62]

The desert in the northwestern frontier has long captured the nation's imagination (see Chapter 1) since the socialist era. When the state farms and the Production Corps were first established in the 1950s, the desert accommodated Mao's campaigns to boost grain production. But Mao's ambition was supported more by revolutionary zeal than by technological capabilities during his time. Now things have changed. With the organizational, technological, and financial might of an assertive CCP state armed with the market, marching into the desert is more attainable than half a century ago, even in times of crisis–or, perhaps–especially in times of crisis. Riding on the national aspiration to sustain production through environmental conservation, the northwest frontier—with its vast and seemingly boundless desert—is physically and administratively expanding to meet these demands.

III Fixing the Defective Desert

Why the desert? As environmental consciousness rose in China, forests and rivers have received increasing attention from conservationists concerned about deforestation and excessive dam building. But environmental damage to the desert induced by mega-sized farming resettlements, in addition to other growth projects like mining, has received much less attention from the conservationists. What is it about the desert that makes the destructive projects seem more acceptable? And what does it take to make the desert bloom and productive?

The answer to the first question lies in the confusion between the desert and the process of desertification. The confusion lends ideological support to the cultivation march into the desert. The answer to the second question comes from the connection between conservation technologies and cultivation expansion. Conservation offers the material means to expand cultivation in the desert. Taken together, the two dynamics build a conservation discourse—in the name of crisis mitigation and combating desertification—to make productive conservation programs acceptable and manageable in the desert.

In the remainder of this Introduction, I will elaborate on these dynamics, starting from the confusion between desert and desertification. Such confusion has been used productively to shape China's campaign of greening the desert.

III.1 Desert and Desertification

The desert is a type of dryland. Drylands are hyper-arid, arid, and semi-arid regions that typically receive between less than 200 to 500 mm average annual precipitation. They are regions with a negative water balance: water loss from evaporation and transpiration exceed water received from precipitation. Deserts as a type of ecological system manifest dynamic climatological and geomorphological processes that hold a long history on earth. Most of the world's great deserts, like the Sahara, date to at least 65 million years ago, predating human life; desert landscapes manifest the action of dynamic climatological and geomorphological processes just like snowy mountains and wet forests.[63] Highly variable rainfalls can make a desert expand, contract, and change its vegetation coverage and land forms. Like mountain ranges or forests, arid landscapes are diverse. They span a spectrum including rangelands, steppes, savannahs, dune fields, salt crusts, piedmonts, sand seas, and gravel gobi. Deserts are also biologically diverse, hosting a great variety of flora and fauna that have developed various ways of surviving and thriving in aridity, such as very long tree roots to reach deep groundwater, and seeds and bulbs that lie dormant in the soil, waiting years for the next rainfall. In short, deserts, just like forests or tundra, are a type of biome that evolve and change.[64]

However, unlike mountains and forests, deserts are popularly seen as a landscape with defects and deficiencies. As a result, deserts are often used interchangeably with the term "desertification" in popular and policy discourse. On the ground, the difference between desert as a landscape and desertification as a process of soil deterioration in arid lands is central to the politics of dryland conservation.

As with the idea of sustainable development, desertification is a concept of global purchase. Definitions of desertification normally emphasize persistent and severe soil erosion and degradation, such as salinization, alkalinization, acidification, crusting, nutrient depletion, patch disruption, and collapse of vegetation production. Soil degradation in the dryland is caused by multiple processes. Compared with many other types of landscapes, drylands are particularly prone to changes in state due to scarce and variable rainfall and low soil fertility. Drylands include a wide range of landscape types, the states of which change more often than other landscape types.[65]

As a result, it is difficult to distinguish between drought-induced changes that sudden precipitation may reverse and more permanent changes associated with prolonged human intervention. There is little consensus among scientists over a timescale of degradation and recovery that can be used to measure the level of desertification: if "desertification" means "permanent undesirable state changes of the dryland," how permanent is permanent? In the drylands, precipitation varies from year to year. Officially designated and fenced-off "desertified zones" where grazing is banned to facilitate grassland recovery are often found to be, in fact, covered with vegetation after several proper rains. Is this really "desertified" land?

This is why geographers David Thomas and Nicholas Middleton (1994)[66] have called the term desertification "elusive." The elusive nature of desertification makes it difficult to parcel out the changes in ecosystem attributes and to identify corresponding climatic and social-economic factors that contribute to the change, such as overgrazing, fire, deforestation, agricultural expansion, as well as urban, mining-industrial, and infrastructure development. As a result, desertification, when defined by soil degradation of the dryland, is often defined qualitatively, such as "is/is not degraded" or "slight/moderate/severe degradation," and applications of the term desertification to particular cases are fraught with ambiguity and inconsistency.

For environmental policy thinkers searching for solutions to the problem of desertification, this challenge is fundamental: the problem itself is difficult to define. And the exact precinct of a "desertified zone" is difficult to draw on the map.

The difficulty of pinning down the moving target of whether and where desertification occurs is further complicated by popular imaginaries of the desert itself.

As mentioned earlier, like snowy mountains and wet forests, desert landscapes manifest dynamic climatological and geomorphological processes. But, unlike mountains and forests that are mostly associated with life and abundance, deserts are often presented in the negative, or in terms of what it lacks. They are perceived as barren and empty, as wastelands.

Environmental historian Diana Davis (2016)[67] has pointed out that since the early period of Christianity, the desert has been seen as the divine punishment for indigenous people's sins. This perception was further reinforced in the 19th and 20th centuries under Anglo-European imperialism. For the imperialists, deserts in the African and Asian colonies were the consequence of the natives' primitive and abusive acts of overgrazing and deforestation. In that discourse that persists to this day, a desert is *de*forested and *de*graded land. It is defective by definition.

III.2 Productive Confusion

The elusiveness of the concept of desertification and the negative imaginary of the desert together blur the boundary between desert and desertification. While the desert itself is considered defective and undesirable, the very term desertification conjures a greater fear about deserts being invasive and "spreading like a disease," as Davis (2016)[68] vividly described it.

Conservation policies in the dryland are derived from this conceptual confusion. Little distinction is made between drylands that have existed for millions of years and require little "improvement," and areas that have only recently been degraded and are in need of properly scaled and well-paced intervention. As a result of such generalizations, drylands of varying states and types in different climatic zones and geological contexts are placed under the universal policy category of area that needs repair and improvement. In this formulation, the area in need of repair indiscriminately includes both desert and recently deteriorated drylands; they are both defective anyway. As a result of the confusion between the desert and desertification, and seeing both as defective, estimates of areas affected by desertification have ranged from 4% to 74% globally.[69] In Mongolia, the range is between 9% and 90%,[70] and in China, between 4% and 28%.[71]

Calling desertification a "myth" that started under European colonialism, Davis (2016) found that the myth continued into the postcolonial era on the international stage. Most notably so in the United Nations' landmark United Nations Educational, Scientific and Cultural Organization (UNESCO) and United Nations Food and Agriculture Organization (UNFAO)'s Arid Zone Programs that began in the 1950s, the United Nations Conference on Desertification (UNCOD) in 1977, and more recently, the United Nation Convention to Combat Desertification (UNCCD) in 1994. The difference between the 1994 UNCCD and its predecessors lies in the identified cause of desertification. Before the UNCCD, the blame was mainly placed on pastoralists, most of whom are ethnic minorities in the border regions of the country in question. The minority pastoralists' overgrazing and deforestation practices were held as the main causes of desertification. The UNCCD added climate change as another important cause of desertification. Nevertheless, the confusion between desert and desertification persisted, and pastoralists continued to be targeted in desertification-combating programs and were relocated in the name of conservation. As international efforts continued to combat deserts, colonial experts became international experts who led the United Nations (UN) commissions to arid regions in former colonies to dispense advice and train local experts.[72]

The prophecies of doom about ever-expanding deserts are popularized by mass media and school educational programs.[73] The sense of urgency in the crisis narrative is undergirded by a simplified explanation of desertification: overgrazing and deforestation. This simplified explanation leads to simplified policy solutions: grazing bans, relocation of herders, and afforestation. The solutions are executed by state bureaucracies whose performance is evaluated quantitatively by the area of pasture enclosed and the number of households removed. The packaged and formulated execution of simplified policy solutions often create detrimental environmental and social consequences in arid lands, which are otherwise more resilient than most people assume.[74]

Under global discourse that confuses desert with desertification, the construction of settlements in the desert in an age of ecological conservation in China is considered an act of fending off the encroaching desert and of improving wasteland. In China's northwest, the resettlements were framed as a reversal of the crisis of "the invasion of sand forcing people to retreat" (*shajin rentui*), to that of "people moving forward to force sands to retreat" (*renjin shatui*). Combating desertification is interchangeable with taming and improving the desert. The goal is to sustain and improve its productivity.

For sure the desert is not easily tamed. Mao's ambitious state farms in the northwest failed spectacularly in productivity leaps, as mentioned earlier. Much of the reclaimed land was abandoned, and the sand did eventually force people to retreat. But China has long since passed Mao's high-spirited but poorly endowed era of the 1950s and 1960s. In the new millennium, armed with technological, financial, and organizational might, China is ready to give it another go.

The determined central state and eager local state leaders of the northwest have conjured up grand plans to fix the defective desert and make the conservation programs productive. One of the measures that help with moving further into the desert is afforestation, along with the accompanied sand-stabilizing infrastructure.

Afforestation has been practiced widely in various dryland regions in the world, in attempts to combat desertification. Since the colonial era, the cures for desertification have been livestock reduction, herder relocation, and tree-planting in the degraded rangeland, all with the goal of returning desertified land to its imagined former state of forested land.

III.3 Greening the Desert

China's antidesertification campaigns have been closely aligned with global trends. The Chinese government has been an active member of the UNCCD since 1994. In 2017, the 13th Meeting of the Parties to the UNCCD was held in Ordos, central IM. It was the first time China hosted the meeting. The meeting was opened by China's Minister of State Forestry Administration (SFA), Zhang Jianlong, who received a Combating Desertification Distinction Award, just as the Minister before him, Zhou Shengxian, had at the 8th UNCCD Meeting in 2002.[75]

Why did the Ministers of Forestry, instead of the Minister of Environmental Protection, represent China in opening the meeting and receive the award of combating desertification? The reason is both historical and structural. During the socialist era, the SFA was one of the most powerful state agencies in China's resource sector. It presided over China's vast swathes of forested land and its resources. It was the master of the socialist land masters of the forest and the overlord of China's timber industry. Under the statist planned economy, the SFA oversaw research and development, training, regulation, management, and the production and distribution of all subsectors related to the forest. The SFA was also commissioned with the task of reforestation and afforestation as early as 1978, when the Chinese government launched the mega project of planting 356.6 million hectares of trees in China, or about two-fifths of China's total land area. The mega project was included in various programs, the most famous one being the "Three North Shelter Forests," or the so-called Green Great Wall.[76] In 1994, as China responded to the UNCCD's call to combat desertification, the SFA won the job by beating the younger and much less resourced Environmental Protection Agency. The SFA became the leader of China's antidesertification machine and received the lion's share of state funding for "sand control." It has since established authoritative antidesertification institutions, including the National Bureau of Combating Desertification, the National Desertification Monitoring Center, the National Training Center for Combating Desertification, and the Institute of Desertification, established by the SFA's research arm, the Chinese Forestry Academy. While the Ministry of Environmental Protection and its local bureaus monitored air and water pollution, the SFA's empire expanded to cover massive areas of land that were, in the eyes of the SFA, ought to be forested. In the age of conservation, the SFA also expanded its portfolio from afforestation and reforestation to restoring wetlands and grasslands. The SFA was the head of China's conservation apparatus, therefore it was appropriate that its leader should address the UNCCD audience.

The leading role of the SFA in combating desertification and in China's conservation machine was further justified by the belief that planting trees is a key measure of conservation in general, and of combating desertification in particular. Behind the devotion to greening by planting trees is the popular perception that a yellow-brown landscape is naked, unhealthy, and aesthetically unappealing and should instead be covered by verdure. In this color-coded approach to conservationism, the color green indicates a healthy environment and brown is the color of illness. The success of conservation is therefore measured predominantly by the density of ground vegetation coverage and the size of forested areas. This belief persisted even after China's restructuring of environmental administrations and renaming of SFA to the State Forestry and Grassland Administration (SFGA) in 2018.[77]

Color-coded conservationism defines what and where is to be cured. To bypass the controversy over defining desertification (*shamohua*), the SFA came up with the term "sandification" (*shahua*) to identify land that is to be greened in both arid and humid areas. The SFA designated over 1.7 million sq. km, or 18% of China's land, as "sandified land", which includes any land surface that is sandy. More than 65% of the sandified land identified by the SFA is fixed or semifixed dune fields and sandy desert, but not necessarily desertified land. Used as a policy tool, sandification has helped to greatly expand the areas in need of afforestation. The expanded area of land that needs afforestation has attracted an increased budget and territorial authority to the SFA. The budget for afforestation in northern China between 2011 and 2020 was US$14.6 billion, compared to a total of US$600 million over the previous 28 years.[78]

Planting trees demonstrates environmental consciousness and a commitment to improving nature. Trees, when successfully established, are also more visually impressive than other conservation measures such as soil quality improvement. Since the 1980s, all levels of the Chinese government have launched tree-planting campaigns. Quotas for tree-planting have been assigned to local government leaders and used in cadre performance evaluations. Leaders from all levels, from the CCP General Secretaries down to township officials, often have a photo of themselves planting trees hanging on their office walls. In the northwest, government employees, school teachers, parents, and students were all mobilized to turn the unsightly yellow landscape into verdure. They were taught to aspire to turn the northern yellow earth to the landscape of the warmer and wetter south. I was taken by surprise when I saw the green landscape on my first visit to the northwest in 2009 (see Figures I.1 and I.2). Expecting to see yellow earth, I was greeted by land covered with trees and seedlings in varied states of health. Many trees had a "nutrition bag" on them, like a patient getting intravenous injections in the hospital, while watering trucks went back and forth between plantations. Planting trees in arid lands is an expensive commitment.

Afforestation has been endorsed in policy and popular discourse worldwide and in China. But the environmental problems created by afforestation in arid lands have received considerably less attention. The problems include the loss of biodiversity, groundwater depletion, loss of soil moisture, and soil salinization and desiccation. Based on a survey of 26 dryland sites globally, Kathleen Farley et al. (2005)[79] reported that afforestation has resulted in a 30% to 100% reduction in annual water runoff, thus causing or intensifying water shortages. Historically, several large-scale afforestation efforts have failed, notably in Stalin's Great Plan for the transformation of nature in 1948, when 30,000 sq. km of trees were planted on the steppe, of which only 2% survived into the 1960s. Also of note are the failures of single-species afforestation of the Green Dam and Green Wall projects in North Africa. In northern China, while the more humid northeast saw greater success in afforestation, the arid northwest experienced a very low survival rate of 15% between 1949 and 2006.[80]

Despite its failures and negative impacts, planting trees and greening the landscape have continued to embody environmental ethics and aesthetics. In 2017, at the 13th Meeting of the Parties to the UNCCD in IM, the 130-plus international participants concluded the meeting by planting 300 seedlings in the new mega town of Kangbashi in the Hobq Desert near the city of Ordos.[81] As long as afforestation remains sacred,

Figure I.1 Greening the yellow earth
Source: Photo credit: Author.

Figure I.2 Greening the desert. The grids are installed to stabilize the sands and help the suosuo seedlings develop (see Chapter 1 for the stories about suosuo).
Source: Photo credit: Author.

the low success rate in planting trees is conceived of as a technical problem that can be improved by choosing drought-tolerant species, more intensive irrigation, and a more elaborate fertilizing and planting regime.

The trees, planted painstakingly at increasing economic and environmental costs, are not just for taste and aesthetics. Forests, even artificial ones, are crucial in making drylands productive.

Forests shelter croplands against sandy wind and modify the microclimate of the planted areas. In China's northwest during the 1950s, after the first few years of poor harvests, state farms in Gansu reportedly tried to grow windbreaks that would reduce wind speed, provide shade, reduce evaporation in the hot and dry months, and raise the temperature by a few degrees in the cold winter. To do so, more than 20% of the cultivation land was devoted to windbreak forests. As the dunes were levelled for new cultivation, trees and bushes were planted along the border between the desert and the farms. The official survival rate of the trees was 43%. The real figure was much lower, reflected in the local idiom that went "in spring trees are planted; in summer trees die; come winter dead trees become fuel."[82] The know-how of planting trees in the desert has grown more elaborate since then. Instead of simple lines of trees, now extended networks of trees and bushes are planted, buttressed by sand stabilizing grids carpeting the mobile dune fields. It is now a multilayered defence system that pins down the sands to protect irrigation channels, settlements, and farmland. The productivity gains are not just on the agricultural front. The forest shelter networks are equally, if not more, important in protecting other infrastructure, such as roads and railways, and production sites, like mines and oil fields, in the desert.

With advancement in technical knowledge and increased investment in afforestation, cultivation—together with other production activities—have penetrated deeper into the desert. If the desert is in need of improvement, planting hundreds and thousands of hectares of trees is a decisive measure for it. In 2019, a report from Xinjiang celebrated the triumphant move of cultivating farmland 25 kilometers deep into the desert, thanks to the shelter forests planted by members of the Xinjiang Production and Construction Corp, the only Production Corp that still operates in China today.[83] A good portion of the trees were fruit trees, like red date and pear trees, which made the 11-km-long and 200-meter-wide shelter forest productive as well.[84] In IM, afforestation campaigns were also celebrated for their service in advancing production into the heart of the desert.[85] What's missing in these triumphant stories, however, was the immense challenge of keeping trees alive and prosperous in the desert. Despite the progress made in technical knowledge and the increase in state investment in afforestation, tree survival rates remained lower than 20% in the 2000s. The northwest was in dire need of a tree species that could effectively and efficiently green the desert.

A desert shrub called suosuo came to rescue. Suosuo has become the superstar in greening the desert of China's northwest, especially since the 1990s. Its stardom owes much to its embodiment as the solution to the mandates of productivity and conservation in a single plant. Suosuo has inspired various conservation actors, including governments at all levels, entrepreneurs of all scales, environmental nongovernmental organizations, herders, farmers, urban consumers, and even Alibaba, China's fin-tech giant. In Chapter 1, I follow this unlikely assemblage of actors to trace suosuo's path to stardom in China's ecological mobilization to green the desert.

Endnotes

1. For a review of China's conservation practices in the 1950s and 1960s, see Muscolino, Micah. 2020. "The contradictions of conservation: Fighting erosion in Mao-era China, 1953–66." *Environmental History* 25: 237–262.
2. For a review on the discourse and politics of resource scarcity, see Mehta, Lyla. 2010. *The Limits to Scarcity: Contesting the Politics of Allocation*. NY: Routledge.
3. Anthropologist Robert Weller and historian Peter Bol (1998) suggested that "the idea that political authority has fundamental responsibility for maintaining harmonious relations between society and environment has a long history in China. On the other hand, this view did not result in the conscious establishment of environmentally sound practices, largely because human utility always received first considerations." They further pointed out that "China is not the only place where a unitary view of nature and society nevertheless supports the human rights to alter that system." See Weller, Robert and Peter Bol. 1998. "From Heaven and earth to nature: Chinese concepts of the environment and their influence on policy implementation." In *Energizing China: Reconciling Environmental Protection and Economic Growth*, edited by Elroy, Michael, Chris Nielsen, and Peter Lyon, p. 473. Cambridge, MA: Harvard University Press.
4. Schmalzer, Sigrid. 2016. *Red Revolution, Green Revolution: Scientific Farming in Socialist China*. Chicago: University of Chicago Press.
5. Historian Lucien Bianco (1967) once commented that the intensive labor input in the Chinese way of farming since the 19th century was akin to home gardening in the U.S. Bianco, Lucien. 1967. *Origins of the Chinese Revolution, 1915–1949*. Stanford: Stanford University Press.
6. Marks, Robert. 2016. "Modern China's agricultural contradictions." *China Dialogue*, September 27. https://chinadialogue.net/en/food/9279-modern-china-s-agricultural-contradictions/. Accessed February 16, 2023.
7. Geertz, Clifford. 1963. *Agricultural Involution: The Process of Ecological Change in Indonesia*. Oakland, CA: University of California Press.
8. Huang, Philip C. C. 1985. *The Peasant Economy and Social Change in North China*. Redwood City, CA: Stanford University Press.
9. Shapiro, Judith. 2001. *Mao's War Against Nature: Politics and the Environment in Revolutionary China*. Cambridge: Cambridge University Press.
10. See, for example, Economy, Elizabeth. 2004. *The River Runs Black: The Environmental Challenge to China's Future*. Ithaca: Cornell University Press; and Smil, Vaclav. 1993. *China's Environmental Crisis: An Inquiry into the Limits of National Development*. NY: M. E. Sharpe.
11. Bianco, Lucien. 1967. Ibid.
12. The rural population, which was mostly made up of peasants and accounted for 64% (or 810 million in absolute numbers) of China's total population in 2000. The percentage of the population that resides in rural areas declined steadily over the ensuing two decades and went down to 37% by 2021. Still, that amounts to a whopping 530 million

people in rural China. See World Bank Group Data, based on United Nations Population Division's World Urbanization Prospects, 2018 update. https://data.worldbank.org/indicator/SP.RUR.TOTL?locations=CN. Accessed November 10, 2022. The urban-rural income disparity in China has grown continuously since current reforms started. See, for example, Zhang, Junsen. 2021. "A survey on income inequality in China." *Journal of Economic Literature* 59 (4): 1191–1239.

13. See Hsing, You-tien. 2012. "No crisis in China? The rise of China's social crisis." In *Aftermath: The Cultures of the Economic Crisis*, edited by Castells, Manuel, João Caraça, and Gustavo Cardoso, pp. 251–277. Oxford: Oxford University Press. In this article, Hsing argues that monetary compensation came to be a measurement of justice in social protest and grievance resolution.
14. See Mullaney, Thomas. 2010. *Coming to Terms with the Nation: Ethnic Classification in Modern China*. Oakland, CA: University of California Press.
15. Fischer, Andrew M. 2015. "Subsidizing Tibet: An interprovincial comparison of Western China up to the end of the Hu–Wen administration." *The China Quarterly* 221: 73–99; Sautman, Barry. 1998. "Preferential policies for ethnic minorities in China: The case of Xinjiang." *Nationalism and Ethnic Politics* 4 (1–2): 86–118.
16. Song, Fuli. 2012. "Neimenggu qiangqu vs fumin: jinnianfupinzijin jiangtu shiyi [Inner Mongolia to strengthen the autonomous region and enrich its people: 1 billion investment in poverty alleviation]." *Economic Observation*, February 22. http://www.eeo.com.cn/2012/0222/221228.shtml. Accessed October 3, 2019.
17. Bai, Liuli. 2015. "Zhuanxingkuayuefazhan fupinkaifagongjian yu shengtai wenmingjianshe xiangjiehe: gansulizushengqing mouzhuanbian [Integrating poverty alleviation-oriented development and ecological civilization: Gansu strategizes to transform]." *China Environment News*, March 27. http://epaper.cenews.com.cn/html/1/2015-03/27/01B/2015032701B_pdf.pdf. Accessed December 11, 2024.
18. World Bank. 2017. "Transcript: World Bank Group Opening Press Conference by President Jim Yong Kim at the 2017 WBG/IMF Annual Meetings." World Bank. October 12. http://www.worldbank.org/en/news/speech/2017/10/12/transcript-world-bank-group-opening-press-conference-by-president-jim-yong-kim-at-the-2017-wbgimf-annual-meetings. Accessed November 29, 2022.
19. See, for example, Zhou, Mingyang. 2017. "Zhongguofupinjingyan zhideshijiejiejian [China's poverty alleviation experience is a model for the world]." *Economic Daily*, October 17. http://www.gov.cn/xinwen/2017-10/17/content_5232241.htm. Accessed November 22, 2022; and Deng, Min. 2017. "Shihang hangzhang jinyong: zhongguofupin jingyan zhidezhongdengshouru guojia jiejian [World Bank President Kim said China's poverty alleviation experience is a model for middle-income countries]." China News Network, October 12. https://news.sina.cn/2017-10-13/detail-ifymuukv1875756.d.html?pos=3&vt=4. Accessed November 1, 2022.
20. Xinhua News, 2017. "Xijinping: Jueshengquanmian jianchengxiaokangshehui duoquxinshidai zhongguo teseshehuizhuyi weidashengli—zaizhongguogongchandang dishijiuci quanguodaibiao dahuishangdebaogao [Xi Jinping: Decisive Victory in Building a Moderately Prosperous Society in an All-round Way and Winning the Great Victory of Socialism with Chinese Characteristics in the New Era—Report at the Nineteenth National Congress of the Communist Party of China]." October 27. http://www.gov.cn/zhuanti/2017-10/27/content_5234876.htm. Accessed December 11, 2024.

21. For example, in Gansu Province, developing a green economy was framed as following Xi's instruction of environmental protection and improvement. See 2016. "Gansu Minqin fupinzhisha lüse yongxu fazhan [Sand control to alleviate poverty and green sustainable Development in Minqin, Gansu Province]." CCTV News, August 7. http://tv.cctv.com/2016/08/07/VIDEF2N4PsRwMuTY4iRexWFA160807.shtml. Accessed November 29, 2022.
22. See, for example, Zhang, Lijie. 2007. *Dongxiangzu pinkun yu fanpinkun wenti yanjiu [Poverty Issue of Dongxiang Ethnic Nationality].* Beijing: Ethnicity Press; and Li, Jian. 2006. *Xinjieduan fupin kaifade chengjiu yu tiaozhan [Achievements and Challenges in the New Phase of Poverty Alleviation-Oriented Development].* Beijing: China Finance and Economics Press.
23. de Silva, Kingsley Muthumuni. 2001. "Colonial expansion and demographic change: The British and Russian experience." *Ethnic Studies Report* 19 (2): 155–168.
24. The Development and Reform Commission, 2016. "Fagaiwei jiedu shengtaibaohubuchang zhuli jingzhuntuopin [The Development and Reform Commission explains ecological compensation and targeted poverty alleviation]." May 25. http://www.gov.cn/zhengce/2016-05/25/content_5076622.htm. Accessed December 11, 2024.
25. Marvier, Michelle, Peter Kareiva, and Robert Lalasz. 2012. "Conservation in the Anthropocene: Beyond solitude and fragility." *Breakthrough Journal.* No 2., 2012. https://thebreakthrough.org/journal/issue-2/conservation-in-the-anthropocene. Accessed May 4, 2025.
26. Dowie, Mark. 2009. *Conservation Refugees: The Hundred-Year Conflict between Global Conservation and Native Peoples.* Cambridge: MIT Press.
27. Fairhead, James, Melissa Leach, and Ian Scoones. 2012. "Green grabbing: A new appropriation of nature?" *Journal of Peasant Studies* 39 (2): 237–261.
28. "nuoqiongwo, gaiqiongye, huanqiongmao, baqionggen" in Chinese. See Ma, Shunlong. 2016. "Gansu liangzhou: yiminbanqian nuoqiongwo, xiashanruchuan chungfulu [Liangzhou of Gansu Province: Migration out of den of poverty, moving down to the flat land to find the road to wealth]." *Gansu Daily*, November 30. http://www.moa.gov.cn/fwllm/qgxxlb/qg/201611/t20161130_5382352.htm. Accessed December 5, 2018.
29. 2016. National Development and Reform Commission. "Quanguo 'shisanwu' yidi fupinbanqianguihua [Thirteenth Five-Year' notice of relocation plan for poverty alleviation]." September 20. https://www.ndrc.gov.cn/xxgk/zcfb/ghwb/201610/t20161031_962201.html?code=&state=123. Accessed November 29, 2022.
30. Croll, Elizabeth. 1999. "Involuntary resettlement in rural China: The local view." *The China Quarterly* 158: 468–483.
31. See Ying, Xing. 2001. *Dahe yimin shangfang de gushi [Stories about Dahe Dam Migrants' Lodging Complaints to the Government].* Beijing: Sanlian Press.
32. See Hsing, You-tien. 2014. "Development as culture: Human development and information development in China." In *Reconceptualizing Development in the Global Information Age*, edited by Castells, Manuel and Pekka Himanen, pp. 116–139. Oxford: Oxford University Press; and Lee, Ching Kwan and Yonghong Zhang. 2013. "The power of instability: Unraveling the microfoundations of bargained authoritarianism in China." *American Journal of Sociology* 118 (6): 1475–1508.
33. Wang, Xiaoyi. 2017. "Shenghuozai Xihaigu: shengtaicuiruodiqi yidibanqiande xinnanti [Living in Xihaigu: New predicaments of relocation in ecologically fragile areas]." *Pengpai News*, February 6. http://www.thepaper.cn/newsDetail_forward_1612858.

Accessed May 31, 2023; "Nanminying yu huanggongde juli: zhengyi huizu musilin yimin [Distance between refugee camps and palaces: Controversies over Muslim immigrants]." 2017. *Duowei News Network*, April 11. https://info.51.ca/articles/527104. Accessed May 31, 2023; Kang, Ning. 2017. "Shenghuozai Xihaigu: shiyingshuikun [Living in Xihaigu: Water shortage]." *Pengpai News*, February 6. https://www.thepaper.cn/newsDetail_forward_1612951. Accessed May 31, 2023; Zhang, Xiaoli and Lu Han. 2016. "Daying tuopingongjianzhan jianshehexie xingfu xinningxia [Win the war of poverty alleviation, build a harmonious and happy new Ningxia]." *Zhongguo Caizheng [China State Finance]*, June 2016. https://www.zgcznet.com/yhfw/gkcx/gkcxzgcz/zgcz1610/zgcz1610wz/202002/20200211/j_2020021112093400015813942370758829.html. Accessed May 31, 2023.

34. 353,000 were relocated between 2006 and 2010, as reported in the 12th Five Year Plan of Gansu Province in 2011 that sums up the delivery of the previous Five-Year Plan "Gansusheng'shierwu'yidefupinbanqianguihua [12th Five Year Plan of Gansu Province]." https://www.gsei.com.cn/html/1312/2012-02-02/content-55352.html. 634,800 were relocated between 2011 and 2015, as reported in the 13th Five Year Plan of Gansu Province in 2016 "Gansusheng'shisanwu'yidefupinbanqianguihua [13th Five Year Plan of Gansu Province]." Office of People's Government of Gansu Province, August 1, 2016. https://www.gsei.com.cn/html/1312/2016-11-15/content-147443.html. The total between 2006 and 2015 is 996,800. According to another report by Xinhua News, by 2015, the cumulative number of relocatees had reached 1.12 million in Gansu, but the report did not specify the starting date. Zhang, Qin. 2016. "Gansu111.6 wan pinkun renkou shixianyidebanqian [1.116 million impoverished people in Gansu have been relocated]." Xinhua News, February 22, 2016. http://www.gov.cn/xinwen/2016-02/22/content_5044534.htm. Between 2016 and 2020, another 499,000 relocatees were added to the list. See Shi, Yaqiao. 2020. "Gansusheng leijijianpin 550wanren yidefupinbanqian 49.9wanren [In Gansu Province, a total of 5.5 million people have been alleviated from poverty, and 499,000 people have been relocated for poverty alleviation]." *People's News*, November 10. http://rmfp.people.com.cn/BIG5/n1/2020/1110/c406725-31925780.html. All links were accessed on May 31, 2023. According to these official and news reports, the total number of relocatees in Gansu was close to 1.62 million by 2020.
35. See Hsing, You-tien. 2010. *The Great Urban Transformation: Politics of Land and Property in China*. Oxford: Oxford University Press.
36. Wang, Yiming. 1988. "Ningxia zhongdao shiqikao [Genesis of rice cultivation in Ningxia]." *Ningxia Agricultural Science and Technology* (6): 15.
37. Marks, Robert. 2011. *China: Its Environment and History*. Lanham: Rowman & Littlefield Publishers.
38. In his research on desertification in China's northwest, Lee, Kang Won (2007) has found large gaps in land area among cultivated, planted and irrigated land in Gansu and Inner Mongolia. In Xinjiang, the discrepancy was much smaller thanks to the Production Corps' extensive hydraulic works. See Lee, Kang Won. 2007. *Samak Jungguk: Junggukui Tojiyiyong Byeonhwawa Samakhwa (in Korean) [Desert China: Land Use Change and Desertification in China]*. pp. 98-103. Seoul: Politeia.
39. Zhangyi Municipal Gazetteer Office, 2016, "Section on agriculture." in Zhangyi dacidian (Zhangyi Encyclopaedia)." May 18. http://www.zhangye.gov.cn/szb/dzdt/njbz/201605/t20160518_51883.html. Accessed December 1, 2022.

40. Wang, Naiang et al. 2002. "Jin liangbai nianlai renlei huodong duiwoguoxibu shengtaihuangjing bianhuade yingxiang [The impact of human activities on ecological environment of western China in the last two hundred years]." *Studies of Chinese Historical Geography* 17 (3): 12–19.
41. The State Council of China, 2011. "Guowuyuanguanyu yinfaquanguozhutigongnengqu guihuade tongzhi [State Council Notification on National Core Function Regional Development Plan (Guofa No.46, 2010)]." The Central People's Government of the People's Republic of China, November 12. http://www.gov.cn/zwgk/2011-06/08/content_1879180.htm. Accessed December 12, 2024.
42. Under this national CFRD Plan, each province was to create a provincial-level Core Function Development Plan based on its assigned role. In each of the provincial-level Core Function Plans, a similar four-category development zoning scheme/structure was planned. The municipalities and counties of the province would be assigned by function as "priority development," "key development," "restricted," or "nondevelopment." This is to ensure that even the provinces that fall under the categories of "restricted development" or "no development" in the national plan have a chance to develop cities in areas marked as "key development" cities within "restricted" provinces.
43. The five Integrated Energy Development bases are: Shanxi Province, Ordos Basin (of IMAR), eastern and southwest Inner Mongolia, and Xinjiang. See the State Council of China, 2013. "guowuyuanguanyu yinfanengyuanfazhan shierwu guihuade tongzhi" (State Council Notification on energy development during the Twelfth Five-Year Plan (Guofa No.2, 2013)]. The Central People's Government of the People's Republic of China. January 1. https://faolex.fao.org/docs/pdf/chn190005.pdf. Accessed December 12, 2024.
44. Turner, Frederick Jackson. 1893. "The Significance of the Frontier in American History" Paper presented at the meeting of the American Historical Association (AHA) in Chicago on July 12, 1893. This essay was published in the *Annual Report of the American Historical Association*, 1893, pp. 197–227. See AHA Archival Document, Archival Resource, Primary Source. https://www.historians.org/resource/the-significance-of-the-frontier-in-american-history/. Accessed December 12, 2024.
45. Zhao, Xiaoli et al. 2014. "Zhongguojinsanshinian gengdibianhua shikongtezheng jiqi zhuyaoyuanyin fenxi [Spatial-temporal analysis of the changes of China's cultivated land in the last thirty years]." *Journal of the Chinese Society of Agricultural Engineering* 30 (3): 1–11.
46. Hsing, You-tien. 2010. Ibid.
47. For transformation of the XPCC since the 2000s, see Cliff, Thomas. 2009. "Neo Oasis: the Xinjiang Bingtuan in the Twenty First Century." *Asian Studies Review* 33 (1): 83–106.
48. When the Xinjiang Production and Construction Corps (XPCC) was first established in the 1950s, its plantations were mostly new reclamations and were deliberately chosen in the mid-reaches of the snow-fed rivers to avoid direct confrontations with existing Uygur settlements in the oases at the lower reaches. Large-scale new reclamation also suit modern mechanized agriculture. The XPCC's farms were supported by extensive water works and aggressive labor recruitment from China proper. In the first 10 to 15 years of XPCC's operation, the plantations were still relatively small and there was sufficient surface runoff left for the Uygur oases in the lower reaches. The water conflicts started in the late 1960s when XPCC's plantations continued to expand to create more "artificial oases," and runoff left for the old oases downstream started to diminish. The Seoul-based geographer Lee, Kang Won (2007) argued that the ethnic conflict between Han Chinese

and Uyghurs is inseparable from struggles for natural resources. But by the time the water conflicts had flared up, the XPCC in Xinjiang had grown much stronger and its territorial power had stabilized compared to its inaugural years. Lee, Kang Won. 2007. Ibid. Chapter 5. Inner Mongolia Corps members reported that the Corps members competed over four things with local Mongolians and Han migrants alike who migrated to Inner Mongolia prior to 1949. Those four things were land, water, mines, and pastures. The competition sometimes led to violence. See He, Lan and Weimin Shi. 1993. *Monanqing: Neimeng shengchanjianshe bingtuan huiyilu [Memoir of Southern Gobi Desert: Sketch of Inner Mongolia's Production and Construction Corps]*, p. 255. Beijing: Law Press.

49. Lee, Kang Won. 2007. Ibid. p. 101.
50. He, Lan and Weimin Shi. 1993. Ibid. p. 255.
51. Even during the politically more stable decade between the mid-1970s and mid-1980s, when the total area of cultivated land was close to 1 million mu, the amount of land that enjoyed "guaranteed irrigation" from any water source was only 100,000 mu, or 10% of the total cultivated land. Another 10% was rain-fed "God-reliant" land (kantian tian), and the rest was cultivated but unplanned and recorded as "unutilized land." The gap between cultivated and planned land was mainly due to water shortages, high salinity of water and soil, and a lack of electric power to operate well-drilling machines for extracting groundwater. Some of the unutilized land might have been cultivated before, but the thin topsoil and salinization led to their abandonment. Out of the total 640,000 mu of Dunhuang State Farm, for example, which was established in 1955, only 18,700 mu, or 2.9%, was planted by 1987. Gansu Provincial Gazetteer Editorial Committee. 1993. *Gansushengzhi nongkenzhi [Gansu Provincial Agricultural Reclamation Gazetteer]* pp. 163–164, 159–190. Lanzhou: Gansu People's Press.

    Lee, Kan Won (2007) also noted that, many of the recruits to the military agricultural colonies between the 1950s and 1970s were southerners with little experience in dryland farming, and they often abandoned the land and moved on to open up another seemingly more promising area. Given that water dried up quickly, sand easily covered the land, and natural calamities were frequent, land was abandoned as much as new land was opened. Lee, Kang Won. 2007. Ibid. pp. 157–158.

    Granted, under-reporting and "hiding the harvest" could contribute to the gap, as the size of registered cultivated land determined the quota that was imposed on state farms to remit part of its harvest to the state. But still, the immense area of abandoned and unplanted land cannot be explained away by under-reporting alone.
52. Pei, Hao, Zongyuan Zhu, and Cunzhu Liang. 2011. *Alashan huangmoqu shangtai huanjing tezheng yu huanjing baohu [The Alxa Desert: Its Environmental Characteristics and Protection]*, p. 118. Beijing: China Meteorological Press.
53. He, Lan and Weimin Shi. 1993. Ibid. p. 255.
54. Ningxia Provincial Gazetteer Editorial Committee. 1995. *Ningxia nongkenzhi [Ningxia Agricultural Reclamation Gazetteer]*, p. 2. Yingchuan: Ningxiao People's Press. For comparison, the area of land that Ningxia Agricultural Reclamation Company controlled in 1988 was more than one-fifth of the total farming and ranching land in the entire state of California, which boasted 24.3 million acres (close to 10 million hectares), operated by 69,600 farms in 2020. See 2021. "California Agricultural Statistics Review, 2020–2021 Report." California Department of Food and Agriculture, p. 2. https://www.cdfa.ca.gov/Statistics/PDFs/2021_Ag_Stats_Review.pdf. Accessed March 11, 2023.

55. Bao, Wen. 2014. "Gansu hexizoulang shulehekaifafupin yiminqunju [Predicaments in development-oriented poverty-alleviation relocation in Shule River basin of Hexi Corridor, Gansu Province]." *Green Earth Volunteers*, June 18. http://chinagev.org/index.php/greenpro/lingyanshumu/4167-shulehekaifayiminkunju Accessed November 3, 2018. This article, published online by an environmental NGO, *Green Earth Volunteers* was no longer available when I revisited it on December 1, 2022.
56. Wang, Lei et al. 2020. "Ershisanwanrende mingyunzhuanzhe—woguozuida yidishengtaiyimin anzhiquede tuopin mima [The fortune change of 230,000 people—poverty alleviation of the largest ecological resettlement in China]." *Xinhua News*, July 27. http://www.xinhuanet.com/politics/2020-07/27/c_1126289780.htm. Accessed February 16, 2023.
57. Fan, Jianrong. 2017. "Tisheng dingjulü, ningxiayidifupin banqiande guanjian [The key issue of Ningxia's 'poverty relocation' is making the relocatees stay in the new settlements]." *China Minzu Cultural Resources*, July 20. Online source. http://www.mzzyk.com/mzwhzyk/674771/682221/682225/728022/index.html. Accessed February 16, 2023.
58. Interview with a China-based researcher, June, 2016.
59. Zhang, Xiaoli and Lu Han. 2016. "Dayingtuopingongjianzhan jianshehexiexingfu xinningxia [Win the war of poverty alleviation, build a harmonious and happy new Ningxia]." *China State Finance*, June 14. https://www.zgcznet.com/yhfw/gkcx/gkcxzgcz/zgcz1610/zgcz1610wz/202002/20200211/j_2020021112093400015813942370758829.html. Accessed June 2, 2023.
60. Mi, Wenbao. 2006. *Ningxia renwen dili [Human Geography in Ningxia]*, p. 27. Hong Kong: China Social Science Research Press; Wang, Yiming. 2005. *Ningxia rendi guanxi yanhua yanjiu [The Evolution of the People-Land Relationship in Ningxia]*, p. 53. Yinchuan: Ningxia People's Press.
61. Interview with a China-based environmental scientist, May, 2018.
62. Ma, Shunlong and Cai, Zeceng. 2016. "Banchuqiongwowo zouxiangxinshenghuo: Tianzhuxian tuijinxiashanruchuan shengtaiyimin gongchengjishi [Moving out from poverty to new life: Tianzhu County's 'moving down to the plains' conservation relocation projects]." *Gansu Daily*, 20 July. http://www.gansu.gov.cn/art/2016/7/20/art_37_280527.html. Accessed October 10, 2018. The link was broken by June 2, 2023. A similar but edited version by the same lead author was available on *Gansu Daily* via this link: http://gansu.gscn.com.cn/system/2016/04/06/011323138.shtml. Accessed June 2, 2023.
63. Davis, Diana. 2016. *The Arid Land: History, Power, Knowledge*, p. 10. Cambridge, MA: The MIT Press.
64. I thank Kurt Cuffey of UC Berkeley Geography for his helpful comments on this section.
65. In addition to what has been referenced in this chapter, more scholarly works on desert and desertification can be found in, for example, Behnke, Roy, Ian Scoones, and Carol Kerven. eds., 1993. *Range Ecology at Disequilibrium: New Models of Natural Variability and Pastoral Adaptation in African Savannas.* London: Overseas Development Institute; Behnke, Roy and Michael Mortimore eds., 2016. *The End of Desertification? Disputing Environmental Changes in the Drylands.* Berlin: Springer; Verón, S.R., J. M. Paruelo, and M. Oesterheld. 2006. "Assessing desertification." *Journal of Arid Environment* 66 (4): 751–763; Verstraete, Michel M., Robert J. Scholes, and Mark S. Smith. 2009. "Climate and desertification: Looking at an old problem through new lenses." *Frontiers in Ecology*

and the Environment 7 (8): 421–428; Reynolds, James et al. 2007. "Global desertification: Building a science for dryland development." *Science* 316 (5826): 847–851; Bestelmeyer, Brandon et al. 2015. "Desertification, land use, and the transformation of global drylands." *Frontiers in Ecology and the Environment* 13 (1): 28–36.

66. Thomas, David. S. G. and Nicholas. J. Middleton. 1994. *Desertification: Exploding the Myth.* Chichester: John Wiley & Sons Ltd.
67. Davis, Diana, 2016. Ibid. p. 21.
68. Davis, Diana. 2016. Ibid. p. 162.
69. Safriel, Uriel. 2007. "The assessment of global trends in land degradation." In *Climate and Land Degradation (Environmental Science and Engineering)*, edited by Sivakumar, M. V. K. and N. Ndiang'ui, p. 18. Heidelberg: Springer.
70. Addison, Jane and Jocelyn Davies. 2012. "A critical review of degradation assumptions applied to Mongolia's Gobi Desert." *The Rangeland Journal* 34 (2): 125–137.
71. Wang, Tao and Xian Xue et al. 2015. "Combating Aeolian desertification in northern China." *Land Degradation and Development* 26 (2): 118–132.
72. See Behnke, Roy and Michael Mortimore eds. 2016. Ibid. pp. 1–34; Orenstein, Daniel E., L. Liang, and S. P. Hamburg. 2011. "An elephant in the planning room: Political demography and its influence on sustainable land use planning in drylands." *Journal of Arid Environments* 75 (6): 596–611.
73. See, for example, Shanahan, Mike. 2017. "Media perceptions and portrayals of pastoralists in Kenya, India and China." In Behnke, Roy and Michael Mortimore eds. 2016. Ibid. pp. 407–425.
74. In this chapter I will not go into the rich literature on environmental resilience. I simply raise questions about the state's measures towards fixing the desert that may not need such intervention. For discussions and critiques of the concept of resilience in the fields of ecology, agrarian studies, and political ecology, see, for example, Holling, Crawford S. 1973. "Resilience and stability of ecological systems." *Annual Review of Ecology and Systematics* 4 (1): 1–23; Carpenter, Steve, Brian Walker, J. Marty Anderies, and Nick Abel. 2001. "From metaphor to measurement: Resilience of what to what?" *Ecosystems* 4 (8): 765–781; Walker, Brian, C., S. Holling, Steve R. Carpenter, and Ann Kinzig. 2004. "Resilience, adaptability and transformability in social–ecological systems." *Ecology and Society* 9 (2): 5; Walker, Jeremy and Melinda Cooper. 2011. "Genealogies of resilience: From systems ecology to the political economy of crisis adaptation." *Security Dialogue* 42 (2): 143–160; and Watts, Michael. J. 2015. "Now and then: The origins of political ecology and the rebirth of adaptation as a form of thought." in *The Routledge Handbook of Political Ecology*, pp. 19–50. New York: Routledge. I thank Nathan Sayer of UC Berkeley Geography for discussion of the concept and reading suggestions.
75. Chen, Shuo and Aiping Li. 2017. "Zhongguo guojialinyejujuzhang huo quanqiu fangzhihuangmohua jiechugongxianjiang [Minister of China's State Forestry Administration received Combating Desertification Distinction Award]." *China News Network*, September 13. http://env.people.com.cn/n1/2017/0913/c1010-29531579.html. Accessed December 1, 2022.
76. Jiang, Hong. 2016. "Taking down the Great Green Wall: The science and policy discourse of desertification and its control in China." In Behnke, Roy and Michael Mortimore eds. 2016. Ibid. pp. 513–531, p. 524.
77. In 2018, following a nationwide institutional restructuring, the SFA was renamed to the State Forestry and Grassland Administration (SFGA) and placed under the Ministry of

Natural Resources (MNR). In the same year, the Ministry of Environmental Protection was renamed to the Ministry of Ecology and Environment (MEE). But the institutional restructuring did not seem to have changed the division of responsibilities between the two bureaucratic systems. While the MEE continues to heed the mandate of environmental protection, the MNR (and the SFGA thereunder) focus on mobilizing resources for productivity gains.

78. Jiang, Hong. 2016. Ibid. pp. 517–527.
79. Farley, Kathleen et al. 2005. "Effects of afforestation on water yield: A global synthesis with implications for policy." *Global Change Biology* 11 (10): 1565–1576.
80. Cao, Shixiong. 2008. "Why large-scale afforestation efforts in China have failed to solve the desertification problem." *Environmental Science and Technology* 42 (6): 1826–1831.
81. Chen, Shuo and Aiping Li. 2017. Ibid.
82. Gansu Provincial Gazetteer Editorial Committee, 1993, *Gansu Provincial Agricultural Reclamation Gazetteer*. Ibid. p. 287.
83. Pan, Ying. 2019. "Zhujianweilizaolüzhou anbiangujiang zhuchangcheng [Turning swords into plows to build oases: XPCC built Green Great Wall to stabilize the borderland and consolidate the frontier]." *Xinhua News*, August 8. http://www.chinanews.org/ruitu/2019/0809/6128.html. Accessed June 2, 2023.
84. Wang, Se. 2017. "Xinjiangshengchanjianshebingtuan diershi ezhishamohelong jianqilüsechanglang [XPCC built green corridors to prevent convergence of two deserts]." *Guangming News*, June 19. https://kknews.cc/zh-my/agriculture/z3bz4bp.html. Accessed June 2, 2023.
85. Zhang, Yunlong and Yunping Li. 2022. "Yikeshujianzheng neimenggu lüsebantu kuozhan [The tree that witnessed the expansion of Inner Mongolia's green landscape]." *Xinhua News*, June 17. http://big5.news.cn/gate/big5/www.news.cn/local/2022-06/17/c_1128750603.htm. Accessed June 2, 2023.

INTRODUCTION to Part I:
PASTORAL POSSIBILITIES IN INNER MONGOLIA'S GOBI DESERT

In the Introduction of this book, I discussed the regime of productive conservation in China's arid northwest and the three-pronged bureaucratic approach to defining the problem, identifying its roots, and devising policy solutions. This approach is to fulfill the Chinese Communist Party (CCP)'s three intertwined political mandates of conservation, poverty alleviation, and social stability.

Part I zooms in on a specific policy solution to the officially defined problem of desertification in Inner Mongolia Autonomous Region (IMAR) over two chapters. Chapter 1, "A Miracle Shrub: Suosuo for Combating Desertification," is led by a plant called suosuo. Suosuo is a desert shrub native to northwest China. Drought-tolerant and sand-stabilizing, suosuo is made a champion in the battle against desertification. Suosuo's success is in large part owed to its productive partner, congrong, a valuable medicinal plant that parasiticides on suosuo's deep roots. Together, suosuo and congrong offer a magical solution to the policy dilemma between conservation and productivity and have become a power couple in China's regime of productive conservation. The power couple leads China's green mobilization across the state and non-state sectors. They have inspired local officials, green entrepreneurs, environmental nongovernmental organizations (ENGOs), and even China's eCommerce giant, Alibaba. These actors join the afforestation effort of expanding suosuo-congrong plantations in the desert. This chapter concludes with a social-environmental assessment of desert under the rule of miracle.

In the synergetic green mobilization under suosuo and congrong, led by the state and urban elite, herders have mostly been seen as the root of the problem of desertification. Herders' role in combating desertification is little more than correcting, or being corrected for, their wrongs. That is, the greedy herders and their hungry herds had created the problem of desertification. Such blaming leads to the policy solutions of relocating herders and reducing herds. That leads to Chapter 2, "Mobility under Restrictions: Ejina Herders Surviving Rangeland Conservation". Drawn mainly from my fieldwork in Xilingol League of central IM and Alxa League in western IM, especially Ejina Banner of Alxa League from 2011 to 2014, this chapter explores herders' coping mechanisms under rangeland conservation programs like pastural decollectivization, destocking, and relocation. None of the programs, framed by containment and restriction, are new to other pastoral regions in the world trying to combat desertification. Yet, few in-depth case studies have been published in English. Through stories about a relocated and destocked pastoral family in Ejina, the most arid and western-most banner of IM, I discuss this family's strategies in identifying Pastoral Possibilities through a new mode of mobility as well as the Impossibilities they encounter. The possibilities they find do not always align with the intention of the state, and the impossibilities they encounter often arise from entrenched dynamics of social inequality that have evolved from eras prior to that of conservationism in the new millennium.

1
A Miracle Shrub: Suosuo for Combating Desertification

In the Introduction of this book, I examined the regime of productive conservation in China's arid northwest frontier in the new millennium. Forceful state intervention has been essential to frontier expansion across places and times. Historians Donald Wurster (1986)[1] and Patricia Limerick (1987)[2] have long dispelled the illusive frontier story framed by individual heroic adventurism. Instead, they demonstrated the decisive role that the state and militaristic forces have played in American western expansion. China's northwest frontier is no exception.

But "state intervention" is easier said than done. Peter Perdue (2005)[3] spent a good part of his *China Marches West* on the daunting challenges of military logistics that the Qing emperors encountered in the process of annexing the New Territory, or Xinjiang in eastern Eurasia. Robert Marks (1998),[4] in his environmental history of late imperial southern China, recounted the "ambiguous legacy" of the Qing emperors' mostly failed attempts to reclaim land in the southern frontier in the 18th and 19th centuries. The officials were neither able to incentivize the peasants to bring more land under cultivation nor were they able to tax the newly cultivated, but unregistered, farms. The challenge of subjugating new frontiers only grew under the pressure of rapid population growth in 18th and 19th century China. By the 19th century, the virgin land that was still available for reclamation was mostly low-yielding hilly dryland that eroded easily after clearance.

The territorial ambition of the emperor does not guarantee successful governance of the frontier. This discrepancy holds true even for the CCP, which is known for its

Conserving China's Northwest Frontier. You-tien Hsing, Oxford University Press. © You-tien Hsing (2025).
DOI: 10.1093/9780191903908.003.0002

unprecedented organizational and mobilizational capacity in Chinese history. But state capacity is not all there is to frontier expansion. Bringing vast and remote terrains under state administration cannot be completed without society's subscription to the idea and participation in the action. To do so, the state needs an agenda in which ideas, actions, resources, and institutions can converge.

The perception of an environmental crisis and the action of mitigating the crisis by expanding tree plantations in the desert contribute to building such an agenda. In this agenda, the relationship between problems and solutions is forged as a given. The unquestionable merits of trees and mass participation in afforestation reinforce one another, making tree-planting a universal moral value in the age of conservationism. Aimed at "turning the desert green," afforestation produces a color-coded notion of conservationism that is shared by both state and non-state actors, including political leaders, private capital, environmental activists, and nongovernmental organizations (NGOs), as well as young, eco-minded urban consumers. Bearing vastly different incentives, these actors agree on the idea that the desert needs to be fixed, and they converge in the remedial action of planting trees, especially suosuo shrubs, in the desert.

The story of suosuo, a drought- and saline-tolerant shrub of the dryland, tells the tale of such convergence of the state, market, and society in the productive conservation programs of China's northwest. I call suosuo a "miracle shrub" because of its phenomenal economic, political, and sociocultural power to mobilize an unlikely assemblage of conservation actors in China today. This humble desert plant has even helped China's e-commerce and fin-tech giant, Alibaba, to maintain its dominance in the market via its financial arm, Ant Financial (renamed Ant Group since 2020). Mobilized by the miracle desert shrub, suosuo, various state and non-state actors with diverse motivations, capacities, and aspirations enable and derail one another in China's campaign of combating desertification. It is the tension created by such enabling and derailing that shapes the processes and results of productive conservation in China's northwest in the new millennium.

Before diving into the tale of suosuo, the miracle shrub of the desert, a prelude thereto about a legendary Chinese scientist's desert dreams in the 1960s will help us appreciate suosuo's mobilizational power in the 2000s.

I A Rocket Scientist's Desert Dream

"Deserticulture," a term which refers to the process of turning desert productive, was coined by the legendary Chinese rocket scientist Qian Xuesen (or Tsien Hsue-shen, b. 1911, d. 2009). Born in China, Qian received his doctoral degree from California Institute of Technology (CalTech) in 1939. Qian's subsequent research and teaching career in the U.S. Airforce, Massachusetts Institute of Technology (MIT), and CalTech ended with prison terms during the McCarthy era. He was later released and sent back to socialist China in 1955. Upon his return, he was involved in China's missile and space programs. A decade later during the Cultural Revolution, Qian escaped, by the width of a piece of hair, the violent purge, disgrace, and death that many other leading intellectuals and scientists suffered, thanks to his political skills and the then Premier Zhou Enlai's intervention. In 1986 during China's market reform, at the age of seventy-five, Qian was awarded China's top job in science as the Chair of the National Science Committee.[5] He is also popularly known as China's Father of Rocketry.

Born and raised in Beijing by a high-ranking Republican official's family, Qian's first encounter with the desert took place in the early 1960s, when he went to the Gobi Desert in Ejina of western IM, to visit the rocket launch base in Ejina.[6] As a physicist with deep social concerns, Qian recalled his excitement when he discovered that the desert was not empty. He was impressed by the diverse fauna and flora of the immense dryland and the abundance of fuel woods and medicinal herbs that local herders collected in the desert.[7]

It is unclear whether Qian made subsequent visits to the desert. But he most definitely had not forgotten about it. In 1984, a few years after he stepped out of the Cultural Revolution and found himself amidst budding market reforms, Qian came up with the term "deserticulture" in English to promote an economy based on resources of the arid lands.

Qian's original vision of deserticulture was to apply modern technologies to transforming solar energy (which is abundant in the northwest) into other forms of energy. He believed that advanced technologies would create a great leap forward in agricultural productivity and would "make the desert serve the people."[8] Deserticulture would help "take back 300,000 sq. kms of desert and turn it into productive woodland and farmland," an objective that was central to the mission of constructing a new socialist China.[9]

What Qian had in mind was to build solar-heated greenhouses and livestock shelters, and to employ water-saving irrigation technologies—all supported by the state's financial, technological, and infrastructure investments. He even advocated for the establishment of a Ministry of Deserticulture at the national level, separate from the Ministries of Agriculture and Forestry, to demonstrate the distinctive significance of the desert in national development.

Qian gave speeches and wrote a few widely cited articles about deserticulture throughout the 1980s and 1990s. But given his experience in two major political purges in two countries within a short interval, it is understandable why Qian shied away from publishing any book-length work to systematically elaborate upon the concept of deserticulture.[10] Meanwhile, in his capacity as Chair of the National Science Committee, the passionate rocket scientist penned thousands of pages of personal correspondences with policymakers and thinkers during the 1980s and early 1990s. These letters covered wide-ranging topics from systems engineering, medical science, biology, and environmental science to architecture, arts, and philosophy, as well as industrial revolutions and national development plans for the next century.[11]

One of the frequently reoccurring themes in these exchanges concerned deserticulture, most of which were with a woman science policy thinker, Liu Shu (1934–). Trained in the Institute of Forestry Engineering in Leningrad, USSR, Liu returned to China in 1960 as a junior researcher with the Glacier and Desert Institute of the

Chinese Academy of Sciences in Lanzhou, Gansu Province. She then became an administrator in the academy. In 1983, Liu was appointed as Vice Governor of Gansu Province in charge of education and research. Halfway through her second term in June 1989 came the Tiananmen Massacre in Beijing. Liu, along with many others who held leadership positions in education and research institutions, was removed from the post. After stepping down from the high-profile government position, Liu developed a new career path for herself advocating for Qian's idea of deserticulture. She co-founded and chaired the semi-official Deserticulture Association and became a board member on the Foundation of Deserticulture that Qian had established with overseas Chinese donations. Liu compiled Qian's lecture notes and letter correspondences, published articles, and edited volumes on theories and policies of deserticulture. She also tried to promote deserticulture through establishing research stations in the Hexi Corridor of Gansu, where she had previously built her career and gained extensive political connections.[12]

In the 1990s, with Qian's leadership status in China's science circle and Liu's advocacy, the concept of deserticulture began to spread. Qian broadened the idea of deserticulture to include arboriculture and mariculture. Furthermore, he embraced the idea of "prataculture" (or, the grass industry), initiated by an academician of the Chinese Academy of Engineering, Ren Jizhou, who was 13 years Qian's junior. Teaching and conducting research in husbandry at the University of Lanzhou in Gansu, Ren had been a leading policy thinker in China's grass industry since the late 1970s.

But during Qian's time, the ideas of deserticulture and prataculture were, for the most part, deliberated amongst only a small circle of elite scientists. In his old age, Qian was disappointed with the fact that the government had mostly talked about deserticulture without taking much action.[13] But soon after his passing in 2009, as fate would have it, Qian's idea of deserticulture started to gain traction.

In 2010, the State Forestry Administration (SFA), the agency that was in charge of China's conservation agenda overseeing responsibilities ranging from afforestation, combating desertification, and wetland restoration to protecting the panda bear and other endangered species (see Introduction), issued the "Opinion on Accelerating the Development of Deserticulture." This was the first national policy document that had adopted the term.[14] The opinion recognized the importance of deserticulture in building "ecological civilization,"[15] restructuring the economy of China's "sand regions" (which include both the arid northwest and west as well as the sandy areas of the humid southeast), and the market and technologies for creating income-generating opportunities for the impoverished people of the sand regions. Following the SFA's landmark policy, the governments of Gansu Province and Inner Mongolia Autonomous Region (IMAR), among other northwest local governments, started to develop deserticultural programs.[16]

These new policies have significantly shaped the productive conservation programs in the northwest. Following national policies, local governments recruited private capital, known in China as "Dragon Head Enterprises," to explore what the desert could offer to promote growth. The Dragon Heads, as the designated engine of growth, were to build up the deserticultural industry and serve as the model for other private enterprises. The government offered them incentives in the form of tax breaks, cheap policy loans, priority in stock listing and bond issuing, and access to land and water. The incentive package was similar to those offered under industrialization initiatives of the 1980s and urbanization initiatives of the 1990s. The conservation-framed development policies in 2010, however, conveyed a stronger sense of political urgency in their emphasis on two priorities: one was sustaining the nation's growth at a time of global economic slowdown, the other helping the poor and their degraded environment at a time of heightened social tension. Under such political discourse of productive conservation, as outlined in the Introduction, Qian's notion of deserticulture was expanded and popularized: ranging from state-sponsored industrial agriculture in the dryland to a wide range of dryland industries, including not just industrial agriculture, but also renewable energy, heritage–and eco–tourism, and urban development.[17]

As the scope of deserticulture proliferated in the new era, entrepreneurial local leaders and private capitalists replaced idealistic policy thinkers like Qian as its main advocates. Qian's bookish term "deserticulture" no longer suited the mood of the new era. From here on, I will switch from the term "deserticulture" to "sand industry," a direct translation of the Chinese term *shachanye*, to register the popularization of productive conservation programs since the 2010s.

II A Power Couple

II.1 Suosuo the Superstar

In the sand industry, suosuo is a shining star. Suosuo, or *Haloxylon ammodendron* (see Figure 1.1), is a dryland shrub native to China's northwest. It is known for its resilience and ability to tolerate drought, salinity, extreme temperatures, and strong winds. Its varieties are found throughout drylands in South Asia, Central Eurasia, and northern Africa. In China's northwest, the suosuo thrives on sand dunes as well as on dried riverbeds, lakebeds, and the alluvial fan in the gravel gobi, where the soil is well drained. Growing between one and five meters tall with a five to ten square meter crown, suosuo has a woody stem and is taller than many other shrubs. A fully grown suosuo shrub looks more like a small-sized tree. Camels and sheep graze on its young leaves and small shoots, and local residents collect its woody branches for construction and fuel. Suosuo wood was used even for building the Great Wall during the Han Dynasty (206 BCE to 220 CE). Suosuo's dense wood also makes for high quality, smokeless fuel and is referred to as the "living coal of the desert." The most authentic, hence the best, Mongolian roast lamb, a local official told me, is roasted in suosuo-fired kilns. Suosuo was likely among the dryland plants that had inspired Qian Xuesen, the aforementioned father of the sand industry, during his historic visit to the desert in the 1960s.

Over 90% of IM's native suosuo forests are found in the plateau of Alxa League in western IMAR.[18] In Alxa's immense territory of 270,000 sq. km (for comparison, the

Figure 1.1 Suosuo and author
Source: Photo credit: Author's host.

total surface area of the UK is 244,820 sq. km), 85% consists of fields of sand dunes and gravel. The official record shows that in the 1950s there were over 1.2 million hectares of native suosuo forests. In these forests, suosuo is mixed with other dryland trees, shrubs, and grasses in various vegetation formations. Suosuo's extensive and penetrating root system stabilizes the sandy land and prevents erosion. Suosuo formations at the edge of the desert create natural windbreaks and sand blockers. Since the 1970s, however, large areas of Alxa's natural suosuo forest have begun to die out. It was estimated that the natural suosuo forest had shrunk from over 1.2 million hectares in the 1950s to 40% thereof by the end of the 1990s, with about half of the original ground coverage.[19] The deterioration of natural suosuo forests exposed the sandy and saline soil to strong winds, deteriorating surface coverage and turned fixed and semifixed sand dunes mobile. The degradation consequently led to more frequent and much larger dust storms in northern China and beyond, especially since the 1990s.

Some China-based scientists argue that the suosuo forests' degeneration was mainly due to the dramatic expansion in irrigated agriculture along the river basin, including the state farms that opened in the 1960s and 1970s and subsequent groundwater depletion.[20] But conservation policymakers placed the blame on overgrazing in the suosuo forests and local peoples' excessive collection of suosuo wood. Following the latter logic, the local government of Alxa League fenced off officially identified "deforested suosuo land" and banned grazing and wood collection in these protected areas. The goal of these measures was to allow deteriorated suosuo forests to regenerate naturally.

But successful regeneration of the natural suosuo forest, like most good things in life, takes time. It also requires perfect timing: the temporal alignment of precipitation for two consecutive years. The first year's precipitation needs to register above the multiyear average to achieve the necessary level of soil moisture. The wet year needs to be followed by timely rains in the ensuing spring and early summer for successful sprouting and the seedlings' survival. But the extremely arid Alxa, which averages less than 100 mm of annual precipitation and over 2,200 mm of evaporation, is known for frequent spring and early summer droughts. The untimely aridity makes it difficult to regenerate young shrubs in the natural forests. In one of the largest natural suosuo forests in Jilantai in eastern Alxa, for example, researchers found that such perfect alignment of precipitation has occurred only five times between 1955 and 1999. In other words, left to God's will, the suosuo forests' cycle of regeneration averages at nine long years.[21] Another research team suggested that if the natural regeneration cycle is supported by planting additional suosuo seedlings in deteriorated areas equipped with artificial irrigation and sand-stabilizing devices, it would still take 10 to 15 years for the restored forest to reach a similar density as forest that has been enclosed for over 20 years without disturbance.[22] In addition, as with restoration projects elsewhere, even when the enclosure-restoration approach succeeds in increasing the suosuo biomass, it takes even longer, if at all, to reach a desirable level of biodiversity and soil quality.

But few local officials can afford the long wait. Tree-planting quotas are assigned and local leaders' responsibility contracts are reviewed annually, much like other measurements of their performance, such as local GDP growth rates. Local leaders serve appointment terms of five years, and they need to prove themselves midway through their terms to prepare for their next career moves. The protracted process to restore forests and local leaders' short evaluation and promotion cycles do not sync up.

An alternative is to build suosuo plantations from scratch. Artificially planted suosuo seedlings grow fast enough to match the cadres' performance evaluation cycle. And suosuo plantations work better than plantations of other species thanks to suosuo's tenacious seedlings. While the native suosuo forest thrives on relatively stable fields of fixed- and semifixed sand dunes, young suosuo seedlings can establish themselves in the precarious, but well-drained, mobile sand dunes that have 5%, or even less, ground coverage, as long as competition is minimal and groundwater is accessible. Within the first two years of sprouting, suosuo seedlings rapidly gain height to avoid being buried by moving sands. Its vertical root trunk grows to 10-times the length of the aboveground stems so that it can stabilize itself in mobile sand dunes. While many other dryland plants share the matured suosuo's feature of drought and saline tolerance, the young suosuo plant's speedy early development is particularly attractive for foresters who are responsible for greening the desert (especially the degraded mobile sand dunes). As large areas of fixed dune fields in Alxa turned into mobile or semi-mobile dunes and were earmarked for afforestation, the adaptive and rapidly growing suosuo seedlings reached higher-than-usual survival rates on mobile dunes within the first two years of planting.

For financial reasons, local leaders have also preferred to establish suosuo plantations rather than restore the natural suosuo forests. The expansion of forested areas has been a top priority for the SFA.[23] The SFA receives the lion's share of the national conservation budget, and, in turn, allocates project-based funding to revenue-poor local governments. In the area of forest conservation, most SFA grants and subsidies to local governments are designated for tree plantations, not to restore natural forests. SFA grants can be used for constructing plantation infrastructure, such as irrigation systems, service roads, and sand-stabilizing devices. Since the agricultural taxes were abolished in the mid-2000s, rural governments have grown increasingly dependent on conservation funding, and tree plantation projects have become an important lifeline for local finance.

Building suosuo plantations is more advantageous than restoring natural forests for spatial reasons as well. Under SFA leadership, China's recent history in planting trees features a persistent pursuit of increasing forest cover through building tree plantations. As early as 1958, Mao declared his goal to "green the entire landscape of our motherland."[24] Despite varying results from region to region, mega-projects like the Northern Shelterbelt Afforestation project that started in 1978 and the Returning Farmland to Forest (also known as the "Grain for Green") project that started in 1999, increased the total area of China's forested land, including artificially planted forests, from about 12% of the national landmass in the late 1970s, to 21.7% in 2018. Today, about 2 million sq. km, or about 90% of China's forested area, is covered by artificial forests, while natural forests continue to decline.[25] In a bid to become the world leader in conservation at a time of global deforestation crises, the head of the SFA announced in 2018 that China would continue its tree-planting efforts to reach new heights of forest coverage of 23% by 2020 and 26% by 2035. These efforts are mostly directed towards China's western and northwestern regions.[26] By 2023, China's forest coverage rate hit 24%.[27]

A vocal environmentalist, Yu Changqing, has questioned the ambiguous official definition of "forested area" as well as the low survival rates of the 2 million sq. km of artificial forests.[28] Nevertheless, the focus on numerical achievements and the budget attached thereto has sent a clear message to local leaders about policy priorities. The ambitious targets to maintain the nation's dominance in creating the world's largest artificial forests are translated into local governments' missions of tree-planting, evaluated by the increase in forest coverage and number of trees they plant. The SFA-issued plantation guidelines also specify the target tree density for plantations, which is much higher than that of natural forests in the arid north. Under criticism about rampant timber harvesting in the rapidly disappearing old growth forests, a forestry official vowed: "for every old tree that is felled, we will plant ten more."[29]

For local officials, the quantified and spatial expansion-driven afforestation policies make suosuo plantations a more desirable option than the restoration of natural suosuo forests. Restoration through the enclosure of native suosuo forests is generally more successful in recovering mother plants' overall height, trunk and crown size, and seed productivity. But young suosuo plants do not compete well with matured plants in the dried-up soil of deteriorated grounds in the natural forests. Even when young plants survive, they normally grow very close to the mother plants—no more than 6 meters away.[30] In other words, a naturally recovered suosuo forest expands very slowly. Therefore, local officials have one more reason to channel their energy and funds to the spatially expansive, high-coverage artificial suosuo plantations.

Lastly, suosuo owes its popularity also to the failure of non-native monocultures in China's long history of afforestation. Since the 1970s, different species have dominated afforestation programs in different regions: firs are common in the south, poplars in the north, red pines in the southeast, and larches in the northwest. Like many other non-native single species afforestation programs in conservation history the world over, these tree plantations have suffered pest infestation, groundwater depletion, loss of soil moisture, as well as soil salinization and desiccation. Often, they fail at the very purpose of planting trees, which is to prevent soil erosion, because of their poor water retention capacities. Some of the species do not support sufficient undergrowth, creating an arid forest environment that leads to more frequent forest fires.[31]

Suosuo, a tough and woody shrub native to the northwest, could be the answer to mitigating non-native species' dominance in tree plantations. Despite the fact that the rest of China continued to plant non-native monocultures, cultivating native suosuo in the northwest appeared to be a more enlightened way of afforestation. Suosuo also contributes to another trend in conservation, namely, an integrated approach that combines trees, shrubs, and grass to generate more effective shelter networks that protect roads, infrastructure, farms, and homes against strong winds and sandstorms.

In short, the combination of suosuo's ability to tolerate the extreme environment, its adaptive young plants that synchronize with the cycle of local government leaders' performance reviews, and its nativeness together make the shrub a champion in the northwest's desertification-combating campaigns.

But in the 2010s, China's northwest needed more than an ecological champion of a plant, and the problem was greater than just combating desertification. What the northwest needed was a miracle plant to serve the triple policy agenda of growth, conservation, and maintenance of social stability in the multiethnic frontier region, as outlined in the Introduction. This is where suosuo's partner, congrong, comes in.

II.2 Congrong the Rainmaker

Suosuo shrubs may be a better option than other species for afforestation, but planting trees in the arid northwest—even with a super-shrub like suosuo—remains an uphill struggle. It is impossible to plant trees and keep them alive in an immense and arid region without the commitment of rural officials and local residents to providing labor and daily care for young suosuo seedlings in high-density plantations.

In most cases, rural officials and locals were reluctant participants in afforestation. Subsidies and grants from the SFA, important sources of local finance as they were, were far from sufficient for grassroots officials to fulfil the assigned quotas for number of seedlings planted and forest area added. Not to mention that these quotas also came with an officially imposed minimum survival rate. In addition to initial funding for irrigation system construction, land compensation and clearance, and the purchase of seedlings, regular maintenance expenses would be needed for labor, water, power, fertilizer, and disease and pest control (especially to combat the rampant rodent infestation caused by soil degradation and biodiversity decline). On top of that, additional funding for repeated replanting to reach the required minimum survival rates was rarely available. These expenses added to poor counties and townships' financial burdens. While "ecological construction" project grants offered a lifeline for grassroots governments, they posed as sugar-coated poison that sent poor and indebted local governments into even deeper debt.[32] In many plantations, after funds or water—or both—ran dry, the young trees were left to die. The problem was particularly severe in the arid region, as the SFA plantation guidelines required a much higher plant density than that of a natural forest. The high-density planting regime created fierce competition among vulnerable seedlings and young trees before they reached a robust state of maturity. Without sufficient irrigation and monitoring, soil moisture is quickly exhausted in arid lands where groundwater replenishment is slow and almost exclusively dependent upon surface runoff rather than on precipitation.

For rural residents, "conservation forests" take up precious land and water. Moreover, afforestation campaigns often drew from village collectives' funds in order to pay for the labor, as it became increasingly difficult to elicit the "voluntary labor" that local infrastructure projects had relied on during the collective era. In the massive Returning Farmland to Forest programs that began in 1999, it was reported that once the cash compensation for "retiring cultivation" was exhausted after the initial period, farmers went back to farming and deforesting the newly forested land again. In other cases, local residents dug holes too shallow for seedlings to survive, did not water the seedlings, planted other competitive crops next to seedlings, and in some cases, even pulled out seedlings after the inspecting officials left, later blaming wandering dogs.[33]

The lack of grassroots support and local sabotage presented a great challenge to afforestation efforts, especially in the arid northwest. But suosuo is different from other plants. Suosuo was one of the few plantation species that grassroots officials and local residents in the northwest were willing to plant and care for. The secret to suosuo's mobilizational capacity lies in its partner: the perennial plant *roucongrong* (*Cistanche deserticola Y. C. Ma*, for simplification I will call it *congrong* from here on), for which the suosuo is the host (see Figure 1.2). Congrong parasitizes on suosuo's extensive and deep roots and grows in a bundle of five to eight sticks of one to three feet long each. Congrong is known as the "desert ginseng" for its beneficiary health effects (especially for male potency in Chinese medicine) and commands a high market price. In the early 2010s, a two-foot-long dried wild congrong could retail for over RMB 3,000 yuan.

Before the 1990s, most congrong sold on the market was wild congrong harvested in native suosuo forests. Herders in Alxa of IM rode camels, and later, motorcycles up and down the suosuo-growing dune fields to find congrong in the windy spring, when the tips of congrong began to peek out above the ground. In the 1990s, just as market demands and prices for congrong began to soar, the supply of wild congrong declined due to the deterioration of natural suosuo forests. Meanwhile, scientists of local SFA branches and state and private pharmaceutical companies began to experiment with micro-propagation of congrong seeds, manually planting them onto suosuo's roots in suosuo plantations. Regular irrigation, seed treatment, fertilization, and pesticide application aided efforts in increasing the productivity of congrong.[34] (see Figures 1.3 and 1.4).

The hardy and restorative suosuo shrubs and its profitable partner, congrong, became a winning pair that has mobilized local officials and rural residents to green the desert. Government leaders in the northwest enthusiastically promoted the power couple for its ability to simultaneously carry out the paired policy priorities of conservation and production (or poverty alleviation in policy language). The expanding congrong market and the lure of conservation grants and loans helped local governments attract private investors to build suosuo-congrong plantations. This in turn helped local leaders to meet the quota of forest land expansion. Some local residents appeared convinced by the power couple as well. TV programs and newspapers featured model suosuo-congrong farmers, who used to be herders in the pre-conservation era, to showcase the magic of the power couple that facilitates both environmental protection and poverty alleviation. After much failure with other drought-tolerant cash crops promoted by the government (such as goji berries, wine grapes, and jujube dates, see Chapter 4), the suosuo-congrong pair has reinvigorated the productive conservation programs in the arid northwest.

III Desert Aspirations

Alxa League of west IM, where large areas of natural suosuo forests have been found, is at the forefront of building suosuo-congrong plantations. Between 1998 and 2016, the Alxa government reported to have doubled its suosuo forests from 5,600 sq. km to over 10,000 sq. km. About 10% to 12% of the suosuo forest, or 1,000 to 1,200 sq. km, was suosuo plantation, which was mostly in Alxa's relatively more humid east.[35]

While the Alxa League government itself established several large suosuo-congrong plantations and invested in congrong-based pharmaceutical companies in order to expand value-added chains, the majority of the suosuo-congrong plantations in Alxa featured investments from private entrepreneurs. In addition to private

Figure 1.2 Wild congrong

Source: Photo credit: Author.

capital, other actors also participated in planting suosuo in the desert with different motivations and approaches. They include one of China's largest domestic environmental NGOs, the Society of Entrepreneurs and Ecology (SEE), and over 300 million urban consumers mobilized by Ant Financial, the financial technology arm of China's e-commerce giant, Alibaba. This section tells the stories about these

Figure 1.3 A natural suosuo field
Source: Photo credit: Author.

Figure 1.4 A suosuo plantation
Source: Photo credit: Author.

key non-state actors who were inspired by the suosuo-congrong duo to try and fix the desert and build a paradigmatic mode of productive conservation in China's northwest frontier.

III.1 Green Entrepreneurs

As mentioned earlier, a paradigmatic shift in China's conservation programs in the 2010s was the openly celebrated involvement of private capital. One can always raise questions about how private China's private capital is, especially in sectors where the government is actively involved, like combating desertification. In many cases, the private and the public are deeply entangled. The stories of two green entrepreneurs who have been involved in the suosuo-congrong business under the umbrella of "sand industry," illustrate the popular policy discourse of Public-Private Partnership (PPP from here on) in China's northwest today.

One of the most active green entrepreneurs in China's sand industry is Wang Wenbiao (1958–). Born in IM to a Han Chinese family, Wang initially made his "first pot of gold" as a construction contractor in the late 1980s, building roads across the desert in IM.[36] But as sandstorms intensified, roads were often buried by sands. Planting shelter forests to protect the roads from sandstorms turned out to be the most challenging part of his business. Wang made a name for himself as much as by planting windbreak forests as by constructing roads. As government contracts for combating desertification increased in the 2000s, Wang expanded his business to building "ecological roads," cash crop plantations, and windbreak shelters in sandy IM and other northern arid lands.

By 2008, Wang was the chair of the Elion Resource Group Company, worth US$16 billion and listed on the Shanghai Stock Exchange. His business empire now included food and feed production and processing, pharmaceutical companies based on dryland herbs from his plantations and contract farms, renewable energy, mining equipment, and resort development. But the core of Elion's business remained to be ecological restoration and construction.

As poor local governments of the northwest received earmarked but partial funds to green the desert, they partnered up with private investors for additional capital and managerial support. In the initial stage, most investors were slow in responding to the call. But the adventurous and visionary Wang, who had significant experience and an extensive socio-political network in IM, dove in. The business of planting trees was highly lucrative. While urban real estate went through cycles of fluctuation, the tree-planting business continued to grow across Chinese cities and the countryside. Since the late 2000s, the Chinese government spent more than US$30 billion on greening cities and about US$23 billion on ecological restoration annually.[37] Much of the conservation funding was used to construct ecological facilities, like parks, irrigation systems, roads, and tree plantations, all of which fell under Wang's business portfolio.

Conservation-framed projects also made a name for Wang's Elion as a socially responsible enterprise. Wang has identified himself as a loyal follower of Qian Xuesen, the rocket scientist-turned father of deserticulture presented in the beginning of this chapter. In 2011, Wang published a ghost-written book *Qian Xuesen and the Sand Industry*. In the book, Wang offered a thorough review of how his investments realized Qian's dream of making the desert serve the people. He also further elaborated upon his own, bigger dream of "leading the global green economy of the desert."[38]

Elion's signature project was the greening of over 11,000 sq. km of the Hobq Desert in West-Central IM, south of the Yellow River Loop.

The Hobq Desert, approximately 16,100 sq. km in area, has recorded an average of less than 200 mm of annual precipitation, but an average of 2,500 mm of annual evaporation over the last three decades. Up until the 1960s, about 80% of the Hobq consisted of fields of 10 to 15 meter-tall mobile and semi-mobile sand dunes, with 1% to 10% natural ground coverage. At the edge of the Hobq were fixed and semi-fixed dune fields that had more than 30% vegetation coverage. Cultivation started to expand in the Hobq in the 1960s, and grazing land was transformed into state or collective farms. The groundwater level dropped, and fixed sand dunes at the edge of the desert turned mobile or semi-mobile. The mobilized sand dunes became the source of sandstorms in the windy spring, destroying homes and fields. The loose dunes also contributed to sediment accumulation in the Yellow River, thus creating floods of greater frequency and magnitude in the river basin in the summer.[39] By the 2000s, planting trees to fix the Hobq Desert seemed more urgent than ever.

Wang planted trees in the Hobq Desert methodically. He followed the four principles of "desert control," by "locking down the borders of the desert, penetrating into the heart of the desert, dividing the desert by roads, and controlling the desert block by block."[40] To date, five desert roads totaling a length of 234 km have been built to divide the Hobq Desert into seven blocks. These roads are lined with windbreaker trees, while the interior of each block is filled with congrong-breeding suosuo shrubs, licorice (*Radix Glycyrrhiza*, or *gancao* in Chinese), which is one of the most widely used herbs in Chinese medicine, and other crops that can be processed for animal feed. The spatially expansive projects that cover an area of over 6,000 sq. km are organized by desert road networks, powered by photovoltaic power stations, and use groundwater-fed irrigation systems. The project in the Hobq Desert also extended to sheltered husbandry, fodder plantation and feed production, renewable energy, and ecotourism.

Wang used assertive language to elaborate his vision of "digging gold in the desert" and "turning ecology into business; demanding dividends from conservation." In one of his media interviews, Wang performed a simple equation: "... 2.6 million sq. km of land in China, more than a quarter of the nation's total, was desertified. If we applied the Hobq model to all of China's desertified land, it would contribute USD $300 billion to China's 'Green GDP' and help reduce poverty for 200 million people in the dryland regions." To attract other investors to the desert, Wang laid great emphasis on the fast return of the ecological restoration business that "does not take two hundred years." With innovative strategies, he stressed, one can "compress the two hundred years into twenty, ten, or even five years."[41]

Wang's ecological projects in the desert has won recognition from China's national leaders. In 2007, the Elion Public Interest Foundation was selected by China's Ministry of Science and Technology, the State Forestry Administration, and the government of the IM Autonomous Region to establish a biannual "Kubuqi Forum" in Ordos, Central IM, with the joint mission of combating desertification and promoting the green economy. The Forum replaced the Mongolian name of the desert, Hobq, with the Chinese pronunciation "Kubuqi" as its official name in English. The biannual Forum is located in a resort complex named the "Seven Star Lake Scenic Area" in Hobq. Developed by Elion on dune fields, wetlands, and lakes in the heart of the Hobq Desert, the Seven Star Lake features ecological parks, botanical gardens, sand surfing arenas, swimming pools, and a luxury hotel mimicking the design of Abu Dhabi's seven-star luxury hotel, Emirate Palace. At the second biannual Kubuqi Forum in 2009, China's Minister of Science and Technology gave a keynote speech and praised the Kubuqi Model for its achievement in "changing from reactive to proactive sand control; shifting from conquering to utilizing nature; reversing from the pattern of 'the sand pushing people back' to that of 'people pushing the sand back' and turning the barren desert into green enterprises."[42]

With recognition from the national government, Wang proceeded to brand the Hobq Model internationally. In 2013, the Kubuqi Forum was formally recognized at the 11th Conference of the Parties of the United Nations Convention to Combat Desertification (UNCCD), the most authoritative international body on the matter, as mentioned in the Introduction. In 2015, UNCCD awarded Wang's Elion Resource Group the Land for Life Award. UNCCD recognized Elion's achievement in "improving the livelihoods of 100,000 farmers and herdsmen in the Kubuqi (Hobq) Desert ... transforming over 11,000 sq. km of degraded land into productive land." Elion's Green Silk Road Equity Investment Fund together with other private enterprises, were also commended by the UNCCD for advancing the environmental restoration project along the Silk Roads.[43] Wang's ecological conservation businesses spread from IM to China's other northern provinces and Central Asia.

Wang was a star on the national and international stage of combating desertification, but he was far from the sole green entrepreneur in China or the northwest. The northwest drylands had bred many smaller-scaled entrepreneurs active at the local level. An official in Central IM reported that almost all the ecological restoration projects in the Hobq Desert were contracted out to over 2,000 private firms, and that they have all found a "profitable business model."[44] Qi Chenghong (1962–) of Alxa League was one such local green entrepreneur. Qi, an ethnic Mongolian born in Alxa Left Banner, started out as a coal miner and then, after graduating from high school, became a mining technician, according to his autobiography.[45] Qi made his fortune by subcontracting a collectively owned coal mine in his home town in 1990 and became a coal boss at the age of 28. During the massive restructuring of collective enterprises in the mid-to-late 1990s, Qi bought failed liquor factories, consolidated the township talcum mines scattered across different villages, and expanded his business into resort tourism in Alxa Left Banner. Qi's business success also earned him quite a few political appointments and honors. He started out as Party Secretary of the CCP youth group in his village after high school. As his business expanded, he became a member of the Political Consultative Conference and of the People's Congress at the Banner level. He also served as the Vice Chair of the Business Association in both Alxa League and Alxa Left Banner. The integration of local economic and political elites in rural China was hardly a new trend in the 2000s. Qi's success in reviving failed collective enterprises and in keeping local jobs during the decline of the collective economy, coupled with his "diligence in paying taxes and fees" to the local government, earned him political recognition as a model businessman in Alxa Left Banner and in Alxa League. As Alxa Left Banner decided to forge a PPP with a private investor in the suosuo-congrong business, Qi was an ideal candidate to assume the role. His various honors and recognitions won him access to policy loans and government grants. By 2016, Qi built close to 700 sq. km of plantations of congrong and suoyang (*Cynomorii Herba*), another dryland medicinal plant, in four locations in Alxa Left Banner and a 2 sq. km-large Sand Industrial Park. Located in Bayanhot, the capital of Alxa League, Qi's Hongkui Congrong Group Company was showcased as the local government's achievement in productive conservation.

The company regularly received visits from inspecting officials, delegations from other provinces, environmental scientists, and journalists.

Qi's experience attests to a two-way convertibility of political and economic capital, framed in the broadly defined PPP scheme. By the end of 2017, China's PPP scheme boasted a planned investment of USD $1,500 billion in 6,808 projects nationwide. Yet it was also recognized as an ongoing experiment that was "making progress in improving managerial transparency."[46]

In the PPP scheme, local governments come up with projects that fit central policy directives and identify possible private partners who will secure policy loans and grants from central or provincial governments. The grants allow local governments to mortgage some of the project area for more policy loans, while the private partner acquires access to bank loans and otherwise restricted land, water, and control of the completed project. It is a financial collaboration between the local state that relies on project-based budgetary transfers and private companies looking for access to state funding and state-controlled resources.

In China's statist market economy, the size of capital corresponds with the rank of the capitalist's governmental partners. All private companies aspire to grow bigger and to be recognized by higher-level governments. As Wang and his US$16 billion behemoth Elion Group received national recognition, Qi's US$500 million operation became the pride of Alxa League, a jurisdiction two levels down from the national level on China's territorial hierarchy.

Regardless of the size of the green entrepreneurs, what makes their political capital essential is not just its convertibility into economic and financial benefits, but also its access to land and water under the regime of conservation. I will focus on land in this chapter and will address the politics of water under the regime of conservation in Chapters 3 and 4.

In the age of conservation, lacking access to sizable land parcels has been the primary barrier to expanding agro-business. Decollectivization and allocation of farmland and pastures have resulted in a highly decentralized structure of de facto land ownership in rural China. Scholars of agrarian studies, such as Philip Huang (2012), Ye, Jingzhong (2015), and Zhang, Qian (2015)[47] have written extensively on Chinese governments' agricultural modernization programs to create large-scale land lease markets aimed at expanding industrial agriculture. These scholars noted that the persistent dominance of small family farms has made it difficult to amass enough farmland for industrial agriculture. Zhang (2015)[48] has also pointed out that the lack of large land tracts has led local officials to turn their attention towards forestland and wetland. Often labelled as "wasteland," these tracts of land had not been subjected to land redistribution during decollectivization of the late 1980s. The "wasteland" in the hands of the local government was often under-demarcated, less fertile, and/or poorly located. But they could be readily mobilized for larger-scaled plantations under the policy calls while evading villagers' scrutiny.

Like their counterparts in other regions of China since the late 1980s, villagers in IM have kept small family farms and pastures, and the fragmented land ownership structure has made it challenging for investors and local governments to assemble land parcels large enough to establish plantations. In addition, environmental regulations and land use restrictions make it even harder to find land for plantations. In Alxa, the entire 270,000 sq. km of the league is divided into sandy desert, gravel gobi, and "desertified rangeland." Alxa league is on the list of "National Key Ecological Zones," and 94% of the League's land is in "ecologically fragile zones" with restricted access.[49] Under such land use restrictions, what is crucial in establishing plantations is the political justification that could unlock the restrictions. The desertification-combating suosuo shrub (often joined by other dryland cash crops) provides such justification.

In addition to its contribution to the environmental conservation cause, suosuo, with its partner congrong, is also considered a key poverty alleviator. In order to build the 6,000 sq. km mega plantation projects in the aforementioned Hobq Desert (10 times the size of Qi's project), Wang's Elion Group signed, through the local government's mediation, land lease agreements with multiple villages and more than 3,000 herder households who lost income to the conservation policies of destocking. For Elion, the wholesale land lease arrangement with multiple villages, not just individual households, helped to consolidate the fragmented land parcels and achieve the scale economy for plantations. Herders received cash compensation from the government for destocking and lease fees from Elion for land. The able-bodied worked as wage laborers on Elion's plantations. Elion also hired migrant workers from poor mountain regions of neighboring Gansu and Ningxia Provinces. In this way, conservation was linked with rural employment. The scheme of employing migrant farmers and herders in the plantations as wage labor, ecological compensation payments, and land lease fees were all included in local governments' calculation of rural families' income improvement under poverty alleviation programs. With these sources of income, Wang proclaimed, "herders would not have to continue overgrazing the pasture and destroying the environment."[50]

With the conservational and social contributions, building suosuo plantations in the name of combating desertification and alleviating poverty wins high-level government approval and endorsement. A government-recognized green entrepreneur would have a much greater chance of eluding restrictions to land and water in the "ecologically fragile zone." In short, the miraculous suosuo opens the door for large-scaled growth projects in a place designated for protection at the height of conservationism.

The Kubuqi model was widely hailed as a win-win solution for all. But Wang Wenbiao himself had a concern. The 3,000 herders' land, which the herders received as household contracted rangeland under rangeland decollectivization policies of the 1980s (see Chapter 2), had a life span of 30 years. The clock started in 1997. Elion leased herders' contracted land parcels and consolidated them into plantations in 2001 and 2002 and obtained the land use rights for the remaining time on the contracts. By 2014, as Elion's business prospered, there were only 13 years left in these land contracts. To protect his investment and control over the herders' contracted land, Wang has advocated fervently for land rights reforms in the desert. In his capacity as a member of the prestigious Political Consultative Committee at the national level, Wang has repeatedly proposed to extend herders' land contracts from 30, to 70, or even 100 years. Contradictory to his earlier claim that the sand industry offers fast returns, he now argued that conservation in the drylands of IM is a long-term commitment that needs the participation of private capital. As such, a stable land rights regime is a prerequisite for drawing more private capital into conservation endeavors. Wang also lobbied for national policymakers to grant private investors who hold contracted land a complete set of land rights, including the rights to use, derive profits from, sell, and mortgage the land.[51] While skillfully avoiding the politically sensitive term "privatization," Wang directed his argument to emphasize the special needs of conservation in the degraded drylands that necessitates a complete package of de facto land privatization.

III.2 An Environmental NGO

Local governments and green entrepreneurs are not the only actors drawn to the miraculous suosuo-congrong pair. Environmental Non-Government Organizations (ENGOs) have also come under its spell. One of the best-known and most well-funded domestic ENGOs in China, the Society of Entrepreneurs and Ecology (SEE), has been actively establishing suosuo-congrong plantations in Alxa since the late 2000s.

The SEE is a high-profile ENGO founded by celebrity real estate chief executive officer (CEO)s in 2004. By 2017, the SEE claimed a membership of over 800 members. While the leading members are real estate tycoons, the rest are entrepreneurs from various sectors of varied scales. The SEE attracts businesspeople who are concerned with the environment or seek membership in a prestigious social club, or both.

Funded by membership dues, the SEE's reputation as an organization of major league businessmen (and a few businesswomen) lends it greater influence compared to other domestic ENGOs in China.[52] In 2014, the SEE inaugurated its signature project to plant 100 million suosuo shrubs in the desert of Alxa.

The connection between the SEE and the miracle shrub suosuo was not love at first sight, however. A brief review of the way the SEE switched from other rural development projects to suosuo helps illuminate suosuo's power.

With leadership from some of China's most formidable real estate tycoons, the SEE has been assertive and vocal. In 2004, the SEE's first president was Liu Xiaoguang, Chairman of the Beijing Capital Group, a large state-owned real estate group worth US$45 billion and comprising of five listed companies that allegedly owned one of China's largest land reserves. Born in 1955 to the Cultural Revolution generation, Liu was one of the millions of Sent-Down youths to the countryside in the 1970s. Liu went on to lead Beijing's Economic Planning Committee in the 1990s before heading the state-owned Beijing Capital Group. He was a "socialist land master," on which I elaborated in my earlier work.[53] At the peak of his career in 2003, Liu traveled to Alxa for an investment opportunity at a desert resort called Moon Lake. A Beijing-based environmental activist, who was present at the time, reported that when Liu saw the desert for the first time, he "kneeled down in the sands under the moonlight, with tears in his eyes."[54] Before the visit, Liu's original idea was to establish a consortium to develop a desert golf course that could "help combat desertification while turning a profit."[55] But he changed his mind soon after. In his poem "Walking in the Desert," Liu wrote, "Rise up, Chinese entrepreneurs! Let us contribute our wealth and talents to our mother and the human race."[56] It is unclear whether the word "mother" referred to Mother Nature or Mother Nation, or both. In any event, under the leadership of the confident CEO of a powerful state-owned development company, the idea of creating a desert golf course was ditched. Instead, Liu decided to create an ENGO to combat desertification. The plan was announced at a preparation meeting among Liu and his entrepreneur friends on Valentine's Day, 2004. Liu was quoted to have called that meeting a "collective elopement" of China's entrepreneurs, as it was unprecedented at that time for entrepreneurs to get together and put money in nonprofit projects.[57]

The groundbreaking move of the SEE got off to a rocky start. Right after the "collective elopement," Liu was under state investigation and taken into custody several times in 2004 and 2005. Each time, he was released without charges. The reason for the investigations was never disclosed, and Liu has kept a low profile since then. Liu's political fall was followed by high turnover in SEE leadership. But the organization has demonstrated impressive perseverance and continued their projects to fix the desert. In 2017, having been diagnosed with cancer, Liu made his last trip to Alxa several months before he passed away at the age of 62. The last publicized picture of Liu shows him planting a suosuo seedling in the desert of Alxa.[58]

Liu's interests in the desert should not be confused with those of Wang and Qi, the green entrepreneurs presented earlier. When Wang and Qi talked about their suosuo-congrong plantations in the desert, it was a straightforward cost-benefit analysis. But Liu and his board members had a vision that was less quantifiable. At his inauguration speech in 2004, Liu declared that the goal of the SEE was to foster "new values, new ideals and new behaviors" of the Chinese people in order to save the environment."[59] The real estate tycoon-turned-desert enthusiast had envisioned an order taller than money.

During its first five years, the SEE devoted its resources to community-based poverty alleviation and alternative energy programs in the Alxa desert. The SEE hired college graduates to work with SEE's local project managers to build dairy cow co-ops, install biogas tanks, and distribute solar panels and stoves to villagers. In exchange, herders agreed to reduce their stock size and to refrain from collecting the wood in natural suosuo forests.

Political scientist Jessica Teets (2014)[60] has used "consultative authoritarianism" to describe the relationship between the state and NGOs in contemporary China. She argues that China's NGOs have found their place in what local governments were obligated, but unable, to do, rather than to provide alternative paths to government policies.

In IM, local governments welcomed the Beijing CEO-backed SEE community projects in Alxa, and they perceived the visiting CEOs as potential investors just as much as environmentalists. Aside from that, the SEE seems to fit Teets' description in many other ways. What the IM government saw as a benefit of the SEE's income-generating programs in the villages, mediated by enthusiastic fresh college graduate-turned-community workers, was the programs' potential to mediate tensions triggered by the government's unpopular conservation policies, such as grazing restrictions, grazing land enclosures, and ecological relocation (see Chapter 2).

A case in point was the SEE's dairy cow co-op project in a relocation village in Alxa. The village had been launching protests and lodging complaints against different levels of the local government prior to the SEE's arrival. The protests were fomented by undelivered promises of water provision and land allocation in the poorly located relocation sites at the edge of the desert under the government's conservation programs.[61]

Dairy cow husbandry was endorsed by local governments and ENGOs to replace open grazing in the deteriorated pastures of Alxa.[62] The young college graduates hired by the SEE lived in the village for months at a time and held numerous meetings with herders at different stages of the project. Under the SEE's design, the dairy cow program was meant to be a collective endeavor aimed at rebuilding the community. But to the dismay of the SEE staff, the "collaborative pastoralism" that they had expected to be a lasting pastoral tradition had long ceased to exist. When pastoral areas were decollectivized in the late 1980s and 1990s wherein stock and grazing land were redistributed among herder households, it triggered a wave of land consolidation into the hands of large and influential families, resulting in uneven land redistribution.[63] The loss suffered by many herder families during decollectivization only raised their suspicion of state-imposed changes. Moreover, the possibility of losing control over their stock, regardless of the labeling—decollectivization, recollectivization, or the fashionable "community building"—only further provoked their agitation. At a meeting about building a dairy cow co-op, a herder asked the SEE staff: "If I join the co-op and put my share in the co-op, how would I find out which leg of which cow belongs to me? And what about the calves that the cows produce? Who owns the calves?" After much compromise and negotiation, the SEE-sponsored dairy cow co-op was established, but not without disputes over chronic deficits, undelivered dividends, and allegedly fraudulent book-keeping. The widening income gap within the village in the rapidly changing rural economy only further deepened the distrust felt by co-op members.[64]

The Beijing-based SEE board was also concerned about project deliverability. The ideal of building community through collaborative projects required endless negotiations between the SEE headquarter in Beijing and its field office in Alxa, as well as negotiations among the SEE field office, Alxa's local governments at various levels, and individual herder families with divided interests and varied capacities. The community development projects that depended on SEE subsidies to attract herders' participation proved to be costly. Just as discerning was the fact that the result of SEE staff's hard work, even if it succeeded, was hardly visible. Like international NGOs that are held accountable to donors, the SEE had hundreds of business-minded members who wanted to see results. These results were not necessarily financial ones. Rather, the members wanted their investment in the desert to deliver measurable social benefits and to win the SEE sociopolitical recognition. By the end of the 2000s, the SEE leadership's patience with the community programs was wearing thin.

In the midst of its internal debates over their future direction, the SEE hired various consulting teams from Chinese research institutes and from the prestigious consulting firm, McKinsey, to perform project evaluations. Coming from different vantage points, these consultants arrived at a similar conclusion that the SEE's community projects had been distractions from its core mission of environmental conservation.[65]

Upon searching for greater deliverability, sociopolitical recognition, and conservation-focused projects, the SEE found the suosuo-congrong pair. In 2009, under new leadership, the SEE started a completely revamped project of planting 2 million mu (about 1,300 sq. km) of suosuo in the desert of Alxa and vowed to create "the largest suosuo forest in the world." In 2014, the SEE made another high-profile announcement that it would plant 100 million suosuo shrubs in 10 years.[66] By shifting to suosuo-led afforestation, the SEE largely abandoned the community projects of the earlier era. To reduce the SEE's financial burden and to sway villagers into buying in, literally and figuratively, the new suosuo project required village participants to contribute more than 70% of the costs in order to qualify for SEE subsidies. By contrast, the community projects, now abandoned, normally required 20% to 30% of matching funds from village participants.

The SEE's new projects with the new financial scheme were implemented at new sites too. This time, they selected villages where most of the villagers had not been subjected to forced relocation, as were the deprived and resentful Mongolian herders at the previous project sites. Rather, the new participants of the new SEE projects were located in villages dominated by second- or third-generation Han Chinese farmers in Alxa, who were descendants of the 1950s famine refugees from the neighboring province of Gansu.[67] At that time, the Han immigrants were granted membership in local collectives, settled in local pastoral villages, and became farmers or herders of camels and sheep. Compared to the recent relocated Mongolians in the SEE's previous project sites, the descendants of these Han immigrants, especially those with financial capacity and political connections, have exhibited much greater willingness to participate in the SEE's suosuo-congrong program.

In the summer of 2015, I went with two dryland environmental scientists to visit one of the SEE's suosuo-congrong project sites in a village in Alxa Left Banner. The village had 120 households and 340 registered residents. The local SEE project manager, a second-generation Han Chinese born in Alxa, told us that the SEE had planted 150,000 mu (10,000 hectares) of suosuo in Alxa Left Banner between 2012 and 2015, half of which were planted in 2015 alone. Thanks to El Niño, which brought heavier-than-usual precipitation in the arid western IM in 2014 and 2015, suosuo-congrong farms in Alxa had been successful. The SEE project manager also told me that "in this village, all those who are able to plant suosuo have done so."

We visited a herder-turned suosuo farmer, Hao. [68] Hao was in his late 50s and was featured in quite a few news reports on the SEE's suosuo-congrong projects in the desert. Also a second-generation Han immigrant, Hao had 10,000 mu of rangeland and 500 sheep and 30 camels in the 1990s. He relinquished most of the livestock under the policy of "retiring pastoralism" and destocking and left home to work in the city in 2005. In 2011, with the rising market price for congrong, Hao returned to the village and built a 7,000 mu suosuo-congrong farm on his contracted rangeland, financed by savings from working in the city and subsidies from the SEE.

Hao also received policy subsidies from other sources. The local SFA office offered him 100 yuan for every mu of suosuo that he planted. The Agriculture and Husbandry Bureau compensated him 10 yuan per mu for his loss in stock reduction. The SEE granted another 25 yuan per mu for suosuo plantation that met the 70% survival rate benchmark in the first year, then another 25 yuan per mu for the second year. Hao invested in earth-moving and hole-digging machines and bore regular expenses like suosuo seedlings, congrong seeds, water, and labor. Every spring Hao hired about a dozen seasonal workers from the neighboring Gansu Province to harvest congrong. His out-of-pocket costs averaged 10 yuan per mu.

The market for Hao's congrong was relatively secure, albeit monopolized, like most contract farming. A pharmaceutical company affiliated with the Chinese Medical University in Tianjin provided him with basic training on how to manually plant congrong seeds on suosuo roots. The company also built a congrong dehydration facility in the village. During the harvest season, the company would send a truck every few days to haul away all the congrong that the village plantations yielded. Hao told me the company was the only game in town and, hence, it dictated the price.

Hao's first harvest in 2014, three years after he started the plantation, earned him over 200,000 yuan net, averaging about 30 yuan net per mu.[69] Hu seemed optimistic about the future and planned on expanding his congrong farm in the coming years.

For Hao, a herder-turned migrant worker who had returned to the village for suosuo farming, investing in a suosuo-congrong plantation was economically more viable than other drought-tolerant policy crops previously promoted by the local government, such as millet or goji berries. In a place like Alxa, where labor is in short supply, the fact that suosuo-congrong farming requires only one-tenth of the labor input compared to that for millet farming is decisive. In the case of goji berries, although they have been in the government development program for over two decades throughout the arid northwest (see Chapter 4), the market is already saturated and has been dominated by the well-networked traders from the neighboring Ningxia Hui Autonomous Region. These Ningxia traders, according to another suosuo-congrong farmer, often blocked market entry of out-of-network producers and pushed down procurement prices. The government's and SEE's subsidies along with rising market demands made congrong a more promising investment for Hao. In a time of grazing land enclosures and grazing bans, growing congrong allowed Hao to continue using his contracted land for profitable production. The technical threshold for growing suosuo-congrong was low enough for Hao, a former herder who had little experience in crop farming. Running his own congrong farm, Hao reflected, also gave him the sense of autonomy that was missing when he labored in the city.

For the SEE, suosuo's stardom in conservation discourse helped improve program deliverability. Villagers' enthusiastic participation in commodity congrong farming made it easier and cheaper to cover a much larger project area in a relatively short period of time with the same amount of investment. Rebranded by the "One Hundred Million Suosuo" initiative, the SEE was able to retain its prominence in China's domestic ENGO world.

For local governments, suosuo-congrong plantations fulfilled the dual mandate of conservation and poverty alleviation, while concomitantly financing the otherwise under-funded task of afforestation in the desert. The profitability of congrong also incentivized local villagers to support afforestation. The consensus among local governments, private capital, and local villagers—at least those who could afford to participate—has helped expand suosuo plantations rapidly. By 2012, Alxa League had about 100,000 hectares of suosuo plantation, 16% of which were suosuo-congrong farms.[70] In the five years between 2016 and 2020, the Alxa League government reported to have added another 300,000 hectares of suosuo plantation.[71]

Encouraged by the suosuo-congrong boom, which is often referred to as "digging gold in the desert,"[72] the government leaders of Alxa League announced more development projects revolving around the power couple. In 2016, at the Alxa Ecological Sand Industry Summit, Alxa's Party Secretary announced his plan to establish a 1,000 sq. km "Ecological Sand Industry Model Development Zone" in the Ulan Buh Desert in eastern Alxa.[73] In 2017, quoting President Xi's statement that "lucid waters and lush mountains are invaluable assets like gold and silver," the governments of Alxa League and Alxa Left Banner hosted the Sand Industry Innovation Tournament, co-organized by China's Ministry of Science and Technology and its six provincial-level bureaus in the northwestern jurisdictions of IM, Ningxia, Gansu, Xinjiang, Qinghai, and Shaanxi. The categories of innovation in the tournament included ecological agriculture, renewable energy, healthcare, and ecotourism. But the event was decidedly organized around the success story of the congrong industry in Alxa. Congrong-related innovations in products and production technologies dominated the tournament statement to exemplify the spirit of innovation and the direction of productive conservation in the future. Sure enough, the team that focused on suosuo-congrong innovation won the championship in the tournament. Winners of the tournament were promised access to land, loans, and grants to set up businesses in Alxa.[74]

One jurisdictional rank below the Alxa League government, the Alxa Left Banner government also announced its own suosuo and congrong-led project, the "Sand and Health Industrial Science and Technology Park" and established "China's first sand industry venture capital." The Park was to attract investors to Alxa Left Banner and add values to congrong, turning raw materials into a variety of pharmaceutical products and health tourism programs. Tapping into China's growing demands for health products, the party secretary of the Banner pledged to "green the desert, increase GDP, improve enterprises' profits and farmers' and herders' income." The suosuo-congrong partnership, which started out in desert "wasteland," was now on a grand mission to "transform the agriculture, restructure the economy, and anchor the ecological construction" of China's dryland and to "improve the natural environment and expand the living space for the entire human race."[75]

III.3 Alibaba's Green Finance

Suosuo's persuasive power and popularity were not lost on the influential and charismatic business guru, Jack Ma. Ma was the executive chairman of the Alibaba Group Holding Ltd., the Chinese IT conglomerate listed on the New York Stock Exchange and one of the brightest stars in global e-commerce of the 2010s.[76] As of January 2018, Alibaba's market capitalization stood at US$527 billion, placing the company in the US$500 billion league together with Facebook and Amazon. Alibaba also became the second Asian company to break the US$500 billion mark, the first being Tencent Holdings Ltd., another Chinese internet conglomerate and Alibaba's primary rival.[77] To facilitate transactions for its hugely successful online shopping platform, Taobao, Alibaba launched a mobile payment platform called Alipay in 2004. It was China's first and largest third-party mobile payment platform. In 2013, Alipay reported US$150 billion in mobile transactions, compared to PayPal's US$27 billion that year, making Alipay the world's largest online payment platform.[78] Riding on the upswing tide, Alipay launched Ant Financial Services in 2014, a micro-lending platform. By June 2020, aided by the rapid growth of Ant Financial, Alipay had accrued over one billion annual users and 80 million merchants, and processed US$243 billion worth of transactions in China over the course of a year.[79]

The seemingly unstoppable Ant Financial was forced to slow down in early November 2020. In less than 48 hours before its scheduled, US$35 billion-worth Initial Public Offering (IPO) (which grew from the 2018 projection of US$5 billion), Chinese regulators suspended Ant Financial's "hotly anticipated" flotation. Stories about the CCP state putting its foot down on China's big capitals are not novel. What is less told is how a non-state financial-technology firm like Ant Financial had expanded in China's statist market economy in the first place. How did Ant Financial grow to the point of being a paramount target of the state disciplinary action in late 2020?

Suosuo played an important role in Ant's bid for global championship in financial technology (fintech from here on). Noting the business success of the suosuo-congrong duo as well as its "green" bona fides, Ma and his strategists found a way to mobilize suosuo for Ant.

III.3.1 Turning a Virtual Game Real

In August 2016, in the midst of the fierce competition between Alipay and WeChat Pay—and between Alibaba and Tencent behind them—Ant Financial released a new app named "Ant Forest." Ant Forest provides Alipay users with a carbon baseline against which users can earn "green energy points" when they reduce their carbon footprint, such as when they pay utility bills, buy movie tickets online, walk or use bike-share services, ride the subway to work, or use Alipay as a cash card for shopping offline. All these activities are carried out on Alipay's platform. Once the users accumulate sufficient green energy points, they are able to plant a virtual tree in the virtual Ant Forest. The tree planted in Ant Forest is none other than suosuo, the star shrub and the ultimate answer to combating desertification in China.

The premise of Ant Forest is similar to that of the addictive social media game "Happy Farm" from the late 2000s. Happy Farm was a massive multiplayer online game that simulated farm management. Predominantly played by users in Mainland China and Taiwan, Happy Farm was developed by a startup called Five Minutes, which was later acquired by Tencent. At its peak, Happy Farm boasted 23 million daily active users who competed with one another to grow virtual vegetables online. But Ant Forest went one step further and turned the virtual game real. Partnering with the aforementioned ENGO, SEE, which is devoted to planting 100 million suosuo in Alxa, Ant Financial converted users' virtual trees into real suosuo shrubs in the Alxa desert. The virtual game became real conservation action. To bring the real-yet-remote forest closer to the urban suosuo gamer-growers, each seedling would come with a certificate that contained a serial number affiliated with individual growers and each gamer-grower received achievement records (Figures 1.5 and 1.6).

On the Ant Forest app, growers can see photos and a live-stream video of the suosuo forests in Alxa (Figure 1.7). The video is accompanied by information about the changing temperature, humidity level, and atmospheric pressure of the forest, updated every 15 minutes, 24/7. Active suosuo growers were invited to visit the actual suosuo forests in Alxa. As visitors reported live updates online from the desert, their voices intermittently broke off as a result of gusty desert winds interrupting their internet connection, which only served to "make it feel more authentic," an Ant Forest gamer commented.[80] As the gamer-growers now felt directly connected with the physical tree plantations in the desert thousands of kilometers away, Ant Forest helped transform a placeless virtual game to place-making action.[81]

By August 2017, a year after the app was launched, Ant Financial reported that over 230 million users (60% of whom were under the age of 28) had signed up for Ant Forest. Together these users had planted over 10 million suosuo shrubs. By Ant's calculation, these online tree growers had also reduced 1.22 million tons of CO_2 emissions.[82]

According to a survey conducted by Ant Financial, 90% of the gamer-growers joined Ant Forest for fun, and 50% joined due to environmental concerns.[83] In 2018, an earnest graduate student from Shanghai told me, "I felt very proud each time I accumulated enough green energy points to sow a suosuo seed on Ant Forest."[84] As he earned more points from using various apps on the Alipay platform, he could watch the seed grow into a small tree and then into a big tree on his smart phone (Figure 1.8). His sense of achievement grew with the tree. Similarly, a Beijing-based

Figure 1.5 Screenshots of the certificate for an Ant Forest gamer/suosuo grower (the name on the certificate is fictional). The top line of the certificate reads "*Certificate for Citizens who have fulfilled their obligation of planting trees voluntarily*." The two red seals read: "*Office of National Greening Committee*" and "*The Chinese Greening Foundation.*" The white text in the green button at the bottom says "Share."

professional in her late 30s was keen on earning carbon-credit-turned-energy-points by walking or taking the subway instead of driving to work. In 2019, she told me that she felt that joining Ant Forest for the environment was the socially responsible thing to do.[85] A young father in Fujian Province planted a virtual-real suosuo when his daughter was born. He believed that his suosuo and his daughter "share the same future."[86]

Most Chinese mobile payment users keep both Alipay and WeChat Pay apps on their smartphones, and most online and offline merchants accept both. However, Ant Forest suosuo growers often have Alipay open most of time to keep track of their energy points after each transaction and to watch their suosuo shrubs grow on their phone screens. Ultimately, it is growing suosuo that keeps customers on Alipay's platform.

Figure 1.6 An Ant Forest gamer/suosuo grower's achievement records shown on their smartphone screen. The text reads, from top to bottom: "New Year's Good Fortune Forest of 2019"; "Thank you, Wang Xiaoming" (fictional name); "You have watered and contributed energy to the Good Future Forest. Together with other growers, you have [collectively] planted 3,962,205 trees in Horqin Right Middle Banner of Inner Mongolia and other places. You have planted new hope in the new year." The circled number is the serial number of the forest guardian (i.e., the gamer/grower). The two figures below the circle indicate that the gamer/grower has accumulated 290 grams of energy and virtually watered the plant 29 times. The text at the bottom of the screen says "Share."

Urban suosuo gamer-growers use Alipay's built-in social media platforms to share tips on how to score higher carbon credits and energy points in order to grow more suosuo seedlings. They also use social media to flaunt their suosuo planting records and to "steal" green energy points from one another, much reminiscent of stealing vegetables on the Happy Farm game. Suosuo mediates interactions among friends on the platform and becomes a source of social capital. Special rankings and awards are granted on a daily basis to honor those who score the most green energy points and who have planted the most suosuo seedlings in that day and week. Suosuo gamer-growers urge friends and families to switch from WeChat Pay to Alipay so as to grow suosuo and save the planet. According to Ant Financial's report, 50% of the 280 million tree growers have recommended Ant Forest to friends and families.[87] Many online games have their ways of turning the virtual real for monetary returns, but growing suosuo elevates gamers to a higher moral ground: for many

Figure 1.7 Screenshots of the live-streamed video of suosuo plantations. The figures indicate atmospheric pressure, UV index and humidity. Numbers 95, 102, 109, and 111 indicate different forests.

gamers, they feel that they are playing for the public good, not just for personal benefit. At a time when heavily polluted air is palpably felt by many Chinese people, the conservation aspect of the game has attracted both gamers and non-gamers alike.

Building on the initial triumph in Alxa, Ant Financial started to expand its Ant Forest to other regions. These included the Hobq Desert in Central IM, where Ant Financial partnered with Elion Resource Group's Wang Wenbiao, the green entrepreneur introduced earlier in this chapter, to expand Ant Forest on Wang's plantations. Ant Forest also diversified from suosuo to other species of dryland plants, including huyang (*Populus euphratica Olive*) and zhangzisong (*Pinus sylvestris var. mongolica Litv.*). But these new species on Ant Forest require 10 to 12 times more green energy points than do suosuo. The much higher thresholds mean that individual Ant Forest tree gamer-growers may need more than a year to accumulate enough credit to grow a single tree—unless they join forces with other player-growers. Ant Forest managers encourage tree growers to pool their carbon credits together in group projects to grow these more "costly", in-vogue species in the new desert sites, see Figure 1.9.[88]

Figure 1.8 Watching your tree grow on the smartphone

When friends in virtual chatrooms and real dorm rooms compare notes, compete, or collaborate with one another to plant trees in the Ant Forest that represents ethical consumption, the fun online game becomes socially rewarding. What is interesting to note is that throughout Ant Forest's campaigns, congrong, suosuo's indispensable partner, would rarely be mentioned. Congrong may be the rainmaker that drives the suosuo fever, but the commercial side of the suosuo story is unlikely to compel the young urban Alipay users.

As suosuo gamer-growers' number of green energy points, sense of achievement, and social connectedness grew, Ant Financial's customer base grew with it. The exploding growth of suosuo growers in the real and virtual Ant Forests also helped place Ant Financial on the global stage of the conservation agenda. In January 2017, Ant Financial Services Group and the UN Environment Program (UNEP) co-founded the Green Digital Finance Alliance, which launched at the World Economic Forum in Davos. That year, Ant Financial also placed sixth out of 56 companies on *Fortune* magazine's "Change the World" list. Ant Financial was recognized as having "changed the world for the positive environmental impact of its Ant Forest, which is now the world's largest platform for tracking individuals' carbon footprint."[89]

Changing the world or not, the fact that a virtual tree-planting app acquired 280 million users in 16 months, and that the app was launched by a company that affiliated itself with the tiny and humble ant instead of the gigantic and majestic dragon that is common in corporate branding, is not to be taken lightly. What is the big deal about a tiny ant?

Figure 1.9 Friends can plant trees together in Ant Forest. The text reads, (from top to bottom): Title text: "Initiate Group Tree-Planting." Dialog: "I can finally plant trees with my boyfriend." "Planting Huyang trees (see Chapter 2) is no longer a dream." (Man on right): "We note our love in green"; (Woman on left): "I can plant trees with my pal." (Second to last line): "Add the color green to Earth; make the sky bluer." The bar at the bottom reads "Initiate group tree-planting."

III.3.2 The Mighty Ant

In 1930, facing detrimental setbacks from the CCP's armed uprisings in the cities, Mao told the pessimistic Red Army leader, General Lin Biao, that "a single spark can start a prairie fire" and decisively shifted the base of the Communist Revolution to the countryside, home to 80% of the Chinese population at the time. The rest, as we know, is not just history. Mao went on to take over China, while the nonbeliever, General Lin, died in a mysterious plane crash in 1971.

Strategies in facilitating a massive number of small transactions—the commercial version of mass mobilization for customer acquisition—were what backed Ant Financial's successful suosuo planting campaign. According to its CEO, Eric Jing, without quoting Mao, whose name was not necessarily fashionable in the world of fintech, the company named itself Ant for its belief in the power of the common people.[90] Starting out in 2004, Alipay—the originator of Ant Financial—was modeled after PayPal and set up to facilitate transactions on Taobao, Alibaba's extraordinarily successful online shopping site for small vendors and shoppers.

A decade later, Alipay grew into the fintech empire Ant Financial, covering a full spectrum of financial services from mobile and online payment, money market funds, wealth management, digital-only banking, credit scoring, a consumer credit portal, insurance services, crowd funding, and cloud technology platforms. But its vision has not changed. Ant Financial aims to construct a galaxy of small yuan transactions by the common people. Calling it "inclusive finance," Ant has taken advantage of China's proliferation of digital and smart devices to meet the "latent demands" of "underserved customers," namely, small businesses and consumers in both the city and the countryside—a market that traditional banks had long neglected.[91]

The online mobile payment platform, Alipay, consistently accounts for over 60% of Ant's revenue streams. In the second quarter of 2016, it boasted 439 million active buyers and 8.5 million sellers, and a gross merchandise volume of US$126 billion. The money market fund, another platform under Ant Financial, attracts users to invest their residual cash flow at interest rates 40% higher than most Chinese banks (but the rates lower after the first 18 months). In the beginning, the money market fund aimed to convince mobile payment users to park their "residual cash" in the fund and allowed users to withdraw funds anytime, thus turning consumers into "invesumers." It has since grown into the world's largest money market fund with a balance of US$165 billion and a user base of 300 million in the first quarter of 2016.[92] Its microlending portal, which offers unsecured and uncollateralized loans to small businesses, boasted 5 million participating small business and individual entrepreneurial users by 2015. The average loan was for US$2,700, but the aggregate volume reached US$130 billion in 2017.[93]

The missing piece in the staggering figures of "inclusive finance" is Ant's risk management. How does the company handle such an astronomical number of small transactions while minimizing fraud? The answer lies in their wealth of data and data-processing capacity.

Alibaba and Ant Finance together offer a wide range of daily service platforms displayed in a neat grid of icons, a set of third-party "mini apps" organized under the Alipay super app. A user does not need to leave the platform to order food delivery, transfer money, hail a taxi, find a restaurant (and coupons), buy movie tickets, get a quick loan, pay back credit debt, top-up mobile phone balances, make doctors' appointments, pay for parking, car insurance, and utility bills, chat with friends, or even buy a new refrigerator online or an onion pancake from a street vendor offline. Alibaba and Ant Financial either directly own, invest in, or partner with these mini-app platforms. The joint power of Alibaba and Ant Financial is likened to "as if Amazon had swallowed the e-commerce companies like eBay, Apple News, Groupon, American Express, Citibank, YouTube, Facebook, Uber, and more."[94] Most importantly, Ant Financial has access to real-time data from all these platforms. As the major platform under Ant Financial, the Alipay super app is an interconnected and increasingly comprehensive "ecosystem" of platforms and data-collection points that help Ant Financial understand, predict, and shape the behavior of its hundreds of millions of users.

Once customers are active on one or two platforms, they are likely to expand to other platforms on Alipay's super app, thus developing customer "stickiness," and accelerating Ant Financial's customer acquisition. As Ant Financial and Alibaba continue to cover more of the "common people's" quotidian operations and incorporate them into the super app, Ant's CEO envisions the company not just being fintech, but as a lifestyle-enabling "finlife" company.[95]

The ever-expanding volume of real-time personal financial, consumption, and social data is further integrated with public data, such as criminal records, citizen identification information, and academic profiles, as well as with data provided by private partners in the car rental and hotel industries. The vast volume of data—of unprecedented breadth and depth—are processed by Alibaba's AI and data analytics platform, AlibabaCloud. Taking the late-mover advantage, Alibaba leapfrogged into adopting state-of-the-art data technologies and now boasts a concurrent processing capability of a record-breaking 120,000 transactions per second at its peak, compared with Visa's 14,000 per second. In addition, Alibaba's low transaction fees are attractive: fees for online payment, footed by the merchant, are 0.6% of the purchase value, far lower than the standard 3% transaction fee in the U.S. [96]

Leveraging the countless number of transactions on Ant Financial and Alibaba and troves of public data, Ant has created powerful credit-profiling capabilities. Its microlending portal can approve a loan in one minute without any human intervention, and it declares a fraud loss rate of one out of every 100,000 transactions, compared with leading U.S. credit card companies' rate of one out of every 100 and U.S. online payment companies' rate of one out of every 1,000.[97] Ant's credit-scoring platform, Zhima (which means "sesame seed" in Chinese) Credit, is the largest comprehensive credit-scoring system in China.

Given the lack of other nationwide credit-scoring systems and Alibaba's reputation as a trustworthy company, Zhima Credit has been widely accepted. High credit scores on Zhima yield benefits and special privileges in daily life, such as renting vehicles or even apartments without security deposits, expedited hotel checkouts, fast-tracked visa applications for international travel, exemptions from asset statement requirements, and the privilege of borrowing an umbrella at convenience stores without a deposit. The higher the credit score, the company proclaimed, "the more trustworthy you are, and the more doors that will magically open for you."[98] Indeed, this is where the name of the platform, "Zhima," or sesame, came from. Like the name of the mother company Alibaba, it evokes the story of Ali Baba and the Forty Thieves, in which the incantation, "open sesame," magically unveils a cave full of treasures.

One of the most telling and unexpected examples of the power of Ant and the extensive sociocultural reach of Ant Financial is the application of Ant's scoring system in China's marriage market. China's One-Child Policy, which started in 1979, has led to sex-selective abortion of female babies. Between 2010 and 2015, the United Nations (UN) Population Division reported that China's sex ratio at birth was 116 boys to 100 girls, far above the natural rate of 105 to 100.[99] This skewed sex ratio at birth has created an immense gender gap of single adults. In 2014, China's National Bureau of Statistics announced that there were 33.76 million more men than women in China. The sex ratio of singles at the age of 45 and older was 206 to 100. For the cohort between 35 and 45, the ratio was 136 to 100.[100] This gender gap, further exacerbated by other factors, including the fact that women are now better educated than their mothers and grandmothers and tend to marry later, if at all, has created a "marriage squeeze" that is historically and globally unprecedented, and even more acute than in India, according to *The Economist.* It was estimated that for every 100 single women expected to marry in 2050 to 54, there could be as many as 186 single men, and over 21% of Chinese men will still be unmarried by age 50 in 2070.[101]

With the marriage squeeze come swindlers who take advantage of men's anxiety and desperation to find a wife. Mistrust of potential matches' online photos and claims is rampant. The anonymity of members on dating sites only further magnifies trust issues in cyberspace. Online chat rooms are flooded with complaints and grievances posted by heartbroken match-seekers who have been catfished by dates whom they met online. Some women have used the site to get men to pay for excessively high-priced drinks and meals at bars that had hired the women as bait. Others turned out to be selling various commodities, including insurance and sex, and still others simply extorted money, favors, and gifts from desperate wife-seekers.[102] The situation was "destabilizing" enough that in 2015, China's Cyberspace Administration launched a campaign to shut down 128 dating sites that "seriously violated the rules and were untrustworthy." The web-based matchmaking industry was discredited. But China still has tens of millions of singles, especially men, looking for a match. And they are not just looking for any match, but marriage-worthy matches who are socioeconomically compatible.

Zhima scoring happens to meet the needs of tens of millions of those navigating the perilous marriage market. Dating and marriage sites have started to require members' Zhima scores to prove their trustworthiness and overall marriageability. Those with high Zhima scores receive more inquiries than they can respond to, while those at the lower end (mostly low-income and migrant workers without a stable address, records of frequent uses of Alipay apps, and/or a continuous credit history) receive few messages from potential dates, if at all.[103] A white-collar male worker in his mid-30s told me: "without a Zhima score over 750, I could not even dream of finding a wife."[104]

The power of Ant Financial lies in its penetrating reach into the everyday lives of 450 million Alipay users, supported by its algorithms in the cloud. The expansion in real and virtual Ant Forests in the desert is a manifestation of such power.

The Ant Forest's army of 280 million suosuo gamer-growers is not just the result of conservation mobilization, as the SEE had tried to launch. Nor does Ant Forest's campaign enjoy tangible products, like congrong, which green entrepreneurs and local governments in the northwest focus on. Instead, Ant Forest's suosuo campaign is a textbook case of a data economy rooted in mass society operating under what anthropologist William Mazzarella (2017) has called the "magic of persuasion."[105] Planting suosuo has caught the public's imagination as a tangible act of environmental protection at the very moment when air quality across China, especially its metropolitan centers, was becoming a pressing concern. Riding on its magic of persuasion, the humble dryland shrub rose up to lead a massive customer acquisition campaign on the ever-expanding super app of an e-commerce empire.

While Ant Forest expanded in cyberspace and physical places across China, Ant Financial strove to build its brand as a visionary fintech leader with a strong sense of social responsibility and environmental commitment. The company has proclaimed that one's personal carbon assets on Alipay, via Ant Forest and Ant's other programs, hold unlimited financial potentials in a future where "everyone will have three accounts: a credit account, a cash account, and a carbon account."[106] Ant was set to make environmental conservation financially productive for the masses.

The statement, catchy as it might sound, should not be dismissed entirely as a sales pitch. According to Cecilia Springer, a researcher on China's carbon market, or carbon dioxide (CO_2) emission trading system (ETS), as the world's largest CO_2 emitter, China could have an immense carbon market.[107] The Chinese government has committed significant resources to building a national carbon market since 2013. The State Forestry Administration, now called State Forestry and Grassland Administration (SFGA), has also monetized the carbon credits associated with afforestation projects, like that of Ant Forest, through other carbon offset programs since 2018. Springer suggests that as China's national carbon market becomes more established, it is possible that Ant Financial could participate in the trade of carbon offsets, called the China Certified Emission Reduction (CCER) program, which makes up a significant portion of the national carbon market. To prepare for the trade, Ant Forest has laid down the groundwork for monitoring, reporting, and verification (MRV), and taken the initial steps to quantify and certify the carbon credits that have accumulated on its super apps and real forests. Of course, Ant still has a long way to go before it can participate in the national carbon trade. The loose requirements of offset projects, which could lead to an oversupply of offsets without reducing carbon dioxide emissions while bringing down offset prices, might be tightened by Chinese regulators.[108] It is also far-fetched to expect Ant's hundreds of millions of carbon credit holders to participate in the offset market as individual traders. However, given the government's desire to build a national ETS with diverse institutional participants, Springer speculated that Ant Financial could get involved as an institutional trader on behalf of the numerous individuals and through its real and ever-expanding Ant Forest. Springer also suggests that Ant Financial might be able to participate in China's carbon trade by lending its operational experience and capacity in managing carbon projects.

In February 2018, less than two years since the launch of Ant Forest, Ant Financial announced its IPO plans to raise US$5 billion, which could value the company at US$100 billion.[109] Around the same time, the Cambridge Analytica/Facebook big data scandal broke.[110] The scandal has led to mounting consumer wariness in different parts of the world and more stringent regulation on data harvesting in some regions. In China, there were concerns over Alibaba's exploitation of big data and its connection with the government's national social credit system. By emphasizing the positive connection among big data, common people, and social equity, Jack Ma seemed to have dodged the bullet.[111] Alibaba and Ant Financial continued to envision big and green, and their numerous "invesumers" continued to bet on Ant's vision. According to the National Key Lab of Urban and Regional Ecology at the Chinese Academy of Science, tree growers of Ant Forest have nearly doubled from 280 million in 2017 to 550 million in 2020. As of early 2020, with the ground support of the SEE and other ENGOs, Ant Forest has planted more than 223 million real trees covering 2.9 million mu, which is close to 200,000 hectares, of tree plantations across China's 11 provinces.[112]

Then came forceful state intervention in late 2020. In less than 48 hours before its scheduled start of trading in Hong Kong and Shanghai on November 5, Ant Financial's IPO was abruptly halted by state regulators on account of its alleged violations relating to "disorderly expansion of capital."[113] Shares in Alibaba that owned a third of Ant tumbled by 8% upon the announcement of the suspension.[114] The halting that turned "the world's biggest IPO" of US$35 billion into "the world's biggest suspended IPO"[115] had dealt a major blow on not just Alibaba and its Ant, but also other non-state financial giants as well as those emergent operators.[116] After the suspension, the outspoken Jack Ma, who was known to be critical of the government's innovation-stifling red tape, disappeared from public view. Ant Financial scaled back its lending operations and dropped the word "financial" from its name and became Ant Group. In July 2021, seven months after Ant's suspended IPO, China's carbon market, the ETS, was formally launched after a decade of planning and delay. By 2022, Alibaba's valuation had fallen by about 70%. Ant seemed to have missed the train.[117]

But the resilience of Ant and the power of Suosuo is not to be underestimated. With a scaled-back lending operation, the rebaptized Ant Group has been holding tight onto its Forest. By 2022, an online report stated that over 600 million Alipay users have contributed to planting 326 million trees over a total area of 3.97 million mu, or 265,000 hectares. It was a 36% increase in afforested area since Ant's IPO suspension two years prior. The author calculated that Ant's online and offline green initiatives have contributed to reducing 12 million tons of carbon annually, and Ant's carbon offset revenue was estimated to be 3 billion yuan per year once it starts to trade.[118] In late 2022, the Chinese government was set to fine Ant Group over US$1 billion. The steep ticket was read as a sign that Ant might be on its way to finally get a financial holding company license, paving the way to relaunch its IPO.[119] On March 28, 2023, after Jack Ma's returned to China after his year-long stay in Japanese hot spring and ski resorts, Alibaba announced its plan to split the company into six units, which was, again, perceived as a precursor to IPO. The next day, the stock price of Alibaba opened at 14% higher than the previous day.[120] While the relationship between the CCP state and big capital continues to evolve, the promise of Alibaba's suosuo-derived green finance lives on.

IV Desert under Miracle's Rule

The spread of suosuo plantations can be explained by local government officials' political motivations, private capital's commercial interests, an ENGO's search for sociopolitical recognition, and some herders' willingness and capacity to participate in the program. Together with its rainmaking partner, congrong, suosuo promised to advance the policy mandates of poverty alleviation, combating desertification, and maintaining social stability in China's northwest. As suosuo turned into an icon on Ant Financial's super app, the magic algorithm of Ant Financial, now Ant Group, brought more people under its spell, which had seemed to outlive the political life of Jack Ma. The desert shrub has become a cultural symbol of China's "ecological civilization." Planting suosuo is an incontrovertible act.

Some online commentators saw Ant Forest as Ant Group's business strategy to increase customer stickiness or to speculate on the carbon market. But they have invariably come to the conclusion that "regardless of Ant's commercial motivations, it never hurts to plant more trees in the desert."[121] Similarly, even the most vocal environmentalists in China, who tend to be critical of the government's environmental practices of building mega-dams and monoculture afforestation, have endorsed suosuo plantations in Alxa desert.[122] The miraculous suosuo shrub seemed to have possessed the moral leverage that could redeem the credibility of greedy capitalists and shortsighted government officials.

But even miracles can be imperfect. For a start, as mentioned in the Introduction, the confusion between deserts and desertification has led to the popular conviction that the desert is naturally defective and, thus, in chronic need of repair. Under the color-coded conservationism and territorial expansionism that has long informed China's regime of afforestation, turning the yellow desert green is both the means and the ends to conservation in the northwest.

Suosuo plantations are deeply entrenched in this conviction. Suosuo's vaunted status in conservation, which is decidedly reinforced by its profitable partner, congrong, has facilitated the expansion of the conservation regime in the desert. Compared with the thirsty poplar tree (nick named "water-guzzler") that was popular in the afforestation programs in much of northern China, suosuo is hailed as a drought- and saline-tolerant northwest native. It is a model species for correcting previous wrongs. The reputation of suosuo as being environmentally correct and corrective has gained suosuo plantations the access to land and water that would have been otherwise highly restricted in the "desertified" area under protection.

Suosuo's sacred status secures its absolute rule in the desert under the regime of productive conservation. Such rule renders the negative impact of suosuo planation invisible and unchallenged. A China-based dryland environmental scientist,

Chen,[123] explained to me the negative environmental impacts of suosuo plantations in the desert. In our conversation, Chen started out by endorsing the practice of planting suosuo between the desert and farming areas as a windbreak to protect the farms. This interface area is where fixed or semifixed sand dunes become mobile due to cultivation expansion. Artificial suosuo forests can contribute to stabilizing the mobile dunes and decelerating wind speed. But in the interior of the desert, the ground's surface—be it the gravel gobi or small-grained sandy soil—has formed a thin crust on top that keeps the loose sand underneath in place. Planting trees, especially on a massive scale and at high density like a suosuo plantation, will cause irreversible damage to the surface crust and topsoil of the dryland. When the surface crust that serves to stabilize the sandy soil underneath it is damaged by the plantations, larger and more frequent sandstorms ensue.

In the Hobq Desert, for example, where Elion's UNCCD-award-winning Kubuqi model was located, the plantations extend far beyond the interface between the desert and villages, where suosuo plantations could help. Instead, they reach the heartland of the desert, where suosuo plantations would damage. Remember, Elion's desert control formula followed the principles of "locking down the borders of the desert, penetrating into the heart of the desert, dividing the desert by roads, and controlling the desert block by block." As mentioned earlier, Elion has built a 234 km-long road network in the Kubuqi Desert. The paved and tree-lined roads are critical for transporting water, seedlings, supplies, and labor to the expansive plantations. Elion's "ecological industrial park" in the desert is also enabled by other construction projects, such as photovoltaic power stations, irrigation systems, and permanent structures for housing, processing and storage facilities; not to mention the resort complex in the desert next to a 6,000 sq. km suosuo plantation. The plantations and auxiliary construction projects have greatly damaged the original ground cover and the topsoil of semifixed sand dunes in the heart of the desert, turning the dunes mobile.

The SEE's "One Hundred Million Suosuo" program in Alxa is similarly worrisome. A large part of the SEE-sponsored suosuo-congrong plantations owned by local herders are built upon the gravel gobi between the dune fields of the Badain Jaran and Tengger Deserts. Before the large-scale suosuo-congrong plantations were established, the coarse and crusty surface of the gobi gravel and its flat, open topography formed a passage to transport airborne sand between neighboring dune fields. This way, the airborne sand would not sink and pile up in the gobi to form new sand dunes; the gravel gobi between dune fields effectively prevents the two vast sandy deserts, Badain Jaran and Tengger, from morphing into a gigantic one. The joint force of the two deserts, once connected and formed a gigantic one, could lead to much more frequent and destructive sandstorms.

The large acreage of high-density suosuo-congrong plantations in the heart of the gravel gobi has disturbed this mechanism. With deep and numerous holes to plant seedlings, the plantation punctures the gobi's otherwise encrusted surface and exposes loose sand underneath. Densely planted suosuo seedlings in the ground decelerate ground wind. Airborne sand falls on the now sandified ground of the gobi and small sand piles accumulate at the feet of each suosuo seedling. It does not take long before these numerous small sand piles merge with one another, forming larger and taller dunes, and eventually amounting to sizable mobile sand dunes, which in turn aggravate sandstorms. The original argument in favor of suosuo rested on its ability to "stabilize the desert." But suosuo planted in the desert interior, at a density at least 10 times higher than in the natural suosuo forest, itself becomes a source of instability (see Figures 1.3 and 1.4).

Planting congrong on the roots of suosuo plants creates an even greater disturbance to the encrusted surface of the gobi. Each suosuo seedling is set in a hole between 1 and 1.5 meters deep, accompanied by three more holes of the same depth around it to sow congrong seeds. In plantations, the drilling is done by earth-moving machines. On average, 11 seedlings are planted for every mu of a congrong farm, creating 44 holes per mu. Hu, the congrong farmer introduced earlier, dug 308,000 holes of 1 to 1.5 meters deep each on his 7,000 mu farm, all in close proximity to one another. In addition to suosuo, other trees are planted to provide windbreaks and to protect the roads and other infrastructure in and around the plantations. Together the new plants and the associated infrastructure cause colossal damage to the tenuous topsoil of the dryland.

Chen observed that since the mid-2010s, as the suosuo-congrong fever escalated, the frequency and magnitude of sandstorms in western IM, which were under better control by the end of the 2000s, have picked up again. This observation was echoed by a journalist's report in 2016, entitled "The return of sandstorms in Alxa."[124]

Water is another concern. Suosuo's reputation as a "drought-tolerant" plant created the impression that suosuo lives only off of air. In reality, the suosuo-congrong farms require heavy watering and fertilizing, just like any commodity crop. The seedlings need regular watering to establish their roots, especially in the high-density plantations. In a natural suosuo forest, when the density of parent and young plants reaches a certain level, some of the young plants die and the forest naturally thins out and the overall health of the forest is maintained. But in a suosuo-congrong plantation, regular watering ensures the growth of the seedlings for the first two years. Then farmers drill holes around the suosuo in order to plant congrong seeds onto the roots of the matured suosuo plants. More watering is needed to ensure the growth of the congrong on the suosuo's roots. The suosuo-congrong farmer Hu explained to me: "each watering helps the suosuo roots and congrong seeds smell and connect with one another under the ground."

Again, the water comes from underground. In both the Kubuqi Model Park and the SEE's "One Hundred Million Suosuo" project in Alxa, there exists a locational advantage of groundwater availability in the initial stage of the projects. Scientist Chen suggested that the Kubuqi Model has been successful thus far because of its proximity to the Yellow River Loop[125] and the relatively high groundwater level south of the Loop, where suosuo-congrong plantations are built. But Chen warned of the negative long-term implications of groundwater depletion. The annual water consumption of the allegedly water-saving suosuo-congrong farms average 100,000 liters of water per mu, compared with corn's 80,000 and alfalfa's 70,000. The amount of water needed to support the millions of mu of suosuo-congrong farms that are already built or planned to be built far exceeds the water reserves and rate of groundwater replenishment in both Hobq and Alxa. Once the groundwater is depleted and/or investment is withdrawn, which has happened in many other dryland areas, the suosuo-congrong farms will collapse and the artificially planted suosuo will die out. In the case of Alxa's suosuo-congrong farms, most of the new farms were built on the alluvial fan, an area where surface runoff feeds the underground aquifers of the watershed. Extracting large amounts of groundwater for the suosuo farms on the alluvial fan would affect the entire watershed.

How do the new plantations gain access to large amounts of water at a time when water use is severely restricted under the regime of conservation? The answer lies in suosuo-congrong duo's lofty reputation as a magical fix for both conservation and poverty alleviation. The suosuo-congrong farms were granted special permits to drill deep wells in areas that were otherwise practicing tight water extraction restrictions. The door had also been opened to allow congrong farming in the natural suosuo forest, which was otherwise sealed off as a protected zone. The expansion of congrong farming has also damaged the natural suosuo forests. The mother plants in the natural suosuo forests are generally healthier and more productive than their counterparts in the suosuo plantation. Plantation managers collect suosuo seeds from protected natural suosuo forests and plant them in plantations, harming the natural forest's regeneration. Other growers have been less patient and do not wait for the young suosuo plants to grow in the plantation, instead planting congrong seeds on the roots of the suosuo plants in the recovered or relatively healthy natural suosuo forests. In order to plant congrong seeds and harvest congrong in natural suosuo forests, congrong growers have drilled 1 to 1.5 meter-deep trenches to expose the suosuo roots. The drilling destroys not only the topsoil but also disturbs the root-level soil and its hydrodynamics, severely damaging the root system of suosuo in the natural suosuo forest.[126] In other words, to make suosuo-congrong plantations productive, the natural suosuo forests and their soil are compromised.

What about the social impact of the suosuo plantations? Has suosuo-congrong farming alleviated poverty? If so, how? Again, even the Holy Grail cannot escape the perennial dilemmas embedded in cash crop development projects.

Like many cash crop projects, suosuo-congrong farming is capital intensive. Only those endowed with sufficient initial capital, like Hu, have been able to run a congrong farm conditioned by the economies of scale. For the first two years, on top of subsidies from the government and the SEE, Hu's annual operational costs amounted to 70,000 yuan for water, power, seedlings, congrong seeds, and fertilizer. This sum also includes the cost of labor provided by his poorer neighbors as well as conservation refugees relocated from the southern Gansu and Ningxia mountainous areas (see Introduction). The initial investment in hole-drilling and earth-moving machines cost another 150,000 to 200,000 yuan. Because it took three years for Hu to see his first congrong harvest in 2014, he also needed enough savings to hold him over. Hu explained that a good portion of the necessary funds came from livestock sales under destocking policies, personal savings from his 10 years of working on construction sites in the city, and his parents' savings.

The high threshold of initial and operating capital is beyond the financial capacity of most of Hu's fellow villagers. The size of land holdings posed another challenge. Hu earned a net profit of 30 yuan per mu in 2014 and 2015, which was much less than planting other cash crops in the dryland in a good year. But the low cash yields per unit of land was compensated by operating a large 7,000 mu farm. For villagers who have much smaller land parcels and cannot achieve an economy of scale on their own, they rent their land out to industrial agricultural operators like Wang's Elion. The able-bodied work as wage laborers for plantations, while other family members try to survive conservation programs in various ways. For rural residents of Alxa, whether and how the suosuo-congrong farm could "alleviate poverty" depended on their capacity to take advantage of the miracle.

To sum up, suosuo, the miracle shrub in combating desertification, has championed China's ecological mobilization. For policy makers, the superstar, suosuo, and its rainmaking partner, congrong, together have produced a miraculous solution for the contradictions between combating desertification and productivity improvement, which few other programs have managed to deliver. It is miraculous also because of the power couple's unprecedented mobilizational capacity. The couple has inspired state and non-state actors alike, including local officials, green entrepreneurs, environmental NGOs, urban middle class consumers, and even China's fintech giant Alibaba—and draw them into a shared vision of greening the desert by expanding suosuo-congrong plantations. The couple's persuasive power miraculously opens the door to otherwise highly restricted access to resources like water, land, and natural suosuo forests in the regime of conservation. Under the rule of miracle that has led to an unlimited expansion of suosuo-congrong plantations, however, the negative environmental and social impacts of the miracle has been grossly ignored in order for the miracle to thrive.

This miracle is mainly maintained by the state, capital, and urban elite in the age of productive conservation. In this suosuo-driven mobilization to combat desertification, herders, especially the small family herders, have played a passive role. In Chapter 2, I will turn to small herding families and look at their strategies of surviving the programs of combating desertification. In that story, suosuo and congrong are also vital. But family herders' congrong are of the wild variety collected from natural suosuo fields, not plantations. Wild congrong generates cash income but performs little miracle for these herding families.

Notes

1. Worster, Donald. 1986. *Rivers of Empire: Water, Aridity, and the Growth of the American West.* Oxford: Oxford University Press.
2. Limerick, Patricia. 1987. *The Legacy of Conquest: The Unbroken Past of the American West.* New York: W. W. Norton.

3. Perdue, Peter. 2005. *China Marches West: The Qing Conquest of Central Eurasia*. Cambridge and London: Belknap Press of Harvard University Press.
4. Marks, Robert. 1998. *Tigers, Rice, Silk and Silt, Environment and Economy in Late Imperial South China*, p. 305. Cambridge: Cambridge University Press.
5. Hua, Xinmin. 2010. "Qian Xuesen ruheduguo wengeshinian [How did Qian Xuesen survive the Cultural Revolution]." *Open Magazine*, January. http://www.open.com.hk/old_version/1009p48.html. Accessed June 2, 2023; 2010. Chinese Academy of Science. "Qian Xuesen: lijingxianzu baoxiaozuguo: huojianzhiwang danbomingyu [Qian Xuesen: Going through hardship to make contribution to the nation: Father of Rocketry cared little about fame]." https://www.cas.cn/zt/rwzt/qxsssyzn/jnwz/201010/t20101031_3000035.html. Accessed January 2, 2025; "Tsien Hsue-Shen Dies." 2009. *CalTech Today*, November 2. https://web.archive.org/web/20100612190920/ http://today.caltech.edu/today/story-display.tcl?story_id=39604. Accessed December 13, 2022.
6. The term Gobi/gobi can be used in two ways. The Gobi refers to the expanse of dryland sandwiched between today's western IM and western Mongolia. The other, lowercase "gobi," is used by my interviewees in western IM (called "gebitan" in Putonghua) to refer to drylands with coarse sand and gravel surface. The Gobi Desert and gobi land overlap in extended areas, but not all, of today's western IM. In this book, I use Gobi to refer to the Gobi Desert, and gobi to refer to "gebitan" in western IM.
7. Hao, Chengzhi and Aijun Liu. 2008. "Qianxuesenyu neimenggushachanye [Qianxuesen and sand industry in Inner Mongolia]." *Ordos Studies*, No 3. Online source. Page numbers unavailable. http://www.caogen.com/blog/Infor_detail.aspx?ID=695&articleId=87531. Accessed November 1, 2016. Link was broken by January 2, 2025. One of the two authors, Hao, Chengzhi, delivered a lecture on the same topic at the University of Science and Technology of China (USTC) in 2011. See the USTC website: https://ses.ustc.edu.cn/2011/1019/c1718a10330/page.htm. Accessed January 2, 2025.
8. Qian, Xuesen. 2007."Letter to Liu Shu dated Oct 12, 1989." 2007. In *Qian Xue-sen shuxin [Compilation of Qian Xuesen Letters]*, edited by Tu, Yuan ji et al., Vol. 5, p. 72. Beijing: National Defense Industry Press.
9. Qian, Xuesen. 2007. "Letter to Liu Shu dated Jan 11, 1990." Ibid. p. 164.
10. Qian, Xuesen. 2012. "Letter to Liu Shu dated May 29, 1994." In *Qian Xue-sen shuxin bubian [Additional Collection of Qian Xue-sen Letters]*, edited by Li, Ming et al. Vol. 4, p. 327. Beijing: National Defense Industry Press.
11. Qian is also known for his role through his protégé, Song Jian, in providing scientific support of China's One Child policy in 1980. Both cases of One Child policy and "deserticulture" manifest Qian and his fellow scientists' approach of marrying "hard" science and engineering with social engineering. See Xu, Tian. 2016. "jihuashengyujinchengzhongde sangeyanjiubaogao (Three research reports in the process of making the planned birth policy)." *Dangshiwenyuan (Literature of Party History)* (02): 52–53; and Greenhalgh, Susan. 2005. "Missile science, population science: The origins of China's One-Child Policy." *The China Quarterly* (2005), 182: 253–276. I thank Ken Pomeranz for this important reminder.
12. Liu, Guoqing. 2015. "Shade gushi: Qianxuesen yu zhongguoshachanye [The story of sand: Qian Xuesen and China's sand industry]." In *Liu Shu's Recollection*, pp. 66–80. Lanzhou: Gansu People's Art Press. Also, Organization Department of Cadre Training

College ed. 1997. *Kexuegongzuo jianmingcidian [Concise Dictionary of Science Commission's Work]*, pp. 279–280. Beijing: Chinese Science and Technology Association.

13. Qian, Xuesen. 2007. "Letter to Liu Shu dated Dec 2, 1996." In *Qian Xue-sen shuxin [Compilation of Qian Xuesen Letters]*, edited by Tu, Yuanji et al., Vol. 10, p. 229. Beijing: National Defense Industry Press.
14. State Forestry Administration of China. 2010. "Guojialinyeju guanyujinyibu jiakuaifazhanshachanyede yijian [Opinion on Accelerating the Development of Deserticulture]." Linshafa [State Forestry Administration]. http://www.forestry.gov.cn/portal/main/govfile/13/govfile_1778.htm. Accessed December 3, 2022.
15. For an analysis of "ecological civilization" in Chinese leaders' green vision, see Rodenbiker, Jesse. 2023. *Ecological States: Politics of Science and Nature in Urbanizing China.* Ithaca, NY: Cornell University Press.
16. Luo, Jie. 2015. "Gansu Hexizoulang shachanye yinqisongping changqiguanzhu, yujianzhongxiya dongjihouchu [Song Ping paid attention to Sand Industry in Hexi Corridor of Gansu, envisioning winter food supplies for central and western Asia]." *Pengpai News*, September 20, 2015. https://www.thepaper.cn/newsDetail_forward_1377121. Accessed June 2, 2023; Jia, Lijun. 2012. "Neimenggu weirao meilizhongguo dazuo shachanye wenzhang [Inner Mongolia elaborated on (Xi Jinpin's) idea of 'Beautiful China' by expanding the sand industry]." *Xinhua News*, November 30, 2012. http://www.gov.cn/jrzg/2012-11/30/content_2278819.htm. Accessed December 8, 2022.
17. A good example of an ecology-framed development zone with multiple functions is the 200 sq. km-large Engebei Ecological Conservation Model Zone in the central-northern part of the Hobq Desert in IM. Established by Ordos Municipal Government in 2010, the Zone covers five types of sand industry, which are, "forest ecology, desert agriculture, science education, cultural tourism, and new energy." http://egb.ordos.gov.cn/zjegb/. Accessed December 15, 2022. Link was broken by January 2, 2025.
18. Alxa is one of the three leagues under IMAR. Administratively, a league is at the same rank as the nine other municipalities in IMAR. Within Alxa League, there are three banners—Ejina Banner, Alxa Right Banner, and Alxa Left Banner. In IMAR, a banner sits at the same administrative rank as a county in other parts of China.
19. Gerile et al. 2014. "Alashan huangmosuosuo ziyuanzhuangkuangyu huifuliyong [Current state and recovery of suosuo in Alxa's Drylands]." *Grass Land and Prataculture* 26 (4): 18–21; Xu, Wenjun. 2016. "Alashanmeng yinlingnongmumin fazhan roucongronghe suoyang chanye [Alxa League guides farmers and herders to develop Congrong and Suoyang industry]." *Inner Mongolia Forestry*. 2016, p. 14. Wang, Weiguan and Guoguang Zheng et al. 2015. "Balidexinqidianhe xinxiwang: yingduiqihoubianhua baokao [New start and Hope in Paris (Agreement): Annual Report on Actions to address Climate Change]," p. 228. Beijing: Social Science Literature Press; Alxa League Gazetteer editorial committee. 1998. *Alashanmeng difangzhibianzhuanweiyuanhui, 1998, Alashanmengzhi [Alxa League Gazetteer]*, p. 343. Beijing: Gazetteer Press.
20. Wang, Jihe and Quanlin Ma. 2013. *Minqin lüzhou rengongsuosuo tuihua xianzhuang, tezhengyu huifu duice [Minqin's Oases: Deterioration and Paths to Recovery]. Northwest Botany.* No. 12, pp. 293–298; Ji, Yong-fu et al. 2010. "Minqin butong lidi tiaojianxia rengong suosuolin shengzhang zhuangkuang yanjiu [Research on suosuo afforestation in

different locational conditions in Minqin]." *Journal of Gansu Forestry Science and Technology* 35 (3): 1–6, p. 34; He, Jiangfeng et al. 2015. "Suosuode yanjiu jinzhan [Progress in suosuo research]." *Xumuyu siliao kexue [Animal Husbandry and Feed]* 36 (12): 94–98.

21. Pei, Hao et al. 2011. *Alashan huangmoqu shengtai huanjing tezheng yu huanjing baohu [Ecology and Environmental Protection of Alxa's Desert]*, pp. 75–76. Beijing: China Meteorological Press.
22. Zuo, Shouyi et al. 1995. "Suosuolinxiufu gongchengyanjiu [A study of suosuo forest restoration]." *Journal of Inner Mongolia Forestry College* 17 (2): 9–18.
23. In 2018, the SFA was renamed to the State Forestry and Grassland Administration (SFGA) after China's restructuring of environmental administrations, as mentioned in Chapter 1.
24. Wang, Hui. 2011. "Yu Changqing: buyaoqingshuaigaizao huangshanhuangdi [Yu Changqing (said): Avoid reconstructing waste land and waste mountains in haste]." *Science Times*, Chinese Academy of Science Website, September 13. https://www.cas.cn/xw/zjsd/201109/t20110913_3347074.shtml. Accessed June 2, 2023.
25. Guo, Xiaohe. 2011. "Saving Sichuan's Trees." *China Dialogue*. https://www.chinadialogue.net/article/show/single/en/4311-Saving-Sichuan-s-trees. Accessed December 8, 2022; Lang, Graeme. 2002. "Forests, floods, and the environmental state in China." *Organization & Environment* 15 (2): 109–130; Liu, Qin. 2014. "Is China's 'Green Great Wall' set to fall?." *China Dialogue*. Feb 2. https://chinadialogue.net/en/climate/6732-is-china-s-green-great-wall-set-to-fall. Accessed March 11, 2023.
26. Gu, Zhongyang. 2018. "2018 nian woguojiang zaolinyiyimu [China will establish 100 million mu of forests by 2018]." *People's Daily*, January 8. http://www.gov.cn/xinwen/2018-01/08/content_5254231.htm. Accessed June 3, 2023.
27. Li, Hongyang. 2023. "China's forest coverage rate hits 24%." *China Daily*, March 12. https://www.chinadaily.com.cn/a/202303/12/WS640d64b0a31057c47ebb3e3f.html. Accessed April 1, 2024.
28. Yu, Chang-qing is a former researcher at the SFA's Research Institute of Forestry. In 1997, he left the SFA and joined an international environmental foundation. In 2011, Yu wrote a lengthy critique in his personal blog, questioning the contradiction in the simultaneous increase in China's forested area and decrease of old growth forests as well as continual soil erosion. Yu, Changqing, 2011. "Fansi zhishuzaolin [reflection on tree plantations]." March 10. http://blog.sciencenet.cn/blog-459318-420742.html. Accessed on December 9, 2018. The link was broken by June 2, 2023. The article could not be found elsewhere online.
29. Interview with a county official in IMAR, 2013.
30. Zuo, Shouyi et al. 1995. "Suosuolin xiufu gongcheng yanjiu [A study of suosuo forest restoration engineering]." *Journal of Inner Mongolia Forestry College* 17 (2): 9–18.
31. Song, Xinzhou. 2007. "Deshizhijiande Zhongguolühua [Greening China: Successes and failures]." *China Dialogue*, February 8. https://www.chinadialogue.net/article/show/single/ch/1195-Greening-China-successes-and-failures. Accessed December 16, 2022; Yu, Changqing. 2011. Ibid.
32. Jiang, Xuecheng et al. 2004. "Zhongzaolin qinghulin yinfagebihuangmo xinshengtaiweiji [New environmental crisis in the Gobi Desert created by afforestation without forest protection]." *China Environment News*. September 13. http://www.china.com.cn/chinese/huanjing/658815.htm. Accessed October 1, 2017. This link was broken and the article could not be found elsewhere online when I revisited it on December 16, 2022.

33. Interview with a researcher in IM, July 2013. For a comparable case, see Peluso, Nancy Lee. 1992. *Rich Forests, Poor People: Resource Control and Resistance in Java.* Berkeley, CA: University of California Press.
34. Tu, Pengfei et al. 2011. "Roucongrong yanjiu jiqi chanye fazhan [Research and Industrial development of Congrong]." *Chinese Pharmaceutical Studies* 46 (12): 882–887.
35. Gerile et al. 2014. Ibid; Xu, Wenjun. 2016. Ibid.
36. Song, Fuli. 2014a. "Shamo taojin [Digging gold in the desert]." *Economic Observer*, November 14. http://finance.sina.com.cn/roll/20141106/233320753098.shtml. Accessed June 2, 2023.
37. Song, Fuli. 2014b. "Mengcaoqishi shengtaizhanluede xiangtuhuigui [Learning from Inner Mongolia's grass industry: Ecological strategies returning to the grassroots]." *Economic Observer*, July 7. http://www.eeo.com.cn/2014/0707/263078.shtml. Accessed June 2, 2023.
38. Wang, Wen-biao. 2011. *Qianxuesenyu shachanye [Qian Xuesen and Sand Industry]*, p. 2. Hohhot: Inner Mongolia University Press.
39. Xue, Xian. 2017. "Desert and Desertification: A Case Study of Hobq Desert." Unpublished manuscript; He, Lan and Weimin Shi. 1993. *Mo nan qing: neimeng shengchan jianshe bingtuan xiezhen [Memoir of Inner Mongolia Production and Construction Corp in Southern Gobi Desert]*, p. 266. Beijing: Law Publications.
40. Wang, Wen-biao. 2011. Ibid. p. 112.
41. See Song, Fuli. 2014c. "Shengtai xiufu shengyilian [Business chains in ecological repair]." *Economic Observer*, December 31. http://www.eeo.com.cn/2014/1231/270919.shtml. Accessed December 16, 2022. Also see Zhang, Xinxin. 2013. "Zhengxieweiyuan weishengtaihuanbao jianshezhizhao: yinjinminzi shichangtuijin [A Political Consultation Committee member's suggestion on ecological construction and protection: Bring in private capital and advance market economy]." *Xinhua News*, March 6. https://china.huanqiu.com/article/9CaKrnJzyy0. Accessed June 3, 2023.
42. Shang, Wenbo. 2009. "Yishengtaiweijichu zaishaqufazhan xinnengyuan [Developing new energy in sand district based on ecology]." *China Green Times*, September 1. http://www.eco.gov.cn/news_info/4588.html. Accessed December 18, 2022.
43. United Nations Convention to Combat Desertification's official website. http://www2.unccd.int/2015-land-life-award-winners. Accessed June 3, 2023.
44. Song, Fuli. 2014a. Ibid.
45. This paragraph on Qi's personal history is drawn from Qi's CV posted on his personal webpage on May 20, 2013, http://www.qichenghong.com/. Accessed December 17, 2022. The link was broken by June 3, 2023; China Central Television's (CCTV) 2015 TV series, "Shengcai youdao [Paths to Wealth]," "Hongkui congrongjituan dongshizhang Qichenghongde chuangyejing [The President of Hongkui Congrong Group Company Qing Chenghong's personal history of entrepreneurship]." CCTV, November 9. http://qichenghong.com/ReadNews.asp?NewsID=55. Accessed December 17, 2022. The link was broken by February 21, 2025. In addition, Hongkui's company webpage "Zhongguo alashan shoujie roucongrong chanyefazhanluntan canhuirenyuan lilin neimengguhongkui congrongjituan canguanzhidao [Participants of the inaugural Alxa Roucongrong Industry Development Forum visit Hongkui Group]." 2016. http://www.honkc.com/readnews.asp?newsid=195. Accessed December 17, 2022. The link was broken by June 3, 2023.

46. Dong, Bijuan. 2017. "Woguo ppp guanli toumingdu buduantisheng [Managerial transparency of China's PPP continues to improve]." *Economic Daily*, December 7. http://www.gov.cn/xinwen/2017-12/07/content_5244987.htm. Accessed June 3, 2023.
47. Huang, Philip C. C., Yuan Gao, and Yusheng Peng. 2012. "Capitalization without proletarianization in China's agricultural development." *Modern China* 38 (2): 139–173; Zhang, Qian Forrest. 2015. "Class differentiation in rural China: Dynamics of accumulation, commodification and state intervention." *Journal of Agrarian Change* 15 (3): 338–365; Ye, Jingzhong. 2015. "Land transfer and the pursuit of agricultural modernization in China." *Journal of Agrarian Change* 15 (3): 314–337; Yan, Hairong and Yiyuan Chen. 2015. "Agrarian capitalization without capitalism? Capitalist dynamics from above and below in China." *Journal of Agrarian Change* 15 (3): 366–391. In their discussion of China's resilient peasantry, Huang et al. (2012) noted the persistent dominance of small but capitalized family farms that have made it more difficult to assemble enough family parcels to make sizable farms for corporate agriculture through the Dragon Head programs. On the other hand, Yan and Chen (2015) and Zhang (2015) argued that the scale of capitalization in agriculture and the influence of industrial and commercial capital in reconcentration of land ownership in the countryside and class stratification in rural China is far more significant than Huang et al. (2012) have recognized.
48. Zhang, Qian Forrest. 2015. Ibid. p. 351.
49. Xiang, Hengyi et al. 2017. "Alashan: shengtaicuiruoqu zhulaolüsedageju [Alxa: An ecologically fragile area reinforces its grand green plans]." *China Forest News*, August 11. http://www.isenlin.cn/sf_1D44BCCE60284F9FAB06F87C6F2A8253_209_isenlinzx.html. Accessed June 3, 2023.
50. Wang, Wenbiao. 2011. Ibid. p. 156.
51. Song, Fuli. 2014a. Ibid.
52. Scholar Judith Shapiro has endorsed the SEE's "highly positive role in promoting public participation around environmental issues." See Shapiro, Judith. 2016. *China's Environmental Challenges*, p. 131. Cambridge: Polity. The UK-based environmental online newsletter, *China Dialogue* (renamed to "Dialogue Earth" in 2024), also praised the SEE for its leadership in China's conservation mobilization. See Liu, Qin. 2017. "Liu Xiaoguang and the Alashan legacy." *China Dialogue*, April 25. https://www.chinadialogue.net/article/show/single/ch/9753-Liu-Xiaoguang-and-the-Alashan-legacy. Accessed February 3, 2020.
53. Hsing, You-tien. 2010. *The Great Urban Transformation: Politics of Land and Property in China*. Oxford: Oxford University Press.
54. Feng, Yongfeng. 2009. *Bianzuo huanbao biansahuang [Protecting the Environment while Telling Lies]*, p. 161. Beijing: Shijie Zhishi Press.
55. Yang, Ping. 2018. "Shinianhuiwang alashan SEE minzhuzhilishiyande chengjiuyuwenti [The past ten years: reflection on the achievements and problems of SEE's experiments in democratic governance]." Gongyi zibenlun [Philanthropy Watch]. April 8. https://gongyizibenlun.com/1613. Accessed June 3, 2023. Yang was the inaugural general secretary of the SEE.
56. Liu, Qin. 2017. Ibid.
57. Xiao, Jin. 2013. *Shengtaibaoyude minzhushiyan: Alashan xingji [An Experiment with Democracy in Conservation: A Travelogue in Alxa League]*, p. 6. Beijing: Social Science Academic Press.

58. Liu, Qin. 2017. Ibid.
59. See SEE Official Website. http://conservation.see.org.cn/about/introduction/. Accessed March 11, 2023.
60. Teets, Jessica. 2014. *Civil Society under Authoritarianism: The China Model.* Cambridge: Cambridge University Press.
61. See Introduction for context on the resettlements in the desert.
62. See Chapter 2 for more on the dairy cow programs.
63. See Chapter 2 for more on the process and impact of rural decollectivization in pastural areas.
64. Xiao, Jin. 2013. Ibid. pp. 97–99.
65. Xiao, Jin. 2013. Ibid. pp. 226–250.
66. Xiao, Jin. 2013. Ibid. p. 303; Zhang, Ke. 2016. "Neimenggumumin jingran yangbuqiyang, yiyike suosuo neng bangshangmangma? [Inner Mongolian herders cannot afford to raise sheep—can one hundred million suosuo help?]." *Diyi Caijing*, May 29. http://www.yicai.com/news/5020100.html. Accessed March 13, 2023.
67. See Introduction to Part III for histories of Han Chinese farming migration to IM.
68. Fictionalized name.
69. The SEE manager estimated that one mu of suosuo plantation produced about 1,000 to 1,500 yuan worth of congrong.
70. Xue, Xian. 2015. "Making desert productive in northern China." Unpublished manuscript.
71. National Forestry and Grassland Administration. 2021. neimenggu zhizhiqu alashanmeng fazhan roucongrong chanye [Alxa League's congrong Industry]." In Linxiajingji fazhandianxinganli" (Model Cases of Agroforestry), a policy report published by National Forestry and Grassland Administration. pp. 18-20. https://www.forestry.gov.cn/html/main/main_5461/20211224164139275849745/file/20211224164220127155731.pdf. Accessed January 2, 2025. The suosuo afforestation projects in Alxa League are located mainly in Alxa Left Banner, the eastern end of Alxa League, where the seat of the League is located and where humidity is higher than that in the western banners of Alxa League. According to a researcher at the Chinese Academy of Science I talked to in 2015, the percentage of suosuo plantations that have turned into suosuo-congrong farms was about 50% in the more humid and politically more important Alxa Left Banner, compared to 16% at the Alxa League level.
72. Song, Fuli. 2014a. Ibid.
73. 2016. "Alashan shengtaishachanyegaofengluntanji xiangmutuijinhui zhaokai [Alashan Ecological Sand Industry Summit opens]." *Alashan Daily News*, January 4. http://www.honkc.com/readnews.asp?newsid=204. Accessed December 20, 2022. The party secretary vowed to develop a Model Development Zone that is "market-oriented, private enterprise-based, processing-led, and science and technology-supported." This link was broken by March 16, 2023. A similar report can be found at http://www.als.gov.cn/art/2022/9/27/art_5_456321.html. Accessed March 16, 2023. Also see Liu, Yunfei and Pengfei Zhang. 2017. "Alashanmeng wulanbuhe shengtai shachanye shifanqu fazhanjishi [Development of Alxa's Ulan Buh Ecological Sand Industry Model Development Zone]." *Inner Mongolia Daily*, September 8. enlin.cn/sf_2C32661715AC4021ABB7A2B975C5F0B4_209_yuyanqi.html. Accessed March 16, 2023.

74. Inner Mongolia Autonomous Region Bureau of Science and Technology. 2017. "2017 shoujie quanguo shachanye chuanxinchuanyedasai yuanmanluomu [2017 Inaugural National Sand Industry Innovation Tournament Closed Successfully]." Ministry of Science and Technology of the People's Republic of China webpage, November 21. https://www.most.gov.cn/dfkj/nmg/zxdt/201711/t20171121_136320.html. Accessed January 2, 2025.
75. Li, Zhuo. 2017. "Alashanzuoqi dazaoguojia shachanye shifanjidi [Alxa Left Banner established National Level Sand Industry Model Base]." *Inner Mongolia News Online*, May 26. http://inews.nmgnews.com.cn/system/2017/05/26/012353698.shtml. Accessed June 3, 2023.
76. Ant Financial regularly makes it onto international financial news. Prior to its aborted IPO in 2020, in 2018, its third attempt to acquire the U.S. money-transfer company, MoneyGram, failed due to the U.S. government's concerns over national security and was widely reported. See Roumeliotis, Greg. 2018. "U.S. blocks MoneyGram sale to China's Ant Financial on national security concerns." *Reuters*, January 2. https://www.reuters.com/article/us-moneygram-intl-m-a-ant-financial/u-s-blocks-moneygram-sale-to-chinas-ant-financial-on-national-security-concerns-idUSKBN1ER1R7. Accessed December 20, 2022; and "China's Ant Financial is obliged to abandon an American acquisition." 2018. *The Economist*, January 6. https://www.economist.com/business/2018/01/06/chinas-ant-financial-is-obliged-to-abandon-an-american-acquisition.
77. He, Laura. 2017. "Tencent is the first Asian company to top US$500 billion in value, joining Apple and Facebook." *Southern China Morning Post*, November 20. https://www.scmp.com/business/companies/article/2120712/tencent-breaches-us500b-valuation-shares-rally-above-hk41460. Accessed December 20, 2022.
78. Heggestuen, John. 2014. "Alipay Overtakes PayPal as The Largest Mobile Payments Platform in The World." *Business Insider*. https://www.businessinsider.com/alipay-overtakes-paypal-as-the-largest-mobile-payments-platform-in-the-world-2014-2. Accessed December 23, 2022.
79. The Stock Exchange of Hong Kong. 2020. H Share IPO Application Proof of Ant Group. p.5. Hong Kong Stock Exchange News. https://www1.hkexnews.hk/listedco/listconews/sehk/2020/1026/2020102600165.pdf. Accessed January 2, 2025.
80. Interview in Beijing, July 2018.
81. I thank Catherine Park of UC Berkeley's School of Education for the discussion of this point.
82. Fenghuang gongyi. 2017."Mayisenlinruwei xingdongzhelianmeng 2017gongyishengdian niandugongyichuangyi [Ant Forest selected for Action Takers 2017 Public Service Innovation Award]." Fenghuang gongyi webpage, November 15. https://gongyi.ifeng.com/a/20171115/44762391_0.shtml. Accessed December 23, 2022
83. Green Digital Finance Alliance. 2017. *Kuodagongminyingdui qihoubianhuaxingdongde guimoxiaoying [Expand the Influence of Citizen Action on Climate Change]*, pp. 15–18. https://wedocs.unep.org/bitstream/handle/20.500.11822/22279/citizen_action_climate_CH.pdf?sequence=2&isAllowed=y. For an English version of the report entitled "Scaling citizen action on climate" see https://docs.wixstatic.com/ugd/3d4f2c_109c450486544f6da883689ccaabe9b3.pdf. All accessed June 3, 2023.
84. Interview in California, May 2018.

85. Interview in Beijing, July 2019.
86. Liu, Chu. 2017. "Shamosannianzhong 50 wanmusuosuo, xiwangyu kunjing bingcun [The hope and predicament of planting 500,000 mu of suosuo in the desert in three years]." *Pengpai News*, April 8. https://www.thepaper.cn/newsDetail_forward_1647994. Accessed December 21, 2022.
87. Green Digital Finance Alliance. 2017. Ibid. p. 18.
88. "Zhifubao mayisenlin zhichihezhongshu, 215 kg huyang buzaishimeng [Alipay and Ant Forest support collaborative tree planting, planting Huyang that requires 215 kg (of energy) is no longer just a dream]." 2018. Kuaikeji (Fast Science and Technology). January 24. http://news.mydrivers.com/1/564/564446.htm. Accessed June 3, 2023.
89. UN Environment Programme. 2017. "Revolutionary digital platform to boost green finance." UN Environment Programme press release online. January 20. https://www.unep.org/news-and-stories/press-release/revolutionary-digital-platform-boost-green-finance. Accessed December 11, 2022; Wang, Yanfei. 2017. "Ant Financial ranked 6th in Fortune environmental list." *China Daily*, September 9. https://web.archive.org/web/20170912165319/http://www.chinadaily.com.cn/business/tech/2017-09/09/content_31776061.htm. Accessed June 3, 2023.
90. Zhuang, Zhengyue. 2014. "Ali mayijinfu jituanliangxiang weishemejiaomayi? [Alibaba's Ant Financial Service: Why is it called Ant?]." *Today Morning News*, October 17. https://yq.zjol.com.cn/system/2014/10/17/020307228.shtml. Accessed June 3, 2023.
91. Zhu, Feng et al. 2018. "Ant Financial (A)." Harvard Business School Case Studies, No. 9-617-060, January 9, pp. 3–4.
92. Xie, Rainny Shuyan et al. 2017. "Fintech and Finance transformation: The rise of Ant Financial Services." The Asian Business Case Center, No. ABCC 2017-021, Singapore: Nanyang Business School, Nanyang Technological University, pp. 3–4.
93. Zhu, Feng et al. 2018. Ibid. pp. 3–4.
94. Hvistendahl, Mara. 2017. "Inside China's vast new experiment in social ranking." *Wired*, December 14. www.wired.com/story/age-of-social-credit. Accessed December 30, 2022.
95. Xie, Rainny Shuyan et al. 2017. Ibid. p. 6.
96. Zhu, Feng et al. 2018. Ibid. pp. 8–9.
97. Xie, Rainny Shuyan et al. 2017. Ibid. pp. 12–14.
98. Xie, Rainny Shuyan et al. 2017. Ibid. p. 11; Zhu, Feng et al. 2018. Ibid. p. 9.
99. "The marriage squeeze in India and China: Bare branches, redundant males." 2015. *The Economist*, April 18.
100. "Zhongguo nannübili shitiao quanqiudiyi [China has the most skewed sex ratio in the world]." 2015. *Sina Finance*, October 30. http://finance.sina.com.cn/360desktop/world/yzjj/20151030/104123630525.shtml. Accessed June 3, 2023.
101. "The marriage squeeze." 2015. *The Economist*, Ibid.
102. Wang, Ying. 2015. "Guojiawangxinban zhankai 'hunlianwangzhan yanzhongweigu-ishixin' zhuanxiang zhengzhi [National Cyberspace Administration establishes special task force to investigate and penalize illegal and dishonest dating websites]." *Xinhua News*, February 12. http://www.cac.gov.cn/2015-02/12/c_1114352948.htm. Accessed June 3, 2023.
103. Geiwoyulimikuangxiangqu, 2018. "Baihewang zhimaxinyong gaodiaoqianshou hunlian-jiaoyou jintuxinyongshidai [Baihe dating site and Zhima Credit join forces, match making enters the era of credit rating]." *Sina News*, February 9. http://k.sina.com.cn/article_6399368038_17d6e9b66001004j0f.html?from=%3Eaccessed#/. Accessed June 4,

2023; Wei, Donghua et al. 2017. "Meinü kenengshinanren, yihunmiaobian danshen—hunlianwangzhanli youduoshaozhenhua? [Pretty women turn out to be men, married people pretend to be single—how trustworthy are dating sites?]." *Xinhua News*, September 20. http://m.xinhuanet.com/gd/2017-09/20/c_1121691462.htm. Accessed March 15, 2023.

104. Interview in Gansu, 2016.
105. Mazzarella, William. 2017. *The Mana of Mass Society*, p. 37. Chicago: The University of Chicago Press.
106. Green Digital Finance Alliance. 2017. Ibid.
107. I thank Cecilia Springer of Global China Initiative at Boston University for the personal exchanges on China's carbon market. Also see Springer, Cecilia. 2020. *China's National Carbon Market: Paradox and Potential.* Belfer Center for Science and International Affairs, Harvard University. Online policy brief. https://www.belfercenter.org/publication/chinas-national-carbon-market-paradox-and-potential. Accessed December 16, 2022. For the global context of carbon finance, see Hamrick, Kelley et al. 2017. "Fertile ground: State of forest carbon finance 2017," a report published by a Washington DC-based NGO, Forest Trends' Ecosystem Marketplace. https://www.forest-trends.org/wp-content/uploads/2018/01/doc_5715.pdf. Accessed January 3, 2023.
108. Xue, Yujie. 2022. "What is the China Certified Emission Reduction scheme and why is it important for Beijing's carbon neutral goal?." *Southern China Morning Post*, January 31. https://www.scmp.com/business/article/3165425/what-china-certified-emission-reduction-scheme-and-why-it-important. Accessed March 19, 2023.
109. Chatterjee, Sumeet and Julie Zhu. 2018. "China's Ant plans equity fundraising at potential $100 billion valuation." *Reuters*, February 9. https://www.reuters.com/article/us-ant-financial-fundraising/exclusive-chinas-ant-plans-equity-fundraising-at-potential-100-billion-valuation-sources-idUSKBN1FT0LA. Accessed December 30, 2022; and Lucas, Louise and Henny Sender. 2018. "Ant Financial seeks $5bn in funding ahead of IPO." *Financial Times*, February 11. https://www.ft.com/content/588ac470-0f94-11e8-940e-08320fc2a277. Accessed January 2, 2025.
110. Confessore, Nicholas. 2018. "Cambridge Analytica and Facebook: The Scandal and the Fallout So Far." *The New York Times*, April 4. https://www.nytimes.com/2018/04/04/us/politics/cambridge-analytica-scandal-fallout.html. Accessed December 30, 2022. Cambridge Analytica was accused of harvesting data from an estimated 87 million *Facebook* users to psychologically profile voters to predict and shape their voting behavior during the 2016 election.
111. Prior to the Cambridge Analytica/Facebook scandal, Jack Ma and his senior management made several statements about Alibaba's respect for its customers' privacy and denied any connection with the Chinese government's project of building a national social credit system. See Hvistendahl, Mara. 2017. "Inside China's vast new experiment in social ranking." *Wired*, December 14. www.wired.com/story/age-of-social-credit. Accessed December 30, 2022.) For big data controversies, see, for example, O'Neil, Cathy. 2016. *Weapons of Math Destruction: How Big Data Increases Inequality and Threatens Democracy*, p. 181. London: Allen Lane. From an opposite direction, Ant Financial's 2016 Sustainability Report entitled, "Moving towards a Better Society for the Future," (https://gw.alipayobjects.com/os/rmsportal/mwUoNtqgLVypRBywLMpU.pdf. Accessed June 4, 2023), envisions social equity through commerce for micro businesses and individual consumers. Where Ant Financial envisioned a connection between big data and

common people as a way to improve social equity, O'Neil argues that hidden algorithms in the insurance industry's calculation of premiums and political consultancies' (like Cambridge Analytica) psychological profiling of voters can increase inequality and threaten democracy. Whereas Ant Financial has flaunted its analytical capacity that "leaves no detail out" (Xie, Rainny Shuyan et al. 2017. "Fintech and Finance transformation." Ibid. p. 8), O'Neil presents a contrasting perspective of micro-targeted citizens under surveillance. And, whereas Ant Financial has boasted about its omnipotent cloud technologies, O'Neil demystifies big data and points out the far-fetched, unexplainable, and just plain wrong correlations and patterns sometimes found by artificial intelligence.

112. "Mayisenlin 2016–2020 nian zaolinxiangmu shengtaixitong shengchanzongzhi (GEP) hesuanbaogao [Report on Ant Forest's Gross Ecosystem Product (GEP) 2016–2020]." 2021. Ecological Environment Research Center of Chinese Academy of Science & International Union for Conservation of Nature (IUCN). *China Science*. March 10. http://www.cnicn.org/h-nd-16959.html. Accessed March 19, 2023.
113. Zhu, Julie. 2022. "China set to fine Ant Group over $1 bln, signaling revamp nears end-sources." *Reuters*, November 23. https://www.reuters.com/business/exclusive-china-set-fine-ant-group-over-1-bln-signalling-revamp-nears-end-2022-11-22/. Accessed December 22, 2022.
114. "Ant agonises: Regulators spoil Ant's party less than 48 hours before it starts trading." 2020. *The Economist*, November 3. https://www.economist.com/finance-and-economics/2020/11/03/regulators-spoil-ants-party-less-than-48-hours-before-it-starts-trading.
115. *The Economist*. 2020. Ibid.
116. See Chapter 8 for the Chinese government's crackdown on China's booming test prep industry that turned into a financial operation.
117. "Alibaba and the 40 officials: Can Chinese big tech learn to love Big Brother?" 2020. *The Economist*, May 7. https://www.economist.com/business/can-chinese-big-tech-learn-to-love-big-brother/21809084.
118. "Chaoliuyirencanyu Mayunde mayisenlincengbei zhiyizaojia rujin zenmele [What happened to Jack Ma's 600 million user-strong Ant Forest that was suspected of falsification?]." 2022. *Digital Finance*, September 5. https://t.cj.sina.com.cn/articles/view/1568309232/5d7a7ff0001011954. Accessed December 23, 2022. "Weilaisishinian zhongguotanshichang guimojinbaiyi, mayisenlin huocheng zuida yingjia [China carbon market will reach 10 billion yuan in the next four decades, Ant Forest could be the biggest winner]." 2021. This article originated from *Tianxie Finance*, reposted on Tanjiaoyi [Carbon Trade] Website, April 24. http://www.tanpaifang.com/tanguwen/2021/0424/77612.html. Accessed March 19, 2023.
119. In November 2022, Reuters reported that the People's Bank of China, China's central bank, was set to fine Ant Group over US1$billion. This would be the largest regulatory penalty imposed on a Chinese internet company since the ride-hailing firm Didi Global was fined $1.2 billion earlier that same year. According to the report, a fine on Ant could help pave the way for the company to secure a long-awaited financial holding company license, seek growth again, and eventually revive its plans for a public market debut. Zhu, Julie. 2022. "China set to fine Ant Group over $1 bln, signaling revamp nears end-sources." *Reuters*, November 23. https://www.reuters.com/business/exclusive-china-set-

fine-ant-group-over-1-bln-signalling-revamp-nears-end-2022-11-22/. Accessed December 22, 2022; Inagaki, Kana et al. 2022. "Alibaba Founder Jack Ma living in Tokyo since China's tech crackdown." *Financial Times*, November 29. https://www.ft.com/content/2f7c7a10-2df3-4f1b-8d2a-eea0e0548713. Accessed December 30, 2022.

120. Wakabayashi, Daisuke. 2023. "Alibaba, China's E-Commerce Giant, Will Split Into 6 Units." *The New York Times*, March 28. https://www.nytimes.com/2023/03/28/business/alibaba-china-e-commerce.html.
121. Zhang, Shisan. 2018. "Mayisenlin beihoude shengyi [The business behind Ant Forest]." Zhihu. March 14. https://zhuanlan.zhihu.com/p/34551222. Accessed June 3, 2023; "Mayisenlin weihuanbaofendou huozhe shangyeliyi [Is Ant Forest aimed at environmental protection or commercial interests]." 2018. Chinese edition of SPUTNIK News, February 3. http://sputniknews.cn/china/201802031024657518/?from=singlemessage&isappinstalled=0(. Accessed Feb 2, 2023.
122. Wang, Chen. 2019. "Can mobile payment apps spur green living?" *China Dialogue*, November 20. https://www.chinadialogue.net/article/show/single/en/11672-Can-mobile-payment-apps-spur-green-living-. Accessed March 21, 2021.
123. Fictional name. Interviews in China 2013, 2014, and 2017.
124. Zhang, Ke. 2016. "Neimenggumumin jingranyangbuqiyang, yiyikesuosuo nengbangshangmangma? [Inner Mongolian herders surprisingly unable to afford to raise sheep, can 100 million suosuo plants help?]." *Diyi Caijing*, May 29. http://www.yicai.com/news/5020100.html. Accessed March 19, 2023.
125. See Chapter 7 on western IMAR's agricultural expansion from the mid-19th to the early-20th century.
126. Wu, Nan et al. 2011. "Alashanmeng roucongrong chanpingongji fuwupinggu [An evaluation of congrong product supplies in Alxa League]." *Resource Science* 33 (7): 1284–1291.

2
Mobility Under Restrictions: Ejina Herders Surviving Rangeland Conservation

Following the previous chapter on the green mobilization led by the state and urban elites, this chapter turns to herders' responses to two key programs of China's productive conservation in pastoral Inner Mongolia (IM) since the early 2000s. One is stock reduction (or destocking), and the other is ecological relocation. Both programs share the principle of "retiring pastoralism," and both are aimed at environmental recovery and poverty alleviation.[1]

In Section I, I review the process of decollectivization of livestock and rangeland in the 1980s and 1990s followed by the contentious destocking and grazing ban policies in the era of rangeland conservation since the 2000s. I tell stories about herders' attempts to survive these policies with highly uneven results. These stories are based on my fieldwork in Alxa Left Banner of Alxa League, Bayannur Municipality, and in the southern banners in Xilingol League[2] (see Figure 5.2) as well as secondary sources, including the works of IM-based scholars.

In Section II, I focus on herders' strategies to survive the ecological relocation programs. I shift the territorial scale, from pastoral IM at large to Ejina Banner of Alxa League, which sits in the westernmost corner of Inner Mongolia Autonomous Region (IMAR). The stories of herders' varied attempts to survive relocation come from my four visits to Ejina between 2012 and 2014. The power couple, *suosuo* and *congrong*, from the previous chapter makes another appearance in this section. But they are not of the plantation variety. Rather, these are the wild congrong that herders collect in Ejina's natural suosuo fields.

Conserving China's Northwest Frontier. You-tien Hsing, Oxford University Press. © You-tien Hsing (2025).
DOI: 10.1093/9780191903903.003.0003

My trip with the relocated Ejina herders to collect wild congrong in the natural suosuo fields opened my eyes to a wide array of herders' strategies for surviving conservational restrictions during different seasons in different places of the immense Ejina Banner. In addition to hunting wild congrong in the spring in the suosuo-growing rangeland, relocated herders also dig semiprecious gemstones during the summer in the Gobi Desert, run ecotourism in their relocation homes in the Fall, and more. Instead of being automatically sedentarized by relocation and victimized by conservational restrictions, the relocated herders have developed a new mode of mobility in the diversifying rural economy of Ejina. Not all are equally successful in their endeavours, for sure. In their search for possibilities under restrictions, Ejina herders have encountered just as many impossibilities. But few can be blamed for not trying.

Allow me to start with the intertwined politics of stocking and destocking.

I Stocking and Destocking in Inner Mongolia

In pastoral societies and economies, livestock builds the foundation for the accumulation and distribution of wealth. The state programs in pastoral IM between the 1980s and the 2010s have left profound impacts on the livestock-based politics of accumulation and distribution. These programs include livestock redistribution in the 1980s, rangeland redistribution in the 1990s, and destocking in the 2000s–2010s. These three programs were initiated under two national policy discourses: livestock and rangeland redistribution programs were implemented at the height of China's rural decollectivization, while destocking was key to China's campaign to combat desertification. The three sequential and consequential programs, as shown in Figure 2.1, form the core of stocking politics in pastoral IM. They have had a profound and cumulative impact on IMAR's social and environmental transformation.[3]

Policy Discourse / Time Period	Rural Decollectivization	Combating Desertification
1980s	Stock redistribution	
1990s	Rangeland redistribution	
2000s–2010s		Destocking

Figure 2.1 Shifts in policy discourse in pastoral IMAR, 1980s to 2010s

To unpack the cumulative effects of China's decollectivization and campaigns to combat desertification, I will first review the role of livestock in IM's pastoral economy.

Livestock, unlike land, multiplies. Livestock is an expandable asset with return rates that far exceed what most savings accounts can offer. Letu,[4] a herder I met in Ejina in 2013, for example, has done well with his camels.

Letu started with a herd of 22 camels, given to him by his mother when he got married in 1993. In the 1990s, camels were on the list of livestock to be reduced for grassland protection. But after the radical decline of camel populations in IMAR, camels became a protected livestock species in China in 2002.[5] Letu's camels were kept in the Gobi, far away from the center of stock reduction campaigns. Letu never "reduced" his camels beyond his own stock management needs.

By 2013, Letu owned 112 camels that were worth RMB 10,000 yuan per head. His camel stock had quintupled in 19 years, not counting the dozen or so camels that he sold over the years. Considering that camel cows have a 14-month gestation period, this pace of expansion was impressive. Letu attributed his good fortune to his kindness: thanks to his kind heart, he said, his cows had reproduced more female than male offspring, which helped the herd to grow fast.

Compared with sheep and cattle, camels, a semi-domesticated animal, require much less herding and daily care. Letu called his camels "god's children." His camels spent summers roaming in the Gobi, foraging on their own. Letu would check on them only once a week or so to make sure that the newborns had access to their mother's milk, since camel cows are not known to be patient mothers. The camels would only return to the home base for water during dry spells when other water sources were too far to reach. During particularly severe droughts when even the home well was exhausted, Letu would have to drive his thirsty camels away, forcing them to search further. In the late fall, camels were gathered and taken to the low-altitude winter rangeland, but they were still mostly left on their own. Letu would visit them to help with birthing or to break the ice on the ground for camels to drink. In the spring, camels were gathered for shearing and branding. The relatively low labor input to keep camels gave Letu and his wife the time to run a roadside diner that served Mongolian-style lamb dumplings to long-distance truckers.[6]

Camels are not homebodies like sheep. But that does not seem to weaken Letu's affection for them. When talking about his camels, his eyes lit up and his voice became animated. Every camel had a name, such as Black Hill, Red Mountain, Golden Yellow, Teapot (who urinated often), Bowl, Iron, and Wood (who moved very slowly). He said that he could identify his camels by their footprints, a skill that comes in handy when tracking his camels in the Gobi. Letu's greatest regret was that his teenage son, who has attended school since the age of seven in Bayanhot, the capital of Alxa League and 700 km away from home, has little interest in and knowledge about the very camels that have helped pay for his costly schooling in the city.

Livestock are not only expandable assets, but also can be liquidated more easily than land. Furthermore, unlike farmers who rely on the fall harvest for cash income, herders enjoy a year-round stream of income from selling livestock of different ages and wool in different seasons. A woman herder in Ejina, who kept 400 sheep and goats in an unrestricted grazing area, told me that she paid cash for a new apartment unit in the town center in 2012 after selling 50 sheep at 2,000 yuan per head.

Another herder sold 10 sheep to pay for his mother's medical bills. After most rural schools were closed in the 1990s and early 2000s in IMAR,[7] many pastoral families, like that of Letu, have relied on their livestock to pay for their children's schooling and high living costs in the township center or in faraway cities. Livestock is also an essential part of a dowry or wedding gift. In normal times and during emergencies, livestock keeps herding families from sinking into high-interest debt, which often befalls farming families. In the agropastoral villages of east IM, families with a sizable herd of sheep have often become the creditors of farming families that rely mostly on cropping.[8]

Livestock as a steadily expandable and easily liquidated asset provides herding families with the sense of financial and psychological security that I seldom observe in small farming families in the rural northwest. For sure pastoralism has its fair share of uncertainty under the market economy and climate change. But even for those with small herds, livestock promises future growth and gradual improvement of financial stability: just give those ewes a few years on a good patch of grass and you will see.

It is important to note that livestock-based wealth accumulation in China's arid northwest is not just a feature of Mongolian culture. Han Chinese herders in western IMAR value livestock just as much. In his ethnographic studies of first- and second-generation Han Chinese immigrant herders in Alxa Left Banner, historian Ding, Peng (2012: 69) found that Han Chinese herding families also prefer herding over cropping. A local Chinese expression illustrates this preference precisely—"After raising sheep for three years, I wouldn't trade it for anything, not even for being a county magistrate."[9] During my fieldwork in different parts of IM, I have also met quite a few full-time, Mongolian-speaking herders who self-identified as Han Chinese. Place makes people just as much as people make place. I will elaborate more on the dynamic relationship between livelihood and ethnic identity in Chapter 8 on Mongol farmers.

Like land for farmers, livestock for herders is the foundation of security and a harbinger of hope that warrants every ounce of effort to hold onto. The conservation policy of stock reduction severs such security and hope. What's more, in practice, stock reduction is not just about numerically reducing the total number of livestock of individual households or in a given jurisdiction. It is, instead, a matter of livestock-based wealth redistribution among herding families, which consequently exacerbates existing socioeconomic disparities in pastoral society. The distributional impact of stock reduction in the 2000s is also cumulative. The seeds of disparity in pastoral IM were sown by the decollectivization policies of livestock redistribution in the 1980s and rangeland redistribution in the 1990s. The conservation-driven destocking program since the early 2000s in and of itself did not create the disparity. But the destocking program, in joint force with climate change and market expansion, has significantly amplified the disparity. For those struggling families at the bottom, it also diminished their sense of security and hope.

The cumulative effect of livestock-related policies from the 1980s to the 2010s proceeded in the following ways.

I.1 Decollectivizing Livestock and Rangelands, 1980s to 1990s

In 1983, under the national policy of rural decollectivization across agricultural, pastoral, fishery, and forest economies in China, IM began to redistribute *gacha* (Mongolian villages) collectives' livestock among gacha households. Depending on the region, each household received between 30 and 40 sheep or goats and/or a few camels or cattle.[10] At this stage, the gacha grazing land remained open for collective use: summer grazing in the higher attitude hillside and meadows; winter grazing in the lower valley and sandy fields; while certain rangeland was reserved for harvesting grass as winter feed.

The redistribution of livestock brought about two social-environmental consequences. The first concerned the economies of scale in herd size. Whether 40 or 400 sheep, each herd required one full-time shepherd. That problem could be resolved by families pooling their small herds and hiring a full-time shepherd. But the collectivist approach could not solve the fundamental problem of production scale at the individual household level. The shrunken herd size could not generate sufficient income for individual households. In Xilingol, for example, it took a minimum of 200 sheep with no less than 90 to 100 reproductive-aged ewes for a household of four to make a living from raising livestock in the 1980s and 1990s.[11] The income from a 40-sheep flock was far from sufficient to sustain a household of four. The rapid rise of production costs at the household level in the era of market reform also contributed to the rise in the minimum herd size needed to make a family ranch economically viable. As a result, families with means purchased additional livestock to reach the threshold. Between 1983 and 1997, most *sumus* (Mongolian townships) saw their herd size expand three- to fourfold. According to the environmental activist and writer Han, Nianyong (2018),[12] the household herd size grew tenfold, or even twentyfold, during this period. The threshold herd size varied from region to region, but most regions shared the trend of a rising threshold size. In Hulunbair League by the early 2000s, for example, it took 400 to 500 heads of sheep for a family of four to cover daily expenses, and even more if schooling and medical expenses were included.[13]

As stock size thresholds at individual household levels rose, the political discourse was also shifting. In the 1980s, the surge in livestock sizes in pastoral IMAR was celebrated as a triumph of market reforms, which incentivized herders to expand their herds and improve rangeland productivity. By the late 1990s, when rangeland deterioration and desertification caught the attention of policymakers, livestock expansion was viewed as evidence of herders' greed and ignorance. In both policy discourses, the issue of herd-size threshold in individualized pastoral economies was seldom discussed, not to mention the uneven results of livestock redistribution. Those with access to cash were able to build up their family herds much faster than those without. Throughout the 1980s, the disparity in stock ownership was less salient, because owners of both large and small herds were able to graze their livestock in collective rangeland. But decollectivization of grazing land in the 1990s, which I will turn to later in this section, has created much greater impact on social disparity.

Another social-environmental impact of livestock redistribution was the loss of collective-based herding expertise, which is particularly critical to pastoralists' adaptive capability in extreme weather conditions, among other uncertainties.

Not all Mongolians are born herders; nor do all herders have the same skill levels or niche expertise in tending livestock. Before decollectivization, each gacha had designated keepers of each type of livestock. Those who were in charge of camels or horses did not necessarily know what to do with cattle or sheep. The experienced expert herders of the gacha would make seasonal plans: where to graze which animal, and how and where to mix them. Using their local knowledge about the ever-changing weather and variable microclimate of the arid steppe, they designed and adjusted grazing paths and calendars every year to ensure the health and growth of the livestock of the gacha. They also worked to minimize livestock loss under natural calamities, such as severe drought and deadly snow and ice storms by strategizing where to lead flocks to water and grass during droughts and where to shelter people and animals during snow and ice storms. In the back of their minds was always an emergency plan for moving livestock of varied sizes and ages and of both sexes to safety, water, and food. Other collective members worked as accountants, runners, croppers, mechanics, woodworkers, drivers, hay cutters, or manure and fuel wood collectors, and most of them had little experience in tending to the animals. During livestock redistribution of the decollectivization era, every family received some livestock to raise on their own, regardless of their expertise. As a result, many of those who had never tended to livestock during the collective era suffered great losses of livestock to wind and snowstorms, severe droughts, predatory wolves, miscarriages, and/or diseases. After losing their own stock, some worked as a full-time shepherd for other livestock owners. Their payment was usually in livestock. But these inexperienced shepherds lost others' sheep as well. A researcher told me that the dismantling of collectively built and shared herding expertise and labor is a key, yet often overlooked, factor in the cause of post-collectivism poverty of small family herders.[14]

Meanwhile, post-Mao economic expansionism had been heating up across China since the 1990s. In IMAR, growth projects are found in every direction and on all scales, including urban and infrastructure construction, dam building, industrial and mining development, commodity cropping, and industrial ranching.[15] All of these growth projects are built on the seemingly boundless frontier territory, materialized through local government-sponsored appropriation of gachas' land. These projects precipitated an extensive array of interconnected environmental depredation to the rangeland, such as wetland and ground cover loss, deforestation, biodiversity reduction, groundwater depletion, air and water pollution, soil salinization, and sandification. In turn, these have led to sandstorms of increasing frequency and magnitude, the decline of local flora and fauna, and the spread of pests and both human and animal diseases. Though these growth projects were the root of environmental deterioration to the northern steppe, it was herders who took the blame. The expansion of flocks in the first phase of decollectivization, which policy makers celebrated in the 1980s as the successful result of the market reforms, was now condemned as the cause of rangeland deterioration owing to herders' unbridled expansion of their livestock. In popular and policy discourses, the collectively-owned rangeland—overgrazed and thus deteriorated—represented a textbook case of the "tragedy of the commons."[16]

To alter the course of the "tragedy," the second phase of the decollectivization policy focused on rangeland redistribution.[17] The policy was first rolled out in the late 1980s and reached its peak in the 1990s. By 1997, more than 80% of IMAR's local jurisdictions reported completion of the redistribution of collective rangeland to individual households.[18]

Mirroring the farmland contracting system implemented across China's farming regions, rangeland redistribution is called "rangeland contracting system" in pastoral China.[19] Because China continues to uphold state and collective land ownership, individual households can contract use rights. In practice and in herders' perception, however, like in the farmland contracting system, the rangeland contracting system (i.e., rangeland redistribution) is the de facto privatization of rangeland.

Also, like in farmland redistribution, rangeland redistribution is calculated based on household size. As such, large households received larger areas of land. Families with several households, such as three brothers who each head a household, can link their allotted parcels together to establish a family-based, multi-household unit of pastoral operation, which allows them to continue practicing small-scale, rotational grazing.[20] They are also able to plan land use jointly so as to preserve a large enough piece of land to harvest hay for winter feeding, to convert some rangeland to plant feed crops for their own livestock, and to sell the rest of the crops to others for cash. Steady cash flows enable these families to rent additional rangeland in dry years when their own land does not produce enough fodder. In wet years, they are able to earn additional income by renting out parts of their rangeland to others to plant and graze. Such families, who own large swaths of rangeland, can afford commercial grass seeds and fertilizers for feed crops, install irrigation systems and mechanize planting, harvesting, and feed processing. They can also invest in durable storage facilities and animal shelters.

In addition to land size, rangeland quality matters just as much. During land redistribution, gacha heads often received more productive rangeland with rich soil and water access. And these gacha leaders often come from large families with multiple male household heads, which in turn helps enhance the families' local influence. The convergence of power, (de facto) rangeland ownership and livestock ownership instigate a virtuous cycle for these families in post-decollectivized pastoral IM.[21]

Small and sociopolitically marginalized families, on the other hand, easily fall into a vicious cycle. Their small pieces of rangeland deteriorate faster due to frequent grazing without being able to afford intervals of grass regeneration. They also lack the option of reserving a part of their rangeland to plant fodder crops or for winter feeding. Consequently, these families rely more heavily on cash-bought fodder. Further, if their rangeland is of low quality and lacks access to water, they also have to invest in tube wells, the cost of which increases as groundwater levels dwindle. Not many small families are able to afford the investment of tens or hundreds of thousands of yuan—in which case, they must truck in cash-bought water from elsewhere. The production costs add up quickly.

Another new and substantial expense in post-land redistribution era is the wire fencing that marks the boundaries of individual family rangelands at the onset of rangeland decollectivization. After the rangelands were parceled out to individual families, there were frequent instances of border infringement and subsequent conflicts between neighboring landowners, which sometimes escalated to physical violence. To make good neighbors, building a fence around the family rangeland was imperative. But fencing-off grassland is far beyond the capacity of cash-poor families. In southern Xilingol in the 2000s, for example, household contracted rangelands averaged around 1,500 mu, or 1 sq. km—equivalent to 140 standard-sized soccer fields.[22] Small by pastoral standards, this is still an immense size when it comes to building a fence around it: with a total perimeter of 4,000 meters and 1.5 to 2.0 meters in height, such a fence would cost tens of thousands of yuan to build. In the arid Alxa League in western IMAR, a small family rangeland averages 3,000 to 4,000 mu, with large family rangelands reaching up to 10,000 mu. Fencing these large expanses of land would cost hundreds of thousands of yuan and take several years to complete. What's more, fence building is not a one-time project. Fences are prone to vandalism by trespassers and require regular maintenance. After a sandstorm or windstorm, they require substantial repair, if not total rebuilding. During my visits to pastoral Xilingol and Alxa Leagues, wherever I went, there were always fence-building and repair projects going on, with large bundles of metal wire standing by half-finished fences or in front of animal pens. Under these conditions, poor and marginalized herding families have two options. They either take out high-interest loans to build fences, or they helplessly watch as their fenceless rangelands are frequented by neighbors' hungry herds, which accelerates the pace of deterioration of their small rangelands.[23] It is, in short, costly to be poor.

Compared to livestock redistribution of the early 1980s, rangeland redistribution of the 1990s was far more detrimental for small herding families. After livestock redistribution, many (though certainly not all) herding families managed to expand their herds to achieve economies of scale. But rangeland redistribution, compounded by long-lasting droughts and deteriorated grassland productivity, accelerated the hike in fodder prices that accounted for no less than half of the total production cost in central and western IMAR in the 1990s. By the mid- to late 1990s, fodder price hikes had forced many families to scale back their herds. Reduced herd sizes meant dwindling cash income and the onset of a vicious cycle: the increasing production costs pushed up the herd size of what was economically sustainable—in many areas by over 100%, from 200 to 400 or more heads of sheep—at the very moment when herders faced the tough choice of reducing their herd sizes in order to reduce their spending on fodder. Family savings that had accumulated during the period of livestock expansion of the

1980s diminished in the 1990s. As the herding threshold went up and small herders' reserves went down, the gulf between herders' capacities and aspirations widened. In their bid to hold onto their remaining livestock before falling beyond the point of recovery, many herders exhausted their family savings and started to take on high-interest loans to purchase fodder. For them, scaling back the herd size was a strategic retreat. Debt exposed them to financial insecurity, but debt also tided them over and kept their hopes of rebounding alive.

To sum up, rangeland redistribution marks the completion of the two-decade-long process of rural decollectivization and a deepening of marketization in pastoral IM. The decollectivization drives of the 1980s and the 1990s have also effectively reinforced herders' perceptions of rangeland as private property and wired fences as a necessity.

The adaptivity of collaborative pastoralism of the previous eras has been traded for individual proprietorship of livestock, land, and water, among other resources and infrastructure in the new era. Under this paradigmatic shift and much increased production costs for individual households, small herding families have been hit the hardest.

It was at this make-it-or-break-it moment for family herders who managed to survive livestock and rangeland redistribution this far, the conservation-framed destocking policy came to pastoral IM.

I.2 Conservational Destocking, 2000s to 2010s

Under the regime of rangeland conservation, livestock reduction was not a strategic retreat for herding families but a forceful government order that threatened to confiscate their "excessive" livestock. During the height of livestock reduction campaigns, especially in the targeted areas, herders sold their "excessive" livestock at a steep financial loss, from which many were never able to recover.[24] Herding families faced an increasingly adverse environment of soaring fodder prices due to conservational rangeland enclosure, more frequent and longer droughts, and overall diminishing forage productivity of the deteriorated rangeland. In the 2010s, fodder accounted for about half of a herding family's total production costs, and that number went up by 70% to 80% during prolonged droughts. To feed 300 sheep in a dry year, the cost of fodder alone could reach 100,000 yuan. According to Han, Nianyong's (2018) survey in 2014 of a gacha in Otog Banner of Ordos Municipality, more than 90% of the herding households in the gacha lived with cyclical debts. What started out as a one-time loan would become cyclical debt traps as the herders borrowed fresh loans to settle their old ones. In another gacha in western Xilingol League, Han interviewed 20 households and found that the average size of household debt was 100,000 yuan, equivalent to the income of a good year. Ninety percent of the debt was incurred from purchasing fodder. At annual interest rates of 24% to 36%, a herder said he felt he was "raising the sheep for money lenders and fodder merchants."[25] After multiyear droughts and chronic reliance on loan-bought fodder, many cyclically indebted families lost their remaining livestock to their creditors.[26] To survive, the herdless herders would lease out their family contracted rangeland to industrial farm investors, like those of the suosuo plantation presented in Chapter 1, or lease out their rangeland to other herding families who had managed to stay in the game. Several researchers have reported on small herding families' downward spiral of losing livestock and falling under the poverty line, step by step and policy by policy from the late 1980s to the 2000s.[27] I myself have met quite a number of herd-less herders in various areas of IMAR in the 2010s. I recall visiting a widowed herder in his late 50s in his home that was built with thin steel sheets and mud bricks. He had no sheep to his name and worked as a hired hand for seasonal work, such as shearing wool in the spring or harvesting hay in the fall.

At the other end of the spectrum, families with large herds and grazing land, many of whom were gacha officials, fared much better under conservation. Under grassland conservation, livestock reduction was calculated based on "carrying capacity," a model that policymakers use as the scientific foundation to calculate how many heads of grazing sheep or cattle a unit area of rangeland can support.[28] For example, according to the "grass-stock balance" guideline in Xilingol League, which was derived from the principle of carrying capacity, a family needed to allot 20 mu for every head of sheep, and 50 mu for each cattle. For owners of large rangeland, it is easier for them to meet the required stocking rate while keeping an economically viable herd size. Under grazing bans and stocking rate restrictions, large families with sufficient cash flow could also lease rangelands from stockless herders and continue to expand their herds and practice rotational grazing between their own rangelands and those that they lease from others. In other words, while the conservation-framed stocking rate tabulation aims at striking a balance between grass and stock, the ability to keep the balance, if at all achievable, is not evenly distributed.

In the summer of 2012 in Xilingol League, I visited a well-to-do herding family that had access to over 15,000 mu of rangeland, half self-owned, half leased. The patriarch of the family, a poised man in his mid-60s, told me that in his sumu, most families had access to 1,000 to 2,000 mu of grazing land. His family was composed of three households headed by him and his two married sons. Together they owned more than a thousand sheep and goats and over one hundred cattle and horses. They also proudly kept a few dozen camels on the side, as the ability to keep the "five Mongolian stocks," namely, sheep, goats, cattle, horses, and camels, is a sign of prosperity and success (I will discuss the mixed herds later in this section). During the summer, his sons and daughters-in-law graze the herds on neighboring rental rangelands, reserving most of their own rangeland for winter grazing. The parents stay in the home base year-round. Their home rangeland is equipped with deep wells and a private connection to power grids. They also have a large and sturdy brick home, as well as a grandiose yurt furnished with a natural gas-heated floor, intricately inlaid and carved wooden cabinets, and embroidered horse saddles imported from Mongolia.

Herding in the age of conservation is not for the faint-hearted. For the most determined or desperately indebted herders, to keep their herd numbers up and fodder costs down, the only viable option is to stick it out with grazing in the open range whenever and wherever possible. Illicit grazing became the norm under the grazing ban. Night grazing and grazing in areas far from paved roads (to better dodge pastoral patrols) were an open secret. On a cloudy morning in June 2013, I witnessed one shepherd who "followed" his hungry sheep through a wired fence to graze in an enclosed grazing land when the patrol crew was out of sight. My host who accompanied my tour of the gacha did not even raise an eyebrow. See Figure 2.2.

Figure 2.2 Hungry sheep defying the fence

Source: Photo credit: Author.

Like rangeland redistribution, which provoked frequent boundary disputes among neighbors, the cat-and-mouse game over illicit grazing creates frequent conflicts and occasionally fist fights between the righteous pasture patrols and resentful herders. Herders often accuse patrol crews of issuing fines only to their personal foes, while letting their own relations get away with grazing in forbidden zones or during grazing ban seasons. The fines for "grazing-land robbery" (*daomu*), as illicit grazing is called in Chinese, help to augment the pasture patrol agency's revenues. One herder suspected that the fines had paid for the patrol's four-wheel drive.[29] For herders, the fines—hundreds of yuan at a time—were yet another weighty item on their list of production costs. They saw the fines as licensing fees that authorized them to graze the livestock in the forbidden zones. This logic is similar to that of Chinese villagers under the family planning policy from late 1970s to mid-2010s,[30] in which families felt entitled to have more children after paying an expensive fine (in the 2000s, it was 5,000 yuan per excessive child in some villages) to village cadres for any children exceeding the birth quota (usually two in rural areas until 2015). For some rural families, their version of "family planning" was to start saving up for the fine even before their first pregnancy. In pastoral IM, the inconsistently issued fines and monetized rangeland governance have triggered frequent conflicts not just between herders and the grassroots regulation enforcers, but also among herders who felt they received unfair treatment in comparison with their better-connected neighbors.

While rangeland enclosures and grazing bans were irregularly executed, the stocking rate restrictions were also routinely breached. I met few herders in IMAR in the 2010s who actually followed the livestock reduction tabulations.[31] Amu, a diligent 38-year-old herder, whom I met in 2012 in southern Xilingol, makes for a good example. Amu, his wife, and his father-in-law owned 60 cattle and 200 sheep. According to local "grass-stock balance" guidelines, the family needed to allot 20 mu for every head of sheep, and 50 mu for each cattle. In theory, Amu would need 7,000 mu of grassland, either self-owned or leased, to sustain his flocks. In reality, his family owned 1,380 mu of grassland, and they leased another 1,000 mu at 10 yuan per mu from a neighbor who had given up herding and left the gacha. Together, the family had access to 2,380 mu of grazing land. Their actual livestock-to-land ratio was three times higher than the official threshold. Amu told me that most of the 38 households in his gacha overstocked (*chaozai*). Amu's father-in-law further suggested that to keep a rangeland healthy, rain matters more than the simple math of the stocking rate. He recounted the family's struggle during a prolonged drought from 2008 to 2011. The rangeland was scorched. They sold off a few more cattle and sheep than usual to keep their fodder expenses manageable, but they persevered and held onto their herds at a sustainable size. To pay for the "gold-like" fodder, they dipped deep into family savings and took out loans from relatives, grinding their way through the three long years. Some of the gacha families, including the one from whom they leased the grassland, did not make it to the third year of the long drought and lost most of their livestock to creditors. But those who survived the three-year drought, like Amu's family, were able to expand their herds in 2012 when several good rains brought the forage back, which reduced their fodder expenses by more than half.

What matters is not just the amount of rain, but also its timing. Well-timed rains in April enable nutritious (and sheep's preferred) perennials like *Xapraha* (in Mongolian, *Jinjier* in Chinese, and *Caragana Fabr* in Latin)[32] to flourish. If the rains come too early—such as in March when the ground temperature is still low—the preferred perennials do not germinate. If the rains come too late, say in late May, grazing lands will be dominated by drought-tolerant but less nutritious annuals that are "useless for the sheep," according to Amu. Amu agrees with his father-in-law that rain matters more than grazing bans and stocking rates in rangeland productivity, a stance shared by other herders and local researchers alike.[33] A local researcher summed up the politics of rain and grazing bans for me: "When the forages are thin and yellow due to the lack of timely rain, government officials blame it on overgrazing and overstocking. In a wet year, say, when the annual precipitation reaches over 360 mm and good grasses are abundant, government officials take credit for it and declare their grazing ban policy a success."[34]

During my visit to pastoral Xilingol in the summer of 2012, I was struck by the magical transformation of the grasslands from brownish yellow to fresh green right after a "good" rain, that is, a rain that could "soak no less than four-fingers deep of the top soil," (four fingers placed parallel to the ground), my host explained. I was equally impressed by the sudden appearance of large flocks of sheep right after the grazing fields turned green. Watching them munch away like there is no tomorrow, I wondered: where were they hiding before the rain?

Undoubtedly, the reach of the Chinese Communist Party (CCP) state, even in far-flung frontier regions, is unprecedented in Chinese history. Still, the question remains to be to what extent can the numerically framed livestock reduction guidelines be executed in the immense, diverse, and ever-changing environments of the northern steppe?

The imperfectly executed policies of livestock reduction and grazing bans have nevertheless brought profound environmental consequences. Of the many impacts that researchers have noted, the negative impacts seem to outnumber the positive ones. Also, as with the social impacts of destocking, the negative environmental impacts are interconnected and cumulative. Among them, soil deterioration, rangeland degeneration, and biodiversity loss of the rangeland have been most salient. These issues are what the conservation policies aim to reverse yet end up reinforcing.

As mentioned earlier, livestock redistribution has led individual families to greatly expand their herds to meet the ever-rising herd-size thresholds. These enlarged herds frequently graze upon fenced-in grasslands, leaving little time for forage regeneration. Rangeland redistribution has also led to a grazing sprawl at the gacha level. Areas that used to be reserved for fodder harvesting in the fall and feeding in the winter, emergency grazing, or spring grazing for the entire gacha are now allotted to individual households for year-round use, leaving little room for seasonal rotation. As grazing intensifies in individual rangelands and grazing activities spread across the gacha, the buffer zones between grazing areas have shrunk. As droughts persist and groundwater levels decline, the heavily grazed rangelands have started to see losses in vegetation cover, exposed surfaces, soil erosion, and sandification. Sandified patches in close proximity are prone to coalescing into large expanses of sandified fields, which start the process of what is usually called desertification.[35]

Conservation-framed rangeland enclosures and grazing bans further accelerate the process of soil deterioration. A significant portion of the rangelands, in many cases about half of a gacha's total and mostly on individually owned rangelands, have been placed under grazing bans. As a result, herding families converge their herds to graze in nonrestricted zones, which are often marginal lands not yet redistributed to individual households. The rangeland redistribution of the 1990s intensified the use of individualized rangelands due to ballooning herd sizes and increased grazing frequency. Whereas grazing bans on individual rangelands since the 2000s have intensified the use of nonrestricted grasslands still in the hands of the gacha collective.[36] As a result of intensive and extensive grazing, forage productivity has continued to decline since the 1980s. Lower and thinner forage means that it takes a much longer time for livestock to graze to satisfaction in the open rangeland, which in turn requires greater labor input. The stock animals are also affected: a low quality and low quantity diet and the lack of exercise in constrained grazing lands and shelters have compromised their growth and health. In Xilingol, for example, the average sheep weight decreased by half from the 1970s to the 2000s, while the duration of ewes' fertility shortened from eight to ten years to five to six years. One old herder gave an explanation: when ewes graze on short grass they tend to take in a lot of sand, which damages their teeth and digestive systems, hindering the ewes' capacity to build up enough body fat to maintain reproductive vigor. Others reported that the inadequate diet also reduces ewes' milk production to the point that herders have to buy carton milk to feed the lambs.[37] The Mongolian Bactrian camels have suffered, too. In the deteriorated rangeland of western Xilingol, without a proper diet, the average weight of eight-year-old camels have declined from their optimal weight of 500 kg to less than 300 kg; their fat-filled humps become limp and droop down.[38]

The rapidly expanding land lease market that comes with the de facto privatization has also hastened rangeland degeneration. Throughout the late 2000s and most of the 2010s, the demand for fodder continued to increase under grazing bans and more frequent and longer droughts that have led to the decline of forage productivity. The rising demand has pushed the fodder price to new heights. To manage production costs, many herding families have chosen to lease grazing lands from others to lower fodder expenses. On the supply side, with more herding families dropping out of herding altogether and struggling families leasing out their land to pay for daily, medical or school expenses, the supply of rangeland on the leasing market is also on the rise.

In the meantime, the increasing supply in the land lease market was met with a changing structure of demand. Herding families were not the only tenants. Since the early 2000s, merchant capital drawn to surging fodder prices have started to lease large areas of rangeland to harvest fodder for sale, offering two to three times the going rate, driving up local land lease rates. In Han's (2018) survey of Central and eastern IMAR, between 2000 and 2015, rangeland rent rates grew at least tenfold, and by the mid-2010s, between 30 and 60% of IMAR's rangelands were under various leasing arrangements.[39]

To make their investment pay, rangeland tenants both big and small work their leased land hard. The semi-oligopolistic fodder merchants bear the reputation of working the rangeland the hardest. They cut the grasses very close to the roots, preventing healthy forage regeneration. The shortened lease terms further distress the rangelands. The increasingly unstable climate and sporadic precipitation patterns in the 2000s and 2010s have made long-term leases too risky for the tenants. During severe droughts, the leased grazing lands yield too little to help ease herding tenants' pressure to buy the "gold-like" fodder; in wet years, paying for a long-term lease is a waste of money because one's own rangeland can produce enough, or at the minimum, the fodder price is lower than leasing fees.

Consequently, the practice of long-term rangeland leases of three to five years in the 1990s gave way to yearly leases of the 2000s, and then to seasonal, monthly, or even daily rentals in the 2010s. The shorter the term, the higher the rent rates, and the more intensively the tenants would graze and harvest the rental land. High turnover renders the rangelands a disposable commodity, subject rental land to the most exploitative extraction under the increasingly unstable relationship between rangeland owners and their tenants. Meanwhile, the frequent turnover disincentivizes caring for the long-term health of the rangelands, by both tenants and land owners. The rental rangelands, most of which are already of substandard quality when they are put on the rental market, therefore deteriorate even faster.[40]

The loss of biodiversity reveals another notable environmental impact of rangeland enclosure. From a vantage point that privileges the color green, or what I call "color-coded conservationism,"[41] policymakers often point to the lush greenery of enclosed rangelands as evidence of ecological recovery and conservation success. But herders and local environmental activist-researchers look at the greenery differently: plant diversity of the rangeland is more important than the color green; plant diversity concerns not just the number of grass species, but the types of forage in a given grazing area. Upon closer inspection of the "recovered" abundance of green vegetation after years of grazing bans, herders found that the rangelands in question were often dominated by forage that "few animals care for."[42] The grazing bans, they explained, have contributed to the decline of both the quantity and quality of edible and nutritious forage that their livestock prefer. Some invasive plants and plants that were formerly nondominant are now dominant and have crowded out the edible ones.[43]

Some herders and local researchers I talked to attribute the dwindling of forage preferred by livestock to the decline in livestock mixing. Under collectivism, most gachas owned large flocks that numbered in the tens of thousands, with most keeping the "five Mongolian stocks," namely: camels, horses, cattle, goats, and sheep. Each herbivore has its own dietary preference, allowing them to co-graze in the same grazing field or to mix in different combinations in different kinds of rangelands during different seasons. In general, cattle and horses are grazers that eat mostly grasses; goats are browsers that prefer the leaves of woody plants, wildflowers, and weeds;

sheep are intermediate feeders that shift their diet among grasses, forbs, and browse. The five types of livestock make complementary contributions to rangeland management. For example, as mentioned earlier, camels require less herding than the others and can largely be left on their own, sparing the labor for other livestock. Sheep and goats make for good foraging partners. Sheep are easily agitated and disperse during windstorms and snowstorms. Goats keep the sheep in the pack, leading them to shelter during storms. In normal times, "lazy" sheep tend to munch in the same patch. But the active goats keep the sheep moving, which helps prevent overgrazing in the same patch. Goats are also the first to sound the alarm when danger approaches, such as wolves. Compared to sheep, goats consume less and are more resilient to drought. On the other hand, sheep, a "warm-mouthed" animal, help their foraging pals as well. During the long and cold winter nights, the sheep's dried dung on the ground and their higher body temperatures and warm breath keep the animal pens warm for the "cold-mouthed" goats, cattle, and camels. Goats often squeeze between sheep or even lie on the back of sheep to keep warm. Large livestock like cattle and horses offer a different kind of contribution. On the winter grazing path, cattle and horses lead the pack by opening a path in the deep snow and by breaking the ground ice so the small sheep and goats can find forage underneath the snow and ice. As mentioned earlier, keeping all five Mongolian stocks came to be a source of cultural pride and a symbol of prosperity.[44]

After livestock redistribution, individual households' small flock size has made it difficult to maintain the five-stock mix at the household level. Under rangeland redistribution, the individual fenced-in grazing lands have made it difficult to keep large animals, like horses and camels that need more space to roam. Conservation policies and stocking rate tabulations, in which one cattle is equal to five sheep (or six goats), one horse to six sheep, and one camel to seven sheep, have further reduced the viability of keeping up both the scale and the mix of animals, resulting in a significant reduction in large-sized horses and camels.

Goats, a small-sized livestock, are also under threat in the age of conservation. Conservation experts and officials accuse goats of being destructive "root eaters" that are responsible for setting sandstorms in motion, as expressed in the aforementioned slogan, "exterminate the goats to defend Beijing" in the campaign to combat desertification. Designed with this perception in mind, grazing bans were particularly strict on goats. For example, grazing bans on sheep usually took place in the spring and lasted between three to six months, while goats often face year-round bans. In the summer and fall, openly grazing sheep miss their foraging pals and shepherds miss their herding assistants, as the active and alert goats are "incarcerated" in shelters, to use one herder's expression.[45]

The reduction in livestock variety has led to a reduction in the diversity, quality, and quantity of preferable and nutritious forage for livestock. As mentioned earlier, each of the five livestock has its favorite plants, and they eat different parts of the same plant. When different animals graze openly upon different types of plants, their manure fertilizes the soil, spreading various kinds of plant seeds. Frequent tramping by hard-hoofed sheep in high-density rangelands might compact the soil and harm forage productivity, but soft-hoofed livestock like camels help stabilize the loosely scattered seeds that may otherwise be blown away in the windy northern steppe, facilitating vegetal germination and growth.

Grazing bans degenerate the rangeland further, as mentioned earlier. Local researchers have found that in the fenced-off rangelands, especially in areas enclosed for over three years, the early-sprouting annual and bi-annual plants tend to dominate. Grazing animals tend to avoid these tough and dry plants. These dominant, yet unappetizing, plants then crowd out the juicier, more nutritious late-sprouting perennials that animals prefer. Long-term grazing bans also trigger near-irreversible plant invasion. For example, news reports often featured a bright, purple-colored flower called *Malan* in Chinese to showcase the beauty of the recovered rangeland. *Malan* is even the title of a popular song that praises the beauty of the pasture. But in Xilingol, my herder host sighed at the sight of *Malan*, whose presence indicates a high level of soil salinization, which inhibits the growth of edible forage. Some grasses that prosper in the enclosed rangeland are even poisonous. One herder in Xilingol told me he lost three cows in a single year to a poisonous plant that has proliferated since the grazing ban was enacted. A researcher reported that in Alxa, a drought-tolerant plant named *zuimacao* ("Drunken Horse") prevailed in the "recovered" rangeland. When sheep, who are not picky eaters during dry years, eat Drunken Horse, they appear drunk and lose weight beyond recovery.[46] *Dazihao* is another plant that thrives in dry summers. Sheep do not like Dazihao. So Dazihao is usually cut for winter feeding when the sheep have few other options. But when consumed in large quantities, dried dazihao causes the ewes' meat to take on a foul flavor.

I.3 Breed Improvement

The conservation-driven livestock reduction and grazing ban programs are accompanied by a productive program that promotes new breeds.

Like seed improvement in agricultural China, breed improvement is not new in pastoral China. Both are integral parts of the socialist science-driven programs of productivity improvement.[47] The breed improvement programs evolved and expanded under market reform and have continued under the regime of productive conservation. In a southern Xilingol banner, a local official told me that each newly appointed banner governor customarily introduces a signature new breed to the local mix, just as local leaders would invest in a new school or bridge to mark their contribution to local development.[48] These new breeds are advertised for their faster growth, shorter reproduction cycle, and/or increased milk, wool, or meat productivity.

New breeds introduce new biopolitics. When various new breeds, some following the national breeding standards and others following local ones, were introduced to improve the local stock, they often mated with the existing local breeds. This process in turn created unclassifiable hybrids. During droughts, herds would frequently move in search of grazing fields and flocks would inevitably mix. The mixed flocks would begin to mate with one another. The purity of the new breeds became difficult to guard and their desirable features hard to preserve. One of the new breeds of sheep, called Sunite in Chinese, for example, is marked by black fur around its eyes and a white-colored body, hence its nickname, the "Panda sheep." Sunite sells for twice the price of other breeds, because its high-quality meat does not have the excessively gamey flavor found in many others. But in southern Xilingol, the director of a banner's Bureau of Husbandry told me that even he could no longer distinguish between purebred and the mixed Sunite sheep.

On the other hand, while the breed might make a difference in the lambs' flavor and their market value, what matters just as much (if not more) is whether the sheep is pasture-raised or feed-fattened in crowded shelters. The distinction is not unlike pasture- versus cage-raised chicken meat and eggs sold in California's supermarkets. Here, the social gap again plays a role. In Xilingol, Sunite sheep or not, the much pricier pasture-raised lamb often comes from owners with large herds and ample grazing land whose sheep spend all day grazing in the open. Lower-priced, feed-fattened lamb often comes from smaller stock- and landowners who rely heavily on sheltered husbandry. The bottom stratum of lamb production is made up of small herding families who resort to subcontracting others' sheep to feed-fatten them over a couple of months before the sheep are ready for market. Meat processing companies that target the high-end market normally reject sheltered and feed-fattened sheep, whose meat is then sold to lower-tier processors at half the price. The segregated meat markets therefore further aggravate the social disparities found in the pastoral economy outlined earlier.

New breeds also bring new managerial challenges. Many herders have reported that the new cattle and sheep breeds are more prone to disease and less tolerant of the droughts and long winters of IM.

In 2012, I met a 43-year-old herder, Enge, in a relocation village in Xilingol. In 2010, Enge had bought three dairy cows of a Dutch breed at over 18,000 yuan each (of which 10,000 yuan came out of his own pocket, with the remaining 8,000 yuan from a policy loan under his name) from the Banner government. Banner officials assured him the cows would produce plenty of milk, which could be sold at a sound profit to the government-sponsored dairy processing station. But these Dutch cows had an appetite five times that of native varieties, and "they did not know how to graze local pastures," Enge lamented. In addition, the new cows often fell sick and constantly needed antibiotic treatment. The cold Mongolian winter brought frostbite to the cows' nipples and caused Bovine mastitis, a mammary gland inflammation that affects milk production. On top of the unexpected expenses and stress, the cows did not reproduce any calves. To cut his losses, Enge sold two of the dairy cows for meat at 5,000 yuan a head. The third cow, an insatiable and indiscriminate eater, accidentally swallowed a plastic bag. After two days of enema at the veterinarian, the cow died. The venture set Enge back 50,000 yuan.

Enge's experiences were shared by many other herders under the regime of productive conservation. Environmental activist Lu, Yan (2014)[49] surveyed herders' financial losses in dairy cows in several Xilingol gachas, finding that the average loss per household was over 100,000 yuan, or about half to two-thirds the average household income in a good year. In Alxa Left Banner, one herder told me about a protest that he joined. He and other herders took the disappointing dairy cows back to the government offices who had sold them the cows, demanding refunds. They succeeded in recovering about half of their investment after gathering hundreds of cows in front of the government building.[50]

One protest reported by Free Asia Radio was on a much larger scale. The case involved more than 250 herders, who claimed damages totaling 27 million yuan. In this case, the protesters did not target lower-level local governments at the sumu or banner level, but rather the IMAR government. The herders' grievances began in 2015 when the Agriculture and Pastoral Administration of IMAR announced its support of a company that planned to bring 100,000 heads of the highly prized New Zealand Angus cattle to IMAR. The IMAR government publicly endorsed the company's program in *Inner Mongolia People's Daily*, the most authoritative official newspaper of IMAR. Through the marketing efforts of the company and its government enablers, herders across six different IMAR subregional jurisdictions signed up and paid a total of 27 million yuan in deposits for the breeding cattle promised by the company. Many herders went into high-interest debt—often on the scale of hundreds of thousands of yuan each—to pay for the deposits. The company never delivered the cattle and vanished from the scene after collecting their deposits. After lodging complaints at the local level in vain, 40 herders from different leagues and banners gathered in front of the "Letters and Visits Bureau" in Hohhot, IMAR's capital in September 2018. They held red banners that read "give back the money we earned with blood and sweat." The report stated that the 40 protestors did not receive much attention from the government. It is unclear whether the case was resolved.[51] What is notable is that while other smaller scale protests involved actual cows—however disappointing the livestock were—this large protest in Hohhot was triggered by hype surrounding the new breed and malfeasance that capitalized upon herders' trust in the IMAR government. In this case, none of the herders who participated in the program ever saw an actual Angus cow. Many of them seemed to have held the notion that while grassroots governments are crafty, the provincial-level IMAR government—the top-tier local government in China's territorial hierarchy—ought to be more trustworthy.[52]

The promotion of new breeds is accompanied by the castration of native species. Both are policy mandates to be executed by grassroots cadres through a quota system, the backbone of China's bureaucratic system of resource allocation and responsibility delegation.[53] Each official is responsible for the sale of a rationed number of new breed cattle or sheep. Grassroots officials are also assigned to perform a rationed number of castrations. The new breed quota is challenging to fulfill. But the castration quota created much greater tension. A banner official from the Husbandry Bureau told me that in 2004 when castration was first imposed, he figured it would be easier to fool the inspecting officials from the city than to force local herders to castrate their native cattle, which were easily identifiable by their smaller size and dark-brown- or black-colored coats. To appease both sides, the official asked herders to hide their cattle's testicles when inspectors would come around. By 2005, his supervisors pushed harder on castration mandates, and his trick no longer worked. The official himself was given a quota to castrate 10 native cattle. He fulfilled the quota by castrating the cattle that belonged to two families. One was the family of his subordinate, who had little choice but to submit to the order of his boss. The other was a local recalcitrant who had offended the official multiple times, to whom the official said bluntly, "If I do not castrate your cattle, whose cattle would I castrate?"[54]

In short, stocking is central to the politics of accumulation and distribution in pastoral IM, and destocking is the key link to its politics of conservation. The tension between stocking and destocking have shaped pastoral IM's transformation from the 1980s to the 2010s.[55] The social consequences of conservation are cumulative and rooted in the previous era of decollectivization. Those who have survived or even thrived under conservation, namely, large and powerful families, have enjoyed a benign cycle of accumulation since the decollectivization of the 1980s and 1990s. The small herding families who were marginalized under decollectivization, on the other hand, have had much slimmer chances of surviving conservation. At each policy turn, the herd-size threshold in herding has gone up, sending small herders into deeper debt and widening the gap between their capacities and aspirations to hold onto their livestock. Many have eventually fallen below the threshold and have dropped out of herding. Through this process of restructuring policy by policy, however, pastoralism did not disappear. Rather, it has been consolidated into the hands of the few: of not just land- and cash-rich herding families, but also merchant capital.

In this cumulative process, social and the environmental consequences produce one another. Social disparity and its uneven impacts on grassland degeneration reinforce one another. Large and resourceful herding families are better positioned to maintain more sustainable stock diversity, stocking ratio, and rotational grazing, thanks to their access to much larger grazing lands. Cash- and land-poor herding families are the most vulnerable to rangeland degeneration due to intensive grazing, trespassings onto their under-defended grazing land, and leasing out their rangeland to exploitative grazing and other land uses. Balancing stock and rangeland is the mantra of dryland conservation in IM and beyond, but the ability to maintain the balance, if achievable at all, is not evenly distributed. Under long-lasting droughts, intensifying state intervention, and accelerating market expansion since the 2000s, the cumulative social and environmental effects make it increasingly difficult for struggling families to maintain any sort of stock-grass balance.

It is important to note that the cumulative consequences are not necessarily inevitable nor sequential. Interruptive events could aggravate, reverse, or reroute the process. In IM from the 1980s to the 2010s, one decisive interruption aggravated social disparity, which was the change in herders' coping mechanism in the face of uncertainty. Uncertainty is a given in pastoral livelihoods in arid lands, or, in any type of livelihood anywhere for that matter.

Prior to the 1980s, labor and resource sharing within the largely lineage-based herding clusters in the pre-CCP era and under CCP's collectivism have been critical to pastoral society and its economy. The collective organizations have helped maintain stock diversity, regularize labor division, and share herding knowledge. These collective mechanisms optimized stock development and minimized the loss of stock to extreme and variable weather. The collective organization of production also helped achieve economies of scale in the sharing of resources, like water and grazing fields, and in infrastructure investments in mechanization, power supplies, and tube well construction. Even during massive agricultural expansion in the 1960s and 1970s, the collectively organized rotational grazing contributed to a relatively slow pace of rangeland deterioration.[56]

Since the 1980s, IM's pastoral society has gone through a paradigm shift from collective to individual mechanisms of coping with uncertainties. Younger generation herders today have only vague memories of and limited exposure to collectivism, while many share negative experiences of decollectivization of the 1980s. The negative experiences have only reinforced their suspicions of CCP-style collectivism. In the meantime, herders have faced increasing uncertainty on multiple fronts: changes in climate, the spread of livestock disease and rangeland pests,[57] hikes in living and production costs and fluctuations in commodity prices, and shifts in policies with variable local implementation, to name just the most obvious.

With a growing sense of distrust in the state and their own neighbors, herders have come to see individually contracted rangeland as the ultimate anchor of family survival. Few families are willing to tear down their fences, which now serve as the most prominent mark of decollectivized pastoral society in IM. Even poor herders feel compelled to build costly fences with high-interest private loans, as mentioned earlier. In southern Xilingol, I met one energetic gacha leader in his 40s who was successful in organizing more than half of his 50-plus fellow villagers into a co-op to purchase fodder and livestock, sell their sheep, and run a village-based ecotourism project. Even so, he was not able to convince his co-op members to take down their fences and pool their grazing land, which would have allowed for more effective and sustainable land use.[58]

As the impacts of climate, policy, and market uncertainties compounded and deepened in the 2010s, even better-positioned families felt threatened. I met one herder in southern Xilingol who had managed to keep a sizable flock of 500 sheep by the late 1990s. But he was unable to hold onto his herd through the prolonged droughts of the early 2010s. The patriarch of the aforementioned well-to-do family in Xilingol, who had over 1,000 sheep, became alarmed, too. He lamented that the wire fences that crisscross the decollectivized grasslands block the grazing paths between his own grazing land and his rental grazing land. He now regularly trucked the herds from pasture to pasture, and also trucked water to rental grazing lands that were of poorer quality and lacked tube wells. During the three years of drought from 2008 to 2011, his fodder expenses went up by 60%. To manage his production costs, he had to sell two times more livestock than he normally would. Compared with most of his neighbors, the 62-year-old man still had plenty to fall back on. But his reserves did little to ease his anxiety in a time of escalating uncertainties.

The increased uncertainty and individualized coping mechanisms together made for a perfect storm that has aggravated social disparities and accelerated the pace of pastoral transformation.

II A New Mode of Mobility in Ejina

Ecological relocation has been another key source of uncertainty for herding families. In IMAR, ecological relocation began in the 1990s, reaching its peak in the early 2000s. Under the paired policies of poverty alleviation and ecological recovery (see Introduction), the scale of relocation varied: from several dozens to hundreds or thousands of households in a resettlement. The programs were initiated by various government units, such as the Development and Planning Committee, Poverty Alleviation Office or Agricultural Development Bureau, at national, provincial, or league and banner levels. The programs were also incorporated into various funding schemes. The involvement of numerous government units in carrying out relocation programs—with varied financial capacities and policy mandates—has led to a large number of resettlements of varied scales, locations, and quality throughout the 1990s and 2000s.

Some resettlements are located at the fringes of townships or cities, providing more employment opportunities for the young and better educated relocatees. Many others are built on remote, inhospitable, and salty land that is unsuitable for cropping or herding. In both types of resettlements, the relocated families have had to come up with cash to pay for various new expenses: completing and improving the construction of government-built housing, home furnishings, and water and electricity bills, as well as dairy products and fodder that used to come from their own pastures. As outlined in the Introduction, ecological relocation has created a long list of predicaments. While almost all resettlements had production and life-supporting infrastructure in their plans, such as the provision of housing, power, tube wells, fodder cropland, and livestock shelters, the execution varied greatly. While some new homes were already built by the time the relocatees had arrived, others were little more than designated sites where relocatees would have to build their own homes from scratch. Tube wells did not always work due to a lack of power or groundwater, or both. Power connections required unexpectedly high installation fees in addition to monthly bills. The quality of the cropland allocated to relocatee families and the size of monetary compensation also varied across leagues, banners, sumus, and gachas.

Compensation packages varied even at the household level within a gacha. The package was often conditioned by one's political position and bargaining skills. Like the massive land appropriations and relocation during China's urban expansion frenzy in the 1990s and 2000s,[59] and like the livestock and land redistribution programs outlined previously, the uneven delivery of relocation housing has also heightened rural residents' sense of unfairness and deepened their suspicions toward the state and their neighbors. Some better-connected villagers gamed the system through under-the-table deals with local authorities; others launched protests to bring officials to the bargaining table where they would advocate for a tailored deal for themselves. The less cunning ones got the short end of the stick and grew embittered and disillusioned.[60]

Environmentally, the high-density, large-scale ecological resettlements supported by deep wells have accelerated groundwater extraction.[61] Resettlements also brought concentrated cultivation of government promoted thirsty fodder crops, like alfalfa. The crops were supported by irrigation and required intense applications of fertilizer and pesticides, which accelerated aquifer degeneration.[62] In addition, infectious diseases spread more easily among cattle and sheep in crowded shelters, prompting regular use of antibiotics in animal feed, not unlike cattle feedlots in the U.S.

Many researchers consider ecological relocation to be the definitive root of the environmental and social predicaments faced by pastoralists. The condition is found not just in IM, but also in other arid lands of sub-Sahara Africa, India, the Middle East, and Central Asia, where herders have also been scapegoated for desertification.[63] A China-based scholar I met in 2011 argued that moving herders into ecological resettlements is the final step in the centuries-long state project to sedentarize Mongol nomads.

It appeared that ecological resettlements are where most sedentarization stories start and end. As I prepared for my first visit to ecological resettlements in pastoral IM, I expected to find entrapped herders there, and perhaps a few better-off herding families that were able to take advantage of government-subsidized programs or were supported by non-farm income, like in the farming villages that I have visited elsewhere in China. But to my surprise, during my visits to eight ecological resettlements of varied scales and conditions in Xilingol and Alxa Leagues in the roasting summers of 2011 and 2012, I saw few of either. Most of the settlement homes were empty, see Figure 2.3.

Figure 2.3 An empty relocation settlement

Source: Photo credit: Author.

One resettlement in Alxa was completely unoccupied. In another resettlement of 56 units in Xilingol, only nine units were occupied. In yet another compound of 40 homes in Alxa, 4 units were rented out to seasonal farmhands, while the others sat empty. Beyond the resettlements, I encountered some relocatees in their twenties who worked in the tourism industry. They donned Mongolian costumes while waiting tables and singing in Mongolian-themed restaurants or acted as mounted archers and Mongolian princes and princesses in tourist resorts. I also met an entrepreneurial herder in his 40s who took advantage of China's widely available delivery services to run a pasture-to-table lamb and beef business from a small city in Xilingol. Still, where are the rest of the "sedentarized" herders?

It was not until 2013 and 2014, when I revisited Ejina banner of Alxa League in different seasons, did I begin to learn that moving to the resettlements was not the end, but the beginning, of the story about sedentarization. The ecological resettlements were central to the state-sanctioned conservation programs of containment and restriction. To survive such restrictions, herders have become more mobile. Some of them even strategically incorporated the resettlement homes into their new modes of mobility in the increasingly diversified rural economy in IM.

My host family in Ejina was well entrenched in this new mode of mobility in the age of restriction. Before telling the story of this family, I will briefly introduce Ejina, their home banner.

Tucked away in the Gobi Desert,[64] Ejina sits at the tail end of Hei River, an inland river that originates in the Qilian Mountains at the southern edge of Hexi Corridor in today's Gansu Province.[65] As the Hei River enters Ejina, it becomes the Ejina River and it feeds the Ejina oases. The oases were a key node in the imperial networks of frontier defense and offense during the Han Dynasty (206 BCE to 220 CE) of the early imperial era.[66] During the Qing Dynasty of the later imperial era, Ejina was the land of the Torghut people, who had a long history of rebellion and defection. Ejina-Torghut Banner, even after being incorporated into the Qing's territory in the mid-18th century, remained outside of Qing Mongolia's territorial core of six leagues and 49 banners.[67] For each successive Chinese court, Ejina was and continues to be a physically remote and administratively peripheral, yet geopolitically strategic, territory. Ejina is expensive to keep but even more expensive to lose. It manifests and tests the state's reach in the frontier.

Today, Ejina is the largest banner of IMAR. It boasts an area of 115,000 sq km, close to the size of South Korea, while also being the least populated banner of IMAR.[68] Compared to South Korea's population of 50 million, Ejina had 35,000 regular residents as of 2020. More than half of the current residents are recent migrants who arrived in the new millennium, and most are Han Chinese.[69] At the moment, about 16% of Ejina's population register as ethnic Mongol, consistent with IMAR's ratio of 17% Mongols. Ejina has an arid climate with an annual average precipitation rate of 40 to 100 mm and an annual evaporation rate of over 2,600 mm. During my four visits to Ejina, I experienced three summer rains, each lasting between five to ten minutes, which invariably compelled people to rush to record and report the historic moment on their cellphones. What's more, no one seemed to own an umbrella.

Since the early 20th century, waves of Han Chinese farming refugees and migrants from Gansu have come to Ejina, expanding cultivation in Ejina's oases.[70] In the 1950s, the Ejina oases underwent massive land use conversion from herding to a mixture of herding and farming. Meanwhile, farming in the mid-reaches of the Hei River expanded at an even faster pace. At the peak of the Great Leap Forward campaign (1958–62), the massive dam building projects in the Hexi Corridor (see Figure 3.1 in Chapter 3) at the mid-reaches of the Hei River blocked much of the runoff downstream to Ejina. As a result of diminishing runoff flows and cultivation expansion, one of Eijna's landmark inland lakes, West Juyan Lake (or Gashuun Nur), went from a size of 267 sq. km in 1958 to becoming completely dry by 1961. Other lakes of varied sizes also either dried up or were greatly reduced in surface area. With diminished runoff and dried up lakes, soil salinization and sandification processes became evident in the late 1970s, and they have accelerated since the 1990s.[71]

The trajectory of soil deterioration due to expansive and intensive farming is also found along the great rivers in China's other northwestern regions of Xinjiang, Ningxia, and Gansu. I will trace in detail the contentious geopolitical and environmental histories of Hexi Corridor in Gansu Province (Part II) and of the three subregions of today's IM from the 18th century to the present day (Part III). For the stories about the relocated herders in Ejina in the current chapter, I focus on the contemporary period from the 1980s to the 2010s.

Throughout the 20th century, Ejina was little known to outsiders except for the archaeologists who studied the Juyan wooden slips (*Juyan hanjian*), which were unearthed in Ejina Oases. The remote and little-known place came into public view in the 1990s when the sandstorms in northern China increased in magnitude and frequency. In 2000, the China Central Television (CCTV) broadcasted a documentary called "Sands from Ejina" (*shaqi ejina*), which was endorsed by the then Premier Zhu Rongji. The state-sponsored publicity stunt turned the formerly obscure Ejina into a household name. The CCTV documentary presents Ejina as the epicenter of desertification, the source of the fast-moving and far-reaching sandstorms that blanket Beijing with yellow grit every spring. Along with being saddled with blame for the demonic sands, Ejina was also subject to prescriptions of antidesertification measures. In the popularized official perception, the problem of desertification stems from three inseparable local elements: Ejina people (i.e., the Mongol herders), Ejina animals (especially, but not exclusively the goats), and Ejina's environment (the desert, which is popularly considered to be deficient by birth, as presented in the Introduction). A primary goal of the prescribed measures was to protect the national capital from the sandstorms, as evident in the Maoist-style militant slogan "eradicate the goats to defend Beijing."

What is it like to live in a remote dryland area that has been pinned as the birthplace of the nation's afflictions?

I first met my host family in Ejina in 2011. The six-member family spans three generations: there is the father, Wuliji (b. 1955), and the mother, Qiqige (b. 1961); two adult sons, Jiri (b. 1979) and Song (b. 1983); and a daughter, Nu (b. 1981), who is a single mother to her son, Talo (b. 2008).

In 2002, when livestock reduction programs came to Ejina, Wuliji was the gacha's accountant, a position just below the gacha head. Wuliji felt obliged to be a model for other gacha members by supporting the government policy. He sold the family's "excessive" sheep and camels at rock bottom prices and moved the family to an ecological resettlement in Dalaihubu Township, the seat of Ejina Banner.

In retrospect, Nu felt her father was naïve and had made too hasty of a move. At that time, many of the 37 families (including four Han Chinese families) in their gacha responded to the destocking policy by waiting it out. They either under-reported the numbers of their flocks or trucked their animals to unrestricted areas until the campaign cooled down. Turns out, that of the 15,000 people in the entire banner of Ejina in 2002,[72] only 1,500 people who resided and herded in the "Key Grazing Ban Zone" in and near Dalaihubu Township were placed under the restriction. Most other families who lived far away from Dalaihubu and the Key Grazing Ban Zone did not reduce their livestock holdings. Beyond the Key Grazing Ban Zone, much of the Banner's jurisdiction in the Gobi was not enclosed.[73] The Gobi did not seem sealable anyway, at least not by an under-funded, low-ranking, and remotely located banner government in charge of a jurisdiction the size of South Korea.

By 2012, Wuliji's family had 22 camels and 50 sheep. The flock size did not warrant a designated shepherd, so the flock joined a relative's herd in the family's home gacha 80 km away from Dalaihubu. The small flock did little to make Wuliji's family—which, at the time, included himself, his wife, and their three unmarried adult children and one grandchild—feel financially secure.

The three adult children had semi-stable jobs, all involving driving motor vehicles. Jiri and Song, with middle school educations, worked as truck drivers. Jiri explained that "Mongolian men do not dig in the coal mine. Those jobs are for the Han Chinese peasants from Shanxi." But the two brothers, along with three of their uncles from their mother's side, did not mind driving water trucks for the coal and iron mines or the oil prospecting teams in west IM. Jiri enjoyed driving fast on the open road. A man of few words otherwise, he recounted in impressive detail his solo 2,000 km road trip in a pickup truck to Qinghai Lake in Qinghai Province and another 2,800 km trip to Hohhot and back. Without consulting a map, he remembered the number of kilometers between the many stops on the long journies. Song, the youngest in the family, previously worked as a long-distance truck driver, hauling coal across the border from Mongolia to IM. But he lost his truck driving license in 2010, after he was caught smuggling otter pelts into IM. Since then, he has worked as a chauffeur for the party secretary of his sumu, which was recently elevated from gacha status to sumu. Nu, Song's older sister and a single mother, had a vocational high school degree and worked as a taxi driver in Dalaihubu. Nu had plans to start a retail business selling frozen Mongolian lamb dumplings and camel meat jerky. But she complained that every time she came up with a business idea, there was always someone else who had beat her to it. In 2014, her newest plan was to plant 20 mu of onions and to build a small suosuo-congrong plantation in the family's winter pasture.

For their compliance with the conservation policies, the family members received ecological compensation in cash from the government. Between 2003 and 2010, they each received 9,000 yuan a year. The monetary compensation is an important source of income for relocatee families who have lost much of their livestock due to relocation and destocking. In the literature on development and poverty, critics have cited government payouts as a factor in recipients' dependency.[74] But a question related to the issue of dependency is whether recipients have enough faith in the government subsidies to fully depend on them. Nu and Song, like their neighbors and relatives I met in Ejina, told me that they did not know for how long the various types of cash compensation dispensed by different government units would last, and in what amounts. It seemed too risky to depend on the state handouts.

Their worries were not unfounded. In IMAR, ecological cash compensation is generally itemized into pastoral compensation, forestry compensation, and livestock reduction compensation from different divisions and levels of the government. These programs follow different compensation calculations for different age groups and local jurisdictions, with varied durations. Over the 2000s and 2010s, some have been abolished while others have been added to the package. In 2011, for example, children's annual subsidies for those registered as pastoral households in Ejina were reduced to 3,000 yuan per person, while that of adults increased to 20,000 yuan.[75] Song speculated that the significant increase in adult compensation was due to "too many protests in the last few years." Nu appreciated the fact that the compensation fund, distributed twice a year, was deposited directly to a designated personal bank account. As a part of the government's transparency program, the direct deposits spare her from queuing up in front of the government office to pick up the checks. She did complain, however, that the funds rarely arrived on time and when they did, there were always various deductions. Some of these deductions, like pension contributions and health plan premiums, were more palatable in her view than others, such as "infrastructure construction fees."[76] Nu's 44-year-old uncle, who would receive the cash compensation via the same route, held a different concern. He felt hijacked by the compensation programs, because "the banner officials could easily block my payments if I stir up trouble for them, like joining a protest."[77]

Land rent supply another source of contribution to many relocatees' income. In the resettlement site, each family is allotted a parcel at the fringes of the resettlement to plant fodder crops like alfalfa and silage corn. In practice, few parcels are used for the policy crops, and few relocatee families farm the allotted land themselves ("We Mongols do not know how to hold a hoe," Song had told me).[78] Instead, most relocatee families rent out their allotted cropland at 300 to 800 yuan per mu (depending on the quality of the parcel) to seasonal migrant farmers from Gansu and other provinces, who plant sweet melons that require much less water than alfalfa. Wuliji's family of five adults received 50 mu of such "fodder cropland." But they were unlucky in their land allocation lottery draw. Their parcel was too salty, rocky, and lacked access to water. It had not attracted any tenants.

The resettlement homes–especially the well-located ones—turn out to be the most tangible asset in herders' relocation packages. My host family had two resettlement units in Dalaihubu. The first one, which came for free, was built in 2003. It is located on the newly developed "Pastoralist Street" in a resettlement compound of 150 housing units near the center of Dalaihubu Township. The unit is a freestanding, one-story brick home of 60 sq. meters in floor area and an 800 sq. meter walled yard. The yard has a built-in animal shelter and a silage tank. Wuliji's family used the animal shelter and the silage tank mostly for storage, or as temporary shelter for a couple of sheep before selling or feasting on them. The house also came with power supplies and a water pump connected to a 30-meter-deep tube well in the yard. In the yard, Nu planted willow trees and vegetables and ran her washing machine.

As the largest banner with the lowest population density of IMAR, Ejina's resettlement homes are the most spacious among all resettlement homes I have visited. Like many families on Pastoralist Street, Wuliji's family expanded the house using their own funds, adding a living room of 26 sq. meters. Other better-endowed families have expanded their units to a total of 100 or even 200 sq. meters. Some have also set up a Mongolian style yurt in the spacious yards for elders who are unaccustomed to living in brick homes.

In 2012, Wuliji's eldest son Jiri received another housing unit from the banner government when he got married. His unit, which is on the 5th floor of an apartment building, measures 86 sq. meters and includes a kitchen, a bathroom, a living-dining area, and two bedrooms. It is in a resettlement compound named "Sunshine Community" at the edge of Dalaihubu Township. The complex's 950 units are housed in 26 five- and six-storied apartment buildings and 40 townhouses. With the new resettlement housing, this area has drawn commercial and private housing development and has been growing fast.

All apartment buildings in Sunshine Community have solar panels, and the compound has a central heating system. The apartment was not free but was heavily subsidized. Jiri paid 20,000 yuan for his apartment, or about 30% of the market rate in Dalaihubu at the time. But the apartment came as an empty shell, with only basic electric wiring and plumbing. The cement walls were unpainted and the floors untiled. The family spent another 60,000 yuan to finish the interior and to furnish the apartment with large screen LCD TV, an L-shaped sofa, dining table and chairs, kitchen appliances, lighting, and a modern bathroom with a flush toilet and a solar-powered water heater. A year later, Jiri's marriage dissolved, but he was able to keep the apartment. Although the apartment is under his name, his whole family has access to it.

With the two housing units, one on "Pastoralist Street" in the town center and the other in "Sunshine Community" in the newly developed area at the edge of the township, and with the rangelands in their home gacha, Wuliji's family rotates among their multiple homes in different seasons for different purposes.

During the winter months from November to March, the family of six stays in Jiri's nicely furnished and well-heated modern apartment in Dalaihubu Township. Come spring, the family decamps from the town and goes back to their home gacha. In the home gacha, Wuliji's family has 10,000 mu of winter rangeland in the basin of the dried-up Guaizi Lake, and another 10,000 mu of spring rangeland in a sandy field 30 km from the dried lake basin. The size of their rangelands, about average in Ejina, is eight times larger than the average size of family rangeland in the neighboring Alxa Left Banner.

Wuliji's family does not go to the family's rangelands to herd, however. They go there to hunt the wild congrong (see Figure 1.2).

II.1 Hunting Wild Congrong in Spring Rangelands

Suosuo and congrong, the power couple that reigns supreme in the regime of productive conservation, as presented in Chapter 1, have origins beyond the plantation. Suosuo is native to western IM and until the 1980s, natural suosuo forests were a signature feature of Alxa's arid landscape.[79] Suosuo's dense and dry wood makes for excellent fuel, as it lasts longer than other fuel woods and produces little smoke. It is a sturdy construction material for animal shelters. Its foliage is also among camels' favorite chews. Suosuo has long been a source of cultural pride in Alxa. As legend has it, during the Qing Dynasty, the prince of Alxa, who spent much of his time politicking in Beijing, would have suosuo wood sent 2,000 km from Alxa to his mansion in Beijing to roast lamb at his famously extravagant banquets.[80] Suosuo's partner, congrong, has been a source of income for local herders since before the collective era. Wild congrong is usually longer and thicker than their plantation cousins and can fetch a much higher price for their perceived greater medicinal potency.[81] Since the 2000s, the policies of livestock reduction and grazing bans have turned more herders into wild congrong hunters.

In mid-April of 2014, I joined Wuliji, Nu, and Nu's son Talo on their wild congrong hunt. Nu took Talo and me in her sedan taxi, and Wuliji followed in his wobbly van. We set out from Dalaihubu and cruised on a paved road for half an hour before the paved road gave way to crisscrossed gullies created by trucks and four-wheel drives over the grainy gobi fields and saline-alkali crusted grounds. Five hours of a bumpy ride later, we arrived at the family's sandy winter rangeland. There, they had a hut of 20 sq. meter built with steel sheets. The hut had a concrete floor, a double bed, a cot, solar-powered light bulbs, and a suosuo wood-fueled cooking stove. It would be the base for the father-daughter-grandson congrong hunting team over the next three months.

Immediately after our arrival, I experienced my first sandstorm. The storm spiralled up from the horizon with little warning. The sky turned from translucent gray to thick ochre. The sandy winds swept across the open field and hit my face hard. Everyone took shelter in the hut. But I was the only one who was visibly scared. The wind died down after 15 minutes. "That was a small one," Nu commented, and went on cooking dinner. The strong spring winds that bring disruptive and sometimes destructive sandstorms help with wild congrong hunting. The wind blows away the surface layer of the sandy suosuo fields to expose the congrong tips to their hunters.

Right before we started eating dinner, Nu's mother, Qiqige, brother Jiri, and Jiri's new girlfriend, Pearl, showed up. They had arrived two weeks earlier and settled in the family's spring rangeland 30 km away from the winter rangeland. The family spreads out between the two rangelands in order to maximize harvest. This is particularly important as the suosuo forests shrink and wild congrong yields have dwindled in recent years. The minute he stepped into the hut, Jiri proudly announced that he had already harvested 6,000 yuan worth of wild congrong over the past two weeks, showing us the photos of his harvests on his cellphone. After dinner, the family assigned me to join Jiri and Qiqige's team in the spring rangeland. So I was on the road again. In the darkness of the night, Jiri drove us in his van at heart-racing speed over the bumpy dune fields. We arrived at the family's spring rangeland just past midnight. There, Jiri had pitched a family-sized camping tent on the sandy ground, furnishing the interior with a double bed, a bunk bed, and a makeshift stove. They also kept a cat that Jiri had found "in the sands." Jiri told me there were plenty of rats around for the cat to hunt (see Figures 2.4 and 2.5).

Figure 2.4 Hunting for congrong on a motorcycle
Source: Photo credit: Author.

In the ensuing days, I rode on the back of Jiri's motorcycle up and down the rolling sand dunes against the howling wind, looking for wild congrong. In the seemingly monotonous landscape of sand dunes between 20 and 70 meters high, Jiri could recognize the spots, to which my uninitiated eyes looked just like any other spot, where he had found a congrong cluster the previous spring. It is customary for local congrong hunters to leave the congrong roots intact, in order to find new shoots in the same spot the following spring. Because it is futile to mark the sandy ground for the

Figure 2.5 Digging wild congrong
Source: Photo credit: Author.

next year, "I just remember their locations in my head," Jiri told me. Jiri had well-honed eyes that could identify the tiniest ivory-white tips peeking out by no more than an inch above the vast, light beige-colored sands. As for me, holding tight for dear life in the back seat of his motorbike, I could hardly keep my eyes open as the sandy winds slapped my face. There were three occasions in which the sandy winds were stormy (at least in my view), but with face and head covers and scarves for protection, my hunter host was not deterred.

Qiqige and Pearl rode separate motorcycles on their hunt. Qiqige's rheumatism was getting worse, so she hunted for only a couple of hours a day and took care of cooking in the camp. Jiri and Pearl worked much longer, from 9 a.m. to 6 p.m., with a lunch break—the length of which depended on how lucky they felt that day. At the end of the hunting season in late May, Qiqige made 5,000 yuan. Jiri made 18,000 yuan, or about 40% of his annual income, which included the ecological compensation cash.

After a week with Qiqige, Jiri, and Pearl, I joined the team of Qiqige's sister-in-law, Alat. Alat's family owned 350 sheep and goats as well as 160 camels—a holding much larger than that of Jiri's family. The difference was reflected in Alat's hunting facilities. On her spring rangeland, which is a 90-minute motorcycle ride from Jiri's (they called each other neighbors), she had a solidly built brickhouse with a storage wing, paved floors, and a built-in brick stove. This spring home was furnished with two steel bunk beds and a wooden dining table. Unlike Jiri's base camp where he drew salty water from a local well, Alat's house had "sweet" water trucked in all the way from Dalaihubu. Alat told me that if she drank the water from Jiri's well, she would have diarrhea. I was relieved to hear that, because I had told myself to tough it out and drink the bitterly salty water from Jiri's well "like the locals."

Alat's team had four other members. They included Alat's cousin and his wife who were in their late 40s. The couple worked in a township government 200 km away from Dalaihubu Township, but they took time off to join the annual congrong hunt. There were also two young men: Alat's 23-year-old son, Hasi, and Hasi's friend of the same age. Neither of the young men held a nine-to-five job.

Alat's team had better vehicles. Instead of the lightweight motorbikes that Jiri and Qiqige used, the three middle-aged and better-endowed hunters used stable, four-wheeled heavyweight motorcycles designed for desert adventure tourism. Among the three motorcycles, Alat's was the newest and best, costing 10,000 yuan. She bought it after her husband's accident. After a night of drinking in 2011, Alat's husband fell off his lightweight motorcycle, triggering a stroke and became semi-paralyzed.[82] That was why he did not join the hunt.

In addition to the congrong hunt, the heavy four-wheel motorcycles were useful for tracking and rounding up the family's camels out in the Gobi. But when it comes to the best gear for the congrong hunt, nothing measures up to camels. Before motorcycles became popular in the 1990s, Alat's cousin told me, people rode on camelback to hunt for wild congrong. Hunters are able to see farther when elevated sitting atop a camel's back. And unlike motorcycles, camels can navigate the paths among dense suosuo shrubs. Camels' slower pace makes it easier for hunters to scout out the tiny tips of congrong shoots in the dune fields. The only drawback of the camels is that, unlike motorcycles, they cannot be worked all day.

Since motor vehicles became popular, however, few camels have been trained and tamed enough to ride. What has also changed in the congrong hunt is the demographic of its participants. Up till the 1980s, hunting wild congrong in the windy and chilly spring was a job mainly for young men. But now, men and women of all ages, with or without regular jobs, join the hunt. On Alat's team, her cousin and his wife take time off from their local government jobs to join the hunt. Song, Jiri's younger brother who works as a chauffeur for the sumu governor also took several days off to make some quick cash before the season ended. In the middle of the hunting season when I went back to Dalaihubu with Jiri and Pearl, I found Jiri's apartment building and the entire "Sunshine Community" compound ghostly empty. In the town center, most shops and restaurants were closed, and there were no taxis on the streets. Jiri told me, "everyone I know is down in the rangeland hunting for congrong."

Jiri and his girlfriend, Pearl, went into town to sell their harvest from the preceding week to wholesale vendors. There were only two congrong vendors in Dalaihubu, and both were Han Chinese. They were licensed by the banner government, practically establishing an oligopolistic operation in town. To maximize his earnings under the oligopoly, Jiri had a plan to deal with each. The first vendor set up his buying station in the front yard of a resettlement housing unit. When I visited, the entire yard was covered by congrong pieces on the ground and on drying racks, and they had already turned from ivory white to dark brown. Jiri used his cellphone to call the vendor, who arrived 25 minutes later in a black Ford with tinted windows. He offered 26 yuan per kilo for Jiri's 73 kilos of smaller pieces. Jiri managed to negotiate to 28 yuan per kilo. The vendor took two bundles of 20-yuan bills from a duffle bag in his trunk and handed Jiri 2,050 yuan.

We then moved on to the second vendor who was known to pay a good price for higher quality products. For this vendor, Jiri reserved his longer and thicker pieces—Jiri deliberately hid these more valuable congrong pieces in the back of the van so the first vendor would not see them—which fetched 40 yuan per kilo, netting another 450 yuan. Jiri told me there used to be a Mongolian vendor in town before the licensing regulation was in place. The Mongolian vendor did not manage to get the license and was forced to drop out of the congrong business.

I had my own reasons for going back to town with Jiri and Pearl: I needed to see a doctor for my fever that would not abate even after taking many Tylenol tablets. Only when I was sick myself did I notice that everyone I met on the congrong hunt brought sizable bags of over-the-counter and prescription medication for various ailments, including toothaches, headaches, conjunctivitis, fever, cough, high blood pressure, rheumatism, and arthritis. Out in the rangeland far from town, congrong hunters needed to take care of themselves.

In Dalaihubu Township Jiri took me to a hospital that specialized in Mongolian medicine.[83] On a Sunday morning inside the clean and modern hospital, I saw a doctor who was Jiri's uncle's high school classmate, and according to Jiri, the best doctor in town. The doctor took my temperature, listened to my lungs, and checked my pulse. Then he suggested that I take a stronger Mongolian medicine instead of the regular, low-priced western medicine available in the hospital pharmacy. I followed the doctor's advice. The medicine came in sizable black pellets sealed in colorful packets. They promised cure and also gave me a glimpse into China's intricate bio-ethnoterritorial map. One packet—for my fatigued lungs—was decorated in Mongolian motifs in red, blue, and yellow, with text written in Mongolian and Chinese scripts. This product came from a Mongolian-medicine hospital's pharmaceutical center located in a Mongolian Autonomous County in Henan Province of central-northern China. As Mongolian medicine is greatly influenced by the Tibetan medicine tradition, the other packet—for my fever and dizziness—was a Tibetan product with Tibetan motifs in gold, blue, and red, with labelling written in Tibetan and Chinese scripts. This was produced by a Tibetan-medicine hospital in a Tibetan Autonomous Prefecture in Gansu Province of northwestern China. The medicine I got was potent indeed: I was knocked out for two days, then my fever ebbed.

Back on the congrong hunting grounds, the competition was getting contentious. Outsiders from neighboring provinces and cities—whom my hosts invariably pronounced to be Han Chinese—trespassed local herder families' immense and indefensible rangelands to hunt wild congrong. On our drive to her family winter grassland at the start of the hunting trip, Nu incessantly pointed to the passing motorcyclists who had wild congrong tied to their backseats, crying: "look at that shameless congrong thief!"

Alat's son, Hasi, had confronted congrong thieves up close. In the spring of 2000, Hasi and his hunting partner caught a group of three congrong thieves on his family's rangeland. They confiscated the trespassers' congrong and took the keys from their motorcycles.

In response, the thieves reached into their bags and brandished long, sharp knives. Unarmed, Hasi and his partner had to retreat. Since then, Hasi told me, he and other young men in the area have always embarked on the congrong hunt girded with knives. Hasi considered the pasture patrol service "useless." The cellphone signal is weak out in the suosuo-growing dune fields. By the time the patrol crew shows up, if at all, the thieves are long gone. Some congrong thieves have appeared in large gangs. Hasi's mother and uncles, too old for fights, would just quickly drive away on their motorcycles whenever they saw congrong gangs on their rangeland.

The congrong thieves hunt differently from the locals, according to Hasi and Jiri. Local hunters keep the congrong's roots for new shoots next year. Thieves cut off the entire plant, including the roots, leaving nothing behind. Also, local hunters leave the flowering congrong plants intact at the end of the harvest season to allow natural seeding. But thieves sneak in after the rangeland owners depart in late May and cut off the flowering plants to collect the seeds that now command a high market price. Not to be outwitted, Hasi and his mother, as well as Jiri and his siblings, now cut all the flowering plants at the end of the season. Jiri's sister Nu and father Wuliji took one step further and planted two dozen government-subsidized suosuo seedlings in their winter rangeland. But they just put the seedling sticks in the sands. No plantation-styled big holes were dug, as presented in Chapter 1. Nu planned to wait and see if the seedlings would survive before using the congrong seeds she had saved from the previous years.

The cutting of flowering congrong plants, the increasing competition among various types of congrong hunters, and the shrinkage of suosuo fields[84] together have contributed to the declining quantity and quality of wild congrong. Almost every hunter I met in the spring of 2014 told me that they now had to hunt for much longer each day. Hasi, for one, was out on his motorcycle for 14 hours a day. He left at dawn and did not come back to the home base until past 10 p.m. After two months of intensive hunting, he made 20,000 yuan in 2014. The year before, he worked about 10 to 11 hours a day and made the same amount.

Hasi was a renaissance man who graduated in 2010 with a polytechnic college degree in applied arts. Upon graduation, he worked for an interior design contractor in Yinchuan City of Gansu Province for two years. When his father suffered a stroke and became semi-paralyzed, Hasi, the only child of the family, returned home to Ejina. Only then did he start to learn how to keep camels. His mother, Alat, took care of the family's sheep flock. Hasi was also a competitive Mongolian wrestler who had won cash prizes at the Naadam festivals, an aspiring keyboard player, and a seasoned photographer. In the summer of 2013, Hasi bought himself a professional camcorder with the cash he made from selling wild congrong. With the camcorder, he produced 20-minute documentary about moving camels from his family's fall rangeland to the winter rangeland in Ejina. Hasi told me that these days people move their camels with trucks, but he wanted to document the traditional way. His cast included nine carefully chosen cooperative camels with elaborately decorated bridles, as well as his parents, grandparents, uncles, and aunts in their Mongolian regalia. In his film, the family loaded the camels up with wooden crates and buckets, rode on the camels' backs, set up and dismantled the yurts, received visitors who came to exchange male camels for mating, enjoyed tea and horse milk liquor, and sang Mongolian songs together. For the film, Hasi also had his mother, Alat, perform the Mongolian ritual of flicking wine drops into the air for earth and heaven in the rosy light of dawn, against the background of smoke billowing out of the tip of a Mongolian yurt. I viewed Hasi's raw footage with him on a computer screen in his family's resettlement home in Dalaihubu. Pointing to the motorcycle at the edge of a frame, Hasi reassured me: "I will cut out this modern stuff in post-production." One of his plans for the near future was to apply for a small business grant to establish a Mongolian-themed wedding photography studio in the large front yard of his family's resettlement home on Pastoralist Street in Dalaihubu. He would stage the studio with a yurt and furnish it with his family's Mongolian-style crates, furniture, and rugs.

II.2 Digging Desert Rose in the Summer Gobi

Hunting congrong in spring was followed by digging desert rose in May and June. Desert rose is the colloquial name for the gypsum or baryte mineral that crystallizes in a rosette growth pattern, and individual "rose" blossoms cluster into compact aggregates. It is formed as water evaporates from the shallow, salty basins of arid and sandy environments. In addition to western IM, it can be found in the Sahara and the southwest of the U.S., among other arid areas. The size of the rosette clusters in Ejina varies widely from 5 to 10 cm to over 200 cm in height and 100 cm in diameter. Tourists buy the smaller pieces, while the large and rare pieces are collector items sold for hundreds of thousands of yuan each.

Song told me about the serendipitous discovery of desert rose in Ejina during the early days of pasture enclosure. The first step to pasture enclosures was to build the fences. When work crews dug the sandy land to install fence posts, they found the semi-transparent, yellow-colored crystal clusters underneath. Today, desert rose and other semiprecious gemstones have become another important source of cash income for relocated herders.

It is not just the Gobi Desert in Ejina that produces gemstones. Badain Jaran and Tengger Deserts in the other two banners of Alxa League—Alxa Left and Alxa Right—produce over a hundred known varieties of semiprecious gemstones under an umbrella name "Alxa curiosity stones" (*Alashan qishi*). These stones are known for their unusual shapes, textures, and vivid colors. The Alxa League government has been promoting the curiosity stones as a catalyst for local economic development in the era of conservation and relocation. By 2005, there were more than 1,000 shops specializing in curiosity stones in Banyanhot, the seat of Alxa League, making the city one of the largest semiprecious gemstone wholesale centers in China.[85]

Gemstones have also generated a network of production in Alxa from excavation, cleaning, sand-polishing, display case construction, artificial treatments of the stones to give them brighter colors or abrade them into specific shapes (such as animals or Buddha heads), and packaging. Actors in the gemstone business vary greatly in scale. In excavation, for example, the dominant players are the mining bosses with both capital and access to the gemstone mines. Prior to the 2000s, curiosity stones were scattered on or near the sandy surfaces across Alxa, and it was easy for individuals with manual tools to collect the stones. In 2002, at the height of retiring pastoralism, a news story broke about how a curiosity stone in the shape of a chick emerging from a half-broken eggshell sold for over 100 million yuan. After this, tens of thousands of outsiders and locals started to sweep the deserts for the curiosity stones. The accessible stones on the ground surface began to thin out and people had to dig deeper. Lured by collectors' growing appetite for larger and rarer pieces, large capital moved in. The mining bosses opened deep and wide pits in the dune fields to excavate curiosity stones with the help of short-term workers, earthmovers, forklifts, trucks, power generators, and pumps. And a production network of different types of labor was formed.

While desert rose does not require much post-excavation processing, other types of raw stones are sent to workshops for cleaning and sand-polishing. This work produces deafening noise and asphyxiating dust and is done in the inner-city neighborhoods of Bayanhot, undertaken by relocated herder families who rent small home-work spaces in the city.[86]

On the circulation front, the new section of Bayanhot city is home to large wholesalers and retailers that deal rare and expensive pieces not just from Alxa's Gobi but also other areas in northwest China and Central Asia. At the bottom of the circulation hierarchy are the small vendors, many of whom are, again, relocated herder families. These small vendors rent small vending stalls in government-designated, indoor and outdoor "curiosity stone markets" to sell cheap and untreated pieces to tourists.

During the summers when the taxi business in town is slow, Song and Nu join a desert rose excavation team. The team is organized by a 50-year-old local dealer, Bayintu. Bayintu's family owns 300,000 mu of rangeland in the dried-up Guaizi Lake basin in the Gobi that is endowed with desert rose reserves. Bayintu hires earthmovers and other machines to open pits that are 40 to 50 meters wide and 1 to 2 meters deep in the sandy land to excavate desert rose and other gemstones. These fields in the dried-up Guaizi Lake basin have high groundwater levels. So, Bayintu installs power generators and pumping systems to drain the pits before starting excavation. Song, Nu, and their fellow workers stay in camping tents or Bayintu's semi-permanent steel sheet huts around the pits for weeks on end during the summer.

Bayintu stores his hundreds of desert rose pieces in a storage shed and displays some of them in the front yard of his resettlement home in Dalaihubu. He sells the stones to wholesalers in Bayanhot, 700 km east of Dalaihubu.[87] In the fall of 2013, I visited Kesi, Bayintu's brother-in-law and a primary client, in Bayanhot city. A native of Alxa Left Banner and a military veteran, Kesi owned a centrally located upscale curiosity stone store. The store's 400-sq.m display space was filled with a dazzling trove of semiprecious gemstones of all shapes, sizes, types, and colors, most of which are from Alxa. Kesi told me that business has slowed down, as both supply and demand of the more profitable large and rare stones ebbed after the initial boom.

Unlike the congrong hunt, the hunt for desert rose is not for everyone. Wuliji and Qiqige, both in their late 50s, never participate in the dig, for example. Jiri, my host in the congrong hunt, has other jobs in the summer too. His main summer task is to check on his family's sheep and camel herds in the Gobi. As droughts became more frequent in the 2010s, Jiri travelled between the Gobi and his apartment in Dalaihubu every week to make sure the camels had access to water. Since summers in Dalaihubu are punishingly hot, especially in his apartment that sits on the top floor of the building, he spends more than half of the summer days in the open, higher-altitude rangelands in the Gobi, where the air is fresh and the temperatures are lower, especially at night. His parents, Wuliji and Qiqige, and Nu's toddler son, Talo, summer in the family's one-story resettlement home on Pastoralist Street in downtown Dalaihubu, which is cooler than Jiri's apartment. Thanks to its proximity to urban services, many of the units in Pastoralist Street are occupied by the elderly who need access to healthcare, as well as by children, who are often accompanied by a parent or a grandparent and need access to schools in town. Some relocatee families run small grocery stores, diners, butcher shops, and motorcycle repair shops on Pastoralist Street. But from what I heard and saw, these low-entry businesses seldom last. Both the butcher shop and the diner that I visited during my visit in 2012 closed the next year. The owner of a small grocery store complained that her business declined substantially since a modern supermarket opened in the new development section of Dalaihubu in 2013. Plus, she added, "How much business can you expect when this town is half empty for six months a year?"

II.3 Running Ecotourism in Autumn Forests

Autumn is a busy time in Ejina. For herding families that still own herds, their sheep need to be fattened up for the long winter, and the camels—"god's children"—that are left on their own in the Gobi during the summer, need to be round up and moved to the lowlands to winter. For Wuliji's family, autumn is tourist season, of which they try to make the best use. The main tourist attraction in Ejina is its huyang forests (see Figure 2.6).

Ejina boasts a large area of old growth Poplar forests found in the arid northwest, called *Huyang* (*Populus Euphratica Oliv*). Huyang is known for its longevity and drought- and saline-tolerance. Camels and sheep graze on huyang leaves; its timber is widely used for fuel and construction. In the fall, huyang foliage turns from dark green to brilliant golden yellow, dramatically transforming the landscape.

But groundwater depletion and droughts have led to a massive death of huyang forests in recent decades throughout western and northwestern China. In 2000, a National Huyang Forest Protection Zone of 390,000 mu (26,000 hectares) was

Figure 2.6 Top: Huyang forest in the spring. Bottom: Huyang foliage in the fall
Source: Photo credit: Author.

established in the heart of the Ejina Oasis, where Dalaihubu Township sits. To make conservation productive, that same year also marked the inauguration of the annual "Ejina Golden Fall Huyang Ecotourism Festival" during the first week of October. Early October is the time when huyang foliage flaunts its most glorious autumnal palette. Nature's calendar synchronizes well with the state's calendar: the first week of October is popularly called “Golden Week” in China. It is a week-long national holiday to commemorate the birth of the People’s Republic of China on October 1, 1949. Domestic tourism in China peaks during the Golden Week, which in turn helps boost Ejina’s Golden Fall Huyang Festival.

Throughout the 2000s and 2010s, over 300,000 visitors would cram into Ejina every October for two weeks. During the brief tourism season, visitors flooded Ejina’s tourism attractions, hotels, restaurants, and souvenir shops in and near Dalaihubu Township, which has about 10,000 regular residents. In addition to the resplendent fall foliage, another Ejina attraction is the dried-up desert lake, East Juyan Lake (*dong juyanhai*), which is now about 20% restored to 30 to 40 sq. km in area and 15 meters in depth. The restored lake is a desert curiosity for tourists from Shanghai and Beijing, and a conservation victory for the government.[88] A third must see in Ejina is the ruins of an ancient walled city, called Heicheng, which was designated as a part of the National Juyan Heritage Protection Zone in 2001. Heicheng was built in the 11th century by the Tangut Empire (Western Xia) and was taken over by Kublai Khan during the Mongol Yuan Dynasty in the 13th century. The ancient walled city is now half buried in sand. Every fall, right before the tourism season starts, trucks and earthmovers are sent to dig out the access roads and ground walkways. To reach the top of the walls, tourists climb up the sand dunes (see Figure 2.7).

Figure 2.7 The Heicheng Heritage Site half buried in sand

Source: Photo credit: Author.

Huyang forest-centered ecotourism during the first two weeks of October highlights Ejina’s regime of productive conservation, in which local residents, local government, and investors are all actively involved.

But Ejina’s “National Huyang Forest Protection Zone,” like most other designated conservation zones the world over, is not empty. Located at the core of the Ejina

Oasis, it offers the best grazing land and has been home to about 500 herding families. The fertile land, with the richest soil and best grasses in Ejina Oasis, was grazed intensively and subsequently deteriorated during the 1980s and 1990s. The area has been placed under the most stringent grazing bans and livestock reduction rules since the late 1990s. Residents were allocated resettlement homes elsewhere, but they were allowed to keep their old homes and much reduced flocks in the animal pens in the huyang forest area.

To augment their income after destocking, many of the families in the huyang forest area started to run family hostels and diners out of their homes during the tourist season. Similar to *nongjiale* ("Happy Farmer's Home"), the agrotourism operations in the suburban villages surrounding China's large cities, these establishments in Ejina's huyang forest area are called *mujiale* ("Happy Herder's Home"). The Happy Herder homeowners invested in new yurts, beds, dining sets and furniture, and expanded their kitchen and enjoyed a golden era during the second half of the 2000s. Characteristic of ecotourism, Ejina's Huyang Festival is short and seasonal, but a hard-working Happy Herder's Home owner family can make a handsome income of 30,000 to 50,000 yuan over the hyper-intensive two weeks in October.

The year 2012 ended the golden era for the Happy Herders' Homes in Ejina. That year, before the annual Huyang Festival began, the Ejina Banner government contracted out its major tourist attractions to a Beijing-based real estate development company called Peak.[89] The banner government and Peak came to a 50/50 profit sharing agreement, in which Peak took over the operation of aforementioned heritage and ecotourism sites.[90]

Peak's first move was to build gates and fences around these sites and to charge high entrance fees for each. For the Huyang Forest Ecotourism Zone alone, a one-day pass cost 170 yuan, and a two-day pass cost 220. The designation of the Zone as a prestigious "national" level ecological protection zone helped justify the high fees. A regime of entry control was established to secure entrance fee revenues. In 2014, I visited the fenced and guarded Huyang Forest Ecotourism Zone. At the box office by the new and grandiose gate, I registered my name and passport number and paid the fees for my pass. I then proceeded to show my passport and the pass to the gatekeeper to prove that I did not split my two-day pass with someone else. Peak recruited work-study students and migrant workers from other provinces to guard the gates of Huyang Ecotourism Zone, fearing that locally hired staff would be too lenient with their visiting friends and relatives and let them in for free. Ejina Banner's Public Security crew joined forces with private guards to reinforce the new order, forming a profitable public-private partnership. The one week of October 1st to 7th in 2013 earned Peak 130 million yuan on ticket sales alone, according to a banner official.[91] By lending state authority to a private company to run the banner's most profitable time and space, the government secured a key source of revenue without the trifling tasks and daunting responsibilities of managing a town inundated by mobs of rowdy tourists and swindlers that outnumber locals by thirtyfold.

Peak and its employees were not reluctant to exercise their borrowed authority. As I rode in Nu's taxi to pass through the checkpoint, the guard pound his fists with full force repeatedly on the hood of Nu's car, shouting: "Your pass and ID!" I asked him not to bang on our car so hard. The young man, in a southern accent, replied: "I can smash your windows if I feel like it!"

Peak seals its turf further by blocking the roads that connect tourist attractions with local Happy Herders' Homes. Tourists in package tours are shepherded from one tourist attraction to the next in tour buses that follow the new road that the Banner government built. The buses bypass the old road and the Happy Herders' Homes, stopping only at the gated tourist destinations and at Peak-contracted hotels, souvenir shops, and restaurants that charge high rates. And though the walkways for the tourists are built right on local huyang forests, Peak stopped hiring local residents for the janitorial jobs that the residents had been promised so as to minimize locals' contact with tourists who might otherwise be lured into the Happy Herders' Homes. The tourists are ushered to see the huyang forests in the Ecotourism Zone, take photos and then are whisked away after half an hour, leaving little more than their garbage in front of local residents' yards.

Peak's moves to monopolize tourism revenue did not go without provoking local contestation. For example, upon the onset of its operation in 2012, Peak banned taxis from entering the tourist destinations in order to protect its tour bus monopoly. Local taxi drivers, many of whom were relocated herders, launched a protest that was "politically too sensitive for the banner government to ignore," according to Nu. Peak conceded and now local taxis drivers like Nu are allowed to enter the tourism sites, but taxis with out-of-town license plates are denied entry.

The Happy Herder's Home owners voiced their grievances too. Jindai, an 80-year-old Happy Herder's Home owner in the Huyang Forest Zone lost almost all his business to Peak in the fall of 2012. In 2013, Jindai led a protest against Peak's monopoly.

Jindai is no stranger to political action. He was among the early generation of Mongolian Chinese Communist Party (CCP) members and of the grassroots party cadres in Ejina. During the era of collectivism, he was made a production team accountant, then promoted to commune accountant in the late 1950s. During IM's racialized and ferocious Cultural Revolution in the late 1960s, Jindai was one of the hundreds of thousands of ethnic Mongolian cadres, military personnel, and state-sector workers who were suspected of being members or sympathizers of the Inner Mongolian People's Revolution Party (*neirendang*) that was accused of betraying Mao, and thus purged.[92] After the Cultural Revolution, Jindai was reinstated and became the Communist party secretary of his home gacha in the late 1970s. Jindai was a keen supporter of China's reform policies in the 1980s. In his yurt, he proudly displayed a photo he took with China's reformist leader, Zhao Ziyang (1919–2005). Zhao Ziyang was China's Premier between 1980 and 1987, and a short-term CCP General Secretary from 1987 to 1989. Zhao lost power and was put under house arrest due to his sympathy towards Tiananmen Square protesters in 1989. Jindai himself was known as an ardent critic of local policies and had mobilized protests more than once. He once led a protest to demand more ecological compensation in the early 2000s. The compensation went up after the protest, but Jindai lost his party leadership position in the gacha as well as his CCP membership. Since then, Jindai told me, he felt even more at liberty to organize protests to "urge local leaders to pay attention to maintaining a harmonious ethnic relationship in a national border region like Ejina."[93] His tactics seemed to work for the most part. Each time he launched a protest, he and his followers received some monetary compensation from the local government.

On October 1, 2013, on the Peoples' Republic of China (PRC)'s National Day and at the start of Ejina's tourist season, Jindai led over 50 residents of the Huyang Forest Zone to block the new road that had killed their Happy Herders' Homes. The well-timed maneuver quickly brought Ejina Banner's governor to the bargaining table. Jindai was invited to the "Commanding Center of Ejina Golden Fall Huyang Ecotourism Festival" located in a hotel in Dalaihubu. At the meeting, the Banner governor offered 20,000 yuan to every affected family as "Huyang Festival compensation." But Jindai did not consider it a victory, because the compensation was still 30,000 yuan short of the 50,000 yuan that he could have earned if it were not for Peak's monopoly. In the end, he and his followers accepted the cash and the festival went on as planned, except that additional Public Security forces and private guards were planted in and around the tourist sites—and outside of Jindai's home.

In any event, Peak's monopoly over business opportunities brought by over 300,000 tourists (337,000 in 2013 according to a banner official) is hardly fool proof. At the height of the Huyang Festival season, there are a substantial number of budget travellers, student backpackers, and adventurous tourists that Peak is unable to capture. Entrepreneurial locals, like Nu and Song, do not sleep on the chance to insert themselves in this niche market. In 2013, before the tourist season started, Nu invested 20,000 yuan in nine single cot beds and new linen sheet sets, turning Jiri's modern apartment in Sunshine Community into a hostel. She also cleaned up her family's centrally located relocation home on Pastoralist Street and prepared seven more beds for tourists.

Song worked the sales front. At the peak of the season when tourists swarmed into town, Song stood by the traffic intersection with a big-lettered sign saying "family hostel" to catch tourists who arrived in small groups in their own vehicles. Song first gauged the supply-demand balance, listening for his competitors' price ranges before quoting the potential customer. After Song sealed the deal, Nu took over and settled the guests in their relocation home-turned-hostels.[94] Over the first four days of October 2013, their family hostels hosted a total of 40 guests, most stayed for one night, at 150 to 200 yuan a night per person. The sister-brother team earned 7,500 yuan from the operation. Nu told me "if I had advertised our hostels on social media like QQ, we could have easily doubled that figure."

The brother-sister team also earned extra income by taking independent tourists to the huyang forest and other attractions via their secret routes, allowing the tourists to dodge the exorbitant entrance fees.

Many locals seemed to have, or at least aspired to find, free access to the Huyang Forest Zone that "the Beijing company" (as Peak was often referred to by the locals) now lorded over. A hotel manager offered to make a phone call for me to get in for free. She later informed me that her contact in the ticket office told her the supervisor was in the office that day, so that backdoor was closed. Then Nu tried to take me into the zone via an unguarded entrance that she found from the previous year. We attempted entry into three such gaps in Peak's entrance control, but all of them had since been guarded. That was how we ended up paying the entry fees and having to deal with the callous gatekeeper, as mentioned earlier.

Upon hearing our story about the gatekeeper, Nu's younger brother Song was outraged. The next day, Song showed us another secret entrance to the Huyang Forest Zone. We found the entrance after crossing a riverbed. The river, called Ang-ci, had dried up after a dam was built upstream. Several pickup trucks, apparently on the same mission, had crossed the riverbed like us and parked by the unguarded entrance. Song said that the Huyang Forest Zone used to have many open entrances like this. But in 2014, as my own experience attested to, Peak had greatly reinforced its border controls, and only those who "really know the forest area well" could find the few remaining openings like the one by the Ang-ci River.

Ejina locals also found other opportunities. Right by the road near the unguarded entrance, I saw a rustic, handwritten cardboard sign that read "Authentic Old Growth Huyang Forest Park." The sign was erected by a local herding family that had huyang trees on their property located immediately outside of the official Huyang Forest Zone. The family-owned Huyang Forest Park offered a bargain entry fee of 30 yuan per person.

The next day, Nu took me in her taxi to see another tourist attraction, the restored Juyan Lake. Like Huyang Forest Zone, the Lake Zone was fenced and gated, firmly within Peak's chokehold. The entrance fees cost 80 yuan per person, half the price of the Huyang Forest Zone. But still, Nu insisted that a penny saved is a penny earned. We passed by the guarded gate on the Lake Zone's southern border, turned right, and drove up north along the long, western fence of the Zone, looking for the unguarded entrance. But after 30 minutes into the pursuit, what felt like a heroic act of defying the state and capital at the start of the drive began to falter. I found myself wondering how much money we would actually save, considering the time spent and the gasoline burnt for the long drive over the bumpy gravel ground of the Gobi Desert. And really, how much longer would we have to drive to find the free entry, if we found it at all? What if the elusive free entry, like those in the Huyang Forest Zone, would now be controlled by ill-mannered guards and we ended up having to pay for the pass anyway? But Nu was in feisty spirits and tried to pump up my morale: "We can't pay that Beijing company any money! No matter how long it takes, we just have to get in for free!" Another 35 minutes later, the seemingly endless fence suddenly ended. We entered the zone from the unguarded northern border of the Zone and saw the legendary restored Juyan Lake. Nu was pleased with herself. I learned my lesson. It was not just about money. It was about *kimoji*, to borrow a popular Japanese term for matters of feelings. The search for a crack in Peak's territorial grip felt like a staring contest. Who would give up first: we, the resentful fee dodgers, or the ruthless outsider Peak that has played the game unfairly? Nu was in good company. On our drive to find the unguarded entrance at the northern border of the Juyan Lake Zone, we saw many tracks left by trucks, four-wheel drives and sedans like Nu's taxi heading in the same direction.

From Peak's perspective, the Juyan Lake might be a conservation wonder, but a partially restored wetland with a few waterfowl is much less photogenic than the spectacular golden foliage of the huyang forest. The Lake pulls in far fewer tourists, and those who do visit pay a much lower entrance fee. A local official explained that Peak's operation in Ejina was organized according to the varying levels of profitability of the tourist sites. The golden-egg laying Huyang Forest Zone conveniently located near Dalaihubu Township was tightly controlled by Peak's real estate branch. The Lake Zone was a second-tier operation of Peak. The low-revenue, high-cost operation of the Lake Zone in the remote and unsealable Gobi might explain the incomplete fence system. It seemed to cost less to let in the few determined fee dodgers like Nu and me than to complete and maintain the fence on the gravel sands. In Heicheng, the ancient ruins under the same management as the Lake Zone, the gate was erected, but locals were hired to work the checkpoints. There, Nu was able to smuggle me in by talking to a gatekeeper who was a relative of hers. This act of defiance saved me 115 yuan. But I paid the price of a brisk, 50-minute walk on a windy late afternoon from the gate to the walled city ruins, while watching the entrance pass holders on Peak's shuttle buses whizz by.

Song told me: "it is easy to make money in Ejina, as long as one is willing to work hard." Working hard Song and Nu were certainly committed to. Nu's cellphone rang constantly during the Golden Week as she ran between receiving tourists in her hostels and shuttling tourists between the town center and tourist destinations. Song, in addition to recruiting customers for their family hostels, took adventurous tourists in his boss's four-wheel drive on sand surfing trips in the dune fields. When their home-hostels were full, Song and Nu spent the night at an internet café in Dalaihubu, where they hung out with neighbors who had also turned their relocation homes into hostels.

Other locals worked hard too. During the Huyang Festival, residents of Huyang Forest Zone brought their tamed camels for tourists to ride and photograph. In the early 2010s, a diligent camel owner could make 8,000 to 9,000 yuan during the Golden Week. Nu told me that camels that grow up in the high-density huyang forest area can be tasked for camel rides, because these camels are accustomed to strangers and to the noise of cars. Nu's family's camels that live in the Gobi, on the other hand, are too wild, and it is too risky to let anyone ride them. When Nu wanted a photo of her son dressed in Mongolian regalia on camelback, she too paid for a camel ride in the huyang forest area.

Outside of the gated Juyan Lake and Heicheng Heritage Tourism Zones, older folks like Nu's aunt and uncle and other relocatee herders from neighboring Alxa Right Banner rented souvenir stands from Peak to sell desert rose, wild congrong, and other semiprecious gemstones to tourists. The vendors set up camp right next to their stands with tents, pickup trucks, and four-wheel drives, and brought foldable chairs, blankets and cooking utensils to settle in for three to four weeks in late

September and the first half of October until the last tourist left town. Over the span of three weeks camping in the windy Juyan Lake area, Nu's aunt netted 1,200 yuan in 2013, after paying 500 yuan to Peak to rent the souvenir stand. "It's better than sitting at home with nothing to do," she told me (see Figure 2.8).

Figure 2.8 Vendors' stands and tents in Juyan Lake Tourism Zone
Source: Photo credit: Author.

The stories from Ejina seem to suggest that the ecological relocation programs do not automatically sedentarize herders, nor do they resolutely confine herders' livelihood strategies. My host family and their relatives in Ejina pool family resources together and keep several residential bases for different income-generating activities in different seasons in different locations. They try to survive the restrictions of resettlement with a territorialized strategy and develop a new mode of mobility. Such new modes of mobility, like pastoral mobility, aligns with seasonal cycles. Yet, it is not exclusively defined by the pastoral calendar. Instead, it follows a new time and space alignment structured by the diversifying rural economy of Ejina in the era of conservation.

Relocated herders' territorialized survival strategies and new modes of mobility drive a theorizing process of what I call "territorialized social analysis." As introduced in the Preface, territorialized social analysis activates the role of territory which shapes social transformation. It is different from the usual "social-spatial analysis," which treats space as a passive container in which social actions take place. I will use the example of Ejina herders' new mode of mobility to elaborate further on the methodological, analytical, and theoretical implications of territorialized social analysis in the Conclusion.

To recap, this chapter traces the broad spectrum of herders' experiences under state intervention and market expansion in the age of productive conservation. What I ask is not just about whether pastoralism has been put to an end by the state, the market, the conservation regime, or all of the above.[95] Rather, I ask *who* in the radically changing pastoral society has and has not survived and *how*. It is a tale of herding families' struggles, resilience, and aspirations under varied conditions and with uneven results. Instead of concluding on a definitive note about the future of pastoralism, these stories offer a glimpse into the diverse pastoral possibilities and impossibilities on the ground in IM today.

Notes

1. Song, Fuli. 2012. "Neimonggu: qiangqu fumin jinnia fupinzijin jiangtou shiyi [Inner Mongolia plans to invest 1 billion yuan in poverty alleviation this year]." *Economic Observer*, February 22. http://www.eeo.com.cn/2012/0222/221228.shtml. Accessed January 29, 2023. The report quoted the governor of Inner Mongolia Autonomous Region (IMAR) having stated that poverty alleviation is not just an economic or social agenda, but also a political one.
2. My fieldwork in Alxa Left Banner was conducted in 2012, 2013, and 2014; fieldwork in Bayannur Municipality was conducted in 2011; fieldwork in Xilingol League was conducted in 2011 and 2012; fieldwork in Ejina was in 2012, 2013, and 2014.
3. For rangeland conservation programs implemented in IMAR and China's other northwestern regions such as Tibet and Xinjiang, see, for example, Li, Wenjun and Lynn Huntsinger. 2011. "China's grassland contract policy and its impact on Herder ability to benefit in Inner Mongolia: tragic feedbacks." *Ecology and Society* 16 (2). http://www.ecologyandsociety.org/vol16/iss2/art1/. Accessed January 23, 2023; Fan, Mingming and Wenjun Li et al. 2014. "Impact of Nomad Sedentarization on social and ecological systems at multiple scales in Xinjiang Uyghur Autonomous Region, China." *AMBIO* 43 (5): 673–686; Aziz, Barbara N. 1978. *Tibetan Frontier Families: Reflection of Three Generations from D'ingri*. Durham: Carolina Academic Press. Blaming the herders for rangeland degradation and seeing destocking and land redistribution as a solution to degradation are also found beyond China's national border in Mongolia, IMAR's northern neighbor. See, for example, case studies of Mongolia's conservation politics by Upton, Caroline. 2010. "Nomadism, identity and the politics of conservation." *Central Asian Survey* 29 (3): 305–319; Sneath, David. 2010. "Political mobilization and construction of collective Identity in Mongolia." *Central Asian Survey* 29 (3): 251–267; Laurie, Andrew et al. 2010. "Biodiversity conservation and the ecological limits to development options in the Mongolian Altai: Formulation of a strategy and discussion of priorities." *Central Asian Survey* 29 (3): 321–343. The similarity between the international donor-driven conservation programs in Mongolia and the Chinese state-driven programs is striking.
4. All the personal names in this chapter are fictionalized.
5. Huang, Haibo et al. 2021. "Zhongguo luotuozhixiang youluotuo buchuiniu [Prosperity of China's camel country]." *Xinhua News*, March 18. https://news.sina.cn/gn/2021-03-18/detail-ikkntiam4491158.d.html. Accessed March 20, 2023.
6. Unlike Chinese dumplings, Mongolian dumplings use unleavened dough for the wrappers.
7. See Chapter 9 for details about school education in rural IMAR.
8. See Chapter 8 for details about the income gap between farming and herding families in IMAR.

9. "*Fangyang sannian, geigexianzhang yebudang.*" Many of the Han Chinese herders in IMAR were descendants of draft dodgers and famine refugees from Minqin County of Gansu Province during the 1930s and 40s. Minqin is the main site for my research on conservation in agricultural regions. See Chapters 3 and 4 of this book. Ding, Peng (2012: 69) recorded a Han herder's comparison between farming and herding: "if the rain and grass are good, raising stock is much less labor-intensive than planting greenhouse vegetables." Under the new policy, the Han herder reluctantly took up greenhouse vegetable farming and complained that it was lots of work: "watering, applying pesticides, thinning the pepper, trimming branches, all are very hard work and I have no free time at all!" See Ding, Peng. 2012. *Hanzu yiminde wenhuashiying yanjiu-yi neimenggu alashanmeng bayanhaotezhen weili [Cultural Adaptation of Han Chinese migrants—a case study from Bayanhot Township, Alxa League, IMAR].* Hohhot: Inner Mongolia University Press. The comments of the Han herder are strikingly similar to those of Mongolian herders to whom I talked. For further discussion on the dynamic relationship between ethnicity and livelihood see Chapter 8 on Mongol farmers in the agropastoral area of East IMAR. For studies of Han Chinese herders in Hailaer of eastern IM in the 1980s, see Pasternak, Burton and Janet Salaff. 1993. *Cowboys and Cultivators: The Chinese of Inner Mongolia,* pp. 170–201. Boulder: Westview.
10. The actual numbers and flock mix vary from place to place.
11. The threshold herd size varies in time and place, depending on the grazing land productivity in wet or dry years, the degree of grazing restrictions, the size of the household, and other factors.
12. Han, Nianyong. 2018. "Chenbaoyu tudizhidu [Dust storm and land system]." In *Duihua chenbao [A Dialogue with (Donald Worster's) Dust Storms*], edited by Han, Nianyong, Shurun Liu, Enhe, and Erdunbuhe, pp. 354–430. Beijing: China Science and Technology Press. Liu and Gao (2007) also noted that a sumu in Alxa Left Banner of Alxa League had expanded its herd of goats from 20,000 in 1982 to 74,000 in 2003, despite the imposition of grazing bans and stocking ratio rules. It was mainly due to the fact that herders were incentivized by the rising price of cashmere. See Liu, Kuili and Bingzhong Gao. 2007. *Alashan shengtaihuanjingde ehua yu shehuiwenhuade bianqian [Environmental Deterioration and Sociocultural Changes in Alxa]*, p. 122. Beijing: Xueyuan Press. This book is based on a research project sponsored by the Society for Environmental Entrepreneurs (SEE,) one of China's most influential domestic environmental nongovernmental organization (ENGO)s. See Chapter 1 for details about the SEE's role in planting suosuo shrub to combat desertification.
13. See Han, Nianyong. 2011. "Yaohaizai chanquan: dangcaoyuan zaoyushichangkunjing [The key role of property rights: The predicament of the market in the pasture]." In *Caoyuande luoji [The Logic of Pastoralism]*, Vol 3., *Xuezhaolinglei shichangzhidu [Searching for an Alternative Market System]*, edited by Han, Nianyong, pp. 31–46, p. 39.
14. Interview with a China-based scholar, 2012 and 2013.
15. See the Introduction for an overview of China's post-Mao economic expansionism and the northwest's role therein.
16. Sun, Wenchao. 2015. "Neimenggumuqu caoyuantuihuade gongdibeijuxianxiang jiqiduice [The tragedy of the commons in Inner Mongolia's pastoral areas and its solution]." *Huanqiushichang xinxidaobao [Global Market Information News]* 8 (43): 63.

17. For a parallel case of rangeland and livestock privatization in post socialist Central Asia, see Kerven, Carol. 2003. "We have seen two worlds: Impacts of privatization on people, land and livestock," and "Agrarian reform and privatization in the wider Asian region: Comparison with Central Asia." In *Prospects for Pastoralism in Kazakstan and Turkmenistan: From State Farms to Private Flocks*, edited by Carol Kerven, pp. 1–26. NY: Routledge.
18. "Neimengguzizhiqu xumuyeting xiuzhibianshi weiyuanhui [Gazetteer editorial committee of the Bureau of Pastoralism, IMAR]." 2000. In *Neimengguxumuye fazhanshi [History of Pastoral Development of Inner Mongolia]*, p. 299. Hohhot: Inner Mongolia People's Press.
19. For a review of IMAR's grassland contracting policies, see Li, Wenjun and Lynn Huntsinger. 2011. Ibid. For a historical review of IMAR's regime of rangeland management in the Mao and post-Mao eras, see Jiang, Hong. 2005. "Grassland management and views of nature in China since 1949: regional policies and local changes in Uxin Ju, Inner Mongolia." *Geoforum* 36: 641–653. For an overall review of socialist and post-socialist Inner Mongolia, see Sneath, David. 2000. *Changing Inner Mongolia: Pastoral Mongolian Society and the Chinese State.* Oxford: Oxford University Press.
20. The organization of collective herding, called "*hot-ail*," has a long history in the Inner Mongolian steppes that continued into the Mao era. According to Enhe (2018: 58–59), in the 1950s, a hot-ail is made of three to five households (in areas with lush grasses) or two to three households (in areas with less productive grazing areas) who may or may not be kin. Members of a hot-ail would share grazing land, animal pens, and wells. They also share the work of herding, shearing, branding, ear-marking, castrating, training draft animals, cutting fodder, cropping, and swapping breeding livestock to maintain the health of the flock. Most importantly, they embark on seasonal movements to different rangelands together. See Enhe. 2018. "Chenbaoxianxiang yu wenhua toushi [A cultural analysis of dust storms]." In *Duihua chenbao [A Dialogue with (Donald Worster's) Dust Storms]*. Ibid. pp. 26–141.
21. Interviews in Hohhot and Xilingol (2012), and Ejina (2014).
22. A standard FIFA soccer field measures 105 m x 68 m = 7,140 sq. meters.
23. Interview with a herder in Xilingol, 2012; also see Han, Nianyong. 2018. Ibid.
24. See, for example, Chen, Jie and Dan Luo. 2009. *Zhongguo caoyuan shengtai zhili diaocha [Survey of Grassland Management and Repair in China]*. Shanghai: Far East Press. The survey was conducted in 2004 and 2005 in four counties and banners of Inner Mongolia, Qinghai, and Ningxia. It focused on the impact of destocking, relocation, and sheltered husbandry on household income.
25. Han, Nianyong. 2018. Ibid. p. 388.
26. For an overview of the increasing debt of Inner Mongolian herding families, see Dalintai and Yisheng Zhen. 2010. "Muquyushichang: Mumin." [Pastoral region and the market: the pastoralists], In *Muquyushichang: Muminjingjixue [Pastoral Region and the Market: Pastoralists' Economics]*, pp. 383–402. Beijing: Social Sciences Academic Press.
27. Li, Tao. 2014. "Dingjujinmu shehuisunshi diaochabaogao [The social impact of sedentarization and grazing bans in Budunhua (Büdüünhua) gacha]."In *Huanjingzainanyu shehuisunshi [Environmental Disasters and Social Costs]*, pp. 180–187. Beijing: Nandu Foundation. http://www.nandufoundation.org/Uploads/file/20141024/5449d2febb5eb.pdf.; Lü, Yan. 2014. "Muqu shengtaiyiminde shehuisunshi diaochabaogao [Social costs of ecological relocation in pastoral areas]." Beijing: Nandu Foundation. http://www.

nandufoundation.org/Uploads/file/20141024/5449d2febb5eb.pdf. Accessed January 23, 2023; Liu, Kuili and Bingzhong Gao. 2007. Ibid. pp. 112–143; Wang, Xiaoyi. 2009. *Huangjingyalixiade caoyuan shequ [Pastoral Communities under Environmental Pressure]*. Beijing: Social Science Academic Press.

28. I thank Nathan Sayre of Berkeley Geography for the discussion on the carrying capacity model. The model has been widely applied in Inner Mongolia's rangeland conservation programs since the early 2000s. University and research institute-based scientists were commissioned to calculate the carrying capacity of different types of rangeland and for different types of livestock so as to determine the stocking rates and grazing ban schedules. The application of the carrying capacity concept to rangeland management started in the American West, where it was formulated to deal with severe grassland degradation as a result of the cattle boom in the 19th century. The assumption was that, if we remove livestock from deteriorated rangeland, vegetation would revert to its earlier composition and density, bringing the relationship between human activity and nature back to a state of equilibrium. The attractiveness of the carrying capacity model is that, compared to another popular concept of "sustainability," carrying capacity can be calculated. Such calculability fits bureaucrats' need to quantify problems, streamline solutions, and evaluate results. For a critical review of the model of carrying capacity, see Sayre, Nathan. 2017. *The Politics of Scale: A History of Rangeland Science*. Chicago: University of Chicago Press; and Sayre, Nathan. 2008. "The Genesis, History, and Limits of Carrying Capacity." *Annals of the Association of American Geographers* 98 (1): 120–134. For a case study in Central America, see Curtin, Charles G., Nathan F. Sayre, and Benjamin D. Lane. 2002. "Transformations of the Chihuahuan Borderlands: Grazing, fragmentation, and biodiversity conservation in desert grasslands." *Environmental Science & Policy* 5: 55–68. For a case study in Africa, see de Leeuw, Peter N. and John C. Tothill. 1993. "The concept of rangeland carrying capacity in sub-Saharan Africa—Myth or Reality?" In *Range Ecology at Disequilibrium: New Models of Natural Variability and Pastoral Adaptation in African Savannas*, edited by Behnke, Roy, Ian Scoones, and Carol Kerven, pp. 77–88. London: Overseas Development Institute, International Institute for Environment and Development, Commonwealth Secretariat.
29. Interview with a herder in Xilingol, 2011.
30. China's one-child policy was formally enacted in 1979, based on policymakers' concerns over overpopulation in China. The one-child policy allowed some exceptions, and ethnic minorities were allowed to have two or more children. In 2015 the one-child policy turned into the two-child policy. In 2021, the three-child policy was introduced, and the government removed all penalties for couples who had more children than allowed.
31. A researcher estimated that on average, herding families exceeded at least 25% more than what their rangelands' carrying capacity allowed (interview in Hohhot, July 2012). Liu and Gao (2007), have also reported on the prevalence of herders' keeping more stock animals than the restrictive policy allowed in Alxa league and other parts of IMAR. See Liu, Kuili and Bingzhong Gao. 2007. Ibid. pp. 112–143.
32. It is a genus under the legume family. See Enhe. 2018. "Chenbaoxianxiangyu wenhuatoushi [A cultural analysis of dust storms]." In *Duihua chenbao [A Dialogue with (Donald Worster's) Dust Storms]*. Ibid. pp. 26–141.
33. Amu's argument is shared by herders in other pastoral areas I visited. The view was also endorsed by a group of IM-based scholars who named themselves members of the

"Pasture School" (*caoyuanpai*), to distinguish themselves from those of the "Agriculture School" (*zhongnongpai*) who supported government policies to "agriculturalize the steppe." The Pasture School is composed of ethnic Mongolian and some Han Chinese university professors, researchers in state institutions, freelance writers and journalists, as well as environmental NGO activists who have been critical of government policies in pastoral IMAR since the 1990s. During their heyday of the 2000s, several members of the Pasture School published important works on the transformation of pastoral IMAR. They also organized an unprecedented conference in Hohhot, in which herders and scholars exchanged views on pastoral policies. But the scholars of the Pasture School have been mostly muted since the mid-2010s as China's political control tightened.

34. Interview 2013 in Hohhot.
35. For a review of the environmental impact of heavy grazing on the global scale, see Asner, Gregory P. et al. 2004. "Grazing systems, ecosystem responses, and global change." *Annual Review of Environmental Resources* (29): 261–299. For works by IMAR and China-based scholars on the social and environmental impact of IM's rangeland decollectivization and conservation policies, see, for example, Enhe. 2005. "Menggugaoyuan caoyuan huangmohuade wenhuaxuesikao [Grassland desertification in Mongolian Plateau: a cultural perspective]." *Inner Mongolia Social Sciences* (3): 136–141; Enhe. 2011. "Caoyuan huangmohuade lishi fansi [A historical reflection of grassland desertification]." In *Neimenggumuqu caoyuantuihua yu shengtai anquandaide jianshe [Grassland Degradation in Inner Mongolia and the Construction of an Ecological Security Belt]*, edited by Liu, Zonglin et al., pp. 136–150. Hohhot: Inner Mongolia University Press; Dalintai. 2011. "Caoyuan tuihuade zhidu yinsu [Institutional factors of grassland degradation]." In *Neimenggu muqu caoyuantuihua yu shengtai anquandaide jianshe [Grassland Degradation in Inner Mongolia and the Construction of an Ecological Security Belt*], edited by Liu, Zonglin et al., pp. 101–113. Hohhot: Inner Mongolia University Press; Gai, Zhiyi. 2008. *Zhidushiyuxiade caoyuanshengtai huanjingbaohu [An Institutional Analysis of the Grassland Ecology and Environmental Protection]*. Shenyang: Liaoning Ethnicity Press; Wang, Jiange. 2006. *Nongmushengtai yu chuantong menggu shehui [Agricultural and pastoral ecology in traditional Mongolian society]*. Jinan: Shandong People's Press; Dalintai and Yisheng Zhen. 2010. *Muquyu shichang: [Pastoral region and Market]*. Ibid; and Shan, Hai. 2008. *Neimenggu quyukaifayu kechixufazhan wentiyanjiu [Studies of Regional Growth and Sustainable Development in Inner Mongolia]*. Hohhot: Inner Mongolia People's Press; and Wang, Xiaoyi. 2009. Ibid.
36. Wang, Xiaoyi. 2009. Ibid. p. 17.
37. Yang, Siyuan. 2009. *Bayintugacha diaocha [A Survey of Bayingtu Gacha]*, p. 107. Beijing: China Economics Press.
38. Interviews in Xilingol, 2012; Han, Nianyong. 2018. Ibid. p. 369.
39. Han, Nianyong. 2018. Ibid. p. 375.
40. Han, Nianyong. 2018. Ibid. p. 376, and interviews in Xilingol, 2012.
41. See Chapter 1.
42. Interview in Xilingol, 2011. I was impressed by the great variety of grasses upon my first visit in the summer of 2011 to southern Xilingol's pastoral region. Where grasslands were still open for grazing, different types of grass are used for a wide range of household needs, not just for feeding the animal. For example, my host showed me a flowering plant called "butter flower," which she used in the process of churning milk into butter.

43. For the negative environmental consequences of grazing bans in different parts of the world, see a review by Weber, Keith and Shannon Horst. 2011. "Desertification and livestock grazing: The roles of sedentarization, mobility and rest." *Pastoralism: Research, Policy and Practice* 1: 19. https://pastoralismjournal.springeropen.com/articles/10.1186/2041-7136-1-19. Accessed March 24, 2023. Based on various research findings, the authors argued that while literature from the 1980s and early 1990s often linked livestock to the degradation of rangelands and hence the environmental policy of rangeland enclosure, studies since the late 1990s have found that prolonged rest leads to even more severe rangeland degradation. These authors therefore questioned the continued use of rest-rotation grazing. One of the problems generated by prolonged absence of herbivory is excessive standing litter accumulations, or "moribund grasses," which are particularly detrimental to grazing-dependent bunchgrasses. Over time, this condition can kill individual grass plants, leaving only patches of bare soil. The authors cited Savory (1999), to emphasize the distinction between the recovery period required by individual plants to minimize or avoid overgrazing, and the episodic, yet high, levels of disturbance both the plants and soil surface require to maintain the health of its biological communities, ensure rapid biological decay, increase organic matter in the soil, and provide soil-covering litter to promote rain-use efficiency. See Savory, Allan and Jodi Butterfield. 1999. *Holistic Management: A New Framework for Decision Making*, 2nd edition. Washington: Island Press. During my fieldwork in Xilingol and Alxa, I heard similar arguments made by herders and local researchers in more plain language: "The good grasses grow better when sheep eat them regularly."
44. Enhe. 2018. "*Chenbaoxianxiang yu wenhua toushi [A Cultural Analysis of Dust Storms]*." Ibid. pp. 64–67.
45. Interview in Xilingol, 2012.
46. Liu, Kuili and Bingzhong Gao. 2007. Ibid. pp. 141–142.
47. For studies on the socialist science-driven productivity improvement programs, see Schmalzer, Sigrid. 2016. *Red Revolution, Green Revolution: Scientific Farming in Socialist China*. University of Chicago Press; and Santi, Ettore, 2023, *Designing a Land Revolution: The Corporate Reinvention of China's Rural Environment*. PhD Dissertation, University of California at Berkeley.
48. Interview in Xilingol, 2012.
49. Lü, Yan. 2014. Ibid. p. 170.
50. Interview in Alxa Left Banner, 2013.
51. Qiao, Long. 2018. "Mainiubeipian nongmumin shangfang qingyuan [Swindled in cow investment, farmers and herders launched petition]." Radio Free Asia, September 6. https://www.rfa.org/mandarin/yataibaodao/renquanfazhi/ql1-09062018093029.html. Accessed Aug 12, 2022.
52. Political scientists Kevin O'Brien and Lianjiang Li (2006) argued that, as peasants' protests in post-Mao China escalated, the government's "fire wall" has been moving upward. Peasants took their grievances to increasingly higher-level local governments. Some eventually reached the national capital. O'Brien, Kevin and Lianjiang Li. 2006. *Rightful Resistance in Rural China*, pp. 1–24. Cambridge: Cambridge University Press.
53. For other examples of the quota system, see Chapter 1 on the assignment of afforestation tasks, and Chapter 9 on the allocation of elite university seats.
54. Interview in southern Xilingol, 2012.

55. Mining and urban-industrial expansion have also profoundly shaped the transformation of pastoral IMAR. But in this chapter, I only focus on the herding families' struggles and strategies under conservational destocking.
56. For analyses of pastoral systems in IMAR during the pre-CCP era, see Wang, Jiange. 2006. Ibid. For Maoist pastoral collectivism in IMAR, see Dalintai and Yisheng Zheng. 2010. Ibid. pp. 39–92.
57. Dwindling wildlife diversity brought infestation of pests like rats due to the disappearance of their natural predators. In 2011, an environmental activist explained that rats spread diseases and contribute to soil erosion and sandification of the rangeland.
58. Interview in southern Xilingol, 2012. For an overview of the organization of village co-ops in IMAR in the 2000s, see Dalintai and Yisheng Zhen. 2010. Ibid. pp. 403–424. During my visit to southern Xilingol in 2012 I met two co-op organizers. One of them identified two major barriers to building a sustainable and substantial pastoral co-op organization in the post collectivist era. One was the resistance of co-op members towards pooling individual contracted grazing land for collective management, as indicated in the text. The other was that once the grassroots-initiated co-op organization was recognized by local governments, co-ops became a policy mandate that requires universal implementation regardless of the highly variable local conditions. The self-initiated co-ops were consequently coopted by local officials. This co-op leader told me that, since his co-op became a model pastoral co-op, most of his time was spent receiving visitors from other gachas and banners, not running the co-op. He also received policy grants from local government. One of the grants, at half a million yuan, was earmarked for building a public bath for local herders.
59. Hsing, You-tien. 2010. *The Great Urban Transformation: Politics of Land and Property in China*. Oxford: Oxford University Press.
60. Interviews in Xilingol (2012) and Alxa (2013). See also Lü, Yan. 2014. Ibid. pp. 162–179.
61. Zhang, Wen. 2016. *Zirande tuoqian: neimengmuqude huanjingyu shehuibianqian [Disembedding Nature: Environmental and Social Change of a Pastoral Area in Inner Mongolia since 1949]*. Beijing: Intellectual Property Rights Press. See also Fan, Mingming, Yanbo Li, and Wenjun Li. 2015. "Solving one problem by creating a bigger one: The consequences of ecological resettlement for grassland restoration and poverty alleviation in Northwestern China." *Land Use Policy* 42: 124–130.
62. According to a Hohhot-based researcher, alfalfa consumes twice as much water as cotton and five times as much as melon. Interview, 2014. Also see Wang, Xiaoyi. 2009. Ibid.
63. See, for example, Behnke, Roy, Ian Scoones and Carol Kerven. eds.1993. Ibid; Scoones, Ian. 1995. *Living with Uncertainty: New Directions in Pastoral Developments in Africa*. International Institute for Environment and Development; and Niamir-Fuller, Maryam ed. 1999. *Managing Mobility in African Rangelands: The Legitimization of Transhumance*. Rugby, UK: Intermediate Technology Publications Limited. See also Turner, M. D. 1999. "No Space for Participation: Pastoralist Narratives and the Etiology of Park-herder Conflict in Southeastern Niger." *Land Degradation and Development* 10: 345–363; and Williams, Dee M. 2000. "Representations of nature on the Mongolian Steppe: An investigation of scientific knowledge construction." *American Anthropologist* 102 (3): 503–519. China-based scholars, such as Enhe (2005), Kuili Liu and Bingzhong Gao (2007), and Dalintai (2011), whose works I referenced earlier, have written about IMAR's relocation policies with similar concerns. I do not disagree with the scholars' assessment of the detrimental social and environmental impacts of the conservation-driven relocation programs

in IMAR and elsewhere, as I have elaborated on in the Introduction. The intention of this chapter is to complicate the story by looking beyond the resettlements in order to understand what herders have attempted to do after they are relocated.

64. The Gobi Desert usually refers to the dryland region between IMAR and Mongolia. But for the locals in Ejina, the term "gobi" is not necessarily a place name, but a specific type of arid landscape covered by small- to medium-sized, white or black colored gravel that is coarser than sand. In this chapter, while Ejina is located in the Gobi Desert, I use the lowercase "gobi" when referring to this type of arid landscape.
65. For the social and environmental history of Hexi Corridor, see Chapter 3.
66. On the offensive, not just defensive, nature of the Great Wall of the Han Dynasty, see Hsing, I-tien. 2022. *Gugediqiu yu qinhan changcheng [Google Earth and the Great Walls of the Qin and Han Dynasties]*. Taipei: Sanmin Press.
67. See Nashunbayier. 2006. "Cong Ejinalishikan neimengguzhengzhiwenhua rentongde xingcheng [The history of Ejina's political and cultural identity]." In *Heishuiyu renwen yu huanjing yanjiu [A Cultural and Environmental Study of the Hei River Basin]*, edited by Shen, Weirong et al., pp. 489–496. Beijing: Renmin University Press. Also, the Qing Dynasty's Alxa included only today's Alxa Left and Alxa Right Banners, not Ejina. See Liang, Lixia. 2009. *Alashan mengguyanjiu [Studies of Alxa Mongolia]*, pp. 5–13. Beijing: Ethnicity Press. During an interview in 2013, a Hohhot-based historian explained to me that Ejina sat at the remote periphery of the Qing empire, and Ejina locals continued to identify themselves as Torghuts more than as Mongols. While such localized identity is found in many subregions in IMAR, the sense of cultural distinction seemed particularly salient in Ejina.
68. "Neimenggurenkouzhizui qingkuangjianxi [A demographical analysis of IMAR]." 2022. Bureau of Statistics of Inner Mongolia Autonomous Region, September 2. http://tj.nmg.gov.cn/tjdt/fbyjd_11654/202209/t20220902_2123238.html. Accessed March 30, 2023.
69. "Renkou minzu [Population and ethnicity]." Ejina Banner Government website. http://www.ejnq.gov.cn/col/col1851/index.html. Accessed March 23, 2023; and 2021. "Alashanmengdiqici quanguorenkou puchagongbao (dierhao) qiquchangzhurenkou qingkuang [The Seventh National Census Report, No 2, regular residents by banner and district]." Bureau of Statistics of Alxa League Government, May 31.
70. Many of the Han Chinese migrants in Alxa come from Minqin County of Gansu Province, a farming area. For the environmental history and conservation politics of Minqin, see Chapters 3 and 4.
71. Yuuki, Kohase (Chinese translation: Xiaochangguyouji). 2005. "Heiheliuyu shengtaiy-imin dekaishi [The origin of ecological relocation in the Hei River basin]." In *Shengtaiy-iming: laizizhongriliangguo xuezhe duizhongguoshengtaihuanjingde kaocha [Ecological Relocation: Investigations of China's Environment by Chinese and Japanese scholars]*, edited by Xinjiletu, pp. 25–38. Hohhot: Inner Mongolia University Press.
72. Yuuki, Kohase. 2005. Ibid. pp. 25–38.
73. Ding, Pingjun. 2014. "Yuanqude muren: Ejinaqi shengtaiyimin diaocha [The disappearing pastoralists: a survey of ecological relocation in Ejina Banner]." In *Huanjingzainan yu shehuisunshi [Environmental Disasters and Social Costs]*. Ibid. pp. 130–161.
74. For debates on the relationship between the welfare state and a "dependency culture," see, for example, two studies on South Africa's social grants: Potts, Rebecca. 2012. "Social welfare in South Africa: Curing or causing poverty?." *Penn State Journal of International*

Affairs 1 (2): 72–90; and Surender, Noble et al. 2010. "Social assistance and dependency in South Africa: An analysis of attitudes to paid work and social grants." *Journal of Social Policy* 39 (2): 203–221.

75. Ding, Pingjun (2014) reported that a family in Ejina received 22,000 yuan annually from 2011 to 2013. See Ding, Pingjun. 2014. Ibid. pp. 130–161.
76. The national policy of "grassland compensation" was calculated on the basis of the size of land that each family forfeits for enclosure and recovery. Given the fact that average family holdings vary from league to league, banner to banner, and village to village, local governments in pastoral areas resorted to paying the compensation sum based on family size. However, in the agropastoral areas such as those in East IMAR where population density is much higher than IMAR's regional average, especially in farming areas (see Chapter 8), ecological compensation for "retiring farming" is calculated by the amount of land.
77. Interview in Ejina, July 2014.
78. In their studies on rural transformation in Alxa League, Liu, Kuili and Bingzhong Gao (2007) reported that some Mongol relocatees did try to cultivate melons. But most of them failed due to the lack of know-how and capital. In the end, they rented out their land to cash crop investors from other provinces who hired experienced farm managers and workers to grow melons. See Liu, Kuili and Bingzhong Gao. 2007. Ibid. pp. 144–145. In Ejina, I met a melon farm manager from Sichuan Province in the summer of 2014. He stayed in Ejina from late spring to early fall and returned to Sichuan after the harvest. He hired seasonal farm hands from Gansu Province, all of whom were middle-aged Han Chinese women. However, whether Mongols know how to hold a hoe is a question less clearcut than what Song has expressed. In Chapter 8 of this book, I will tell stories about Mongol farmers and their critical role in the expansion of intensive farming in eastern IMAR during the 19th and 20th centuries.
79. It is important to note that what makes a native plant "native" is subject to debate. Also, while suosuo may be native, its partner congrong may not be. According to a local researcher, the species of congrong planted in many plantations in western IM today is native to Xinjiang in western China. The Xinjiang species is said to be tougher and easier to sprout than the Inner Mongolian variety. Interview in Alxa Left Banner, July 2013.
80. "CCTV documentary: Changchengneiwai (175) Alashan kaoquanyangjiyi [The Two Sides of the Great Wall (episode 175): The Craft of Alxa's Roast Lamb]." 2016. CCTV. June 24. http://tv.cctv.com/2016/06/24/VIDEMEGZs90IEwiul0s8PmhI160624.shtml. Accessed March 30, 2023.
81. Mongolian herders hunted wild congrong for sale. But few of them consumed the medicinal plant that is believed beneficial for male potency because, according to a congrong hunter, "only Han Chinese men need the help of congrong." Interview in Ejina, April 2014.
82. Strokes plague quite a few Mongolian men (and one woman) I met in IMAR. Most people I met in IM blamed it on heavy drinking.
83. In addition to bilingual schooling for students of large and geopolitically important minority nationalities such as Mongols, Tibetans, and Uyghurs (see Chapters 5 and 9), ethnic medicine is another key component of China's ethnicity policy.
84. See Chapter 1 for details about the shrinking natural suosuo forests.
85. He, Yuling et al. 2005. "Alashanmeng chengweiquanguo zuidadeqishijiaoyide zhiyi [Alxa League has become one of the largest curiosity stone wholesale centers in China]."

Sina.com. December 19. https://news.sina.com.cn/o/2005-12-09/12227666550s.shtml. Accessed on October 1, 2024; and Bao, Xiuwen et al. 2009. "Alashanqishichanye nianjiaoyiyuyiyuan [Alxa's curiosity stone exceeds 100 million yuan in annual sales]." Xinhua News, May 1. http://news.sohu.com/20090501/n263722257.shtml. Accessed March 31, 2023.

86. Xue, Qing. 2011. "Jinmuxiade caoyuan: Alashanmumin diaocha [Grassland under grazing ban: a survey of Herders in Alxa]." In *Caoyuande luoji [The Logic of Pastoralism]: Guojia shengtaixiangmu youlaiyu mumin neishengdongli [The Success of the State's Environmental Protection Programs Depends on Pastoralists' Motivation]*, edited by Han, Nianyong. Ibid. Vol. 4, pp. 1–45, p. 14.
87. At the end of my visit, Bayintu asked if I would be interested in joining him to launch a trading company in the U.S. to sell desert rose stones from Ejina. I declined the offer.
88. See Chapters 3 and 4 for a more detailed story about the politics of reviving a dried-up lake in Minqin, Gansu Province.
89. Fictional name.
90. Interview with an Ejina Banner official, October 2013.
91. Interview with an Ejina Banner official, October 2013.
92. The Cultural Revolution in IMAR, similar to that in Tibet Autonomous Region, was heavily racialized and violent. In 1966, Ulanhu, the prominent Mongol Communist Party leader who facilitated the establishment of IMAR in 1947 (the CCP's first minority-named autonomous region), was purged. Ulanhu's fall was followed by a witch hunt called "*wa-su*," which means "expose and eradicate" in Chinese. It was an abbreviation of "exposing Ulanhu's underground gang and eradicating Ulanhu's poisonous influence." Under the iron-fisted command of the Peoples' Liberation Army (PLA), General Teng Haiqing, who was dispatched from the Beijing Military Region to IMAR, the Cultural Revolution turned into massive ethnic persecution and terror in IM. The violent witch hunt of "*wa-su*" criminalized ethnic Mongols and led to atrocious torture, injuries, incapacitation, and fatalities. The official report cites that more than 346,000 Mongol party cadres, military officers, and soldiers, government officials, workers, intellectuals, religious leaders, and villagers were persecuted for their alleged connections with the Inner Mongolian People's Revolution Party (*neirendang*). Neirendang was active in the 1920s during the heyday of modern Mongol nationalism, but the party lost its influence starting in the 1930s. During the Cultural Revolution, the name "neirendang" was brought back to label alleged Mongol separatists and to justify the political purge. For an overview of wa-su, see Qi, Zhi. 2010. *Neimongwengeshilu: "minzufenlie" yu"wasu"yundong [Records of the Cultural Revolution in Inner Mongolia: Ethnic Fissure and Wasu Campaigns]*. Hong Kong: Tianxingjian Press. Also see Yang, Haiying. 2017. "The truth about the Mongolian Genocide during the Chinese Cultural Revolution." *Asian Studies* 6: 1–65. Center for Research on Asia, Faculty of Humanities and Social Sciences, Shizuoka University; and Sneath, David. 2000. *Changing Inner Mongolia: Pastoral Mongolian Society and the Chinese State*, pp. 114–115. Oxford: Oxford University Press. For a Mongolian villager's personal account of wa-su in eastern IMAR, see Chapter 8.
93. Interview in Ejina, 2013. Retired cadres played a similar role in peasants' protests elsewhere in rural China in the 1990s and 2000s. These local cadre-turned mobilizers possessed local influence and knowledge of the inner workings of the state, both of which were essential to grassroots mobilization. This phenomenon is not new. In Chapter 8 on eastern IMAR's agricultural frontier, I recount low-ranking Mongolian banner officials

leading armed uprisings against the Qing State's land reclamation in the 19th and early 20th centuries. These local elites have a dual role that could support or disrupt the political order at the grassroots level. In Chapter 9, on Mongolian students in China's college race, I elaborate on the geopolitical significance of managing the frustration of Mongolian college graduates, the future local elites, in China's territorial governance of IMAR.

94. Tourism was part of the developmental relocation program in Ejina. Herder families decorated the façades of the relocation units built on the main roads with the intention of turning their relocation homes into hostels and restaurants. But the capacity to run tourism businesses varied greatly among relocated families. The official "ecotourism development zone" in the outskirts of Dalaihubu Township was much less popular among tourists compared to those near the town center.
95. For a review of the transformation of pastoralism in Inner Asia, see Humphrey, Caroline and David Sneath. 1999. *The End of Nomadism? Society, State, and the Environment in Inner Asia.* Durham, NC: Duke University Press. The authors found that pastoral nomadism has survived the market economy in parts of the Mongolian Steppe in Chinese, Mongolian, and Russian territories.

INTRODUCTION to Part II: AGRICULTURAL FUTURES OF GANSU'S SALTY SOIL

Farming, with its various modes of dry and irrigated farming, has had a long history in China's northwestern drylands. The northwest's agrarian histories are made of resource struggles and conservation contradictions just as contentious as those in pastoral Inner Mongolia presented in Part I.

Part II, Agricultural Futures of Gansu's Salty Soil, draws upon materials from my fieldwork in Minqin County of Gansu Province in 2013–16. Minqin is an oasis sandwiched by two deserts, Badain Jaran and Tengger, in the Hexi Corridor of Central Gansu. It has long been tucked away in the geopolitical periphery and stuck in cycles of soil salinization. By the 1990s, Minqin was portrayed in the media as a hopeless place that would soon be buried by the two encroaching deserts. Then in the new millennium, Minqin soared from being an hopeless swamp to landing on the frontpage of every news story on China's successful campaign of combating desertification. How did this happen? Chapter 3, "Hope of the Hopeless: Recharging the Dried-up Qingtu Lake in Minqin," chronicles Minqin's dramatic ascent that brought interbasin water transfers, unprecedented state funding, and media attention. This story is contextualized in Minqin's agrarian and geopolitical histories from the imperial era to the present moment, especially since the 1950s.

Much of the doom and hope in agrarian Minqin is dictated by water. Chapter 4, "Opportunity in Scarcity: Building a National Model of Water Conservancy" uses ethnographic materials to examine Minqin's water conservancy regime during the 2000s and 2010s. Local officials, entrepreneurs, and farmers (who were often called "ecological refugees" in popular and policy discourse) strategized how to implement, survive, and thrive in the restrictive water conservancy policies like farmland reduction, well closures, groundwater metering, and water price hikes. Local actors also navigated government programs designed to turn scarcity into opportunity, like installing drip irrigation, planting drought-tolerant cash crops, and building capital-intensive industrial farms. Contradictions and tensions are found between officially constructed water scarcity and actual lived scarcity and between constructed and lived opportunity. The tension is illustrated by the story in the last section about a three-generation "ecological refugee" family's strategies to survive current conservation while striving for a future beyond Minqin's salty soil.

3

Hope of the Hopeless: Recharging the Dried-up Qingtu Lake in Minqin

In an essay entitled "Where is Minqin, the county of sand and wind, today?" posted on a China-based website *ScienceNet*, a concerned writer presented Minqin as a place on the verge of disappearance: "... the desert is devouring farms and villages, the oases are rapidly shrinking .... relocation is inevitable."[1] Similar tones about Minqin's demise are adopted in a number of other journalistic, academic and policy reports on the present and future of Minqin.[2] Geographically, Minqin is sandwiched between two "encroaching" deserts of Badain Jaran and Tengger in Central Gansu Province, and Gansu is a province whose GDP per capita ranked the second lowest among China's 31 provinces throughout much of the post-reform era. Long before that, Gansu was known as the home of famine refugees fleeing neighboring provinces. Under the jurisdiction of Gansu, Minqin, which means "tenacious people" in Chinese, is a place where people have to work tenaciously to, hopefully, survive its predestined environmental crises.

The root of the crises, according to contemporary policy and journalist reports, is water scarcity. Minqin rains about 100 mm a year, but its annual evaporation rate averages 2,600 mm. The rivers that used to feed Minqin's oases are diminishing. Desperate local farmers have extracted an unsustainable amount of groundwater, sending the arid place on a downward spiral from an ill birth to a slow death.

I went to Minqin for the first time in the summer of 2013. I was first led by my local host to see the site of a former village that featured empty and dilapidated farmhouses, so that I could take photographs of a "typical sight in Minqin." Except the homes were not destroyed by sandstorms, but rather razed by bulldozers under the conservation program of farmland reduction. In the "shrinking oases," I saw abandoned farms and

Conserving China's Northwest Frontier. You-tien Hsing, Oxford University Press. © You-tien Hsing (2025).
DOI: 10.1093/9780191903908.003.0004

sealed wells, marking the era of water conservancy. In these villages, most young people had left. I met quite a few "left-behind" peasants in their 70s and 80s, who served me tea that tasted bitterly salty. The picture did seem bleak. But in other villages of Minqin, I saw newly paved roads that led to massive plantations of cash crops and industrial sheep and cattle farms. There, I found myself amidst the lively presence of farmers trying to predict the market price of the onion, the most profitable crop at the time, but also a thirsty crop. There were few signs of scaling back and much speculation and hope for its future.

I came to realize that Minqin, a county-level jurisdiction of 300,000 people and of 16,000 sq. km in the northwest of China, is not going to be written off so easily, as newspaper headlines suggested, after all. Minqin's crises and scarcity, once recognized by the state, could produce salvation and abundance. In 2004, Premier Wen Jiabao visited Minqin and vowed to rescue Minqin from the invading deserts. Minqin has since been lifted from a geopolitical periphery to the center of China's "ecological civilization,"[3] the Chinese Communist Party (CCP) state's version of environmentalism in the new millennium. It has transformed from a destitute place to a stage where the state demonstrates its capacity for crisis management. In the era of conservationism, Minqin's hope hinges on its hopelessness.

Minqin's agrarian history does not start from Premier Wen's historic visit in 2004. In this chapter I first briefly review Minqin's history of irrigated farming since the early imperial Han Dynasty (206 BCE to 220 CE), when the area was a farming colony for border defense and military offensives. This is a history of turning lowland swamps into farms, which led to increasingly salinized soil and local farmers' adaptive techniques to work the salty soil. Located at the lower reaches of the river basin and in the remote frontier far from state-invested infrastructure, Minqin farmers have confronted both geopolitical and hydrosocial marginality since the late imperial era of the 18th century. With accelerating desertification in the 1990s, the county had been expected to fall off the national map at any moment. Then came state-marshalled environmentalism in the 2000s. Minqin made a triumphant comeback in leading the CCP state's campaign to combat desertification and was enthroned as the site for demonstrating the state's capacity to resolve problems and avert crises. With such fame came unprecedented financial support from the state, interbasin water transfers, and an intensified regime of neoliberal water conservancy cloaked in the language of scarcity.

Minqin's unexpected change of luck may or may not serve as a template for other places in a similar situation. Yet, there is little question that its status as a demonstration site for productive conservation has had profound impacts on life and livelihoods in the ostensible margins of the northwest frontier. Such an "atypical" case, in terms of the attention and resources that have been poured onto Minqin since the 2000s, also helps show the possibilities and limits of strong state intervention in the age of productive conservation. (I will elaborate on the analytical and theoretical implications of place-driven stories in the concluding chapter, Telling Place -Driven Stories.) This chapter on Minqin's rise to conservation championship sets the stage for the next chapter on Minqin farmers' strategies for surviving conservation.

I Once Upon a Swamp

Although synonymous with water scarcity in China today, Minqin was once a swamp with lakes, streams, and springs in the early imperial era. During the 2nd century BCE, Minqin was known as Zhuyeze (a "Frontier of Congregating Waters").[4] Shiyang, one of the largest inland rivers in China, traversed north from its origin in the Qilian Mountains for 90 kilometers before concluding its journey in the endorheic lakes in Zhuyeze's alluvial basin. Streams, springs, and lakes congregated in Zhuyeze, intersecting with woodlands and pastures where steppe peoples grazed their livestock. Environmental historian Li Bingcheng (1993) estimated that the surface area of the two largest lakes in Zhuyeze then measured 540 sq. km.[5] The environmental and social transformations of Zhuyeze over the millennia are shaped by waves of territorial conquest, retreat, settlement, and resettlement.

I.1 Turning Swamp into Farms

The swampy wetland of Zhuyeze was incorporated into the Han territory in 121 BCE and placed under the jurisdiction of Wuwei ("martial might" in Chinese) Prefecture, along with the rest of the Hexi Corridor (Figure 3.1). To consolidate his territorial control, the emperor established military colonies in the Hexi Corridor and recruited farmer-soldiers to defend the frontier while establishing farms for food supplies. At its height, the mid- and lower reaches of the inland river basins of the Corridor were home to half a million farmer-soldiers. Sitting at the tail end of the Shiyang River, Zhuyeze's fertile alluvial soil and dense networks of streams, springs, and lakes made it an ideal site for the military farming colonies. By the early 3rd century BCE, the area under cultivation in Zhuyeze was estimated at 14,800 hectares.[6]

In the post-Han Dynasty era, Zhuyeze and the rest of the Hexi Corridor went through more than 10 centuries of regime shifts among various Han Chinese and non-Han steppe powers, as well as periods of substantial cultivation expansion and contraction. When agrarian Han Chinese-dominant regimes were stable and expanding, waterways in the lower basin shrank with the expansion of farming. At times of frequent warfare, or when the non-Han pastoral powers dominated the Shiyang Basin especially during the Mongolian Yuan Dynasty (1271 to 1368), agriculture in the Corridor was reduced to a negligible level. When farming in the upper reaches of the Shiyang was reduced, a great volume of surface runoff flowed down to Zhuyeze, expanding the size of the endorheic lakes. New swamps and ponds were formed, and old ones refilled.[7] What came with the dynamic environmental and geopolitical shifts in the Hexi Corridor watersheds, Zhuyeze included, was the mixing and shifting of herding and farming livelihoods.

At the fall of the Mongolian Yuan Dynasty and establishment of the Ming Dynasty (1368 to 1644) by Han Chinese, Zhuyeze was incorporated into a military colony called Zhenfan.[8] Zhenfan means "conquering the barbarian," which says much about the aspirations of the Ming court. The confident emperors of early Ming, who had just

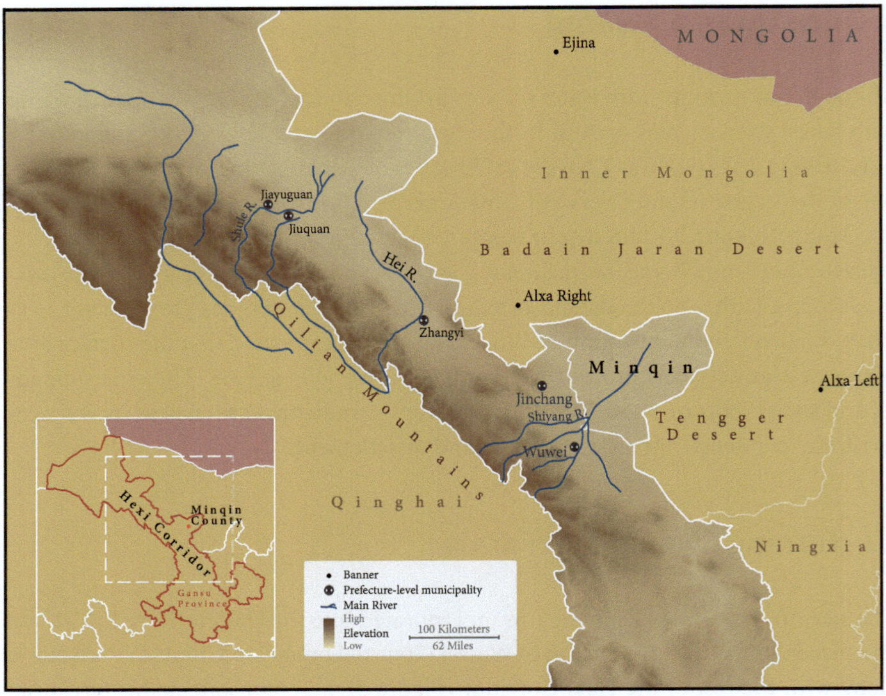

Figure 3.1 Map of contemporary Hexi Corridor

Source: Cartographer: Alan Pong.

defeated the Mongols, resumed the territorial project of consolidating the frontier by reviving military-farming colonies and expanding cultivation throughout the Hexi Corridor. By this time, the ancient military colonies from the Han and subsequent dynasties had long been abandoned and buried under the sand. The new military colonies of the Ming shifted eastward and grew to twice the size of the Han-era colonies at 26,600 hectares.[9]

The succeeding emperors of the Ming Dynasty, weaker and poorer than the Dynasty's founders, conceded much of the frontier territory to other steppe powers and took a more defensive stance. They built the Great Wall with durable masonry and brick instead of the rammed earth used for Han era fortifications (see Chapter 10). The Ming Great Wall ran along the southern edge of Zhenfan, which was much further south than the Han-era fortifications, indicating the Ming emperors' contracting territorial command and ambition. Cultivation in the Ming border colonies was kept to the south of the Great Wall, in today's Dam District and Huanhe District of Minqin, while Lake District, the largest irrigated district in Minqin today, sat north of the Great Wall (see Figure 3.2).

The Ming Dynasty was succeeded by the Manchurian Qing (1644 to 1911), the last dynasty of imperial China. With a semi-pastoral background, the Manchu Qing emperors controlled both sides of the Ming Great Wall and extended the empire west to Central Eurasia.

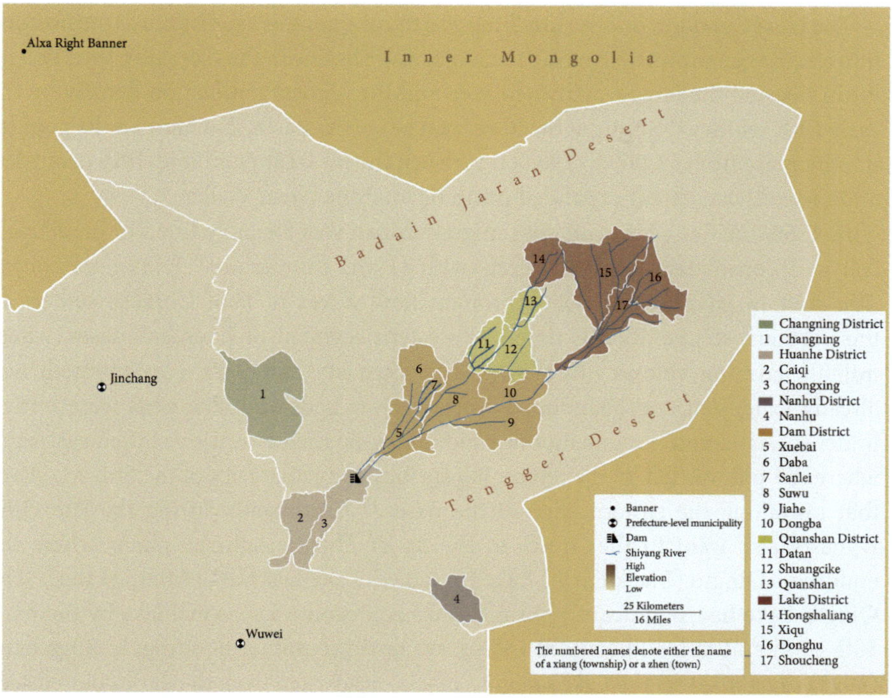

Figure 3.2 Map of Minqin's contemporary irrigation districts
Source: Cartographer: Alan Pong.

During the Ming-Qing transition period, a large number of Han Chinese war and famine refugees fled to the north of the Ming Great Wall. Fearing the loss of Manchu identity to the Han Chinese, the Qing court decided to close off Manchuria to Han immigrants in 1740. The Manchu Qing-controlled Mongol territories were also closed off to Han Chinese to prevent ethnic collision and collusion (see Chapter 6). In the meantime, the Qing government itself actively recruited settlers from south of the Great Wall to farm the nine military-farming colonies along the Hexi Corridor to support the court's military actions in central Eurasia in today's Xinjiang. Among the nine military-farming colonies, the one in Zhenfan was the largest, which boasted more than 2,600 settler households working on 120,000 mu of farmland, compared to other colonies measuring only a few thousand mu each.[10] The government's labor recruitment programs made it impossible to guard the border against self-initiated migrants, because undocumented settlers often forged travel documents to cross the border passes. So northbound migration continued. Han Chinese farmers trekked up north from Shaanxi, Shanxi, and Henan Provinces, as well as from the Gansu mountains to Hexi Corridor. In 1760, following the Qing's successful subjugation of Jungar territory in today's Xinjiang, the military significance of the Hexi Corridor declined. Soldiers of the Hexi Corridor's farming colonies were dispatched further west to guard the new frontier in Xinjiang, leaving the Hexi Corridor to civilian cultivators.

The Hexi Corridor, once a launching pad to conquer the "barbarians," transformed into a settler community. Among the major river basins in the Corridor, the Shiyang Basin boasted the largest cultivated area and the highest population density by the early 19th century.[11] Sitting at the lower reaches of the Basin, Zhenfan saw its population increase from 11,000 to 190,000 between the mid-18th and mid-19th centuries, and the cultivated areas expanded north beyond the Great Wall.[12]

In 1860, the Qing government's migration ban was formally lifted to proactively "fill and consolidate border regions with (Han) immigrants" (*yimin shibian*).[13] The shift in government policy brought new waves of Han Chinese settlers to the northern steppe. By this time, the western segment of Zhenfan's oases, where military-farming colonies from the Ming Dynasty had been concentrated, was already exhausted and abandoned. Former river beds and lake beds were buried under the sand and became mobile sand dunes. So the cultivation shifted eastward, where the soil was fed by the remaining springs and tributaries of the Shiyang River that ran along the eastern edge of the oases.[14] Cultivation during the late Qing Dynasty also went further north to the tip of Zhenfan alluvial plains where the endorheic Qingtu (Black Earth) Lake (in today's Lake District in Minqin) sits.[15] The Qingtu Lake had significantly shrunk and had become a seasonal lake by the mid-18th century. But it still covered 140 sq. km during summer flooding. Li Bingcheng (1993) suggested that the Lake's name, "Black," originated from the dark-colored sediment in the lakebed that was exposed as the lake shrank. The exposed lakebed, with its rich soil was repurposed for farming and grazing.[16] For water, the crop fields relied primarily on scattered ponds filled by summer floods and off-season upstream surface flows. Before the sowing season started in early spring, farmers channeled fresh surface water to flood the fields, then drained them to wash away excessive salinity and alkalinity in the soil. The flood irrigation to "settle the seeds" with fresh surface runoff, a local farming method to adapt to water shortage and salinity, was practiced only once a year. For the rest of the growing season, dryland farmers in Zhenfan developed various labor-intensive techniques to maintain soil moisture for crop development.

Farmers in China are well recognized as hard workers. Historian John McNeill (1998)[17] has called China's landscape "hyperanthropogenic," noting its terraces, rice paddies, polders, dikes, dams, and canals constructed at an intensity unparalleled in human history. Robert Marks (1998, 2011)[18] summarized China's environmental history as a process of upward and outward cultivation expansion, often from more humid to drier soil and from gentle to steep slopes. Such a sculpted landscape is the work of intensive labor input, and its productivity depends on constant and vigilant maintenance of an unusually high degree. Any disruption or neglect of China's hyperanthropogenic landscape could lead to a significant dip in production and productivity.[19]

Farmers of China's arid northwest have had their fair, if not larger, share of vigilant work to maintain the hyperanthropogenic landscape. Farming in the northwest is characterized by short growing seasons, harsh winters, low and highly unpredictable precipitation. Most of all, high evaporation rates of the dryland accelerate saline-alkaline accumulation in the soil and water, which is exacerbated by irrigation that channels salt from deeper underground levels up to the root zone. Soil moisture conservation and saline and alkaline content management are two interconnected and pressing tasks for dryland farmers. It takes not just arduous labor, but also local knowledge to make a living in an increasingly adverse farming environment. The agricultural history of Zhenfan, now called Minqin, is that of farmers battling the salty soil with toilsome labor and know-how in dryland farming. Battling the salty soil has been imperative since imperial times, and some of the ancient practices of farming in salty soil continue to this day, which I will turn to in the next section. I will use Zhenfan's modern name, Minqin, in the remaining text, with notes on time periods when necessary.

I.2 Battling the Salty Soil

Saline soil, found in about one-fifth of China's cultivated land, is a common feature of the arid north, west, and northwest regions. In Minqin, soil in and around the former lakes has high saline content. It is predominantly the crusted clay soil that cracks and, thus, accelerates moisture loss. To improve soil structure and minimize moisture loss, farmers first break the caked soil and transport sand from the edge of the oases or silty sediment from the bottom of ditches to mix with the clay soil so as to reduce cracks and improve soil permeability. In areas of sandy soil at the edge of the desert and in sandified patches of the oases, farmers improve the soil's water-holding capacity by mixing the sand with clay and silt, which they often have to carry in from afar. Having been a frontier military base since early imperial times, Minqin is home to quite a few Great Wall ruins, including the Wall foundation, beacon towers, and watch towers from the Han and Ming Dynasties.[20] Fragments of the ancient structure, made of rammed earth mixed with organic materials such as twigs and straw, are also used to improve soil fertility and structure. Some farmers believe that debris from the ancient structures can also bring good fortune.[21]

The work of maintaining the right balance between the soil's permeability and water-holding capacity is followed by building alternating mounds and furrows on flat lands and terraces as well as creating banks on slopes. These measures trap water around the plants, limit runoff, and retard erosion. Multiple rounds of plowing, smoothing, and rolling over the fields are also crucial. The topsoil must be dense enough to minimize evaporation and resist being blown away by strong winds, but also loose enough to allow healthy sprouting. To reduce evaporation, farmers spread as much as four to five inches of gravel or sand mulching over the fields during off seasons. Frequent weeding is another way of maintaining soil moisture in Minqin's drylands.[22]

Much of the success of moisture conservation relies not just on the strenuous physical labor of plowing, spreading mulch, or weeding. Moisture conservation also requires vigilance and knowledge. With highly unpredictable rainfalls and temperature changes in the dryland, farmers must constantly monitor and assess the amount of moisture present (or absent) and be ready to respond promptly. Different levels of soil moisture at different stages of a crop cycle require different combinations of tillage, smoothing, and rolling over. The impact of a dry spell during the sprouting season can be mitigated by rolling a small-sized stone wheel lightly over the fields to seal the soil's surface and induce deep soil moisture to rise up via capillary action.[23] Untimely heavy rainfall right after plowing and before sowing, or during the growing season, may compact the soil, causing crusting, cracking, and loss of soil moisture. As a result, the soil has to be loosened and smoothed again several times immediately after the rain.

Managing soil salinity and alkalinity is another major task in dryland farming. Salinity and alkalinity exist in all naturally occurring bodies of water. But in hot and dry climates, regular water evaporation leaves a large amount of salt accumulation in the soil and sediment. The natural occurrence of salt in the soil is called primary salinity. In arid lands, salinity can be found in wetlands and lakebeds, as in Minqin. Irrigation induces secondary salinity through the following processes: the removal of deeply rooted native dryland vegetation and the introduction of shallow-rooted annuals increases water leakage into the groundwater system, which leads to groundwater rise. When groundwater rises within about two meters of the soil's surface, salt is lifted into the root zone and the soil surface, thus accelerating the salinization of irrigated fields. To work with the increasingly salty soil, farmers need more water to flush away the salt. But more irrigation water brings more salt up to the root zone and surface soil, creating a vicious cycle of ever-increasing demands for labor and water.

The long history of irrigated agriculture in China's northwest river basins, where primary salinity is already higher than that of most other regions, has created a chronic challenge with secondary soil salinity. Agricultural historian Min Zongdian (1989) summed up nine major techniques of saline and alkaline soil management that northern Chinese farmers have developed since the early imperial era. These nine techniques include biological, chemical, and mechanical approaches to "remove (*paiyan*), flush (*xiyan*), prevent (*fangyan*), suppress (*yiyan*), block (*duyan*), avoid (*duoyan*), tolerate (*naiyan*), resist (*kangyan*), and convert (*gaiyan*)" the salinity and alkalinity of the soil.[24]

A number of these techniques have been practiced as early as the Han dynasty in the 2nd century BCE. One such example is *yu-guan*, a technique that involves flooding salinized land with silt-laden surface runoff to cover the infertile soil with a layer of silt, so that the silt filters out excess salt. The silt also helps improve soil fertility and keeps the saline from rising up the soil through the roots of the crops. Developed in 246 BCE during the late Warring States period in today's Shaanxi Province, this method peaked during the Song Dynasty (960 to 1279 CE) and spread to other areas in northern and northwestern China and continued into the late imperial Ming and Qing Dynasties.[25] But this method is more effective when the supply of surface runoff is sufficient. With reduced surface water, silt needs to be transported manually from the bottom of ditches, as is the case in Minqin today.[26]

Another common technique developed during the 19th century, when the diminished surface runoff rendered the traditional method of flooding the field less attainable, was "plow deep and bury the salty soil" (*shenfan woyan*). Min (1989) quoted a folk saying: "in the sandy land, wet soil can be found one foot under; in the saline land, sweet soil can be found one foot under."[27] This method entails raking and plowing salty topsoil under, raising the less salty soil to the top, and then mixing the two types of soil to dilute the salinity.

The Minqin Gazetteer recorded two saline management measures that were practiced in the Republican era. Plots with differing levels of salinity required different treatments. For soil of lighter salinity (*fujiandi*), the treatment entailed shoveling away the saline topsoil and replacing it with a layer of sandy silt collected from the bottom of ditches and mixing the two through deep plowing. For soil of heavy salinity (*laojiandi*), a method of revamping (*daodahang)* was applied. Revamping the soil was a daunting, multiphase project. First, the topsoil needed to be meticulously inspected for living plant roots in the soil. If so, the soil was "alive." The "living" soil would be carefully separated from the "dead" soil bit by bit, and then placed back. The painstaking process of sifting the soil to separate the "living" from the "dead" would then be followed by mixing in new soil with the living soil and deep plowing at least 60 cm deep, while keeping the dense clay at the bottom in order to prevent saline from rising up through capillary action.[28]

In Minqin, soil with the highest levels of salinity is found in the northern edge of the alluvial plain in and around the drained lakebeds. This area has high groundwater levels, and groundwater at the vadose zone is prone to salinization. The soil of former lakebeds is also prone to pests and weeds. To manage the multiple challenges, farmers would leave this parcel of land to fallow for one summer every few years. During the fallow, farmers alternate mounds and furrows. Mounds are plowed down to make furrows, and furrows are built up to make mounds. This way all the *yin* soil (the soil buried under the mound) is sterilized through exposure to the summer heat, and thus transformed into *yang* soil. After four to five days, the field is plowed again—this time to shift the orientation of the mound and furrows by 90 degrees, turning them from a vertical to horizontal direction. After four to five rounds of such shifts of both the architecture and orientation of the mounds and furrows, the rejuvenated soil promises "three consecutive years of harvest," according to folklore.[29]

As they tried to improve soil quality, farmers also maximized uses for the soil. Historian Lillian Li (2007)[30] wrote that during the Qing Dynasty, in Zhili, the capital region around Beijing (in today's Hebei Province), the relatively drought- and saline-tolerant crops of wheat, barley, millet, sorghum, and beans were the main crops. Inter-planting and rotational cropping would bring three harvests of grain crops in a two-year cycle. The diverse and rotational cropping pattern reduced climatic risks and maintained soil quality. For example, the tall, robust sorghum plant is flood-resistant during the summer growing season, while millet is drought-tolerant, and growing wheat in the winter helps prevent summer flooding. Unlike farms in Europe, northern China's soil received few breaks from farming, and Chinese farmers spared little downtime throughout the year.

Minqin farmers grew drought-tolerant corps similar to those grown in Zhili during late imperial times recounted by Li. Minqin farmers also planted small quantities of other grains, such as buckwheat, highland barley, flax for oil, and a variety of vegetables and fruits mostly for subsistence use. They practiced inter-cropping, wherein two or three crops were planted adjacently, and rotational cropping. They used the soil just as intensively as those in Zhili. But the cold winters in Minqin could not support winter wheat, so there was only one primary grain harvest a year in Minqin.[31]

Sandification has posed another challenge to farming in Minqin since the late imperial era. As more cropland sandified, more labor was required to build wind shelters made from long grasses, tree branches, and twigs collected from near and far, and to carry heavy loads of dirt from other areas to build grids to lock down the loosened sand dunes around the farms. This practice of sand control continues to present day and removing sand that blankets around the field is still part of the springtime routine that takes place before irrigation and sowing.

The sorting, removing, replacing, and mixing of large quantities of soil, as well as intercropping, frequent weeding, and deep and multiple plowings were measures taken to maximize productivity of poor and easily exhausted soil. In Minqin there is an old adage: "seven plowings fill the stomach."[32] But not every household has the sufficient work force to deep plow the fields seven times every year. Poor households with little human or animal power have limited ability to improve the soil. While draft animals are able to drive deep plows, that is not an option for families who cannot afford draft animals in the first place.

Agricultural machinery began to appear in Minqin in the 1950s and 1960s, but only in the few large state farms, which accounted for less than 5% of the total cultivated land in Minqin at the time.[33] For the rest, human labor had to toil away with wooden and iron hand tools, some were aided by draft animals, until the 1980s.[34]

Despite working hard and working the land hard, yields remained low. During the first half of the 20th century, the average harvest of spring wheat was 40 to 75 kg per mu, compared to the 150 to 160 kg of wheat per mu of dry farmland, and 600 to 700 kg of wheat per mu of irrigated farmland elsewhere in mid-20th century China.[35] Since the 1980s, as the level of soil and water salinity has increased at an accelerated rate, Minqin villagers have shifted to tougher crops: from wheat to sunflower, cotton and melon; then again onto alfalfa and fennel. They also tried hybrid corn species that are more drought- and saline-tolerant.[36] Rotational cropping annually or biannually continued to be a coping method in the face of salty soil and water.

Farming in the northwest is also vulnerable to extreme climatic events. Droughts occurred frequently in late imperial era Minqin: "for every four years, there are three years of droughts, one year of severe drought;" and severe droughts could "send the old and the weak begging, and women and children eating plant roots."[37] Natural calamities such as floods, frost, hail, dry and hot winds, dust storms, pests, and epidemics occurred almost annually. Sandstorms that swept over the area could wipe out the year's harvest. Epidemics killed or paralyzed the able-bodied and the weak indiscriminately. Natural calamities were further compounded and/or created by man-made crises of warfare and the loss of men and animals drafted by the military.

Peasants' lives were further strained by erratic and excessive taxation by local authorities, armed forces, and landlords as well as raids from Han and non-Han bandits and rebels in the multiethnic frontier. The frequent natural and manmade cataclysms wreaked havoc on the livelihoods of Minqin farmers in unpredictable ways.

To mitigate the impact of low yields and high unpredictability, Minqin farmers continuously reclaimed new cropland when conditions permitted in order to offset the bad years, and whenever and wherever possible, to produce extra yields hopefully beyond the reach of tax collectors. The customary term for land reclamation is "moving the sand dunes" (*yi-qiu*). Drawing groundwater reserves from under dried-up lakebeds, farmers blasted sand dunes with water through a system of water tanks, pumping devices, graded channels, and trenches to power-wash the dunes and channel sandy flows to raise the lowlands.[38] The flattened and leveled "raw" fields required follow-up work to meet desired soil composition and fertility, as illustrated earlier. Different crops were planted in scattered parcels of varying planting conditions across different sites. With the highly variable microclimate and soil qualities in the region, spatial spread and crop diversity were ways of improving food security. A destroyed spring wheat harvest could be partially salvaged by planting beans or sorghum later in the same or different parcel. But the success of turning raw soil into cropland "to fill the stomach" is subject to the same, if not more, natural and man-made adversities. Locals have called land reclamation "venturesome cultivation" (*chuangtian*),[39] which aptly describes the precarity and uncertainty behind the promise of land reclamation.

II Dual Marginality

Minqin's unforgiving planting conditions demand diligence and vigilance from farmers. The adversity farmers face is further exacerbated by its geopolitical position at the national level and its hydrosocial position at the regional level. Living in unstable terrain at the military frontline, Minqin farmers had long been left out of state infrastructure investment plans since imperial times until the rise of 21st century conservationism. Minqin's geopolitical marginality is compounded by its hydrosocial marginality.[40] Located at the tail end of the Shiyang River Basin, Minqin is also at a disadvantage in its competition for water with upstream farming settlements.

II.1 Geopolitical Marginality

The northwest, despite its strategic location for national defense, and *because of* such a location, was rarely at the center of state investment plans. Imperial courts at different times have sent troops and recruited cultivators to create a buffer zone stretching along the border lands. But as historian Alexander Woodside (2007) maintains, China's borderlands have been too big and too varied for any political center to control. The empire may have been united from time to time, but it was never fully centralized.[41]

In addition to the varied conceptualizations of the empire's boundary,[42] another important explanation for the discrepancy between the ideal of a fully centralized empire and the reality of the emperor's limited reach lies with money. The cost of maintaining the state's presence in the frontier was prohibitively high. When the emperor could barely pay for military expenses, investment in developmental projects—such as major regional water works or a rail system to connect China proper with the frontier—remained aspirational, if not rhetorical.[43]

China's northwest frontier was, after all, a territory in flux that has changed hands frequently among China's emperors and other continental powers of various ethnicities. Major state investment in waterworks for productivity and taxation gain was not to be prioritized in this region, unless the central ruler felt confident about its command over the immense border territory and its diverse peoples of dubious loyalty.

The gap between the aspiration and the reality of the state's reach persisted into the warring Republican years (1911–49). During its first half, Republican China saw the rise of regional warlords as well as Chiang Kai-Shek's military campaigns to consolidate the Nationalists' power. The second half of the Republican era was preoccupied with the Second Sino-Japanese War, the main act of the Second World War in East Asia that was intertwined with the civil war between Chiang's Republican and Mao's Communist forces until Mao took over China in 1949. Throughout the Republican era, the northwest frontier was a major battlefield. Power over the Hexi Corridor shifted among Han and Chinese Muslim warlords and Chiang's Nationalist forces, and between Chinese and Japanese rule, all while the Chinese Communists expanded their base in the area.

The Hexi Corridor's instability did not help improve its geopolitical status in Republican China. In 1936, a Columbia University-trained Chinese economic historian Chi Ch'ao-ting (1903–63), published his doctoral thesis, "Key Economic Areas in Chinese History: As Revealed in the Development of Public Works for Water Control."[44] Deeply influenced by Karl Wiffogel's thesis about hydraulic state-building,[45] Chi added a geopolitical angle by reviewing the Chinese state's shifting geographical focus in water works investment. Chi identified several "Key Economic Areas" as the regional centers of water work investment that had ensured the emperors' territorial power: the Lower Yellow and Yangtze River Basins, and two subregions of the Basin of Sichuan in the Central-West, and the southern basins of Guangdong and Guangxi (see Figure P.1). Under different dynastic reigns, one particular area became the most favored, or the "Key Area," wherein state investment in irrigation and water transport networks were concentrated. Chi's historical review of the relationship between water and state power was clearly aimed at mapping out China's territorial structure and state investment plans for the future.

The northwest was nowhere to be found on Chi's map of China's past or future. Serving as a financial advisor in Chiang Kai-shek's Nationalist inner circle during the Second Sino-Japanese War, Chi's view could reflect China's geopolitical reality and Chinese policy thinkers' siege mentality during the warring time. It was advisable to leave the unstable northwest off the map of state investment and focus instead on the "key areas" in China proper.[46] In addition, the geopolitical status of different frontiers was uneven. During the Republican era, the northwest was strategically less important than the western border of Xinjiang, which was under direct threat from Russia (and later the Soviet Union), as well as the northeastern border of Manchuria, which was the base of Japan's invasion. On this national geopolitical map, Minqin, tucked away in a corner of the Hexi Corridor in northwest China, became even less visible. It was too far from the state's reach, and too risky for the state to try to reach it.[47]

II.2 Hydrosocial Marginality

Minqin's marginality at the national level is duplicated at the regional level, especially when it comes to agricultural development supported by irrigation infrastructure. Minqin is located disadvantageously downstream of the Shiyang River Basin, one of the main river basins of the Hexi Corridor. Since the 18th century, local state and non-state actors have developed extensive irrigation networks in the mid-reaches of the major river basins of the Hexi Corridor at the expense of the lower reaches. The continuous damming of surface runoff to feed expanding cultivation in the middle reaches of the Shiyang Basin around its leading city Wuwei, significantly reduced flow to Minqin, and, thereby fomented fierce water conflicts, disputes, and violence.

Since as early as the 17th century during the Ming Dynasty, litigation records from local authorities in Minqin and Wuwei recounted episodes of fierce water competition and armed fights between cultivators of the two places. In the ensuing Qing era, water-related litigation was prevalent enough to warrant a special chapter in the *Zhenfan Gazetteer*.[48] Within Minqin, water conflicts also erupted at every level of the irrigation hierarchy: among farmers whose farms were serviced by the same irrigation system but located in different canals of the system, or between farmers with land located at the head and those at the tail ends of shared irrigation canals.

The drawing-down of resources and the "elimination of ecological buffers," to use John McNeill's (1998)[49] term, continued to intensify during the socialist era. As cultivation undertaken by state farms and villager collectives along the Shiyang Basin expanded, resource competition between upstream Wuwei and downstream Minqin escalated.

Water competition was particularly violent during times of drought; local leadership was made and unmade by water wars. One of the legendary water battles between midstream Wuwei and downstream Minqin in the socialist era occurred in 1962, a year of extreme drought, right after the infamous, nationwide "three years of famine" (1958–61), during which more than 30 million Chinese people perished. In Gansu Province alone, the death toll of the three-year famine was estimated at over 1 million.[50] In the spring of 1962, to save local harvests in what looked like a fourth-year famine in the making, Wuwei's water resource bureau dammed more surface runoff, leaving little water for Minqin. The CCP party secretary of Minqin at the time was Li Yuxin. A Minqin native and a staunch leader, Li was known for his heroic act of blocking the provincial grain collection truck from entering Minqin during the previous famine. This time, Li made an even bolder move and led a group of Minqin peasants to Wuwei. On his truck, Li loaded two bags of explosives and a coffin. The explosives were to destroy the dam in Wuwei that was causing Minqin crops to die of thirst. The coffin was for Li himself, attesting to his commitment to a life-or-death water battle. There are two endings to this local legend. In one, Li was stopped by troops sent from Wuwei before he reached the dam. In the other, he managed to reach the dam and install the explosives, only to be arrested before being able to set off the explosives. What is certain was that, for his heroic act, Li lost his job and party membership. While Li spent the next two decades in exile in IM, the incident led the governments of Wuwei and Minqin to reach a water sharing agreement.[51]

This story shows what it takes to bring Wuwei to the negotiation table. But implementing a water sharing scheme is more difficult than reaching an agreement on paper. Sharing a river among multiple jurisdictions is a matter of partitioning moving water that flows across jurisdictional boundaries through uneven terrain. Physically, water flowing downstream loses volume through soil absorption in unpaved canals and leaks in poorly paved ones. Extremely high evaporation rates in the dryland also take another big toll. Many other mechanisms work to further complicate a water sharing scheme: the multi-stream waterways change course over time and their volume varies across the seasons and years. Geopolitically, even with a water sharing agreement, leaders of the upper stream jurisdictions are often reluctant to share the precious water and breach the agreement regularly. The physical advantage of the upper reaches is reinforced by their territorial dominance in the river basin. The political center of the Shiyang Basin, Wuwei, is located in the middle reaches of the river, and the government of Wuwei commands the entire Shiyang Basin and supervises the lower-ranking Minqin County government downstream. Such jurisdictional hierarchy that coincides with the uneven access to water between Wuwei and Minqin makes it politically risky for Minqin County leaders to challenge the governor of Wuwei over water allocation in the event Wuwei keeps more water than its agreed-upon share. As a result of Minqin's hydrosocial marginality, the under-delivery of surface flow to Minqin, even after a water sharing scheme was reached, continued into the 1990s and 2000s.[52]

It was not the case that the new CCP state did not make any attempts to improve Minqin's hydrosocial woes in the 1950s. Gansu's provincial authority did pay attention to repairing and improving the war-torn irrigation infrastructure in the Hexi Corridor. But the disruptive political campaigns and technical and financial constraints had brought mixed results.

One prominent water project in Minqin built during the first decade of socialist China was the Hongyashan (HYS) Reservoir. In 1957, at the onset of Mao's Great Leap Forward campaign, the construction of the HYS Reservoir and a new irrigation main called "Leap Forward" Canal was launched to improve water supplies in

Minqin. The HYS reservoir, which boasted being the largest desert reservoir in Asia, took eight years to complete (1957–64). Located at the southern end of Minqin, the HYS Reservoir stored every bit of surface runoff discharged from Wuwei's dam. The endorheic lake of the Shiyang River, the Qingtu (Black Earth) Lake, dried up soon after the reservoir was completed. The HYS Reservoir had become the new endorheic lake of the Shiyang River.

The new reservoir was a milestone in Minqin's hydro history, as it completely cut off flow to areas below it along the northern tail of the basin (see Figure 3.2). Journalist Yan Shide (2010)[53] reported on an elderly man's recollection of the pre-HYS Reservoir days. Growing up in a village north of the reservoir, the elderly man recalled his childhood experience in the 1940s before the reservoir was built, when groundwater level was high:

> We kids used to play a game called "frying the pancake" in the spring. Several kids would stand together, each hooking one foot with the next kid's foot to make a circle. We hopped in circles with the other feet. After we hopped for a while, a round mound would appear under our feet, like an onion pancake. We used our fingers to poke the mound until water dribbled out around the mound, like oil encircling a pancake when you fry it.

Even in the early 1950s, locals remembered that the wetlands around the Qingtu Lake had reeds "taller than men, and their feathery plumes fell like snow." The lake was home of a variety of "very noisy water fowls" and such an abundance of fish that "one could just take off his clothes, jump into the water and catch the fish easily." By 1959, as the Qingtu Lake had been dried up by the reservoir, the elderly man recalled, he watched his home village and fields turn sandy.

While successful in cutting off surface flows to northern Minqin and draining the endorheic lake, the HYS Reservoir did not deliver what the dam designers had hoped. Built on gentle slopes like most other hydro projects in the Hexi Corridor, sediment accumulated fast in the HYS Reservoir. Also, located on a sandy site during the feverish years of the Great Leap Forward, which hastened project completion for political recognition, the dam structure suffered chronic cracking and seepage. While the first phase of the reservoir was finally declared complete in 1964 after eight years of construction, it did not start operating until 1966 and only reached one-third of its designed capacity. This was not before several incidents occurred, including a retaining wall failure in 1958 that destroyed 1,500 workers' tents and killed 11 local and Sent-Down youth workers, according to official records.[54]

Despite its shortcomings, the landmark project of the HYS Reservoir received an annual average of 500 million cubic meters of surface water from upstream flows during the early years of its operation.[55] However, as more tributaries of the Shiyang River were dammed in the middle reaches to feed Wuwei's expanding farms, flows to the HYS Reservoir dwindled. By the mid-1970s, seven of the eight major tributaries of the Shiyang watershed were completely dammed in the mid-reaches, cutting the flow to Minqin by half.

Acceleration of groundwater extraction in the mid-1970s marked yet another turning point in Minqin's hydro-environmental history. The acceleration was powered by two co-productive events. One concerns the designation of the Hexi Corridor, Minqin included, as a National Base for Commodity Grain Production. "Commodity grains" is a term commonly used in China's planned economy to refer to staple grains that are collected and distributed through the state distribution system to provide food for non-food producers (e.g., urban residents, industrial workers, military personnel, and government employees). Those who "eat the commodity grain" were often the envy of farmers. Unlike farmers who needed to feed themselves because of the rural "self-reliance" policy doctrine, these state-supported "commodity grain eaters" enjoyed a guaranteed food supply. The designation of national and subnational "commodity grain production bases" in the rural areas was the socialist state's spatial strategy for managing its welfare programs for state-sector employees in the city.

Tasked with producing commodity grains for the nation and pressured by the heavy production quota, local governments in the Hexi Corridor began to aggressively expand cultivation in their jurisdictions. Previously uncultivated, poor-quality marginal land was opened to plant grains, and more water was extracted to feed the expanded fields. Minqin farmers, while mobilized to produce more for the state, also felt entitled to reclaim additional land on the side to produce more for themselves. It was a time when production expansion was hailed as being heroic and patriotic. Both local officials and farmers participated in a surge of land reclamation, thus pushing Minqin's cultivation from the oases into the surrounding dune fields. Under a positive and productionist framing, the new farms built on the ecologically fragile dune fields were given a neutralized name, "artificial oases," in policy and research papers which has persisted through present-day.

The other event that had accelerated groundwater extraction in Minqin was the introduction of new technologies for groundwater extraction, namely, tube wells and sunken pumps. Extracting water from underground was nothing novel in Minqin's long history of battling for water. The high groundwater levels and widespread springs and boreholes in the alluvial plains made it possible for farmers to dig shallow wells with rudimentary tools. In 1965, Minqin had approximately one hundred shallow wells in total, each no more than five meters deep. New extraction technology since the 1970s has made it possible to withdraw beyond the shallow vadose zone of salinized water, and extract fresh water in the saturation zone from as deep as 80 to 300 meters below ground level. The adoption of new technology proved to be the point of no return. As discussed earlier, irrigation accelerates soil salinization, and salinized soil needs more water to flush away the salt. Watering crops with groundwater only aggravates saline accumulation. By 2000, Minqin had more than 10,000 wells, 250 of which were deeper than 300 meters. As such, total groundwater withdrawal from 1965 to 2000 exceeded 500 million cubic meters.[56] That number was close to the volume of surface water Minqin had lost to farms upstream. In other words, the surface water that was siphoned off from Minqin was made up for by Minqin's groundwater reserves. Minqin, long suffering from its physical location downstream of the river basin and its inferior territorial status at the bottom of the administrative hierarchy, found salvation deep under its own turf.

With salvation came new challenges. With a decrease in surface runoff, irrigation canals' reinforced pavement prevented water leaking into the soil along the waterways and massive withdrawals of groundwater greatly outpaced groundwater replenishment. As a result, groundwater aquifers dwindled. The water table in Minqin dropped from an average of 2.7 meters deep between 1960 and 1969, to 3.6 meters between 1969 and 1979, and 7.65 meters between 1979 and 1989. That was just the era prior to China's development frenzy in the 1990s. With a decollectivized rural economy and rising prices of commodity grains, the 1990s saw another great leap in land reclamation and groundwater extraction. In Minqin, the average water table reached 12.98 meters deep by the late 1990s. In 2000, the HYS Reservoir in Minqin recorded having received 86 million cubic meters of water channeled from Wuwei. It was an 83% reduction from the 500 million cubic meters of the 1960s. Minqin's groundwater extraction hit a new high, and groundwater levels sunk to a record low, down another 7.54 meters to 20.52 meters on average annually between 1999 and 2008. In some areas in northern Minqin where groundwater was most heavily drawn out, groundwater levels measured 50 meters below by 2009. All in all, from 1960 to 2009, Minqin's water table plummeted between 0.5 to 1 meter per year on average.[57] The saline and alkaline content of soil also increased from less than 1 gram/liter in the 1960s to 5 grams/liter or even higher in the 2000s in the northern end of the farming areas, leading to long-term farmland abandonment.[58] As cultivation expanded into the buffer zone between semifixed sand dunes and farms, groundwater levels declined and vegetal ground cover loss accelerated. The topsoil of abandoned farmland and the destroyed semifixed sand dunes became loose, leading to increasingly frequent and severe sandstorms in spring. This is the genesis of what the China-based environmental scientists Xue, Xian et al. (2005) and Wang, Tao et al. (2015)[59] have called aeolian desertification, the primary type of soil degradation in Minqin and in China's north and northwest in the past half century.

The two thousand years of Minqin's intertwined environmental and geopolitical history witnessed the exhaustion of Minqin's soil and water. But unlike in popular imagination, the "encroaching deserts, disappearing villages, and fleeing villagers" have not wiped Minqin off the face of the earth. Rather, the crisis set the stage for a recharged flurry of conservation actions embarking on a rescue mission. Once a swamp at the geopolitical periphery of the nation and the hydrosocial periphery of the Shiyang River Basin, Minqin now found itself at the forefront of state-marshalled environmentalism of the 21st century China.

III Turning the Hopeless Hopeful

In 2001, with China's environmentalism on the upswing, the amount of water flowing into the HYS Reservoir of Minqin hit a historic low. China's then Premier Wen Jiabao, who was responsible for the widely hailed (albeit temporary) halt of the Nu River

Dam project,[60] publically declared that he "will not allow Minqin to become another Lop Nor."[61]

What does Lop Nor, located in the Tarim Basin of Xinjiang in western China, have anything to do with Minqin? Lop Nor was a giant salt lake that once covered more than 10,000 sq. km in surface area. By 1931, the lake still measured 1,900 sq. km. As a result of massive expansion in irrigated agriculture in Xinjiang by the CCP military colonies since the 1950s, however, Lop Nor shrank rapidly. By 1962, the total surface area shrunk to 660 sq. km. A decade later, it had completely dried up.[62] Lop Nor gained international fame primarily due to its tragic death. As environmental consciousness grew in China, the death of the great lake became a subject of national shame.[63] During the 2000s, state investment poured in to revive Lop Nor. In the early 2010s, a segment of a tributary of the Tarim River that used to feed Lop Nor was restored by interbasin water transfers, but the legendary Lop Nor itself was beyond resurrection.

Qingtu Lake of Minqin presented a second chance for China to recover its tarnished global reputation in environmental conservation. This time, under Premier Wen's determined intervention, the phoenix must find a way to rise from the ashes. For a start, the Shiyang River Basin Water Resource Bureau was established in 2001. It was a resolute push to institutionalize water allocation arrangements between the upper and lower reaches of the River across local jurisdictions, which had never happened in the Basin before. Following that, Gansu's provincial government negotiated with the Yellow River Water Resources Commission to initiate an interbasin water transfer program, set to deliver 61 million cubic meters of water annually from the Yellow River to Minqin's HYS Reservoir. After traveling 200 km through the desert, pumped up and flowing downhill, 46.7 million cubic meters of water from the Yellow River, China's Mother River, reached Minqin's HYS Reservoir. But by 2003, due to intra-bureaucratic disputes over the payment for the costly water from afar, the Yellow River Water Resource Commission stopped sending water to the HYS Reservoir, and Qingtu Lake remained dry.[64]

In June 2004, the HYS Reservoir completely dried up. With unprecedented crisis came unrivalled opportunities. This time, Premier Wen vowed to fill both the reservoir and Qingtu Lake. A national rescue mission to Minqin was launched. Under political pressure from above, the Yellow River Water Resources Commission resumed its commitment and channeled 30 million cubic meters of water from China's Mother River to rescue Minqin's dying crops. Wuwei, in the mid-reaches, topped it off by sending another 3 million cubic meters of Shiyang runoff to Minqin's HYS Reservoir. But the 33 million cubic meters of water from the two sources, especially after long-distance travel, was far from enough. To make up for the deficit, another 12 million cubic meters of groundwater was extracted locally under a special program that overrode the groundwater extraction restrictions. Water from far and near, above and below kept Minqin's crops alive in the spring of 2005.[65] But the patchy rescue package, achieved through much arm-twisting, was not as sustainable as Premier Wen would have liked to see. The HYS Reservoir dried up once again the following year, foreshadowing a crisis that was becoming the new norm. Premier

Wen pushed harder for a longer-term solution by making Minqin a model case for China's answer to global water scarcity and desertification. In 2007, sponsored by national leadership, Gansu's provincial government released an unprecedented "Strategic Management Plan of the Shiyang River Basin." It was an ambitious, 300 million yuan-worth watershed management plan.[66] In the same year, Premier Wen made a highly publicized visit to the remote, rural county of Minqin to launch the plan. The restoration of the dried-up Qingtu Lake seemed now no less significant than the protection of the endangered panda bear in showcasing China's "ecological civilization."

One of the most transformative elements of the 2007 Strategic Management Plan of the Shiyang River Basin concerns the interbasin water transfers from the Yellow River to Minqin on a regular basis beyond the sporadic and unreliable rescue missions. The amount of water released by the head gate control station of the Gansu division of the Yellow River Resource Commission gradually increased from 50 million cubic meters per year in the inaugural year of 2007 to double that amount in 2014. By 2017, the amount of water released reached 120 million cubic meters a year. Water was extracted using 11 large-scale pumping stations and ran through three canals constructed exclusively for this project. More than one-third of its 200 kilometer-long journey traversed the Tengger Desert. Of the 120 million cubic meters of water that left the head gate of the Yellow River, 80 percent made it to Minqin that year. In the meantime, more surface runoff was released from the mid-stream point of the Shiyang River, raising the total surface water inflow to Minqin from the low point of 86 million cubic meters in 2000 to an annual average of 260 million since 2010, bringing it back to the level of the 1970s.[67]

Out of the 120 million cubic meters of water drawn from the Yellow River, 33 million cubic meters were labelled "ecological water," an underdefined category in environmental policies, meant to be channeled directly to Qingtu Lake.[68] In 2010, three years after the interbasin water transfer program had started, it was reported that for the first time in half a century, Qingtu Lake had three sq. km of its surface filled. The recovery steadily improved to a triumphant 26 sq. km by 2016. Minqin's Qingtu Lake did not, after all, become another Lop Nor.

Although irrigation water accounted for more than 75 percent of the 260 million cubic meters of the water sourced locally and beyond, it was the 33 million cubic meters of "ecological water" that revived Qingtu Lake that dominated the media reports.

The HYS Reservoir, Asia's largest desert dam that completely dried up in 2004, had been also replenished. To accommodate the increase in water supplies to rescue Minqin from its demise, in 2016 the HYS Reservoir received national government funding to expand the dam's capacity by 49%, from 99 to 148 million cubic meters. The "medium-sized" dam in China's official classification would now be upgraded to a taller, "large-sized" dam. The upgrading project also included plans to clear out the sediment that had accumulated inside, effectively taking up a third of the dam's capacity prior to the expansion, and to plant large areas of sand-shelter forests around the dam.[69]

Tucked away in the periphery of the periphery and stuck in the vicious cycle of soil deterioration, Minqin soared in the new millennium from being an exhausted swamp to landing on the frontpage of environmental recovery. Such triumphant transformation was driven by its role as a showcase example of the state's capacity for crisis management. Minqin's hope, in other words, hinged on its hopelessness. The greatly augmented water supply was framed in policy discourse as a mission to rescue Minqin, a place of crisis and scarcity in dire need of relief. The rescue mission was on the order of national ecological security: the encroaching deserts surrounding Minqin threatened to devour the oases, desertify the rest of northern China, and expose the entire country to the threat of dust storms. This discourse of a crisis-and-rescue mission has worked in favor of the Minqin government.[70] State-recognized victimhood endowed Minqin with fresh water supplies that the county had not seen since the 1970s. On the other hand, to keep water flowing in from afar, Minqin needed to maintain its narrative of scarcity and crisis. The slogan, "Minqin is at the top of the world's water scarcity crisis," was written on banners hung across streets, painted on walls along the roads in towns and villages, and on the bathroom mirrors of county government office buildings, schools, and local hotels. The politics of water conservancy in Minqin that have existed since the 2000s are structured by the paradox of scarcity and the abundance rallied by scarcity, as well as the aspiration to generate opportunity from scarcity. It is the interplay of scarcity, abundance, and opportunity that have fortified the regime of productive conservation in Minqin. But such an official framing, central to the regime of productive conservation as it is, is only a part of the story. What have been Minqin farmers' experiences on the ground and their response to scarcity, abundance, and opportunity? In the following chapter I will trace Minqin farmers' survival strategies under the regime of scarcity and opportunity.

Notes

1. Wu, Guolin. 2014. "Fengsha Minqinxian jinanzai? [Where is Minqin, the county of sand and wind, today?]." *Sciencenet.* http://blog.sciencenet.cn/blog-447363-838876.html. Accessed on May 2, 2018. The link was broken by April 16, 2023.
2. CCTV News. 2007. "Zhengzai xiaoshide cunzhuang [A disappearing village]." CCTV.com, April 9. https://news.cctv.com/society/20070410/103791.shtml. Accessed January 5, 2025. Also see He, Xueping. 2005. "Yazhouzuida shamoshuiku hongyashan yinheliuduanliu mianlinganhe [Asia's largest desert reservoir Hongyashan faces a complete dry out]." *Western Commercial News*, June 27. http://news.sina.com.cn/c/p/2005-06-27/03177051902.shtml. Accessed April 25, 2023; CCTV News. 2008. "Wen Jiabao zongliminqinjixing (Premier Wen Jiabao's visit to Minqin)." CCTV.com, June 16. http://news.cctv.com/china/20080616/104052.shtml. Accessed April 28, 2023.
3. For analysis of China's ecological civilization, see Rodenbiker, Jesse. 2023. *Ecological States: Politics of Science and Nature in Urbanizing China.* Ithaca: Cornell University Press; and Rodenbiker, Jesse. 2021. "Making ecology developmental: China's environmental sciences and green modernization in global context." *Annals of the American Association of Geographers* 111 (7): 1931–1948.

4. Li, Bingcheng. 1993. "Zhuyezejiqi lishibianqiankao [Zhuyeze and its transformation]." *Geographica Sinica* 48 (1): 55–59. Li also references the prominent historian, Gu Jiegang's, interpretation of the word "*zhu*" as "where waters converge," so "Zhuyeze" refers to wetlands in general. A well-known China-based investigative journalist, Zhou, Youdi (2008; 2016), cited the popular belief that the word "*zhu*," which means "pig" in Chinese, implies that wild boars once roamed the wetlands. But there is little research on whether wild boars have been found in Minqin 2,000 years ago. See Zhou, Youdi. 2016. "Houwang Shu [Looking Back]." In *Xibeiqueshui beihoude zhenshi [The Truth Behind Northwest's Water Shortage]*, pp. 157–200. Beijing: United Publishing Company. The book was first published in 2008, by Zhongxin Press in Beijing.
5. Li, Bingcheng. 1993. Ibid. p. 56.
6. Xie, Yaowen, Fahu Chen, and Naiang Wang. 2004. "Jin liangqian nianlai gansu minqin pendillüzhoude kongjian bianhua [Spatial transformation of Minqin oases in the past two thousand years]." *ACTA Geographica Sinica* 59 (5): 662–670.
7. Xie, Yaowen et al. 2004. Ibid; and Li, Bingcheng. 1990. "Minqinxian jinsanbainianlaide renkou zengzhangyu shamohua guocheng [Population growth and desertification in Minqin County in the past three hundred years]." *Hexi Population* 11 (2): 29–33.
8. Xie, Jicheng et al. 1825. *Zhenfan Xianzhi [Zhenfan County Gazetteer] 1825 Edition (the 5th Year of Qing Dynasty's Daoguang Emperor)*, p. 65. Reprinted by Taipei: Chengwen Publishing Company.
9. Xie, Yaowen et al. 2004. Ibid.
10. Li, Bingcheng. 1993. Ibid. pp. 55–59.
11. Li, Guoren and Caixia Wei. 2012. "lungudai hexizoulang tuntian dui lüzhoushengtaide yingxiang (The environmental impact of military colonies in Hexi Corridor) 2012-2-24," *China Economic History Website*. http://economy.guoxue.com/?p=5031. Accessed April 15, 2023.
12. Li, Bingcheng. 1990. Ibid. pp. 29–30. Li also noted that the population peaked and started to decline in the mid-19th century, mainly due to the intensive land use that had led to soil deterioration.
13. Cheng, Chongde. 1991. "Qingdaiqianqi duimenggude jinfengzhengce yu enkou, kaifaji shengtaihuanjingde guanxi [The policy of border control in early Qing and its impact on development, population, and ecological environment of Mongolia]." In *Qingshi Yanjiu [Studies of Qing History]*, Vol. 2, pp. 26–31; and Vermeer, Eduard. 1998. "Population and ecology along the frontier in Qing China." In *Sediments of Time: Environment and Society in Chinese History*, edited by Elvin, Mark and Ts'ui-jung Liu, pp. 235–279. Cambridge: Cambridge University Press.
14. Feng, Shengwu. 1963. "Minqinlüzhoude shuixi yanbian [Evolution of Minqin oases' hydrological system]." *ACTA Geographica Sinica* 29 (3): 241–249.
15. Xie, Yaowen et al. 2004. Ibid.
16. Li, Bingcheng. 1993. Ibid.
17. McNeill, John R. 1998. "China's environmental history in world perspective." In *Sediments of Time: Environment and Society in Chinese History*, edited by Elvin, Mark and Ts'ui-jung Liu, pp. 31–49, p. 38. New York: Cambridge University Press.
18. Marks, Robert. 1998. *Tiger, Rice, Silk, and Silt: Environment and Economy in Late Imperial South China*. Cambridge: Cambridge University Press; Marks, Robert. 2011. *China: Its Environment and History*. Lanham: Rowman & Littlefield Publishers.

19. For further elaboration on the relationship between agricultural labor and development in pre-reform China, see Philip Huang (1985, 1990). Huang applies Clifford Geertz's (1963) concept of "agricultural involution" to China's agrarian history to explain why the production growth from intensive labor input did not improve productivity growth and development. See Geertz, Clifford. 1963. *Agricultural Involution: The Processes of Ecological Change in Indonesia.* Oakland, CA: University of California Press; Huang, Philip C. C. 1985. *The Peasant Economy and Social Change in North China.* Stanford: Stanford University Press; and Huang, Philip C. C. 1990. *The Peasant Family and Rural Development in the Yangzi Delta, 1350–1988.* Redwood City, CA: Stanford University Press. Ken Pomeranz (2000), on the other hand, upon comparing China with Europe, suggests that until 1800, China was much less involuted than what was generally believed. See Pomeranz, Kenneth. 2000. *The Great Divergence: China, Europe, and the Making of the Modern World Economy.* Princeton: Princeton University Press.
20. Minqin County Gazetteer Editorial Committee. 1994. (based on the 1985 edition)." *Minqin Xianzhi [Minqin County Gazetteer]*, p. 182. Lanzhou: Lanzhou University Press and Xinhua Bookstore of Gansu Province.
21. For stories about the relationship between the Great Wall ruins and local villagers who live by the Wall ruins, see Chapter 10.
22. Jiang, Delin. 1944. "Jiangdelin peitongmeijiguwen luodemin kaochaxibeishuitubaochi zhuangkuang baogao [Report on my trip with American consultant Lowdermilk to the northwest to investigate the state of soil conservation]." In *Kangzhanshiqixibeikaifa danganshiliaoxuanbian [Selected Historical Archives on Development of the Northwest during the Sino-Japanese War]*, edited by Ma, Zhendu et al., pp. 127–139. Beijing: Chinese Social Science Press.
23. Minqin County Gazetteer Editorial Committee. 1994. Ibid.
24. See Min, Zongdian. 1989. "Woguogudaide zhiliyanjianjishu [The saline-alkaline management techniques in ancient China]." *Nongshi yanjiu [Studies of Agricultural History]* No. 8: 104–112.
25. Min, Zhongdian. 1989. Ibid. pp.106-107. Min commented that the success of "yuguan" was conditioned by the season, and its application required taking other hydraulic factors, such as river navigation and flood control, into consideration. Pierre-Étienne Will (1998) has elaborated on the dynamic relationship between clear water and muddy water in facilitating and blocking irrigation systems in Shaanxi in the late imperial period. See Will, Pierre-Étienne. 1998. "Clear waters versus muddy waters: The Zheng-bai irrigation system of Shaanxi Province in the late imperial period." In *Sediments of Time*, Ibid. pp. 283–343.
26. Interview with a farmer in Minqin, 2013.
27. Min, Zongdian. 1989. Ibid. p. 109.
28. Minqin County Gazetteer Editorial Committee 1994. Ibid.
29. Minqin County Gazetteer Editorial Committee 1994. Ibid. p. 180.
30. Li, Lilian. 2007. *Fighting Famine in North China: State, Market, and Environmental Decline, 1690s–1990s.* Redwood City, CA: Stanford University Press.
31. Xie, Jicheng et al. 1825. Ibid. p. 191; Minqin County Gazetteer Editorial Committee 1994. Ibid. pp. 101–105; Wang, Zhichen. 1967. *Minqin Xianzhi [Minqin County Gazetteer]*, pp. 38–100. Taipei, Taiwan: Xuesheng Publisher. This 1967 edition was a reprint of a handwritten manuscript first published in 1926 during the Republican era; it was reprinted again in 1970 by Chengwen Press in Taipei, Taiwan.

32. Minqin County Gazetteer Editorial Committee 1994. Ibid. p. 180.
33. Interview with a local researcher in Gansu, 2013.
34. Minqin County Gazetteer Editorial Committee 1994. Ibid. p. 192. In the late 1960s and early 1970s, there were several official reports on the "iron maiden" land reclamation team of Minqin. These iron maidens were teenage girls aged 14 to 17 who were praised for their devotion to "removing sand to build crop fields" (*yisha zaotian*). The propagandistic tone of these accounts aside, what is important to note is the amount of manual labor involved. According to a report, the iron maidens "brought tons of long grasses on their back from far away to build wind shields" and they "carried on their shoulders heavy soil to build the dirt grids to stabilize the sand dunes around the farms." Jiao, Xisheng. 2008 [1977]. "Yiminqintuanjiedadui tieguniangdui [In remembrance of the Iron Maiden Team in Minqin]." In Committee of the History of Education, *Science and Culture of Wuwei Municipality: Wuwei wenzhi [Culture and History of Wuwei]*, Vol. 4, pp. 101–106. Also see 1973. "Zhanfengsha zaoliangtian: jigansusheng minqinxian hongliuyuan gongshe tuanjiedadui tieguniangdui, [Battling sand and wind to build fertile farms: The iron maiden team of the United Brigade, Hongliuyuan Commune in Minqin County, Gansu Province]." *Gansu Province Gansu Daily*, July 25.
35. Minqin County Gazetteer Editorial Committee. 1994. Ibid. p. 135.
36. Interview with a local researcher and a seed trader in Minqin, 2014.
37. Minqin County Gazetteer Editorial Committee. 1994. Ibid. p. 148.
38. Interview with a local researcher in Minqin, 2014.
39. I have heard two interpretations of *chuangtian*: one refers to any form of reclamation in the drylands; the other is more specific, referring to taking advantage of the melted snowturned-summer floods that gush down from the high mountains to hydrate the soil for seed germination and seedling development. It can be done only during the flooding season in the summer. In both cases, chuangtian is about seizing windows of opportunities in the highly uncertain planting environment of the drylands. Interviews in Gansu with village elders in 2014 and in Xinjiang in 2010 with a former state farm (Xinjiang Production and Construction Corps) worker retelling his father's tales of the 1950s and 1960s.
40. For an elaboration on the hydrosocial dynamics, see a special issue of *Geoforum* on hydrosocial cycles, edited by Jessica Budds et al. 2014. *Geoforum*, Vol. 57.
41. See Woodside, Alexander. 2007. "The center and the borderland in Chinese political theory." In *The Chinese State at the Borders*, edited by Larry, Diana, pp. 11–28; pp. 13–19. Oakland, CA: University of California Press.
42. See, for example, Hsing, I-tien. 1991. *Tianxiayijia: Huangdi, guanliao yushehui [All Under Heaven are of One Family: Emperor, Bureaucracy, and Society]*. Beijing: Zhonghua Press; Ge, Zhaoguang. 2004. Songdai zhongguoyishede tuxian:guanyujinshiminzuzhuyi sixiangdeyigeyuanyuan [The emergence of the concept of China in the Song Dynasty: the distant origin of nationalism], *Wenshizhe [Journal of Literature, History and Philosophy]*. No.1 (Serial No. 280). pp. 5–12.
43. See, for example, Kinzley, Judd. 2018. *Natural Resources and the New Frontier: Constructing Modern China's Borderlands*. Chicago: The University of Chicago Press. Focusing on Xinjiang from the late Qing to the 1960s, Kinzley argues that the state's reach was extremely limited even in the geopolitically important frontier of Xinjiang. As a result, Xinjiang's local governors collaborated with the Russians for financial support from the late Qing through the Republican era.

44. Chi, Ch'ao-ting. 1936. *Key Economic Areas in Chinese History*. This book was first published by George Allen & Unwin of London under the auspices of the American Council Institute of Pacific Relations. It was reprinted by Paragon Book Reprint Corp of New York in 1963, the year Chi passed away at the age of 59.
45. Wittfogel, Karl. 1957. *Oriental Despotism: A Comparative Study of Total Power*. New Haven: Yale University Press. Wittfogel's work triggered heated intellectual and political debates from the 1960s to the 1980s. But the debates are beyond the scope of this book.
46. It has been widely held that Chi had secretly been a CCP member since his twenties and was a spy for the Communist Party while trusted by the Nationalists' leader Chiang Kai-shek during the 1930s and 40s. After his death in 1963, Chi was remembered mostly for his controversial role in the debate over "who lost China to the Communists," rather than his book. For a review of Qi's political career, see MacKinnon, Stephen. 2009. "Losing the Mainland: Chen Hansheng and Ji Chaoding in the 1940s." In *Yijiusiling niandaide zhongguo [China in the 1940s]*, pp. 955–966. Division of Republican History of Chinese Academy of Social Sciences and College of History and Culture of Sichuan Normal University. Beijing: Social Sciences Academic Press.
47. It is important to note that, during the Republican era, especially since the Mukden Incident in 1931 when Japanese forces escalated its territorial ambition in China's northeast, which led to the establishment of Manchukuo, there had been much enthusiasm in Republican policy and intellectual circles about defending and developing China's northwest frontier. Beijing-based geographers Zhang, Xiangwen and Gu, Jiegan and their writings in the 1910s and 1930s on Wang, Tongchun, the hydro turfdom builders in Hetao (see Chapter 7), for example, was a case in point. Yet much of the discussions remained either a Chinese nationalist aspiration or focused mainly on resource extraction and land reclamation in the northwest. Little state investment in irrigation infrastructure was found, as the story about Wang Tongchun in Chapter 7 shows. For further elaboration of northwest development as Chinese nationalist discourse, see Tighe, Justin. 2005. *Constructing Suiyuan: The Politics of Northwestern Territory and Development in Early Twentieth-Century China*, pp. 92–118. Leiden: Brill. I thank Ken Pomeranz for the discussion of this important point. Further research on infrastructure investment made by regional warlords in Hexi and Minqin is needed.
48. Xie, Jicheng et al. 1825. Ibid. pp. 214–218.
49. McNeill, John R. 1998. Ibid.
50. Cao, Shuji. 2005. *Dajihuang: 1959–1961 niande zhongguorenkou [The Great Famine: China's Population in 1959–1961]*. Hong Kong: Guojishidai Publisher.
51. Minqin County Gazetteer Editorial Committee 1994. Ibid. p. 195.
52. Sun, Xuetao. 2004. "Minqinlüzhou shuiziyuan liyongdelishi xianzhuangheweilai [The history, current state, and the future of water resources in Minqin Oases]." *Zhongguo gongcheng kexue [Engineering Science of China]* 6 (1): 1–9.
53. Yan, Shide. 2010. "Minqin shengyusi [Life and Death of Minqin]." *Economic Observer*, April 30. http://finance.sina.com.cn/roll/20100430/21427862196.shtml. Accessed April 22, 2023.
54. Minqin County Gazetteer Editorial Committee 1994. Ibid. p. 36.
55. Xue, Xian et al. 2015. "Policies, Land Use, and Water Resource Management in an Arid Oasis Ecosystem." *Environmental Management* 55 (5): 1036–1051. Chen, Li-juan et al. (2012) reported a larger amount of 620 million cubic meters. See Chen, Li Juan et al. 2012.

"Minqinluzhou dixiashuihuanjing dongtaiyanjiu [The groundwater hydrodynamics of Minqin oases]." *Journal of Arid Land Resources and Environment* 26 (7): 8–13, p. 8.

56. Chen, Li Juan et al. 2012. Ibid. p. 8.
57. Chen, Li Juan et al. 2012. Ibid. p. 10; Zhang, Ruijin et al. 2012. "Minqinxian 2000-2009 nianlai shuiziyuan shengtaihuangjing yalifenxi [Water resources and environmental pressure in Minqin County 2000–2009]." *Zhongguo shamo [Journal of Desert in China]* 32 (2): 558–563, p. 559.
58. Sun, Xuetao. 2004. Ibid. p. 5; Ding, Hongwei et al. 2003. "Hongyashanshuiku jingliuliangjianshao yu minqinshuiziyuanfenxi [Reduction of Inflows to Hongyashan Reservoir and Minqin's water resources]." *Zhongguo shamo [Journal of Desert in China]* 23 (1): 84–89, p. 86.
59. Xue, Xian et al. 2005. "The desertification development and its causes of agropastoral mixed regions in North China." *Journal of Desert Research.* Vol. 25: 320–328; and Wang, Tao et al. 2015. "Combating Aeolian desertification in northern China." *Land Degradation and Development* Vol. 26: 118–132.
60. For the politics of damming the Nu River Valley, see McDonald, Kristen. 2007. *Damming China's Grand Canyon: Pluralization without Democracy in the Nu River Valley.* Doctoral dissertation. University of California at Berkeley.
61. "Wenjiabao kaochajishi: juebunengrang minqinchengwei dierge luobubo [Wen Jiabao's Visit to Minqin: (We) will not let Minqin become another Lop Nor]." 2007. State Council of the PRC website. October 2. http://www.gov.cn/ldhd/2007-10/02/content_767479.htm. Accessed April 23, 2023.
62. Wang, Naiang et al. 2002. "Jinliangbai nianlai renlei huodong duiwoguoxibu shengtaihuanjing bianhuade yingxiang [The impact of human activities on ecological environment of western China in the last two hundred years]." *Studies of Chinese Historical Geography* 17 (3): 12–19.
63. The demise of Lop Nor revealed a lakebed abundant in a key mineral resource: potash. On the immense bed of the dried-up Lop Nor stood one of the world's largest potassium mines. By 2015, the mine produced an annual 1.5 million tons of the key mineral to fertilize China's nutrient-depleted soils. Potassium (potash) is one of the most important types of fertilizer and is on the official list of the top seven strategically important minerals in China. Estimated to hold over 100 million tons in reserves, the Lop Nor mines were expected to reduce China's heavy reliance on imported potash. Regardless of the environmental problems derived from fertilizer run-off and overuse, the establishment of the mega potash production complex on the dried-up lakebed was celebrated for its significant contribution to reinforcing China's resource security and China's bargaining position in the international potash market. See "Luobubode mimi: siwangzhihai ruhechuangzao jiayanqiji [The secret of Lop Nor: How did the 'Sea of Death' create a potash miracle]." 2006. Diyicaijing website. January 27. https://www.yicai.com/news/4744875.html. Accessed April 27, 2023; Huo, Youguang. 2013. "Luobubo tedaxingjiayankuang: jiayanjiujing shifushihuo [The mega potash factory on Lop Nor: good or bad news?]." ScienceNet website. November 12. https://blog.sciencenet.cn/blog-533560-741172.html. Accessed April 28, 2023.
64. Interview with a retired official in Gansu Province, 2014. Sun, Xuetao (2004) also reported that the water transferred from the Yellow River lasted for only one year. See Sun, Xuetao. 2004. Ibid. p. 7.

65. Ma, Weikuan. 2005. "Yazhouzuidade shamoshuiku Hongyashan shouciganhehou chongxinxushui [Asia's largest desert reservoir Hongyashan filled again after complete dryout]." Xinhua Net. January 15. http://tech.sina.com.cn/d/2005-01-15/1329505378.shtml. Accessed April 28, 2023.
66. Water Conservancy Department and Committee of Development and Reform of Gansu Province. 2007. "Shiyangheliuyu zhongdianzhiliguihua [Strategic Management Plan of Shiyang River Basin]. The plan was initially called the "Comprehensive" Management Plan. The daunting task of implementing comprehensive management of the entire basin was later downscaled to a "strategic" management plan, with a selected set of targets and a focus on restoring Qingtu (Black Earth) Lake. Interview with a provincial official in Gansu, 2016. For a review of the implementation of the Plan, see Mao, KuoRay and Qian Zhang. 2018. "Dilemmas of state-led environmental conservation in China: Environmental target enforcement and public participation in Minqin County." *Society and Natural Resources* 31 (5): 615–631.
67. Shi, Lei et al. 2017. "Ganhanqueshuiqu minqinxianshuiziyuan chixugaoxiaoliyong cuoshiyanjiu [Research on sustainable and efficient utilization of water resources in Minqin, an arid region with water shortages]." *Water Resources Protection* 33 (4): 20–25.
68. Wang, Heng et al. 2017. "Gansu conghuanghediaoshui jishamozhikun [Gansu Province transfers water from the Yellow River to rescue the desert]." *Xinhuanet*, January 3. http://www.xinhuanet.com/politics/2017-01/03/c_129430456.htm. Accessed April 23, 2023.
69. Lian, Zhenxiang. 2016. "Yazhouzuida shamoshuiku gansuhongyashan kuorongbaoshengtai [Asia's largest desert reservoir Hongyashan expands its capacity for environmental protection]." *Xinhuanet*, February 19. http://www.xinhuanet.com/politics/2016-02/19/c_1118093365.htm. Accessed April 28, 2023.
70. For an illuminating case in India, see Sainath, Palagummi. 1996. *Everybody Loves a Good Drought.* Delhi: Penguin India.

4
Opportunity in Scarcity: Building a National Model of Water Conservancy

As presented in the previous chapter, the new millennium has witnessed Minqin's rise from doom to fame, and from despondency to hope. Peripheral Minqin, left by the tail end of a drying-up river, now leads China's green future. Minqin's ascendant political status in the era of state-marshalled environmentalism has brought money and water. It has also brought greatly tightened water regulation. The old-fashioned view of unlimited nature has now given way to the new global discourse on resource scarcity.

But what is scarcity? Like desertification examined in the Introduction and Part I, the increasingly popular and consequential concept of scarcity warrants closer scrutiny. In her studies on arid western India, sociologist Lyla Mehta (2005)[1] used the term "constructed scarcity" to refer to the official paradigm of water scarcity. Constructed scarcity helps justify state intervention and helps local officials obtain drought relief and hydro project funding. The other side of constructed scarcity is the *lived* scarcity of the villagers. Unlike the standardized and quantified official version of constructed scarcity, lived scarcity varies from site to site, parcel to parcel, year to year, and season to season. Lived scarcity is not just about the physical lack of water. It also concerns villagers' adaptation to social and environmental uncertainties in dryland agriculture and pastoralism. Mehta has argued that in neglecting

Conserving China's Northwest Frontier. You-tien Hsing, Oxford University Press. © You-tien Hsing (2025).
DOI: 10.1093/9780191903908.003.0005

villagers' lived experiences and strategies for coping with uncertainties, the state "downplayed the inherent potential of the land to sustain viable forms of dryland agriculture." Geographer Jessica Barnes (2014)[2] has also examined constructed and lived water scarcity, in both material and discursive aspects, in her ethnography of irrigated farming along the Nile River in Egypt.

Both Mehta and Barnes built their analyses on the critical distinction and contradictions between constructed and lived scarcities. In this chapter on farmers' strategies to survive not just water scarcity but also the water conservancy regime in Minqin, I extend their framing in three directions.

First, in addition to the distinction and contradiction between constructed and lived scarcities, I also look at the co-productive relationship between them. State-constructed scarcity legitimizes restrictive policies. On the other hand, villagers' coping strategies also condition the ways in which the restrictive policies are negotiated and executed on the ground. The key link in this co-productive relationship is the grassroots officials at the bottom of the bureaucratic hierarchy who serve as brokers between the state and the peasantry.

Second, I see scarcity—both constructed and lived—as only half of the story. To make scarcity-informed restrictions like cropland reduction and well-closing politically sustainable on the ground, scarcity must be paired with opportunity. Cropland reductions and well-closing policies have significantly aggravated social tensions in Minqin. In order to abate the tension, the local government has promoted greenhouse farming and drought-tolerant cash crops to harness new opportunities in the age of conservation. As hopelessness generates hopefulness for Minqin (see previous chapter), scarcity breeds opportunity. And like scarcity, opportunity also has two faces: there is the opportunity that is officially constructed, and then there is the *lived* opportunity of the villagers trying to survive the state's opportunity projects. Most of all, the dynamics of constructed and lived opportunities, like those of scarcity, are shaped by interactions between local officials and farmers.

Third, in addition to the villagers and the local officials, another key local actor are the agricultural investors wearing the hat of green entrepreneurs under the regime of productive conservation. Green entrepreneurs of varied capacities find their niche of opportunity in conservation under the "Public-Private Partnership" schemes outlined in Chapter 1. Together, the local officials, the villagers, and the green entrepreneurs shape the dynamics of scarcity and opportunity and enable the regime of productive conservation in Minqin today.

In what follows, I will first examine the politics of scarcity, followed by that of opportunity. With scarcity in Section I, I tell the tales of implementing the two key programs derived from constructed scarcity. The first program is called "Sealing Wells and Reducing Croplands," and the second program concerns the pricing of surface water and the metering of groundwater. In Section II, I review the key programs that were designed to bring opportunities to the land of scarcity. These opportunity programs include installing water conservancy infrastructure, such as greenhouses and drip irrigation systems; promoting drought-tolerant cash crops, such as goji berries, red jujube dates, and wine grapes; and building conservation spaces like model ecological parks and cash crop plantations. While the ideas behind these programs are far from novel, their execution on the ground was nothing short of ingenious and resulted in far-reaching environmental and social consequences. Finally, in Section III, I zoom in on two Minqin farming families and look at their coping strategies and future aspirations in the age of productive conservation.

I Scarcity

In governmental policy reports, local officials regularly framed Minqin's water scarcity in two directions. First, they wrote about diminishing surface water flows from upstream over the past half a century: in the 1950s, the annual flow from midstream Wuwei to downstream Minqin averaged 500 million cubic meters. By the early 2000s, it had dropped to less than 100 million cubic meters. Then, the officials wrote about the other side of Minqin's water scarcity: the depletion of groundwater and the consequential soil degradation and desertification. Framing scarcity as a hereditary disease and measuring scarcity by the quantitative gap between the projected supply of and demand for water, policymakers have focused on curing the symptoms of the scarcity disease by closing this gap between supply and demand.[3]

But scarcity is as much a question of distribution as it is of supply and demand. And the definition of scarcity, so often predetermined by its policy remedy, is as much a discursive agenda as it is a quantitative one. In 1994, the outspoken environmental journalist Zhu Youdi, of the state news agency Xinhua, demystified the popular misconception about water scarcity in the Hexi Corridor. He asserted that the Corridor, in fact, was blessed with abundance, not scarcity.[4] Despite low precipitation and high evaporation rates, the Hexi Corridor is surrounded by high mountain ranges. The mountain ranges, which stand 2,000 to 5,000 meters above sea level, effectively capture the atmospheric moisture brought by the prevailing west wind. Melted snow from the southern highlands feeds into three great inland river systems through more than 60 major tributaries in the Corridor. As the great rivers, fed by melted snow, run through slopes and enter the flat lands in the north, the dramatic drop in altitude creates many alluvial fans at each level, thereby creating more tributaries that overlap with alluvial fans of various scales, and finally forming springs and filling up groundwater aquifers. The multiple river valleys and streams create pasture-ready land at higher altitudes on the slopes and fertile cropland at the fans. Zhu argued that both surface and groundwater reserves in the Hexi Corridor would have been much higher than the national average per capita, had it not been for massive deforestation upstream, dam construction and irrigated farm expansion in the middle reaches that drained the streams and depleted the aquifers at the lower reaches. The cause of desertification in Minqin, Zhu argued, is excessive resource extraction—mostly state-sponsored and policy-driven—in the upper- and middle-reaches of the Shiyang River Basin since the 1950s.

Assigning historical responsibility, however, is touchy business. For the lowly Minqin County officials, they would be better advised not to dwell on their grievances over their supervising Wuwei municipal government's damming of more than 80% of surface runoff in the middle reaches, as presented in Chapter 3. Instead, Minqin County leaders chose to accept Minqin's water scarcity as a given and tried to turn their vulnerability into opportunity. Local political energy was channeled towards bargaining with the provincial and central governments for financial support to combat the scarcity problem. The slogan "Minqin has the worst water scarcity problem in the world" anchors Minqin's political identity and branding strategy in the era of conservationism. The historic "Key-Issue Management Plan of Shiyang River Basin" ("Key-Issue Plan" from hereon) of 2007 identified two key solutions to keep Minqin from being swallowed up by the two encroaching deserts. One of the solutions was to increase surface water supply through interbasin water transfers from the Yellow River and to improve the intra-basin water sharing scheme from upstream, as outlined in Chapter 3. The other solution, much less publicized than the first, was to restrict groundwater extraction. But the question is, which place and actor should swallow this bitter pill of having to reduce water use? In terms of place, the issue of Minqin's water scarcity and soil deterioration concerns the entire watershed and beyond. But in the policy document, the root cause of the issue was localized within the county jurisdiction of Minqin. In terms of actors, it was the farmers—Minqin's major water users—to whom blame was assigned. Localized blame localizes the responsibility. Just like Inner Mongolia (IM)'s herders who were blamed for desertification and hence were placed under restrictive policies of grazing bans and destocking (see Chapter 2), Minqin farmers were subjected to restricted water use.

The prescription for scarcity is formulated in two programs in Minqin. One is "sealing wells and reducing croplands." The other is pricing water with a focus on improving the apparatuses for water fee collection and groundwater metering.

I.1 Sealing Wells and Reducing Croplands

The primary goals of the provincial Key-Issue Plan, as presented in Chapter 3, were to seal 3,000 wells (about one-third of Minqin's total number of licensed wells in 2003), and to reduce 439,990 mu of cropland (out of the county's total registered cropland of 900,000 mu in 2003)[5] within five years between 2006 and 2010. The Key-Issue Plan also aimed to reduce annual groundwater extraction from the 2003 baseline of 517 million cubic meters to 89 million cubic meters by 2010. As the cropland reduction scheme increases surface water inflow and reduces the demand for irrigation water, the plan prescribes further reductions in Minqin's annual groundwater extraction to 86 million cubic meters by 2020.

These target figures for reductions in cropland and groundwater extraction were to be achieved by a land and water quota system applied to the 248 villages across Minqin's 18 townships, where average land distribution was 5 mu per capita. The new regime permitted each villager to keep 2.5 mu, and required them to retire the rest. Irrigation water allocation was set at 410 cubic meters per mu, including both surface water and groundwater, with local variations in different irrigation districts, conditioned by the level of soil salinity (see Figure 3.2).[6]

In 2011, the county water bureau reported the results of the five-year campaign of sealing wells and reducing cropland. A total of 3,018 wells were successfully sealed, which cut off the water supply to 441,800 mu of cropland that had been retired. Like most official reports on policy deliverables, both counts slightly exceeded the targets. By 2012, the county reported that groundwater extraction was reduced to 85.15 million cubic meters, thereby meeting the target of 86 million cubic meters by 2020—8 years early.[7]

The county water bureau kept a detailed record of all 3,018 wells that were sealed between 2006 and 2010. The record, broken down by township and year, registers each of the 3,018 wells with a serial number and the geographic coordinates of its location. The meticulously compiled dataset also includes the various types of wells that were sealed during the campaign: those that were individually and collectively owned; licensed and unlicensed; old wells built in the 1970s and 1980s, as well as newer wells built in the mid-1990s during the feverish years of land reclamation.

But inconsistencies and omissions, often found in multiyear data compiled at the grassroots level, are also found in this data set.[8] For example, one of the most critical data points, the depth of the sealed wells, was incomplete. Out of the five recorded years, only data from 2006, the inaugural year of the well-sealing policy, registered the depth of the sealed wells. After 2006, the "depth of well" data point disappeared from the register.

What's absent is just as telling as what's present. The depth of the sealed wells matters greatly, as deep wells are critical for conserving groundwater at the saturated zone, which cannot be replenished easily, if at all. Thus, deep wells have been at the heart of environmentalists' concerns over groundwater extraction. But sealing deep wells can potentially incite the most fierce opposition. A 100 meter-deep well costed about 30,000 yuan to build in the 2000s, about half to one-third of a Minqin farming family's annual income from cash cropping in a good year. The price tag for a 300 meter-deep well is 10 times higher at 200,000 to 300,000 yuan per system. Deep wells typically produce a steady supply of sweeter water, and in Minqin they are often joint ventures between several households of the same lineage, or owned by those with more capital and political connections. The stakes of sealing deep and productive wells could be too high for most local officials.

It was challenging enough for grassroots officials to seal an old, low-yielding, and relatively shallow well of 30 to 60 meters deep. It would have been unfathomable to permanently shut down a recently constructed 200 or 300 meter-deep well. A researcher estimated that Minqin had no less than 350 wells of 300 meters in depth. In 2006, the only year for which the data shows the depth of the sealed wells, only two out of the 500 wells that were sealed that year were 300 meters deep and both were located in the Lake District, the most scrutinized epicenter of the crisis zone in the northern tip of Minqin County. What happened after 2006?

Where the official data leaves off is where our story picks up.

In the inaugural years of the well-sealing campaign, the political mandate to "rescue Minqin from encroaching deserts" was pushed ahead with great zeal. Next to each sealed well, a concrete stele of 1.0 × 0.8 meters (or, for a smaller size, 0.6 × 0.8 meters) was erected. Each stele was inscribed with the character *guan*, meaning "sealed," in large, bold script painted in red, and highlighted by a red circle. Each stele also featured a serial number and the date when the well was sealed, completed by the authoritative signature of "The People's Government of Minqin County," carved across the bottom. The stele was erected to commemorate the state's historic act of conservation (see Figure 4.1).

Figure 4.1 A sealed well in Minqin. The red paint on the stele from 2006 had faded by 2013 when the photo was taken. But faint traces of red color could still be discerned.
Source: Photo credit: Author.

But the actual process of sealing wells was not nearly as stately as the steles might have suggested. A retired county official recounted the mobilization work at the outset of the campaign to seal wells in Minqin. Hundreds of county, township, and village cadres who would be the foot soldiers of the massive campaign attended trainings at the party school to learn about the policies. These foot soldiers were each assigned "responsibility villages," where they would visit villagers' homes one by one to conduct "thought work"—i.e., working on the minds of villagers to persuade them to seal their wells. Policy fliers were sent to every household to "raise their awareness about the water crisis". Premier Wen's quote "We will never let Minqin become another Lop Nor" was painted on the walls of village homes. Banners that read "sealing wells and reducing croplands to save Minqin and the world" hung across streets in town and village centers. These measures were meant to affirm the priority of the well-sealing policy. More importantly, they conveyed the government's determination to execute the policy.[9]

The moment of truth came when targeted wells were to be physically sealed. How is one to seal a well without radicalizing its agitated owner or escalating social tensions that were already high in the villages? There have been cases wherein villagers took their grievances to the municipal and even provincial government, complaining that local officials executed the well-sealing policy in a way that "did not leave us peasants with anything to eat." Some audacious villagers took a more radical approach, threatening to take their own lives by drinking pesticides in front of the well-sealing crew, if their wells—the source of life and livelihoods—were destroyed. An ill-handled case of such "disruption to social order," especially if circulated on social media or exposed by the Central TV station as a "negative example of local governance," could cost officials their chance at promotion or even their jobs.

County and township officials learned to take a less provocative approach. While they assigned each village a quota of wells to be sealed and a set acreage of cropland to be retired each year, the officials let the villagers identify which wells to seal and which parcels to retire, as long as they fulfilled the quota. Village leaders understandably strove to choose the least productive wells and parcels for retirement, focusing particularly on collective wells. The depth of the well mattered greatly in this case.

The 2006 data show that close to 80% of the sealed wells were between 60 and 80 meters deep, and in some townships most of the sealed wells were built at the onset of the reform in the 1970s and 1980s. But even shutting off these shallower, older, and lower-yielding wells was not to be taken lightly. In some cases, crews were instructed to avoid using explosives so as not to completely destroy the wells. Instead, under the watchful eyes of the villagers, the crew would merely crack the top portion of the well's wall, no more than three or four meters deep. After a cement cap was placed on top, the well was declared sealed and duly recorded in the official report. Officials and villagers alike knew that it would still be possible to resuscitate the well when the campaign of sealing wells dwindled down, like all the other campaigns that have come and gone.

Officials also sought support from other government units. To fulfill the quota, especially during crunch time at the end of the five-year campaign of sealing wells in 2010 when the achievements were to be evaluated, many wells on public property, like government offices, state-owned timber plantations and farms, and abandoned school sites that were unlikely to trigger much resistance, were sealed. Large areas of unregistered land of lesser quality in the dune fields were slated for retirement, and their unlicensed wells were sealed and duly recorded.

In the eyes of the villagers who had already lived with diminishing surface water supplies and soil and groundwater salinization since the 1970s, they now faced a new type of scarcity brought about by conservation regime's restrictive access to water and land. To cope, villagers found "phantom" water and land, that is, water and land circulated on the black market that are created, ironically, by the water and land quota system. The aforementioned Key-Issue Plan allocates land quota at 2.5 mu per registered villager. A four-person household (the average household size in Minqin) would have a family farm of 10 mu with a fixed water allocation of 410 to 485 cubic meters per mu. The water quota varied across different irrigation districts (see Chapter 3), depending on soil quality. Districts with high salinity soil, like that in the Lake District, were allocated more water than those with less salty soil, like Dam and Quanshan Districts (see Figure 3.2).

For retired land, detailed criteria for cash compensation were formulated. But the compensation, even when fully delivered, was far from sufficient to maintain villagers' livelihoods. Most villagers looked for extra water and land beyond the quota allowance. The primary source of the extra water and land came from their absentee neighbors' unutilized quotas.

Like many other rural residents in China since the 1990s, Minqin villagers were reluctant to withdraw from their village residency status, as maintaining village residency was the way to keep claims over village land and water. For local residents who were relocated from Minqin under the government's ecological relocation program,[10] their counter strategy was to divide one household into two. One household would move their residency to the new settlement in order to receive government-allocated housing, and land, and access to water. The other half of the original household would retain their residency in the home village, in order to retain their land and water quota there. Other families who moved out of Minqin entirely would still try to keep their residency status intact. As a result, the gap between the figure of village residents in the official record and that of people actually living in Minqin villages was sizeable. In 2008, two years into the Sealing Wells and Reducing Croplands campaign, the Poverty Alleviation Office of the Minqin county government conducted a survey of the residents who were registered in the county books. They found that 14,000 "agricultural residents" had moved out for more than five years but still retained their residency in Minqin. Among the 14,000 absentee residents, 8,813 of them—or 63% of the total—were residents of the Lake District, the center of Minqin's crisis zone with the most severe soil and water deterioration.[11]

Under the quota system, these 8,813 absentee Lake District villagers, who retained their residency and entitlement to land and water, together had the rights to 22,032 mu of cropland, more than 10% of the total in the district. As each registered mu of cropland is entitled to 485 cubic meters of water, the absentee villagers also retained their rights to about 10 million cubic meters of water each year. In Xiqu Township alone, the epicenter of the crisis in the Lake District, close to 5,000 absentee residents claimed over 12,500 mu of land to which they were entitled, but not working on. In the entire county of Minqin, at least 35,000 mu of such phantom land and 15 million cubic meters of phantom water were allocated to the absentee residents.

The phantom land and water did not lay idle, however. Villagers actively, albeit informally, traded water and land quotas. Water and land could be traded together or separately. Villagers who remained in Minqin would rent the absentee neighbors' land and/or purchase the neighbors' water quota to expand their own farms.

Informal trade of land rights within villages has been common in post-decollectivization rural China. Minqin was no exception. One reason was that, as collective land was divided into small parcels for individual households in the late 1980s and early 1990s, each household often received quite a few small parcels scattered throughout the village. Tiny and irregularly shaped parcels made it almost impossible to use the plowing, sowing, and harvesting machines that have been popular since the 1990s. To a certain extent, parcel swapping and trading among villagers helped consolidate the highly fragmented parcels, and saved time and labor. Other factors being equal, the actual size of the parcels effectively conditioned its unit price on the informal market. The lease fee of a 1.5 mu parcel, for example, would be much higher than that of three 0.5 mu parcels in disparate locations.

The Minqin county government has tried to consolidate the fragmented allotment of land and water rights and to take control of the phantom water and land. In the late 2000s, the county government even offered cash compensation to those who were willing to forfeit their residency, and the land and water claims attached thereto. But villagers in Minqin, like their counterparts elsewhere in rural China, were reluctant to give up their residency status, not least because the government's compensation rates were significantly lower than what the land and water rights fees could fetch on the informal market.

Thus village land and water rights remained fragmented throughout the 2000s and 2010s. The discrepancy between the nominal and actual users of the land and water continued to belie official records. The phantom land and water allowed villagers to plant beyond the quota limits. In the meantime, the usual cat-and-mouse games between villagers and the water patrols persisted. Villagers were reported to have tried to revive sealed wells and tamper with water meters attached to the wells, especially during the hot and dry summers. A water bureau official admitted that he spent most of his days (and often nights as well) "resolving water conflicts." When the villagers were caught stealing water, they were charged a fine. As the monetary mechanism mediated both behavioral disciplines (fining violators) and resource allocation (pricing water, which I will talk about later in this section), villagers saw the fines as another form of water fee that entitled them to use more water.[12]

Grassroots governments' financial constraints also precluded a full execution of the cropland reduction program. By 2016, some farmers in off-the-beaten-path villages still worked the cropland that had supposedly been retired nearly a decade prior. The villagers explained to me matter-of-factly that they did so because the government had not been able to pay them the cash compensation for retiring the land. In other cases, earmarked parcels were duly retired as required, but then revived a couple of years later because the promised compensation was not delivered.

The highly unpopular measures of restricting water use triggered villagers' counter tactics and elevated social tensions. Most grassroots officials had limited capacity or incentive to "disturb the beehives." Indeed the state has its limits. But China's market reformers have prided themselves on "walking with two legs"—that is, combining state regulation with market mechanisms in policy design and implementation. The two-legged principle applies to water conservancy in Minqin as well. In this case, the regulatory leg is the well-sealing and cropland reduction policy, the market leg is pricing water.

I.2 Pricing Water

Following the neoliberal logic, China's policymakers began to bring in price-based market mechanisms to resource management in the early 2000s. Aligned with global sentiment at the time, they believed that water scarcity could and should be mitigated by raising the price of water in order to reduce demand and induce more efficient use of water. This logic has led to a much-increased water tariff for irrigation water, which accounts for about 64% of the total water use in China today.[13]

Since the beginning of market reforms in the 1980s, China has charged farmers directly for surface water. But the charges were minimal in the first two decades of the reform period. As conservationism rose to prominence in the new millennium, the Ministry of Water Resources formally introduced market-pricing mechanisms in 2003. Citing the need for water conservancy, the new water pricing scheme aimed at a "full recovery of the cost of water supply." Policy thinkers argued that market-price irrigation water could "incentivize farmers to use the water more efficiently and to grow water-conserving and high-value cash crops."[14]

Yet pricing irrigation water is easier said than done. Compared to industrial and domestic water, raising tariffs on irrigation water to recover the production costs has been more controversial and less successful in many parts of the world, including in industrialized countries like the U.S., Australia, and Japan. In China, a 2004 survey of five central and northern provinces found several technical and financial challenges to pricing irrigation water. For a start, it was costly to install volumetric facilities on numerous micro irrigation canals, many of which were in dire need of repair and maintenance before any metering devices could be installed. A flat rate for water that was based on parcel size only encouraged farmers to use more water, not less. Payment collection presented another challenge for local water bureaus: only half of water tariffs dues were collected successfully, according to the survey. Last but not least, the rising tariffs on surface water only encouraged farmers to abstract more groundwater, as access to groundwater was still open in many regions, despite the water management law that required all wells to go through an approval and licensing process.[15]

Surface water and groundwater are intimately connected in a hydrological system. The challenges in regulating surface water are intertwined with issues in regulating groundwater. In Minqin, where farmers use both types of water, the regulation challenges were more than doubled. There were two types of irrigation districts in Minqin. One was a conjunctive irrigation district that used both surface water and groundwater. The other type used groundwater exclusively. At the center of Minqin's crisis zone were conjunctive districts, namely, the Lake, Dam, and Quanshan Districts (see Figure 3.2). In the 1990s, more than 70% of irrigation needs in the conjunctive districts were fulfilled by groundwater. With surface water supply having started to increase since 2006 (see Chapter 3), groundwater averaged about half of the total irrigation water use in these districts by 2015, according to a local researcher.

Although surface and groundwater are integrated hydrologically, they work with different spatial and social orders. These differences produce distinctive modes of regulation and sets of politics between regulators and farmers. In Minqin, as in many other agricultural areas in China, surface water is charged at a flat rate based on the acreage of irrigated land. The challenge in marketizing water mainly lies in collecting the much increased water fees. In the case of groundwater, the charge is volume-based, putting groundwater abstraction metering to the test.

I.2.1 Collecting Surface Water Fees

China's surface irrigation, like its territorial system, is organized hierarchically. Regional-level irrigation systems that can feed 10,000 mu of fields or more, called "macro irrigation systems," (*dashuili*) are managed by provincial and municipal-level water bureaus. Main canals bring water from large reservoirs down the irrigation hierarchy to smaller reservoirs at the local levels, or the "micro irrigation system," (*xiaoshuili*), and further down to the village and sub-village levels through the last mile of the waterways to the fields.

During the collectivist era, the last mile of the irrigation networks was managed by village and sub-village collectives.[16] Under rural decollectivization of the 1980s, individual households divided the villages' collective land. The water fee system also changed in two directions. First, the paying unit shifted from the village collective to individual households, and the fee was calculated by the size of the farm at a flat rate. The role of the village head shifted from that of a mediator between the village collective and the water bureau, a key role in grassroots water management, to a water fee collector who has little influence in coordinating local water allocation. Second, since the 2000s, as rural decollectivization deepened, villagers no longer contributed obligatory labor to maintain local waterworks as they did under collectivism. What remained unchanged was the time-honored practice of paying the water fee after use. That is, farmers use water during the spring-summer growing season, but they are not required to pay for it until after they sell their harvest in the fall.

The change in paying unit from the village to individual households at a flat rate triggered a chain reaction.

In irrigation, like in land, location matters. Surface water needs to be transported from where it is stored, such as a reservoir or a tank, through branched canals, before it reaches individual fields. Farmers' parcels are located in different sections of the canals, and the canals traverse uneven terrain. The all-too-familiar conflict between the upper and lower reaches of a river basin repeats itself at every level and at every segment of the irrigation network—among villages at different sections of a main canal, between different sub-village groups at different sections of a lateral, and among households whose fields are located in different sites along the same micro-canal.

Entangled land rights further complicate an already labyrinthian process to access water. As a result of the decollectivization of village farmland, land rights structures had become highly fragmented. In order to make the division of collective land more equitable, each household gained rights over multiple small parcels located in different sites with varied soil quality and water accessibility. Consequently, along any segment of the irrigation network there were many water users, and every user would have vested interest in multiple channels within the village's irrigation system. When the paying units of irrigation water changed from the collective to individual households, such variations in water access brought their conflicts of interest to the surface. The fragmented and varied weighing of household interests ironically created a shared sense of unfairness across village households. For different reasons, almost everyone felt they were getting the shorter end of the stick. Figure 4.2 helps visualize this shared sense of unfairness stemming from divergent roots.

Two locational factors dictate a parcel's accessibility to water: one is the distance between the parcel and the reservoir; the other is the elevation of the parcel in relation to the reservoir.

Elevation / Distance	Lower than reservoir	Higher than reservoir
Close to reservoir	**Type A** Highest water accessibility	In-between cases
Far from reservoir	In-between cases	**Type B** Lowest water accessibility; needs more energy to pump water and canals to deliver water

Figure 4.2 Locational advantages and disadvantages of parcels fed by an irrigation canal

Source: Author's adaptation based on Jiao, Changquan (2011).

Sociologist Jiao, Changquan (2011)[17] observed that the incompatibility between fragmented land rights and interconnected irrigation networks has made it almost impossible to divide water fairly between Type A and B water users at every level of the irrigation hierarchy, and many of those in between.

This structure represents a major challenge in designing a fee schedule that is acceptable to all village households that have parcels scattered across different parts of the irrigation network.

When surface water was priced according to the size of the parcel rather than its location-based access to water, it was deemed unfair by both types of water users. Type A users complained about having to pay too much for the electricity used to pump water and canals given how little they used the facilities. Type B users were aggrieved because their parcels received water last and often missed the critical window for irrigation during the sprouting season. Type B users also received less water overall, especially during the dry years when there was less water to go around. The aging pumping devices were rarely powerful enough to deliver water to the last few parcels at the most distant, higher end of the water routes. To complicate things further, in dry years it was hard for Type A users to resist the temptation to dig a small and temporary side ditch to divert water into their fields when it was Type B users' turn to irrigate.

When folded into a collective payment plan and when water charges were negligible, the locational difference was less contentious. Even if there were a few late payers, the village collective's funds could cover the payment. But things are different in a decollectivized economy of scarcity. Water is now conceptualized and institutionalized as a commodity. The new policy of fully recovering the cost of water supply has been consequential. Now the local water bureau included, in their calculation of water fees, line items such as water purchased from the regional reservoir and the construction of infrastructure that stores, transports, and controls water into its cost-benefit analysis. Consequently, water tariffs grew between five- and tenfold from the 1990s to the 2000s. The latent problem of the location-neutral water pricing regime bubbled to the surface. Everyone felt pinched by the water charges and was reluctant to pay the universal flat fee. As a result, water fee collection became a constant challenge for local water bureaus.

The problem of fee collection is made worse by the annual water bill being due only after farmers have used the water and sold their harvests in the fall. In bad years, villagers felt justified in not paying for what ultimately brought them little yield. In poorly funded villages, even when fees were successfully collected, however partially, the funds collected by village heads on behalf of the water bureau were often apportioned to other more urgent payments. This shift of funds in turn initiated a vicious cycle. The water bureau would shut off the water to the entire village or a sub-village irrigation unit that failed to pay. To ensure the punishment was felt, they would shut the water off during irrigation season. But within a village or sub-village unit that shared a channel, some households did pay for water while others did not; some paid in full, others only a fraction. Cutting off water at the village head gate affected all paying and nonpaying households alike. Indiscriminate punishment easily fueled tension in the village. Enraged villagers would often accuse the village head of embezzling the water fees; sometimes lodging complaints with the county or municipal government. Villagers who had paid the fees were resentful of their free-riding neighbors. Friction over uneven fee payment led to more villagers withholding their payments. The snowball effect led to a less than 50% success rate of water fee collection in the aforementioned survey.

The conflicts over water fee collection had further repercussions. Since the 2000s, villagers were no longer obligated to contribute labor to regular maintenance or emergency repair work, and local water bureaus lacked sufficient funds to properly maintain the micro-waterworks. As a result, the irrigation system—especially the last mile of it—decayed rapidly. Tired of the fee disputes, leaky canals, and broken pumps, increasing numbers of individuals and groups of villagers decided to drill their own wells, install their own micro-irrigation systems, and withdraw from the collective irrigation network altogether. In some areas in China, the massive exodus of water users created an upward chain reaction, forcing some regional-level reservoirs to shut down. Sociologists Chen, Bofeng and Huihuang Lin (2011)[18] termed this spiraling effect the "tragedy of privatization," the antithesis of the "tragedy of the commons." In

2013, a member of the Communist Party School of Xiangtan Municipality in Hunan Province reflected on the frequent crop failures in Hunan and other southern agricultural regions. He maintained that, although crop failures were often conveniently blamed on droughts and floods, the root cause of the failures was the de facto privatization of irrigation systems. The collapse of the micro-irrigation works, in his view, has been the "most devastating mistake in China's rural reforms."[19]

Minqin farmers shared a similar tragedy of privatization and locational dilemma in their local irrigation networks. In the hot and dry summer of 2016, the relationship between the water bureau and Keli Village[20] in Minqin's Lake Irrigation District came to a standstill. One 66-year-old villager told me that though he had already paid the water fees and applied fertilizer to his five mu of sunflower fields, he was unable to water the crops. It was because several of his neighbors who shared the same lateral did not pay the water fees, and no one in the village could coordinate among the rest of the neighbors to negotiate with the water bureau. As a result, the water bureau refused to open the head gate, and more than 40 villagers watched their crops wither under the roasting sun.

In addition to the locational conflicts arising from fragmented land usership under shared irrigation networks, Minqin farmers faced other woes. In drylands, fresh surface water is critical for flushing out the mineral content in saline soil. But because the water travels a long distance to Minqin, the new principle of pricing water to "fully recover the cost of production" has made water more expensive for its users. Minqin farmers pay 100 yuan per mu for surface water, while their counterparts in Wuwei at the upper reaches of the Shiyang River pay only 40 yuan per mu, the difference representing the extra cost to deliver water all the way to Minqin, which sits at the tail end of the water channels. Within Minqin, the mineral content of the soil varies from district to district. Soil in the Lake District has the highest mineral content, and hence needs more surface water to flush it out. But the Lake District is also located furthest from the Hongyashan Reservoir (see Figure 3.2) and the distance would translate into a 60% higher water fee than other irrigation districts in Minqin. Also, within individual irrigation districts, soil structure varies across villages and parcels. Sandy soil with low moisture-holding capacities needs to be watered more frequently and for longer durations each time, dividing the interests among village households even further. Those who had parcels with poor quality sandy soil and low water accessibility, which were often connected, felt doubly pinched. While the yield of their land was already lower than average, they were stuck with a water bill that was unfairly higher than their lucky neighbors within and beyond Minqin. In Keli village, both the water fee-paying and nonpaying villagers resented one another to the extent that no one would budge. Only the sunflowers lowered their heads in defeat.

What about the groundwater that fed the other half of Minqin's cropland? In many other places, the price jump for surface water forced farmers to turn to unregulated groundwater. But farmers under Minqin's water conservancy regime did not have this option. After over 3,000 wells were sealed, the remaining 8,300 working wells were closely monitored by the county government under a quota system. An electronic metering apparatus was installed on every borehole to register the water flow and to charge the owners at incremental rates.[21]

I.2.2 Metering Groundwater

The significance and the challenge of metering Minqin's groundwater can be better appreciated in the context of rising interest in groundwater regulation worldwide.

Groundwater is estimated to constitute 97% to 98% of all nonfrozen freshwater on earth.[22] But unlike surface water streams and lakes that are mostly visible and normally confined to known and definite channels and reservoirs, and which can be released or blocked via controllable outlets, groundwater is concealed, spatially scattered, widely accessible, and amenable to private, local, and on-demand abstraction. The spatial features of groundwater lead to prohibitively high costs in regulating its abstraction. All of the key aspects of groundwater regulation, including licensing, monitoring, and metering are technically, financially, and administratively more demanding than those for surface water regulation. While state authorities have the option to control surface runoff—itself a daunting task—groundwater control is often left to individual discretion.[23] China has a long history of state authorities building large-scale hydraulic infrastructures to tame the major rivers for economic and territorial control of China's core regions. Beyond the core regions in the peripheries, land reclaimers, local bosses, war and famine refugees, and tax evaders have dug their wells out in the open.

The hydrogeological characteristics of groundwater further disincentivize state intervention. Groundwater is theoretically everywhere, yet always elusive. The transmissibility, permeability, and storage capacity of aquifer systems are shaped by highly dynamic geomorphological and climatological processes at the local, regional, and global levels. The complex and ever-changing processes, due to both human and non-human activities, create immeasurable variation in the reserves and exploitability of groundwater within and across aquifers.[24] The fact that surface water and groundwater are tightly interconnected in a hydrological system only complicates the processes further. The elusiveness of groundwater often frustrates state planners and investors alike, whose operations are built on projections about the extent of available reserves and their exploitable amounts. Hydrogeologists Karen Villholth et al. (2007)[25] concluded that although groundwater reserves on earth are estimated at billions of cubic meters, "very little about groundwater is known locally and globally." The cost of knowing more about these numerous, scattered, and moving targets is high and does not always pay off.[26]

The "secret, occult and concealed"[27] existence and movement of groundwater deters centralized control up until the moment groundwater's abundance seems to be shrinking and when water competition expands from surface water to groundwater, leading to escalating water conflicts and soil degradation. Karen Villholth et al. (2007) aptly summed up this moment of reckoning: "you never miss your water until your well runs dry."[28]

To appreciate the challenges in regulating groundwater that the Minqin government faced, it is useful to look at solutions that the state of California in the United States has attempted in recent decades. Like Minqin, California is an important agricultural producer with a large portion of its territory in a semi-arid region. Known for its extensive groundwater depletion problems, California suffers one of the most severe cases in the world.[29] Groundwater supplied "well over half" of California's water in dry years to feed its 9 million acres of irrigated farmland between the early 1970s and the late 1990s.[30] But California's first groundwater law was not ratified until 2014, at the end of the state's fourth year of drought, which had triggered another unbridled wave of deep well construction. The new law divides California into more than 500 aquifer basin districts, with management agencies that coordinate, plan, and monitor groundwater abstraction. The law triggered heated debates over whether and how the mandatory flow meters—the basis of groundwater regulation—could be installed on wells that have long been associated with the mystified independent spirit of the American West. In addition, questions arose over how the hundreds of new aquifer-based groundwater management agencies would draw their judicial boundaries to align with the boundaries of river basins and local government jurisdictions. Others wondered who, if anyone at all, would pay for the colossal costs of regular data collection on groundwater volume at each meter (if successfully installed) and in each basin, measuring recharge and extraction rates, and finally processing, interpreting, and storing these data in a unified database for overall abstraction monitoring and planning. Even if money were no issue, the work of coordinating among such fragmented control points is daunting, as each of the hundreds of groundwater management agencies presides over its own localized definition of sustainable yields, to say nothing about the long Californian tradition of seeing well drilling and groundwater flow logs as private information.[31]

In other places where the history of groundwater regulation is longer than that in California and where the cowboy mentality is less pronounced, regulators are still routinely frustrated. Upon reviewing the institutional and technical challenges in monitoring and planning groundwater abstraction in more than a dozen countries in both the developed and developing worlds, the environmental legal scholar Kerstin Mechlem (2016)[32] concluded that even where laws and regulations are in place, most of them remain unimplemented or ineffective.

Groundwater seems to have a way of slipping through the grip of regulators. Worldwide, state control of groundwater remains more of an aspiration and a mobilizational platform than an apparatus that delivers reliable results.

China shares this inability to govern groundwater, perhaps even more so than other countries. While surface water engineering boasts a long history of thousands of years in China, the state's attempts to regulate groundwater only started in the 1990s when dwindling water tables and the acceleration of soil deterioration began to surface in policy discourse. With the rise of conservationism and an ever more fervid resource race at global, national, and local levels, the state's hands-off approach gave way to calls for tightening control over groundwater abstraction. But shifting policy discourse and serious attempts by the state to curb groundwater exploitation did not automatically bring success.

The fragmented structure of groundwater regulation offered little help. In China, the task is undertaken by nine central-level ministries and their numerous subsidiaries at the subnational levels, which further diffuses the responsibility and complicates coordination across government agencies and the administrative hierarchy.[33]

Widespread and under-regulated groundwater extraction goes hand in hand with a spectacular jump in groundwater usage in China. China's annual groundwater consumption increased from 57 billion cubic meters in the 1970s to 100 billion cubic meters in the 2000s, while the number of registered tube wells doubled from 2.3 million in the 1970s to 4.7 million in 2003, when groundwater contributed to about 19% of irrigation water use nationwide. At the subnational level, groundwater is unevenly distributed between the humid south and arid north. While possessing only 30% of the national reserve, the north uses 70% of the country's abstracted groundwater, mostly for irrigated farming. Peking University-based hydrologists Wang, Jinxia et al. (2007)[34] estimated that 68% of irrigation water in northern China was supplied by groundwater by the early 2000s. Based on two surveys in 2004 and 2005 of six northern provinces where 75% of the 448 surveyed villages relied on tube wells for irrigation, the authors concluded that although northern China has effectively taken control of most of its surface water, groundwater was "almost completely unregulated." Less than 10% of well owners had obtained a well-drilling permit before drilling, despite regulations having been in place since 1993. Well owners were not charged for groundwater in any of the surveyed villages, nor were they subject to volumetric limits. Wang, Jinxia et al. cited the interwoven financial, administrative, and technical constraints in China's groundwater regulation, which is similar to that in California.

The ungovernability of groundwater, on the other hand, has been seen as a tool for alleviating rural poverty.[35] In their analysis of the "groundwater economy" in India, Tushaar Shah et al. (2003),[36] for example, noted that while surface irrigation systems tend to create "islands of affluence," groundwater is spatially more diffuse and can sustain the livelihoods of a larger number of small farmers. The authors suggested that, 55% to 60% of the population in India depended on groundwater drafted from 19 million groundwater structures as of 2000. As groundwater's spatial extensiveness frustrates regulators, this same characteristic is a boon to small farms in arid land.

In arid northern China, the dilemma between regulating groundwater and alleviating poverty has produced an impasse: grassroots officials are frustrated in their efforts to monitor the numerous scattered boreholes, and even when they succeed, it is only counterproductive to the other priority policy—that of poverty alleviation. As a result, the most viable option for grassroots officials seems to be to do nothing. Little wonder that well licensing remained unimplemented in northern China for 12 years after the birth of the policy.

But governance impasses do not stop history or the market force. The rapid increase in groundwater exploitation and the dwindling aquifers draining the shallow boreholes yielded increasingly saltier water. As groundwater availability shrank, informal groundwater markets in northern China, like in India, expanded quickly.[37] By 2004, 44% of well owners of various scales in northern China sold their water for profit. As the water tables fell, it also cost more to pump water from the deep zone, which in turn raised the water price. The ownership structure of wells in rural northern China changed too, from predominantly collective to 70% private ownership.[38] After all, groundwater is not just a "common pool" type of resource,[39] but also an unequally pooled resource. High density drilling often takes place in areas with lesser reserves, and only those who can afford to tap water from the deep zone or buy water can stay in the game. Large industrial farmers' numerous, deep, and networked boreholes in an aquifer system leave small farmers in the dry. The drier the time and place, the higher the political and economic stakes of groundwater abstraction. Heightened stakes, in turn, intensify social contention, or to use Chinese policy language, threaten social stability.

The intimate link between water competition and social instability has kept Minqin water regulators on their toes. As aquifers dwindled and social tensions rose, more vigilant management would be needed to keep conflict in check. The pressure for local officials to perform grew even more acute after Minqin rose to being the showcase model of China's conservationism. High-ranking provincial government leaders in Gansu, officials from other regions, and journalists from the state media poured in to learn from this model case.[40] Groundwater control in Minqin had to work. In 2007, Minqin officials took advantage of their special water conservancy grants to install Integrated Circuit (IC)-operated flow monitoring systems on each of the county's 8,300 remaining, registered wells. This was unprecedented in agricultural China, where most local governments were too indebted to finance such a large-scale project.[41] Once the monitoring apparatuses were installed on every well, farmers purchased an electronic key card from the county's water bureau. Each pump was set with a predetermined amount of water output per unit of time. The prepaid and rechargeable key card would be loaded with a preset amount of time to operate the pump.

The electronic key card enables a precise reading of the water yield from individual wells, and water fees are calculated accordingly. Using price to manage demand, water tariffs are calculated in two segments. One segment is the standard water allotment for the 2.5 mu of subsistence land that each village member is allowed to retain. The groundwater charge for 2.5 mu of land rings up a universal flat rate of 2 yuan per mu per year. If a farmer used 200 cubic meters of groundwater per mu per year, the prefixed quota, the fee would amount to an affordable rate of 0.01 yuan per cubic meter. If a farmer used water above the quota, which most did, the price would jump. Each irrigation district has its own ceiling for the additional water that farmers are able to purchase, and the above-quota rates vary across irrigation districts. The three irrigation districts that were designated as the "crisis zone" in Minqin, had the lowest ceilings, and the above-quota rate was forty times higher than the standard rate. Outside of the crisis zone, water use restrictions were more relaxed: the ceiling for extra water use was six times higher than that in the crisis zone, and the above-quota water rate was only one-sixth of what farmers in the crisis zone had to pay. In other words, under the dual mechanisms of water quota and tiered pricing schemes to control demand, farmers in the crisis zone were allocated the least amount of water while paying the highest rates. To compensate for the fact that the soil in the crisis zone contained the highest mineral content and required more water to flush out the salt, the surface water quota in the crisis zone was 20% higher than in other districts. But again, farmers in the crisis zone paid 60% more per cubic meter of surface water than their counterparts in noncrisis zones.

The implementation of the IC metering system marked a milestone in the Chinese state's attempt to regulate the seemingly ungovernable groundwater. With more precise readings of water yields, officials were able to charge volume-based water fees. Interestingly, while farmers in the crisis zone were subjected to higher fees than those outside the zone, they still considered the individualized groundwater metering system to be more equitable than the collective surface irrigation networks, because "you pay for exactly what you use."[42] The new system of direct payment using a smart key eased villagers' worries that corrupt village heads would siphon off the water fees to pay for other expenses. This borehole-based and individualized groundwater pricing system became a socially acceptable way to moderate villagers' resentment against surface water fee systems, which had been widely perceived to be unfair, as presented earlier.

Local officials congratulated themselves for the technological advancement in metering and the added benefit of reducing villagers' sense of unfairness. But what really made local water bureau officials embrace the electronic metering apparatus was its prepaid mechanism.

As mentioned earlier, despite rounds of water pricing reforms starting from the 1980s, the time-honored practice of "use before payment" in agrarian China continued. It was customarily practiced not only for water charges, but also in the seed and fertilizer trades in the private sector. There were often lapses in harvest-contingent payments in bad years, leading to a proliferation of debt through the supply chain, including the water and electricity bureaus. The lapses constantly created conflicts among farmers, traders, and local officials.

The prepaid electronic key card of the pumps helped secure payment *before* use and to synchronize water and electricity fee payments. To turn on the irrigation pumps, farmers must first load the key card and pay both fees regardless of the year's harvest. This method saved transaction costs for local water and electricity bureaus, secured fee collection, and eased the bureau's financial predicaments.

But the borehole-based electronic metering was far from a perfect policy solution and was plagued by technical and administrative challenges from the outset. Governance requires constant and continuous maintenance, especially with a moving target like groundwater. One of the major issues in Minqin was hardware maintenance. In 2016, a recently retired engineer told me he worried that many of the electronic monitoring and metering devices in Minqin were not working properly. The system was installed in haste in 2007 at the inauguration of the water conservancy campaign, in preparation for Premier Wen's historic visit (see Chapter 3). By 2016, these systems were a decade old. Some had had problems from the start. Others malfunctioned due to the muddy groundwater, which damaged the meter's water sensor and short-circuited the system. Fluctuating voltage problems in the villages led to measurement errors, interruptions to pump operation, and even caused meters to combust. These well-known problems presented villagers with a smokescreen for tampering with the meters. Reduced readings could be blamed on unstable power supplies and the low-quality and aging metering devices. Though the thousands of metering systems were badly in need of an upgrade, there was little budget for maintenance after the initial installation funds had been exhausted. In an interview with another official in 2016, I asked about this problem. The official responded that the water bureau had recruited a 660-strong patrol crew to inspect the wells and the pumps "at least twice a month" to ensure that the meters were working properly to prevent villagers from stealing water. While I was unable to verify the astonishing figure of 660, it seemed clear that the smart key card may have changed the cat-and-mouse game, but it has not put an end to it.

II Opportunity

To make restrictive conservation programs politically sustainable, the government also needed to create opportunities to offset the restrictions. As an integral part of the regime of productive conservation, the opportunity project employs science and technology aimed at improving productivity and raising villagers' income level (at least compensating for their income loss), all while using less water. In Minqin, opportunities have been harnessed through building water conservancy infrastructure like greenhouses and drip irrigation; promoting drought-tolerant cash crops like red jujube dates and goji berries (which were believed to require less water and command high market prices); and creating conservation spaces such as model ecological farms. These "constructed opportunities," as mentioned earlier, co-produce "lived opportunities," just as constructed and lived scarcities do.

II.1 New Infrastructure

In Minqin, the most widely promoted opportunity infrastructure has been greenhouse farms and drip irrigation. Qian Xuesen, the rocket scientist and father of China's sand industry introduced in Chapter 1, built his theory of "deserticulture" on photosynthesis. Greenhouse farming and drip irrigation were at the center of Qian's vision of a solar energy-powered future for China's drylands. As Qian's deserticulture turned into a populist "sand industry" in the northwest in the 2000s, the paired solutions of greenhouse farming and drip irrigation were in every local governments' toolkit of productive conservation.

The idea behind the paired solutions was to reduce water waste and improve water use efficiency. Measured in monetary terms, the traditional method of using flood irrigation to flush salt out from the saline soil was deemed wasteful and inefficient. As water prices went up, villagers were to plant cash crops with higher market values. The point was not just to reduce the total use of water per se, but also to introduce more cost-effective uses of water via greenhouse farming.[43]

To promote greenhouse farming, the provincial government of Gansu set an annual target for constructing greenhouses each year, measured by acreage and the number of greenhouse structures. This policy was similar to afforestation with a targeted acreage of forested area and number of planted trees, as presented in Chapter 1. The target for greenhouse acreage was divided and assigned to individual municipalities in Gansu Province. Each municipality then allocated the municipal quota down the jurisdictional hierarchy to counties, then counties to townships, townships to villages, and finally villages to sub-village groups.

At the bottom of the ladder, each village subgroup needed to fulfill its assigned quota for a certain number of greenhouse structures, each with a minimum size requirement. In 2007, Minqin County received the quota assignment from its supervisory government, Wuwei Municipality. In three years, every village household was required to build at least one greenhouse, each of which had to be at least two mu.

The top-down quota allocation scheme met a number of implementation barriers on the ground. For starters, the cost of building a greenhouse was prohibitively high. On average, a 9 by 60 sq. meter greenhouse (about 0.75 mu, including the 1.4-meter-thick walls) cost about 20,000 yuan to build in 2007. As an incentive for the villagers, the county government provided a subsidy of 5,000 yuan and a low-interest loan of 7,000. The township government provided another 1,000 yuan. The remaining 7,000 yuan needed to come from villagers' own pockets. If this scheme were fully realized, the total subsidies for building greenhouses would have equaled the budgetary revenue of the entire county.[44] None of the actors involved—the county, townships, villages, or individual households—had the means nor the will to carry out the assignment, at least not in full.

While villagers hesitated, the market swiftly reacted to the new program. As the Minqin government pushed hard to build the greenhouses to fulfill the quota before the deadline, the cost for greenhouse building materials rose by 30% between 2007 and 2008, which largely cancelled out the government subsidies and added to villagers' share of the expense. By the summer of 2010, a villager recalled, to build a standard-sized greenhouse with a powered rollup canopy would cost 50,000 yuan, more than half of her household's income in a good year.

Construction costs were not the only concern. A villager told me that he would be happy to go into debt to invest in a greenhouse if it were indeed profitable. But after witnessing the failure of those who responded to the government's call to build greenhouses in 2007, he became reluctant. In those greenhouses, the villagers experimented with growing mushrooms, a novel crop in the northwest endorsed by the county government for its higher market value. However, few knew how to grow mushrooms in the dryland and the harvest was poor. The pioneers suffered a big loss and were unable to pay back the loans, which made the local banks reluctant to fund villagers' greenhouse construction projects the following year.

Market fluctuations for cash crops created yet another barrier. Contemporary Chinese farmers have been well versed in market fluctuation of cash crops since the late 1970s when rural reforms started. But the level of financial risk associated with investment in greenhouses was higher than usual. In addition to high construction costs, greenhouse farming requires greater input of labor, water, electricity, and fertilizer to support high-density and year-round cropping. The warm and humid greenhouse environment also requires more frequent applications of fungicides and pesticides. As their land quota was reduced to 2.5 mu per head under the policy of retiring farmland, villagers were even more reluctant to risk their shrunken farms for the greenhouse venture. One villager told me that if she used the family savings to build a greenhouse, she would not be able to send her children to school.

As the apple of the national government's eyes, Minqin was now a must-see stop for state media journalists and inspecting officials from Beijing and the provincial capital. To hold on to this privileged status, the municipal government of Wuwei, the supervising government of Minqin County, pressed hard to build greenhouses. To encourage Minqin villagers to build greenhouses, the Wuwei municipal government launched a campaign of "thought work" mobilization, much like for the aforementioned Sealing Wells and Reducing Croplands campaign.[45] 12,000 employees from municipal, county, township, and village governments were sent to visit thousands of village homes and attempted to persuade the villagers to build greenhouses. An online post depicted Wuwei's greenhouse campaign as a "war zone without the smoke and smell of explosives."[46] Under pressure to fulfill the quota, some village heads resorted to a lottery system to decide which village households would be responsible for building the greenhouses. The households who made unlucky draws (or, to use a villager's expression, "those whose hands were 'stinky' on the day of drawing the lottery") were forced to take out bank loans and build the greenhouses. The greenhouses were deliberately built to line the main road within clear view of officials conducting inspections from their moving cars. Because the greenhouses were built reluctantly—mainly to meet the quota obligation and to achieve a visual effect—the sites chosen for the greenhouses were not always conducive to cropping. To minimize the cost, the greenhouse walls were thin, the canopy fragile, and the irrigation system inadequate, resulting in low yields. The poor performance of these "model" greenhouses did not make a strong case for greenhouse farming in persuading other villagers to follow suit.[47]

While most villagers' enthusiasm for greenhouses remained low, the leader of Harvest, a township in the heart of Minqin's crisis zone, stood out for his exceptionally successful promotion of greenhouses. In 2013, Harvest Township's party secretary, Xu Xingwen, was featured in the local official newspaper for his success in mobilizing villagers to build the impressive number of 1,300 greenhouses. But Harvest's success needs a bit of contextualization. Villagers in Harvest began building greenhouses on their own accord long before the government's greenhouse campaign. In the 1990s, as the cash crop prices spiked, most villagers of Harvest shifted from grains to more profitable sweet melons. The sweet and juicy melons grown in Harvest's sandy soil and sunny climate were profitable enough for villagers to accumulate the capital to invest in greenhouses, which helped to extend and regulate the harvest time for the regional and national market. By the time the governments launched the greenhouse campaign in the 2000s, Harvest easily claimed the championship in Minqin.

Xu's acclaimed leadership ran aground just a few months after his success hit the news. In the cold winter of January 2014, a social media post about him went viral. In photos and video clips, Xu was shown leading a group of men inside a greenhouse and smashing 600,000-yuan worth of crops inside.

The crops were not melons. They were two-week-old onion sprouts. Unlike melons, onions have been banned in Minqin since 2008 because they were considered a thirsty crop. But Harvest farmers needed a way to recover the greenhouse construction costs by using the greenhouses all year round. During the winter months after the end of the sweet melon season, villagers rented out their greenhouses to farmers and traders to sprout onions. In December and January, as nighttime outdoor temperatures dropped to minus-20 degrees Celsius, the greenhouses remained at 2 to 3 degrees and nurtured the onion spouts, preparing them for spring planting in the open fields. While onions were banned in Minqin's crisis zone, onion sprouting was not, provided the sprouts are planted outside of the zone.

In late January 2014, right after Lunar New Year day, the Wuwei municipal government tightened up on the regulation and announced a new ban on onion seedlings in all greenhouses in all of its sub-municipal jurisdictions, Minqin included. But the ban came after the onion seeds had already been sown in the greenhouses, and sprouts were already two weeks tall. Village greenhouse owners took their chances and bet on the government officials' good holiday mood, expecting that the township leader would allow them to keep the sprouts until they were ready to be transplanted elsewhere.

On the third day of the New Year, still an official holiday, Harvest's party secretary Xu took the villagers by surprise when he showed up unannounced in a village with shovels, accompanied by over 50 (another source says 80) men. Xu reportedly had his men destroy eight greenhouses and the onion sprouts therein. The images of him brandishing a shovel while three village women attempted to hold him back from destroying their crops went viral on the internet.[48] Xu disappeared from the public eye after the incident. Rumor has it he was transferred to a lesser office. While official media sources remained silent about the scandal, local villagers in Minqin have not forgotten about it. During my fieldwork in 2015 and 2016, I repeatedly heard about the incident in different villages, with an unusually high degree of consistency across the recounts.

The incident in Harvest Township was not accidental, nor was party secretary Xu the only one to blame. Xu, the greenhouse champion who ended up smashing greenhouses, was simply executing the conservation policy that bore the contradictory mandates of scarcity-framed restrictions and opportunity-framed production expansion, which clashed with one another when it came to the greenhouse projects.

Drip irrigation created more glitches in delivering opportunity. Drip irrigation and plastic sheeting were touted for being able to minimize moisture loss in soil. While villagers happily accepted the government-subsidized, affordable plastic sheeting, they were less enthusiastic about drip irrigation. Drip irrigation transports water through a micro system of water tanks, pumps, main and lateral pipes, filters, valves, water pressure regulators, flush pipelines, and plastic driplines placed along rows of crops. The driplines release water slowly through tiny emitters placed close to the root zone of each crop to minimize evaporation. Fertilizers and pesticides can be mixed with the water and reach individual crops through the same system as well. This controlled and targeted application of water and other inputs, widely extolled for its efficient use of water, was promoted by water conservancy programs in various dryland agricultural regions around the world, notably Israel and India, with varying levels of technological sophistication and success. The cost of installing and maintaining the system has been a major barrier towards its adoption, however. In California, for example, despite severe water shortages, only 39% of irrigated acreage was equipped with drip irrigation systems by the early 2010s.[49]

In China, drip irrigation had been adopted since the 1980s to support cotton plantations in the Xinjiang Production and Construction Corps (XPCC). XPCC is a formidable institution that has established para-military, mega-scale farming colonies across China's western frontier since the 1950s.[50] Minqin, by contrast, did not start promoting drip irrigation until the mid-2000s under the regime of productive conservation. Researchers and policymakers believed drip irrigation to be more efficient than traditional flood irrigation that inundates entire fields, which results in more than 30% water loss to local waterways in unleveled fields. The high costs of installing and maintaining drip irrigation systems, however, has been a challenge. Only high-value cash crops can justify the costs. Drip irrigation is also scale sensitive. It is only suitable for large farms of monocrops, such as the cotton plantations in the state farms of the XPCC that have a unified schedule for watering and pesticide and fertilizer application. Heavily salinized soils in the dryland complicate the opportunity project further. Drip irrigation systems require relatively clean water. The emitters' waterways are tiny: ranging from 0.2 to 2.0 mm in diameter, thus easily clogged. In addition to usual sediment, fertilizer deposits and dissolved chemicals, and salinized soil with high mineral content also clog the emitters frequently. In addition, drip irrigation tends to promote soil salinization in the root zone through capillary action, thus accelerating soil deterioration.

Most farms in Minqin are far from ideal candidates for drip irrigation. Minqin features highly fragmented land usership, and cropping patterns among neighbors are hard to coordinate to achieve economies of scale. The installation and maintenance costs are prohibitively high for most small farmers, even when partially subsidized like the greenhouse program. Sediment from Minqin's salinized soil easily clogs irrigation nozzles, even with filtration devices. The government-subsidized, low-quality plastic driplines leak and need constant replacement. Most of all, several farmers told me that the drip system cannot replace the tried-and-true flood irrigation method. In the spring before sowing, flood irrigation is indispensable, as the freshwater flushes out excess salt that accumulates over the long winter, especially for crops like cotton and sunflowers.

As a result, Minqin's drip irrigation could hardly claim success. Exactly to what extent Minqin's farms have been equipped with working drip irrigation systems is anyone's guess. A local official told me that drip irrigation has been installed in half of the total irrigated land in Minqin. In 2014, a local researcher estimated that drip irrigation systems had been adopted in "less than one-third" of the local farms. But in the two dozen family farms in different irrigation districts of Minqin that I visited between 2013 and 2016, I failed to find a single fully operating drip irrigation system. Instead, I was often greeted by partially installed drip systems awaiting completion, or systems that were installed but unused.

II.2 New Crops

Another opportunity project concerns drought-tolerant cash crops. In Minqin, three crops, called the "Three Reds"—goji berries,[51] red jujube dates, and wine grapes—were promoted in the early 2010s for Minqin's remaining cropland. The photo below (see Figure 4.3) depicts the county government's billboard that visualized Minqin's agricultural future with the "Three Reds" and greenhouses.

Figure 4.3 A billboard showing Minqin's agricultural future with the "Three Reds" policy crops and greenhouses. This billboard was placed in front of Minqin's Museum of Combating Desertification. The text on top reads "Implement the Three Key Strategies"
Source: Photo credit: Author.

Promoting the Three Reds was again implemented through the quota allocation mechanism from county to townships, down to villages and village households. To fulfill the quota, every village household was required to plant three mu of goji berries. The villagers felt further squeezed. The restriction policy of retiring farmland left them with a meager piece of land, 2.5 mu per head, or an average of 8 to 10 mu of land per household. To ask each household to devote 3 mu to growing a cash crop without guaranteed market was a tall order.

Farming goji berries was hardly a novel idea in China's northwest. The small, bright red-colored,[52] sweet berry is ubiquitous in Chinese, Korean, and Vietnamese medicine. Considered a super fruit, goji berries have also gained popularity in U.S. health food stores since the 2000s. China has been a key supplier of goji in the global market, and Ningxia Hui Autonomous Region (NHAR) in China's northwest, where Chinese Muslims concentrate, has grown more than half of China's total. In 2019, NHAR produced 15.5-billion-yuan worth of goji berries, contributing 4% of the autonomous region's total GDP that year.[53] The seemingly small percentage is not insignificant. Sitting at the third from the bottom in China's provincial GDP ranking, every bit counts in the poor NHAR. Moreover, goji berries have been the backbone of Ningxia's poverty alleviation programs, especially in the minority Muslim Hui-concentrated areas. Zhongning County, located in northern Ningxia's Yellow River floodplains, is Ningxia's, therefore China's, epicenter of goji berry industry.

Goji berries have long been a staple in Zongning County government's economic development policy. The small berries spearhead the growth programs of Zhongning County through its extensive networks of goji investors, growers, processors, wholesale and retail traders of varied scales and ownership structures; disease control researchers; and new seed and product development in university labs, government institutions, and private pharmaceutical companies. Goji also plays a central role in poverty alleviation and social stability maintenance programs in Zhongning. By the late 2010s, the goji berry industry in Zhongning had bred a growing number of local entrepreneurs and provided more than 200,000 jobs to local and migrant workers.[54] Beyond Zhongning, traveling goji berry traders, many of whom are also Muslim Hui, are active in Ningxia and neighboring Gansu. Also, Hui women in the relocation villages (see Introduction), who customarily do not leave home with their husbands and fathers to work in the city, stay in the resettlements and pick goji berries for much-needed cash income.[55]

Ningxia's long history of cultivating goji berries (some claim to have started since the 16th century) and its pioneering role in developing goji berry breeding infrastructure since the 1960s has turned Ningxia goji into a brand name, recognized by its large, plump, and vibrant red. Ningxia is China's goji king, period. By the time Gansu started to expand its goji berry production in the late 2000s, it was up against not just the goji king, but also several second-tier goji lords of the northwest, such as Xinjiang and Qinghai. The market for goji berries, the so-called "red diamonds," has already been saturated with high-quality products by established early mover producers. Thus, Minqin's small goji berries of lesser quality faced an uphill battle in penetrating the saturated market. Little wonder Minqin villagers were reluctant to venture into the risky business of competing with the king and the lords. Market risks aside, production costs constituted another deterrent. Compared to other cash crops like sunflowers and corn which can be harvested by machines, harvesting goji berries is a labor-intensive endeavor, for the fruits need to be hand-picked. Labor costs, which were on the rise throughout the 2010s, have made farming goji berries even less appealing to Minqin's family farmers.

Red jujube dates and wine grapes faced similar obstacles to goji berries. The lack of marketing channels greatly weakened their popularity among Minqin villagers. When compelled, villagers would plant a few red jujube date seedlings along the village's dirt roads, yet pay them little attention. I would often spot small piles of dried red dates lying abandoned in the corners of villagers' courtyards. One villager told me that "even the sheep do not care for them" (see Figure 4.4). Wine grapes faced an even greater challenge. Again, Ningxia championed viniculture promotion in the northwest and has declared modest success.[56] But Minqin farmers were not equipped to participate in this opportunity program. It was not just because of their lack of know-how and financial and cultural capital in wine production. A villager in 2014 emphasized that it was also because planting grape vines is, again, highly labor-intensive, as the vines need to be buried under the soil to winter, in addition to many other types of intensive work throughout the growing and harvest seasons.

Despite these barriers, the Minqin County government reported that the County had planted over 30,000 hectares of the Three Reds between 2010 and 2015.[57] Information gaps aside, how did the government manage to achieve such impressive results? The Harvest Township party secretary's aggressive approach in carrying out policies, as mentioned earlier, was far from exemplary for other grassroots officials to emulate. Violent repression would not be practical. It is because, unlike destroying banned crops, growing policy crops requires more of peasants' cooperation and participation, as the story of suosuo in Chapter 1 demonstrated.

To coax villagers into growing the Three Reds, grassroots officials had a few sticks and carrots at their disposal. One stick that came handy was the IC-operated key card used to operate groundwater pumps introduced earlier in this chapter. The key card for groundwater pumping and metering was also an implementation tool for other programs. Villagers were eligible for water allocation and could get their IC card loaded only if they participated in the policy crop programs. The water bureau collaborated with village and township officials to enforce the Three Reds. In exchange, the latter helped collect surface water fees for the water bureau.

Land was the carrot used to entice villagers into planting the Three Reds. Villagers received an additional land allowance beyond the 2.5 mu per head limit to plant the Three Reds. Some of the additional land came from parcels that were slated for retirement but were never actually retired, as the local government lacked the funds to pay for compensation. Now under the Three Reds program, these nominally retired croplands assumed a new life under a new name, "ecological land." The ecological land remained active and was repurposed for water conservancy crops like the Three Reds.

Similarly, some wells that were earmarked to be sealed remained open or were re-opened to feed the policy crops. Villages were also allowed to reclaim land parcels at the edge of the village farming areas, which were otherwise strictly prohibited, for the policy crops. One villager told me that her household of five was granted the

Figure 4.4 Red jujube dates that "even the sheep do not care for"
Source: Photo credit: Author.

right to reclaim 0.5 mu of land per head to plant goji berries, so the household had a total of 2.5 mu of extra land under the opportunity program. In another village, every household was allowed to reclaim 3 mu of land to grow red jujube dates. The county water bureau also allotted additional "ecological water" to feed these added croplands.

But the additional allotments of land and water, tempting as they were, were useless if they could only be used for unmarketable goji berries and red dates. To get the program off the ground, officials sweetened the deal by allowing villagers to double crop for the first three years of the Three Reds program. Between the young goji seedlings, villagers could use the "ecological land" and "ecological water" to grow their preferred crops like sunflower, alfalfa, corn, or cotton. Villagers often placed the distance between goji seedlings as wide as possible to leave room for their preferred crops.

The plot thickened with additional commercial entanglements.

When the goji program was launched in 2011, the county leader requested township governments to provide free goji seedlings to villagers. But the officials of Rise Township,[58] where I visited in 2014, sold the seedlings to villagers, promising to reimburse them later.

It turned out the goji seedlings were a source of revenue for the cash-strapped townships. In China, the seed business in traditional crops like corn and sunflower had long been carved out by international, national, and regional seed-breeding companies and distribution networks. Corn seeds, for example, have been dominated by a joint venture of DuPont's seed breeding subsidiary in China, DuPont-Pioneer and another Chinese firm. In the 2010s, the DuPont-Pioneer's drought- and saline-tolerant varieties of corn were planted on 43 million mu of land, about 9% of China's corn fields—a large share given the highly fragmented market. Other international, national, and regional companies with different patented seed varieties have also established their strongholds throughout China's northeast, north, and northwest corn regions.[59] There left little room in the corn or sunflower seed businesses for newcomers. But the business of policy crops like the Three Reds was open for bidders. In 2015, a seed trader told me that unlike corn and sunflower seeds, the goji program allowed local officials to profit from brokering the seedling trade (the most profitable link in the supply chain) through negotiating directly with suppliers from Ningxia, China's king of goji.

But the scheme, again, had glitches. When I revisited Rise Township in 2016, the township government still had not delivered the compensation for land retirement nor the promised reimbursement for the goji seedlings to villagers. One villager told me that because the township government owed her tens of thousands of yuan in compensation and reimbursement, she felt entitled to continue using both the land that she was supposed to retire, and the extra 2.5 mu of land that was earmarked for goji for her preferred crops of sunflower and alfalfa, even though the three-year grace period for double-cropping had long expired. While the total acreage of her family's cropland had increased, the goji shrubs withered in the shade of other thriving crops in the nominal "goji" fields.

In short, under the Three Reds program, retired land for ecological recovery was revived and rechristened as ecological land. A significant portion of the ecological land, designed to grow drought-tolerant crops, were occupied by villager-preferred crops instead. Most of these practices were daily cat-and-mouse games between villagers and grassroots officials, and between grassroots officials and their supervisors. But carrying out the assignment to promote policy crops, upon which local officials' career futures were contingent, was too important to leave solely up to a game of cat-and-mouse. Villagers' Three Reds crops being scattered across a quarter mu here and half a mu there could do only so much to help with the aggregate sum that local leaders need for their performance evaluations. Patches of depressed goji shrubs and undernourished red date trees struggling for their lives could hardly impress visiting supervisors and photojournalists from the provincial and national capitals. To excel in opportunity programs, local state leaders needed grander, signature projects. They needed a new type of space.

II.3 New Space

Larger-scale and photogenic "model ecological parks" were a vehicle to demonstrate local leaders' diligence and capacity. Built on the decade-long programs of large-scale "Dragon Head" farming in the villages, as introduced in Chapter 1, green entrepreneurs were brought in to develop the opportunity projects. Like their counterparts elsewhere in China, Minqin's green entrepreneurs took advantage of their access to policy loans, land, and water that were otherwise restricted in Minqin's officially designated ecological crisis zones.

Visitors can see model ecological parks adjacent to the major roads in Minqin and along the roads that connect Minqin with large cities in the Hexi Corridor. Large signs that read Husbandry Science and Technology Park, Sheep Breeding Base, Sand Industry Model Park, Ecological Sheep Husbandry Zone, Ecological Cattle Husbandry Park, Crop Breeding Base, Red Date Model Park, Gojiberry Model Orchard, Wine Grape Model Vineyard, and more are hung at the entrance gates of these parks. Placed next to the gates are billboards that detail the site plan, the size of land and investment in the model park, irrigation facilities installed in the park, and the sponsoring government unit. Given the conservational nature of these model parks, an environmental research institute would be listed on the billboard as well.

While there are many such model parks, only a few appeared to be active during my visits. In 2016, I visited an unusually busy goji farm that was established in 2013 (see Figure 4.5). The investor was from Zhongning, the center of China's goji kingdom in Ningxia, as mentioned previously. Armed with extensive trading networks, the Zhongning investor took advantage of government subsidies in land, water, and capital for goji farming in Minqin. Fifty plus middle-aged women from Henan Province in northern China were picking the berries, earning around 100 yuan a day on piece rates, with room and board provided by the employer. The site manager, who was also from Zhongning, told me that his boss had established goji farms throughout the northwest on leased "ecological land," and his other plantations were at least four to five times larger than this Minqin one of "only 200 mu."

But to build industrial farms of a few hundred or even a couple thousand mu, the challenges remained in fragmented land rights in Minqin, where family land holdings ranged between 6 and 12 mu. How did local officials assemble land tracts large enough to build model ecological parks? As mentioned in the Introduction, the arid northwest that was considered to be immense but empty had been assigned multiple tasks by the national development planners. All these tasks, be it energy production base or ecological zone, require land allocation. For national and provincial planners, designating land tracks for various uses was a matter of drawing up color-coded land use maps at the aggregate level. For local officials, however, it took a great deal of tweaking and scouting on the ground for large enough tracts of land in order to materialize the multiple ministries' various initiatives, plans, and programs.[60]

The first step towards assembling large land tracts was to pool small parcels together, which was promoted through the "Dragon Head" programs designed for rural land consolidation.[61] In Chapter 1, I introduced the green entrepreneur Wang,

Figure 4.5 A Goji Ecological Park in Minqin
Source: Photo credit: Author.

a super "dragon head" investor who managed to lease rangeland from 3,000 herder families to build his mega Kubuqi Ecological Park for suosuo plantations and other "sand industry" projects in the Hobq Desert. Here in Minqin's ecological crisis zone, the magnitude of the dragon heads' investment was more modest. While many villagers were reluctant to part with their land, others did lease their land to local dragon heads or to outside investors to build ecological parks. Take the aforementioned 200-mu goji farm for example. The villagers who leased their land to the Zhongning investor, most of whom were over the age of 50, felt that since they themselves had neither market access nor the political connections to secure ecological policy loans, land, or water, they had few options but to lease the land to those who did. As they leased the land to the goji investor, they also leased out their water rights attached to the land, as outlined earlier.

Negotiating piece-by-piece with dozens or sometimes hundreds of villagers to get a tract of land sizeable enough for a plantation is a trying task. Many such plans have failed. In 2015, a Minqin fertilizer trader, Zhang[62] with a peasant family background recounted his attempts to invest in a model park. In 2014, Zhang identified a 400-mu parcel in the Lake District, the heart of the crisis zone, jointly owned by 28 households in a sub-village unit. Zhang mobilized his local networks and negotiated with each of the 28 households and the sub-village head to lease their land. Midway through the protracted negotiations, another competitor intervened with the support of the township government and offered a higher land and water lease price. The villagers quickly learned that their bargaining position was stronger than they had previously thought. Some households launched a protest in front of the township government to demand a higher lease price that the bidding parties were unwilling to pay; others took a more passive position and decided to wait for a higher bidder. Given that these hardened bargainers' parcels were the critical link to maintain contiguity of the land tract in question, the deal fell through for both contenders. Similar stories were found in other villages. The so-called "nail households," or the holdouts, were often those who owned the parcels that could make or break the contiguity of the land tract. The location critically conditioned the bargaining position of the villagers. While villagers may or may not carry sentimental attachment to their land, they were well attuned to the market value and locational advantage of their parcels.

The predicament of pooling small parcels resulted in modest-scaled ecological parks in Minqin. Most of the ecological parks in operation that I visited in the former farming area were between 80 and 150 mu, much smaller than the 1,000 mu-parks that the county leader had vowed to build.[63]

Squeezing land parcels out of the "canny and greedy" peasants, as the frustrated fertilizer trader and aspiring ecological park investor Zhang described them, was just one way of scouting land tracts for ecological parks. In Minqin's immense county jurisdiction of 16,000 sq. km, of which more than 90% is categorized as wasteland or desert land, local officials were limited only by their creativity. Two sets of grassroots officials' strategies in finding large enough land tracts for opportunity projects are notable. One is to activate formerly unregistered land, which I call "land without identities"; the other is locating multiple projects on a single parcel, which can be called "land with multiple identities."

II.3.1 Land without Identities

One source of large land tracts was the unregistered land invisible to the state. In his studies on the Dragon Head Program in central China, sociologist Zhang, Qian (2015)[64] found that the lack of large land tracts for industrial farms in central China led local officials to set their sights on hilly land and wetlands, or in an underdefined term, "wasteland," in the official discourse.[65] The underdefined and under-demarcated wastelands were often infertile and poorly located. It was not subject to redistribution to villagers during decollectivization, and hence remained on the books of village collectives. In the 2010s, the fact that most of the wastelands attracted less scrutiny from villagers made it easier for local officials to turn the wasteland into larger-scaled industrial farms for policy crops.

In addition to wastelands, there are also the so-called "black lands," or land that had been appropriated for state farms, factories, or research stations during the socialist era but subsequently abandoned. Some of these sites were turned into farmland and divided up by villagers during decollectivization, while others remained in the hands of the village collective. While the wasteland may or may not appear in the official register due to its ambiguous definition, black land was deliberately left out of the official inventory records for village leaders' discretional allocation. Black land is common in the history of rural China. It was used to stash harvests away from the emperor's tax collectors. It was also commonly used throughout China's collective era. At different times, the unregistered cropland and hidden harvests helped peasants survive famines, especially after the disastrous Great Leap Forward. The Beijing-based sociologist Zhu, Xiaoyang (2011) has estimated that by the 1980s, no less than 10% of all farmland in China was black land.[66]

Minqin villages had their fair share of under-defined wasteland and unreported black land. In these cases, the official data of the land tract's existence, location, size, boundary, and changes of use were nebulous, if there were any data at all. These were land tracts without identities.

A lot of Minqin's inventory of land without identities also came from villagers' land reclamation, a common practice in the arid northwest frontier. During waves of land reclamation in the 1950s, 1970s, and the 1990s, most of the efforts to reclaim land were organized and led by sub-village production teams. The reclaimed land was considered shared property of those who participated in reclamation. Reclaiming land was back-breaking. It involved flattening sand dunes to build fields and shaping the sand into shelter walls, drilling wells, building water storage tanks, improving soil quality by mixing clay with sandy soil, and breaking down the hardened saline soil.[67] What motivated villagers to endure the toil was the prospect to keep most, if not all, of the harvest to themselves. While villagers responded to the government's call to "march in to the desert to open up farms," the actual amount of the reclaimed land was rarely reported in full to the government.[68]

The reclaimed land without identities were a product of the arid environment and its ever-changing growing conditions and uncertain access to water. A reclaimed tract might be abandoned before the tax collectors even become aware of its existence. Or, even if the regulators were aware of it, the yields might be too low to warrant the administrative cost of tax collection. It usually takes at least three years for newly cleared land to mature and start producing. Oftentimes, cultivated and sown land requires three to five years of rest before it can be sown again. When the land is resting or maturing, its ambiguous identity may lead to its classification as wasteland, subject to state appropriation for other projects.

The identity of land in Minqin, therefore, is ambiguous and in flux. A parcel might be sown one spring but buried by a dust storm the next spring, registered or not. Part of the buried parcel might be recovered two years later, but unsown for another two years due to droughts, with the harvest ultimately destroyed by a late frost in the third year. As a result of the highly variable growing conditions and the constant shifts in land use, the size of cropland (defined as land that has been plowed and sown at any given time) and "sown land" (defined as land that is actively planted in a particular crop cycle) fluctuates significantly from year to year, and the ratio of one to the other could be as large as 10 to 1 in any given year for a village.

The rural decollectivization of the 1980s further complicated the vacillating state of land use in Minqin. During decollectivization, village land of higher quality was contracted out to individual village households, while other, less desirable parcels were left unclaimed. For the contracted land parcels, some were registered in the government's book, but others have remained black land inherited from the collective era. And almost every household retains parcels of privately reclaimed black land that are not included in the village's land redistribution scheme. To be fair to members of the collective, some villages have conducted several rounds of land readjustment by taking back contracted land from those who have left the village or who have passed away and reallocating the land to new village members. During such times of readjustment, some of the village land reserves were also redistributed. However, land readjustment was not implemented consistently across villages in Minqin. In some villages, land readjustment never took place. The institutional and natural variations have made Minqin villages' land inventory, for the most part, a black box to regulators at the county level and above.

The repeated campaigns of reducing farmland for environmental conservation did little to improve the accuracy of official land counts. In the late 1990s, the nationwide Grain for Green campaign was launched to convert farmland back to forests, followed by the Sealing Wells and Reducing Croplands campaign in the late 2000s, as presented earlier. These programs accelerated land use changes on the ground and created an even greater gap in information. Higher levels of government rely on satellite imaging technologies for a bird's eye view of land inventory, but even satellite imaging could not distinguish, for example, the forbidden, thirsty crops of cotton and onions from the policy crops like the Three Reds. The devilish details, or, to use the term from remote sensing, the "ground truths" were still bound to village officials' own books.

The fluidity of land uses and land rights as well as the gaps in land bookkeeping have created room for village heads to identify additional tracts of land, often of lesser quality, to accommodate large projects imposed by higher levels of government. They could also initiate large projects themselves, under the condition that they identify the investors. The patterns of alliance and negotiation among different levels of local government follow territorial hierarchy. Under the county authority, townships and villages may collude to deal with demands from the county, while keeping some "ground truth" to themselves. Under the township's authority, individual villages and sub-village groups do their best to keep their books from the township head. The decision of which land tracts are to be taken from which villages' inventory of unidentified land is subject to such a hierarchy in information gaps and alliance-building.

II.3.2 Land with Multiple Identities

The information gap between the high-level authority's bird's eye view and grassroots officials' ground truth has produced what I call "land without identities." These land tracts can be activated for ecological model parks. The information gap also works in grassroots officials' favor in a different direction. One land tract could acquire multiple identities that stretch over time and/or overlap in physical space in order to accommodate multiple programs on the same site.

One such strategy concerns recycling and repurposing land tracts for different policies from different eras. As a conservation veteran, Minqin has experienced quite a few waves of conservation campaigns over the last four decades. Land tracts used for conservation programs have been recycled multiple times. For instance, under the afforestation campaigns in the 1980s and the Green for Grain campaign in the 1990s, Minqin built large artificial suosuo forests at the edge of the desert (for details on suosuo, see Chapter 1). The suosuo forests shielded expanding farms from sandy winds. But the artificial forests started to fail in the early 2000s, due to the destructively high density of the suosuo forests and farm expansion that led to groundwater depletion. In the late 2000s, the land from failed suosuo forests was repurposed as a Red Date Model Park and a Goji Model Farm, together greatly boosting the official record of total acreage of the Three Reds farms in Minqin by more than 2,000 mu. More recently, some of the cropland that was retired during the 2006–10 Sealing Wells and Reducing Croplands campaign also underwent an identity shift from retired cropland to ecological land, and thus gained eligibility to become a model ecological park. In fact, the prospect of turning retired cropland into ecological land for large model parks was what incentivized grassroots officials to push for cropland reduction in the first place. The new life and new identity of the parcel would have been planned even before its old life ended. Whether a parcel was suitable for "retirement," a retired official told me, was determined not necessarily by its level of soil degradation, but its location and compatibility with future ecological park projects. That is, whether it could contribute to producing contiguous land tracts for cash crop plantations in the name of the ecological parks that would draw investors. Isolated parcels of jagged shapes were normally low on the priority list for retirement. In other words, while national policymakers envisioned a conservational logic of retiring degraded land for recovery, local officials have implemented the policy with an opposite logic—retiring land for new uses and marketability. On the ground, it was the future prospects of the parcel for sale that conditioned its present status in conservation.

Crops planted on retired-cropland-cum-newly-established ecological parks would also transform. After planting policy crops, like red jujube dates or sweet sorghum (sweet sorghum was a policy crop in the arid northwest that was meant for the industrial production of animal feed), for the first couple of years, and after passing numerous inspections for loan approval, investors would switch back to tried-and-true commodity crops, such as corn and melon. If necessary, they would double crop like the villagers did, only on a grander scale. When double-cropping, villagers' preferred crops that were shorter in height, like pumpkins, melons, and corn would be planted behind the outer rings of tall-stalked policy crops, like sweet sorghum. The wall of sweet sorghum created a visual façade and appeased the inspectors of policy crop programs. From their moving cars, inspectors would only see the walls of policy crops and assume that entire fields were devoted to them.

In this way, retired farmland was first transformed into ecological land for policy crops, and ultimately made a full circle return to cultivating corn, cotton, and melons—the very same crops that were planted there before the land was retired. But history proceeds in a spiral rather than in a flat circle. In the new conservation spaces of the "Sweet Sorghum Model Farm," "Model Goji Berry Park," or the "Model Red Date Park," the revived-yet-hidden melon and corn fields were at least 50 times larger than small family farms and were controlled by larger agricultural capital, or to use a villager's words, by "those who have connections with the top to get policy loans." While the consolidation of small family farms through the decade-old Dragon Head programs has progressed slowly, the incessant waves of conservation campaigns to retire croplands—fortified by conservation ethos and subsidies—seem to have increased the average farm size in Minqin more effectively.[69] A single site, in this case, held multiple identities as retired land and ecological land. And different actors identified it differently. For visiting officials, it was an ecological park for policy cash crops; for investors, it was ultimately a plantation for non-policy yet marketable cash crops; for grassroots officials, it was a solution to accommodate multiple policy demands of production, conservation, and social stability (see Introduction). Last, but not least, for local farmers, it was a "model" park that justified their own cat-and-mouse game with grassroots officials: if the officials could play tricks, so could they.

Finally, there remains the wide-open desert awaiting improvement. The time-worn practice of land reclamation in the northwest, rendered illegal under the regime of restrictive conservation, found its way back through programs of productive conservation. But large-scale land reclamation required serious capital. When a particularly well-endowed investor—most of the time it means a well-connected investor with access to large policy loans—or an exceptionally significant flagship project initiated by a high-level government office needs a sizeable chunk of land, the local government would be granted special permission to reclaim desert land for the project. As outlined in the Introduction, the productive confusion between the desert and desertification and the rapidly growing land demands in the northwest has helped justify the expansion of new development projects into the seemingly boundless desert. Dune fields, gravel gobi, pastures, and fallow land have been categorized as "wasteland" in need of improvement via projects like "Model Red Date Parks" or "Crop Breeding Bases." Again, a land tract's designated role in production defines its status in conservation.

It took strenuous and creative effort by grassroots officials to manipulate land tract identities to fulfill the quota of building ecological parks for policy crops. But this strategy would have little purchase in the dryland if there was no water. Thankfully, Minqin now had plenty of water. As mentioned in the previous chapter, since Minqin became a conservation star, surface water that flows into its reservoir has more than tripled from 84 million cubic meters in 2001 to an annual average of 260 million cubic meters since 2010, reaching 320 million cubic meters in 2014.

The surface water sent from the Yellow River and the upper reaches of the Shiyang River, had two primary uses in the official plan: agriculture and ecology. The additional supply of agricultural water helped replace a portion of groundwater used for irrigation so that groundwater abstraction could be reduced. The extra supply of surface water, together with the Sealing Wells and Reducing Croplands campaign, has managed to reduce Minqin's total groundwater abstraction from 660 million cubic meters in 2007 to 125 million cubic meters in 2014, an 80% reduction. The official data also showed an impressive 65% reduction in agricultural water use over the same period, from more than 700 million to 250 million cubic meters, thanks to the policies of farmland reduction and thirsty crop bans. Overall, based on the official data Minqin's total water use has been halved, from 760 million cubic meters in 2007 to 360 million cubic meters in 2014, and the percentage of agricultural water shrank from more than 95% of 760 million in 2007 to 70% of 360 million cubic meters in 2014.[70] With the reduced agricultural use of water in Minqin and the additional supplies of surface water since the mid-2000s, Minqin now had a *surplus* of 195 million cubic meters of surface water.

What was the 195 million cubic meters of water used for, and where did it go? The water was named "ecological water," and it was earmarked for ecological recovery. Like the new category of "ecological land" in land use planning, "ecological water" was a new category in water management. Similar to "ecological land", which was under-defined in land use laws, "ecological water" was legalistically ambiguous but politically potent. Out of the 195 million cubic meters of Minqin's ecological water, 33 million cubic meters went straight to Qingtu Lake to revive the dried-up swamp.[71] Ecological water has contributed to achieving the goal of "not letting Qingtu Lake become another Lop Nor" (see Chapter 3). By 2016, the surface of Qingtu Lake measured 26 sq. km. Overall, 100 sq. km of wetland was recovered and the water table around the Lake has risen by 0.8 meters since 2007.[72]

After filling up Qingtu Lake and soaking the surrounding wetlands, however, there was still more than 160 million cubic meters of ecological water left. The precious ecological water needed to be used productively and profitably, not least because the water from afar was not free. The county water bureau had to pay the Yellow River Resource Commission 40 million yuan a year for 120 million cubic meters of water from China's Mother River, for which the provincial government chipped in 15 million yuan. The rest had to be covered by water sales. Individual farmers were one type of buyer of ecological water. They received a set quota (an additional 15% of their agricultural water quota) of ecological water to water their policy crops. But the major buyers of ecological water have been various kinds of ecological parks, afforestation sites, and cash crop plantations. In the age of scarcity, as "agricultural water" became a politically incorrect type of water use, the more legitimate "ecological water" now contributed to the productive conservation programs.

With the water from afar feeding the dryland, a mega conservation space emerged in Minqin. In 2016, I saw an impressive red jujube date ecological park, boasting a total of 16,000 mu, according to the billboard by the gate, built on a sandy site at the interface zone between the farming area and the sandy desert. Inside the park, plump sweet melons outgrew the neighboring rows of red date seedlings. By the gate of another ecological park, an outsized billboard read, in red characters: "Ten Thousand Mu Red Date Base." Two rows of date trees lined the new roads around the Base. The rest of the Base was populated by rows of squash, sunflowers, and corn, contracted out to villagers to farm.

Of an even grander scale was the seemingly infinite afforestation expanse stretching from the exterior edge to the interior of the desert. The program of "Afforestation and Sand Management" (*zhisha zaolin*) took the form of building sand-stabilizing grids made of black plastic mesh or dried corn and wheat stalks, then planting suosuo seedlings, the miracle desert shrub introduced in Chapter 1, in each cell of the grids (see Figure I.2). Since the early 2010s, Minqin has been learning from the Kubuqi model, and suosuo-congrong plantations have dominated Minqin's opportunity-themed programs. The Minqin County announced that they had built 120,000 mu of sand-stabilizing grids as of 2015. With the help of the grids, airborne sand was blocked from burying the young suosuo seedlings. With such measures, 70,000 mu of suosuo shrubs were planted, of which 40,000 mu were suosuo-congrong plantations.[73] As suosuo-congrong plantations expanded in Minqin, they also brought new environmental problems with them. These included the acceleration of groundwater depletion and the destruction of topsoil and crust of the sandy land, as reviewed in Chapter 1.

As government officials scouted for large land tracts for ecological parks, what did the villagers in the crisis zone do? The usual path of migrating to work in the city was hardly an option for most middle-aged farmers who were in their 50s or older and who lacked the educational and the physical edge to compete in the urban labor market. Some younger farmers in their 30s and 40s did try. However, many returned to their farms in Minqin after a few years, citing the discriminating job market and urban society, as well as the poor working condition in factories, mines, and construction sites. By 2016, Minqin still had close to a quarter of a million residents with agricultural residency status, with at least half still relying on farming as the primary source of family income. And there is only so much of the cat-and-mouse game that the villagers could play to dodge conservation restrictions. To sustain livelihoods and secure a future for their families, Minqin villagers looked for water and land beyond the crisis zone.

III Moving from Scarcity to Opportunity

In this last installment of the tale about Minqin's scarcity and opportunity, I follow the Jins,[74] a three-generation family in Minqin. Aspiring to move up the social ladder and leave the drudgery of tilling land, the Jins ventured beyond the crisis zone to plant cash crops in the unrestricted areas of neighboring counties. The story of the Jins is situated within the long history of northwestern farmers' mobility. Land reclamation and migration to less populated areas as a steam-release valve strategy has long been a crucial part of state policy and non-state initiatives since the late imperial era. I will elaborate on this process in Part III on Inner Mongolia's three agricultural frontiers. For the remainder of the current chapter, I take a closer look at the Jins' lived scarcity and opportunity beyond Minqin's crisis zone.

I will start the Jins' story with Jin Three.[75] Jin Three was an onion farmer in his late 40s when I first met him in 2014. He lived with his parents, his wife, and two teenage sons in the Dam District. Like the nation's reform that "walks on two legs," Jin Three's strategy for surviving conservation had two legs as well. One was a short-term spatial strategy of spreading out, the other a longer-term social inspiration for moving up.

III.1 Spreading Out

Jin Three received a poor deal in the collective land redistribution of 1990. As mentioned earlier, to adjust to the demographic changes in village families, villages were expected to practice land allocation readjustments every few years after the initial decollectivization of the late 1980s. For example, upon the marriage of a daughter or the death of an elderly, the land allocated to them would be returned to the village land pool to be redistributed to the village newborns. In reality, however the frequency of land readjustment varied greatly from region to region, and from village to village. In Jin Three's village in Minqin, there was only a one-time land readjustment in 1990. During initial land redistribution in 1987, Jin Three's family had four eligible members with village residency and each received four mu of land, totaling 16 mu. In 1990, as the village was ready to readjust land allocation, Jin Three's two brothers had already left the village, and their village residency status moved with them. So the two brothers' parcels were returned to the village pool. Jin Three's family was left with half of the land they used to farm, which amounted to eight mu, scattered across 10 locations in the village. Jin Three got married in 1993 and had two sons. But there were no more land readjustments, so his sons did not receive land under their names as they otherwise would have if land readjustment had taken place after their birth. Under the program of Cropland Reduction, the Jins' small family land holding of 8 mu was further reduced to 6 mu. Luckily, the Jins and their fellow villagers in the Dam District, unlike many in the Lake District, did not have to relocate. Jin Three supplemented his income by driving an old, eight-seater shuttle between the village and the long-distance bus stop at the town center and by taking on temporary construction jobs around town and in nearby villages. Jin Three also grew onions.

Onions had been the most important source of cash income for Jin Three and his fellow villagers since the early 2000s. Corn and sunflowers commanded a relatively stable price, but small parcels of such crops with low profit margins could barely support the family. It was onions that had helped local farmers build new homes, pay their medical bills, and send their children to school in the city. But under the restrictive regime of water conservancy, onions were officially deemed a thirsty crop and were banned. Several fellow villagers continued to plant onions in areas that were tucked away from the main road. Many more, Jin Three included, set out to rent farmland in the neighboring jurisdiction of Jinchang Municipality.

Sitting at the mid-reaches of the Shiyang Basin, Jinchang hosts one of the world's largest nickel reserves. Back in the 1970s when Minqin and Wuwei reached the water sharing agreement, as mentioned in Chapter 3, Jinchang was the third stakeholder in the agreement thanks to its advantageous status as a national center for nickel mining. Farms surrounding Jinchang's mining industrial complex benefited from the large share of surface runoff dammed for the entire area. Compared to Minqin, Jinchang enjoyed a much lower price for irrigation water, and onions were not banned in Jinchang. In addition, job opportunities in Jinchang city and its mining industry have lured Jinchang villagers away from the farms. Absentee Jinchang villagers pooled their fragmented parcels into larger contiguous tracts and rented out their land and water access as well as the vacated farmhouses to farmers from neighboring Minqin.

Jin Three started renting land to grow onions in a village in Jinchang in 2007. Between early spring and late summer each year, he made the two-hour drive each way in his old van between the family home in Minqin and the rental land in Jinchang. During the planting and harvest seasons, he would stay in a rental house for one to two week stretches. For the rest of the growing season, he would travel back and forth every week, staying in Jinchang for two or three nights during each visit to water, weed, and apply fertilizers and pesticides.

The land and the farmhouse were rented on a yearly basis. In 2015, Jin Three rented 30 mu in a Jinchang village to grow onions. His investment was about 4,000 yuan per mu for onion sprouts, water, land lease fees, fertilizers, pesticides, labor,[76] and fuel for his commute, for a total annual investment of 120,000 yuan. If everything went well, the harvest could sell for 8,000 yuan per mu, so the profit rate would be 100%, not counting Jin Three's own labor.[77]

2015 was a good year for onion farmers in Jinchang and in other areas along the Hexi Corridor. That year, fields in Shandong Province, the center of China's onion production, were attacked by pests and suffered severe drought. The poor onion harvest in Shandong raised the price of onions and benefited producers elsewhere in China. But that year, Jin Three battled a local problem. Out of his 30 mu of onions, 10 mu were infested by pests. Under the roasting sun in July 2015, I went with Jin Three on his trip to rescue the failed onion crops. The yellowed leaves of the infested plants had lost their strength to stand upright and were toppling onto one another on the ground. Jin Three pulled out the dying crops to show me the rotten roots. Trying to contain the infestation, Jin Three decided to apply more pesticides. As he walked along rows of remaining crops with a heavy tank of pesticide solution on his back, he said he would rent a different parcel next year.

Constant moves from one rental farm to another was common for Minqin's commuting farmers. Rotational cropping was necessary if one is to minimize infestation in onion crops. Since Jin Three rented cropland on a yearly basis, he simply rotated the cropping sites instead of the crop. I asked him whether he could tell if the land he rented had been an onion farm the prior year. He said he routinely asked around in the village to gather information about the conditions of particular parcels and inspected the soil to check for debris from the previous harvest. Despite taking such precautionary measures, one-third of his 30 mu of onions still failed in 2015, missing a well-priced year for onions, as mentioned earlier. In 2016, upon my third visit, Jin Three had leased 20 mu of farmland to grow onions in a different village in Jinchang.

The onion price had dropped below the 2015 level, but his onions were not infested that year. He moved his onion farm to still yet another site in 2017. But by 2017, the onion ban had been lifted in Minqin's Dam District, so he also grew 4 mu of onions on his own land as well. Jin Three had told me he was determined to keep growing onions until both his sons graduated college.

Another migrant farmer, Xiao Liu,[78] whom I met in 2015, came from Minqin's Lake District, a district with the most stringent conservation restrictions in Minqin. In 2007, at the age 29 with two young children and only 2.5 mu of land to his name after the cropland reduction program, Xiao Liu started looking beyond Minqin. With little initial capital, he first rented 80 mu of land on the outer fringes of the Minqin Oasis to grow corn for three years. But the low-quality land yielded little. So he moved to Jinchang in 2011, investing all his savings in renting 200 mu of land to plant sunflowers. But his entire crop became infested, setting him back 100,000 yuan, a significant loss in a place where the annual household income in a good year was about 50,000 yuan at the time. Xiao Liu blamed it on the untrustworthy Jinchang folks. Like onions, but unlike corn and fennel, sunflower fields require rotational cropping every two to three years to minimize pest infestation. Xiao Liu suspected that his rental farm had been used for sunflowers for many years in a row before he took over, and the cunning landowner had plowed the soil deep after the last harvest to erase the land's cropping history.

After his failed attempt in Jinchang, Xiao Liu traveled further in search of cheaper and less depleted land, before settling down in 2013 on his current farm in Alxa Right Banner of Alxa League in western Inner Mongolia (IM), about 150 kilometers north of Minqin. Originally he had wanted to lease a larger parcel, but another Minqin farmer beat him to it. He settled for a farm totaling 120 mu on a three-year lease—an affordable arrangement given that land rent in IM was only a third of the rate in Jinchang. Xiao Liu's farm was fed entirely by groundwater. But the farm is in Alxa Right Banner of IM, not Minqin. Groundwater in Alxa Right Banner came at a low tariff, with few restrictions on irrigation, and best of all, no IC key-controlled groundwater meters.

The only problem was that the water was salty, even when drawn from a 100-meter-deep tube well. Thus, Xiao Liu and his wife grew saline-tolerant fennel and sunflowers and bought drinking water from the owner of a sweet water well 45 kilometers from their rental farm. Compared to onions, fennel and sunflowers were less capital- and labor-intensive, and they enjoyed a relatively stable market price. In an unrestricted area with low land rent and water fees, the Lius ran a larger farm to offset the lower profit margins of the crops. During the harvest and planting seasons, the young couple trucked in four to six farm hands from Minqin to work for a couple of weeks at a time, for whom the Lius provided room and board. In 2014, Xiao Liu netted 50,000 yuan from his sunflowers and another 30,000 yuan from the fennel. When I met him in the summer of 2015, Xiao Liu was hopeful for the year's harvest, ensured by a "sufficient amount of pesticides" that he had applied. He also told me that if he were to come out in the red in 2015, he would quit farming the next year. The following summer, I went back to Xiao Liu's rented farmhouse, only to find a new family there.

All in all, small family farmers were much affected by Minqin's scarcity-framed conservation restrictions while benefitting little from the opportunity-framed growth programs. To make a sustainable living, those who stayed in farming had to spread out beyond Minqin to dodge the restrictive conservation policies.

Jin Three faced a two-hour-long commute between his home and the rented farms in a neighboring city within Gansu. Xiao Liu, who was less well-endowed, had to sojourn further to the more marginal and cheaper land in western IM. While Jin Three commuted on a weekly basis, Liu and his wife spent five continuous months in Alxa Right Banner during the growing season from May to September, and returned to their home village in Minqin after the harvest.

The puzzle here is not just how the farmers keep moving in order to continue farming, but what is there to hold onto in farming and in the home village situated in a crisis zone that promised so little? Given the daunting odds in farming the increasingly salty soil, why didn't Jin Three and Xiao Liu just quit farming altogether, as had 300 million other Chinese rural-urban migrant workers?

As mentioned earlier, Jin Three and Xiao Liu had few other options. It was difficult to find worthwhile jobs in the city, especially in the post-financial crisis era. Quite a few Minqin villagers indeed went to the city during their twenties, in the 1980s and early 1990s. Many of them returned to their home villages after a decade or so, as they aged, and as urban job markets tightened. Jin Three and Xiao Liu faced similar constraints on the urban labor market. But they also had another reason for retaining strong ties to Minqin: their children's schooling.

III.2 Moving Up

Minqin was known for two things. At the national level, it was known to be at the center of China's environmental crisis. Within Gansu Province, Minqin was recognized for its unusually high-performing K-12 schools. Most rural schools in China, especially those in poor regions, were losing out to urban schools and had been closing down since the 2000s.[79] But Minqin's public school system, against all odds, has continued to send a disproportionate number of high school graduates to China's top universities, including Peking and Tsinghua in Beijing. Minqin's middle and high schools, and even its primary schools, are considered among the best in the Hexi Corridor, second only to schools in the provincial capital of Lanzhou.

For village parents with school-aged children, staying in Minqin meant remaining eligible for attendance in Minqin's high-performing public schools. While some attributed Minqin schools' exceptional records to their unique literati tradition since the late imperial era, the Minqin County leaders preferred to see them as the success of government policies. With few other things to show for in a county of low GDP, the county government has formulated its policy mandate as "strengthening the county through investing in education," (*jiaoyu lixian*) and focuses its resources on maintaining the their schools' competitive edge. But most people I talked to in Minqin believed that the success should also be given credit to Minqin parents' willingness to devote their resources to children's schooling. "Children's academic success is these farmers' only hope for social mobility," a high school English teacher in Minqin told me.

But attending schools in Minqin, even though they are all public schools, requires substantial financial commitment. The best schools were located in the county seat of Minqin, not in the townships or villages where most farmers lived. In the mid-2000s, under the policy of "abolishing villages and merging townships" (*chexiang bingzhen*), most village schools in rural China were closed. Since then, village children have been attending schools in townships and county seats far away from their village homes. The spatial, social and economic impact of school consolidation has been particularly palpable in the rural northwest, given the immense terrain and low population density of the region. In Minqin, primary and middle schools in the county seat, usually located even further away than township schools from most village homes, are generally believed to offer higher quality education, hence better preparing children for the star high schools. High-ranking high schools in the county seat promise admission to high-ranking universities in big cities. To increase their children's chances of getting into prestigious universities, which promise urban white-collar jobs, many parents would pass up the inferior township schools and send their children to star schools in Minqin's county seat starting from a young age (see Chapter 9). The younger they were, oftentimes starting at ages six or seven, the greater their chance to "win at the starting line." One parent or grandparent would move with the young school-aged child to the county seat, which added to living costs and reduced available labor at the home farm. School expenses, after-school tutoring fees, and the cost of urban living were all major household expenditures for peasant families.

Jin Three's sons were 10 and 12 years old when I first met them in the summer of 2014. Both boys attended schools in Minqin's county seat. To accommodate their need to stay close to school and to attend after-school tutoring sessions that often ran until ten o'clock in the evening, Jin Three, who worked hard and saved even harder, managed to purchase a small apartment unit in the county seat that was a 40-minute car ride from their village home. His wife stayed with their two sons in the apartment while school was in session, and returned to the village during summer and winter breaks. The two sons' schooling and living expenses in the county's urban center cost about 50,000 yuan a year, more than one-third of Jin Three's annual earnings in a good year. Jin Three was also beset by another issue: his older son had been experiencing acute pain in his right knee and calf for three years. Each of their dozens of visits to the hospital in the provincial capital, Lanzhou, cost a few thousand yuan, and the boy's condition was worsening. These education and medical bills had to be paid for by the forbidden crop of onions.

The other farmer, Xiao Liu, had a similar aspiration but a much smaller savings account to invest in his children's future. When I met them in 2015, Xiao Liu's son was 17, and his daughter was 10. The children also attended public schools in the Minqin county seat, while the parents worked 150 kilometers away on their sunflower farm in western IM. Xiao Liu could not afford to buy an apartment in Minqin's county seat for his children, nor could anyone from the family move with the children to the county seat. Instead, the children stayed in the school dormitory, a less desirable option because the children would receive limited attention there. The cost for two children's schooling and living amounted to 20,000 yuan a year, about 35% of Xiao Liu's annual income. This percentage is consistent with a 2012 survey of 110 households in four Minqin villages.[80] The survey shows that the cost of school fees, tutoring sessions, and urban living often accounted for between a third to half of total household expenditures in rural Minqin. Parents led frugal lives to save money for their children's schooling. With such heavy investment in schooling, Minqin parents aspire for their children to secure a good job upon graduation from a high-ranking university. Preferably, the job would be one in the state sector in a metropolitan center like Lanzhou, the provincial capital of Gansu, or even better, further away in the national political and economic centers of Beijing, Shanghai, Shenzhen or Guangzhou. The family's future, in other words, lies beyond the salty soil of Minqin, and their success is measured by the distance they manage to move away from it.

School children seemed receptive to the expectations. Many of my visits to villagers in Minqin took place during children's summer recess from school. While I talked to the parents, their primary schoolers did their summer homework with impressive concentration. The young children sat at the table working on math problems and writing compositions, undistracted by the adults' chatter. It is one thing for parents to invest in schooling and push their children to study hard, but it is another to see seven- and eight-year-olds sitting still and doing homework for an hour-long stretch without having to be nagged. It is telling that the biggest family celebration in Minqin, one that warrants a whole roasted lamb banquet, is not for a wedding nor for a grandparent's birthday, but a high school graduate's admission to a prestigious college in a big city.[81]

Their children's education was the primary reason for Jin Three and Xiao Liu to keep roots in Minqin while breaking their backs laboring on farms outside of Minqin. This strategy of spreading out is formulated along spatial and temporal axes. Spatially, the village home and the farm are separated, and farmers move their farms from site to site in the neighboring region beyond the reach of conservation restrictions. Temporally, keeping the home in Minqin for schooling, while farming in places with greater land and water accessibility, was a bid to not just sustain the livelihood in the present, but also elevate future generations out of farming. The short-term spatial arrangement is motivated by aspirations to improve the family's social standing in the long run. In many cases, this long-term goal would take multiple generations to reach, if at all.

In Jin Three's family, at least three generations have engaged in this aspiration for upward social mobility, starting with Jin Three's father, Old Jin.

Old Jin was born in 1946 in Minqin, in the same village where Jin Three still lived. Old Jin was the third in a family of five sons and a widowed mother. Their family plot was too small to support the five growing sons. To support their own families, some of the sons had to make a living elsewhere. In 1971, at the age of 25, Old Jin was recruited to work as a messenger in a government office in Tianzhou County, located in the mountains of southern Gansu. Old Jin got the job because he was known as a daredevil in the village. The Tianzhou office needed a young man gutsy enough to ride a horse on the winding, unpaved, and extremely windy mountain trails between dispersed villages and townships, to deliver governmental documents. After working as a messenger for a few years, Old Jin was promoted to a safer job as a cook in the county's party school and guest house. A quick learner, he turned himself into an electrician, then moved up to being an electricity fee collector, and then was promoted further to a buyer position in the county's electricity bureau. Eventually, Old Jin made it onto the state payroll and became a low-ranking state employee. He had made a decisive step up from peasantry into the state sector, albeit in a mountainous county that was even more peripheral and more poor than Minqin. His transformation from a "dirt-eating" peasant to an eater of "commodity grain" (see Introduction) provided by the state, which came with his state-sector job, made him the object of many fellow villagers' envy at the time.

Old Jin got married and had three sons in the mountain county of Tianzhu. In 1981, at the outset of village decollectivization, Old Jin's wife and their three sons moved back to Minqin to secure their share of redistributed village land. Old Jin stayed on at his job in Tianzhu. His state employee status prevented him from re-establishing his residency in the village, so he lost his entitlement to land allocation. As a result, the Jins had four officially recognized village residents, and they received a total of 16 mu of land. It was far from enough to support the family's three growing sons. Each of Old Jin's three sons followed a distinct career path. Each of which are representative of Chinese peasants' options for upward mobility.

Old Jin's eldest and brightest son, Big Jin, tried the academic route. Big Jin graduated from the reputable Northwestern Normal University in Gansu's capital city of Lanzhou. It was a respectable achievement for his background. China's provincial Normal Universities train middle and high school teachers, and graduates were guaranteed teaching jobs at that time. Many graduates went on to work in the government after a few years of teaching. Normal universities, thus, trained not just teachers, but also bureaucrats. Provincial Normal Universities were an initial step for hardworking farm boys and girls to move out and up (see Chapter 9).

But upon Big Jin's graduation, by Old Jin's account, the Jin family's social connections were too weak to secure Big Jin a desirable post. Old Jin's marginal position in a county office in the remote mountains was only sufficient to land Big Jin a teaching job in a middle school in another poor county, of which Gansu Province has quite a few. The year was 1993, right after China's reformist leader Deng Xiaoping's legendary visit to the south in 1992. Deng's visit to China's pioneer region of open-door policies in the south signaled the state leader's commitment to deepening market reforms, and the country was basking in optimism for the future. Not long after starting, Big Jin left his secure but unpromising teaching job in a poor county of a poor province in the poor northwest. He went to the booming southern coastal city of Guangzhou to work in a rubber factory, a job that paid three times more than his middle school teaching job in Gansu. However, the bookish Big Jin did not get along with his coworkers or his manager who came from other provinces and subsequently lost the job. He circled back to the northwest to work for a metal refinery, and then an interior design contractor. Coming to terms with the reality that manual labor was not his strength, the former middle school teacher studied hard and passed the basic-level civil service exam to become a state employee and was assigned a marginal position in Zhangyi Municipality, the largest city in the Hexi Corridor. Again, according to Old Jin, Big Jin's meager income was insufficient to buy his way into a better government job in Zhangyi, which eventually dampened his career ambitions. Big Jin, the best educated of the three Jin brothers, is now back in the Tianzhu Mountains, where he was born, teaching in a local high school and holding private tutoring classes to supplement his income. As Old Jin recounted his eldest son's life history to me, he made a passing comment that Big Jin did not join the Communist Party, hinting at the correlation between Big Jin's lack of party membership and his rocky career path in the public sector. Old Jin did not get into the details about whether Big Jin was unwilling or unable to join the Party, and I was reluctant to probe the old man's regrets any further.

Old Jin's second son, Jin Two, however, did join the Communist Party. Jin Two also joined the army, another quintessential route Chinese peasants take to move out and up. Jin Two's original plan was to gain some technical skills in the army, such as telecommunications or engineering, and use those skills to earn a living after separating from the army. Unfortunately, Jin Two spent six years in a parachute unit that did not involve much training in marketable skills. Meanwhile, he was dispatched on a rescue mission during the infamous super flood event along the Yangtze River Basin in the summer of 1998. The assignment deeply distressed Jin Two's mother. Throughout her son's heroic mission fighting the super flood in the south, she was "glued to the TV screen" at home, following every update about the flood and praying for her son's safe return. Jin Two left the army soon after that mission. Old Jin spent all his social (and some economic) capital on securing Jin Two a state-sector job at the water resource bureau in Tianzhu, his own career base, before his own retirement. But Jin Two, then in his mid-20s, was too restless to stick to a low-paying job in the mountains. He took a leave of absence and ventured out. He first invested his savings from the years in the parachute unit in an earth mover for hire in land reclamation sites and quarries. He then dipped into a gold mining venture in southern Gansu, and later joined a tube well construction crew that traveled through the Hexi Corridor. But none of these ventures took him far enough. So, Jin Two, the adventurous veteran parachutist, like Big Jin, returned to his old government job inherited from his father in mountainous Tianzhu in 2010, and settled in the place where he was born.

The youngest son, Jin Three, the onion farmer, was born in 1978. Jin Three did not show much academic promise nor ambition to venture outside of the farm. He stayed in the village to work the family farm. In the early 1990s, a period of high optimism in China, while the college-educated Big Jin abandoned his teaching job and tried to make it in the southern city, local leaders in the northwest mobilized peasants to "open up wasteland" in the desert. Minqin villagers responded to the call with great enthusiasm. After Jin Three graduated from middle school, he, too, caught the "fever of land reclamation" in Minqin in 1995. Jin Three told me it was his chance to make up for the land the family had lost during the 1990 land readjustment, as mentioned earlier. At the age of 17, carrying a water pump and a tank of diesel fuel, Jin Three set off with a group of relatives on tractors to open new farmland. They went to the upper reaches of the Shiyang River Basin, about 80 kilometers southwest of the Minqin Oasis. Their destination was in the dune fields, locally known as *shawozi*. *Shawozi* is a type of lowlands in between semi-mobile dunes at the edge of the desert, where the water table is high and groundwater is free for abstraction. *Shawozi* soil is also more conducive to cropping. It normally has higher clay and silt content than the sandy soil around it, and its topsoil is thicker than the gravel gobi further west. Out of the 100 mu of land that Jin Three's group had reclaimed in 1995, Jin Three received a share of 14 mu, on which he grew melons and sold the melon seeds. He netted 25,000 to 30,000 yuan a year for the next five years. At the time, labor and inputs for farming were relatively cheap, and market demand was high. Jin Three managed to save enough money for his wedding, which took place a few years later.

But the 1990s were also a time when the frequency and magnitude of sandstorms in China's northwest were on the rise. On May 5, 1993, two years before Jin Three went off to reclaim land in the *shawozi*, Minqin was hit by a super sandstorm that destroyed over 300,000 mu of farmland. Since then, major sandstorms have been recorded multiple times each spring, with numerous minor storms interspersed on a weekly basis. Of his time opening land, Jin Three recalled the toil of leveling the sandy terrain with earth movers and hand tools, drilling wells, and plowing the *shawozi* in the stormy springs. He slept in a teepee-shaped shed and only after two years did his group manage to build a small mud house, and they lived with cracks in their walls and sand in their rice bowls.

In 2000, the fifth year of Jin Three's melon farming in the *shawozi*, the Returning Farmland to Forest—or the "Grain for Green" campaign—was launched in the Hexi Corridor. Peasants who were previously encouraged to reclaim land were now forbidden from working the reclaimed land. Jin Three's reclaimed land was in an area earmarked for retirement to fill the local "Grain for Green" quota. Local officials gave Jin Three two options: he could either forfeit his 14 mu of reclaimed land, or he could keep the land in exchange for growing the policy plants of suosuo and red willows instead of his preferred melon on the land. For the latter, he also needed to take up the responsibility of keeping the seedlings of the policy plants alive until they passed the inspection. Jin Three chose to forfeit the land and let his cousin take it over and deal with the officials' demands. He felt that he had made the right decision, because by 2016, the farming ban in that area was still in place and his cousin was stuck with the land. What Jin Three was not aware of was that in 2001 an archaeological research team reported that the area near his reclaimed land in the *shawozi* was a part of the famous "Shajing Culture" area from 2,500 to 3,000 years ago. The official confirmation of the historical value of the area led to a discussion of designating and enclosing the area for heritage preservation. This would have only further dampened the prospects of farming the reclaimed land ever again, had Jin Three kept his reclaimed land back in 2000.

After Jin Three forfeited his 14 mu of reclaimed land in the *shawozi* under the "Grain for Green" campaign in 2000, he lost another three mu in his village during the Sealing Wells and Reducing Croplands campaign in 2007. To cope, Jin Three worked hard on the rented land in Jinchang. To make his heavy capital investment pay off, he worked the rented land hard. More challenges arose: the deteriorated soil of the rented land required an increasing amount of fertilizers and pesticides; and the cost of the chemical inputs, water, seedlings, labor, and land lease fees continued to soar.

The pressure for Jin Three's two school-age sons to move out and up could not be any greater. Old Jin, the grandfather, tried his best to break out of the village, yet only reached the bottom rung of the state bureaucracy in a remote mountain. Old Jin's three sons—Big Jin, Jin Two, and Jin Three—tried to seize the opportunities of their times, but none of them went very far. Now it was Jin Three's two sons' turn to take the baton in the relay.

In the summer of 2016, upon my third visit to Jin Three's home, Jin Three's older boy was not there. He was sent to Big Jin's home in Tianzhu for the summer. Now that Big Jin had returned to teaching high school, he organized tutoring sessions for students in Tianzhu, where parents were also eager to move their children out of the mountain villages through investing in children's education. Jin Three's son was sent to Big Jin's tutoring class for the summer to prepare for the upcoming high school entrance exam.

Looking ahead, Jin Three's investment in his two sons' education and the family's future is far from risk free. In rural China, this exit strategy seemed to have worked for the first two decades of market reform, if the mushrooming new apartment buildings in the Minqin county seat serve as any evidence. Successful Minqin students who landed good jobs after college bought apartments in the county's urban center for their hardworking parents. The parents may or may not move into in these apartments, but simply owning an apartment in the city that their children bought for them was an important sign of a family making their first step towards a metropolitan future.

The barrier of entry for this exit strategy has been rising, however. Since the mid-2000s, the average university tuition rate in China has increased twentyfold, while the national average income has increased only fourfold. On average, education expenses account for more than 30% of total expenditures for peasant households, and many poor families fall deep into debt to pay for school fees and schooling-related urban living expenses. In the post-financial crisis economy, tuition hikes have been followed by rising unemployment rates of college graduates.[82] As schooling took an increasingly larger bite into the household budget throughout the 2000s, parents who had planned to pay back the education debt after their college graduate children found high-paying jobs were stuck with lofty debts.[83] As many college graduates from Minqin were unable to land desirable white-collar jobs in the big city, some returned to Minqin to teach in K-12 schools, an increasingly competitive option. Like Big Jin, they also tried to supplement their income by tutoring students who, like the returned college graduates themselves, aspired to leave the hard life of farming one day. The dream was getting harder to materialize, but the alternatives seemed harder still to find.

To sum up the politics of scarcity and opportunity in contemporary Minqin, the "ecological refugees" of Minqin have strategized to survive not just environmental deterioration, but also the state programs of environmental conservation. Minqin was lifted from a forgotten corner to the center of the state's attention in the age of conservation. What came with such attention were the extra funding, water transfers, and policy exemptions to turn Minqin into a national model of conservation success. The story of Minqin's rise to stardom and the resources that came with the fame may not be representative of rural China's environmental predicaments today. However, Minqin's exceptional circumstances also reveal much about what it takes to materialize the regime of productive conservation on the ground, and what such a regime can and cannot deliver even in best-case scenarios. Most of all, while Minqin stood out in the eyes of state leaders in Beijing, it has not escaped the everyday politics of resource struggles in rural China.

Minqin's unique policy status and its villagers' entrenched resource struggles reveal the contradictory and co-productive relationship between constructed and lived scarcity, and between constructed and lived opportunity.

In terms of scarcity, under the official framing, the village farmers' "wasteful" water use and "disordered" land reclamation have made it necessary for the state to launch the programs of sealing wells and reducing croplands. On the ground, villagers' lived scarcity was shaped by both ongoing water struggles in the dryland and the politics of surviving water conservancy restrictions. To minimize tensions that could aggravate social instability, local officials executed the contested policies by avoiding permanent damage of the sealed wells and by diffusing the responsibility of which wells to seal to village collectives. As a result, the majority of the sealed wells were low-yielding ones, hence making the least impact on water conservancy. Such implementation gaps are not just a compromise. They are, in fact, what has enabled the unpopular conservation programs. Local officials and villagers also navigated the groundwater metering system, another scarcity-induced measure in water conservancy. Local officials used the IC-metered water pumps to enforce villagers' compliance with planting policy crops, while villagers would tamper with the water meters to evade mounting water charges. In both cases of well-sealing and metering, the constructed scarcity and the lived scarcity enable and derail one another. Such a contradictory yet co-productive relationship is mediated by the local officials who need to answer to their superiors while keeping a lid on the mounting hydro-social tensions in Minqin.

As for constructed opportunity, projects like promoting the unpopular crops of the Three Reds, local officials offered both sticks (i.e., withholding irrigation water) and carrots (i.e., granting extra land and water) to win villagers' cooperation. For villagers, their lived opportunities materialized through bargaining for more carrots, evading the sticks, and seeking land and water on the black market. As with the everyday politics of scarcity, it is a cat-and-mouse game in which frictions are never far away.

In the politics of opportunity, there is yet another actor, agricultural capital of varied sizes. Under conservationism, agricultural investors presented themselves as green entrepreneurs. Under the national government's drive to modernize agricultural sectors, local officials have tried to partner with green entrepreneurs to build capital-intensive industrial farms. In Minqin, these green entrepreneurs have actively shaped the opportunity programs on the ground through ecologically branded land consolidation. The capital-intensive plantations are built on retired land-turned "ecological land," and fed by "ecological water" from interbasin water transfers or specially granted access to groundwater. While the green entrepreneurs took advantage of access to otherwise restricted funds, land, and water to build large plantations, they did not always plant the officially promoted drought- and saline-tolerant crops. As green entrepreneurs were instrumental in enabling conservation programs in Minqin, they also veered off from conservationism's main goal.

Together, Minqin's local officials, villagers, and green entrepreneurs tell a place-driven story about scarcity and opportunity. As these actors converged in Minqin and interacted with one another under Minqin's regime of water conservancy, they collaborated, negotiated, evaded, and/or competed with one another. Their multidirectional interactions with intended and unintended results have blurred the usual dichotomic division between an oppressive state and an oppressed (or resistant) society.

In addition, a place-driven story is not a story confined to a bounded space. The conservation programs in Minqin are sustained by itinerant farmers spreading their intensive farming to neighboring areas that were not zoned for conservational restrictions. In their response to the call for modern industrial farming, local state-sponsored green entrepreneurs extended their large-scaled plantations into the heart of the desert. At different spatial scales and through divergent paths, these state and non-state actors shared the territorial strategy of expanding cultivation beyond the heavily regulated conservation zones. Under the regime of productive conservation, it was the expansion of production that enabled restrictive conservation. Meanwhile, production expansion in the drylands has derailed environmental protection. From such territorial tension between expansion and restriction, between enabling and derailing, and between co-production and counter-production arises the agricultural futures of the salty soil in China's northwest.

Notes

1. Mehta, Lyla. 2005. *The Politics and Poetics of Water: Naturalizing Scarcity in Western India*, p. 196. New Delhi: Orient Longman.
2. Barnes, Jessica. 2014. *Cultivating the Nile: The Everyday Politics of Water in Egypt*. Durham, NC: Duke University Press.

3. Water Conservancy Department and Committee of Development and Reform of Gansu Province. 2007. "Shiyangheliuyu zhongdianzhiliguihua [Strategic Management Plan of Shiyang River Basin]." https://www.ndrc.gov.cn/fggz/fzzlgh/gjjzxgh/200806/P020191104623858217901.pdf. Accessed January 8, 2025.
4. Zhu, Youdi. 2015 [1994]. "Xibeiqueshuibeihoude zhenshi [The real story behind northwest's water shortage]." In *Houwangshu [Book of Looking Back]*, pp. 158–200. Beijing: Lianhe Publishing Company.
5. Like other figures of cultivated land, this "900,000 mu" in the official reports and government leaders' speeches should be seen as a concept. It is cited not for its statistical precision, and government reports are often inconsistent. In the 1994 edition of the *Minqin County Gazetteer*, for example, the "900,000 mu cultivated land in Minqin" was cited (p. 193) but late in the chapter. When the figures were listed district by district, the Hongyashan district alone, which is the largest in Minqin and the center of the water crisis, had 980,000 mu (p. 200), exceeding the county's reported total of 900,000. Both figures were from 1985. Since then, Minqin's cultivation area has much increased, especially at the height of land reclamation in the 1990s. A local researcher estimated that Minqin's actual area of cultivation could be around 1.0 to 1.2 million mu before the reduction policies started in 2007. The gap between the official and actual figure is no less than 100,000 mu, one-ninth of the total. This information gap suggests the widespread phenomenon of "phantom land," on which I will elaborate later in this chapter. The gap also suggests that in the arid region, cultivated land, registered or not, is often abandoned or let to rest after the thin top soil is exhausted, or water has run out. It is therefore difficult to keep track of the total amount of land that is cultivated but not planted or land that is planted but not irrigated regularly. The restrictive policies and growth projects under the regime of productive conservation complicate bookkeeping even further.
6. According to a local official I interviewed in the summer of 2016, the quota system works as follows. In Lake Irrigation District, where the soil is most salinized, the quota is 485 cubit meters per mu; in Dam District it is 480 cubit meters per mu; in Quanshan District, it is 450 cubit meters per mu. Three-fifths of the allocation is composed of surface water, two-fifths is groundwater.
7. Wu, Jianfu et al. 2015. "Qiantan minqinxian shuiziyuan guanli qingkuang [A preliminary discussion of Minqin's water resource management]." *Gansu Agriculture* 17 (395): 58–59. The authors were engineers in Minqin County's water resource bureau.
8. Another example is that, in the records of the first two years of the campaign when momentum was high, each sealed well was associated with a figure of cropland size reduction. But for the remaining three years of the campaign, these figures—a critical indicator for the success of water conservancy campaign—were absent.
9. Interview of Minqin officials, 2013; also see He, Haining. 2010. "Gansuminqin shishangzuiyanlide jieshuizhisha [The most rigorous measures of water conservancy and sand control in Minqin's history]." *Southern Weekend*, April 17. http://www.infzm.com/content/43298. Accessed July 2, 2023.
10. For parallels, see the Introduction and Chapters 1 and 2 for details on ecological relocation programs in pastoral regions.
11. The breakdown of the absentee residents in the four townships was 518 in Hongshaliang, 1,153 in Shoucheng, 2,638 in Dongzhen, and 4,976 in Xiqu. Xiqu is the epicenter of Minqin's crisis zone. It is also where most of Minqin's "ecological relocatees" came from. But Xiqu's residents still kept their residency in Xiqu after relocation in order to maintain their entitlements to land and water.

12. See Chapter 2 for a similar situation in the enforcement of grazing bans in the pastoral area. China-based researchers have labeled this mode of governance, which can be found in many areas of regulation enforcement from environmental and traffic regulation to family planning, "substituting penalty for governance," or *yifa daiguan*). See, for example, Huang, Pei. 2016. "Yifadaiguan xingzhengzhifafangshi shengchengde zhidujiliyanjiu [Substituting penalty for governance: A study of the structure of regulation enforcement]." *Politics and Law* 5: 13–25.
13. Rutkowski, Ryan. 2014. *The Economics of H2O: Water Price Reforms in China.* Washintgon D. C.: Peterson Institute for International Economics. July 22. https://piie.com/blogs/china-economic-watch/economics-h2o-water-price-reforms-china. Accessed June 16, 2023.
14. Sui, Fumin, Taichang Wu, and Li Wu. 2007. *Gansu Wuwei Huangyangzhen chengxiangfazhan yitihua fazhanzhilu [The Path towards Rural Urban Integrated Development in Huangyang Township, Wuwei, Gansu]*, p. 97. Beijing: China Social Sciences Press.
15. Liao, Yongsong et al. 2008. "China's water pricing reforms for irrigation: Effectiveness and impact." Comprehensive Assessment of Water Management in Agriculture, Discussion Paper 6. Colombo: International Water Management Institute.
16. In some areas, as irrigated land expanded, municipal and county-level water bureaus would build pumping stations for groundwater and channel the groundwater into irrigation networks to supplement surface water. But, overall, this hierarchy of irrigation systems is built around surface water.
17. Jiao, Changchuan. 2011. "Nongtianshuilijiufen yu xiangcunzhixu: ezhong W cun diaocha [Conflicts over irrigation water and social order in the rural areas: Investigation of village W in central Hubei Province]." *Law and Social Sciences* No 8: 1–26.
18. Chen, Bofeng and Huihuang Lin. 2011. "Nongtian shuilide fangongdi beiju yanjiu [Tragedy of the anti-commons in irrigation systems]." *Renwen Zazhi [Journal of Humanities]* No 6: 144-153. In his studies of the irrigation system in rural Hubei Province, Luo, Xingzuo (2006) also found that the increasing conflicts over individualized water fee payment and rotational water use among village households had contributed to the collapse of local irrigation operation, which in turn led to man-made droughts. See Luo, Xingzuo. 2006. *Zhishui: guojiajieruyu nongminhezuo [Water Governance: State Intervention and Peasants' Collaboration]*. pp.63-71. Wuhan: Hubei People's Press.
19. Chu, Guoliang. 2013. "Nongcun gaigeyilai zuidade shiwushi shuili—guanyu 2013 nian zhongguonanfangdahande zhexue sikao [The most devastating mistake of China's rural reform is in irrigation infrastructure: A philosophical reflection on the 2013 great droughts in southern China]." This piece was posted by blogger "Bohantadie" on March 28, 2015. http://www.360doc.com/content/15/0328/08/12847660_458640320.shtml. Accessed September 21, 2018. The link was broken by June 28, 2023.
20. Fictional name.
21. Shi, Lei et al. 2017. "Hanhan queshuiqu minqinxian shuiziyuan chixugaoxiaoliyong cuoshiyanjiu, [Research on measures for sustainable and efficient utilization of water resources in Minqin County, an arid and cold area with water shortages]." *Water Resources Protection* 33 (4): 20–25.
22. For an estimate on global groundwater reserves see Fetter, C. W., Tom Boving, and Dave Kreamer. 2018. *Contaminant Hydrogeology*, p. 1. Long Grove, IL: Waveland Press; Dunne, Thomas and Luna B. Leopold. 1978. *Water in Environmental Planning*, p. 192. San Francisco: WH Freeman and Company; UN World Water Development Report.

2003. "Water for People. Water for Life." United Nations World Water Assessment Program. United Nations Educational, Scientific, and Cultural Organization (UNESCO) and New York: Berghahn Books.

23. For writings on groundwater extraction in different world regions, see, for example, Custodio, Emilio. 2002. "Aquifer Overexploitation: What does it mean?." *Hydrogeology Journal* Vol.10: 254–277; Miliband, Wesley. 2015. "Regulating groundwater in California: Will groundwater sustainability agencies change the landscape?" *Environmental Law Reporter* 12 (45): 11104–11111.
24. Dunne, Thomas and Luna B. Leopold. 1978. Ibid. pp. 193–211.
25. Villholth, Karen and Mark Giordano. 2007. "Groundwater use in a global perspective—can it be managed?" In *Agricultural Groundwater Revolution: Opportunities and Threats to Development*, edited by Villholth, Karen and Mark Giordano, pp. 393–402, p. 331. CABI and Colombo: International Water Management Institute.
26. Mechlem, Kerstin. 2016. "Groundwater Governance: The role of legal frameworks at the local and national level—established practice and emerging trends." *Water* 8 (8): 347. https://doi.org/10.3390/w8080347. Accessed June 17, 2023.
27. Mechlem, Kerstin. 2016. Ibid. The quote is from the legal case of Frazier vs Brown, 12 Ohio St. 294 (1861), which stated: "The existence, origin, movement and course of groundwaters and the causes which govern and direct their movements, are so secret, occult, and concealed, that an attempt to administer any set of legal rules in respect to them would be involved in hopeless uncertainty, and would be, therefore, practically impossible."
28. Villholth, Karen and Mark Giordano. 2007. Ibid. p. 393.
29. For an account of groundwater-fed farming in the American West during the 20th century, see, Reisner, Marc. 1986. *Cadillac Desert: The American West and Its Disappearing Water*. New York: Viking Penguin.
30. Lund, Jay, Josué Medellín-Azuara, and Thomas Harter. 2014. "Why California's agriculture needs groundwater management." California Water Blog, online publication by https://UC%20Davis%20Center%20for%20Watershed%20Sciences. May 26. https://californiawaterblog.com/2014/05/26/why-californias-agriculture-needs-groundwater-management. Accessed June 11, 2023.
31. Weiser, Matt. 2018. "As California Groundwater regulation unfolds, some feel left out." Water News Network, San Diego Water Authority. January 22. https://www.newsdeeply.com/water/articles/2018/01/22/as-california-groundwater-regulation-unfolds-some-feel-left-out. Accessed Nov 15 2018. The link was broken by July 17, 2023. Wee, Heesun. 2015. "Well water metering? Not on my land, say California landowners." NBC News, May 7. https://www.nbcnews.com/storyline/california-drought/well-water-metering-not-my-land-say-california-landowners-n358296. Accessed July 17, 2023.
32. Mechlem, Kerstin. 2016. Ibid. p. 347.
33. Sun, Ronglin et al. 2009. "Urban and rural groundwater use in Zhenzhou China: Challenges in joint management." *Hydrogeology Journal* 17: 1495–1506, p. 1499.
34. Wang, Jinxia et al. 2007. "Agriculture and groundwater development in northern China: Trends, institutional responses and policy options." *Water Policy* 9 (1): 61–74.
35. Villholth, Karen et al. 2013. "Smallholder groundwater irrigation in sub-Saharan Africa: An interdisciplinary framework applied to the Usangu Plains, Tanzania." *Hydrogeology Journal* 21: 1481–1495.

36. Shah, Tushaar et al. 2003. "Sustaining Asia's groundwater boom: An overview of issues and evidence." *Natural Resource Forum* 27: 130–141, pp. 131–132.
37. Shah, Tushaar et al. 2003. Ibid.
38. Wang, Jinxia et al. 2007. Ibid.
39. Elinor Ostrom (1990) identified groundwater as a common pool resource. It is a public good with finite, or subtractive benefits. When one user uses more, less remains for the others. When there is no incentive for users to constrain their resource use, the self-interest of the individual users easily leads to over-exploitation. See Ostrom, Elinor. 1990. *Governing the Commons: The Evolution of Institutions for Collective Action.* Cambridge: Cambridge University Press. Also see Custodio, E. 2002. "Aquifer Overexploitation: what does it mean?" *Hydrogeology Journal* 10: 254–277.
40. See Chapter 3 for Minqin's rise to stardom in China's campaign to combat desertification.
41. Zhang, Lijuan and Jinxia Wang. 2005. "Zhineng IC-ka xitongzai jidianjingguangaizhongde yingyongjiyingxiang [Impact of using Integrated Circuit (IC) card for monitoring tube well water extraction]." *Shuili Jingji [Water Resource & Economy]* 23 (2): 42–44.
42. Interview in Minqin, 2016.
43. Sui, Fumin, Taichang Wu, and Li Wu. 2007. Ibid. p. 97.
44. Wang, Zenong. 2007. "Minqinjieshuijishu biangehanqunongye [Minqin's water saving technology transforms dryland agriculture]." News release on Minqin government website, November 8. http://www.minqin.cn/html/lyfq/200711/08-1710.html. Accessed June 30, 2018. The link was broken by June 17, 2023.
45. Political scientist Yuen Yuen Ang (2016) has argued that the so-called "weak institutions" like China's campaign-style policy implementation has the advantage of mobilizing local energy to focus on targeted policy goals. Under high political pressure and with limited resources, campaign governance is an effective and improvisational approach for local bureaucracy to deliver results. See Yuen Yuen Ang, 2016. *How China Escaped the Poverty Trap*, pp. 171–173. Ithaca: Cornell University Press. A further investigation at the grassroots level over a longer time period in different policy domains and geographical areas may help illuminate the sustainability and efficacy of campaign governance.
46. "Shiyanghe shengkai shengtaijiushuzhihua:shiyangheliuyu riguangwenshi jianshetuixingdiaocha [Flowers of 'ecological salvation' bloom by the Shiyang River: Investigation of promoting greenhouse construction in the Shiyang River Basin]." 2009. Online news posted at http://szb.gsjb.com/jjrb/html/2009-11/19/content_13847.htm. Accessed November 2, 2014. The link was broken by June 17, 2023.
47. Han, Chuanhao. 2008. "Zhengfulitui nongmindizhi, riguangwenshi chujingtaiganga [Government pushes hard and peasants resist hard: Greenhouse farms' thorny situation]." *Jingji cankaobao [Economic Reference News]*, May 26. http://finance.people.com.cn/nc/GB/7,293,283.html. Accessed June 22, 2017. The link was broken by June 17, 2023.
48. The story of the Harvest Township greenhouse incident came from interviews in 2015 and 2016 and online posts. One of the most informative posts is: "Wangyou tucao: gansuminqin shouchengxiang dangweishuji Xuxingwen daitouhuihuaidapeng zhishinongminsunshi shangbaiwan, weiguanzhecheng zhenxiangbutong [Netizen complaint: The party secretary Xu Xingwen of Shoucheng (Harvest) Township in Minqin of Gansu led a gang to destroy peasants' greenhouses and caused more than a million yuan of damage. Onlookers said, '(we) really cannot figure out (why he did this).']" 2014. Online

posting on *Baidu* website. February 16. http://tieba.baidu.com/p/2871966881. Accessed June 22 2016. The link was broken by June 17, 2023.

49. Johnson, Renée and Betsy A. Cody. 2015. "California Agricultural Production and Irrigated Water Use." Report prepared for members and Committees of Congress. Congressional Research Service. June 30. https://sgp.fas.org/crs/misc/R44093.pdf. Accessed April 11, 2024.
50. See Chapter 5 for an ethnoterritorial comparison among China's three major minority autonomous regions, namely, Xinjiang Uyghur Autonomous Region, Tibet Autonomous Region, and Inner Mongolia Autonomous Region.
51. Goji berry, or gouqi in Chinese, is also known as wolfberry. Most of the goji berries produced in China are from the Lycium barbarum L. shrub.
52. There is also a black-colored variety that has gained increasing popularity among Chinese consumers since the 2000s. But the scale of production of black goji is much smaller than that of the red variety.
53. Wen, Shuping et al. 2022. "Woguogouqishichang yuchanye diaochafenxibaogao [Survey and Analysis of China's Goji market and industry]." Report from Bureau of Market and Information, Ministry of Agriculture and Rural Affairs. Posted on Zhihu. April 12. https://zhuanlan.zhihu.com/p/349,217,058. Accessed June 20, 2023.
54. Cui, Jianling. 2020. "Dianliang ningxiazhihong—zhongninggouqide pinpaishijian [Ningxia red: Branding Zongning's gojiberry]." *Nongchanpin Shichang [Agricultural Market]* 14: 8–15; Wan, Majia et al. 2018. "Ningxiazhongninggouqide qianniangujin [A thousand years of Ningxia's goji]." *Guangming Daily*, September 20. https://news.gmw.cn/2018-09/20/content_31270740.htm. Accessed June 20, 2023; Sun, Qing. 2007. "Zhongninggouqi yingxiaozhutide fanzhanxianzhuang, cunzaiwentiji duiceyanjiu [Production and marketing of Zhongning's goji: Problems and solutions]." *Journal of Hebei Agricultural Sciences* 11 (3): 80–81, p. 88.
55. Further research is needed to understand the ethnoterritorial and socioeconomic organization of the goji industry.
56. For Ningxia's attempts to break into the high-end wine market, see Fan, Jiayang. 2018. "Can Wine Transform China's Countryside?." *The New Yorker*, March 12. https://www.newyorker.com/magazine/2018/03/12/can-wine-transform-chinas-countryside. According to Fan, while a select few boutique wineries in Ningxia won international awards, most of the aspiring wine makers—state and private—struggled to stay afloat.
57. According to the report a local official shared with me in 2016, Minqin had planted 138,500 mu of wine grapes, 224,000 mu of red dates, and 102,000 mu of goji, between 2010 and 2015. Altogether there were 464,500 mu, or over 30,000 hectares of the Three Reds.
58. Fictional name.
59. Chen, Longjiang and Qiquan Xiong. 2012. "Zhongguo zhongyekaifang shiyunian huiguyufansi [Reflections on China's seed industry since the opening of the market over a decade ago]." *Journal of South China Agriculture* 7–17.
60. A popular saying likens grassroots officials' juggling numerous demands from above to "pushing a thousand threads through one needle."
61. See Chapter 2 for China's rural land consolidation through similar Dragon Head programs in the pastoral areas. Also see Huang, Philip C. C. et al. 2012. "Capitalization without Proletarianization in China's Agricultural Development. Modern China." 38 (2); and Yan, Hairong et al. 2015. "Agrarian Capitalization Without Capitalism? Capitalist

dynamics from above and below in China." *Journal of Agrarian Change* 15 (3): 366–39, on whether and how post-Mao decollectivization and market expansion in rural China make a case for "capitalization without proletarianization." The trend of land rights consolidation to make industrial farms was key to this debate. For works on the socioeconomic impact of land consolidation since the late 1990s, see, for example, Jiao, Changquan and Feizhou Zhou. 2016. "Zibenxiaxiangyu cunzhuangde zaizao [Capital's move to rural areas and village restructuring]." *Chinese Social Sciences [Zhongguo shehuikexue]* 1: 100–116.

62. Fictional name.
63. Interview with a township official in 2014. The official recalled a public speech given by Minqin County's party secretary in 2013.
64. Zhang, Qian Forrest. 2015. "Class differentiation in rural China: Dynamics of accumulation, commodification and state intervention." *Journal of Agrarian Change* 15 (3): 338–365, p. 351.
65. According to Elizabeth Grinspoon's (2002) study of rural Sichuan's land use and land rights change during the 1990s, when "wasteland" was to be decollectivized and auctioned out to private investors, the definition and designation of "wasteland" was highly flexible. To accelerate the pace of decollectivizing and leasing out the land to private investors, some of the working farms and productive forests were labeled as "wasteland" in order to be eligible for wasteland auctions. See Grinspoon, Elizabeth. 2002. "Socialist Wasteland Auction: Collective Forest Land in China's Economic Transition." PhD dissertation. University of California at Berkeley.
66. Zhu, Xiaoyang. 2011. *Xiaocungushi: dizhiyu jiayuan [Stories of a Small Village: Local History and Homeland]* p. 76. Beijing: Peking University Press. For Zhu's other related work on rural land politics, see Zhu, Xiaoyang. 2008. "Heidi, bingdi, shidi—dianchixiaocunde dizhiyu siketejinlude wenti [Black land, sick land, and lost land—a village in Kunming (Yunnan) and a critique of (James) Scott]." *Journal of China Agricultural University (Social Science edition)* 25 (2): 22–48.
67. See Chapter 3 for details on turning salty soil into cropland. Also, see Chapter 8 for the history of Mongol farmers' land reclamation in eastern Inner Mongolia.
68. See, for example, Di, Jinhua and Zhangbao Zhong. 2014. "Bianqianzhongde jicengzhiliziyuan jiqi zhilijixiao: jiyuhubeixinan hecun heididefenxi [Transformation of local governance: A case study of black land in He Village in southwest Hubei Province]." *Shehui [Chinese Journal of Sociology]* 34: 148–174. The authors reported that during the land reclamation campaign in the village studied in 1953, a production team reported only 200 mu out of the actual 500 mu of reclaimed land (p. 155). A similar story was told by Jin Three, a Minqin villager who had participated in Minqin's land reclamation in the 1990s. See the last section of this chapter for stories about Jin Three and his family.
69. Case studies from elsewhere indicated that some of the government-subsidized industrial farms had shifted to agrotourism, and only a very small portion of the land was used for agricultural production. See, for example, the studies of Hubei and Chongqing by Jiao, Changquan and Feizhou Zhou. 2016. "Zibenxiaxiangyu cunzhuangde zaizao [Sending down capital to the countryside and village reconstruction]." *Chinese Social Science* 1: 100–116. But Minqin had little potential for agrotourism development. It is far from metropolitan centers and its soil erosion was not dramatic enough to build disaster tourism like areas where the Yellow River cuts through the Loess Plateau and creates spectacular trenches that can be over a hundred meters deep.

70. Shi, Lei et al. 2017. "Ganhanqueshuiqu minqinxian shuiziyuan chixugaoxiaoliyong cuoshiyanjiu [Research on the sustainable and efficient utilization of water resources in Minqin, an arid region with water shortages]." *Water Resources Protection* 33 (4): 20–25.
71. Wang, Heng et al. 2017. "Gansu conghuanghe diaoshui jishamozhikun [Gansu Province transfers water from the Yellow River to rescue the desert]." XinhuaNet. January 3. http://www.xinhuanet.com/politics/2017-01/03/c_129430456.htm. Accessed April 23, 2023.
72. Zhang, Xuejiang. 2018. "Yashaqiushui-wuweiminqin qingtuhu chongxianbibo [Suppress sand and search for water—Qingtu Lake reappears in Minqin of Wuwei Municipality]." *Meiritoutiao [Daily Headlines]*, May 30. https://kknews.cc/other/ne24p8g.html. Accessed June 22, 2023.
73. Interview with a local researcher in 2016.
74. Fictional name.
75. Fictional name.
76. In the summer, Jin Three hired two local workers to weed once every three days, for 100 yuan per person per day. During the planting and harvesting seasons, he would recruit workers from Minqin. When there was labor shortage in the harvest season, he turned to traveling farm hands from Henan Province. Like several other villagers I met in Minqin, Jin Three considered Minqin workers to be more diligent than migrants from other provinces.
77. During the interviews, farmers rarely included their own labor when calculating the overall production costs.
78. Fictional name.
79. See Chapter 9 for the consolidation of rural schools in China since the 1990s.
80. Unpublished survey results, shared by a local researcher in 2015.
81. As a part of the gift-exchange economy, the banquet also serves to raise funds for the child's college education. The guests would gift the host with cash in red envelops to payback or to accumulate "debts of interpersonal feelings" (*renqingzhai*). See Chapter 9 for a Mongol farming family's experiences.
82. See Chapter 9 for China's expansion in higher education since the 1990s and the rising unemployment rates of college graduates since the 2000s.
83. Liu, Xinwu. 2010. "Minqinjiaoyu huibuhuibu huiningdehouchen? [Will education of Minqin follow the (bad) example of Huining?]." Online publication on a Minqin-focused website. April 26. http://www.minqin.cn/html/whjy/201004/26-5240.html. Accessed on May 12, 2018. The link was broken by June 24, 2023.

INTRODUCTION to Part III:
AGROPASTORAL ENTANGLEMENTS OF INNER MONGOLIA'S TURBULENT STEPPES

In the previous two parts, I consider pastoralism and agriculture separately in order to tell legible stories about complex places and times. But life and livelihoods in northern arid lands are rarely clear-cut. My third ethnographic base, Horqin Right Front Banner (Horqin RF) of Hinggan League in eastern Inner Mongolia Autonomous Region (IMAR), affords an opportunity to look into the mixes and shifts of ethnoterritorial relationships and livelihoods in the dryland environments of Inner Mongolia's steppe, hence the title of Part III, "Agropastoral Entanglements." To disentangle the entanglements in Horqin RF, I first place IMAR in the broader ethnoterritorial map of China today (Chapter 5). Then I trace the tumultuous geopolitical, ethnoterritorial, and environmental histories of cultivation expansion in the three subregions of IMAR over the past three centuries (Chapters 6 to 8). Notes of this Introduction are located at the end of Chapter 5.[1]

Inner Mongolia's Ethnoterritorial Structure in Comparison

In Chapter 5, entitled "Mongols as China's Triple Minority: A Comparison with Tibetans and Uyghurs," I outline the ethnoterritorial dynamics between Han Chinese, China's 91%-strong majority, and Mongols, what I call China's "Triple Minority" at the national, regional, and local levels, in IMAR today. To show the distinctiveness of Mongols as a Triple Minority in their name-sake region, I compare them with Uyghurs in Xinjiang Uyghur Autonomous Region (XUAR) and Tibetans in Tibet Autonomous Region (TAR).

IMAR's ethnoterritorial distinctiveness became evident early on in my fieldwork. Quite a few Mongolian scholars whom I met expressed their misgivings about there being "too many Han Chinese" in IMAR compared to China's two other major minority-named autonomous regions, XUAR and TAR. The statistics are telling. By 2020, Mongols accounted for 17.7% of IMAR's total population of 24 million, while Han Chinese stood at 78.7%, rendering Han Chinese a dominant majority in the Mongol-named Autonomous Region. By contrast, 3.14 million Tibetans have registered their residency in TAR, constituting an 86% majority in TAR's total population of 3.65 million as of 2020, while Han Chinese accounted for 12%. In the same year, the Uyghur population accounted for 45% of XUAR's total of 25.85 million, while Han Chinese accounted for 42.2%.[2] In the latter two cases, Han Chinese weigh much lighter demographically as it does in IMAR.

But what has made these scholars feel as though there are "too many Hans" in IMAR is not just Han Chineses' demographic weight. It is also the omnipresent Han Chinese who are "everywhere," they contend. Unlike Han Chinese in TAR and XUAR who are concentrated in large cities and military-administrative centers, Han Chinese in IMAR are dispersed across IMAR's cities and countryside, creating mosaics of ethnically mixed urban neighborhoods and rural villages alike. In other words, not only does IMAR host a distinctively weighty presence of Han Chinese, compared to TAR and XUAR, it also features an ethnoterritorial structure in which Han Chinese are widely distributed and the ethnic mix penetrates to a much more granular level.

Why does the ethnoterritorial structure matter? For a start, political scientist Erin Jenne (2007)[3] suggested that territorially concentrated ethnic groups are more likely to mobilize around separatist demands than those who are spread out widely and intermixed with other ethnicities. Referencing Jenne, Enze Han (2011)[4] suspected that the low concentration of Mongols, among other factors such as limited overseas connections, explains the fewer protests in IMAR in recent decades compared to in TAR and XUAR, hence a more "tamed" Mongol population. A Hohhot-based scholar I talked to in 2013 believed that IMAR's granular ethnoterritorial structure helped explain, if only partially, the Chinese Communist Party (CCP)'s successful incorporation of IMAR into Communist rule as early as 1947, two years prior to the establishment of the People's Republic of China (PRC), a stark contrast to the formal incorporation of TAR in as late as 1965 and XUAR in 1955. Not that Mongols did not put up a good fight against the Han Chinese-dominant CCP regime. During the first half of the 20th century, many modern Mongol nationalist leaders campaigning for IM's independence came from East IM, where the Mongol population was most concentrated since the early 20th century. The "barbarian bandits," as the Mongol resistors were called by the CCP, staged numerous acts of sabotage in the first few years of the Communists' takeover of IMAR. But their resistance was quickly quashed, unlike the bloodshed of the protracted armed struggles in TAR and XUAR that lasted the first two decades of PRC's establishment in 1949.

Ethnoterritorial structures, it appears, can make a difference in ethnic identity-based mobilization. More research is needed to examine the connection between ethnicity-based mobilizations and ethnoterritorial demands, and whether and how minority protestors' grievances coincide with their ethnic identification. More importantly, unlike what the CCP state presumes, not all minority nationalists (or minority nationals for that matter) are separatists. And unlike what western media often portrays, not all protests in Xinjiang, Tibet, or IM are rooted in exclusively "ethnic" conflicts.[5] Still more investigation will help illuminate not just why and how a minority group mobilizes but also why it does *not* mobilize, as is often the case.[6]

It is beyond the scope of this book to track the mobilizational implications of IMAR's ethnoterritorial structure. Instead, in Chapter 5, I analyse the ethnoterritorial mix and ask: how does IMAR's granular ethnic mix play out at each of the three territorial levels of the national, the regional, and the local, compared to two other minority-named autonomous regions, TAR and XUAR? Such a comparison of ethnoterritorial mixes in China's three major autonomous regions under the CCP may shed light on the question of mobilization. More immediately, the comparison provides geopolitical context for my current inquiry into the agropastoral entanglements in the northern steppe.

Inner Mongolia's Three Agricultural Frontiers from the early 18th Century to the present

Following Chapter 5 on IMAR's ethnoterritorial structure in comparison with XUAR and TAR, I move to disentangle the agropastoral entanglements through the histories of IMAR's cultivation expansion in Chapters 6, 7, and 8.

Cultivation expansion in the Mongolian steppe started from the relatively warmer southern belt immediately north of the Great Wall and moved further to the progressively higher, colder, and dryer north. Along IM's east-west axis stretching over 2,400 kms, cultivation emerged in central IM as early as the 17th century and expanded during the 18th centuries. Next came irrigated farming in the arid west, mainly in the Yellow River Loop Plains, which took off in the mid-19th century. Finally, in the cold-temperate and relatively more humid eastern IM, rain-fed farming has expanded rapidly since the early 20th century and continues to this day. The processes of cultivation expansion across IM's immense and variant terrains of 1.15 million sq. km that sprawl up from its lower southern belt have not been even or eventual. Instead, it has triggered eventful, diverse, and often contentious geopolitical and environmental processes that have taken place over the past four centuries. Different types of territorial dynamisms have evolved in different agricultural frontiers of the northern steppe with lasting ethnoterritorial, environmental, and sociocultural impacts.

The state certainly matters in cultivation expansion in the northern steppes. But the way and the extent to which it matters are conditioned by territorial dynamisms, that is, the interaction between the state, semi-state, and non-state territorial actors in a place at a specific historical juncture. In IM from the 18th to the 20th centuries, the state actors shifted from the imperial court to the Republican and then to the Communist regimes, and the semi-state and non-state actors ranged from Mongol nobles, land barons, warlords, and Catholic missionaries to exiles, bandits, secret societies, and most of all, droves of migrants and refugees of diverse ethnicities. The confluence of these actors has shaped the processes and consequences of cultivation expansion in the Mongolian steppe and its agropastoral dynamics until this day.

To tell the multivocal stories about IM's agropastoral histories, I divide IMAR's immense and diverse terrain into three subregions—the Central, the West, and the East—and present them as three agricultural frontiers in three successive chapters.

In each of these subregion-focused chapters, I focus on the critical time period when large-scale cultivation took shape through different territorial dynamisms under different leading territorial actors.

Chapter 6, "Land Commodification: Emperors and Princes in Central IM in the 18th–19th Centuries" reviews the geopolitical and environmental politics of labor supply, land rights transfer, and land use conversion from the early 18th century to early 19th century. The politics of labor and land were shaped by gaps in policy implementation on the ground. The imperial court of the Manchurian Qing had banned Han Chinese farmers' northbound migration as well as unauthorized commodification of the Mongolian manorial land. However, famines in the south forced open the gate and hordes of Han refugees trekked across the Great Wall to labor in the northern steppe as farm hands. Meanwhile, two territorial powers of Central IM, one the Manchu emperors' Mongol ally, the other the emperors' foes, followed separate yet converging paths of land commodification and financialization that inaugurated the first wave of intensive and expansive farming in late imperial IM.

Chapter 7, "Hydro Turfdoms: Barons, Priests and Bandits in West IM in the 19th–20th Centuries," focuses on the expansion of irrigated farming in Hetao, the Yellow River Loop Plain between the mid-19th and mid-20th centuries in West IM. A pair of rivalrous non-state territorial actors lead the story: the Han Chinese land-water barons and the Belgian Catholic missionary of the Congregation of Immaculate Heart of Mary (*Congregatio Immaculati Cordis Mariae*, CICM). These two actors, or what I call "hydro turfdom builders," divided up the Yellow River Loop Plain where and when state presence was scant. They commanded over large expanses of land, hydraulic infrastructure, capital, labor, and armed forces. As they consolidated their territorial control, they were entrenched in the violent time and place that involved other territorial actors like warlords, bandits, and secret societies. These hydro turfdoms, built on vastly different brands of territorial entrepreneurship, fit neither Wittfogel's model of hydraulic empire nor Geertz's irrigation society.

Chapter 8, "Mongol Farmers: Massacre Refugees in East IM in the 20th–21st Centuries," concerns cultivation expansion in East IM from the early 20th century to the present era. The region boasts the largest concentration of ethnic Mongols in China today. And most Mongols in rural East IM today are farmers, not herders. And many rural Mongol families have been farming for two centuries or even longer. Yet, Mongol farmers hardly exist in the popular imaginary of Mongols. Museums of Mongolian culture and history, even in the heavy agricultural region of Hinggan League in East IMAR, are dominated by displays of Mongol herders on horseback surrounded by flocks of sheep. The policy discourse today has also placed an emphasis on pastoral areas and pastoralists. As a result, farmers and farming areas in IMAR received much less state investment and fewer subsidies. Mongol farmers have fallen through the historical cracks, discursively and politically. To bring Mongol farmers back to the story, I trace the tempestuous history of resource violence and massacre refugees' escape routes that propelled ethnoterritorial and livelihood mixes and shifts across East IM. With ethnographic materials, I zoom in on Horqin Right Front (HRF) Banner of northern Jerim (today's Hinggan) League, then look further into HRF's three sub-banner zones. This ethnoterritorial and environmental history at multiple territorial levels helps contextualize the stories about two Mongol farming families' survival strategies over three generations. By distinguishing "agropastoral" from "pastoagricultural" livelihoods on the ground, I found multiple conservation contradictions arising in HRF's mixed livelihoods in East IM's changing rural economy.

Stories from the three IM agricultural frontiers break from the imaginary of Mongols as perpetual nomadic pastoralists. They also diverge from the usual explanatory model that sees "external stimulation" as the motor behind the northern steppe's transformations. In Chapters 6 and 7 on Central and West IM, I emphasize the interaction between various outsiders and multiethnic locals, not just the reaction of a homogeneous local to a singular outside force. The ethnographic and archival details from East IM in Chapter 8 help to tell more nuanced stories about such variations and spotlight the farming Mongols who transformed the frontier from within. Driven by resource violence and ethnic massacre, the Mongol refugee farmers fled from the early agricultural frontier of Central IM and tried to settle in East IM as inside-outsiders. During the stormy first half of the 20th century, their eastward moves and confrontations with various frontier authorities, Han Chinese settlers and eastern Mongol natives show the entanglements of peoples, identities, and livelihoods in the frontier. Like other stories in this book, these Mongol farmers tell a place-driven story, on which I will elaborate in the concluding chapter of this book.

The three agricultural frontiers that have evolved since the 18th century are important also for their close connections with environmental conservation today. Throughout most of China's imperial period from the 10th century BCE to the 17th century CE, the ever-shifting northern frontiers went through successive rounds of agricultural advancement and withdrawal, precipitated by steppe power shifts and climate changes. Agricultural expansion since the 18th century, however, charged northward with few setbacks, especially as steppe temperatures have been rising since the early 19th century.[7] IMAR's current politics of resource struggle and conservation is to be understood in this broader context of the persistent agrarian transformation since the 18th century. It is also important to note that on the ground, this transformation has not been an absolute or linear transition from pastoralism to agriculture. Instead, it has created mixed and shifting livelihoods in what Chinese policymakers have called the "Interwoven Belt of Agriculture and Pastoralism" (*nongmu jiaocuodai*) spanning 650,000 sq. km in China's continental frontiers. Close to 70% of this swathe of the Interwoven Belt is in today's IMAR, manifesting as a distinctive territorial dynamism of resource struggles, ethnoterritorial relationships, and social and environmental contradictions.

Mapping Inner Mongolia (Supplement to Chapters 6, 7, and 8)

The three Inner Mongolian agricultural frontiers reviewed previously assume different geopolitical positions and follow divergent routes of cultivation expansion.

Figure P.III.1[8] shows IM's three subregions of West, Central, and East and a subdivision of the Central between Central-West and Central-East. This mapping reflects the geopolitical and environmental dynamics of IM since the 18th century and guides the story of Chapters 6, 7, and 8. Jurisdictional boundaries of the northern steppe have been drawn and redrawn multiple times during the long 20th century under the late Imperial, Republican, Japanese, and CCP regimes. For consistency, I use the jurisdictional boundaries and place names of the Qing era in this map. During the Qing, IM included six leagues, two banners west of Hetao and Chahar. Hulunbuir in today's northeast IMAR was not part of IM during the Qing, so it was not included in this map. I pair this Qing-era map with the contemporary jurisdictional map of IMAR in Figure P.III.2.[9]

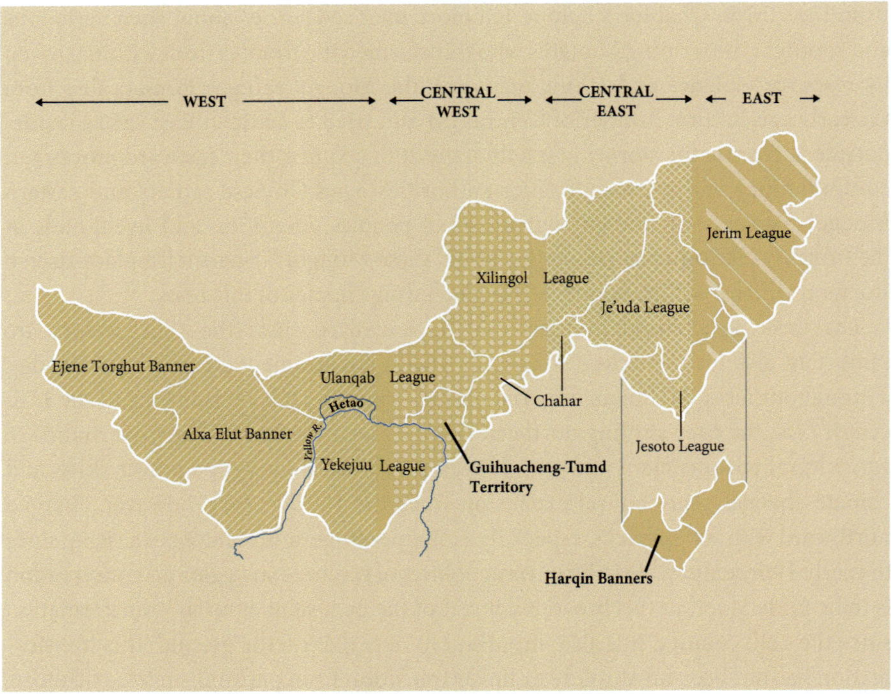

Figure P.III.1 Map of Inner Mongolia's three agricultural frontiers during the Qing Dynasty

Source: Cartographer: Alan Pong, based on Tan, Qixiang et al. 1987.

I draw IM's three agricultural frontiers with the following considerations:

Central IM, the focus of Chapter 6, is divided into Central-West and Central-East.

Central-West IM includes the eastern portions of Ulanqab and Yekejuu Leagues, as well as the Guihuacheng-Tumd territory. These areas were part of Suiyuan Province during the Republican era, and they are divided among Baotou, Ordos, and Hohhot Municipalities and Ulanqab League today. Half of my story in this chapter focuses on the Guihuacheng-Tumd territory of southeast Suiyuan (today's Hohhot), which sits in the center of the Tumd Plain. The dense networks of streams and

Figure P.III.2 Map of contemporary Inner Mongolia Autonomous Region

Source: Cartographer: Alan Pong, based on 2012. *Neimengguzizhiqu ditu [Map of IMAR]*.

fertile soils of the Tumd Plain made it ideal for grazing. But fertile pastures were also the most desirable croplands. The Plain is generally perceived as the earliest site of cultivation in the northern steppe, beginning in the early 16th century.[10]

Central-East IM includes Xilingol League in its eastern half, called Chahar Province during the Republican era, and Je'uda and Jesoto Leagues in its western half, which were part of Rehe Province during the Republican era. Most of Je'uda is included in today's Chifeng Municipality of IMAR, and most of Jesoto is divided among southern Chifeng Municipality and northern Liaoning and Hebei Provinces. Another half of my story in Chapter 6 focuses on Harqin Banner of Jesoto League. Central-East IM has been the site of cultivation expansion since the 17th century and boomed in the 18th century.

West IM mainly refers to Ejene Torghut and Alxa Elut Banners—both of which were incorporated into Ningxia Province during the Republican era—as well as the western portion of Ulanqab and Yekejuu Leagues. Ejene Torghut and Alxa Elut Banners are part of today's Alxa League, the setting for my pastoral stories in Chapters 1 and 2, in which I recount the state and non-state actors' efforts to "fix" the desert and the social and environmental impact of rangeland conservation programs in the contemporary context. In Chapter 7 on Hydro Turfdoms, I focus on the Hetao Plains of Yekejuu, nestled in the northwest pocket of the Yellow River Loop and is incorporated into today's Bayanur Municipality.

East IM is the site of Chapter 8. It mainly refers to Jerim League. In the Republican era, Jerim League was divided into Heilongjiang, Fengtian, and Jilin Provinces, and was redrawn under the Japanese Manchukuo. Today, Jerim League is divided into Hinggan League in the north and Tongliao Municipality, Jilin and Liaoning Provinces in the south. Jesoto, Je'uda, and Jerim Leagues are customarily called the "Three Eastern Leagues" (*dongsanmeng*) of IM. But for the sake of clarity in my stories about the three agricultural frontiers in IM and Mongol farmers' migration from Jesoto and Je'uda to Jerim, I divide the Three Eastern Leagues into "Central-East" (Jesoto and Je'uda) and "East" (Jerim).

5

Mongols as China's Triple Minority: A Comparison with Tibetans and Uyghurs

As the first step towards disentangling Inner Mongolia Autonomous Region (IMAR)'s agropastoral entanglements, this chapter examines what IMAR's ethnoterritorial structure looks like today, and how it differs from that of Tibet Autonomous Region (TAR) and Xinjiang Uyghur Autonomous Region (XUAR).[11] I conclude that the distinctiveness of IMAR's granular ethnoterritorial structure reflects the geopolitical dilemma and ethnoterritorial afflictions that the IM political leaders were confronted with upon the establishment of the autonomous region under the CCP regime.

Let me begin with the role of autonomous regions on CCP China's ethnoterritorial map.

With the political mandate of building a unified country upon the ideal of multinationalism, China has officially classified and recognized 55 minority nationalities since 1954.[12] By 2020, the Han Chinese majority accounted for 91.11% of the nation's population, while the 55 minority nationalities made up the rest, or 8.89% of the total.[13] Small in percentage, the absolute size of China's minority population—125.47 million—is nevertheless approximately double the population of the United Kingdom.

Nationality registers Chinese citizens' relationship with the state. On the citizen identification card, the cardholder's nationality, be it the majority Han or the minority Uyghur, is encoded next to one's headshot, name, gender, date of birth, and address, and concludes with an 18-digit ID number running across the bottom of the card. The nationality defines the citizens' access to resources and sometimes presumes guilt in the case of "separatist" Tibetans and "terrorist" Uyghurs. In the aftermath of the 2008 Lhasa unrest, for example, a Tibetan ID card was sufficient proof of the cardholder's threat to national security, and possession of such an ID would often lead to humiliating interrogations in public and denial of hotel accommodations. The internment of Uyghurs in Xinjiang since 2017 is another blatant case of presumed criminality. Such minority status also enjoys perks: nationality serves

Conserving China's Northwest Frontier. You-tien Hsing, Oxford University Press. © You-tien Hsing (2025).
DOI: 10.1093/9780191903908.003.0006

as the basis for preferential policies in education, employment and promotion. Specific minority benefits in areas like medicine, marriage and birth, land entitlements, among others, have also been created (see Chapter 9 for the evolution of China's minority education policies and their implementation in IMAR).

The ethnonationality classification is territorialized and reinforced by jurisdictional design. This jurisdictional design, like language, education, legal and cultural institutions, is crucial in stabilizing ethnic classification, shaping ethnic identification, and defining ethnic relationships according to the ethnoterritorial order of the nation.

Almost all of China's 20,000 kilometers-long terrestrial national borders are historic homelands of minority nationalities. The minority populations of China, while accounting for about 9% of the total national population, occupy 64% of China's territory. Today, minority territories are organized into five autonomous regions, 30 autonomous prefectures, and 120 autonomous counties and banners. These immense territories are also endowed with rich natural resources. From Beijing's point of view, China's border security and national development are conditioned by the geopolitical relationships between the CCP and the nation's minorities.

But not all minorities are equal in the eyes of state leaders. The territorial significance of minority nationalities in China has followed a hierarchical order, depending on their perceived threat to China's national security.[14] Preferential policies for minorities, such as financial transfers and investment, larger birth quotas, accommodation of minority languages, and preferential college admissions, are tailored accordingly.

Size matters in minority ranking. In 2020, the largest nationality, Zhuangs, had about 19.5 million registered members. Other large minority nationalities, such as Miaos, Yis, Manchus, Huis, and Uyghurs count around 10 to 11 million members each. As for Mongols and Tibetans, the count was 6.3 million and 7 million, respectively.[15] These large nationalities are all ranked high in their political significance.

What matters more than population size is the geopolitical status of the minority nationality. Among the large minorities who occupy large territories, those inhabiting China's Central Asia frontiers, especially Mongols, Uyghurs, and Tibetans have been particularly crucial in the eyes of the state leaders. In this vast region, China, Russia, Japan, and the U.S. have clashed since the late 19th century, escalating during conflicts that include the Second World War in the 1930s to 40s, the Korean War of the 1950s, and the Sino-Soviet border conflicts from the 1960s to mid-1970s. Tensions among Russia, Mongolia, Central Asia, Northeast Asia, and China have persisted through present day.[16]

All three autonomous regions named by their major ethnic nationalities of Mongols, Uyghurs, and Tibetans are home to multiple nationalities with multilayered ethnoterritorial relationships. In the remainder of this chapter, I focus mainly (but not exclusively) on the relationship between the Han Chinese majority and each region's namesake minority nationality. I begin with Mongols of IMAR, where the presence of Han Chinese spreads the widest and permeates the deepest, rendering Mongols not just a minority at the national level, but also a minority at the regional and local levels. I therefore call Mongols a "Triple Minority" in China.

I Mongols: A National, Regional, and Local Minority

Mongols hold a distinct position in the CCP's ethnoterritorial order. Compared to Uyghurs and Tibetans, Mongols have been seen as being more cooperative with the CCP, hence less threatening to China's border security. But unlike how it has been presented in the official history, the cooperation between Mongols and the CCP was hardly an inevitable, natural course of ethnic assimilation. Between the end of imperial rule in 1911 and the establishment of the PRC in 1949, Mongol elites of IM were deeply divided in their ideological inclinations and political affiliations with different neighboring and occupying powers, including the Russians, the Japanese, the Chinese Nationalists, and the Chinese Communists. By the mid-1940s, after much political maneuvering, the Mongolian Communists who had collaborated with the CCP succeeded in consolidating their power in IM.[17] The Mongolian Communists, under the leadership of Ulanhu (Yun Ze), were said to have "delivered" IM to Mao, facilitating the establishment of IMAR in 1947, two years prior to the establishment of the PRC. Growing up speaking Chinese, not Mongolian, in a farming village of Central-West IM, Ulanhu was an icon in China's multinational polity and a model minority leader unmatched by any other minority Communist figure.[18]

By contrast, the CCP's attempts to consolidate Xinjiang and Tibet were met with fierce resistance from the get-go. The Red Army's intense battles and the CCP's protracted negotiations and persuasion work with local "bandits" and "rebel" leaders to "peacefully liberate" the vast frontier territories continued long after the establishment of the PRC in 1949. The government of Xinjiang Uyghur Autonomous Region under the PRC was not established until 1955. The government of Tibet Autonomous Region was established even later, in 1965, only a year before the start of the Cultural Revolution, which produced egregious atrocities in all three autonomous regions.

In many observers' eyes, including in those of Mongol nationalists, Mongols have been more "tamed" by the Han Chinese-dominant CCP in comparison to Tibetans and Uyghurs. In fact, the relationship between Mongols and Chinese state power, featuring collaboration more than competition and compliance more than defiance, had developed long before the CCP came to power. Historian Nicola Di Cosmo (1998)[19] noted that during the Qing Dynasty, Mongolia enjoyed a special status with the Manchu rulers because of Mongol elites' military support of Qing imperial expansion. In contrast to eastern Turkistan (today's XUAR) and Tibet, which were also annexed by the Qing, Mongolia maintained its political autonomy under a Mongolian aristocracy and local administrators and was not occupied or closely watched by the Manchu military.[20]

The political elites' collaboration has defined ethnoterritorial relationships between Mongols of today's IMAR and Chinese state power since the 17th century. At the grassroots level, massive Han Chinese northbound migration is often cited as the cause of IMAR being diluted with Han Chinese at the present. All five Autonomous Regions in China today share a history of Han Chinese population influx under state and non-state initiatives since the late imperial era. The scope and scale, however, of the in-migration-led ethnoterritorial restructuring varies significantly in each of the five Autonomous Regions. Among TAR, XUAR, and IMAR, IMAR is the most accessible from south of the Great Wall and received the largest number of Han Chinese migrants. By contrast, Buddhist Tibetans in the distant high mountains of TAR and the Muslim Uyghurs in the oases separated by immense stretches of desert and mountain ranges have had much shorter histories of mixing with Han Chinese migrants.

The sharp contrast in demographic weight between Mongols' 17.7% and Tibetans' 86% in their namesake Autonomous Regions at the present moment, however, is not just the result of Han Chinese migration. An equally important explanation comes from ethnoterritorial restructuring through jurisdictional realignment, most notably at the inauguration of the CCP regime. Under the CCP overlord, ethnoterritorial boundaries were redrawn and homelands of various minorities were included or excluded in each Autonomous Region at the time of their establishment. Such jurisdictional restructuring has created different territorial dilemmas that Tibetan and Mongol leaders have had to confront. Tibetans' status as a predominant regional majority in TAR under the CCP is the result of the territorial partition of the Qinghai-Tibet Plateau. Mongols' status as a minority within the nominally "Mongolian" IMAR is the price that Mongol political leaders paid for their success in reunifying the historic Mongolian territories in the 1950s.

Allow me to elaborate.

The immense Mongolian territory that traversed China's northern border during the Qing Dynasty measured approximately 2.7 million sq. km. This territory was divided into north and south Mongolia. The Soviet-backed Mongolia to the north declared independence in 1922, while southern Mongolia—today's IMAR—remained in the hands of warlords and Mongol aristocrats who maneuvered among competing Chinese forces as well as Japanese and Russian imperial powers. In 1928, the Chinese Nationalist Party leader, Chiang Kai-Shek, declared the successful unification of warlord-run northern China. In Chiang's territorial scheme for a unified northern China, southern Mongolia was divided into three provinces of Rehe, Chahar, and Suiyuan. The name "Mongolia" was erased from the national map, as was Mongols' claim to their ancestral land.

Ever since the partition of southern Mongolia, reunifying the divided homeland has been a shared aspiration for Mongolian nationalists. Despite the great divergence in Mongolian elites' political affiliations with various geopolitical powers, these elites shared the Mongolian nationalist agenda wherein territorial recovery and reunification were priorities for southern Mongolia.[21]

Among the geopolitical powers competing for Mongolian land in the 1930s and 1940s, only Mao of the CCP took Mongolian nationalists' yearning for territorial unification seriously. During his depleting, yet enlightening Long March across the perilous border regions in the northwest and southwest in 1934–35, Mao learned the geopolitical necessity of building coalitions with leaders of the diverse ethnic groups in these immense and resource-rich territories. In 1935, the lowest point of the Communist Revolution, Mao, in his attempt to secure Mongol leaders' support for his fight against the Japanese imperialists and the Chinese nationalists, issued the Declaration to the Mongol People. In this declaration, which Mongolian nationalists frequently cited, Mao promised that the CCP would return the historic southern Mongol territory to the Mongol people. Mao listed the lands to be returned: the six leagues, 24 sections (*bu*), and 49 banners; Chahar, two sections of Tumd, as well as the three special banners in Ningxia. He also promised to abolish the three Republican-era Provinces of Rehe, Chahar, and Suiyuan that had erased Mongolian history from the Mongolian homeland.[22] In 1956, Mao's promise was delivered. This reunified territory of southern (today's Inner) Mongolia under the name of Mongolia is one of Ulanhu's most celebrated achievements.

But the recovery of the lost Mongolian homeland came at a steep price. Anthropologist Uradyn Bulag (2010)[23] has pointed out that the more land IMAR incorporated into its jurisdiction, the more Han Chinese were brought into (via the redrawn jurisdictions) historic Mongolian lands. The result was a decrease in Mongols' demographic weight in post-unification IMAR.

The official announcement of IMAR's unification was followed by negotiations of territorial consolidation, province by province and subregion by subregion in the immense terrain. The negotiations began in 1949 in East IMAR, where the IMAR government was first established. East IMAR had the largest Mongol presence in IMAR at that time, averaging about 40% of the local population. As territorial consolidation progressed westward, more Mongol land with a much smaller Mongol presence (and greater Han Chinese presence) was incorporated into the IMAR jurisdiction. In Rehe Province, for example, 88% of the local population was Han Chinese in the late 1940s. By incorporating the land and residents of Rehe into IMAR, it significantly lowered the Mongol-to-Han Chinese ratio in IMAR. Similarly, when Chahar and Suiyuan Provinces were triumphantly reclaimed by IMAR government as part of IMAR territory in 1952 and 1954, the two provinces reported 67% and 91% of their populations as Han Chinese, respectively.[24] After much arm twisting and negotiation with former provincial leaders who were reluctant to let go of their turfs, the reunification project was finally completed in 1956. By then, only 12% of the 9.36 million in the newly reunified IMAR, or 1.1 million people, were registered ethnic Mongols, and Han Chinese accounted for close to 87%.[25]

The much-celebrated territorial recovery effectively reduced Mongols from a significant minority that accounted for 40% of the total population in a smaller territory of East IMAR, to a decidedly diluted 12% minority in the much-expanded, reunified territory of IMAR. By 2020, Mongols' weight went up to 17.7% of the total population of IMAR, which had grown 2.5-fold since 1957, or 24 million in absolute numbers.[26]

II Tibetans: A Regional and Local Majority

Mongols' territorial reunification in 1956 was built upon bringing the Han Chinese-majority jurisdictions back into a reunified Mongolian land, reducing Mongols to a small minority of the reunified and expanded IMAR. By contrast, Tibetans retained their regional majority status in TAR through excluding other Tibetan areas of the Qinghai-Tibet Plateau.

The Qinghai-Tibet Plateau stands over 4,000 to 5,000 meters above sea level and is surrounded by imposing mountain ranges. Historically, the plateau has been divided into three regions: the Lhasa-centered Ü-Tsang (or Central Tibet) in the west, Kham in the southeast, and Amdo in the northeast of the plateau.

Centralizing territorial authority over the entire plateau has been at the forefront of Lhasa's political and religious elites' aspirations since the 7th century. But such aspirations have not fully materialized even after the establishment of the Lhasa-based Tibetan government, Ganden Phodrang, in the 17th century. Local resistance in Kham and Amdo against Lhasa government's tax collectors and labor drafters persisted, and at times escalated into armed conflicts. In the first half of the 20th century, the three Tibetan regions' contentious relationships, and their separate connections with external powers, such as Chinese warlords and British colonialists, continued to fuel regionalism in each of the three regions. Despite its concentration of great monasteries that made Lhasa the ultimate pilgrimage destination, the Khampas and the Amdowas resented the Lhasapas' arrogance and Lhasa aristocratic and religious elites' abusive treatment of people in and from Kham and Amdo. The feeling was mutual. Lhasapas saw eastern Tibetans as uncultivated, despite the fact that the 14th Dalai Lama was born in Amdo.

In the 1950s, as Mao proceeded to "liberate" the entire Qinghai-Tibet Plateau by sending the People's Liberation Army to Kham, and later to Lhasa, the historic tensions between Central and Eastern Tibet was reconfigured under a pan-Tibetan nationalism against the common rival—the Chinese Communist regime and its soldiers.[27] While regionalism never completely dissipated, many of the Central and Eastern Tibetan elites felt an urgency to advocate for a united front.

But a united Tibet was the last thing Mao needed for his territorial consolidation project. For the CCP, a rising pan-Tibetan nationalism necessitated the time-honored strategy of divide and conquer. After 15 years of militaristic suppression and political maneuvering, TAR was established under CCP control in 1965, 18 years after the establishment of IMAR.

Against the wishes of the pan-Tibetan nationalists and exploiting the regional schism, TAR under CCP mapping included Lhasa-centered Ü-Tsang (Central Tibet), but excluded the two eastern regions of Kham and Amdo. As a result, TAR maintained its ethnic majority at the cost of foregoing its territorial claims over the eastern half of the Qinghai-Tibet Plateau. The newly established Tibet Autonomous Region is confined to Central Tibet, and its Tibetan majority live with the imposing presence of the People's Liberation Army (PLA). At the time of TAR's establishment in 1964, 97% of its population of 1.25 million was Tibetan, much higher than the current count of 86% out of the total population of 3.65 million. Paralleled with the CCP's heavy-handed control, TAR has also been the most heavily subsidized provincial-level jurisdiction in China over the past half a century.[28]

But this is only half of the story of Tibetans in China. An additional 3.76 million Tibetans—more than half of the total registered Tibetans in China today—live beyond the boundary of TAR in the two eastern regions of the Qinghai-Tibet Plateau that are now under the jurisdiction of four neighboring Provinces of Qinghai, Sichuan, Yunnan, and Gansu. Eastern Tibetans of Kham and Amdo dwelling in these Han Chinese-dominant provinces were turned into a miniscule minority within each of the provinces, mixing with Han Chinese and many other minority nationalities.[29]

Inclusion and exclusion, after all, are two edges of the same territorial slicing tool. In jurisdictional mapping, what is not included is just as, if not more, important as what is included in the jurisdiction in question. And both ethnoterritorial concentration and fragmentation can be instrumental for minority governance. If Central Tibet-based TAR is a case of ethnoterritorial concentration contained by jurisdictional maneuvering, Kham and Amdo make a case for ethnoterritorial fragmentation, governed by the principle of "divide, mix, and rule."

After the establishment of TAR, Kham and Amdo were incorporated into five provincial-level jurisdictions. The Kham territory, where about 2 million Tibetans lived—or 25% of all Tibetans in the PRC—[30] was divided amongst TAR, Qinghai, Sichuan, and Yunnan Provinces; Amdo territory, with about another 2 million Tibetans, was incorporated into the two neighboring Provinces of Qinghai and Gansu. The Kham and Amdo territories in TAR and the four neighboring provinces were delineated as Autonomous Prefectures and Autonomous Counties. In parallel with China's hierarchically ordered jurisdictional organization, the Autonomous Region (AR), Autonomous Prefecture (AP), and Autonomous County (AC) constitute the three basic tiers of jurisdiction in minority regions. AR ranks at the same level as province in nonminority areas. The jurisdictional hierarchy dictates the scale and scope of territorial authority, that is, leader officials (who are also ranked) of the higher-ranking jurisdiction hold the ultimate authority over those at the lower ranks. Under this tiered territorial order, when a minority-named AP is under the jurisdictional authority of a nonminority province, as is the case in Kham and Amdo, which have been turned into several Tibetan APs under four different provinces, these Tibetan-labeled APs are subject to the authority of the supervising, majority-dominant provincial government in almost every aspect of territorial governance.

Also, similar to territorial politics elsewhere in China's nonminority jurisdictions, the APs compete with one another for provincial governments' budgetary transfers, project grants and investments, and local official promotion quotas. The fact that five out of the six Tibetan APs within Qinghai Province are in historically Amdowa speakers' territory, and the sixth Tibetan AP in Qinghai Province is in historically Khampa speakers' territory adds an ethnic layer to the already fierce competition among the prefecture-level governments of the same province. In another case from the Kham territory, the core of the historical Kham area was brought under Sichuan Province, a jurisdictional design that the CCP inherited from the late imperial and Republican eras, while the western Kham territory makes up another autonomous prefecture under TAR.[31] Consequently, leaders of the partitioned Kham territory report to different provincial-level authorities and are subject to different policies and resource allocation schemes, creating different territorial orientations and political interests among the Khampas. The jurisdictional design, in short, not only reinforces existing differences, but also draws new boundaries and creates new ethnoterritorial dynamics.

Further down the territorial ladder, the politics of ethnoterritorial mix and division become progressively complex within both Kham and Amdo regions. Historian Jack Patrick Hayes (2014)[32] has attributed the highly decentralized politics of the eastern Qinghai-Tibet Plateau to the isolation of peoples imposed by the physical geography of high mountain ranges, deep gorges, impenetrable forests, and unnavigable rivers. Such physical barriers create divergent micro polities and complex ethnoterritorial relationships among Tibetans and other nationalities, like Qiangs and Yis.[33] The jurisdictional design reflects and shapes such fragmentation. For example, the Kham territory that has been incorporated into Sichuan Province is further divided into three jurisdictions at two jurisdictional ranks among three minority nationalities. The first jurisdiction is Garzê (Ganzi) Tibetan Autonomous Prefecture (GTAP); the second jurisdiction is also a prefecture but named by two nationalities, that is, Ngawa (Aba) Tibetan and Qiang Autonomous Prefecture (NTQAP). The third jurisdiction is a county, one level below prefecture, that is, Muli Tibetan Autonomous County (MTAC). MTAC, a Tibetan-named county, is placed under yet another minority-named prefecture, Liangshan Yi AP. Historically, the relationships among Tibetans, Qiangs, Yis and their subgroup were far from a peaceful or neighborly sort. Incorporating them into the same jurisdiction complicates grassroots ethnoterritorial politics further. For example, in NTQAP, as of 2020, Tibetans accounted for 59.9% of the total population, Qiangs for 18.6%, and the rest being mainly Han Chinese.[34] Han Chinese, Tibetans, and Qiangs engage in multidirectional competition and collaboration in NTQAP under the Han Chinese dominant Sichuan provincial government. In MTAC, a jurisdiction that sits one level below the Yi AP, the government officials are subject to the authority of two higher-level supervising governments: the Han Chinese-dominant Sichuan provincial government and the Yi-privileging Yi AP government. In some jurisdictions, there are also Autonomous Townships below the county, extending the multiethnic politics further down the territorial hierarchy.

To sum up, the jurisdictional design in the eastern Qinghai-Tibet Plateau is built on three sets of ethnoterritorial governing tools. The first tool is dividing a given minority territory into separate jurisdictions under different reporting lines, such as in the case of the Kham territory being split between TAR and Sichuan Province, which produces divergent territorial orientations and political interests among the Khampas. The second tool is mixing different nationalities into one jurisdiction, as in the case of Sichuan Province which includes both Kham and Amdo territories; or in the case of Aba AP, which includes Qiangs, Khampas, and Han Chinese. The third tool is ethnic division and mixing across territorial ranks, such as in the case of MTAC under the Yi AP within Sichuan Province, in which the intergovernmental and ethnoterritorial relationships complicate one another.[35]

In his studies of the CCP state's ethnic classification in Yunnan in 1953–54, historian Thomas Mullaney (2011)[36] observed that the CCP's ethnic classification involved creating new ethnic orders more than affirming existing ethnic differences. Similarly, these jurisdictional configurations in the Qinghai-Tibet Plateau were geared towards creating new ethnoterritorial orders more than following existing ethnoterritorial boundaries which, for sure, were not always clear nor stable. After several generations, like state-sanctioned ethnic classification, the state's demarcation of minority-named jurisdictions began to feel natural and was perceived as a historical given. The interconnected projects of ethnic and territorial mapping contributed to stabilizing the nation's ethnoterritorial order in the frontier.[37]

The CCP state did not invent the ethnoterritorial diversity and complexity of the Qinghai-Tibet Plateau. But the diversity has been well exploited by the CCP and its imperial predecessor, stabilizing fluid variations into ordered fragmentation. Such fragmented polities also explain the aspirations of pan-Tibetan nationalism. For pan-Tibetan nationalists, including the 14th Dalai Lama in exile and his followers, the fragmented polity and its vulnerability to CCP manipulation are exactly what needs to be changed.[38]

Bapa Püntsok Wangyel (1921–2014), one of the most prominent Tibetan communist leaders, believed that Tibetan autonomy would not be possible without unification of the Tibetan lands. Born in 1921 in Kham and schooled in China, Bapa Püntsok Wangyel became an underground revolutionary for the cause of pan-Tibetan unification in 1940, joined the CCP in 1949, and played a key role in the CCP's "peaceful liberation" of Tibet in the 1950s. Like many other minority communist leaders, including aforementioned Ulanhu of IM, Bapa Püntsok Wangyel was purged from political campaigns during the Cultural Revolution, and imprisoned for his alleged promotion of "local nationalism." Between 1960 and 1978, he spent 18 years in the infamous Qincheng Prison, known for incarcerating the country's top "enemies of the people," including Mao's wife Jiang Qing. In 1985, after his political rehabilitation, he served eight years as Vice Chair of the Ethnicity Committee of National People's Congress, China's top job in minority affairs reserved for leaders of strategically important minority nationalities. And the old soldier never dies. In his retirement, between 2004 and 2008, Bapa Püntsok Wangyel wrote four letters to Hu Jintao, the then top leader of the CCP, to advocate for the reunification of the Tibetan land. In his last letter written in 2008, six years before he passed away, Bapa Püntsok Wangyel reassured the CCP chief that the 14th Dalai Lama was not a separatist and that a unified Tibet does not mean an independent Tibet. Territorial unification is just a prerequisite for a truly autonomous Tibet under Tibetan rule, as Mao had once promised.[39]

It is unclear how Bapa Püntsok Wangyel might have gauged the interests of eastern Tibetans and the many other non-Tibetan minorities, such as Qiangs, in the Qinghai-Tibet Plateau in his proposal of pan-Tibetan unification. Even if eastern Tibetans and non-Tibetans in the Plateau agreed to join the Lhasa Tibetan-centered territorial unification, Wangyel would still have the "Inner Mongolia dilemma" to ponder. Like IMAR, the project of Tibetan territorial unification, if it happens, would have to include more Chinese-speaking Tibetans, Han Chinese, and other ethnonationalities of varied degrees of sinicization into the unified "Tibetan" territory and hence a reduction of Tibetans' demographic weight in the Tibetan land.

But time is running out for the pan-Tibetan unification cause. Since the post-reform era, restrictions on migration to TAR have been significantly relaxed and the region has witnessed a massive influx of Han Chinese. Unlike the lower-altitude river valleys in eastern Tibet that have attracted Han Chinese settlers since the 17th century, TAR of Central Tibet was under strict migration restrictions until recently. Geographer Emily Yeh (2013)[40] noted that Han Chinese migrant workers have been pouring into Lhasa since the mid-1980s to work on government construction projects, joined by an increasing number of Han Chinese farming migrants who have been renting parcels from state farms or Tibetan villagers in Lhasa's peri-urban areas to grow greenhouse vegetables for Lhasa's growing urban consumers. In the aftermath of nationalist demonstrations in Lhasa in 1987 and 1989, thousands of Han Chinese "Aid-Tibet" officials were sent to Tibet, and more Han Chinese and Hui migrants moved to Lhasa to set up businesses, including selling khataks, the widely used ceremonial Tibetan scarves. As a result, clusters of Han Chinese migrants grew rapidly in Lhasa's commercial core and in the urban-rural interface areas where vegetable greenhouses were concentrated. Yeh suggests that, if the estimated 200,000 unregistered Han Chinese migrants were counted in official figures (in addition to Lhasa Municipality's total population count of 475,000), it would raise the Han Chinese population from 80,000 to 280,000 and would render Tibetans a much smaller majority—57% in Lhasa, rather than the official figure of 82%. Accordingly, the Han Chinese population would grow from 17% to 41% of the total population, not counting military personnel, whose presence is not included in any official data.[41] In TAR as a whole, Tibetans' demographic weight declined from 92.2% in 2000 to 86% in 2020 while the total population of TAR increased from 2.61 to 3.65 million.[42]

The influx of Han Chinese into TAR since the 1980s seems to repeat IMAR's ethnoterritorial history. Yet there is an important difference between the two autonomous regions in terms of their ethnoterritorial structures. In TAR, recent Han Chinese migrants tend to be concentrated in the urban core and fringe areas of Lhasa, while Tibetans remain the dominant majority in the vast rural hinterland. Han Chinese in IMAR, on the other hand, have settled across both cities and the countryside throughout the entire autonomous region, and have deeply penetrated into townships and villages, rendering Mongols a minority even at the grassroots level. While Tibetans of TAR (but not Tibetans outside of TAR) maintain their status as a national minority but a regional and local majority, Mongols of IMAR are a Triple Minority at the national, the regional, and the local levels.

The different ethnoterritorial structure between TAR and IMAR can be further illuminated by the third case, Xinjiang Uyghur Autonomous Region (XUAR), which represents an in-between scenario.

III Uyghurs: A Local Majority

XUAR has experienced a similar surge in Han Chinese population since the 1950s. In 1953, Uyghurs accounted for 75% and Han Chinese 6% of Xinjiang's total population of about 5 million.[43] By 2020, the percentage of Han Chinese jumped to 42.24%, while the Uyghur population dwindled to 44.96%, and the total population in XUAR increased more than fivefold to 25.85 million. Of the 25.85 million, about 2 million were Han migrants who moved to XUAR between 2010 and 2020. Today, while Uyghurs have managed to retain their status as the largest nationality in XUAR by a thin margin, Han Chinese come in at a very close second. The rest of XUAR's population, 12.80% of the total of XUAR, is comprised of more than 30 other minority nationalities, including Kazakh, Hui, Mongol, Kyrgyz, Tajik, Tibetan, Sibe, and Russian peoples, among others.[44]

Despite their status as the largest nationality in number, Uyghurs' majority status in XUAR is fragile because of their thin and narrowing margin over Han Chinese. Uyghurs' statistical majority is also a contingent one, due to the three-way ethnic structure that includes Uyghurs, Han Chinese, and a significant portion of other nationalities who do not necessarily share ethnoterritorial interests with Uyghurs. Han Chinese and non-Uyghur minorities together make up more than half of the population in XUAR, and the multilateral ethnoterritorial politics could destabilize Uyghurs' majority status at various jurisdictional levels in XUAR, as presented in the previous section on TAR.

Uyghurs' ethnoterritorial weight is further constrained by their spatial distribution. XUAR's 1.66 million sq. km boasts the largest subnational jurisdiction in China. It is composed of two large basins separated by the east-west running Tianshan mountains. Uyghurs congregate in the oases around the Tarim Basin south of Tianshan, while Han Chinese and some of the major minority nationalities, like Huis, Kazakhs, and Mongols, are largely concentrated in the northern half of XUAR around the Junggar Basin. In the northern half, large Han Chinese-dominant cities were built around administrative centers and paramilitary plantations of the formidable Xinjiang Production and Construction Corps (XPCC), established in 1954. Among these major cities is XUAR's capital, Urumqi, where 71% of its 2.2 million residents were Han Chinese as of 2018. Another major city in northern XUAR is Shihezi, which used to headquarter the XPCC, and still headquarters one of the XPCC's largest Divisions, the 8th Division. In 2018, 94% of Shihezi's 592,500 residents were Han Chinese. In Changji, yet another city built around paramilitary plantations, 73% of its 1.3 million residents were Han Chinese and 17% were Hui as of 2019.[45] In these military-farming and administrative centers in northern XUAR, Uyghurs' presence is minimal and dispersed.[46]

In brief, Uyghurs' demographic presence in XUAR is outweighed by Han Chinese and other minorities combined, and their territorial presence is mostly confined to the southern half of XUAR. For these reasons, despite their status as the statistically largest nationality in XUAR, Uyghurs are more of a regional minority in XUAR by an ethnoterritorial account.

On the other hand, at the local level in southern XUAR, where the XPCC's presence is less concentrated compared to in the north, Uyghurs' ethnoterritorial weight is undeniable. In an area of 542,300 sq. km, about one-third of the entire XUAR, three major subregional prefectures of Hotan, Aksu, and Kashgar together are home to more than 8 million Uyghurs. In 2018, in Hotan Prefecture, 2.46 million (about 97%) out of a total 2.53 million local population were Uyghur. In Aksu, 2.09 million (82%) out of a total 2.56 million local residents were Uyghur. In Kashgar Prefecture, which is located at the western end of southern XUAR and shares borders with Tajikistan, Afghanistan, Pakistan, and India, 4.29 million (93%), out of the total local population of 4.63 million were Uyghur. The concentration of Uyghurs, ranging between 2 and 4 million in each of these subregional jurisdictions, make them a significant subregional, or local, majority. Beyond southern XUAR, there are several smaller, yet still sizable Uyghur clusters, such as in Turpan, a prefecture-level municipality in eastern XUAR. In 2018, Turpan boasted near half a million Uyghur residents, counting for 77% of the total local population.[47] The Uyghur clusters at the local level in XUAR is significantly larger compared to Mongols' congregation in IMAR, which counted from a few hundred to no more than 20,000 each.

Uyghurs of XUAR, therefore, are a minority at the national and regional level, but a significant local majority in southern XUAR. For the CCP, the large number of Uyghur congregations in southern XUAR means that its job is far from complete. To trim the large Uyghur clusters, the CCP has used a territorial tool of dividing the prefectures into cities and counties in the rural hinterland, rendering Han Chinese a much larger presence in the urban centers of southern XUAR. For instance, Aksu Prefecture is divided into Aksu City and eight rural counties. While Han Chinese took up a small 18.6% minority in the prefecture as a whole, they weighed 43.2% in Aksu City as of 2018.[48]

A more nuanced story of the ethnoterritorial dynamics in TAR and XUAR at the regional and grassroots levels remains to be told. The statistical sketches in this chapter, however, help reveal the different ethnoterritorial structures of the three autonomous regions. Tibetans of TAR are a national minority but a regional and local majority within TAR. Uyghurs of XUAR are a national and regional minority, but a local majority in southern XUAR. Mongols of IMAR, on the other end of the spectrum, are a "triple minority" at all three territorial levels: the national, the regional, and the local. In addition, while Han Chinese in TAR and XUAR are concentrated in cities, administrative centers, and military bases, in IMAR they percolate far and wide beyond the traditional strongholds of the state.

As mentioned in the Introduction to Part III, IMAR's granular ethnoterritorial structure could carry critical implications for Mongols' mobilizational capacity. To better understand such capacity and before entering the debates on how "tamed" IMAR's Mongols are, it will be useful to first trace the processes of the making of IMAR's ethnoterritorial structure. IMAR's current ethnoterritorial structure is shaped by a tumultuous geopolitical history of inter- and intra-ethnic collusion and collision intertwined with a contentious environmental history of resource struggles. It is an eventful history fraught with violence, atrocities and dispossession. Yet this history is too often buried under the presumed political compliance and sociocultural assimilation of Mongols under CCP rule. In the next three chapters, I will trace the geopolitical, ethnoterritorial, and environmental histories in Central, West, and East IMAR from the 18th century to the present.

Notes

1. Historically and geographically, Inner Mongolia (IM), as a part of the Mongolian Plateau, is better understood as southern Mongolia. The history of territorial restructuring of the Mongolian Plateau between today's Mongolia as an independent country and IMAR as an autonomous region of China, and the partition of the southern Mongolian territory between IMAR and other Chinese provinces warrants a much more extensive elaboration beyond the scope of this book. I use the official Chinese term "Inner Mongolia Autonomous Region" (IMAR) in this book to define my study area. I also use IM in my discussion of the geopolitical and environmental history of today's IMAR. I recognize the sinocentric bias implied in the term "Inner" Mongolia and the fact that many people prefer to refer to the territory as "South Mongolia." I choose to use "Inner Mongolia" in this book simply for consistency. Similarly, I adopt the official spelling of League and Banner names of today's IMAR, as shown in texts and Figures 5.1 and 5.2. I also adopt the official spelling of the names of mountains and rivers in today's IMAR. When it comes to the names of Mongolian authors, I follow either the spelling that the authors themselves use (such as Burensain Borjigin and Uradyn Bulag), or the Putonghua spelling (based on Chinese transliteration) if the authors do not specify (such as Enhe and Shuangxi). Some Mongolian authors use their Chinese names in Chinese publications (such as Bai, Meirong and Wang, Yuhai).
2. The ethnic labels used in this chapter, like "Han Chinese," "Mongols," and "Tibetans," refer to China's officially classified nationalities. I will explore the fluidity and the politics of ethnic identification, not just identity, in the context of Mongol students' college and job races in Chapter 9. The population statistics of the three autonomous regions are from the following sources:
Statistics Bureau of Inner Mongolia Autonomous Region. 2021. "Neimengguzizhiqudiqiciquanguorenkoupuchagongbao [The 7th population census of Inner Mongolia Autonomous Region]." Statistics Bureau of Inner Mongolia Autonomous Region, May 20. http://www.nmg.gov.cn/tjsj/sjjdfx/202,105/t202,10526_1596820.html. Accessed August 6, 2023;
Statistics Bureau of Xinjiang Uygur Autonomous Region. 2021. "Xinjiangweiwuerzizhiqudiqiciquanguorenkoupuchagongbao [The 7th population census of Xinjiang Uyghur Autonomous Region]." Statistics Bureau of Xinjiang Uygur Autonomous Region, June 14.

https://tjj.xinjiang.gov.cn/tjj/tjgn/202,106/34c32383b11042c7836ff5a8b78d3345.shtml. Accessed August 8, 2023;
Statistics Bureau of Tibet Autonomous Region. 2021. "Xizangzizhiqudiqiciquanguorenkoupuchazhuyaoshujugongbao [The 7th population census of Tibet Autonomous Region]." Statistics Bureau of Tibet Autonomous Region, May 20. https://www.xizang.gov.cn/zwgk/zfsj/ndtjgb/202,105/t20210520_202889.html. Accessed August 8, 2023.

3. Jenne, Erin. 2007. *Ethnic Bargaining: The Paradox of Minority Empowerment.* Ithaca: Cornell University Press.
4. Han, Enze. 2011. "The dog that hasn't barked: Assimilation and resistance in Inner Mongolia, China." *Asian Ethnicity* 12 (1): 55–75.
5. In Inner Mongolia, for instance, many of the recent protests in pastoral areas were triggered by ecological relocation and land rights appropriation that concerned both the Mongolian and Han pastoralists. These protests stemmed from struggles over resources that have greatly complicated the "ethnic conflicts" generated by purely ethnicity-framed interests. See Qiao, Long. 2018. "Neimenggumumindaibiao beijingshangfang zaojiefangkongzhi [Inner Mongolian herders' representatives were obstructed [by authorities] on their way to Beijing to file grievances]." Radio Free Asia, June 29. https://www.rfa.org/mandarin/yataibaodao/shaoshuminzu/ql2-06292018100910.html. Accessed July 8, 2023. Also, Qiao, Long. 2018. "Mainiubeipian nongmumin shangfangqingyuan [Cheated herders and farmers in a case of cattle purchase lodged complaints and filed grievances (in Hohhot)]." Radio Free Asia, September 6. https://www.rfa.org/mandarin/yataibaodao/renquanfazhi/ql1-09062018093029.html. Accessed July 8, 2023.
6. Fearon, James and David Laitin. 1996. "Explaining Interethnic Cooperation." *American Political Science Review* 90(4): 715–735.
7. Zhu, Kezhen. 1972. "Zhongguo jinwuqiannianlai qihoubianqiande chubuyanjiu [A preliminary study of climate change in China in the past five thousand years]." *Kaoguxuebao [Journal of Archaeology]* 1: 168–189.
8. This map is based on Tan, Qixiang et al. 1987. *Zhongguolishi tuji—qing shiqi [The historical atlas of China, The Qing period].* Beijing: China Cartographic Publishing House. Vol. 8, pp. 57–58.
9. This map is based on 2012. *Neimenggu zizhiqu ditu [Map of IMAR].* Beijing: Xingqiu dituchubanshe [Planet Cartographic Press].
10. Although the Central-West in this map is in the geographical center of contemporary IMAR, it is customarily considered western IMAR. The Central-East subregion in this map is customarily identified as being part of eastern IM, or the "Eastern Three Leagues" (those are, Je'uda, Jesoto, and Jerim Leagues) of Inner Mongolia during the Qing era. I frame Central-West and Central-East as two subregions to organize my stories in the following chapters and to avoid confusing customary perception with the jurisdictional map of IMAR today.
11. The analyses in this chapter are mostly based on my readings of existing literature and compilation of government data. It is meant to offer an ethnoterritorial context for the later chapters on agropastoral mixes and shifts. The complex geographies and rich histories of all three immense regions and their peoples, a vast and dynamic field of study, are beyond the scope of this book.
12. For an overview of the CCP state's evolving minority policies and the establishment of the autonomous regions, see, for example, Dreyer, June Teufel. 1976. *China's Forty Millions: Minority Nationalities and National Integration in the People's Republic of China.*

Cambridge, MA: Harvard University Press; Mackerras, Colin. 1994. *China's Minorities: Integration and Modernization in the Twentieth Century.* Oxford: Oxford University Press; and Elliott, Mark. 2015. "The Case of the Missing Indigene: Debate over a "second-generation" ethnic policy." *The China Journal* 73: 186–213. For investigations of the fluid and constructed ethnic boundaries of both the minorities and the majority of China, see for example, Wang, Minke. 2003. *Qiangzaihanzang zhijian: yigehuaxialishi bianyuande lishi [Qiangs between Hans and Tibetans: A Historical Anthropological Study of China's Peripheries].* Taipei: Lianjing Press; Harrell, Stevan. 1990. "Ethnicity, local interests and the state: Yi Communities in Southwest China." *Comparative Studies in Society and History* 32 (3): 515–548; Bulag, Uradyn. 2010. *Collaborative Nationalism: The Politics of Friendship on China's Mongolian Frontier.* Lanham, MD: Rowman and Littlefield; and Mullaney, Thomas et al. eds. 2012. *Critical Han Studies: The History, Representation and Identity of China's Majority.* Oakland, CA: University of California Press. For the fluctuation of minority population size under shifting minority policies, see, for example, Hoddie, Matthew. 1998. "Ethnic identity change in the People's Republic of China: An explanation using data from the 1982 and 1990 census enumerations." *Nationalism and Ethnic Politics* 4 (1–2): 119–141. According to Hoddie, from 1982 to 1990, the size of the minority population grew from 10 to 24 million. The fertility increase accounted for about 10 million. The rest, 4 million, came from individuals converting their ethnic identity from Han to minority nationalities in order to take advantage of the preferential policies stipulated in the new laws that started in the mid-1980s. For the CCP state's ethnic classification that forms the foundation of organizing China's plurality under the Han majority-dominant CCP's singular rule, see Mullaney, Thomas. 2011. *Coming to Terms with the Nation: Ethnic Classification in Modern China.* Oakland, CA: University of California Press. For critiques of the Chinese government's shift from treating ethnic minorities as "nationalities" to "minority groups" that have only nominal autonomy, see Bulag, Uradyn. 2010. "Alter/native Mongolian identity: From nationality to ethnic group." In *Chinese Society: Change, Conflict, Resistance,* edited by Perry, Elizabeth and Mark Seldon, 3rd edition. pp. 269–287. London: Routledge.

13. National Bureau of Statistics of China. 2021. The Seventh National Population Census. Online source. May 11. https://www.gov.cn/guoqing/2021-05/13/content_5606149.htm. Accessed August 8, 2023.
14. Zhou, Mingliang. 2004. 'Minority language policy in China: Equality in theory and inequality in practice." In *Language Policy in the People's Republic of China: Theory and Practice Since 1949*, edited by Mingliang Zhou and Hongkai Sun, pp. 719–795, p. 82. Boston, MA: Kluwer Academic Publisher.
15. National Bureau of Statistics of China. 2021. "Population by Ethnic Groups and Gender," section 2-22. China Statistical Yearbook. http://www.stats.gov.cn/sj/ndsj/2021/indexeh.htm. Accessed April 12, 2024.
16. For detailed accounts of the geopolitical relationships among Mongolia, China, and other world powers during the first half of the 20th century, see Liu, Xiaoyuan. 2006. *Reins of Liberation: An Entangled History of Mongolian Independence, Chinese Territoriality, and Great Power Hegemony, 1911–1950.* Redwood City, CA: Stanford University Press; and Liu, Xiaoyuan. 2003. *Frontier Passages: Ethnopolitics and the Rise of Chinese Communism, 1921–1945.* Redwood City, CA:Stanford University Press.
17. Atwood, Christopher. 1992. "The east Mongolian revolution and Chinese communism." *Mongolian Studies* 15: 79–83; Hudagula. 2007. *Temuerbagen deyisheng [The life*

of Temürbagana]. Hohhot: Inner Mongolia People's Press. The author Hudagula is Temürbagana's daughter and was Associate Professor of History in the University of Inner Mongolia at the time of publication; and Mo'ergen. 2015. *Wode aba Hafeng'a: jiyizhongde lishi [My Father Khafungga: History in Memory].* Hong Kong: Zhongguo Yanhuang Publisher. Both Khafungga and Temürbagana were Mongolian nationalists with a pro-Inner Mongolia independence stance during the 1930s and 40s. Like many of the east Mongolian revolutionaries who later joined the IMAR government, they were purged, imprisoned, and tortured to death during the Cultural Revolution.

18. Like many other minority communist leaders, Ulanhu was attacked and stripped of power during the highly racialized Cultural Revolution. See Chapter 8 on the devastating impact of his downfall on IMAR.
19. Di Cosmo, Nicola. 1998. "Qing colonial administration in Inner Asia." *The International History Review* 20 (2): 287-309.
20. There were local exceptions to this general statement. Guihuacheng-Tumd, a pacified rebel's territory, for example was put under direct central control and military occupation under the Manchu Qing. See Chapter 6.
21. For historical accounts of Mongolia's division and Mongolian nationalism during the first half of the 20th century, see, for example, Liu, Xiaoyuan. 2006. Ibid.; Liu, Xiaoyuan. 2003. Ibid.
22. The Declaration, issued on December 20, 1935, is entitled "Zhonghuasuweiai zhongyangzhengfu duimenggurenmin xuanyan" [Declaration to the People of Inner Mongolia by the central government of the Chinese Soviet], CCP Central Secretariate ed., 1981, *Liudayilai dangnei mimiwenjian [Classified Documents of the CCP since the Sixth National Congress].* Beijing: People's Press, Vol. 1 (2 volumes total), pp. 732–733. Most Mongolian nationalists of the 1940s, despite the internal split between the western (represented by Ulanhu) and the eastern (represented by aforementioned Khafungga and Temürbagana) fractions, embraced the declaration and counted on Mao's support of minority regions' self-governance. See, for example, Hudagula. 2007. Ibid. pp. 92–94, about the CCP's endorsement of the establishment of East Mongolia People's Autonomous Government in 1945–46. The declaration had been a key reference, albeit with divergent interpretations in the discussion of IMAR's autonomy. See for example, Li, Yuwei. 2007. *Neimenggushixian minzuquyu zizhide lilunyushijian [Theory and Practice of Ethnic Autonomy in Inner Mongolia]*, p. 114. Hohhot: Inner Mongolia University Press.
23. Bulag, Uradyn. 2010. Ibid. pp. 266–267.
24. These figures were as of 1937, according to Bulag, Uradyn. 2010. Ibid. pp. 266–267. Also see Yan, Tianling. 2004. "Saiwaimenghan zajugejude xingchengyu menghan shuangxiangwenhuaxishou [Formation of Mongolian-Han Chinese mixed settlements and their two-way acculturation]." *Journal of South-Central University for Nationalities (Humanities & Social Science edition)* 24 (1): 80–85. Yan suggested that by the 1930s, Mongols counted for only 7% of Rehe, Chahar, and Suiyuan Provinces, while Han Chinese counted for 93%. Meanwhile, the Mongolian population declined in the first half of the 20th century. The explanations that Yan listed included wars, epidemics, natural disasters, and the Buddhist practice of celibacy.
25. Renqin. 2015. "Shilunneimenggu siqing yundong [The Four Cleansings Movement in Inner Mongolia]." As web post on Wengeyu dangdaishi yanjiu [Studies of Cultural

Revolution and Contemporary History], June 26. https://www.difangwenge.org/forum.php?mod=viewthread&tid=11368. Accessed November 13, 2023.

26. Statistics Bureau of Inner Mongolia Autonomous Region. 2021. The 7th population census of Inner Mongolia Autonomous Region. Government website. May 20. http://www.nmg.gov.cn/tjsj/sjjdfx/202105/t20210526_1596820.html. Accessed August 6, 2023.
27. Buffetrille, Katia. 2019. "The increasing visibility of the Tibetan borderlands." In *Frontier Tibet: Patterns of Change in the Sino-Tibetan Borderlands*, edited by Stéphane Gros, pp. 85–113. Amsterdam: Amsterdam University Press.
28. China Tibetology Research Center. 2009. "Zhongguozangxueyanjiuzhongxinxizangjingjishehuifazhanbaogao [Report on Economic and Social Development of Tibet by China Tibetology Research Center]." Government website. March 30. https://www.gov.cn/jrzg/2009-03/30/content_1272056.htm. Accessed August 9, 2023; Source of 2020 population size: Statistics Bureau of Tibet Autonomous Region. Bulletin on the main data of the 7th national population census of the Tibet Autonomous Region. government website. May 20. https://www.xizang.gov.cn/zwgk/zfsj/ndtjgb/202105/t20210520_202889.html. Accessed August 9, 2023. For review of central subsidies to TAR before 2012, see Fisher, Andrew. 2015. "Subsidizing Tibet: An interprovincial comparison of western China up to the end of Hu-Wen administration." *The China Quarterly* 221: 73–99. For the connection and disconnection between the subsidies and local needs, see Jinba Tenzin. 2014. "A grassroots association on the Sino-Tibetan border: The role, agendas and beyond." *The China Quarterly* 217: 99–120.
29. Sources of demographic data are the following: Tibetans in Sichuan Province: as of 2021, 1.63 million Tibetans accounted for 1.79% of Sichuan's provincial total of 90.9 million, see 2023. "Sichuanshengqingdeqing [Sichuan Provincial statistics]." In *Sichuan Yearbook*, 2022 edition. http://www.scdfz.org.cn/scdqs/scsq/content_12038. Accessed August 9, 2023. Tibetans in Gansu Province: as of 2021, about half a million Tibetans counted for 2% of Gansu's provincial total of 25 million (430,000 in Gannan Tibetan Autonomous Prefecture; close to 70,000 in Tianzhu Tibetan Autonomous County. See Statistical Data on Economic and Social Development of Minority Areas. 2022. "Gannanzangzuzizhizhou2021nianguominjingjiheshehuifazhantongjigongbao [Gannan Tibetan Autonomous Prefecture 2021 National Economic and Social Development Statistical Bulletin]." October 25. https://www.neac.gov.cn/seac/c103544/202210/1159376.shtml. And 2022. Tianzhu Tibetan Autonomous County Government. "Tianzhuzangzuzizhixianjibenqingkuang [2021 Basic Situation of Tianzhu Tibetan Autonomous County]." http://www.gstianzhu.gov.cn/art/2022/4/7/art_3510_566580.html. Accessed August 9, 2023. Tibetans in Yunnan Province: as of 2020, 148,000, or 0.3% of Yunnan's provincial total of 47.2 million. See Yunnan Provincial Bureau of Statistics ed. 2021. *Yunnantongjinianjian [Statistical Yearbook of Yunnan Province]*, p. 357. Beijing: China Statistics Press. In Qinghai Province, Kham and Amdo-based Tibetans have had a much stronger demographic presence, of 1.51 million, or 25.48% of Qinghai's 5.92 million in 2020. See Qinghai Provincial Bureau of Statistics. 2021. *Qinghaitongjinianjian [Statistical Yearbook of Qinghai Province]*, pp. 74–75. Beijing: China Statistics Press. It is important to note that the Tibetan-dominant sub-provincial jurisdictions in Qinghai Province are divided into six Autonomous Prefectures between the Kham and the Amdo areas. Also, in addition to Tibetans' very small presence in each of the provinces listed previously, the fact that these neighboring provinces are home to more than 20 other minority nationalities further complicates Tibetans' influence at the provincial and sub-provincial level jurisdictions.

30. Gros, Stéphane. 2016. "Introduction to special issue, Frontier Tibet: Trade and boundaries of authority." *Cross Currents: East Asian History and Culture* 19: 1–26.
31. It is important to note that the boundary of the "Kham" territory was never clearly marked, nor did it ever constitute a single administrative entity. For detailed discussion see Gros, Stéphane. 2016. Ibid.
32. Hayes, Jack Patrick. 2014. *A Change in Worlds on the Sino-Tibetan Borderlands: Politics, Economies, and Environments in Northern Sichuan*. New York: Lexington Books.
33. For a review of the construction of the "Qiang" nationality, see Wang, Minke. 2003. Ibid.; for a collection of studies of the construction of the "Yi" nationality, see Harrell, Stevan. 2001. *Perspectives on the Yi of Southwest China*. Berkeley: University of California Press.
34. National Ethnic Affairs Commission of PRC. 2022. "Abazangzuqiangzuzizhizhou 2021nianguominjingjiheshehuifazhantongjigongbao [Aba Tibetan and Qiang Autonomous Prefecture 2021 National Economic and Social Development Statistical Bulletin]." October 21. https://www.neac.gov.cn/seac/c103544/202210/1159326.shtml. Accessed August 9, 2023.
35. Wang, Minke. 2003. Ibid. pp. 30–34. Wang observed that the competition within and among minority groups in Aba Tibetan-Qiang AP (AAP) took place even down to the sub-village level. At the Prefecture level, the Gyalrong Tibetans dominated the minority leadership positions, but below the prefecture level in several counties where the Qiang people concentrated, Qiangs held more influence.
36. Mullaney, Thomas. 2011. Ibid.
37. See for example, Harrell, Stevan. 2008. "L'état, c'est nous, or We have met the oppressor and he is one of us: The predicament of minority cadres in the PRC." In *The Chinese State at the Borders*, edited by Diana Lary, pp. 221–239. Vancouver: University of British Columbia Press.
38. Goldstein, Melvyn. 1990. "The dragon and the snow lion: The Tibet question in the twentieth century." In *China Briefing*, edited by Anthony Kane, pp. 129–168. Boulder, CO: Westview Press. Goldstein reported that in 1982, when the Dalai Lama's government-in-exile sent a delegation to Beijing, the delegation insisted that any settlement on the Sino-Tibetan relationship must address the issue of reuniting the ethnic Tibetan areas in Qinghai, Sichuan, Gansu, and Yunnan Provinces with Tibet proper, and that all Han troops should be withdrawn from the region (p. 145). Goldstein noted that in the Tibetan exile community in Dharamsala, India, Khampas and Amdowas had different views and separate organizations from the Lhasapa-dominant exile government. To ensure unity among the Tibetan communities in exile, the Dalai Lama nevertheless needed to emphasize his point of a unified Tibet. In 1988, at the European Parliament at Strasbourg, the Dalai Lama reasserted that Tibet and ethnic Tibetan areas in the four neighboring provinces should become a self-governing, democratic political entity under a single government apart from the rest of China (p. 160).
39. Goldstein, Melvyn et al. 2004. *A Tibetan Revolutionary: The Political Life and Times of Bapa Püntsok Wangyel*. Oakland, CA: University of California Press.
40. Yeh, Emily. 2013. *Taming Tibet: Landscape Transformation and the Gift of Chinese Development*, p. 3. Ithaca: Cornell University Press.
41. Yeh, Emily. 2013. Ibid. pp. 99–105.
42. 2021. "Xizangzizhiqudiqiciquanguorenkoupuchazhuyaoshujugongbao [The 7th population census of Tibet Autonomous Region]." Ibid. Accessed August 8, 2023; China Statistics Information. 2001. "Xizangzizhiqu2000niandiwuciquanguorenkoupuchazhu

yaoshujugongbao [Bulletin on Main Data of the 5th National Population Census of Tibet Autonomous Region in 2000]." China Statistics Information website, March 29. https://www.cnstats.org/rkpc/201112/xczzq-2000-qpfoo.html. Accessed August 9, 2023.

43. Toops, Stanley. 2004. "The demography of Xinjiang." In *Xinjiang: China's Muslim Borderland*, edited by Frederick Starr, pp. 241–263, pp. 246–248. Armonk: M. E. Sharpe.
44. Statistics Bureau of Xinjiang Uygur Autonomous Region. 2021. "Xinjiangweiwuerzizhiqu diqiciquanguo renkoupuchagongbao [The 7th population census of Xinjiang Uyghur Autonomous Region]." Government website, June 14. https://tjj.xinjiang.gov.cn/tjj/tjgn/202106/34c32383b11042c7836ff5a8b78d3345.shtml. Accessed August 8, 2023.
45. Bureau of Statistics of XUAR. 2020. "Gedi, zhou, shi, xian(shi)fenminzu renkoushu [Population by ethnic group by region, state, city, county (city)]." government website. June 10. https://tjj.xinjiang.gov.cn/tjj/rkjyu/202006/3b1eef1049114b0c9cf9e81bf18433ef.shtml. Accessed August 9, 2023.
46. The concentration of Han Chinese population in northern Xinjiang is paralleled with state investment in modern infrastructure for resource extraction in northern Xinjiang throughout the 20th century. See Kinzley, Judd. 2018. *Natural Resources and the New Frontier: Constructing Modern China's Modern Borderlands*, p. 16. Chicago: University of Chicago Press.
47. Ibid.
48. Ibid.

6

Land Commodification: Emperors and Princes in Central IM in the 18th–19th Centuries

Cultivating the northern steppe concerns both labor and land. The state matters on both counts. The Qing court put in place a pair of frontier policies from early on: one tried to regulate Han Chinese northbound migrant labor; the other centered on allocating land rights to the emperor's Mongol allies and stripping land rights from the emperor's Mongol foes. But how and how much these state policies worked on the ground and over time is a different story.

I Imperial Ambivalence

The Qing state's policy towards Han Chinese migration to the Mongolian steppe was anything but consistent. The Qing court archives present the three emperors of the High Qing—Kangxi (r. 1661–1722), Yongzheng (r. 1722–35), and Qianlong (r. 1735–96)—as fervent border defenders against Chinese northbound migration and the migrant-fueled cultivation expansion in the northern steppes. In practice, however, theirs and that of the proceeding reigns followed a see-saw pattern of opening and closing Great Wall passages for migration, in addition to various exemptions to the bans on land use conversion and land rights transfer.

On paper, the segregation mandates stayed in place for 250 years until the last few years of the Qing, which ended in 1911. In reality, the Inner Mongolian steppe saw unceasing cultivation expansion from its southern to northern terrains and from its central to western and eastern reaches throughout the Qing period. In the

Conserving China's Northwest Frontier. You-tien Hsing, Oxford University Press.
DOI: 10.1093/9780191903908.003.0007

mid-18th century, the Guihuacheng-Tumd territory in Central-West Inner Mongolia (IM) (see Figure P.III.1), for example, hosted no less than half a million Han Chinese migrants, greatly surpassing the native population. Over 80% of the land in this territory was turned into crop fields for drought- and cold-tolerant wheat, barley, flax, and buckwheat in its north, and drought-tolerant (but less cold-resistant) crops like mung bean, millet, and sorghum in its south. Han Chinese migrants continued to pour in throughout the 19th century, and their migration patterns evolved—from single men's seasonal migration to permanent settlements of farming households. In Central-East IM's Jesoto and Je'uda Leagues, between the mid-18th to the mid-19th centuries, the Han Chinese population quadrupled from 200,000 to 800,000, rendering Mongols a 30% minority in the area.[1]

Why did the emperors insist on the migration ban, and why didn't it work?

The rationale behind the Manchu Qing emperors' migration bans was mainly geopolitical. By the early 18th century, Sino-Mongolian sociocultural assimilation was visible in the Mongol land. The Han Chinese settlers were said to have been "assimilated by the Mongols" as they appended to land-owning Mongolian families, spoke the Mongolian language, followed Mongolian customs, adopted Mongolian names, joined Mongolian Banners, and married Mongolian women. Meanwhile, mixed villages of Mongols and Han Chinese had sprouted up widely north of the Great Wall.[2]

The Manchu emperors worried that Sino-Mongolian sociocultural assimilation and physical proximity could lead to a political alliance between the two and threaten Manchus' dominance in the northern steppe. To keep Mongols and Han Chinese from getting too cozy with each other and positioning Manchus as the "laughing third,"[3] the emperors repeatedly issued border crossing bans in the 18th and 19th centuries. Han Chinese seasonal migrant laborers were not permitted to stay on after autumn harvest nor were they allowed to bring families and build permanent housing in the Mongolian steppe. Migration bans were reinforced by severe penalties on unauthorized land rights transactions between Mongols and Han Chinese in the northern steppe.[4] To disentangle the two peoples living in mixed villages, the Qianlong emperor went as far as to order Mongols and Han Chinese to swap their homes and farms and to move in with their own people so that the Mongol and the Han Chinese settlements would be physically and socially segregated.[5]

But throughout the 250 years of the migration ban, the emperors' repeated prohibitions were repeatedly breached. And ethnic segregation via border control and territorial containment remained mostly a political aspiration. Han Chinese continued to arrive to Mongol lands in droves, and farmland continued to expand, creating a mosaic agropastoral landscape in the steppe.

Three territorial contradictions were responsible for the emperors' unsuccessful attempts to keep Han Chinese out of the northern steppe.

The first contradiction was geopolitical. The inauguration of the Qing reign in 1644 did not automatically end the turf wars in the northwest frontier. While most Mongolian tribal leaders collaborated with Manchus in their conquest of China, other territorial powers remained defiant. During the first century of the Qing between the mid-17th and the mid-18th centuries, the most pressing threat to the Manchu Qing came from the Zunghars, who launched unyielding attacks in the Qing's northwestern frontier. To secure the frontier, farming settlements were crucial to creating a defensive buffer zone between Qing China and the steppe powers.

Cultivation expansion in the frontier also served to facilitate a military offense. At the height of the Qing court's migration bans during the first half of the 18th century, the Yongzheng and Qianlong emperors were preparing to launch military campaigns to pacify the Zunghars in the west. As Peter Perdue (2005)[6] points out, the logistical challenges of military campaigns to central Eurasia were daunting. It was nearly impossible to transport food, war horses, and other supplies from south of the Great Wall and across the arid and rugged terrain to equip the hundreds of thousands of soldiers on their march west. These essential provisions had to be sourced en route. While unauthorized migration and cultivation were banned, the emperors made an exception for large-scale, military-farming colonies in central and western IM, for which the court actively recruited farm labor from the North China Plain. Documented farm labor recruits from south of the Wall were joined by counterfeit paper carriers heading north, who followed the military's westward advance and opened farmland under the protection of the military. As a result, the emperors' vision of ethnic segregation was compromised by the logistical needs derived from their own geopolitical ambitions for westward empire expansion.

The second territorial contradiction was rooted in social-environmental predicaments in North China. Since the early 16th century during the Ming Dynasty, Han Chinese settlers—including captives of Mongols' raids, prisoners of war, disserted or demobilized soldiers, draft evaders, convicts, and exiles—had been reaching the northern steppe. By the late Ming, hardships in the frontier had led to widespread defection by low-ranking military officers and soldiers of the Ming's border defense force. Organized by secret societies, these Ming defectors often sought asylum to the north of the Wall. The asylum seekers found company in the large numbers of refugees from Northern China. The ferocious wars during the dynastic transition from the Ming to the Qing destroyed livelihoods and created swarms of war and famine refugees. In addition, during the first years of the Qing, many noble Manchu families moved from their northeast homeland to Beijing and the surrounding region of Zhili in today's Hebei Province. These Manchu noble families were granted swaths of fertile land in the North China Plain, driving out local peasants. The dispossessed peasants joined the war and famine refugees fleeing north. In the 18th century, floods and droughts in the North China Plain sent still more waves of refugees across the Great Wall to the northern steppe. Upon these occasions, the Qing emperors had to order the Wall gate keepers to not turn the refugees away.

The northbound movement of dispossessed peasants and refugees of war and famine was not just a hiccup in history, and the northern steppe's role as a depository for disaster refugees from the south of the Great Wall was more than an ad hoc solution. Northbound migration was predicated on a history of dramatic population growth and a soaring man-to-arable-land ratio in China's heartland. Between the mid-17th to the mid-19th centuries, China's population almost tripled from

152 to 436 million.[7] In the short span between 1753 and 1812, the average size of land access per person declined from 6.89 to 2.19 mu, which was below the minimum subsistence level of 4 mu at the time.[8] The land squeeze in northern China was compounded by soil exhaustion and deforestation. The Yellow River, which was crucial to northern China's dry farming, silted up easily from soil erosion and routinely created destructive floods.[9] These socioecological predicaments resulted in a ceaseless movement of seasonal, short- or long-term migrant farmers, traders, craftsmen, and poachers across the gates of the Great Wall.

Not all migrants departed voluntarily. James Reardon-Anderson (2005)[10] calls the migrants from northeast China to the northeastern frontier in Manchuria "reluctant pioneers." Many were coerced laborers. For those who voluntarily moved north, they often did so in an ambivalent manner, as they were met with suspicious hosts, an unforgiving climate, and resistant soil waiting at their journey's end. Moving north, in any event, was not a choice, but the lack thereof. Northbound migration peaked at moments of great disaster in the south—flooding, drought, famine, and war—and such calamities transformed the reluctant migrants into desperate refugees who had no home to return to and who were willing to work just for food. The popular expression about the refugees' ventures to the northern frontier, "seeking food beyond the Great Wall" (*jiushi guanwai*), evinces a motivation little greater than dodging starvation.

Thus, the emperors saw the steppe as a spatial fix for the escalating socioecological crises to the south of the Great Wall. In addition, farm expansion north of the Great Wall offered financial benefits to the court, which introduces the third territorial contradiction that explains the emperors' unsuccessful migration ban. It turned out that the steppe did not just passively absorb northern China's refugees. Instead, commodity grains produced in the steppe proved indispensable for food security in Beijing, the empire's capital in the midst of soaring land and food prices in northern China. By the early 18th century, millet cultivated in the steppe cost only one quarter of what was produced in the North China Plain.[11] Generally speaking, farming settlements also created a productive and manageable tax base for the emperors. Cultivation expansion across the Great Wall into the northern steppe extended the state's administrative grip on a taxable frontier. Many refugee migrants were recruited by military-farming colonies, but the majority found their way to farms scattered across areas under the control of local state agencies, banner elites, and private farms of varied scales.

The lure of turning the northern steppe into farms was hard to resist. In the early 18th century, the Kangxi emperor visited the Great Wall's Gubei Pass, located northeast of the capital. As he looked north, the emperor was gratified at the sight of his empire that was "legible by identical landscapes near and far," and that "the barren mountains north of the Great Wall were thoroughly converted into crop fields."[12] For the Qing overlord, it was the densely populated farming settlements, more than the pastoralists' mobile yurts and herds, that would better serve to unify the territorial order on both sides of the Great Wall.

So, the ambivalent emperors could not hold the line to keep Han Chinese migrants out of Manchu and Mongol homelands; massive and continuous migration from south of the Great Wall provided the necessary labor for cultivation expansion in the northern steppes. Across the North China Plain from west to east, migrants traveled the shortest possible distance, moving directly north from their hometowns in Shanxi, Shaanxi (west of the North China Plain), Hebei (central), and Shandong (east) Provinces and ending up in West, Central, and East Inner Mongolia (IM).

Central IM, the geographical focus of this chapter, tells stories about the geopolitics of land commodification and financialization during the 18th and 19th centuries.

II Geopolitical Divergence

Among IM's three agricultural frontiers (see Figure P.III.1), the Central was the first to see significant expansion in intensive farming. It was also the closest to the Qing capital of Beijing. Its proximity to the "emperor's feet" foregrounded the geopolitical dynamics between central and local authorities, that is, between the Manchu Qing emperor and the Mongol Banner princes, in this story. Such central-local dynamics have shaped the processes of commodification of steppe land and labor and prepared the ground for agricultural expansion in Central IM and beyond.

The geopolitical map of Mongolia, as far as the Manchu Qing emperors were concerned, consisted of two types of Mongol tribes: those who had fought the Manchus but failed, and those who had joined the Manchus' successful conquest of China. During the Qing era, pacified Mongol resisters were put under the direct control of military regiments and central administration. The ally tribes, on the other hand, were rewarded with large land grants and territorial autonomy like a "petty sovereign."[13]

Both types of tribes can be found in Central IM. Located in Central-West IM were the Guihuacheng-Tumd Banners, where the pacified resisters (and, hence the emperors' foes) resided.[14] In Central-East IM were the Harqin Banners, where the trusted allies, and hence the emperors' friends, resided. With their vastly different geopolitical standings and degrees of local autonomy, these two territories embarked on divergent paths of cultivation expansion during the 18th and the 19th centuries.

II.1 Emperors' Foes in the Central-West

The core of the Guihuacheng-Tumd territory in the Central-West was in the fertile Tumd fluvial delta between the Yellow River and the Black River in today's Hohhot. Compared to its neighboring areas,[15] the Tumd Plain enjoyed fertile soil, a warmer climate, and proximity to northern China, a steady source of migrant labor. These conditions gave early rise to cultivation in the early 16th century during the mid-Ming era, after the warring Ming emperor and the Mongol Khan signed a peace agreement. By the inauguration of the Qing in 1644, the Tumd Plain had already seen large-scale farming for over a century.

Guihuacheng-Tumd's strategic location and its local leaders' position as distrusted former rebels brought the Qing court's forceful intervention in the area. The defeated Guihuacheng-Tumd tribal chiefs were made to prove their loyalty by surrendering to the Manchu overlord with land, a predicament called "*daidi toucheng*." To consolidate the Manchus' physical presence in the subjugated rebels' territory, the court enclosed massive land tracts and established military horse farms, garrison complexes, and commanding headquarters, in Suiyuan City, for the Manchu Banner military regiments. To fund these military projects and feed the large forces, additional land tracts were allocated to the military units in the form of estates that operated as land holding trusts. The court also enclosed large swathes of land to establish imperial, noble, and official estates, turning Mongol tribal lands into Manchu Qing state-owned land. The estate land tracts were used for grazing and cropping—a base for food supplies and a source of revenue for imperial families, Manchu nobles, and government agencies.[16] On these estate farms and ranches, bannermen and Han Chinese migrants were recruited as estate workers with hereditary land use rights. In exchange for the land use rights, estate workers paid rent and taxes and provided labor to the estate.[17] By the mid-18th century, after the century-long cultivation period in the pre-Qing era and the state-sponsored projects during the first century of the Qing era, more than 80% of the 500,000 hectares of rangeland in Guihuacheng-Tumd territory was converted to farmland.[18] Large Han Chinese farming settlements, shops, and temples peppered the landscape, surrounding the Han Chinese craftsmen-built palace of the Khan and the homes of his Mongol subjects. Meanwhile the garrison-turned trading town, Guihuacheng City, stood as the major commercial center in the region.

Compared to the heavy presence of the Qing state in Guihuacheng-Tumd territory, Harqin Banners of the Central-East enjoyed much greater local autonomy.

II.2 Emperors' Friends in the Central-East

Located in Central-East IM, the three Harqin Banners of Jesoto League, especially Left Harqin and Central Harqin Banners in the south, saw the rise of intensive farming no later than the mid-18th century.

Unlike Guihuacheng-Tumd territory of the Central-West, these eastern tribes did not produce a political leader capable of mobilizing unified resistance against the Manchu forces in the 17th century. Also, the eastern tribes of Jesoto faced a greater threat than the Manchus: the Chahar tribes. The absence of a unifying leader from within and the inter-tribal conflicts propelled the Jesoto tribes, along with tribes in the neighboring Je'uda and Jerim Leagues, to form a political alliance with the Manchus and to join the Manchus' military campaigns to establish the Qing Dynasty.

To reward the eastern Mongol tribal leaders' prior contributions and to secure their future loyalty and military service, the Manchu court granted eastern Mongol nobles large land tracts. The Manchu royalty also established multigenerational marriage partnerships with its Mongolian allies, regularly marrying off Manchurian princesses to eastern Mongolian noble families.[19]

Major Mongol princes were appointed by the Qing court as administrative chiefs, or *jasaghs*, of the banners. The jasaghs held both traditional manorial authority over bannermen and banner land as well as Qing court-endorsed administrative authority over the banner jurisdiction. The jasagh and other ranked banner nobles received land grants as their personal renumeration. The jasaghs were also entrusted with estates that served as sources of revenue for the banner's administrative and military expenditures.

Commoner banner members who served in the military, banner units, temples, and estate farms were also allocated hereditary and nontaxable banner land on a smaller scale, which formed the main source of income and wealth of banner households. Banner land was associated with banner membership and could not be sold to non-banner members. Bannermen were bonded to the nobles and could not move at will. If caught fleeing the banner, one was subject to fines, severe physical punishment like flogging, or even exile. Overall, banner land of varying scales was granted to banner units to finance the banner military and administrative operations, reward the banner elites, and sustain bannermen who served in the military or worked for the banner elites. Circulation of land was restricted within the banner and under the tight control of the jasagh.[20] In short, according to banner rules, land and labor were administratively allocated and territorially managed resources; neither were freely tradable commodities.

III Socioeconomic Convergence

During the 17th and 18th centuries, while the subjugated yet still untrusted tribes of Guihuacheng-Tumd territory in Central-West IM were dominated by state-military institutions, the allied tribes of the Harqin Banners in Central-East IM maintained their autonomy under the rule of banner aristocracies. But the geopolitical distinction between the emperors' foes and friends begins to fade when we switch our lens from geopolitical to socioeconomic affairs, and from institutional design to everyday practices. Shaped by different territorial dynamics, the two territories nevertheless converged in large-scaled land commodification and financialization in the 18th century, which paved the way for cultivation expansion in Central IM and beyond.

III.1 Commodifying State Land in the Central-West

The Guihuacheng-Tumd territory was administered directly by the Qing state-military institutions. While state-military control was centralized, the actual physical locations of military operations in the immense frontier were dispersed widely. The garrison-post system is a case in point. Since 1692, the Kangxi emperor had built five garrison-post systems along the Great Wall.[21] Intended to ensure the Qing court's centralized control of the peripheries at times of war and in peace, the garrison-post systems integrated the functions of military base, frontier governance, and the transmission of materials and information—emperors' policy ordinances, warfare commands, military materials and personnel, as well as monetary transfers from the capital to the frontier outposts. They also served to facilitate military and governance reports and material submissions from the frontier to the capital. In addition, the garrison-post stations were obligated to host traveling royalty, including the emperor himself occasionally, as well as officials who traveled with sizable entourages of soldiers, staff, servants, family members, and horses—all needed food and accommodations.

The five garrison-post systems in the northern frontier were part of the Qing's unprecedented extension of fortification that encompassed the continental empire's northeast, north, northwest, west, and the southwest frontiers.[22] By the mid-18th century, the garrison-post system traversed approximately 3,500 km from Beijing to the southwest frontier, and over 6,000 km from Beijing to the western frontier.[23] In the Xinjiang, Tibet, and Mongolia frontiers, the garrison-post stations stretched long distances over rugged and expansive terrains. To sustain such fiscally draining projects, the empire needed to be financed from the ground up. A significant portion of the burden was placed on local state units, making the local branch stations self-reliant, using corvee labor like exiles and convicts, and building farming colonies staffed by local recruits.

Peter Perdue (2005)[24] has pointed out that, in comparison with the military-farming colonies attempted by previous imperial reigns, the Qing operation was more successful: it lasted longer and covered a much greater area of the border terrain. Comparatively successful as it was, applying a self-reliance model to a prohibative number of operation sites over an expansive territory thousands of kilometers away from the capital was still a centralist's nightmare. The garrison-post system was established to govern the frontier, but how does one govern the governing system itself?

The five garrison-post systems in the Mongolian frontier had 71 stations along networked routes, measuring over 3,400 km.[25] The western-most garrison-post system of the five was called Shahukou, named after a pass of the Ming Great Wall, and was built upon Guihuacheng-Tumd and its neighboring Yekejuu territories. According to Liu, Zhonghe (2017),[26] the Shahukou garrison-post system, the most extensive among the five, comprised of 12 local stations connecting Beijing with the territory west of Yekejuu via two major routes, with a total length of 1,500 km. Each of the 12 station complexes included many structures, such as watch towers, walls, granaries, offices, living quarters, and Lamaist temples. In addition, large tracts of land surrounding the station complex were enclosed as estate land for grazing horses, camels, and other livestock, and for farming to support the operations of the station. Each of the Shahukou stations were staffed by 50 soldier households, the majority of them Guihuacheng-Tumd Mongols. Thus, across the 12 Shahukou stations, there were no less than 550 Mongol soldier households at the time of establishment. However, none of the soldiers were on state payroll. Under the "*daiti toucheng*" scheme for the subjugated rebel tribes, the Guihuacheng-Tumd soldiers who staffed the Shahukou stations were expected to prepare their own supplies and mounts and to serve the military without compensation.

To make this punishing policy of self-reliance viable on the ground, low-ranking Mongol officials found a solution in the garrison-post station land, called "*taizhandi*." Station heads leased out the land to pay for the station's overhead costs, while individual soldiers rented out their salary-substitution parcels for subsistence needs. Most of these arrangements were carried out at the station chiefs' discretion. During the second half of the 18th century, with the successful pacification of the Zunghars, and hence the diminished strategic significance of the Mongolian frontier, more station land, rangeland, and temple land of various sizes were leased out on various terms by station chiefs, soldier families, and Lamaist monks. With settlements and farms sprouting up and expanding around the garrison-post stations, they also became trading centers along the northern border.

Similar cases are found in the war horse farms north of the Tumd Plain. The 10 horse farms under the command of the Eight-Banner Horse Farm covered an area larger than 180,000 sq. km and were designated to support the Manchu Banner calvary units stationed in Guihua City. Although the Manchu calvary did not have to prepare their own mounts and supplies like their Mongol counterparts, they were not on state payroll either. Heads of the horse farms were responsible for overhead costs and soldiers' salaries. Again, they found the solution in leasing out the rangeland under their command. Like at the garrison-post stations, at the vast horse farms, parcels were leased out to migrant farmers by estate managers, workers, and soldiers, in varying parcel sizes and leasing terms. Between the late 18th and early 19th centuries, three rounds of rangeland lease sales had transferred a total of close to 50,000 hectares[27] of land for cultivation. And this is only the official figure. Additional rangeland was leased out on numerous occasions on a smaller scale by Guihuacheng-Tumd Mongol herders, whose land was within or sandwiched between military horse farms.[28]

Thus, estate land that was nominally owned by the state and used and managed by garrison-post stations and military horse farms was effectively privatized and commodified. Through land brokers, parcels of privatized land were transferred from individual land users-turned de facto owners to cultivators. Since most of the transfers were illicit, these transactions were carried out under the pretense of long-term or permanent tenancy, called pledging (*yongdianquan*), to avoid direct violation of the law that prohibited the outright sale of estate land to non-banner members. Pledging was also a way for the original owners to retain some rental income after they lost their actual use rights indefinitely. Land rights transfers could take place between Mongols within the state system and those outside of it. Hugejile (1990)[29] noted that Guihuacheng-Tumd soldiers treated their informally assigned shares of the garrison-post station land as inheritable family assets. Station soldiers customarily allocated a parcel of land as part of their daughters' dowry for when they got married. These soldiers' daughters often married men from local Mongol families, and the station's estate land was hence returned to local families through such informal transfers.

As a result of privatization through multigenerational and under-reported land rights transfers, the land tenure system grew increasingly entangled.

Xu, Yonghe (2017)[30] has studied one of the 12 Shahukou post-stations in Dongsuhai, located in Junghur Banner of Yekejuu League (in today's Ordos Municipality), another heavily regulated territory of Central-West IM. Xu found that, in addition to land for station facilities, the post station also included an 80 sq. km estate rangeland for postal horses, draft camels, and cattle and sheep, as well as five Lamaist temples. Since the station was staffed by local Junghur officers and soldiers, and the boundary between the station's estate land and Junghur banner land was never clearly demarcated, the land allocated to the station estate was at the discretion of the banner leader, who also served as the station chief. In the mid-18th century, the Dongsuhai station chief started to recruit Han Chinese refugee migrants from Shanxi and Shaanxi Provinces to turn the rangeland into farms. The chief lamas of the five temples around the station, each with its own allocated temple estate land, also recruited refugee migrants to farm the temples' estate land. By the early 19th century, there was a sizable cluster of Han Chinese settlements around the station.[31]

To sum up, in Guihuacheng-Tumd territory, under the self-sufficiency model of frontier fortification, the widespread military garrison-post stations and military horse farms ventured into a slippery slope of privatization and commodification of estate land.

III.2 Financializing Banner Land in the Central-East

If strong central control did not stop local military and state institutions in Guihuacheng-Tumd in the Central-West from leasing out estate land to settlers, the highly autonomous Harqin Banners in the Central-East faced even fewer constraints in profiting from land lease sales. Here the official rules against land commodification were weakened by the emperors' own needs to court the Mongol aristocracy. During the 18th century, the Mongol princes' political and military support was too critical to border security for the Qing emperor to impose restrictions around land rights sales and land use conversion. The influx of migrants and rising demand for land only accelerated the opening and commodification of manorial land in Harqin.[32]

Taking advantage of their territorial autonomy and the emperors' tolerance, Harqin banner elites had been making bold moves and initiated rounds of large-scale banner land sales since the early 18th century. Again, the transaction agreements used leasing and rental terminology, but the nature of these transactions was more akin to outright sales. The reigning jasaghs, who wore two hats as both the tribal chief and local government head, exercised their discretionary authority to lease out land tracts in their jurisdictions, paying little attention to the official distinctions between their personal land grants and the banner's estate land.

Land revenue was vital to the jasaghs and other high-ranking banner elites to maintain their power and status. A critical item on their list of expenses came from politicking in Beijing. Many of the Mongol princes who married Manchu princesses set up residence in the capital city of Beijing. Land lease sales were indispensable to fund the operations at their home bases in IM as well as their cosmopolitan lifestyles in Beijing. Aristocrats with administrative appointments who did not marry Manchu royal daughters were not allowed to set up residency in Beijing, but they were still required to travel regularly to the capital. On these visits, they brought luxury gifts for their political contacts in Beijing and an entourage of staff, family members, soldiers, servants, and horses, all of whom stayed in the capital for months on end. The court's financial subsidies for these regular visits and part-time residencies in Beijing were far from sufficient.[33] The cost of traveling, living, and politicking added up quickly. The inheritance of a noble title, for example, could not be accomplished without a substantial bribe of as high as 200,000 taels.[34]

It was financially draining for the Mongol princes and noble-officials to maintain operations in the capital. Many of the noblemen subsequently incurred heavy debt from their long-distance travels and their need to maintain a sociopolitical presence in Beijing. Such debts were pervasive and substantial enough to warrant a special name—*jingzhai* ("debt incurred in the capital"). Most Mongol nobles incurred hundreds of thousands of silver taels of *jingzhai* and came to count on income from land leases to pay them off.[35] With their sovereign-like power, jasaghs came to be the most formidable land suppliers of the Harqin Banners. Their geopolitical capital as the emperors' allies was converted into financial capital via large-scale land lease sales.

The jasaghs would mortgage banner land for loans, lease out land tracts to land brokers, or reclaim land by recruiting Han Chinese migrants as tenants or wage workers to clear the land for cultivation. In return for their labor, the migrants received the aforementioned "permanent tenancy" of a parcel at a fixed rent rate. The "permanent tenancy" effectively turned banner land into private holdings that could be leased out in fragments to "permanent tenants" (*yongdianhu*). As the migrant farmers turned the "raw" land to "cooked" land, they also increased the overall supply of marketable land and contributed to the expansion of the estates' and banners' revenue base.

In addition to their land under permanent tenancy, tenants followed the customary practice of clearing more land than their original tenancy agreements stipulated. One of the most critical and contentious stipulations in a tenancy agreement was that the parcel in question "would never be re-measured" (*yongbu zhangdi*). The stipulation, often insisted upon by the commercially savvy Han Chinese tenants, was to help the tenants avoid rent increases when they expanded the cropland beyond the originally leased area. In fact, many of the parcels were barely surveyed or measured at all by the original banner land holders at the time of transaction. As such, the parcels under the agreements tended to be larger than the agreed-upon size, and they grew even bigger after several years. These extra undocumented parcels further increased the amount of land in circulation. Private land clearance also stretched beyond the estate boundaries and even Banner jurisdictions in under-demarcated, so-called "wasteland," areas. In the absence of systematic cadastral land surveys, the line between where banner land ended and where unincorporated "wasteland" began remained ambiguous and fluid. Land tracts in the marginal areas—predominantly sandy patches and salty swamps—were less fertile. But they could be reclaimed by those who were determined and resourceful enough to transform these tracts into cropland, albeit with low productivity. To compensate for the low productivity per unit of land, the cultivated area would be expanded wherever possible, and tax and rent would be dodged whenever possible.

The jasaghs' land sales were not the only game in town. While the jasaghs controlled large-scale land lease sales, there were many more small- and medium-sized land suppliers in the market. Within the banner, lower-ranking noblemen and Lamaist priests received land grants. Below the ranks of the noblemen and priests, banner officials and common bannermen with hereditary banner membership were allocated banner land as compensation for their administrative, military and labor services. Banner land was also distributed as a form of welfare provision and livelihood support to banner members. These land allotments were designed as perpetual trusts that could not be sold to non-banner members. The trustees of the banner land could work on the land themselves or recruit tenants who would pay taxes, rent, and grains in return. Banner land holders also recruited wage workers, bond servants, slaves, or convicts to farm their land in exchange for wages, food, and shelter.

In theory, none of these land trustees were allowed to sell their land allotments. But when banner chiefs leased out large tracts of land, the secondary noblemen, banner officials, and smaller land-holding banner households followed suit. As a result, the land market was stocked with parcels of varied sizes. While some landholders sold the land to migrant tenants directly, others found tenants through land and labor brokers. By the mid-18th century, many Mongol bannermen of varying statuses and endowments relied on land rents as their primary source of income.[36] The multiple suppliers on the land market offered parcels of assorted sizes and lease conditions to match the needs of different land buyers/lessees. The fragmented process of land commodification in which banner members across ranks took part was fundamental to IM's cultivation expansion.

Similar to the process in China's heartland, land commodification in IM proceeded in conjunction with land financialization, thanks to a binary land rights system.

In China's heartland, where the man-to-arable-land ratio was high and land competition fierce, many landowners were small owner-cultivators and part-time tenants. These small owner-cultivators were extremely reluctant to part with their land, however humble their holdings were, in fear of falling further down the ranks to the most vulnerable, landless class. But small landholders were also under the greatest financial pressure to sell their modest holdings because of the very thin margin of survival. Falling into the landless class was often just a bad harvest, an illness, a funeral, or a wedding away. One common strategy to deal with the precarious condition was to separate the "bone" from the "skin" of the land rights—the "bone" being the ownership rights, and the "skin" the use rights. There were many ways in which the two types of rights were combined and separated. The exact configuration of bone and skin rights was subject to the bargaining positions and skills of the two parties.

In IM, where Chinese migrant-tenants were often more skillful bargainers than the small Mongol landowners, the land rights arrangements were practically land sales. In its common practice of "permanent tenancy" or "pledging," the bone-rights holder—the small Mongol landowners—would retain the right of first refusal and receive a leasing fee upon signing the land lease contract while still collecting a small annual rent from the Chinese tenant. The bone-rights holder could neither nullify the contract without the consent of the skin-rights holder, nor could the bone-rights holder increase rent rates unilaterally. Meanwhile, skin-rights holders had the use rights to cultivate and garner profits generated from the land, as well as to lease out all or a part of the parcel to a third party or even to mortgage the skin rights without the bone-rights holders' consent. The skin-rights holders could also dig wells, build graveyards, plant trees, and build houses and shops on the leased land. This type of arrangement effectively rendered the "bone-rights" a highly restricted variant of ownership rights, while "skin-rights" lent itself to a much broader set of rights beyond the typical scope of "use" rights. Used mainly as a way to skirt the prohibition ordinance against selling banner land to non-banner members, the majority of small Mongol landowners retained extremely restrictive bone-rights in these arrangements that resembled land sales more than tenancy arrangements.[37]

The binary land rights system paved the road to land financialization. As bone-rights and skin-rights could be traded and mortgaged separately in an increasingly commercialized rural economy, their market values were determined by interest rates on the money market. Liu, Kexiang (1986)[38] found that by the late 19th century in Central-East IM, the relationship between land sellers and buyers was akin to the financial relationship between debtors and creditors. The precious commodity of land could be liquidized as a dividable financial asset. Payments to landowners were divided into two segments—the lease fee and the rent. The lease fee was similar to cash payments a borrower would receive from a money lender as if the parcel were used as collateral for a loan, whereas annual rent payments were the equivalent of the interest that sellers would earn if they loaned out the leasing fees. As such, the going interest rate on the money market determined the land rent, which could be formulated as: lease fee (X) = rent (Y)/interest rate (Z). Of the 11 cases of land rights transfer that Liu examined between 1838 and 1908, the leasing fees ranged from three to six times the annual rental payments, equivalent to interest rates of between 17% and 35%, which was consistent with the range of interest rates on the money market during the same time period in the region. In other words, far from upholding the ideal, the enclosed manorial system that the early Qing emperors had designed did not manage to prevent the most productive land in Central IM from being privatized and commodified any later than the early 18th century. And the commodified land was financialized no later than the mid-19th century. This process involved local state agents and banner elites, land and money brokers, banner members across a wide spectrum of social standings as well as Han Chinese migrant farmers.

In short, the convergence of the commodification of land, commercialization of agriculture, and the dismantling of the manorial system were the key ingredients in the agrarian transformation of Central IM during the 18th and 19th centuries. As Reardon-Anderson (2005)[39] pointed out, commodified land and commercialized agriculture constitute the most salient distinction between the Qing and Romanov (Russia) empires' frontier expansion and governance. Both empires set out with a similar approach to govern their peripheries during the 17th and 18th centuries. At a time when frontier regions were surrounded by unfriendly and often aggressive neighbors, both the Qing and the Romanov built up bureaucratic governance and agrarian economies in these thinly populated but potentially arable border regions and offered land grants to hereditary elites in exchange for the their loyalty and service to the state. Both empires also built large standing armies to guard the borders and to support a system of enforced labor. But unlike the deep-rooted agrarian manor system that had existed in Muscovy since the 14th century, which could be transplanted to the border, the Qings' manor system in the northern steppe was highly experimental. Moreover, the Mongol and Manchu elites were unfamiliar with intensive cultivation and the management of a large agricultural labor force. Eventually the manor system in the Qing frontier gave way to a commodified land system that had long been practiced south of the Great Wall. Thus, the Qing state's frontier governance was facilitated, if not hijacked, by merchant capital by the 19th century. By contrast, the ongoing manor system in Russia enabled a strong Russian state in the 19th century, in a much less commercialized Russian economy and agricultural sector, with a small and weak Russian merchant class.

The supply of migrant and refugee labor, the commodification and financialization of land, and commercialization of agriculture saw its genesis in Central IM and spread to other parts of the northern steppe. Now, what about capital, another key factor in commodity crop production, and water, an indispensable component in dryland farming, not to mention the social institutions that organize them all? In late imperial IM where farm labor consisted largely of refugees, what social institutions were in place to transform them from unaccountable drifters into manageable workers, rent-paying tenants, and tax-paying subjects? In a land market in which land suppliers and buyers came from distinct cultural-linguistic backgrounds and held disparate perceptions of the meaning and value of land, what social institution could regulate cross-cultural land transactions? In the remote and arid frontier where there was chronic state deficiency, what social organizations were in place to build critical infrastructure such as irrigation networks so that commercial farming would take root and expand? Last but not least, throughout the tumultuous period between the mid 19th and mid 20th centuries, the northern frontier was infested with endemic armed banditry, local militias, and state military forces, whose exploits were often indistinguishable. What territorial governing mechanisms were in place to ensure a basic level of safety and stability for settlers to farm?

In IM's agricultural frontiers during such turbulent times, some of these questions were answered by two non-state actors—land-water barons and Catholic missionaries who organized the economy, polity, society, and territory in the agricultural frontier. While these two actors could be found in many other agriculturalizing areas in the northern steppes, their influence was most notable in the Yellow River Loop Plain of West IM, where the climate is the driest in IM and the state's presence the faintest. Land-water barons and missionaries, along with refugees, bandits, and warlords will lead the story of cultivation expansion in Chapter 7 on West IM.

Notes

1. Zhou, Qingshu. 1964. "Shilunqingdai neimenggude nongyefazhan [Agricultural development of the Qing's Inner Mongolia]." *Journal of University of Inner Mongolia (Social Science edition)* No. 2: 35–63; Wang, Yuhai. 2000. *Fazhanyu biange: qingdaineimenggu dongbu youmuxiangnongde zhuanxing [Development and Change: Eastern Inner Mongolia's Transformation from Pastoralism to Agriculture]*, p. 21. Hohhot: University of Inner Mongolia Press; Huang, Jianying. 2009. *Beifang nongmujiaocuodaibianqian duimengguzu jingjiwenhualeixingde yingxiang [The Transformation of the Agricultural-Pastoral Interwoven Belt of Northern China and its Impact on Mongols' Economic and Cultural Typology]*, p. 51. Beijing: Central Ethnicity University Press.
2. Yan, Guangliang. 2006. *Qingdaineimenggu dongsanmengshi [History of the Three East Leagues of the Qing's Inner Mongolia]*, p. 93. Beijing: China Social Science Press.
3. Uradyn Bulag (2012) called this a strategy of creating distrust between Mongols and Hans, so that the Manchu rulers could be "*the laughing third*," adopting George Simmel's term "*tertius gaudens*." See Bulag, Uradyn. 2012. "Rethinking borders: Empire and nation at the foot of the Willow Palisade." In *Frontier Encounters: Knowledge and Practice at the Russian, Chinese and Mongolian Border*, edited by Franck Bille, Grégory Delaplace, and Caroline Humphrey, pp. 33–53, p. 49. Cambridge: Open Book Publishers. Yet, at the end, Manchus had become more of an "anxious third" than a "laughing third," as depicted in Elliot, Mark. 2001. *The Manchu Way: The Eight Banners and Ethnic Identity in Late Imperial China*. Redwood City, CA: Stanford University Press.
4. Zhou, Qingshu. 1964. Ibid.
5. Wang, Yuhai. 2000. Ibid. p. 9.
6. Perdue, Peter. 2005. *China Marches West: The Qing Conquest of Central Eurasia*. Cambridge, MA: Harvard University Press.
7. Cao, Shuji. 2000. *Zhongguorenkoushi [History of China's Population]*, Vol. 4, *The Ming Period*, pp. 451–452. Shanghai: Fudan University Press; Cao, Shuji. 2005. *Zhongguorenkoushi [History of China's Population]*, Vol. 5, *The Qing Period*, pp. 703–704. Shanghai: Fudan University Press.
8. Liang, Fangzhong. 1980. "Zhongguolidai hukoutianditianfutongji [Statistics of households, land, and land taxation in Chinese history]." *Shanghai People's Press*, 10–11; Xing, Long. 1992. "Renkouyaliyu qingzhongye shehuimaodun [Population pressure and social conflicts during the mid-Qing Dynasty]." *Zhongguo lishiyanjiu [Studies of Chinese History]* No. 4: 51–58, p. 52. It is unclear, however, what the mortality rate was during this period when the average size of land access per person dropped to below the subsistence level. I thank Ken Pomeranz for pointing out this critical missing link.
9. For recent publications on the environmental histories of the Yellow River of different time periods, see Pietz, David. 2015. *The Yellow River: The Problem of Water in Modern China*. Cambridge, MA: Harvard University Press; Muscolino, Micah. 2015. *The Ecology of War in China: Henan Province, the Yellow River, and Beyond, 1938–1950*. Cambridge: Cambridge University Press; and Ling, Zhang. 2016. *The River, the Plain, and the State: An Environmental Drama in Northern Song China, 1048–1128*. Cambridge: Cambridge University Press. It is important to note that it is not just the Yellow River, but also other major river systems that have played important roles in northern China's economy, society, and polity. See, for example, Lü, Zhiru. 2015. *Genzhihaiheyundongyu xiangcunshehui yanjiu, 1963–1980 [A Study of the 'Fixing the Hai River' Movement and Rural Societies,*

1963–1980]. Beijing: People's Press; and Wang, Zhiguo et al. 2018. *Jindaihuiheliuyu ziranzaihaiyu xiangcunsheyui yanjiu [A Study of Natural Calamities and Rural Societies of Modern Huai River Basin]*. Hefei: Anhui University Press.

10. Reardon-Anderson, James. 2005. *Reluctant Pioneers: China's Expansion Northward, 1644–1937*. Redwood City, CA: Stanford University Press.
11. Wang, Yuhai. 2000. Ibid. p. 15.
12. "bantukeshitongxiaer, saiwaihuangshanjinpitian," see He, Shen and Guozhi Liang. 1983. *Qinding Rehezhi [Imperial Authorized Rehe Gazetteer]* 92: pp. 11–12. Taipei: Taiwan Shangwu Publisher. This gazetteer is a part of Qinding Sikuquanshu [Imperial Collection in Four Treasuries] compiled under the Qianlong reign between 1772 and 1783.
13. Lattimore, Owen. 1934. *The Mongols of Manchuria*, p. 78. New York: The John Day Company.
14. Guihuacheng-Tumd of the Central-West is not to be confused with the Tumd Banners in Jesoto League of the Central-East. Guihuacheng-Tumd has had a long history of intensive farming that started no later than the early 16th century, and its people were considered the most sinicized among Mongols. The ancestors of some Mongols in Guihuacheng-Tumd were Mongolianized Han who were captured and brought to the steppe by Mongol raiders. See Liu, Zhonghe. 2008. "Zouxikou lishi yanjiu [The History of Han Migration to West Inner Mongolia]." Doctoral dissertation. University of Inner Mongolia, p. 27.
15. To the west of Guihuacheng-Tumd was Yekejuu League in the arid Ordos Plateau sandwiched between two deserts. To its northwest was the cold and sandy Ulanchab League. While all three areas saw land reclamation during the Qing, it was the Guihuacheng-Tumd territory that had seen the earliest and largest expansion of cultivation.
16. The condition of Guihuacheng-Tumd was similar to its neighboring Chahar that also boasted a charismatic leader, Ligdan Khan (d. 1634). Ligdan Khan fought the Manchu Qing but failed. Chahar tribes were subsequently forced to yield its territories to create large horse ranches granted to Manchu nobles and estate farms that provided tax revenues directly to the royal families. See Zhao, Bing. 1990a. "Qingmo suiyuancheng baqimuchang fangkentanshu [Land reclamation projects of Eight Banner horse ranch in Suiyuancheng in late Qing]." In *Neimenggu kenwu yanjiu [Studies of Land Reclamation in Inner Mongolia]*, edited by Liu, Haiyuan et al., pp. 141–153. Hohhot; Inner Mongolia People's Press.
17. Liu, Zhonghe. 2008. Ibid. pp. 28–29; Reardon-Anderson, James. 2005. Ibid. p. 32; Zhao, Bing. 1990b. "Qingmo shahukou taizhandi fangken lunshu [Land reclamation projects of garrison complexes in the late Qing]." In *Neimenggu kenwu yanjiu [Studies of Land Reclamation in Inner Mongolia]*, edited by Liu, Haiyuan et al., pp. 154–165. Hohhot: Inner Mongolia People's Press.
18. See Liu, Zhonghe. 2008. Ibid. p. 30 for the figure 75,000 Chinese qing. I converted the figure using a rate of 1 Chinese qing for every 100 mu. Therefore, 75,000 qing x 100 = 7,500,000 mu = 500,250 hectares (1 mu = 0.0667 hectare). The actual size of Chinese mu varied in different areas at different time periods, with different measuring tools. The size of 1 mu was usually larger in northern China than it was in the south because of the lower productivity per unit of land in the north. As a result of the varied definitions of mu, the conversion rate between mu and qing also varied. For discussion of the variations in land measurement during the Qing era, see Guo, Songyi. 2010. *Minmingsuoxi: qingdaidenongyehe nongmin [Anchor of People's Lives: Agriculture and Peasantry of the Qing]*, pp. 446–464. Beijing: Chinese Agriculture Press.

19. For the political alliances and marriage partnerships between Qing royalty and eastern IM banner nobles, see Yan, Guangliang. 2006. Ibid. pp. 58–84.
20. Reardon-Anderson, James. 2005. Ibid. For analyses of the Qing's banner system, see Elliott, Mark. 2001. *The Manchu Way: The Eight Banners and Ethnic Identity in Late Imperial China*. Redwood City, CA: Stanford University Press; and Porter, David. 2023. *Slaves of the Emperors: Service, Privilege, and Status in the Qing Eight Banners*. New York: Columbia University Press.
21. Liu, Zhonghe. 2017. "Shahukouyizhan gujin dimingyanjiu [A study of place name changes in Shahukou garrison posts]." *Shuofang luncong* [*Shuofang Collection of Research Papers*] No. 6: 192–204. Hohhot: University of Inner Mongolia Press.
22. Liu, Wenpeng. 2002. "Lunqingdai dongbeiyizhan gongnengdefazhan [Development of the function of garrison posts in the northeast during the Qing era]." *Songliao Journal (Humanities and Social Sciences edition)* 6: 49–54.
23. The price tag on this empire consolidation project was about 3 million silver taels a year, according to Liu, Wenpeng. 2020. "Yizhantixiyu qingdai yuanjuli guojiazhilide youxiaoshixian [The post system and effectiveness of long-distance governance during the Qing]." *Guangming Daily*, January 13. https://epaper.gmw.cn/gmrb/html/2020-01/13/nw.D110000gmrb_20200113_1-14.htm. Accessed August 13, 2023.
24. Perdue, Peter. 2005. Ibid.
25. Jin, Feng. 1979. "Qingdaineimenggu wuluyizhan [Five garrison-post systems of the Qing era]." *Journal of Inner Mongolia Normal University (Social Science and Philosophy edition)*. No 1. Page range unavailable. Reprint by Association of Mongolian Language and History in Hohhot, IMAR. 1984. Menggushi lunwenxuanji *[Selected Papers on Mongolian History]* No. 3: 333–354.
26. Liu, Zhonghe. 2017. Ibid. pp. 192–204.
27. I converted the figure using a rate of 1 Chinese qing for every 100 mu. Therefore, 7,300 qing x 100 = 730,000 mu = 48,691 hectares (1 mu = 0.0667 hectare).
28. Zhao, Bing. 1990a. Ibid. pp. 141–153.
29. Hugejile. 1990. "Lunqingmo Hohhot-Tumd diqude kenwu [Analysis of land reclamation in Hohhot-Tumd area in the late Qing]." In *Neimenggu kenwu yanjiu [Studies of Land Reclamation in Inner Mongolia]*, edited by Liu, Haiyuan et al., pp. 166–177, p. 171. Hohhot: Inner Mongolia People's Press.
30. Xu, Yonghe. 2017. "Qing dongsuhaiyizhan de fangken yu dalamayaozi cun [Reclamation of Dongsuhai garrison post station and Dalamayaozi village in the Qing era]." *Baotou Daily*, June 10.
31. The Han Chinese settlers had built a Chinese Guandi temple in the Dongsuhai post-garrison station complex. According to a local official's report in 1829, Chinese settlers pooled their funds to invite a Chinese folk opera group to perform for three days in front of the Guandi temple at the end of the fall harvest, a performance that attracted two hundred male and female spectators. See Xu, Yonghe. 2017. Ibid.
32. Philip Huang (1985) found a similar situation in northern China's manorial estate of the Manchu Banners. He suggested that the manorial system in northern China collapsed as early as the mid-18th century as a result of serf population growth beyond the capacity of enclosed estate land. See Huang, Philip. 1985. *The Peasant Economy and Social Change in North China*, p. 87. Redwood City, CA: Stanford University Press.
33. Li, Wenqi. 2011. "Qingdaiwaifan mengguwanggong zaibeijingde huodongjingfeiyu juzhuqingkuang [Waifan Mongolian nobles' funding for activities and residency

in Beijing during the Qing]." In *Shoudu bowuguan luncong [Essay Collection of the Capital Museum]*, October 31, pp. 173–181; Mao, Liping. 2019. "Jinzhiyuyeyu shouzhikunju: Qingdaizhonghouqi gongzhu jingjijingyukaocha [Financial predicaments of the princesses during the mid-late Qing era]." *Lishi Yanjiu [Historical Research]* No. 4: 61–76.

34. Li, Jingtang. 1995. "Daerhanwangqi chuhuangshimo [History of land lease sales of Daerhan Banner]." p. 26. Published by the Committee of Culture and History under the Political Consultation Committee of Horqin Left Middle Banner.
35. Information on the banner elites' land lease sales in the next three paragraphs is based on Li, Jingtang. 1995. Ibid. p. 7 and Wang, Yuhai. 2000. Ibid. p. 107.
36. Li, Keren. 1990. "Qingdai wulanchabumeng kenwu chutan [A preliminary analysis of land reclamation in Wulanchab League during the Qing]." In *Neimenggu genwu yanjiu [Studies of Land Reclamation in Inner Mongolia]*, edited by Liu, Haiyuan et al., pp. 128–140, p. 131. Hohhot: Inner Mongolia People's Press.
37. Liu, Kexiang. 1986. "Qingdairehede mengdikaikenhe yongdianzhidu [The permanent tenancy system in Rehe's reclamation during the Qing]." *Studies of Chinese Economic History* 3: 49–69.
38. Liu, Kexiang. 1986. Ibid. p. 62.
39. Reardon-Anderson, James. 2005. Ibid. pp. 91–93.

7
Hydro Turfdoms: Barons, Priests, and Bandits in West IM in the 19th–20th Centuries

Two non-state actors were responsible for organizing agricultural expansion in the Yellow River Loop Plain, commonly called Hetao in Chinese, of West Inner Mongolia (IM) (see Figure P.III.1) between 1850 and the 1930s. Hetao refers to the area in the northwest stretch of the Great Bend (the loop) of the Yellow River in today's Bayannur Municipality of IMAR (see Figure P.III.2).[1] The two non-state actors were Chinese land-water barons and Belgium Catholic missionaries. Although both actors were also active in Central and East IM, they thrived in IM's remote, arid west where the state's presence was the weakest. The two actors held different motivations and pursued conflicting interests in Hetao. Yet, they converged in their push for the area's dramatic agrarian transformation in the 19th and 20th centuries.

What is a land-water baron? Compared with land merchants who brokered land and money in northern China and in other regions of IM, the land-water barons in arid West IM commanded much more centralized territorial authority anchored upon the extensive irrigation systems they built and/or controlled. They also boasted a greater level of territorial autonomy in a place and time of limited state presence.

Conserving China's Northwest Frontier. You-tien Hsing, Oxford University Press. © You-tien Hsing (2025).
DOI: 10.1093/9780191903908 003.0008

Thanks to their command over land, water, capital, and armed forces, land-water barons centralized control of the frontier economy, polity, and society like a lord of local turf. They ran the turfdom with a brand of territorial entrepreneurship built on pragmatism with little ideological predisposition. Such territorial setup does not transpire in either a state-centered Wittfogelian hydraulic empire[2] nor a decentralized Geertzian irrigation society.[3] Instead, what the barons had built was what I call "hydro turfdoms."

Catholic missionaries, especially the Belgian Congregation of Immaculate Heart of Mary (*Congregatio Immaculati Cordis Mariae*, CICM from here on), were another formidable turfdom builder in West IM's agricultural frontier from the mid-19th to mid-20th centuries. After the Opium Wars of the mid-19th century when China reopened to western religions, CICM missionaries set out to convert Mongol souls. However, they found readier apostles in the Han Chinese refugees trying to dodge starvation in the northern steppe. To expand their church-settlement compounds in an over-militarized and under-governed frontier, the Belgian missionaries found themselves preoccupied with pursuits similar to that of the Chinese land-water barons, that is, gaining access to land and water, organizing the settler society and space, and confronting violence with violence. The missionaries tried to leverage transitory powers and play the role of intermediary between warring parties in the frontier. Their brand of territorial entrepreneurship was characterized by political brokerage. Yet as deeply vested territorial actors themselves, they were far from being a neutral third party in violent resource struggles at such a tumultuous time in Hetao.

In this chapter I tell the stories of these two non-state territorial entrepreneurs and their strategies of establishing and defending their hydro turfdoms built on water, land, and guns in the Hetao Plain of West IM. The two rivalrous turf builders sported two distinctive brands of territorial entrepreneurship, but unwittingly converged on their zealous push to expand irrigated farming in the arid northwest frontier from 1850 to the 1930s.

I Land-Water Barons

Land-water barons, one of the two leading organizers of Hetao's agricultural expansion since the mid-19th century, grew out of "land merchants" (*dishang*). In the northern frontier, land merchants played multiple roles as land investor/speculator, money lender, and grain trader, not unlike rich landlords in other parts of rural China. But the scale and scope of IM's large land merchants were much grander in comparison with even the richest landlords in the North China Plain during the late imperial era. Among the land merchants of the northern steppe, the largest and most powerful ones became what I call land barons.

In the early 19th century, few regular or sizable farming activities were carried out in Hetao due to the Yellow River's frequent flooding. The year 1850 saw the Yellow River shift its course, creating a historical opportunity to expand irrigated farms in the former riverbed. It was also a time when merchant capital, which had been defeated by foreign traders and bankers in the post-Opium War era, was searching for investment outlets. The will of the Yellow and the wealth of the merchants together produced land barons, some of the largest private landholders in the late imperial northwest frontier.

Despite the difference in scale and scope between land merchants and land barons, they shared similar geopolitical roots. To understand the land barons, it is useful to first trace the making of the land merchants.

I.1 Frontier Merchants

Land merchants of the northern frontier started out as caravan traders of agricultural and pastoral goods between China and Mongolia. During the 17th and 18th centuries, as the Qing emperors led their military expeditions westward against Galdan Bushugtu Khan, the defiant steppe leader in Central Eurasia, frontier traders provided essential logistical support. Headquartered in the garrison-turned-trading-centers Guihua City and Baotou in Central-West IM,[4] these traders coordinated extensive networks of pushcart peddlers and shoulder-carriers, as well as camel teams and horse farms to ensure that the emperor's soldiers were fed, clothed, and equipped during their long march across the perilous frontier. The logistical barriers, as historian Peter Perdue (2005)[5] pointed out, were what had prevented China's previous emperors from penetrating and conquering Central Eurasia since the 3rd century BCE. By the mid-18th century, thanks to the caravan merchants and military-farming colonies, among other factors, the Qing successfully doubled China's territory to the scale at which we know it today.

To motivate and reward the merchants' contributions to the Qing's unprecedented conquests, the court granted lead merchants official titles and trade monopoly rights between the agricultural base in the south and pastoral Mongolian banners up north. The trade business continued to flourish after the emperors' military campaigns concluded. With successful territorial conquest came the even more daunting task of empire maintenance. A strong military presence was critical to guard the newly annexed eastern Turkistan, today's Xinjiang, and the merchants' logistical support of border defense forces became more indispensable than ever.[6]

As border trade flourished, a portion of merchant capital was channeled towards land trade. Well-endowed merchants would lease large tracts of pasture from landholding Mongol princes, Lamaist priests, and estate managers, as presented in Chapter 6. Having accumulated substantial wealth from generations of grain and fur trades, the merchants established commercial and financial networks with landowning Mongolian elites across the steppe. Many Mongolian banner chiefs, noblemen, and officials were the merchants' debtors and suppliers. Sociocultural cross-pollination was also an integral part of the frontier. Frontier merchants, many of whom had Han Chinese ancestry, were immersed in Mongolian diets, clothing, and worship customs. They spoke Mongolian, adopted Mongolian names, and married Mongol women. Some even earned Mongolian banner memberships and became bannermen themselves, which gave them direct access to banner land.

These were no paltry land deals. The land merchants' political and sociocultural capital enabled them to negotiate with Mongolian elites for large tracts of banner and estate land on long-term leases. The merchants would conduct land surveys and create subdivisions. Then they leased subdivided parcels to cultivation organizers who worked with labor brokers to recruit tenants and farm workers. Most of the land merchants were Han Chinese, as mentioned earlier. There were also entrepreneurial Mongolian banner noblemen, officials, and rent collectors who brokered land transfers of various scopes and at various scales.[7]

While well-endowed and -embedded land merchants negotiated with banner chiefs and estate managers over large land deals, there were many lesser landlords who doubled as land merchants. They brokered smaller parcels released by lower-ranking banner elites, impoverished banner members, and small owner-cultivators and even tenants who rented land from the Mongol or Han Chinese landlords and held tradable permanent tenancies (see Chapter 6 for details).

The growing social gap between large landowners and landless peasants ensured a steady supply of farm labor, which further contributed to the expansion of land merchants' land holdings. As mentioned in Chapter 6, for small landholders who often doubled as tenants in order to meet their own subsistence needs, a flood, drought, illness, or wedding or funeral could force them into having to sell their holdings and move down the social strata, thus becoming completely landless tenants. Similarly, poor tenants were at risk of being pushed to sell their tenancy rights, sinking them even further below the margin of survival. Refugees' margin of survival was thinner still. Land merchants were among the few suppliers of farming tools, food, and cash for the desperate refugees in the frontier. The annual interest rates on loaned tools, food, and cash, which ranged from 20% to 30% to an extremely usurious rate of 100% or even higher,[8] created cyclical debt. This cyclical debt in turn tied debtors to land merchants and kept the discounted and collateralized land ownership and tenancy rights in the hands of merchants who would put the land back onto the rental market. Land merchants also traded grains, which were tightly linked to their other business interests. When tenants could not pay their land rent, water fees, or other debts in silver, which happened routinely, land merchants were happy to take their payment in grain, especially when grain prices were high.

Through their various channels of amassing land and accumulating capital, West IM land merchants' landholdings outpaced that of their counterparts elsewhere. In Central-East IM, where agricultural expansion had begun more than a century earlier than in West IM, for example, the largest holdings were reported to range between 300 and 1,700 hectares.[9] The scale was greater than that of the "rich landlords" in 18th century northern China, where the majority of rich landlords held between 7 and 33 hectares, while a few super landlords held over 80 hectares.[10] The large holdings of rich land merchants in Central IM in the 18th century, however impressive by northern China's standards, were dwarfed by a new class of land merchants that emerged in mid-19th century Hetao of West IM. By the late 19th century, one of the largest land merchants in Hetao, a man named Wang, Tongchun, controlled no less than 67,000 hectares[11] of irrigated land, surpassing his counterparts in Central IM and northern China by a vast margin. More importantly, what land merchants in Hetao controlled was not just dry farms. Instead, more than one-third of Wang's land was fed by extensive irrigation networks, boasting 10 times greater productivity than that of northern China's rain-fed farms. Also, unlike the decentralized irrigation systems in northern China, the extensive water works in Hetao were in the hands of just a few super land merchants, and about three dozen smaller ones. Access to water and land in Hetao, in other words, was significantly more centralized than that in other parts of IM's agricultural frontiers and the North China Plain during the late imperial era.[12] The scale and scope of their control over resources and the intensity of their territorial command put these oligarchs in a different league than what the term "land merchant" connotes. I therefore call them land-water barons.

I.2 Shifted Yellow River Meets Displaced Capital

The land-water barons emerged in Hetao at a moment when two critical ingredients for agricultural expansion, water and capital, converged in Hetao.

During the two Opium Wars (1839–42; 1856–60), the Qing were repeatedly defeated by the British, French, and Russian armies and navies, among other foreign military forces. The Opium Wars reshaped border geopolitics and weakened Chinese merchants' monopoly over cross-border trading. The defeated Qing were forced to open treaty ports and domestic markets to foreign commercial interests, on top of paying an astronomical indemnity. Foreign capital poured into China, pushing out domestic capital—including the aforementioned frontier merchants in West IM. One Tianjin-based British trading firm, for example, set up a branch in Guihua City (today's Hohhot), thereby pushing out Chinese merchants from the fur business in Mongolia and monopolizing both the raw materials and imported goods markets in the region. Similarly, in Guihua, a large Siberian tea merchant drove dozens of Chinese tea merchants out of business.[13]

A good number of Chinese merchants in the trading cities of Guihua and Baotou went bankrupt. Many were reduced to working as clerks for foreign trading houses. Others started to explore alternative outlets in the rural hinterlands where foreign capital had yet to reach. While merchants were involved in land trade prior to the Opium Wars, as mentioned earlier, land was largely used to diversify investment portfolios. It was a side hustle. But after the Opium Wars, merchants redirected their capital to rural land as a decisive retreat from urban commerce.

Other factors also drew the former Chinese tea and fur merchants deep into the rural land trade. The social, ecological, and political turmoil of the second half of the 19th century drove up the price of food and land. And, as mentioned before, recurrent droughts, floods, and famines in northern China during the same period sent waves of refugees to IM, depressing labor costs in the northern steppe to a bare minimum. Together with the availability of cheap refugee labor and the promise of rising profits from food and land made for sound business prospects for merchant capital to invest in land in the frontier.

But of all places in IM, why Hetao?

The size of the Hetao Plain measures about 400 km in length and 60 km in width. With an arid and semi-arid climate similar to that of Minqin (see Chapters 3 and 4), annual precipitation rates in today's Hetao range between 100 and 200 mm, while its annual evaporation rate exceeds 2,000 mm, with 130 to 140 frost-free days a year. Unlike dry farms in Central and East IM that could count on surface runoff and an annual precipitation of 300 to 500 mm, regular farming in arid Hetao is unfeasible without irrigation. Water was crucial for plant growth and draining the excessive saline and alkaline in the soil, which would prevent the relentless summer sun from hardening and cracking the soil beyond any possibility for cultivation.

Hetao holds a distinctive place in China's agricultural and hydraulic history. As early as 200 BCE during the Western Han (206 BCE–9 CE) era, as the ambitious Emperor Wu warred with steppe powers, Hetao saw substantial investment from Emperor Wu put towards constructing irrigation canals to support military farming colonies. It was estimated that the early imperial irrigation system was sufficient to support military colonies of up to 200,000 people in Western Han's northwest frontier.[14] With the power shifts in the steppe after the Western Han period, the substantial irrigation systems in the military colonies deteriorated, while annual flooding of the Yellow River continued and pastoralism dominated the area.

During the 18th and early 19th centuries, Hetao was an occasional fishing ground for Han Chinese seasonal migrants. Some attempted to plant crops with improvised methods and devices. To plant in the spring, resourceful migrant farmers would spot areas of soil that had been flooded during the previous fall and remained moist enough for seedling development. The farmers would build leverage devices to collect water from nearby ponds created by the flooding and channeled the water to fields.[15] In some cases, straw-and-mud embankments were built to retain flood runoffs. However, these rudimentary water works were suitable mainly for small fields, and most of the structures lasted for only one planting season. Large-scaled and more durable irrigation required much more substantial investment. Yet the Qing emperors were reluctant to take on costly projects in the remote West IM where the Zunghars continued to raid. An ambivalent emperor made for a reluctant investor, and the Yellow River's destructive floods prevented large-scale farming on the otherwise rich soil.

Then the Yellow River shifted its course in 1850. The Yellow River is well known for being prone to siltation, flooding, and course shifts. In Hetao, prior to 1850, there were two major tributaries of the Yellow River that ran east-west, called the North and the South Rivers. The North River, which traversed the low-lying terrain, was wider and more voluminous. It moved more slowly and accumulated more sediment than the South River, and its bed continued to rise. In 1850, after yet another torrential flood, the North River was completely silted up. The surface runoff meandered off, entering the South River and other smaller tributaries. The North River's drained bed, with its high groundwater levels and fertile sediment, became ideal for cropping. More importantly, the riverbed-turned-fields located in areas of lower elevation could now be irrigated by the South River at the higher elevation. The low-lying fields in the north and the elevated source of water in the south made irrigation canals financially and technologically feasible. The irrigation system would run in a south-north direction to support unprecedented large-scale farming on the fertile, low-lying northern fields. Blessed by a confluence of factors in one place at the right time—the shift of the river course and the warming up of the post-Little Ice Age era—Hetao was poised for agricultural take off.[16]

For displaced merchant capital looking for alternative outlets, the shifted course of the Yellow River in Hetao was a match made in heaven. In arid lands where "people follow the land, and land follows water" (*rensuidizou, disuishuizou*), the use and exchange values of land parcels depended upon access to water. Now that water was available, the fertile and virgin alluvial plain of Hetao had the potential to be more productive and valuable than that of the exhausted soil of the Loess Plateau in northern China.

To create commercial value for land, land merchants doubled as water lords. Taking advantage of the shifted river course, arming themselves with long-term leases on large land tracts thanks to their entrenched sociocultural connections with banner elites, and maximizing the use of abundant and cheap refugee labor, land merchants set out to build irrigation networks to direct flows from the South River to northern fields and created large and congruous commercial farms.[17] Operating on largely uncultivated land with less entangled land tenure arrangements compared to Central IM and the North China Plain (see Chapter 6), some entrepreneurial and well-endowed land merchants in Hetao were able to expand their turfs rapidly, ultimately becoming land-water barons.

Most of the barons started out by forming consortia to invest in irrigation systems, dividing the canals and irrigated land in proportion to their respective shares. Most of the systems took several generations of merchant families to complete.[18] By the dawn of the 20th century, Hetao boasted eight major, and no less than 31 smaller, canal systems.[19] Connecting the drained bed of the North River and the newly expanded course of the Yellow River in the south, these systems were made of about 900 km of mains and 500 km lateral channels and furrows across 316 branches.[20] The far-reaching networks of canals also functioned as waterways to transport grains from rural hinterlands to the trading center of Baotou.[21]

I.3 Dragon King of Hetao

Among the leading land-water barons in Hetao, a man named Wang, Tongchun (1851–1925) has been the most legendary. At the height of his power in the late 19th century, Wang controlled five out of the eight major canal systems in Hetao and amassed unparalleled holdings of no less than 67,000 hectares of irrigated land, as noted earlier. Baron Wang's hydro turfdom tells the tale of the ways in which resources, economy, society, and violence were organized in the strongman polity of the frontier. Wang was not just a formidable land-water baron, he was an epic turfdom builder, a territorial entrepreneur in 19th-century Hetao.[22]

Born in 1851 in Zhili (today's Hebei Province) to a poor peasant family, Wang Tongchun was never schooled and could not read. By the age of 16, he was on the run from a homicide charge at home. Following the hundreds of thousands of other migrants and fugitives from northern China, he teamed up with a martial arts master and crossed the Great Wall on foot with a pushcart. Wang ended up in Hetao and joined a canal construction crew under a local land-water baron. An enterprising and heavy-built young man of six feet, Wang worked his way out of the labor lot and rose to manage a canal construction site for his baron boss, then married his boss's daughter. With the support of his father-in-law, he started building his own canals and expanded his canal-fed land holdings.

It is unclear how skillful a farmer Wang was. But he was unanimously recognized in various accounts as a gifted hydraulic engineer. Wang did not have today's modern affordances: bulldozers and earth movers for terraforming the landscape to accommodate ruler-straight channels or electrical pumping stations for propelling the flow of water against gravity. Instead, Wang fit his canals to the contour of the earth and designed the routes of the channels' course by painstakingly customizing the depth, width, and orientation of each waterway, section by section.

The hydraulic engineer-turned-hydraulic historian Cheng, Erdong (1988)[23] reported Wang's ingenious methods of following the contours of the terrain. For instance, one account relayed how he took 10 baskets painted in white and hung them on 10 posts of the same height. Ten men then held the posts and stood in a straight line, spaced at equal intervals. The posts, the baskets, and the post holders were thus devices that Wang could use to trace the land's contours. If the surface of the land was flat, the distance between the men would appear greater; if the land surface was uneven, Wang would arrange the post-holders closer together to mark the points of variation in surface level. Once all the white baskets were in perfect alignment, Wang would compare the original and adjusted configurations in which the men were positioned and then map out the contours of the land's surface to design the depth of each canal section. A simpler version of this method could be performed at night, with three lanterns lined up on the ground.[24]

To create effective canal slopes and routes to facilitate stable flows throughout the entire system, Wang rode on horseback for weeks to survey the contours of the land and map out where and how the canal mains and tributaries would run and turn, widen and narrow. He then designed the canal's sections at different elevations to elevate or lower the water level to ensure stable and far-reaching flows. As legend has it, the slopes and sections of Wang's canal system could send water to the farthest end of the waterways even during dry years yet would not flood the fields close to the main gate during wet years. He knew how to space out and angle the turns of the waterway so as to maximize the ferocity of the flow while avoiding abrupt surges caused by having too many turns in any one section, which could break the embankment. Wang knew his local geology well. He was said to be able to orient himself anywhere in Hetao in the dark simply by inspecting the dirt under his feet. He could also gauge groundwater levels by examining the moisture level of the soil around holes dug by rats.

Wang's mastery in hydroengineering made him a folk hero. Like other folk heroes, he was credited by the local people with the divine ability to perform miracles the way the Dragon King, the folk god that controlled rain and water, could. After he passed away, Wang's children built an ancestral hall in his honor. Locals regarded the ancestral hall as a temple for Dragon King Wang. During droughts or floods, they would bring offerings to the hall and float lanterns in the canal, praying for Wang's divine power to bring rain or halt floods.

The water works also shaped the turfdom's social and spatial configurations. Wang's irrigation systems were made of hierarchically structured mains, branches, lateral channels, and furrows. They were built, maintained, and accessed by a parallel social and territorial order of 70 villages—with a total of over 20,000 settler households. Appointed by Wang, the head of each segment of an irrigation system held the jurisdictional authority over each irrigation zone. Managers of irrigation jurisdictions were ranked in parallel with the hierarchy of the irrigation system. These ranked water managers were also responsible for allocating land tenancy and water rights, scheduling rotational water use for different sections, collecting land rents and water fees, as well as organizing the work of building and maintaining the waterways. They also arbitrated civil disputes and even criminal charges in their jurisdictions.

How does this hydro-territorial order that Wang established in Hetao speak to the debates around the "irrigation society"? Scholars have written on the irrigation society in different times and places, including Geertz's (1980) 19th century wet-rice cultivating in Bali and Han's (2006), Xing's (2006), and Zhang's (2006) 16th to 20th centuries dry farming in the arid environment of China's northwestern provinces, Shaanxi and Shanxi.[25] These irrigation societies were organized by grassroots social and ritual networks, in which the state played a symbolic and/or irregular and extractive role. These irrigation societies were opposite of the hydraulic state proposed by Karl Wittfogel (1957)[26] who saw centralized state authority and the state's forceful intervention as inevitable to develop irrigated agriculture-based civilizations.

But neither the hydraulic state nor the irrigation society model seems to fit Hetao: the hydraulic state was clearly absent in Hetao in the late Qing and the Republican periods. And the irrigation society—built upon centuries-long and decentralized irrigation associations at the grassroots level in either the wet environment of Bali or the dry environment of Shanxi—find few parallels in the highly transient migrant society of 19th and 20th century Hetao.[27]

How about the gentry class that historian Chang Chung-Li (1955),[28] among others, have employed in their analyses of local governance in late imperial China? Could we consider Baron Wang a member of the gentry class in 19th century Hetao? A textbook definition of the gentry is that of a broker between the state and the peasantry, a local elite that fuses significant landholdings with political influence and leverages local penetration with state recognition. The gentry was a vital link of state extraction, and a central figure in civil organization for infrastructure construction, disaster relief, prevention and even local militia organization.[29] While some scholars view the gentry as agents of the state, others see them as guardians of the local community. Still others, such as Prasenjit Duara (1988) and Vivienne Shue (1988),[30] perceive them as brokers between the state and peasantry—some of whom are more predatory than others. When it comes to the role of the gentry in hydro-social order in the dryland, the aforementioned scholars Han and Xing have applied the concept of gentry to their studies of Shanxi and Shaanxi, calling the canal chief–an influential and inherited position—the "canal gentry" (*qushen*).[31]

Baron Wang might be somewhat reminiscent of the canal gentry. Yet, if the gentry, or "canal gentry," is mostly about brokering between the state and the peasantry, how much brokering did Baron Wang perform? Late 19th-century Hetao was marked by feeble state presence and a transient society made up of refugees, fugitives, and recent migrants. In such a frontier of the frontier, the triangular power structure in the heartland of rural China, in which the gentry mediates between a well-established state administration and a deeply rooted peasant society, seems less fitting.

If neither the irrigation society nor the triangular structure of state, gentry, and peasantry fits Hetao's hydro-social order, then what does?

In spring 1914, Zhang, Xiangwen (1867–1933), the founder of China's Association of Geographers and a political activist during the Republican Revolution, visited Hetao and met with Baron Wang. Deeply impressed by Wang's command over the extensive irrigation networks, farming settlements, and irrigated fields in the frontier, Zhang crowned Baron Wang as a "kingdom builder" (*jianguozhu*).[32]

Zhang's visit to the northern frontier took place at a moment when the scramble for power after the 1911 Republican Revolution had reached a new height, and Republican China's inaugural congress, of which Zhang was a member, had been dissolved by the military strongman, Yuan Shikai. As a modernist scholar and disillusioned Republican politician, Zhang was fascinated by the territorial order that "Dragon King" Wang had managed to establish in the frontier. The absence of the state does not preclude, and in fact often creates the space for, non-state or para-state territorial actors. In any event, a hydro-social order cannot be built without a corresponding territorial order.

If Zhang's term, "kingdom," sounds a bit too lofty, what Wang Tongchun did build in Hetao was nothing less than a hydro turfdom. The hydro turfdom was physically defined by the reach of hydraulic infrastructure. Within the turfdom, Wang was more of a forceful defender of territorial autonomy than a brokering gentry between the state and the peasantry. In addition, with his socioeconomic, political, and military command (which I will turn to next), the power structure of his hydro turfdom was decidedly more centralized and authoritarian than it was in a gentry-based irrigation society.[33] The territorial order of the hydro turfdom in Hetao featured territorial autonomy vis-à-vis external powers as well as centralized and authoritarian rule from within.

To build and maintain such hydro-territorial order, Dragon King Wang needed more than hydroengineering talent: he also needed to assemble a formidable militia.

I.4 One-Eyed Dragon's Militia

Growing up in bandit-ridden Hebei in the 1850s and 1860s, Wang was no stranger to violence. He himself had killed someone—the predicament that had propelled him to leave home at the age of 16. Dragon King Wang was known as "One-Eyed Dragon" (*duyanlong*), as he had one eye gouged out by a rival during a fierce turf fight.[34] He was also said to have scooped out both eyes of a rival baron before killing him.[35]

To build an armed force, Wang recruited those who were likewise familiar with violence. Once a fugitive, Wang learned firsthand how tenuous the line separating hungry peasants from fearless bandits can be. He was also immersed in martial boxing and swordsmanship that proliferated in 19th-century northern China, as well as the martial arts virtue of self-reliance.[36] And, as mentioned earlier, on his initial journey from Hebei to Hetao, Wang's traveling companion was no other than a martial arts master from his hometown. Northbound refugees, who had in their midst martial arts masters and combatants, draft evaders, disbanded soldiers, exiles, and seasonal and career bandits, provided a reservoir of potential recruits for Wang's militia.

There were many occasions that called for militia action in the second half of the 19th century in Hetao. With continued expansion of cultivation, more irrigation channels were built, and water competition grew fierce. Skirmishes between settlers during the dry season would escalate to armed feuds between competing land-water barons. To guard his waterways and to expand his hydro-territorial control, Baron Wang industriously organized his territory, such as his military-farming colony that was guarded by one of the most formidable militias in Hetao. He acted as a generous patron toward his skillful and loyal militia recruits—especially martial arts masters—by granting them land and finding them wives,[37] a significant feat given the grossly skewed sex ratio in the frontier society. His tenant-fighters swore allegiance to him, and he trained these peasant-fighters in combat skills during off seasons. Many of his combatants were equipped with not just spears and swords, but also modern firearms, like front-loading shotguns and rifles.[38]

Baron Wang also dispatched his armed men to intimidate and suppress Mongols who would not be persuaded otherwise to accept his land lease sales terms. According to one account, Wang intimidated a Mongolian nobleman into signing a land lease on a 10,000-year term. On another occasion, Wang's militia successfully crushed a resistance mobilized by a Mongol banner leader.[39]

Internally, Wang did not hesitate to use violence to enforce his authority. Not unlike the authoritarian structures of secret societies in northern China of his time, Wang's words were law, and he held the power of life and death over his subordinates. He was feared just as much as he was revered by his tenants and followers. Wang showed little mercy in his torture methods inflicted upon disloyal followers and captured rivals. For example, victims were said to be bagged and tossed into the Yellow River—this particular method of torture was called "dropping dumplings" (*xiajiaozi*). Another method involved dumping victims in a deep hole drilled into a frozen canal, then sealing the hole—and this was sardonically dubbed "living in a roofed house" (*zhudingpeng fangzi*). In one year, Wang had allegedly executed a horrific toll of 3,500 people.[40]

Land, water, refugee labor, and violence formed the backbone of Baron Wang's hydro turfdom in Hetao. But Baron Wang and other barons did not monopolize the agricultural frontier in West IM. At the peak of Wang's territorial power during the last few decades of the 19th century, another formidable turf builder, the Catholic missionary, was closing in on competing with him for water and land in Hetao.

II Catholic Missionaries

The most active missionary group in IM in the 19th century was the Belgian CICM.[41] CICM missionaries set out to convert Mongol souls but drew readier converts in Han Chinese refugees fleeing the famines and military drafts of northern China. Regardless of their aspirations, the missionaries found themselves preoccupied with pursuits similar to those of the land-water baron, those being, gaining access to land and water, organizing settler society and space, and confronting violence with violence. The CICM mission built a series of concession-like farming colonies in IM. Among CICM's three apostolic jurisdictions in the vast northern steppe, the Apostolic Vicariate of Southwest Mongolia boasted the largest congregation and the greatest number of establishments. Hetao sat at the heart of the CICM's Southwest Vicariate.

How did the Belgian missionaries end up in IM in the first place? The story starts with the spread of Catholicism in China.

II.1 Catholicism in China

According to sociologist Richard Madsen (1998),[42] Catholic missionaries' activity in imperial China went through several waves. The latest wave, starting in the 16th century and continuing to shape Catholicism in China today, was influenced by upheavals in Catholicism in Europe at that time. During the Catholic Reformation in 16th-century Europe, counter-Reformation missions, like the Jesuits, Franciscans, Dominicans, and Paris Foreign Missions Society (MEP), took advantage of the new routes that had opened during the Age of Exploration and set out to China to win converts to make up for their losses in Europe under the Reformation.

The Counter-Reformation Catholic missions in China followed an episcopal hierarchy that was even more elaborate than in medieval Christianity. Incidentally, the episcopal hierarchy fit in well with 16th- and 17th-century China. The Jesuits, led by

Matteo Ricci, convinced the Ming and early Qing emperors that their episcopal hierarchy could reinforce Chinese imperial hierarchy. The Jesuits also managed to attract Chinese political and intellectual elites with their knowledge of Western science and technology. Most importantly, they were willing to accommodate Chinese cultural traditions, including ancestral worship and folk religion. Ricci himself was known to discard his Jesuit outfit and dress as a Buddhist monk when he first entered China. Later on, he changed his wardrobe again to that of a Chinese scholar and finally got it right: the scholar-officials of the court made an even better ally for the missionaries than did the Buddhist monks.[43]

One of the Jesuits, Ferdinand Verbiest, became a personal friend and advisor to Emperor Kangxi (r. 1661–1722) of the Qing Dynasty. Although Kangxi did not convert to Catholicism, he issued an edict of tolerance in 1692. All was well for the Jesuits in China, as missionaries mingled with imperial elites and enjoyed success in the capital during the early Qing period. By the early 18th century, however, the Jesuits' Catholic rivals—notably the Dominicans, Franciscans, and MEPs—began to gain political momentum in the Vatican. These rival orders criticized the Jesuits for accommodating Chinese folk practices, such as worshipping "false" gods, like ancestors and folk gods. The Jesuits' Catholic rivals eventually convinced Pope Clement XI, who issued an edict condemning the Chinese rites in 1704. The century-long "Chinese Rites Controversy" ended with Pope Benedict XIV's termination of the Jesuit mission to China in 1742. In return, Emperor Kangxi and his successors declared Catholicism a heterodox sect and proscribed foreign missionary activity in China. Most European missionaries withdrew from China by the late 18th century. But they left behind a small contingent of European-trained Chinese priests, seminarians, preachers, lay leaders, and congregants who kept their Catholic networks underground and passed down the faith for generations.

After the Opium Wars in the mid-19th century, foreign missionary activities resumed. The expansion of Christianity and imperialism in 19th century China (and other parts of the world) went hand in hand. British and American Protestant missionaries, for example, served as translators in all treaty negotiations after the imperialist invasion of China.[44] What was not lost in translation were the clauses protecting missionaries' rights to travel, proselytize, build churches, own property, and recover property confiscated by the imperial court after the Rites Controversy.

One decisive change in Catholicism in post-Opium Wars China was its spatial shift from urban to rural areas, and its social shift from the elite to the peasantry. While the Jesuits of the 16th- and 17th-centuries focused on political and intellectual elites in the city, the prohibitions in the 18th century drove Catholic activities underground and to the countryside far away from the capital city and the emperor. These activities were led by the Chinese priests, since most foreign missionaries were expelled from China. After the Opium Wars, the Catholic missionaries returned to China. Catholic families and infrastructure that were scattered across the countryside from a century ago were reactivated and served as seedbeds to sprout new opportunities for Catholic expansion in China. In the meantime, the famine, warfare, and banditry that plagued the rural hinterland of 19th-century China proved to be fertile grounds for spreading the gospel. When neither the state nor local gentry could provide relief to the pauperized peasantry, missionaries were eager to deliver this-worldly help and next-worldly hope. The Catholic churches' rural inclination, a state-avoidance strategy of the 18th century, was reinforced by the large pool of potential rural converts in the 19th century.[45] The number of potential converts in rural China was unparalleled. Between 1870 and 1913, about 300 to 350 million people lived in China's countryside, about 80% of China's total. To contextualize this count, 14 plus western European countries recorded 190 to 260 million residents in total during the same period.[46]

Populous China's re-opening to Western religions after the Opium Wars inspired a new generation of European and American proselytizers from both Catholic and Protestant churches. Setting out to explore the immense potential of episcopal expansion, post-Opium Wars missionaries arrived in China with recharged fervor and emboldened ambitions. Among the Catholic churches in China were both traditional orders (such as the Jesuits and the Dominicans, who had been in China since the 16th century) and the newly established orders of the 19th century. The Belgium-based Congregatio Immaculati Cordis Mariae (CICM) was among the latter.

II.2 Congregatio Immaculati Cordis Mariae (CICM) in Rural Inner Mongolia

Founded in 1862 by the Belgian priest Theophiel Verbist (1823–68) in Scheut, a town near Brussels, CICM was established specifically to spread the faith in the newly reopened China.[47] To avoid head-on competition in the treaty ports dominated by missions from major imperial powers like France, Britain, Germany, and the U.S., and hoping to distance themselves from the militaristic imperialism for which those allied nations were criticized, CICM went for China's periphery.[48]

In the fall of 1865, Verbist, a determined priest in his early forties ready for a career breakthrough, embarked with four other missionaries[49] on a 103-day-long journey along the spice trade route, from western Europe via Alexandria, Aden, Singapore, and Hong Kong, finally reaching China's northern treaty port city, Tianjin. From Tianjin, they trekked the overland route to Beijing to obtain travel permits from the French government's extraterritorial office. With the permission of the French occupying force in China, the Belgian missionaries headed north to present-day Inner Mongolia (IM) in the bitter winter. Endorsed by the Vatican, CICM took over the episcopal jurisdiction of its predecessor, the French Congregation of the Mission (CM) in Xiwanzi in Central-West IM (see Figure P.III.1) and set out to consolidate the missions in China's western and northern frontiers of Xinjiang and IM.[50]

In Xinjiang, the Muslim communities proved to be hard to penetrate, let alone convert. Over the span of almost four decades from 1883 to 1922, the number of Catholic converts grew from 100 to 300, most of whom were from Catholic Han Chinese families deported to the western frontier from China's heartland during the persecution era of the 18th century. The frustrated CICM missionaries lamented their work in Xinjiang as "the most unfruitful mission in the world."[51]

In IM, the missionaries also encountered barriers to their attempts to convert Mongols. Verbist and his colleagues did their best to make friends. They learned the Mongolian language and ate and dressed like Mongols. But the Mongol banner aristocracy and Lamaist monks were not impressed. The Mongol ruling elites considered the missionaries competitors for local labor and temple donations and prohibited missionary activities among banner subjects. In the end, few Mongols were converted.[52]

But when God closes a door, he opens a window. The massive number of Han Chinese refugees in IM made for a readier pool of potential converts, as Ivo Stragier, a CICM missionary wrote in 1891, "famine brings harvest to God."[53] Another CICM missionary commented that Han Chinese refugees demonstrated a "much more open mind."[54]

In 1874, CICM missionary work expanded westward from Xiwanzi to Hetao. With its large Han Chinese refugee population (and, hence, potential converts), Hetao grew to be the center of Catholicism in IM under CICM, with a cathedral in Sanshenggong, today's Dengkou County of Banyannur Municipality (Figures 7.1, 7.2, and 7.3).

Figure 7.1 Renovated Sanshenggong Cathedral, exterior

Source: Photo credit: I-tien Hsing 2015.

The gateway to the refugees' souls in Hetao, however, was not God's word but land and water. Without land and water to attract and keep the refugees, there would be no souls to fill the church. As on other occasions where people convert to Christianity primarily for food, medical services, or other benefits, many of the converts

Figure 7.2 Renovated Sanshenggong Cathedral, interior

Source: Photo credit: I-tien Hsing 2015.

Figure 7.3 The original Sanshenggong Cathedral

Source: The photo was put on display at the cathedral, copied by I-tien Hsing in 2015.

in Hetao were, after all, "rice Christians." Or, in Hetao's context, "millet Catholics" (*mizi jiaoyou*). Lyrics from a folk song about millet Catholics in Hetao are telling:

Holy God and Virgin Mary, my warm body kneels down on the cold ground.
(I ask:) Father, where to get land allocation?
(Father replies:) Oh, come to Hongshengyi and plant your crop!
Why do you join the church?
For two strings of copper coins;
Why do you learn the bible?
For three "sheng" (Chinese liters) of millet.[55]

Like the Chinese land-water barons, the Belgium CICM missionaries leased land tracts from Mongol landowners. For water, the mission's rank and file equipped with engineering skills would design irrigation canals and hire refugee labor to build them. But the waterworks built by the church were of a much smaller scale—378 km in total and serving about 10,000 hectares of irrigated land[56]—compared to the land-water barons' over 1,300 km of waterways that fed no less than 87,100 hectares of land.[57] To stretch beyond their own irrigation turf, missionaries provided loans to land owners in exchange for access to their waterworks and irrigated land. For example, between 1917 and 1927 the CICM mission provided a loan of more than 140,000 silver taels in a canal project built by the Yangs, a local land-owning family. It took three generations of the Yangs to complete the canal system, and the mission ended up claiming 30% of the irrigated land.[58]

The loan of 140,000 silver taels was not a trivial sum, and especially so considering the fact that the CICM mission itself had a meager start. Back in 1865, when Verbist and his fellow missionaries first arrived in IM, their finances relied on a Shanghai-based French mission's subsidies and some rental income, which totaled about 7,000 Belgian Francs.[59] The revenue could barely cover the missionaries' own logistical needs, especially after the 30% exchange discount between Shanghai's silver taels and rural IM's copper cash.[60] The heavy debt of over 36,000 Belgian Francs that CICM inherited from the CM mission, whose episcopal jurisdiction CICM took over, only set them back more. The mission was running a deficit twice the size of its revenue and could hardly deliver disaster relief in the immense, calamity-ridden, and impoverished rural IM. The challenges to spreading faith in the Mongolian steppe greatly exceeded what Verbist had expected. In a letter to a colleague, Verbist, who would later die of typhoid fever two years after arriving in IM, wrote about the vast contrast between the optimistic accounts of China depicted in Belgian newspapers and China's, especially IM's disappointing reality of unimaginable penury.[61] Unlike his affluent congregation back home in Belgium, few converts in rural IM were able to donate any amount of their earnings to the church. Quite the contrary, they came to the mission hoping to dodge starvation. The financial demands to respond to local poverty was overwhelming. Realizing that the funds that the Vatican had promised would be slow to materialize, Verbist even made plans to exploit a local mine, which never took off. At the height of desperation, he resorted to borrowing from local Chinese loan sharks at annual interest rates of 30% to 40%.[62] It was, as historian Patrick Taveiren called it, "mission impossible."[63]

How did the mission's financial standing take such a remarkable upturn—from that of a client of loan sharks to holding court in the local money market in a few short decades in an impoverished land?

The missionaries' financial acumen helped. And, the Boxer Indemnity was pivotal. The Boxer Indemnity was the outcome of the Boxer Uprising in northern China from 1899 to 1901. The Boxer Uprising started as a poor peasants' movement led by martial arts experts fighting against foreign forces. It ended with the Eight Nation Alliance's military invasion and the defeat of the Qing, followed by the ruinous Boxer Indemnity, which was perceived as the final straw that broke the Qing, China's last dynasty.[64]

The Boxer Uprising was rooted in peasants' deep enmity toward foreign forces that had been brewing since the Opium Wars of the mid-19th century. After the Wars, missionaries returned to China upon imperialism's upswing. Unlike the Jesuits of the 17th century, post-Opium Wars missionaries were much more assertive of their moral righteousness. By papal decree, Catholic missionaries took an oath to not accommodate any traditional Chinese customs, including traditional marriage arrangements and funerary rites, and most important of all, ancestral worship, the foundation of Chinese spiritual and social values.[65] For most Chinese, this rule radically broke with the "culture of the past and community of the present" and was difficult to accept.[66]

On the other hand, joining the foreign church conferred benefits that were essential for survival and future prospects of the peasants. The wide-ranging benefits included access to land, water, loans, seeds, farming tools, relief grains, schools, clinics, as well as social belonging and political protection. In northern China, at the height of church influence in the late 19th century, missionaries were able to enhance the power of tenants in relation to their landlords or money lenders.[67] Similarly in IM, missionaries also extended their own rights of extraterritoriality to those under their tutelage, which enabled Chinese converts to enjoy immunity from Chinese law. The missionaries' use of political influence to protect converts triggered social conflicts, which were frequent enough to warrant the category of "church-related litigation cases" (*jiao-an*) in official judicial logs and a separate chapter in local gazetteers. In Hetao, one of the many cases of "church-related litigation" involved CICM missionaries sheltering a group of congregants who had killed nine people from a rival village over land-water disputes, and who had used the church as an extraterritorial space that local officials could not enter. In another case, a bandit was jailed. His family went to the missionaries for help. The missionaries baptized the bandit's family members before negotiating with a local governor to get the bandit released.[68]

Abandoning traditional Chinese customs and receiving protection and benefits from the foreign church, Chinese converts were brought into a privileged social-political clique that was separate from, and deeply suspected by, local non-followers.

Widespread and prolonged famine in northern China further inflamed the rural poor's hostility towards privileged foreign missionaries and Chinese converts.

Meanwhile, after the military invasion by the Eight Nation Alliance, the defeated Qing were forced to sign the Boxer Protocol in 1901. The Protocol included the infamous Boxer Indemnity of 450 million silver taels, which was the equivalent of about 18,000 tones of silver, or US$333 million at the exchange rate of the time, to be paid over the course of 39 years.[69]

The restitution funds were a decisive contribution to the boom in Christianity in China in the decades following the Boxer Uprising.[70] Belgium was not a full member of the Eight Nations Alliance, but Belgium did contribute to the alliance's military exploits and was thus awarded 1.89% of the indemnity sum—a sum that equated 9 million silver taels.[71] The Boxer Uprising resulted in great damage and fatalities in different regions in IM, especially in Central-West and West IM. According to the CICM's report, eight foreign missionaries and close to 3,000 converts were killed during the Boxer Uprising in IM. Twenty-five churches, three orphanages, and more than 3,000 village homes were looted and burned. Woman and child captives were brought to neighboring Ningxia and sold, and more than 20,000 congregates were displaced.[72] Based on the self-report, CICM missionaries successfully claimed their share of the Indemnity of more than 2 million silver taels,[73] which fuelled CICM's rapid growth in IM. Between 1896 and 1911, the number of church settlements in Vicariate grew from 14 to 36, and the number of baptized converts in these settlements more than quintupled from 3,635 in 1896 to 20,010 in 1911.[74] The Southwest Vicariate counted 72,000 converts by 1940. That year in IM as a whole, the CICM congregation reached 220,000, a remarkable growth from 14,000 in 1883.[75]

The Boxer Indemnity benefitted not just the mission's treasury but also its inventory of land. The Qing court had spread the colossal burden of the Boxer Indemnity among provincial and sub-provincial governments. The cash-poor local authorities, obligated to pay restitution to missions in their jurisdictions, negotiated with missionaries to pay their indemnity obligations with land. A significant portion of the CICM's land holdings was therefore within the category of "Indemnity land" (*peijiaodi*). Ridden with violent conflicts to which I will turn in the next section, Indemnity land negotiations between the missions and local authorities added more than 200,000 hectares to CICM's holdings.[76] That was, however, just the official figure. Missions allegedly extended their land holdings beyond what was officially conferred. In one case, a mission was allocated 2,000 qing (13,340 hectares) of Indemnity land but enclosed 10,000 qing (66,700 hectares), or five times the official allocation.[77]

With deepened pockets lined with Indemnity payouts, the church was able to expand its land holdings through other channels as well. Some of the CICM's holdings were direct purchases from small land holders, especially during droughts and floods when the cash-poor peasants had few options other than liquidizing their parcels. Other holdings were loan collateral retained after debtors defaulted. As mentioned earlier, the church also obtained land by providing loans to irrigation canal builders in exchange for irrigated land upon completion of projects. As CICM's land holdings multiplied, embittered and excluded locals nicknamed the church "the Holy Hall of Landlords" (*dizhutang*), and the missionaries "land rakes" (*dipazi*).[78] As a formidable landlord in Hetao, the missionaries did what landlords do: they collected land rent, water fees, and interest from their tenant-debtor-congregants, and used the irrigation networks in their control to transport and trade grain.[79] In sum, CICM's transformation from a humble debtor to a formidable creditor—as well as its unprecedented expansion in early 20th-century Hetao—had the Boxer Indemnity to thank.

II.3 Fortifying God's Home on Earth

While China-based scholars have criticized the missionaries' imperialistic land grabs in Hetao,[80] the missionaries themselves offered a different take on the matter. In his memoire, CICM missionary Van Melckebeke (1898–1980), who worked in China's northwest from 1927 to 1952, emphasized that a good portion of the mission's land holdings came from voluntary donations by Chinese converts. Better endowed settlers offered land parcels and invited missionaries to build churches in their villages. While Van Melckebeke celebrated the settlers' pledges as a sign of their religious devotion, he also acknowledged the pragmatic motivations behind such pledges.[81] Parcels were donated in exchange for the church's political capital and defense might, which protected settlers against the widespread banditry in Hetao.

Rampant banditry was a defining feature of the 19th century and the first half of the 20th century on both sides of the Great Wall. The successful Republican Revolution in 1911 that ended China's imperial history did not automatically bring social order or political stability. In Hetao, the convergence of disbanded soldiers from various sides, warlords, opium cartels, secret societies, and foreign interests—aggravated by the multiple and constantly shifting centers of authority—created an over-militarized yet under-governed region.

Armed men in bands of tens, hundreds, or even thousands alternated between banditry and serving as soldiers. Under unfavorable political circumstances the raiding bandits would surrender and change hats to "safeguard" the vicinity for local authorities who were too weak to eliminate banditry outright or to discipline its own law enforcers and armed forces. Often the bandit-turned-soldiers resumed banditry when career prospects of the old trade improved. Disbanded soldiers carried firearms to rob and kidnap for ransom. Village-based militia members who performed seasonal banditry would turn into permanent banditry, and vice versa, depending on the social and political conditions of the moment and their leaders' vacillating plans. In their interchangeable roles as soldiers and bandits, armed men rampaged through villages to either collect levies or to loot, and often both. In local terminology, banditry and soldiers represented the twin fiascos of "bandit disaster" (*feihuo*) and "soldier disaster" (*bingzai*).

Church establishments stood as one of the most reliable organizers of local defense against the armed aggression of bandits and soldiers in Hetao. Missionaries were known as effective builders of fortification and were equipped with modern firearms. The scale and scope of the church-centered safe havens reflected both the magnitude of the banditry infestation and the church's capacity for guarding its turf. One of the major Catholic bases in central-west IM after the Boxer Uprising, for example, was reinforced into a rammed-earth and crenelated bulwark that was 1,600 meters long, 5 meters tall, and 4 meters thick at its base, complemented by 16 batteries and four watch towers.[82] In the church compound of Xiwanzi, CICM's commanding center in West IM, its strong fortification had a former artillery unit commander from the Belgian army, named Arthur Wittamer, to head its armed forces since 1900. Wittamer led the effort in building fortifications and trenches, manufacturing weaponry and ammunition, and providing military trainings to church villagers. The Xiwanzi compound was said to have owned 400 rifles and six cannons.[83]

In various church bases, CICM missionaries organized the villagers into patrol and combat squads and distributed firearms to church militia members when bandit-soldiers came to the gate. The mission's fortification and militia provided much-needed protection and maintained stability for villagers to carry on farming. During severe drought or other disasters when banditry was particularly rampant, villagers would stay inside the walled fortification at night and work in fields close to the fortification during the day.

Donating land to build Catholic villages proved to be a win-win strategy: better-off settlers could leverage the Church's political influence and defense might for safety, while the mission was able to expand its episcopal territory. Land donations added to the mission's overall holdings in addition to the aforementioned sources—the Boxer Indemnity, land purchases, and retainment of land collateral—all of which contributed to the mission's land stock. The large land stock meant more than a numerical triumph. It also bears critical territorial implications. The massive landholdings helped consolidate otherwise scattered and isolated land tracts, bringing them into congruous and connected territorial expanses. It is the physical foundation of a turfdom. With territorial consolidation over a vast expanse of land, the mission was able to launch relocation projects on its own turf and establish new Catholic farming settlements to support the growing congregation. Unrestrained by the immediate survival needs of the present, the mission now held enough territorial sway to plan its future growth. Such a future-oriented aspiration and action shows a territorial vision far beyond keeping to scattered and isolated Catholic enclaves. The mission, God willing, is here to stay and to expand. Of the 59 new Catholic settlements built in the early 20th century, the 12 largest ones were home to more than 54,000 settlers. The largest among the top 12, Shanba, established in 1907, housed 20,000 settlers by 1940. Others varied between 300 and 8,000 each.[84]

Territorial consolidation and physical fortification of Catholic concessions were further bolstered by the Catholic congregation's moral discipline. Life in the Catholic villages followed the mission's regimented orders, and livelihoods were organized around the principle of social and economic self-sufficiency. In addition to land and other agricultural input, church-organized social services, such as relief grain, elderly homes, orphanages, cemeteries, clinics, postal services, and schools, were made available exclusively for the congregation. Family added another layer to the church's soft power and the Catholic villagers' social solidarity. Unlike urban-based protestant proselytizers who saw their converts as individuals, CICM missionaries in rural Hetao set about to build Catholic families. Congregants married one another under the blessing and guidance of the missionary and were buried together in church cemeteries. The baby girls adopted by the mission's orphanages helped to expand the Catholic socio-religious orbit. Between 1870 and 1910, according to the church's bookkeeping, more than 8,500 babies were brought into CICM orphanages in western IM. Baby girls were disproportionately represented in the orphanages due to frequent abandonment of female newborns in the impoverished region. At times of crisis, baby girls were the first to be left on the church's doorstep by parents who chose to keep their boys who could carry on the blood line. This practice in turn created a highly skewed sex ratio in marriage-aged cohorts. With a very high mortality rate even after adoption, orphaned girls who managed to reach marriageable age were sought-after brides. For the large number of poor, single men in the northern frontier who possessed neither matchmaking social networks nor the capacity to pay the prohibitively high bridal prices, joining the Catholic congregation afforded the critical benefit of marriages arranged by the missionary.[85]

Catholic families stocked the Catholic villages. Few non-Catholics lived in these villages. The patriarchal church, to which converted families adhered, was the anchor of their tribal identity. Richard Madsen (1998) has likened Catholicism in rural China to an ethnicity, suggesting that it was "less a faith of personal choice than an ascribed status of inherited membership in a community."[86] The Catholic community expanded further over time by producing Chinese priests and lay leaders. Chinese priests, most of whom had grown up in Catholic families and church villages and studied in Catholic schools, were the critical link that enabled the reach of foreign missionaries across China's immense territory. They played a critical role ever since the prohibition years of the 18th century, as mentioned previously. In the post-Boxer era, as the CICM mission expanded, the number of Chinese priests also grew rapidly, filling mostly lower-ranking positions.[87] CICM missionaries, Chinese priests, and Chinese converts together forged a strong sense of solidarity that reinforced their physical fortifications in Hetao.

Catholic land concessions in Hetao, in sum, were consolidated by fortifications, cultivation expansion, and community solidarity—all under the steadfast command of the missionaries. Catholic villages were among the best governed and most resolutely guarded turfdoms in Hetao during the turbulent early 20th century.

II.4 Violent Purity

The grassroots-based Catholic mission was no immersion program, however. Quite the contrary, missionaries aspired to establish a pure and secluded Catholic community untainted by nonbelievers. Their goal was not to mingle with the locals, but to install purity in a land of vice. In his brief recount of the history of CICM in China, Fr Leo Van den Berg reflected that the Catholic church had tried to build an ideal, virtuous house of God, the "Civitas Christiana," in different corners of the world, like in the Jesuits' church collective farm-villages in Paraguay and in the secluded and remote medieval European seminaries. Such Catholic spatial aspirations of purity proved to be hard to establish and even harder to maintain. But the ideal of an unadulterated Catholic community unexpectedly materialized in 19th century IM, where Chinese refugees filled the church settlements modeled after both the Paraguayan collective farms and medieval European seminaries.[88]

A pure and holy land in the tumultuous 19th to 20th century IM, however, could not be secured without violence. Sturdy fortitudes were essential not just to protect converts, but missionaries themselves against antimission forces that surrounded Catholic villages. And the best defense is a good offense.

Hetao of the late-19th century was the frontier of the frontier. Refugees from northern China and other parts of IM congregated and escalated resource struggles in Hetao. Armed conflicts over land, water, and fuelwood, among others, were frequent between families, between factions of a village, between villages at different reaches of an irrigation channel, or between neighboring canal systems. To strengthen one's edge in the competition to survive, political coalitions were essential. Sworn brotherhoods, secret societies, and sectarian cults were popular, all of which were intertwined with militias and bandits. Sending a family member to join a militia or a bandit group served not just economic but also political ends: it was a way to enlist political backing for the family amidst the violence of everyday life.

CICM missionaries were far from an innocent external force that was dropped into Hetao. Rather, like other territorial actors in Hetao, they were an integral part of the resource struggle and violence. As a powerful and determined contender, the missionaries fanned the flames, but also got burned themselves quite a few times.

In the years after the Opium Wars, as the missionaries raked in land parcel after land parcel, resentment towards them also grew. There were many other wealthy landlords and moneylenders around. The missionaries did not charge more than the going rates for rent and interest. And the price they paid for purchasing land was no less than other land dealers. Still, peasants were particularly resentful of the missionaries for the latter's use and abuse of their unparalleled political clout. CICM held extraterritorial authority that was protected by its political patron, the French occupying force in Beijing. The French authorities stepped in on behalf of CICM whenever disputes with local authorities arose. Locally, missionaries exhibited little hesitation to lend their political capital to converts in land or water conflicts with non-followers. Without the backing of local authorities, who were often too timid to lend support, non-followers often lost out in disputes with the converts. The missionaries' influence and discriminatory practices added another explosive fault line in a society that was already deeply fractured by ethnic, class, and territorial divides.

The unbalanced power between local authorities and the missionaries did not go unnoticed by settlers. To gain the upper hand against their rivals, entire families, villages, or even factions of a secret society would convert en masse in exchange for the unconditional support offered by CICM.

As land and water struggles became increasingly fierce, the vicious cycle of aggression and retaliation brought the local society's resentment towards converts and their political patron, the CICM missionaries, to a boiling point. One of the deadliest feuds between the Catholic congregation and local society in Hetao occurred at the height of the Boxer Uprising in 1900. The conflict was triggered by a land dispute and resulted in 300 Catholic converts raiding a rival village, slaughtering nine villagers, and tossing their corpses into the Yellow River. The lead murderers subsequently took refuge in a church compound called "Twenty-Four Qing of Land" (*Er'shisiqingdi*). Located in today's Baotou Municipality, the church and its surrounding villages were a CICM stronghold in West IM. The General of Suiyuan, the lead regional governor appointed by the imperial court, was an advocate for taking a firm stance against the foreign powers. He sent in troops equipped with modern rifles and heavy cannons to attack the church fortification. Over 2,000 combatants, comprised of Mongol banner calvary, Chinese secret society members, and Boxers, joined the battle. The church fortification was shattered, leading to a death toll of over 900 church villagers and the capture of the ill-reputed missionary Ferdinand Hamer (1840–1900), who locals had nicknamed "Old Devil Head" (*laomotou*). According to the Chinese Jesuit priest, Li Tai's (1840–1911) account published in 1905, on the fatal day of July 23, 1900, Hamer was hung by his feet. His lower body was charred, his hands and feet dismembered, and his ears and nose mutilated. His heart was eviscerated, boiled, and fed to a child beggar who received a monetary reward of 500 *wen* for swallowing the "Old Devil Head's" heart.[89] Hamer first set foot in IM in 1865. At 24, he was the youngest of the mission to China led by CICM's founder, Theophiel Verbist, who had passed away two years after arriving in IM. Hamer carried on the CICM mission and was ordained Bishop in 1878 as CICM expanded in IM. Five years later, he was appointed by the Pope to head the apostolic vicariate of Southwest Mongolia, CICM's largest operation in IM.

It is difficult to verify the gruesome details of the end of a veteran mission leader's life as reported by Li Tai, a Chinese priest. Li's narrative, based the recollection and writings of CICM missionaries, who may or may not have witnessed the event, could be Li's way of showing the non-followers' barbarism. His figures of the damages and death tolls were based on CICM's registry, which served as the basis for the retribution negotiation with the Qing court, could also be inflated.[90] The passage describing the torture in Li's report nonetheless reflects the extraordinary level of antagonism present in the unmitigated resource struggles and violence of 19th- and 20th-century

Hetao. Embarking on a global mission of purification, the Catholic proselytizers' work in the embattled Hetao was tainted with blood.

III Territorial Entrepreneurs

Baron Wang and CICM missionaries were territorial rivals. During the late 19th and early 20th centuries when both were in expansion mode, Wang and other land-water barons shared the anti-missionary stance while the missionaries saw the well-armed and well-endowed barons as impediments to CICM's grand mission. The two territorial contenders eventually parceled out Hetao between themselves. CICM grew to dominate the western half of Hetao, thwarting Wang's attempts to purchase land in the church's domain. Baron Wang, on the other end, resolutely guarded his turf in central and eastern Hetao, where no Catholic villages could be found.[91]

But the two hydro turf builders, rivalrous as they were, had more in common than they would probably care to admit, especially when it came to their territorial logic. They both established their bases in the periphery, away from the center of competition in China's heartland. The barons started off with merchant capital displaced by foreign trading powers before eventually finding an outlet for capital in the northern frontier. The Belgian CICM, a minor league contender in the missionaries' overseas expansionary race, which was dominated by established churches of the major imperial powers, avoided the highly competitive treaty port cities and went for the untouched territory of the northern frontier.

The two hydro turf builders also shared a similar set of strategies for territorial consolidation. They amassed large amounts of land and money, then consolidated their territorial control by building and/or investing in extensive irrigation works, recruiting refugee labor, and organizing farming settlements. Both built up armed forces to ensure territorial autonomy and authority. Though their goals diverged—the missionaries aimed to save souls, while the barons aimed to harvest crops—their methods were surprisingly similar, and the means and the ends often became entangled along the way.

The two hydro turf builders were non-state territorial actors who organized the frontier economy, society, and space with what I call "territorial entrepreneurship" at a time and in a place of palpable state deficiency. Although they divided Hetao into two rival turfdoms, what they created in Hetao was one uninterrupted expanse of agricultural frontier, leaving few rocks unturned. The territorial rivals unwittingly converged in their enterprise of cultivation expansion in West IM.

On the other hand, the shared territorial strategies built upon land, water, and guns did not lead the two turf builders onto a common path in the next phase of their territorial projects. After all, these key ingredients—land, water, and guns—were not a fixed set of tools, but rather, part of evolving territorial dynamisms in Hetao. And these ingredients could not ensure eventual nor perpetual success in territorial consolidation. Territorial dynamisms entailed contingent territorial struggles fraught with friction, setbacks, realignments, and detours. These territorial dynamisms set the paths of the barons and the missionaries apart as other formidable territorial contenders appeared on the scene at the dawn of the tumultuous 20th century.

III.1 Barons under the Predatory State

The Boxer Indemnity allowed the CICM mission to thrive in the early 20th century. The Indemnity also clipped Baron Wang's hydro turfdom. The astronomical sum of the Indemnity led the desperate Qing court to launch a frantic search for new sources of revenue. After offloading some of the fiscal burden to local governments, the Qing court was still left with a hefty sum. The pressure was mounting as foreign powers threatened more military action for late payments. The Hetao area, which had been left to Mongol princes and Han Chinese land-water barons for most of the previous century, and which had now been transformed into vast expanses of irrigated farms, promised new tax and rent revenues to replenish the state treasury.

In 1903, the Qing court established the Land Reclamation Bureau in Hetao and set out to conduct cadastral surveys and register land that had been cleared and cultivated, which were now deemed taxable. But in the post-Boxer era, CICM's properties in Hetao were beyond the reach of the court's Reclamation Bureau. Indemnity-related land disputes and conflicts between Hetao locals and CICM were already too inflammatory for the Reclamation Bureau to get involved. So the Bureau went for land outside of CICM's claims. For sure the non-mission lands were not empty. There, Bureau officials and their armed surveyors and troops were met with fierce resistance from the poor and the rich alike: Mongol noblemen, Chinese land-water barons, merchants, as well as small Chinese and Mongol land holders and tenants—all of whom were agitated by the new taxes and land lease fees imposed by the Reclamation Bureau. Poor tenants were squeezed the hardest, as they were now responsible for fees and rents to both their landlords and the Reclamation Bureau.

The key to imposing the new, hugely unpopular state taxes and rents while also quelling the resistance was to rein in the most powerful local boss-cum-super-land-water barons like Baron Wang. To remove this weighty roadblock, the newly appointed head of the Land Reclamation Bureau in Hetao marshalled hundreds of armed soldiers to visit Baron Wang at his residence. Wang eventually agreed to turn over his canals to the Reclamation Bureau, which marked the beginning of the end of Dragon King Wang's hydro turfdom. To remove Wang's influence further, the local governor threw Wang in jail in 1906 on charges of murdering a rival land baron in 1902. Although he was most likely responsible for the murder in 1902, Wang was not made responsible for it until the political climate was no longer in his favor in 1906. Hoping to reduce his jail time, the illiterate Wang agreed to sign a written agreement that transferred much of his land and canals to the Reclamation Bureau.

The political winds shifted again in 1911. Upon the demise of the Qing Dynasty and the establishment of the Republican regime, Baron Wang was released from prison. He was subsequently commissioned by the newly established Republican authority in Hetao to organize a local militia and was decorated for successfully thwarting a raid by a northern Mongolian banner.[92] But Wang had lost much of his land by then, and more importantly, his control over the irrigation canals. The Republican authority that took over the land and the canals was more interested in land rents than in maintaining the canal systems, however. The canals, fed by the easily silted-up Yellow River, deteriorated quickly for want of regular dredging and repairs.[93]

After Dragon King Wang passed away and his hydro turfdom was largely dissolved, his third son, Wang Ying, carried on the family legacy with the militia. Like father, like son: Ying was a charismatic leader, and there was no shortage of drifting armed men in Hetao to recruit. At one point Wang Ying's force boasted over 10,000 men. Embroiled in frontier politics of the early 20th century where few boundaries existed between the formal and the informal, Wang Ying was enlisted by the regional warlord-backed Republican army in the 1920s and served as a regiment leader. It was a political move for the declining Wangs to set foot in the regional power circle. However, growing up as the heir of the formidable Dragon King, Wang Ying never learned to take orders from his military superiors, who pressed him to squeeze silver taels out of the remaining Wang family coffers. After a failed attempt at a coup d'état, Wang Ying became an exile in Tianjin, a port city in northern China.

Baron Wang's daughter, Er'laocai, was no more docile than her brother. Despite having bound feet, Er'laocai was said to have carried a rifle at a young age while supervising canal construction workers. After her father's death and while her brother Wang Ying was away with the Republican army, Er'laocai was in charge of a 4,000-strong militia in the Wangs' home base, Linhe County, today's Bayannur. Known as the "Mu Guiying of Hetao,"[94] she successfully drove off a raiding bandit gang that threatened to loot and kill all in Linhe.[95]

Under the predatory state and semi-state powers, Baron Wang's turfdom was completely dissolved by the 1930s. Er'laocai was jailed on charges of sheltering criminals. The farming settlements that Baron Wang established were incorporated into three county jurisdictions under the Republican-warlord regime. And the Wangs' private militiamen resorted to banditry. Legend has it that most bandit gangs in Hetao and its northern neighboring region, Chahar, in the 20th century can trace their origins to the Wang family's militia.[96]

III.2 Missionaries amidst Bandits and Warlords

In the western half of Hetao, where CICM dominated, the proselytizers' work in the post-Boxer era was hardly smooth sailing. The signing of the Boxer Protocol in 1901 may have ended the full-blown military invasion of the Eight Nation

Alliance to China, but it did not allay the boiling socioeconomic tensions, nor did it ease the widespread antipathy towards the foreign missions. In IM, foreign missions' recharged moral righteousness and elevated political prestige after the Boxer Uprising added fuel to their already strained relationship with non-followers. A new chapter of violence and increasingly frequent anti-missionary conflicts kicked off in the aftermath of the Boxer Uprising.

Land and water, again, were key. Much of the Indemnity land conferred to the church was neither empty nor "wasteland," as logged on the official registry. With more than a century-long history of farming, most parcels in Central-West IM and Hetao had carried convoluted histories of ownership and tenancy arrangements intertwined with multi-phased reclamation and subdivisions of land and water access. When local governments designated such "wasteland" as Indemnity land to the CICM mission in various locations, it immediately ignited head-on conflicts between CICM converts and deprived land holders and tenants alike. These converts were led by self-righteous missionaries to take control over the Indemnity land.

Rubbing salt into the wound, the Qing court began to tighten its grip over land in Hetao, in hopes of finding new sources of revenue for the depleted state treasury. As mentioned earlier, the court set up a Land Reclamation Bureau in Hetao in 1903, two years after the Boxer Protocol, to enforce land registration and tax and fee collection, targeting the area outside of the mission's immediate reach. With both the extractive state and the emboldened mission pressing for more land and land rents, resource violence surged to new heights. The demise of the Qing and the fragmented polity of the ensuing Republican-warlord era only created more predatory local strongmen in Hetao. The fact that the best soil was devoted to opium, the most profitable crop, inflamed the conflicts further still. Opium depleted the soil's nutrients, and capital-intensive opium plantations widened social inequality. More land was diverted from grain to opium cropping, which reduced grain reserves for drought and flood years. Opium became the major tax base for local authorities and a convertible currency. Opium addiction across class and age spread with its cultivation. The vicious cycle of the opium economy lead to even more endemic banditry.[97]

Banditry reached historic heights in the 1920s and 1930s. Large bandit leaders were indistinguishable from mini warlords. Despite their strong defence, the affluent and highly visible mission compounds were some of the few places around that were worth looting and became prime targets for bandit strikes. A growing number of missionaries were killed or kidnapped for ransom, which usually entailed demands for silver taels, horses, firearms, and opium. By Van Melckebeke's account, during the eight decades from 1865 to 1945, more than two hundred missionaries lost their lives in IM. One hundred and twelve of them died during the two decades between 1910 and 1930, long after the Boxer Uprising. The two leading causes of the missionaries' demise were banditry and endemic disease.[98]

One such banditry incident was reported in an English newspaper published in Shanghai. In March 1925, news broke about a CICM missionary who was kidnapped by a bandit band led by the formidable Su Yu-seng.[99] On an unspecified day in late February 1925, the band razed the mission in aforementioned Er'shisiqingdi church compound, one of the most fortified Catholic bases in the Vicarate of Southwest Mongolia. Bandit chief Su captured a CICM missionary, Father de Clippele. de Clippele was dragged around by Su's band over the next 78 days. On March 8, hiding in a dust storm, 400 of Su's men swooped in and ambushed another Catholic village. In addition to the looting, the bandits captured yet another missionary to "provide companionship" for the captive de Clippele. In the following days, as the band charged on towards the outskirts of the provincial capital of Suiyuan, they laid siege to several other Catholic villages along the way. On March 13, Su led 100 men in attacking a Catholic village 60 km south of Suiyuan, killing the grand catechist and the church comprador and burning homes and the school within the walled compound. The bandits left behind them a sack that contained three heads and two hands of decapitated victims. Three days later, on the night of March 16, a much-expanded band of over 1,000 men armed with rifles forced their way into another mission fortification. Houses and schools were burned. Missionaries and converts took refuge inside the church until March 18, when a relief force finally arrived to repel the bandits. There were deaths and injuries on both sides. But like in most cases, only Christian losses were reported: four dead, a dozen wounded.

Republican armies did make attempts to stop Su's rampage. But often when soldiers dispatched by the local authority arrived at the scene, the bandits simply ran across the frozen-over Yellow River to another jurisdiction, which was under a different local authority. On one occasion, a group of soldiers was sent to a besieged Catholic village, but they suddenly withdrew upon the start of the battle. On another occasion, an earnest officer, Colonel Yu, led a regiment of cavalry to pursue the bandits. The bandits "lured the Colonel into the recess of a temple and captured him and used him as a shield against the government troops," according to a government report cited by the newspaper. Colonel Yu, like Father de Clippele, was paraded around from place to place by the bandits. In his captivity, the fearless Colonel was said to have "snatched the revolver from one of the guards" at an opportune moment and killed several bandits before he shot himself.

The incident in the winter of 1925 was not the first time bandits kidnapped missionaries in IM, nor was it the last. But 1925 carried special territorial and historical significance. It was the year when one of the most powerful warlord-generals in Republican China, Feng Yuxiang, began to rule Central-West IM. In the early 1920s, Feng fought other warlords and supported the founding father of the Republic of China, Dr Sun Yat-sen, and later became the military pillar of Dr Sun's fragile Republican government. Feng was also known as the "Christian General," as he was baptized by the Methodist Episcopal Church early on in his military career in 1914. When Feng took over Central-West IM he, unlike his predecessors, swore to eradicate the mission-raiding bandits. He delivered on his promise by waging vigorous campaigns against the bandits. It was under Feng Yuxiang's reign that the military governor of Suiyuan sent the heroic Colonel Yu, the one who committed suicide during captivity, to confront the bandits. The unfavorable political climate of the time drove many bandit groups to surrender to local authorities and gain admittance to local military regiments. For these armed men, enlistment was a survival strategy that allowed them to continue on a similar career path with greater political legitimacy. For authorities who aspired to eradicate banditry and restore territorial control, however, they had to think twice about lending such legitimacy to former bandits. Such political dilemmas played out in full in 1925 with bandit chief Su's raids on Catholic villages. Su's motivation, in addition to the usual looting, was said to have been to press local authorities into granting his band admission into the government's armies. According to coverage in *The Shanghai Times*, Su attacked the missionaries because the local Republican authority had already taken in hundreds of armed bandits from other bands, and Su felt it was unfair that his men were left out of the deal. Thus, the news article emphasized that the bandits' outrage was "solely against the Chinese authorities," despite the fact that they exclusively targeted church missions and villages. Su was quoted to have said, "If they won't take us into the government army we will burn down every Catholic church until the authorities take action."

Assuming the quote of Su's words was close enough to what actually happened, Su's strategy of raiding the missions to bring local authorities to the bargaining table suggests that the Catholic mission was far from an accidental outsider, but a weighty player in frontier geopolitics. CICM's local influence also lasted longer than that of Baron Wang. The mission stayed in West IM until 1949 when it was expelled by the newly established Chinese Communist regime.

III.3 Branding Territorial Entrepreneurship

Both the barons' and the missionaries' turfdoms in the tumultuous frontier over the second half of the 19th century were built upon water, land, and guns. Their paths then diverged in the 20th century when other territorial contenders gained prominence in Hetao. Baron Wang's hydro turfdom was broken apart by the predatory state, while CICM's political prestige proved to be both an asset and a liability in the era of warlords and banditry. In their rise and fall, the two hydro turf builders navigated the volatile Hetao with their own brands of territorial entrepreneurship.

I use "territorial entrepreneurship" to highlight the spatial dimension of the two lead actors' political maneuvers. Their strategies of establishing authority and maintaining autonomy shaped and were shaped by the territorial dynamics of the place and time. These two non-state territorial entrepreneurs had built their turfdoms following the territorial logic of consolidation and expansion of resource control, tract by tract, canal by canal, while guarding their domains with guns. Under this shared territorial logic, however, they each developed a distinctive brand of territorial entrepreneurship.

Baron Wang's territorial entrepreneurship evinces a peasant brand of political pragmatism that involved little ideological dogma. In the context of the debate over Chinese peasants' revolutionary capacity, historian Lucien Bianco (1967, 2001) argued that for Chinese peasants of the 19th and 20th centuries, neither nationalism nor communism could save them from starvation or other rural miseries. For the peasants, the urban intellectuals' debates over various "isms" for China's future stood far from China's rural reality in which "survival was the ultimate heroism."[100] Peasants' survival strategies were not all passive, though. They could be predatory and aggressive, such as by engaging in armed feuds and taking up banditry, as Elizabeth Perry (1980) has examined. Yet peasants' political vision rarely went beyond preserving family livelihood and fending for local autonomy. Few actively challenged the emperor's "mandate of heaven."[101]

Baron Wang did not challenge the emperor's mandate of heaven, for sure. But he did try to borrow political legitimacy from the emperor. During the Qing, Wang attempted the usual path of upward mobility from landlord to gentry, and regularly donated grains to the government's drought relief programs. He had also led his militia to drive out invading Mongols. He was awarded an official title by the court for his contributions.[102] But this usual route of legitimacy-borrowing did not take Wang very far during dynastic decline and transition. To diversify his political portfolio at the transient moment of regime change, Wang also provided financial support to the Republican revolutionaries who overthrew the last Qing emperor in 1911. He was subsequently commissioned to organize a militia for the new Republican government in Hetao. Wang was, in other words, an indiscriminate borrower of political legitimacy from the multiple and shifting authorities. Wang did not exhibit any particular sentiment for ethnic nationalism either. Wang's visitor Zhang Xiangwen had projected him as a heroic defender of China's national border, as mentioned previously. Yet, in his heyday, Baron Wang was known for his ruthless suppression of uncooperative Mongol landowners and Chinese tenants alike. He was also hailed as a generous business partner by his Mongol noblemen collaborators. He even once took refuge in a Mongol ally's home when he was pursued by a rival Chinese baron. Baron Wang, in short, appeared to sport a peasant brand of territorial entrepreneurship that features political pragmatism with little ideological predisposition.

In comparison, the CICM missionaries' territorial entrepreneurship can be seen as being of a broker brand. As social contempt against the mission and its congregation ran high, missionaries tried to maintain their political relevance and reduce antagonism through diplomacy with local elites. At a time and place where centers of power were elusive and transitory, the CICM missionaries strived to position themselves as a neutral third-party between any two clashing forces in the evolving local politics. During the Republican Revolution in the first decade of the 20th century, for example, the battle between Republican soldiers and the Qing-backed banner army in Hetao concluded with the banner army's surrender under CICM's mediation. During the Republican era when local authority in Hetao was fragile, newly appointed county officials would seek shelter within church fortifications to evade robbery by armed secret society gangs.[103]

The mission itself was not immune to armed aggressions, as illustrated earlier. Yet, compared with the fleeting Republican government and its representatives in the frontier, the mission proved to be more organized and committed to holding onto its turf. Also, as local governance in Hetao was incapacitated as a result of ethnic fault lines between the Mongolian banner and Chinese county authorities, the mission was often brought in to arbitrate the disputes between Chinese and Mongolian authorities and their constituencies, or even to mediate ceasefire negotiations between the local militia and bandit bands during protracted armed conflicts.[104] In his eyewitness account of the rise of Communism in China in the 1930s, the American journalist, Edgar Snow, reported that the CICM missionaries in Suiyuan had a "vast estate" sandwiched between the "communist Red's" territory on one side and the "Republican White troops'" on the other. The Reds negotiated a treaty with the missionaries, in which they promised to protect the mission's property in exchange for permission to organize anti-Japanese societies among the tenants within the mission's "fiefdom."[105]

As a deeply vested outside-insider with special political privileges and as a formidable landlord, money lender, and armed force, the mission managed to carve out their political niche—a mediator of territorial contestation between various raging forces, be they the imperial and revolutionary armies, Republican authorities and local bandits, Chinese and Mongolian jurisdictional authorities, or Communist and Republican warlord-led troops. They were a broker-style territorial entrepreneur with a territorial agenda of their own, that is, expanding and keeping God's home standing for as long as possible in IM, however tumultuous.

What also set the two brands of territorial entrepreneurs apart is their discursive powers. Missionaries were men of letters. They were well-versed in the text-based Catholic bureaucracy of bookkeeping, reporting, and publishing. Supported by the imperial and institutional might of Catholicism, missionaries embarked on a civilizing mission with propaganda skills and infrastructure that Baron Wang lacked. Like missionaries elsewhere, CICM missionaries in IM left reams of detailed records enumerating their accomplishments. Their scrupulous bookkeeping included event logs, lists of property possessions, records of personnel changes, figures indicating congregation expansion, and lists of construction projects and social service provision by establishment and by year. The regimented bookkeeping apparatus, enriched by missionaries' letters, memoirs, and biographies, built an immeasurable wealth of textual materials in European languages and in Chinese. "Print Catholicism"[106]—though its texts should be read intertextually and contextually—has nevertheless contributed to the durable and visible presence of CICM in China. The rich archives serve as an authoritative source of references for both the mission's supporters and critics alike to this day.

It is not just the European missionaries who diligently wrote their own histories. Chinese priests were also essential contributors to "print Catholicism" in China. The aforementioned priest Li, Tai who authored *Quanfeihuojiaoji* ("Catholicism under the Boxer Bandits' Attack") in 1905, makes for an telling example. The Chinese priests were also essential in spreading God's word in the Chinese language. Father Jacobi Tchang (1856–1935), a Chinese clergyman of the CICM mission in IM serves as another example. According to Tchang's biographer, Father

Rondelez, Tchang had published no less than 14 books and booklets that covered topics ranging from elaboration of bible verses to guidelines for church financial management. To reach a broader audience, his works were written in vernacular Chinese instead of Classical Chinese, an uncommon practice in the publishing world at the time. Between 1908 and 1928, at least 180,000 copies of Tchang's works, printed in Shanghai by the same printer of Li Tai's book, were circulated nationwide. The most celebrated one among his publications was a book entitled "*Xiezheng-likao*" [*Investigation of the Evil and the Virtuous*], boasting eight editions and 70,000 copies.[107]

While missionaries were well-equipped to fashion their own stories and spread their gospel, Baron Wang relied on others to tell his life stories and interpret his legacy. Unschooled and illiterate, the pen was not in Wang's toolkit for building socio-political legitimacy and territorial authority. Wang's children erected an ancestral hall in his honor after his death, and Wang's best-educated son wrote a biography of him, but with very limited circulation. In any event, propaganda work was not in the family enterprise, and Wang was remembered mostly in brief entries in local gazetteers and folk tales. Stories about Wang were fragmentary and incoherent, exemplified by the fact that the two most coherent versions of Wang's biography recorded two dates of his death eight years apart. Also, while one biographer reported that the One-Eyed Dragon lost an eye during a fight, another attributed it to a chicken pox infection from when Wang was five years old.[108]

One of the most coherent biographies of Baron Wang was authored by Gu, Jiegang (1893–1980), an eminent historical geographer. In 1934, seventeen (or nine, depending on whom you read) years after Baron Wang passed away, Gu visited Hetao. It was two years after Japan established its colony, Manchukuo, in northeast China. Chinese intellectuals' anxiety over national survival and reinvigoration was running high. Scores of writers, journalists, academics, photographers, and filmmakers took to traveling to the northwest and southwest frontiers, producing a wide array of textual and visual works on China's borderlands. In his search for inspiration and hope for the nation in the northwest frontier, Gu heard about Dragon King Wang. Inspired by the Dragon King's legendary achievements in Hetao, Gu wrote a biographical essay of Baron Wang based on eyewitness accounts, folk tales, litigation records, gazetteer entries, and the recollections of those who had met the Dragon King, including geographer Zhang Xiangwen. For Gu, a socially and politically concerned scholar from Beijing, Wang's hydro kingdom in the northwestern frontier was nothing short of a stronghold that protected the nation's territorial integrity against foreign aggressors. Gu concluded his essay by crowning Wang a hero who "fought to defend every inch of the nation's territory."[109]

While Gu Jiegang, like Zhang Xiangwen before him, enthusiastically foregrounded Wang's nationalistic sentiment, missionaries hardly acknowledged Wang's existence. In his well-circulated memoir, the CICM missionary, van Melckebeke (1947), proclaimed that CICM was the "sole pillar of civilization" in IM.[110] Were it not for the missionaries' diligence and self-sacrifice, IM would have been a "barren land." Van Melckebeke did briefly mention Baron Wang's waterworks. But the one-line recognition was followed by van Melckebeke's dismissal of Wang's "lack of organization" and his "selfish motivations" in contrast to the mission's altruism.[111]

Van Melckebeke's point about the Catholics' trademark organizational capacity is of great relevance. For a start, it enabled the CICM mission to successfully and consistently recruit new blood from Europe during the turbulent Republican era, making up for the mission's high death toll in IM. CICM's local operations also methodically and systematically produced Chinese clergymen to carry on and expand the mission in IM. The mission was sustained by a mega organization with global vision and local resilience.

On the other hand, once Baron Wang's locally entrenched family enterprise succumbed to the predatory state, it crumbled into rebel and bandit bands. While rebel forces could spark wildfires across vast terrains, their long-term political impact, in this case revolutionary potential, was contingent on an organizational center. In 20th-century China, that ultimate organizational center was the Communist Party, which consolidated and expanded in the midst of the Second Sino-Japanese War in the 1930 and 1940s.[112] But that is a story beyond the scope of this book.

In brief, the land-water baron and the missionary, two non-state territorial entrepreneurs in Hetao between the mid-19th and the early 20th centuries, were the primary organizers of the agricultural frontier in Hetao of West IM. During their rise in the mid- to late-19th century, they shared a similar set of territorial strategies for controlling land and water and consolidating said control with arms. To weather the turbulent 20th century, both fought against various emerging territorial contenders in Hetao. Baron Wang conceded his hydro turfdom to the revenue-thirsty state, and his once-consolidated armed forces fragmented into banditry gangs. The CICM mission, on the other hand, maintained its post-Boxer expansion while battling constant bandit attacks as social tensions in Hetao continued to boil. In their separate struggles to maintain territorial autonomy and authority, the CICM mission and Baron Wang developed two distinctive brands of territorial entrepreneurship in the near absence of the state. Baron Wang was a pragmatic borrower of political legitimacy. Coming from the fugitive lot of rural northern China, he followed the conventional route of purchasing and borrowing political legitimacy from established authorities without adhering to any specific political ideology. But his marginality in national and regional politics, which was to his advantage in the 19th century, made him vulnerable to the predatory state in the early 20th century. The missionaries leveraged their insider-outsider position by brokering various rivals emerging from the ever-shifting political configuration of Hetao. But the missionaries could hardly maintain their own neutrality in resource conflicts, nor were they immune to violence. Territorial entrepreneurship involves risks, not unlike other types of entrepreneurship. Territorial entrepreneurship in the precarious frontier at a turbulent time carried just that much higher of a risk.

In any event, with their similarities and differences, and with their rise and demise, the two territorial entrepreneurs in Hetao decidedly transformed the agricultural frontier of West IM from the mid-19th to mid-20th centuries. As the drama of West

IM's agricultural frontier continued to unfold, a new farming frontier was taking shape in East IM in the early 20th century, along with a new set of territorial actors and territorial dynamisms. This takes us to Chapter 8 on Mongol farmers.

Notes

1. Hetao is also known as Houtao (the "Rear Yellow River Loop") at the northwest section of the area surrounded by the Great Bend. The area east of Houtao is sometimes called Qiantao (the "Front Loop"). In this chapter I follow the common usage, and refer to the northwest section of the Yellow River Loop as Hetao as indicated in Figure P.III.1 and Figure P.III.2.
2. Wittfogel, Karl. 1957. *Oriental Despotism: A Comparative Study of Total Power*. New Haven, CT: Yale University Press.
3. Geertz, Clifford. 1980. *Negara: The Theater State in Nineteenth Century Bali*. Princeton, NJ: Princeton University Press.
4. See Chapter 6 and Figure P.III.1.
5. Perdue, Peter. 2005. *China Marches West: The Qing Conquest of Central Eurasia*. Cambridge, MA: The Belknap Press of Harvard University Press.
6. Zhang, Zhihua. 1990. "lüelun hetaodishang [A preliminary analysis of land merchants of the Yellow River Loop]." In *Neimenggukenwuyanjiu [Studies of Reclamation in Inner Mongolia]*, edited by Liu, Yuanhai, pp. 81–99. Hohhot: Inner Mongolia People's Press.
7. Wang, Yuhai. 2000. *Fazhanyubiange: qingdaineimenggu dongbu youmuxiangnongde zhuanxing [Development and Change: Eastern Inner Mongolia's Transformation from Pastoralism to Agriculture]*, pp. 78–79. Hohhot: University of Inner Mongolia Press.
8. See Bianco, Lucien. 1967/1971. *Origins of the Chinese Revolution, 1915–1949*, p. 103. Redwood City, CA: Stanford University Press. The rates varied considerably, depending on the season, whether one borrowed from the landlord or a professional moneylender, whether it is in cash or in grain. Bianco did not specify the geographical area of rural China from where the interest rate figures were collected. According to Liu, Kexiang (1986), the interest rate during Qing's Rehe, of Central-East IM, ranged between 17% and 35%. See Liu, Kexiang. 1986. "Qingdai rehede mengdikaikenhe yongdian zhidu [The permanent tenancy system in Rehe's reclamation during the Qing]." *Studies of Chinese Economic History* No. 3: 49–69.
9. In Rehe of Central-East IM, among the earliest agricultural areas in IM, land merchants' holding could be 100–200 Chinese qing (200 qing x 100 = 20,000 mu; 20,000 mu x 0.0667 = 1,334 hectares), and the largest could be 400–500 qing (500 qing = 3,335 hectares). See Liu, Kexiang. 1986. Ibid. p. 67.
10. Long Xing and Phillip Huang have written about the increasingly fragmented land ownership in northern China since the late imperial era. Xing (2008) suggested that in the North China Plain the average holding per person was less than 5 mu (0.33 hectare) in the 19th century, down to less than 4 mu (0.27 hectare) by early 20th century, and further down to slightly over 3 mu by the 1930s–40s (p. 646). Huang (1985 and 1990) suggested that big landlords have disappeared from the Yangtzi River Delta or reduced to less than 10% of total planted areas in the North China Plain because of population growth, equal division of inherited land among sons, and the landlord-upper gentry class's move to the city. In northern China, even those who owned more than 200 mu would rent out

some of their parcels to small peasants rather than turn the large holdings into modern managerial farms. Also, large land holdings were accumulated over many generations. Huang (1985: p. 104–105) noted that the largest landlord in Huolu County of Hebei, whose holding of 500 mu, or 33 hectares, was the result of over 144 years of accumulation, via 105 transactions. See Xing, Long. 2008. "Jindaihuabeinongcun renkouxiaozhang jiqiliudong: jianlun Huang Zongzhi meiyoufazhande zengzhangshuo [Population growth, decline and mobility in modern rural northern China: A commentary on Philip Huang's theses of agricultural involution in China]," pp. 636–652. Collection of Research Papers of the College of History and Culture. University of Shanxi. Taiyuan: Beiyuewenyi Press; Huang, Philip C. C. 1990. *The Peasant Family and Rural Development in the Yangzi Delta, 1350–1988*. Redwood City, CA: Stanford University Press; Huang, Philip C. C. 1985. *The Peasant Economy and Social Change in North China*. Redwood City, CA: Stanford University Press.

11. Accounts of the total area of irrigated land under the control of land-water barons in late 19th century Hetao and the size of individual land-water baron's holdings vary greatly. Gu, Jiegang (1935) put Wang Tongchun's holdings of irrigated land at "over 10,000 qing," which equals about 67,000 hectares (based on the conversion rate of 1 Chinese qing to 100 mu, 1 mu equals 0.0667 hectare). Wang, Jiange (2001) suggested a much larger sum of 27,000 qing, or 180,000 hectares. Zhang, Zhihua (1987) listed the land size served by each of the eight major irrigation systems, and the numbers added up to no less than 13,000 qing, or 87,100 hectares, in Hetao's total irrigated land. Zhang, Zhihua did not mention anything about the 10,000 hectares of irrigated land controlled by the CICM missionaries. Assuming Zhang only counted land-water barons' waterworks in Hetao, Wang's own holdings of irrigated land (which were fed by five out of the eight major irrigation systems) would be around 54,400 hectares. Given the under-regulated nature of cultivation in Hetao at the time, such vast discrepancies among different estimates is not surprising. Another possible explanation for the discrepancies could be the confusion between regularly irrigated and planted land and land that was reclaimed but irregularly planted with irregular water supplies. In short, the scale of irrigated area in Hetao by the early 20th century is anywhere between 87,100 and over 180,000 hectares. Wang Tongchun's own holdings can be anywhere between 54,440 and 180,000 hectares. A further study of the scale of the irrigation systems in late 19th century Hetao is much needed. In this chapter, I use Ge, Jiegang's estimate of Wang Tongchun's holdings, which is 67,000 hectares. See Gu, Jiegang. 1935. "Wangtongchun kaifahetaoji [A brief history of Wang Tongchun's development of Hetao]." *Yugong banyuekan [Yugong Bi-Monthly]* 2 (12): 2–14; Wang, Jiange. 2001. "Qingmohetaodiqude shuilizhiduyu shehuishiying [The hydraulic system and social adaptation in Hetao during the late Qing]." *Jindaishi Yanjiu [Studies of Modern History]* No. 6: 127–152, p. 132; Zhang, Zhihua. 1987. Ibid. p. 91.
12. In her studies of dryland farming in Shanxi of north China, Han, Maoli (2006) noted the significantly varied scale of irrigation canals. One county had more than 40 small-scale canal mains, each serving between 3 and 13 villages, none of which extended beyond county boundaries. In Zhang, Junfeng's (2006) case study of an unusually large spring-based irrigation network in central Shanxi during the late imperial eras, the system fed between 1,300 and 3,000 hectares of dry farms from the late 16th to early 18th centuries. See Han, Maoli. 2006. "Jindaishanshaandiqu jicengshuiliguanlitixitanxi [Grassroots-level irrigation management in modern Shanxi and Shaanxi Provinces]." *Research on Chinese Economic History* 1: 119–125; and Zhang, Junfeng. 2006. "Mingqingjiexiushuianyu

difangshihui—duishuilishehuide yixiangleixingxue fenxi [Water disputes and folk society during the Min and Qing in Jiexiu (of Shanxi): A typology of irrigation society]." In *Quyushehuishi bijiaoyanjiu [Comparative Studies of Regional History]*, edited by Xing, Long and Nianqun Yang, pp. 77–93. Beijing: Social Science Academic Press. Impressive as it was for the time and place, the scale of the irrigation works that Zhang, Junfeng (2006) reported, which were among the largest in central Shanxi, was in a different league from that in Hetao. Each of Hetao's eight major canal mains fed over 6,000 hectares; the largest among them irrigated over 24,000 hectares of cropland (see Zhang, Zhihua. 1987. Ibid.).

13. Liu, Hanming et al. 1983. *Mengguji menguren [Mongolia and the Mongols]*, Vol. 2. p. 94. Hohhot: Inner Mongolia People's Press. Translation of Pozdneev, Aleksei Matveevich. 1896–1898. *Mongolia and the Mongols.* St. Petersburg: The Imperial Russian Geographical Society.
14. Liang, Bing. 1991. *Yikezhaomeng tudidekaiken [Land Reclamation of Yekejuu League]*, pp. 14–22. Hohhot: University of Inner Mongolia Press.
15. A common method of channeling water is called "*jiegao qushui*." This method employs levered posts and pails to deliver water to the fields surrounding the water source. This method has had a long history since China's Spring and Autumn Period (770–476 BCE). See Du, Jingyuan. 2012a. "Nongmujiaocuodidaide shuilikaifayu yiminshehui—neimenggu hetaodiqude lishirenleixueyanjiu [Hydraulic development and migrant society in China's agricultural-pastoral interwoven belt in the Hetao Plain of Inner Mongolia: A view from Historical Anthropology]." Doctoral dissertation. Guangzhou: Zhongshan University, pp. 44–45. Gu, Jiegang (1935) reported that during the second half of the 18th century, this method was still used by seasonal fishermen who tried to plant in Hetao. See Gu, Jiegang. 1935. Ibid.
16. For a review of the rise in temperature and northbound march in pursuit of farming, see Zou, Yilin. 1995. "Mingqingshiqi beibunongmuguodudaide tuiyi heqihouhannuanbianhua [Shift of agricultural-pastoral transitional belt and temperature changes in northern China during the Ming and Qing Dynasties]." *Journal of Fudan University (Social Science edition)* No.1: 25–33.
17. Wang, Jiange. 2001. Ibid. p. 131.
18. It is important to note that in some areas of Hetao, notably in Urad Front Banner on the Ordos Loop of the Yellow River in western IM, there were irrigation works built by Mongol landowners during the early 20th century. These irrigation works served more than 10,000 hectares (1,500 qing) of land. See Yang, Zengzhi et al. 1934. "Syuyuansheng fenxiandiaochagaiyao, [Survey of Suiyuan Province by county]." "Mengqi diaochagaiyao [Survey of Mongolian banners]." Suiyuan Provincial Bureau of Mass Education. Reprint in "Minguoshiqi saiwaisisheng shiliaowenxianhuibian [Compilation of historical documents of the four provinces north of the Great Wall during the Republican period]," No.15, p. 540. Published by Chuanguotushuguan wenxianweisuofuzhi zhongxon [National Center of library collection reprints and microfilms]. More research on the Mongol-built hydro-social systems in Hetao is much needed. In this section, I only focus on the Han Chinese land barons' waterworks.
19. Chen, Erdong. 1988. *Hetaoguanqu shuilijianshi [History of Hetao Irrigation District]*, p. 51. Beijing: Shuilidianli chubanshe [Hydraulic and Electrical Power Publisher].
20. Zhang, Zhi-hua. 1987. Ibid. p. 91. Zhang also reports that the total length of the mains was 1,543 Chinese li, which I converted into km with the following formula: 1 li = 0.576

km; 1,543 x 0.576 = 888.8 km. For the estimates on Hetao's total irrigated areas during the late 19th century and early 20th century, see note #11.

21. The irrigation networks built by land barons transformed arid Hetao into a breadbasket. The extensive waterworks built in the late 19th century laid the foundation for the Chinese government's hydraulic construction drives in the post-1949 era. In the new millennium, with modern technologies and massive government investment, Hetao's irrigated area expanded from the estimated 87,100 hectares in the early 20th century to reportedly over 660,000 hectares (10 million mu) by the late 2010s. See Deng, Jun. et al. 2020. "Research on Protection and Utilization of Irrigation Works Heritage in Hetao Irrigation District in Inner Mongolia." In *E3S Web of Conferences*, EDP Sciences 218, 04028. https://doi.org/10.1051/e3sconf/202021804028. Accessed April 13, 2024. In 2019, Hetao Irrigation System was recognized as a World Heritage Irrigation Structure (WHIS) by the International Commission on Irrigation and Drainage (ICID). Mingmei. 2019. "Two ancient Chinese irrigation sites added to World Heritage Irrigation Structure list." Sourced from *Xinhua News*, September 5. http://www.xinhuanet.com/english/2019-09/05/c_138367847.htm. Accessed September 11, 2023.
22. Unless otherwise noted, the story about Wang Tongchun is based on the following sources: Wang, Wenxi et al. 1931. "*Linhe Xianzhi [Linhe County Gazetteer]*," publisher not identified; Gu, Jiegang. 1935. Ibid.; Zhang, Xiangwen (written in 1915, according to Gu, Jiegang, 1935). The entire collection was published in 1929–1935. In *Nanyuan Conggao [Nanyuan Manuscript Collection*], Vol. 7, pp. 52–53. Peking: Zhongguodixuehui [Chinese Geographical Society]. Reprint in Wu, Yugan et al. 1996. *Minguocongshu [Compilation of Publications of the Republican Era]*, Vol. 5, p. 98. Shanghai: Shanghai Books; Zhang, Weihua 1936. "Wangtongchun shengpingshijifangwenji [History of Wang Tongchun: An interview (with Wang Tongchun's daughter)]." *Yugong Bimonthly* 6 (5): 119–137; Wang, Jiange. 2001. Ibid.; see Zhang, Zhihua. 1987. Ibid.; and 1990, Ibid.; and Du, Jingyuan. 2012a. Ibid.
23. Chen, Erdong. 1988. Ibid.
24. The geometry behind this method is adjusting the baskets as visual targets until they are all on the same horizontal plane. Assuming Wang had a way of establishing a horizontal line (like using a flask of water marked with gradations), then the distances from the baskets to the ground could be subtracted from one another to give the true elevation difference between the spots where the post-holders were standing. I thank Kurt Cuffey of UC Berkeley Geography for explaining this method.
25. See Geertz, Clifford. 1980. Ibid. pp. 45–85; Han, Maoli. 2006. Ibid.; Xing, Long. 2006. "Conggongxiangdao zhengduo: Jinshuiliuyushuiziyuan riqukuifadelishikaocha [From sharing to competition: A historical inquiry into water scarcity in the Jin River Basin]." In *Quyushehuishi bijiaoyanjiu [Comparative Studies of Regional History]*, edited by Xing, Long and Nianqun Yang, pp. 3–18. Beijing: Social Science Academic Press; Zhang, Junfeng. 2006. Ibid. In their studies of Hetao of the 19th century, Du, Jingyuan and Max Woodworth (2011) suggested that Hetao was a case closer to Geertz's irrigated society of Bali than Wittfogel's hydraulic state, due to the negligible state involvement in Hetao. See Du, Jingyuan and Max Woodworth. 2011. "Irrigation Society in China's northern frontier, 1860s–1920s." *Cross Currents: East Asian History and Culture Review* 1 (1): December 1. https://escholarship.org/uc/item/48r0n6ps. Accessed August 24, 2023.
26. Wittfogel, Karl. 1957. Ibid.

27. Clifford Geertz (1972) compared farming in wet Bali and dry Morocco and found that while the irrigation of the former case was collectively organized, the latter depended on individual acts of collecting water from scattered springs. Geertz's dryland farming in Morocco seems closer to the pre-Hydraulic Turfdom era of Hetao. See Geertz, Clifford. 1972. "The wet and the dry: Traditional irrigation in Bali and Morocco." *Human Ecology* 1 (1): 23–39.
28. Chang, Chung-Li. 1955. *The Chinese Gentry: Studies on Their Role in Nineteenth-Century Chinese Society.* University of Washington Publications on Asia; other classics on late imperial Chinese gentry includes Hsiao, Kung-Chuan. 1960. *Rural China: Imperial Control in the Nineteenth Century.* University of Washington Publications on Asia; Ch'ü, T'ung-tsu. 1962. *Local Government in China under the Ch'ing.* Cambridge, MA: Harvard University Press; Esherick, Joseph and Mary Rankin eds. 1990. *Chinese Local Elites and Patterns of Dominance.* Oakland, CA: University of California Press.
29. Philip Kuhn pointed out that the gentry is not just a local political-economic elite, but also a local militia leader. See Kuhn, Philip. 1970. *Rebellion and Its Enemies in Late Imperial China: Militarization and Social Structure, 1796–1864.* Cambridge, MA: Harvard University Press.
30. See Shue, Vivienne. 1988. *The Reach of the State: Sketches of the Chinese Body Politics.* Redwood City, CA: Stanford University Press; and Duara, Prasenjit. 1988. *Culture, Power and the State: Rural North China 1900–1942*, pp. 51–57. Redwood City, CA: Stanford University Press.
31. For the role of the gentry in building and managing hydro infrastructure in the wet climate of the Yangzi Basin in China's heartland, see, for example, Peter Perdue's (1987) account of the dike-building projects around Dongting Lake of the mid-Yangzi Basin in his book, *Exhausting the Earth: State and Peasant in Hunan 1500–1850.* Cambridge, MA: Harvard University Press. The hydro-social order of the villages is inseparable from its hydro-political order. Zhang, Junfeng (2001)'s study provides a glimpse into villagers' political life that was built around the hydro order. In arid, rural Shanxi, the marriage circle was defined by the political relationship among villages. Daughters and sisters would be married to ally villages to seal inter-village collaboration over water allocation. On the other hand, it would be out of the question to build a conjugal bond with rival villages. The boundary between friends and foes, defined by hydro-political interests, was drawn and guarded. See Zhang, Junfeng. 2001. "Shuiquan yu difangshehui—yimingqing yilai shanxisheng wenshuixian ganquanqu shuian weili [Water rights and folk society: A case study of Ganquan Canal of Wenshui County in Shanxi Province in the Ming and the Qing eras]." *Journal of Shanxi University (Social Science and Humanities edition)* No. 6: 5–9.
32. Zhang, Xiangwen. 1915. Ibid.
33. In his study of Shandong and Hebei of the North China Plain, Philip Huang (1985) argued that the Qing imperial state institutionalized the divorce of land ownership from administrative, judicial, and military power of the local elite in order to control peasant society. See Huang, Philip C. C. 1985. Ibid.
34. See Gu, Jiegang. 1935. Ibid. p. 8. It was unclear whether Wang lost an eye during the fight or after he was brought to his knees and captured by the rival land baron. In Zhang, Weihua's account based on an interview with Wang's daughter, Wang lost an eye to chicken pox when he was five years old (see Zhang, Weihua. 1936. Ibid. p. 121).

35. Zhang, Yu. 2015. "Qisumuanyu baolixingshengcunjingzheng fangshi [The case of Qisumu and the violence in survival competition]." *Journal of University of Electronics Science and Technology (Social Science edition)* 17 (2): 76–80.
36. For the martial tradition in bandit-infested Shandong and neighboring Hebei in the 19th and the first half of the 20th century, see Esherick, Joseph. 1987. *The Origins of the Boxer Uprising*. Oakland, CA: California University Press.
37. See Sui, Xixian. 1989. "Wangtongchun: hetaoshuilikaifade jiechurencai (Wangtongchun, an outstanding contributor to irrigation work in Hetao)," in IMAR Committee of Historical Archies ed., *Neikonggu wenshiziliao [Inner Mongolia historical achieves),*" Vol. 36. Wangtongchunyu hetaoshuili [Wangtongchun and Hetao's Irrigation]. pp. 43–91. p. 63. According to this source, if martial arts master, Liu, Tian-you were to join Wang's Militia, Wang would offer him a pretty wife. But Liu did not accept the offer. Also see Gu, Jiegang. 1935. Ibid. p. 6. Gu mentioned that Wang offered not just wives, but also 100 or even 1,000 mu of land to his recruits. Gu did not specify whether these recruits were for the militia, but it is hard to imagine that Wang would make such generous offers to the refugees who needed to pay Wang land rent and water fees.
38. See Perry, Elizabeth. 1980. *Rebels and Revolutionaries in North China, 1845–1945*, p. 75. Redwood City, CA: Stanford University Press on the lucrative business of fire arm production by ironsmiths for private use in rural Henan and Anhui during the 19th century. The tumultuous 19th–20th centuries in bandit-ridden northern China made it necessary for villagers to arm themselves. Banditry was also a part of the aggressive survival strategy and a career choice for the peasants, especially during the off-season of the winter time and in the late summer before harvest. Villages were fortified and would often organize semi-permanent or permanent militia. Joseph Esherick (1987. Ibid. pp. 13–37) reported on the widespread banditry in Shandong and Hebei. My late father, Hsing, Fuying (1919–2023) had vivid memories of the frequent bandit attacks during his childhood when growing up in the rural area of eastern Shandong Province in northern China. The armed violence and the arms trade go hand in hand. In the next section on the missionaries, I will elaborate more on banditry in Hetao.
39. Zhang, Zhihua (1990. Ibid. p. 94) noted that Chinese archives tend to emphasize Wang's contribution to Hetao's irrigation works, while keeping Wang's brutality and deceptive tactics in his grabbing of Mongolian Banner land vague or completely absent. Zhang suspected that the Mongolian records, which he was unable to consult, would provide a fuller story. The violent resource competition between Mongolian banner land holders and Han Chinese land barons is also reported in Li, Keren's (1990a, 1990b) two informative case studies in Yekejuu and Ulanqab Leagues in the 19th century. In Yekejuu, many second-tier banner aristocracy (*taiji*) lost much of their land to the Banner's top leaders during the reclamation rush of the early 19th century. So, these taijis resorted to farming the remaining land tracts or leasing them out. They also sharpened their skills in lease negotiation and farm management while collaborating with land merchants to broker land lease sales. By the mid-19th century, these entrepreneurial taijis had become formidable landlords themselves in the commodified land market. In Ulanqab, by contrast, Banner aristocracy across all ranks were much less savvy in land lease negotiation and often lost out to land barons. The trickery in land lease negotiations often led to armed conflicts in Ulanqab. See Li, Keren. 1990a. "*Qianxiyimeng wanggongguizudui guankende taidu* [The Yekejuu League noblemen's attitude towards official reclamation projects]." In *Neimenggukenwuyanjiu [Studies of Reclamation in Inner Mongolia]*, edited

by Liu, Yuanhai, pp. 109–111. Hohhot: Inner Mongolia People's Press; and Li, Keran. 1990b. "QingdaiWulanchabumeng kenwuchutan [An analysis of land reclamation in Qing's Ulanqab League]." Ibid. pp. 128–140, p. 131.

40. Gu, Jiegang. 1935. Ibid. p. 10. The staggering, yet unverifiable, figure suggests that an important ingredient in Baron Wang's territorial rule was fear.
41. Niu, Jingzhong and Zhong Ren. 2010. *Jindaisuiyuandiqude shehuiwenti [Social Issues of Modern Suiyuan Area].* Hohhot: Inner Mongolia University Press. Suiyuan area includes today's Ulanqab, Hohhot, Baotou, Bayannur, and Ordos in Central and West IM.
42. Unless otherwise noted, most of the historical accounts of Catholicism in China in this section is drawn from Madsen, Richard. 1998. *China's Catholics: Tragedy and Hope in an Emerging Civil Society*, Oakland, CA: University of California Press.
43. Bianco, Joseph Lo. 2009. "Intercultural encounters and deep cultural beliefs." In *China and English: Globalization and the Dilemmas of Identity*, edited by Joseph Lo Bianco et al., pp. 23–55, p. 29. Toronto: Multilingual Matters.
44. Esherick, Joseph. 1987. Ibid. p. 75.
45. The Catholic institution's focus on the rural since the 18th century has shaped Catholicism in China ever since. According to Madsen's (1998. Ibid. p. 51) estimate, at least 80% of Chinese Catholics still lived in the villages by the 1990s. Madsen commented that Saint Austin's *The City of God* ought to be renamed *The Village of God* in the Chinese context.
46. Historian Ho, Ping-ti (1959) has stated that "The century between 1851 and 1949, despite the availability of various figures, is practically a demographers' vacuum." Ho, Ping-ti. 1959. *Studies on the Population of China, 1368–1953*, p. 97. Cambridge, MA: Harvard University Press. It is even more challenging to try to compare China's population with other regions during this period. Here I just use the figures to make the point about the irresistible size of the religious market in rural China, adopting a common presumption that about 80% of China's population during that time period was rural. The figures of country population come from Maddison, Angus. 2006. *The World Economy: Volume 1: A Millennial Perspective* and *Volume 2: Historical Statistics*, p. 636. Paris: OECD Publishing. As an example of significant variations in the demographical figures of the tumultuous era, Maddison's figure of China's total population in 1870, 358 million, is smaller than John Durand's (1960) figure of 432 million in 1851 (see Durand, John. 1960. "The population statistics of China, A.D. 2–1953." *Population Studies* 13 (3): 209–256, p. 240.
47. For the history of CICM in West IM, see Taveirne, Patrick. 2004. *Han-Mongol Encounters and Missionary Endeavors: A History of Scheut in Ordos (Hetao) 1874–1911.* Leuven University Press and Ferdinand Verbiest Foundation K. U. Leuven. Taveirne is a Belgian CICM missionary and a Leiden-trained sinologist. There are also quite a few memoirs, biographies, and reports authored by CICM's IM-based missionaries that were published mostly during the first half of the 20th century, albeit far less thorough than Taveirne's work. These church-based publications have been criticized by China scholars for their Church- and Euro-centric views. For the critics' works, see, for example, Dai, Xueji. 1960. "1900 nian neimengguxibudiqu gezurenminde fandidouzheng [The anti-imperialism struggle of various peoples in West Inner Mongolia]." *Lishiyanjiu [Historical Studies]* 6: 27–44; and Dai, Xueji. 1964. "Xifangzhiminzhezai hetaoerduosi dengdidezuiehuodong-diguozhuyiliyongtianzhujiao qinlue zhongguodeyigeshili [Criminal activities of western imperialists in Hetao and Ordos: A case of Imperialists' invasion of China via Catholicism]." *Lishiyanjiu [Historical Studies]* 5–6: 67–96. More recently,

a new generation of China-based historians revisited the debates and broadly consulted church publications, Qing government archives, as well as local gazetteers. They have arrived at a diverse set of conclusions. One of the most thorough accounts can be found in Zhang, Yu. 2006. "Wanqingshiqi shengmushengxinhui zaineimenggudiqu chuanjiao-huodongyanjiu 1865–1911 [CICM's Activities in Inner Mongolia during the Late Qing Period]." Doctoral dissertation. Guangzhou: Jinan University. Other examples include: Tang, Kaijian and Jinlian Zeng. 2011. "Zhongguoxibeidiqu tianzhujiaojijiduxinjiaoshi yanjiuxianzhuangyushiliao [Status and historical sources on the history of Catholicism and Protestantism in northwest China]." *Northwest Journal of Ethnology* 71: 103–121; and Mi, Chenfeng. 2001. "Congershisiqingdi jiaoan riqidefenqi kanjiaohuishiliaodejux-ian [The limitation of church archives: The case of the controversy over the date of ershisiqingdi riot]." *Studies in Qing History* 4: 75–84; The debates over the church's contribution to and/or exploitation of IM during the century before the establishment of the PRC is beyond the scope of this book. But I will allude to it when necessary. I will also return to this question in the last section of this chapter, where I compare the discursive power of the two territorial entrepreneurs—the land-water barons and the CICM missionaries in 19th century Hetao.

48. See the Chinese translation of "Françoise Aubin's Quelques Echos des Prêtres Chinois dans les Missions de Scheut (Mongolie-Intérieure et Chine Occidentale], Dix-Neuvième-Vingtième Siècles." In Ku, Weiying ed. 2002. *Saiwai chuanjiaoshi [Mission beyond the Great Wall]*, pp. 319–352. Jointly published by Ferdinand Verbiest Foundation in K.U. Leuven, Belgium and Kuangchi Cultural Group in Taipei, Taiwan; and the Chinese translation of Fr Leo Van den Berg's "Scheut in China," in Ku, Weiying ed. 2002. Ibid. pp. 281–310.
49. One of Verbist's team members was Ferdinand Hamer, CICM. Hamer arrived in China at the age of 24 and later became a monsignor for his service in IM. He was killed during the Boxer Uprising in Hetao in 1900. See details later in this chapter.
50. In the 16th to 17th centuries, two traditional Catholic orders in China, the Franciscans and the Paris Foreign Missions (MEP), had tried to spread the faith in IM. But their work left limited impact. During Catholic prohibition of the 18th century, the immense northern steppe saw few missionary activities. CM built the first Catholic seminary in IM in the early 19th century. See the Chinese translation of Fr Daniël Verhelst's "Th. Verbist and CICM Pioneers." In Ku, Weiying. 2002. Ibid. pp. 125–214; and the translation of Fr Valeer Rondelez's "Vita Patris Jacobi Tchang,." In Ku, Weiying ed. 2002. Ibid. pp. 215–280.
51. See Gorissen, Bert. 2003. '"The Most Unfruitful Mission in the World': CICM father Frans and Jozef Hoogers in Xinjiang, 1895–1922." In *The History of the Relations between the Low Countries and China in the Qing Era (1644–1911)*, edited by Vande Walle, Willy and Noël Golvers, pp. 325–342. Leuven University Press and Ferdinand Verbiest Foundation K.U. Leuven; and Tang, Kaijian and Zhanjun Ma. 2005. "Qingmomingchu shengmushengxinhui xinjiangchuanjiaokaoshu 1883–1922nian [CICM in Xinjiang during the end of Qing and early Republican era, 1883–1922]." *Xiyuyanjiu [Studies of Western Frontier]* (2): 63–74.
52. See Zhang, Yu. 2006. Ibid. pp. 44–49 and Taveirne, Patrick. 2004. Ibid. p. 256 for the reasons for CICM's unsuccessful recruitment of Mongolian followers.
53. In Stragier's original words: "la famine est une bonne moisson pour le Bon Dieu." See Patrick Taveirne. 2004. Ibid. p. 345, note 33.

54. The Chinese translation of Fr Leo Van den Berg's "Scheut in China." In Ku, Weiying ed. 2002. Ibid. pp. 281–310, p. 292.
55. The Chinese lyrics are: "天主聖母玛利亞, 熱身子跪在冷地下。神父!哪里撥地呀?噢来!红盛義去種吧!你为什么進教?我为銅錢兩吊。為什麼念經?為了黄米三升." See Zhang, Yu. 2007. "Wanqingshengmushengxinhui xinanmenggujiaoqu chuanjiaolunshu [CICM in the Apostolic Vicariate of Southwest Mongolia during the late Qing]." *Journal of the Second Northwest University for Nationalities*, No. 74: 75–81.
56. Mgr. C. Van Melckebeke CICM (1945), "En Mongolie: L'action sociale de I'Eglise Catholique," tran. Mingyuan Fu in 1947 with a Chinese title *bianjianggongjiao shehuishiye [Catholic Social Enterprise at the Frontier]*, pp. 23–24. Peking: Shangzhi Press. In what follows I will use "C. Van Melckebeke, 1945, tran. 1947, Ibid." for this reference.
57. See note #11.
58. Du, Jingyuan. 2012a. Ibid. p. 30.
59. Verhelst, Daniël. In Ku, Weiying ed. 2002. Ibid. pp. 159–160.
60. Taveirne, Patrick. 2004. Ibid. p. 216.
61. Verhelst, Daniël. In Ku, Weiying ed. 2002. Ibid. p. 145.
62. Verhelst, Daniël. In Ku, Weiying ed. 2002. Ibid. p. 151.
63. Taveirne, Patrick. 2004. Ibid. p. 247.
64. The eight nation forces included American, Austro-Hungarian, British, French, German, Italian, Japanese, and Russian troops. In addition, the Netherlands, Belgium, and Spain participated on the side.
65. Madsen, Richard. 1998. Ibid. p. 32.
66. Esherick, Joseph. 1987. Ibid. p. 86.
67. Esherick, Joseph. 1987. Ibid. p. 91.
68. Niu, Jingzhong and Ren Zhong. 2010. *Jindai suiyuandiqude shehui wenti [Social Issues of Modern Suiyan Region]*, p. 104. Hohhot: Inner Mongolia University Press; Niu, Jingzhong. 2001. "Jindaisuiyuandiqude minjiaochongtu—yeshuoyihetuanyundong baofadeyuanyin [Conflicts between local people and the church in modern Suiyuan: The cause of Boxer movement]." *Journal of Inner Mongolia University (Humanities and Social Sciences)* 33 (4): 90–95.
69. Ji, Zhaojin. 2003. *A History of Modern Shanghai Banking*, p. 75. Armonk, NY: M. E. Sharpe.
70. Madsen, Richard. 1998. Ibid. p. 33.
71. Ji, Zhaojin. 2003. Ibid. p. 75.
72. Zhang, Yu. 2006. Ibid. p. 129. Zhang also noted that some of the figures in the missionary-prepared damage reports for the purpose of restitution were inflated.
73. Zhang, Yu. 2006. Ibid. pp. 150–151.
74. Calculated on the basis of Taveirne, Patrick. 2004. Ibid. pp. 637–638.
75. C. Van Melckebeke, 1945, tran. 1947, Ibid. p. 5. The author did not specify whether these figures refer to catechumens or baptized Christians. The gap between the two categories could be significant.
76. Zhang, Yu. 2006. Ibid. p. 151. Zhang calculated that the Catholic church received a total of 30,503 qing of Indemnity land. The calculation is as follows: 30,503 qing x 100 = 3,050,300 mu; 3,050,300 mu x 0.0667 = 203,455 hectares.
77. Pan, Fu. 1923. "Diaochahetao baogaoshu [Survey Report of Hetao]," edited by Dubanyunhe gongchengzongju bianjichu [Publication Unit of Bureau of Canal Construction], p. 174. Beijing: Jinghuayinshuju [Jinghua Book Printing Service].

78. "Catholic church" in Chinese is "*tianzhutang*," literally, "the holy hall (*tang*) of the Lord (*zhu*) in the heaven (*tian*)." Here, the character "*tian*" was substituted with "*di*" (earth or land). "*Dizhu*" means land lord in Chinese. See Zhou, Zhiping. 2007. "Jidujiaochuanboyu jindaisuiyuanshehui [The spread of Protestantism and modern Suiyuan society]." Master's thesis. Hohhot: University of Inner Mongolia, p. 19.
79. Niu, Jingzhong and Ren Zhong. 2010. Ibid. p. 106.
80. See, for example, Dai, Xueji. 1960, 1964. Ibid.; Chen, Yuning. 1982. "Jindaie'erduosi diqugezurenmin fanduijiaohuiqinluededouzheng [The struggle of different peoples' resistance against the missions' invasion in modern Ordos area]." *Inner Mongolia Social Science* 4: 67–73; Zhao, Kunsheng. 1985. "Jindaiwaiguotianzhujiaohuizai neimenggu qinzhantudiqingkuang jiqiyingxiang [Foreign Catholic missions' land grab in modern Inner Mongolia and its impact]." *Inner Mongolia Social Science* 3: 61–66; Bo, Yanhua. 2002. "Hanmoliyu ershisiqingdi jiaotang [Ferdinand Hamer and Ershisiqingdi Church]." *Journal of Inner Mongolia Normal University (Philosophy and Social Science edition)* 31 (2): 93–96.
81. C. Van Melckebeke, 1945, tran. 1947, Ibid. p. 15 and p. 36.
82. The walls measured 1.5 *zhang* tall and 1.2 *zhang* thick. I use the following conversion formulas: 1 *zhang* = 10 *chi*, 1 construction *chi* =32 cm; 120×10 x 32 = 38,400 cm = 384 meters. CICM built 76 fortifications in IM. See C. Van Melckebeke, 1945, tran. 1947, Ibid. p. 54 and p. 58.
83. Tiedemann, Rolf Gerhard (Chinese name Di, Deman). 2002. "Yihetuanminyu tianzhujiaotuzai huabeidewuzhuangchongtu [Armed conflicts between Boxers and Catholic congregations in North China]." *Lishiyanjiu [Historical Studies]* No.2: 79–93, p. 90. Although he focused on northern China, Tiedemann noted the CICM's strong fortification in Xiwanzi.
84. C. Van Melckebeke. 1945, tran. 1947. Ibid. p. 35.
85. C. Van Melckebeke. 1945, tran. 1947. Ibid. p. 98. Niu, Jingzhong and Ren Zhong. 2010. Ibid. p. 360.
86. Madsen, Richard. 1998. Ibid. pp. 53–57.
87. This does not mean that there were no conflicts between European missionaries and their Chinese colleagues. Richard Madsen (1998, Ibid. p. 128) noted that when missionaries returned to China after 1842, they often clashed with local lay leaders *(huizhang)*, who, in the century when the missionaries had been expelled because of the Rites Controversy, exercised strong control, especially financial control, over local Catholic communities. The European missionaries eventually reasserted their control. In the 1930s, during the Japanese occupation, Catholic missionaries who came from countries that had declared war against Japan during the Second World War were imprisoned by Japanese forces in China. Again, the church operation was left to Chinese church leaders and congregation. European missionaries' dominance over Chinese priests were also implicitly mentioned in Fr Valeer Rondelez's "Vita Patris Jacobi Tchang." In Ku, Weiying ed. 2002. Ibid. pp. 215–280.
88. See the Chinese translation of Fr Leo Van den Berg's "Scheut in China." In Ku, Weiying ed. 2002. Ibid. pp. 281–310, p. 292.
89. Li, Tai. 1905. *Quanfeihuojiaoji [Catholicism under the Boxer Bandits' Attack]*, p. 257. Shanghai: Tushanwan Book Printing Service.
90. See also Mi, Chenfeng. 2001. Ibid. for a detailed comparison between Li Tai and other missionaries' recounts and the local officials' reports on the incident.

91. Niu, Jingzhong and Ren Zhong. 2010. Ibid. p. 123.
92. Gu, Jiegang. 1935. Ibid. p. 8.
93. Pan, Fu's (1923. Ibid. pp. 53–54) survey of Hetao's waterways in the early 1920s showed that "more than half" of the canal systems in Hetao had dried up and that the irrigated areas had shrank considerably. The Yongji Canal, the crown jewel of Hetao's eight major canal mains, for example, was recorded to have fed over 4,000 qing of land in the late 19th century (see Zhang, Zhihua. 1987. Ibid.). By the early 1920s, it covered only 771 qing according to Pan. Zhang, who visited Hetao in 1936, also noted the gravely deteriorated canals. See Zhang, Weihua. 1936. Ibid. pp. 119–137.
94. Mu Guiying is a heroine in Chinese folktales, operas, and dramas, who fought beside her military leader husband to guard the frontier against West Xia and Liao forces during the Northern Song dynasty (960 to 1127 CE).
95. Gu, Jiegang. 1935. Ibid. p. 9.
96. Gu, Jiegang. 1935. Ibid. p. 19.
97. Niu, Jingzhong and Ren Zhong. 2010. Ibid. pp. 201–202.
98. C. Van Melckebeke. 1945. tran. 1947. Ibid. p. 6.
99. The recount of this event is based on the following news clippings from *The Shanghai Times*: "Belgian's Priest's Rescuer Is Trapped By Bandits," published on March 16, 1925; "Christian Village Raided by Bandits, Priest Shot Dead," published on March 25, 1925; "Bandits Terrorize Catholic Villages in Mongolia by Raids," published on March 26, 1925; "Church and Schools burned in new bandit attack on Catholic center in Mongolia," published on April 1, 1925. Also, see "Bandits burn town and Kill Two Residents," *The China Press*, published on March 25, 1925. C. Van Melckebeke (1945, tran. 1947. Ibid.) also briefly mentioned the incident (p. 55).
100. Bianco, Lucien. 1967. Ibid.; and Bianco, Lucien. 2001. *Peasant Without Party: Grassroots Movements in Twentieth-Century China*. New York: M. E. Sharpe.
101. Perry, Elizabeth. 1980. Ibid., and Perry, Elizabeth. 2002. *Challenging the Mandate of Heaven: Social Protest and State Power in China*. New York: M. E. Sharpe.
102. See Philip Huang's (1985) analysis of the landlord-gentry connection in note #33.
103. Niu, Jingzhong and Ren Zhong. 2010. Ibid. p. 113.
104. Niu, Jingzhiong, and Ren Zhong. 2010. Ibid. pp. 112–115.
105. Snow, Edgar. 1938. *Red Star Over China*, p. 362. New York: Random House.
106. This is a paraphrasing of Benedict Anderson's concept of "print capitalism." Anderson argued that the printing business facilitated the rise of the nation-state in modern Europe. See Anderson, Benedict. 2006 [1983]. *Imagined Communities: Reflections on the Origin and Spread of Nationalism*, pp. 37–46. New York: Verso.
107. Chinese translation of Fr Valeer Rondelez's essay. In Ku, Weiying ed. 2002. Ibid. pp. 239–245.
108. Gu, Jiegang (1935. Ibid.) wrote that Baron Wang died in 1917. Zhang, Weihua (1936. Ibid. p. 134) dates Baron Wang's death to 1925. Gu recorded that Baron Wang lost an eye during a fight (p. 8). In Zhang's recount, based on his interview with Baron Wang's daughter, Wang lost an eye to chicken pox at the age of five (p. 121).
109. Gu, Jiegang. 1935. Ibid. p. 28.
110. C. Van Melckebeke. 1945. tran. 1947. Ibid. p. 32.
111. C. Van Melckebeke. 1945. tran. 1947. Ibid. p. 21.
112. Bianco, Lucien. 1967. Ibid.

8
Mongol Farmers: Massacre Refugees in East IM in the 20th–21st Centuries

In the popular discourse on Inner Mongolia (IM)'s agricultural expansion, Mongols are said to have dismounted their horses and picked up their hoes under the influence of Han Chinese. While some writers attribute the shift to an inevitable process of civilization, others charge Han Chinese for excessive resource extraction and the consequential deterioration of Mongolian pasture land and pastoral society and culture. The two contrasting assessments of IM's agriculturalization, either as progress or regress, however, share the assumption that Mongolian agriculturalization was Mongols' passive response to external, Chinese stimulation.

There is little doubt that Han Chinese settlers, refugees, and merchant capital contributed to cultivation expansion in the northern steppe, as shown in the previous two chapters on Central and West IM's agricultural frontiers. But that view from outside accounts for only half of the story. The other half involves Mongol farmers and the internal dynamics that have shaped the processes and results of agricultural expansion in the northern steppe. While Han Chinese farmers dominate the historiography of IM's cultivation expansion, in this chapter I bring Mongol farmers back to the history of East IM's cultivation expansion. I look at Mongols' internal migration from Central-East to East IM (see Figure P.III.1) and the ways Mongolian farming migrants and refugees transformed local livelihoods and complicated inter- and intra-ethnic relations in East IM throughout the 20th century. It is an inside-out story.

This is also a bottom-up story. In the previous two chapters on Central and West IM, the leading actors were mainly powerful elites—the likes of Qing emperors,

Conserving China's Northwest Frontier. You-tien Hsing, Oxford University Press. © You-tien Hsing (2025).
DOI: 10.1093/9780191903908.003.0009

Mongol princes, Chinese land-water barons, warlords, and Belgian missionaries. In this chapter, I take the view from those at the bottom of rural society—the farming Mongols, many of whom were refugees pushed out of Central-East IM by resource competition, ethnic violence, and massacre and fled to East IM. This story about East IM's agricultural frontier during the 20th century, in many ways, is even more turbulent than those in Central and West IM of the previous centuries. This internal migration is also what led to East IM hosting the largest concentration of ethnic Mongols in China today.

The intra-regional Mongol refugee-migrants who became "inside-outsiders," or whom I call "outlander Mongols" in East IM, lead the story of this chapter. Most of the outlander Mongols came from multigenerational farming families in Central-East IM who started intensive farming in the 18th century, as presented in Chapter 6. The outlander Mongols in East IM defy the presumed ethnicity-livelihood division between Chinese farmers and Mongol herders. They also embodied multidirectional processes of agricultural transformation in the steppe of East IM. The outlander Mongols transformed much of East IM's rural livelihoods towards intensive farming. But it was hardly a clearcut transformation from a homogeneous form of pastoralism to that of agriculture. Instead, there were multidirectional shifts that created varied modes of livelihood mixes. These Mongol farmers, or the outlander Mongols in East IM, did not carry the transformation single-handedly either. Instead, the outlander Mongols intermingled with various locals—both Chinese and East IM natives, both settlers and land and livestock owners of different ethnicities—and contributed to mixed rural livelihoods of herding, cropping and beyond. Within East IM, the massacre refugee-turned-outlander Mongols moved from the western to eastern and from the southern to northern ends, and they shaped East IM's ethnoterritorial structure. The new structure has impacted the politics of resource struggles and conservation of East IM that continue to the present day.

This inside-out and bottom-up story is mainly based on oral histories and ethnography I conducted in Horqin Right Front Banner (Horqin RF) of today's Hinggan League in East IM between 2017 and 2022. Interviews during the Covid pandemic years were conducted online. These stories are local and often personal. To contextualize these stories historically and geographically, I consulted local gazetteers, memoirs, news clippings, historical atlases, and scholarly works. What has been particularly helpful is the publications by historians and ethnologists of East IM origin who used their home villages and banners in their case studies.[1]

A place-driven story about migrants inevitably involves multiple places: how and where they move from and to; the tension and friction arising from their multi-stop odyssey, their repeated attempts to settle in new homes in different locations, and the successes and failures of such attempts. I now follow the itinerant Mongols' journey, beginning in their home turf in Jesoto and Je'uda Leagues in Central-East IM in the late 19th century. Figure 8.1 below depicts the three East Inner Mongolia Leagues during the Qing era.[2]

Figure 8.1 Map of three East Inner Mongolia Leagues during the Qing Dynasty
Source: Cartographer: Alan Pong, based on James Reardon-Anderson. 2005. p. 44.

I Itinerant Mongols of East Inner Mongolia

During the Qing era, Mongols moved across banners and leagues from the warmer south to the colder north regions of IM, and from Central IM to its eastern and western lands largely due to war, land loss, or climate change, and often all of the above. Internal Mongol migrants trekked along three major routes: the central route went from Chahar to Xilingol in the north; the western route from Yekejuu to Alxa in the northwest; and the eastern route went from southern Je'uda and Jesoto to Jerim in the east[3] (see Figure P.III.1).

Among the three primary migratory routes, it is the eastern route that has produced the greatest impact on IM's agrarian transformation. This was due to the large-scale movement of farming Mongols over a prolonged period of time of the eastward migration. The move stretched over two centuries, transpiring in two phases and three places. From the mid-18th century to the late 19th century, farming Mongols fled from their home banners in southern Je'uda and Jesoto of Central-East IM to southern Jerim of East IM; and since the late 19th century, the Je'uda and Jesoto Mongols have been pushed out again from south Jerim to the mountainous north Jerim. To avoid confusion, in this chapter I use Jesoto as an umbrella term for all the Mongol migrants from Central-East to East IM.[4]

As IM's earliest converts to intensive farming, the Jesoto Mongols played a pivotal role in pushing the agricultural frontier further north and east to Jerim. Their moves were fraught with disruption and violence. After being uprooted repeatedly, Jesoto Mongols acquired an identity in Jerim that was neither native nor settler. They had lost most of their connections with their banner of origin after two or three generations, yet they were not fully accepted in Jerim wherein they tried to make a new home. They were the perpetual outsiders with low social and economic status. The majority of the Jesoto outlanders were Harqin Mongols who, in the popular imaginary, came to represent all farming Mongols in the eyes of other, farming-averse Mongols—so much so that the tribal and territorial name *Harqin* was adopted as a generic term for all farming Mongols. Farming Mongols were also mocked as "*oyudung*" Mongols, or "short" Mongols: that is, Harqins traded their Mongolian riding robes for short, Chinese peasant-style blouses.[5]

This chapter tells the tale about these outlander Mongols from Jesoto who pioneered farming expansion in East IM. In what follows I will first trace the conditions that had pushed Jesoto Mongols' move from Jesoto to southern Jerim, followed by their subsequent move from the lower-altitude southern Jerim to higher-altitude northern Jerim. Every step and stop along this journey was marked by fierce resource competition and brutal resource violence at an extraordinarily turbulent time.

I.1 Massacre Refugees from Jesoto

As outlined in Chapter 6 on Central IM, banner noblemen and commoners alike leased out manorial and estate land—often illegally to land brokers and cultivators—in exchange for rent. While the banner noblemen with large land endowments could live well on land revenue alone, low-ranking banner commoners with small allotments could not. With shrinking grazing land, many low-status banner commoners turned to intensive "Chinese-style" farming. The Harqin Banners of Jesoto League in Central-East IM (see Figures P.III.1 and 8.1) witnessed similar changes. By the late

18th century, many Harqin Banner families had been practicing intensive farming for over a century.

In the process of banner land privatization and commodification in Jesoto, large tracts of the banner's estate land and commoners' land allotments were appropriated by banner elites. Princes and Lamaist priests consolidated their holdings and sold land leases or used land as collateral for loans. As many defaulted on their loans, these land tracts eventually fell into the hands of moneylenders and land brokers, many of whom were Han Chinese, a few were Mongolian banner officials. Land brokers often doubled as moneylenders, with clients from all ranks of banner society. Many banner commoners with small holdings were subsequently dispossessed due to banner nobles' land grabs and/or creditors' repossession.

Tax burdens and rampant land rent delinquency further burdened banner commoners. Jesoto's cultivation and population expansion attracted the attention of imperial tax collectors early on. To expand its tax base, the Qing court carved out chunks of banner territory, incorporating them into county jurisdictions where there were significant numbers of Han Chinese immigrants. Most of such territorial partitions took place in populous farming areas. In Harqin Banners, the county and the banner formed a dualistic administrative system, which in turn created jurisdictional competition and rivalry over tax revenues. Under the dualistic system, the banner government held jurisdiction over native Harqin Banner members, while the county governments held authority over Han Chinese settlers. As Han Chinese (who mostly held tenancy) and Mongols (who were mostly landowners of varied scales, or landowner-cultivators) often cohabitated in the same or neighboring villages, they were subject to two competing jurisdictional authorities. When Han Chinese tenant-settlers began to outnumber Harqin natives by the middle of the 18th century, the emboldened Chinese tenants, many of whom were members of secret societies, evaded rent payments, refused to return land at the end of their tenancy, and even leased out their tenancy and excessively expanded cultivation without permission from the banner landholders and authorities.

Combing through Harqin Banners' Mongolian archives, historian Shuangxi (2011) and ethnologist Bai, Meirong (2016) found numerous cases of litigation between small Harqin landholders and their Chinese tenants over delinquent rent payments and abuses of tenant rights. Disputes between Mongols and Chinese were mostly handled by the county courts, where authorities almost always favored the Chinese. One case from a Mongol village in Harqin Banner shows the reversal of the skewed power dynamics wherein the Mongol landowners held the shorter end of the stick when dealing with their Chinese tenants. In this village, every Mongol banner member held a "subsistence land" allotment of 25 mu, which they customarily leased out to Chinese tenants. The Chinese tenants paid less than one-third of the officially set rent but provided loans to their cash-poor landlords. (See Chapter 6 on financialization of land). Having the tenants as creditors weakened the small landowners' bargaining position. So, the Chinese tenants' rent delinquency persisted, while the Mongol landowners continued to accrue interest on the loans they took out from their Chinese tenants. The county authorities would not intervene despite repeated appeals and litigation by the Mongol villagers over the course of 16 years. Meanwhile, the small Mongol landowners held little more than nominal ownership of the land. At the end of their wits and with great resentment towards the Chinese tenants, these small Mongol landowners decided to "donate" the land to a local Lamaist temple. Since the small landowners could not fight their Chinese tenants, they instead let the more influential lamas collect rent from the Chinese tenants. In return, they received modest compensation from the lamas.[6]

Other Mongol landholders took a more proactive approach. In response to Chinese tenants' rent delinquency, some Mongol landowners would transfer the lease from the nonpaying tenant to a new tenant, collecting lease fees from the latter without informing the former, subsequently igniting a three-way feud among the original tenant, the new tenant, and the Mongol landowner. Or, to curb Chinese tenants' excessive reclamation beyond the original agreement, Mongols—either small landowners or the banner authority—would press hard to conduct land surveys to reassess rents or tax dues. Chinese tenants responded with armed riots, often organized by local secret societies. Mongol landowners' attempts to assert their ownership rights only escalated the conflicts further.

The banner government did not do any better. The conferral of the most taxworthy banner land to county jurisdictions significantly eroded the banners' fiscal base. To cope with the loss, banner leaders opted to squeeze more labor service and taxes in kind and in tael from the banner commoners. To dodge the excessive tax and draft burdens, many Harqin commoners fled their home banners.[7]

Running away from one's home banner was not a light decision to make. Banners were military and territorial units installed by the Manchu Qing regime in Mongolia. Hereditary banner membership was a part of what historian Christopher Atwood (2012)[8] called the "appanage community," which qualified members' access to banner resources like land, water, fuelwood, among others. Along with these entitlements came tax, labor, and military obligations to banner nobles and lamas. The appanage system aligned with banner jurisdiction. Banner members were obligated to stay in the banner's jurisdiction to stabilize banners' tax revenue and labor/soldier supplies. Those who attempted to escape their home banners received 100 counts of flogging, while the responsible banner official paid a penalty of as much as 100 horses if a member ran away. On the other hand, those who captured runaways were awarded livestock.[9] For those runaways who made it to Jerim, they could still be hunted down by tax collectors dispatched from home banners in Jesoto.[10]

But the risks of flogging and tax hunters' pursuits were outweighed by hardship brought on by the banner elites' land grabs and labor drafts, moneylenders' repossession, as well as Chinese tenants' rampant tenancy abuses. The number of escaped bannermen continued to increase; those who stayed behind were made to pick up the tax and labor obligations left by the deserters, feeding a vicious cycle of escape. The precarity experienced by banner commoners in Jesoto and their longing for Jerim is acutely expressed in a farewell blessing to deceased young children: "Wish you were reborn in Horqin (of Jerim), so that you could eat the delicious fried millet."[11]

Cross-banner migration from Jesoto to Jerim accelerated in the 19th century as home conditions in Jesoto deteriorated further. In the post-Opium Wars era of the mid-19th century, the Qing government began to compete with private capital and banner authorities for land rents by initiating large reclamation projects in Jesoto and Je'uda Leagues, similar to the situation in Hetao, as presented in Chapter 7. In response to their dwindling revenues, banner leaders squeezed their subjects even harder. The exorbitant tax burden pushed poor banner commoners to "hang themselves after their own parents had starved to death and their children were sold to pay for the tax they owed to the jasagh."[12]

Tensions between banner elites, banner commoners, and Han Chinese settlers culminated in increasingly frequent tax and rent riots in Jesoto and Je'uda. In 1853, for example, the bannermen of Tumd Right Banner revolted against the banner jasagh's excessive tax and labor demands. The resistance lasted for almost two decades until 1870, when its leaders were captured. Around the same period, numerous other similar tax and draft revolts organized by Chinese and outlander Mongol tenants against banner nobles occurred in the neighboring Tumd Left Banner and other banners, the scale of which ranged from several hundreds to tens of thousands of rioters and lasted for months or years.

Other types of resource conflicts likewise provoked ethnoterritorial clashes in Jesoto and Je'uda. One reported case concerned a fishing ground in Hexigten Banner of Je'uda League (see Figure 8.1). A Han Chinese who was a former militia head from Shandong Province occupied the fishing ground without permission from the banner landowners. Prolonged conflicts between banner members and the Chinese trespassers eventually led to the formation of a 2,000-strong band of Chinese bandits. The bandits rampaged Mongol settlements in various banners in Jesoto and Je'uda for over three decades between the late 1850s and the early 1890s, until the leader, who had declared himself the Master of Pacifying King (*pingwang tangzhu*), was captured by the emperor's army.[13]

Another conflict took place in a gold mine in the hills of Ongniud Banner of Je'uda League (see Figure 8.1) in the mid-1840s, where a Chinese gang recruited over 12,000 miners and militarized the mining turf against Mongol "trespassers." According to the French Catholic missionary Evariste Régis Huc (CE) (1850)[14] the banner's jasagh was too timid to attempt to chase away the mining gang. Tensions exploded one day when the jasagh's wife passed by the mining site on her way to visit her ancestral burial ground. The jasagh's wife was stopped by the gangsters and was forced to surrender her jewelry before being allowed to leave. The humiliating incident finally compelled the jasagh to dispatch his cavalry to the mining hills. After protracted battles, the banner cavalry broke the mining gang's defense line and began to slaughter the miners. When the banner soldiers found out that some Chinese miners took refuge in a mining tunnel, they blocked its entrance with large rocks. The trapped miners' cries for help could be heard for days until they perished. As for live captives, the jasagh ordered for their eyes to be gouged out before being released.

Fuelwood, humble as it may sound compared to gold, was the most common trigger for resource agitation and conflicts.[15] Due to deforestation in the cultivation area, fuelwood became a precious resource. As with most other resource conflicts, the issue was not just about scarcity, but access.[16] As retribution against the increasingly aggressive Han Chinese settlers, banner officials evoked the banner rule of blocking non-banner members' entry to the timberland. Han Chinese had to purchase fuelwood from banner members who enjoyed unlimited access to the timberland and its products.

Fuelwood, like grain, was a matter of life and death. In a plea to the banner jasagh to ease the ban against Chinese settlers, a local official in Ongniud Banner wrote: "... the fuelwood collection ban threatened to starve and freeze the 30,000 plus Chinese peasants who could not survive without the wood to cook their meals and heat their beds in the freezing winter."[17] Yet this was precisely the strategic thinking behind the fuelwood ban: by cutting Han Chinese peasants' fuelwood supply, the banner chief, now facing a shrinking number of banner servicemen to patrol the timberland, hoped that Han Chinese would have few options but to depart voluntarily.

Under the stringent rules, Han Chinese who were caught selling or collecting fuelwood were subject to harsh flogging and fines, and their tools, ox carts, and harvests would be confiscated.[18] The discriminatory and retributive restriction on Han Chineses' access to fuelwood, built upon ethnoterritorial rivalry amidst escalating resource competition, incited frequent fistfights and even armed conflicts. On top of discrimination was the banner noble families' excessive abuse of power. Adding insult to injury, even lowly slaves and servants of the noble's court could reprimand and cane Chinese fuelwood thieves in public. The everyday fuelwood conflicts, arbitrary punishments, and public displays of humiliation deepened Chinese settlers' resentment towards Mongols.

The fact that Han Chinese had become the majority in Mongol land only further inflamed the ethnoterritorial tension. By 1872, the Chinese population in Jesoto and Je'uda was close to one million, while Mongols accounted for less than 200,000, or about 15% of the total.[19]

However, population size by itself does not automatically amount to commensurate power. The masses need to be organized. Han Chinese settlers joined secret societies and sectarian cults that were popular in the North China Plain and spread to the northern frontier during the late imperial era. It was estimated that by the late 19th century, "nine out of ten Han Chinese settlers" in Jesoto belonged to one of the sectarian organizations. While many joined the sectarian cults voluntarily, others were drafted from poor peasant households by powerful sectarian organizations.[20]

At a time of boiling tensions and pervasive violence, the distinction between sectarian cults, secret societies, militias, and banditry was nebulous. As mentioned in Chapter 7 on Hetao of West IM, the northern frontier was a heavily militarized yet under-governed place during the late 19th century. Central-East IM was no exception. The banners of Jesoto and Je'uda were territorially truncated and financially stripped by the expansion of county jurisdictions and by the continuous loss of tax-paying and military/labor-serving bannermen. The Han Chinese-dominant county governments in the far-flung frontier, on the other hand, were often staffed by under-supervised and rent-seeking officials with an ever-increasing populace from whom to extract. The dualistic administrative system with overlapping jurisdictions also turned county and banner authorities into structural and perpetual rivals. It was a time and place where tenants, even with signed contracts and officially-registered title documents in hand, had to be escorted by armed men during their first visits to their newly leased parcels.[21] The law was validated and violated by everyday violence. As such, the frequent skirmishes over land rights and fuelwood, when mishandled by local officials and provoked by secret society organizers and their militia wings, could easily swell into outsized armed clashes.

One of the most ferocious ethnic clashes, known as the Jindandao Massacre in 1891, recorded a death toll of 100,000 to 200,000, with an estimated ratio of 1:4 between Han Chinese and Mongols.[22] The year of the massacre started with a series of devastating floods followed by famine and numerous incidents of "cult bandit" (*jiaofei*) insurgencies in Jesoto and southern Je'uda Leagues. Local officials were neither alarmed nor incentivized enough to rein in the insurgents or to alert their superiors, and when they did, their warnings fell on deaf ears. By fall 1891, the Aohan Banner of Je'uda League, where the banner Duke was known for his merciless treatment and exorbitant taxation of Han Chinese settlers, became the target of the Han Chinese-dominant cult sect, Jindandao. The followers of Jindandao, similar to the peasant followers of the Boxer uprising (see Chapter 7), believed that their leaders possessed supernatural powers against deadly weapons and could transfer such powers to them. After months of preparation—recruiting and organizing combatants, purchasing weapon and supplies, and gathering intelligence—the Jindandao leaders led over 2,000 Han Chinese rioters to launch an all-out attack on the Duke's mansion in the deep of the night on October 9. The mansion was plundered and burned down. The Duke and his family, guards, and staff were slaughtered, and their corpses burned. The raging rioters proceeded to ransack the Duke's ancestral tombs, setting fire to the remains of the deceased—the ultimate expression of hatred and the gravest act of vengeance. The pillage of Aohan Banner rippled across 10 banners in Jesoto and southern Je'uda. In the following two months, the armed insurgents—15,000 to 25,000 men in total and divided into three regiments of 5,000 to 8,000 men each—advanced along three routes to the east, west, and north from Aohan Banner. As the armed Jindandao rioters rampaged villages along the way, chanting "*death to the Mongols!*," Han Chinese villagers, hooligans, and local militiamen joined to loot neighboring Mongol homes and villages. More than one thousand Mongol settlements and several commercial centers across 10 banners and eight counties of Jesoto and Je'uda Leagues, an area that stretched over 100,000 sq. km, were besieged.

One of the most-cited witness accounts of the massacre was penned by Wang, Guojun (1853–1921) in 1918. Wang was born in Harqin Right Banner (see Figure 8.1). Wang's ancestors originally came from Shandong Province in northern China during the Ming Dynasty (1368 to 1644) and settled in the border zone north of the Great Wall, where they took advantage of their multilingual skills to serve as interpreters for the invading Manchu Qing troops. Upon the establishment of the Qing, Wang's family was granted banner membership and held high posts in the Harqin Right Banner government for seven generations. Wang himself was part of the literati and fluent in Mongolian, Chinese, and Manchurian, and served as an official archivist for Harqin Right Banner. Perceived by most scholars to be a more objective observer than his monolingual Chinese contemporaries, Wang reported on the brutality of the Jindandao attack on one Mongol settlement that he witnessed. The attackers raped women, slit their genitals, and left them bleeding to death. They killed children with spears. They beheaded men, and the blood of Mongolian men overflowed the dozens of stone mangers in the village. In that single killing field, among hundreds of other such fields across the 10 banners that were under siege, the entire village of more than 2,000 people were ruthlessly slaughtered.[23] The pogrom lasted for 48 days, and ended in December 1891, when the top leader of Jindandao, Yang Yuechun, was captured by imperial troops from his refuge in a mining pit after intentional delays and diversions of the military commander who sympathized with the Han Chinese rioters.[24] Upon apprehension, one of the Chinese riot leaders confessed that his original motivation to join the Jindandao cult was to wreak vengeance upon Mongols after he had been maliciously battered and publicly humiliated for collecting fuelwood in the banner's woodland.[25]

The capture of the Chinese cult leaders and the official end to the Jindandao Massacre did not end the violence, however. Instead, it set off Mongols' blood vengeance against Han Chinese. The vicious cycle of ethnic rivalry deepened and spread further. The massacre also aggravated frictions between the authorities of Mongol banners and Chinese counties, rendering them even less capable of curbing the post-conflict proliferation of Mongolian and Han Chinese banditry. These bandit bands rampaged across Mongolian-governed banners and Chinese-governed counties, alternating between taking refuge in each, as neither government would chase them across jurisdictional lines.[26]

In explaining the extraordinary violence of the Jindandao Massacre, the Chinese Communist Party (CCP)'s official line stressed the class struggle of Mongolian feudal society between the exploitative class of landowning banner nobles and Chinese moneylenders on one camp and the exploited Han Chinese and Mongol peasants on the other.[27] East IM-born and Japan-based historian Burensain Borjigin (2004)[28] diverged from that view and suggested that Jindandao was a quintessential ethnicity-motivated massacre, not a class struggle. It was because the target of the Han Chinese rioters was Mongols at all ranks and classes. By Wang Guojun's (1918) account, in most cases, it was Han Chinese peasants slaughtering Mongolian peasants. But a catastrophic bloodbath like the Jindandao Massacre is unlikely to have a single root; both class and ethnicity in resource struggle played a role. Tensions between Mongol elites and Mongol commoners, or between Chinese moneylenders and poor Chinese and Mongol borrowers could be class-based; while contestations between Mongol landowners and Chinese tenants denote an entangled ethno-class source of violence.

Territoriality adds a third nexus to the resource violence, most visible in the ethnoterritorial tensions between Mongol natives and Han Chinese outsiders, escalating at a time of massive Han Chinese population influx that exacerbated resource competition in Jesoto.

To start, the Qing state institutionalized the otherwise porous frontier identities through their dualistic jurisdictional system. The ethnicity-based jurisdictional system that separated the governance of Mongols and Han Chinese turned their respective authorities into rivals. The unbalanced power relationship between the neighboring Mongol and Chinese jurisdictions led to discriminatory treatment of Mongol residents who registered under Mongol authorities. The discriminatory treatment also emboldened the Chinese settlers and enraged native Mongols, which was then countered by imposing banner membership-only resource access restrictions. Territorial conflicts, in turn, amplified class- and ethnicity-based violence.

Ethnoterritorial violence produced ethnoterritorial consequences. The Jindandao Massacre in 1891 prompted an exodus of Mongols from Central-East to East IM. It was estimated that about 400,000 Mongol refugees escaped home banners in Jesoto and Je'uda since the time of the massacre and continued on till the 1930s. Out of the 400,000 refugees, more than 300,000 fled Central-East IM in the immediate aftermath of the massacre.[29] Some refugees went straight up north to seek refuge, but the majority headed northeast to Jerim League. Considering that the total Mongol population in the late Qing was only about 1.2 million, the 80,000 to 160,000 Mongol fatalities and 300,000 refugees meant that the massacre had directly affected between one-quarter and one-third of the total Mongol population by the end of the Qing.[30]

Burensain Borjigin (2004)[31] considered the Jindandao Massacre a watershed moment in Central-East and East IM's agrarian histories. The massacre and the massive exodus of Mongols marked a decisive end to the manorial land, labor, and military system in the banners of Jesoto and its neighboring leagues in Central-East IM. The land left behind by the victims and refugees of the massacre did not stay vacant for long. After the dust had settled, land merchants moved in and subsequently leased out the parcels to Han Chinese settlers. On the receiving end of the migration, the massacre refugees also accelerated the opening up of the new agricultural frontier in East IM in the 20th century. In many ways the making of the new frontier of Jerim League in East IM looks quite similar to that of the earlier frontier in Central IM two centuries prior. But when history repeats itself, geography helps avoid an identical story.

Here, the geographical question is: why Jerim? What was in Jerim that drew Jesoto refugees?

I.2 Trudging across Jerim

It turns out that the Jesoto refugees who fled to Jerim in the late 19th century were not the first Jesotos in Jerim. During the first half of the 18th century, the banners of Jesoto—who were strong military allies of the Manchu Qing—sent thousands of soldiers to join the Manchu military campaigns against Zunghars in the west. These Jesoto soldiers, many of whom came from farming families, provided indispensable labor in the military-farming colonies in the frontier. When the war was over by the mid-18th century, Jesoto veterans were not sent back home, where land competition was already fierce. Instead, the Qing government settled the Jesoto veterans in the much less populated southern Jerim, which was blessed with fluvial plains created by dense river networks. Jesoto veterans were allotted land parcels and tasked with teaching Jerim Mongols farming skills, so as to expand grain production in Jerim. Jerim Banner leaders welcomed the tax and rent revenues from farm expansion, especially because they were required by the emperor to be self-sufficient in producing grain for disaster relief. So, Jerim banner leaders actively recruited Jesoto farmers to work the southern Jerim fields. Jerim leaders preferred Jesoto farmworkers over Han Chinese migrants, whom they feared would dilute the Mongol population and create conflicts like what had happened in Jesoto.[32]

In addition to the state's resettlement of war veterans and local elites' recruitment of farmers, another channel for Jesoto Mongols' cross-banner migration before the Jindandao Massacre was through marriage exchanges between banner nobles. Customarily, nobles did not marry within the same banner, and they established multigenerational marriage partnerships with specific banners. Many Jesoto nobles maintained such marriage partnerships with Jerim noble families. When marrying Jerim banner princes, Jesoto princesses brought their dowry of servants, slaves, craftsmen, and staffers to southern Jerim. Each cross-banner marriage started out with dozens of households of dowry servants and staff. After several generations of marriage exchange with the same partner banners, and with the natural population growth of the servant households, dowry entourages grew into farming villages of one to two hundred households each.[33]

The 18th century state-organized Jesoto migration to Jerim was accompanied by self-initiated migration. At a time when arable land was plentiful and competitors few in southern Jerim, the self-initiated Jesoto migrants worked as tenants or farmhands while opening up more land of their own. The hard-working Jesoto families were more adept at intensive farming in comparison to Jerim natives and, thus, managed to build up their own land holdings. Thanks to inter-banner marriages that were popular not just among nobles but also low-ranking officials and their extended families, many Jesoto migrants were blessed with in-law networks in Jerim. Well-connected and entrepreneurial Jesoto migrants leased large parcels from host banners, recruited farm hands and tenants from Jesoto, and became labor and land brokers themselves.[34]

Jerim had become Jesoto farming Mongols' new frontier. The success stories from the first wave of Jesoto migrants in Jerim and Jesoto migrants' tight social networks attracted more Jesoto migrants to Jerim, a familiar pattern evident in many other migration histories. By the early 19th century, Jesoto migrants had built a vibrant peasant economy in southern Gorlos, Horqin Left Rear, and Horqin Left Front Banners of southern Jerim. These Jesoto migrants included the early movers who held land of various sizes and the recent arrivals who worked as day laborers and farmhands.

During the second half of the 19th century, resource struggles and ethnoterritorial tension soared in Jesoto, as presented earlier. An increasing number of Jesoto families escaped exploitation and dispossession in their home banners by joining their relatives in Jerim. The continuous trickle from the 18th century turned into sizable waves of migrations. By 1891, in the midst of the catastrophic Jindandao Massacre in Jesoto, the waves of migration gushed into torrential swarms of hundreds of thousands of distraught massacre refugees scrambling to find their way to Jerim. There were now many more Jesotos in Jerim, and the most recent arrivals, the massacre refugees, were much more desperate than their predecessors.

In the meantime, the conditions in the host banners of southern Jerim were changing fast.

For a start, the overall population in southern Jerim had surged. The massive influx of Jesoto Mongols coincided with an influx of Chinese refugees fleeing recurrent famines and chronic banditry in the east of the North China Plain. As both Chinese and Jesoto refugees poured in, resource conflicts escalated in south Jerim. The south Jerim hosts who originally favored the Jesoto migrants over Han Chinese now felt threatened by both. They turned hostile to all outsiders, including Jesoto migrants. Any pan-Mongol empathy, which was tenuous to begin with, quickly gave way to banner-centered territorialism. With the change in locals' attitude towards all outsiders, Jesoto Mongols were increasingly made the subjects of native Jerim Mongols' suspicion and mockery. For instance, Jerim natives considered migrants from Tumd Left Banner of Jesoto, known as "Legin" Mongols, to be penny pinchers. The hard-working Legin migrants, especially those early migrants who managed to buy land and lead better lives than those of the south Jerim natives, were ridiculed by jealous natives with satiric tales such as the following:

> A Legin Mongol family had a pickled cabbage hung under the ceiling. The family would eat their tasteless meal while looking up at the hanging cabbage and consumed the flavorful pickle in their imagination, so that the precious pickled cabbage would last longer. When a child looked at the cabbage too many times, his parents would warn him: "Quit doing that! If you look at the cabbage one more time, you will start coughing!"[35]

South Jerim natives also despised Legin Mongols for their sycophancy, which, if extant at all, might have developed as, what historian Bai Meirong (2016) suspected, a survival instinct honed from the precarious life of the refugee. Jerim natives circulated tales about the "crafty and sweet-tongued" Legin Mongols, whom they also derogatorily named the "short Mongols" as mentioned earlier. The fact that some Jesoto Mongols shifted their banner and ethnic affiliations in order to survive made it even harder for them to earn respect from the Jerim natives. The southern belt of IM had long been a breeding ground for identity mixing and shifting. Many Jesotos were the descendants of Chinese progenitors who were Mongolianized during the Ming and early Qing eras. But they either switched back to their ancestral Chinese identity and registered with the county authorities when Han Chinese became dominant in the 19th century, or they kept their Mongol banner memberships but not the Mongolian tongue. They were, in Jerim natives' views, untrustworthy transients with little allegiance.

Jesoto Mongols in Jerim were subject to not just mockery and prejudice. They also became targets of territorial discrimination and contempt. As non-banner members, Jesoto migrants were burdened with excessive taxation and labor drafts in exchange for their rights to stay in the southern Jerim banners. But their land tenancy was still subject to host banner officials' arbitrary termination. In an oral history account recorded by Bai, Meirong (2016),[36] a 77-year-old man, who was a third-generation Jesoto migrant in Jerim, recalled his grandfather's plight in Gorlos Front Banner (See Figure 8.1), one of the most popular destinations in south Jerim for Jesoto Mongols. In addition to imposing heavy taxation and labor service on the Jesoto outlanders, the Gorlos Front Banner officials would invite themselves to the homes of relatively well-to-do Jesoto settlers and stay for days. The host was expected to serve the visiting officials feasts, alcohol, and pretty women. At night, the officials played card games lit by lamps that burned precious sheep fat. Shuangxi (2011)[37] also found a Mongolian record of a group of Jesoto Mongols' petition to the Gorlos Banner jasagh who threatened to expel the outlanders and confiscate their homes, animals, and land. The outlander petitioners cited that they were pushed to the point of having to sell their children to fulfill their taxation obligation to the jasagh. And they were never as cunning as the Han Chinese settlers who routinely evaded taxes and rents and made trouble for the host banner. But now the jasagh rewarded their compliance by ordering them to go back to their home banner, where despair awaited.

The Jesoto migrants did not always remain an acquiescent bunch, however, especially when they began to outnumber the natives. By the middle of the 19th century, there were already 3,600 households of Jesoto Mongols in Gorlos Front Banner, greatly outnumbering Jerim natives and Han Chinese migrants. As Jesoto migrants became the majority in south Jerim, they also became more assertive. Skirmishes between Jesoto migrant tenants and Jerim native landowners flared up regularly. But as was the case with Chinese migrants in Jesoto, the large number of agitated Jesoto migrants in south Jerim first needed to get organized into effective combat units. In 1863, an entrepreneurial Jesoto outlander led hundreds of fellow Jesoto Mongol settlers in making an audacious proposal to the jasagh of Gorlos Banner. The proposal was to establish a concession for Jesoto settlers, like what the Han Chinese settlers were granted in Gorlos Banner. The proposal was believed to have drawn inspiration from, if not direct support of, the Eight Arrows and the Elderly Council, the Mongolian secret societies that were responsible for the armed tax revolts against the jasaghs in Jesoto in the 1850s.[38]

The Jesoto settlers' demand for a concession outraged the jasagh of Gorlos Front Banner. The Chinese concession was established under the emperor's order; who did these ungrateful Jesoto drifters think they were, demanding a piece of Gorlos territory? But the Jesotos would not take no for an answer. They traveled to the regional capital, presented their case to the regional governor, and lobbied to various authorities—all to no avail. When the lobbyist delegation finally returned to Gorlos after their two years' sojourn in the political centers, the infuriated jasagh requested that the regional governor send 500 calvary troops to Gorlos to teach the Jesoto troublemakers a lesson. Upon the arrival of the calvary troops, the emboldened jasagh ordered all Jesoto migrants to take leave immediately, or their homes would be set on fire and their livestock confiscated. No bloodshed was recorded, but tens of thousands of Jesoto settlers who overstayed their welcome were evicted at gunpoint.[39]

The territorial rifts between south Jerim natives and Jesoto Mongol outlanders were complicated by a third player, the Han Chinese settlers. The ostracized and sinicized Jesoto Mongols, most of whom no longer spoke Mongolian, chose to settle in areas closer to Han Chinese settlements than to native Jerim Mongol settlements. Meanwhile, Jesoto and Han Chinese settlers—old foes back in Jesoto but now sharing outsider status in south Jerim—found themselves fighting side by side in rent and tax riots that involved hundreds or thousands of tenant farmers against the Jerim Banner authorities and native landowners.[40]

The outsiders' alliance across ethnic divides was far from stable, however. The coalition of Han Chinese and Jesoto Mongol settlers in one battle did not preclude their collision in another. In the end, resource politics in late 19th century southern Jerim bore a three-pronged structure composed of banner natives, Jesoto Mongol settlers, and Han Chinese settlers. Upon this structure developed variant configurations of ethnoterritorial alliance and rivalry. Jesoto tenants would join their Jerim landowners to drive away lurking Chinese reclamation gangs; native Jerim landowners would get organized to attack both Chinese and Jesoto settlers who refused to pay rent and/or reclaim land without permission. The three-way ethnoterritorial resource conflicts climaxed in the early 20th century, as the desperate last emperors of the Qing launched reclamation programs in south Jerim on an unprecedented pace and scale, followed by the land exploits of the regional warlords of the ensuing Republican era.

The predatory state's reclamation campaigns in south Jerim can be better understood in the broader geopolitical context of China's northeast on both sides of the Great Wall. East IM and northeast China in the early 20th century stood at the center of a power scramble at the national and international levels. Nationally, the turbulent final decade of the Qing empire was followed by the precarious infancy of the new Republic that was hijacked by regional warlords, especially in the north. Internationally, the new Republican regime's social-economic and political fragility was further threatened by lurking foreign powers—the Japanese and the Russians along China's northern borders. Power scrambles at the international and national levels in the northern borders trickled down to south Jerim in the form of turf wars.

Turf wars on the ground in south Jerim, in turn, transpired via a land reclamation rush. Unlike earlier phases of cultivation expansion that were dominated by local bosses, the new rounds of land grabs were spearheaded by a succession of state and para-state actors. These actors included the last, desperate reign of the Qing, the shifting Republican authorities, and the revolving slate of regional and local warlords. All of them tried to finance their military buildup by carving out tracts of land and selling them for quick cash in the new agricultural frontier of Jerim. Accompanied by armed soldiers, their reclamation crews conducted cadastral surveys, marked the boundaries of the reclamation zones, graded the land tracts, and assigned leasing fees and tax obligations accordingly. As the reclamation race proceeded from regime to regime and from one reclamation authority to the next, reclamation sprawled from the southern plains to the northern hills, and from fertile soils to sterile sandy fields, reaching far-flung corners of Jerim.

These state and para-state reclamation projects invariably started from the relatively more productive land for their higher market value. More importantly, these areas were usually where the settlers were concentrated. The settlers—be they Han Chinese or Jesoto Mongols—held the weakest levels of social legitimacy and political support, and hence the thinnest land proprietary claims, making them an easy target for reclamation officials. The better-located, productive land also held long cultivation history that featured numerous transactions over many generations, hence creating highly convoluted tenancy and ownership relationships. In the eyes of reclamation officials, however, almost all landholder and tenants, regardless of their ownership status, owed the state taxes and lease fees for the land they cleared, farmed, bought, sold, and rented. For tenants, state reclamation added a third layer to their already heavy financial burdens. Prior to reclamation programs, they already bore tax obligations to the banner authority and rent to landowners. State reclamation did not replace the existing taxes but instead added to it.

Settlers were not the only ones affected by the reclamation rush. State reclamation authorities' targeting the most productive land also chipped away at the banner elites' key revenue base and stripped banner commoners' land allotments, on which the commoners relied for rental income. In other words, unbridled state land grabs struck just about everybody in southern Jerim banners, and social tensions soared to an unprecedented level. The additional tax burden triggered widespread anti-reclamation riots by settlers across south Jerim.

Some of the most persistent and widespread Mongolian anti-reclamation insurgencies were led not by grieved settlers and commoners, but second-tier banner elites. Reclamation had triggered internal schisms among banner elites. Jasaghs, the banner prince-governors, often collaborated with the state reclamation office to share the profits and keep themselves in power. But second-tier nobles, lower-ranking banner government and military officers often lost much of their land to state reclamation. They were also excluded from sharing the reclamation profits. The uneven distribution of profits set off bickering competition among banner elites of different ranks. The resentful mid-to-low ranking banner elites who lost out in reclamation, but still possessed the sociopolitical legitimacy to call on followers, became leaders of the insurgencies.

Two of the best-known armed revolts of such genre took place in Jalaid Banner in 1902 and in Gorlos Front Banner in 1907. The former was mobilized by Choghdalai, a military officer. His force eventually halted the state's reclamation project in Jalaid. The latter was led by the legendary Engkhoilegttin Togtokh (1864–1922, *Taoketaohu* in Chinese).[41] Togtokh and his bannermen killed the state reclamation chief official and continued to attack reclamation sites for three years. After being crushed by the

Qing army in 1910, Togtokh retreated to Russia.[42] As state reclamation moved further up north of Jerim in the proceeding years, more insurgencies erupted in the north as well. In these cases, Han Chinese settlers in the newly established state reclamation zones also became targets of the Mongol insurgents' attacks.

After the Qing's demise in 1911, the Republican-Warlord era saw even greater aggravation of anti-reclamation insurgencies. In 1929, the northeast warlord Zhang Xueliang launched a new round of reclamation in Horqin Left Central Banner in south Jerim. With the collaboration of the banner jasagh, Zhang commenced land enclosures. As a result, thousands of low-ranking banner officials and commoners were dispossessed. A former banner military officer, known as Ɣada Meyiren (1892–1931, *Gadameilin* in Chinese), led a thousand-strong insurrection. The insurgents attacked the reclamation bureau's field stations, killed the survey crew, destroyed the boundary posts, and burned the tax records. To dodge the banner authorities' pursuits, Ɣada Meyiren's band roamed across banner boundaries in south Jerim and mounted guerilla attacks in various reclamation sites in the region. Topping the local authorities' most wanted list, Ɣada Meyiren was captured at one point. Legend has it that Ɣada Meyiren's equally fearless wife, Mudan, led a group of combatants to storm the prison and freed him. The guerilla warfare continued for another two years until the warlord's 4,000-strong troop, joined by the jasagh's calvaries, crushed Ɣada Meyiren's force in 1931.

It was no coincidence that the commander who had led the warlord's troops to crush Ɣada Meyiren was a Jesoto Mongol, an outsider from within, went by a Chinese name: Li, Shouxin. But Li was more than a sinicized Jesoto Mongol. Tracing back further in his family history, Li's ancestors were once outsiders from the outside of the Mongolian land. They came from Shandong Province in northeastern China during the late Ming, in the 16th or 17th century. Like many other Han Chinese migrants at the time, Li's ancestors were Mongolianized and managed to obtain Mongol banner membership. But by the time Li's father was born in a farming village in 19th century Jesoto, the ethnopolitical wind had shifted and the Li family switched to Han Chinese ways. Under social pressure, however, they did not abandon their banner membership nor register with the Chinese county authority, a despicable act in the eyes of their Mongol neighbors. Instead, the Lis separated from the banner, but appendaged themselves to the Lamaist temple, an allegedly more neutral sociopolitical space. By the time Li Shouxin was born, his family no longer spoke Mongolian.[43] As a man with political entrepreneurship and an aspiring military career, Li Shouxin served the warlord and built up his credentials during the battle against the undefeatable Ɣada Meyiren. In the 1930s he rose to command the armed forces of Prince Demčugdongrub (1902–1966, *Dewang* in Chinese). Prince Demčugdongrub led one of the most important IM independence movements of the 20th century and was the symbol of Mongolian nationalism. He was also seen, fairly or unfairly, as a traitor by Chinese nationalists for his connection to Japanese forces.[44] The Li family's shifting ethnic-cultural associations and Li Shouxin's oscillating political alignments represent the identification politics of the borderland. It does not adhere to fixed ethnic labels, nor does it predetermine political allegiance.[45] I will spend Chapter 9 on ethnoterritorial identification politics in contemporary East IM. For now, I will go back to the Jesotos' itinerary in 20th century East IM.

II Outlander Mongols in North Jerim Hills

The Jesoto settlers were pushed out of south Jerim by their increasingly hostile hosts, the disruptive state reclamation projects, and the anti-reclamation insurgence that turned many of them into fugitives. As the Jesoto settlers took to the road again, they had few options but trekking to the chilly hills of north Jerim, today's Hinggan League.

Sandwiched between the Daxing'anling Mountains to its northwest and the Songnen Plain to its southeast, north Jerim had 95% of its 60,000 sq. km territory covered by forested hills at 150 to 1,800 meters above sea level. The annual average temperature is 4 to 6 degrees Celsius. Summer lasts for no more than two months, while winter takes up five to six months of the year. The growing season is short, with only 120 to 140 frost-free days annually. Its highest northwest mountainous area skips the summer altogether, with only 51 frost-free days a year.[46]

North Jerim, in other words, was far from a settlers' dream destination. Within its vast territory the only promising land is found in the narrow strip along the southern border. At a lower altitude this belt is blessed with relatively warmer temperatures, arable river basins, and rich, albeit thin, fluvial soil. But this area was not vacant when the Jesotos arrived in the early 20th century. By then, the precious arable land was already claimed by earlier settlers, some were early Jesoto migrants, but most were Han Chinese. And some of these early settlers had become landowners or landowner-cultivators. Thus, the latecomers took up tenancy or worked as farmhands for the early settlers in the southern lowlands of north Jerim.

At first, banner leaders of the southern belt in northern Jerim had no objections to hosting the farming Jesoto migrants. Harboring deep suspicions of Han Chinese, they preferred the Jesotos who were able and willing to farm just as hard.[47] Like what they did in south Jerim before, Jesoto settlers enabled north Jerim banners to expand their grain production and sources of revenue. The Jesoto farming migrants also made another fiscal contribution to northern banner authorities. Under the dualistic administrative system of Chinese counties and Mongolian banners in Jerim, banner authorities were largely excluded from the tax and land lease revenues that Chinese tenants submitted to the county government. But the taxes and fees that Jesoto farming settlers paid were considered Mongolian affairs and hence went to the banner treasury.[48]

This win-win arrangement for the Jesoto migrants and their north Jerim hosts, however, did not last. Not before long, heavily armed state reclamation crews showed up in north Jerim, again starting from its most lucrative—the relatively warmer and lower southern plains. And a new round of land grab and dispossession began.

Like elsewhere, state reclamation in north Jerim was supported by local banner leaders who collaborated with the Qing state to secure their own appointments and to enjoy a share of the land conveyance fees. But unlike the earlier era, state reclamation in 20th century north Jerim relied more heavily on speculative merchant capital. Long gone were the days of commodified manor land, which took place in a piecemeal manner at varied scales and by all banner ranks, like in Central IM in the 18th centuries (see Chapter 6). At the dynastic end of the early 20th century in East IM, land reclamation and land sales were of a much larger scale. To boost their own performance records, which were evaluated by the size of land reclaimed and sold, state reclamation officials skipped the retail mode and actively leased out sizable tracts to large land merchants at low conveyance charges. Yet, even at low fees, the merchants rarely paid in full.[49] These well-connected land speculators made a windfall by selling the subdivisions to second-tier land/money brokers and tenant recruiters, who in turn found Han Chinese migrants to sign on to clear and cultivate the land.

This model of state-initiated, large-scale land reclamation carried out through joint forces with speculative capital was common across IM during the late 19th and early 20th centuries. But this formula glitched in the hilly north Jerim. Interests in taking up tenancy in the hills waned with the rising altitude. Han Chinese settlers, normally eager to gain access to state-sanctioned reclamation zones, were reluctant to venture into the chilly northern hills.

The cold and dry climate in the northern highlands was a decisive deterrent, but it was not the sole reason that made Han Chinese settlers hesitate. Safety was a bigger concern. Throughout the first decades of the 20th century, the havoc wreaked by state land grabs and subsequent dispossession brought anti-reclamation riots across Jerim, from its southern banners to the north. Han Chinese settlers who took up tenancy in reclamation zones were often targeted by these rioters.

Some rioters were captured and executed; many more went on the run and found a safe haven in the under-governed and forested north Jerim hills. The remote and rugged terrains came to be a hub of Mongol fugitives from different eras and places of reclamation, including those who had revolted against banner jasaghs and those who had attacked state reclamation crews. Increasingly, the northern hills of Jerim also hosted hordes of dispossessed south Jerim natives as well as Jesoto migrants, both of whom were dispossessed by state reclamation in south Jerim.

The refugees, the fugitives, the drifters, and the dispossessed in the northern hills made for a reservoir of potential recruits for multiethnic rebel bands. At times of extreme deprivation and sociopolitical upheaval, it seems futile to distinguish heroic guerilla combatants from bandits who fed upon extortion and raids. Even legendary leaders of anti-reclamation revolts, like the aforementioned Togtokh and Ɣada Meyiren who had become Mongolian folk heroes, were said to have financed their armed forces via various channels, including "borrowing food" from better-endowed settlements and livestock owners. Their actions may have been motivated by redistribution, as in what Eric Hobsbawm (2000) has called "social banditry."[50] Or they could represent the cause of Mongolian nationalism, as Burensain Borjigin (2007)[51] has argued. They might also exemplify heroism in class struggles against greedy imperialists, exploitative merchant capital, and the feudalistic Mongolian aristocracy, an image that the Chinese Communist Party (CCP) regime has continued to cultivate and popularize via film, musical theater, and TV drama productions to this day.

However Togtokh, ɣada Meyiren and their peers were portrayed—as heroes or looters—and whatever their causes may have been—social redistribution or otherwise—one thing was clear to Han Chinese settlers at the time: their settlements out in the remote mountains would be prime targets for the flourishing "barbarian bandits" (*hufei*). It was an area beyond the reach of the Chinese-staffed county governments in south Jerim. Even the government officials themselves would not venture into the woody hills without the protection of legions of armed and mounted soldiers. And if Chinese settlements were raided, settlers knew they would receive little sympathy from the local banner authority.

Where Han Chinese settlers were reluctant to venture, the Jesoto migrants, who had fewer options, filled the gap. The rent was far more affordable in the undesirable hills. In fact, there was an inverse correlation between rent rates and altitude—the higher the altitude, the lower the rent.[52] But for many refugees, the low rent was still beyond their reach. So they went even higher up to areas beyond the state reclamation zone to work as day laborers or farmhands for native herders. Following the frontier tradition, they also cleared land for themselves wherever and whenever possible. In place of Han Chinese settlers who populated other IM agricultural frontiers, Mongol farming refugees and migrants from the early agricultural frontier of Jesoto pioneered cultivation expansion in the new frontier of the northern Jerim hills.

The multi-stop migration of Mongols from Jesoto to south Jerim, and onto north Jerim left a lasting impact on East IM as a new agricultural frontier of the Mongolian steppe in the 20th century. It is a new frontier not just in chronological terms. It is new also in its ethnoterritorial configuration. The cold and hilly north Jerim had grown into a hub of itinerant Mongols from various places of origin and identities. Under the label of "Mongols," there arose diverse territorial identities among northern Jerim Banner natives, refugees from southern Jerim banners, as well as Jesoto migrants driven out of banners of southern Jerim. Reclamation and massacre refugees from Jesoto and Je'uda Leagues also found their way to the cold and hilly north Jerim, sometimes bypassing the tumultuous south Jerim. The congregation of various kinds of "Mongols" has profoundly shaped the demographic structure of north Jerim through present-day Hinggan League. Today, Mongols of kaleidoscopic ancestral and ethnoterritorial backgrounds, now all under the nationality register of "Mongol," account for 42% of the 1.6 million residents in Hinggan League, or 672,000 in absolute numbers, making Hinggan League the largest cluster of ethnic Mongols outside of Mongolia. As presented in Chapter 5, this local concentration of Mongols in East IM, which was much higher than Mongols' weight of 17% to 18% in Inner Mongolia Autonomous Region (IMAR)'s total population, was built on Mongols' massive intra-regional migration of the early 20th century.[53]

In the remainder of this chapter, I will use the term "outlander Mongols" to register the various kinds of Mongol refugees and migrants who have congregated in north Jerim since the early 20th century. The territorially defined term "outlander Mongols" denotes their shared status as internal outsiders as well as their shared histories of repeated uprooting, dispossession, and aspirations to find new homes. In the northern hills of Jerim, outlander Mongols' territorial status as outsiders further reinforced their derogatory tag as "short" Mongols in the eyes of north Jerim's native pastoralists who despised farming and farming Mongols.

II.1 Mixes and Shifts in the Hills

Most outlander Mongols in north Jerim took on the drudgery of clearing and cultivating land in the cold and hilly terrains. But their arrival did not bring a finite shift from herding to cropping. Rather, the outlander Mongols contributed to the livelihoods in the hills that were always highly heterogeneous, including varied modes of herding, cropping, foraging, and hunting. What the outlander Mongols did bring to the northern hills of Jerim, though, was a shift to new modes of mixed livelihoods.

Mixes and shifts are nothing new in dryland livelihoods at large. Between China's roughly divided pastoral northwest half and agricultural southeast half, there has long existed an immense buffer zone that China-based scholars have named the "Interwoven Belt of Agriculture and Pastoralism" (*nongmu jiaocuodai*).[54] This Interwoven Belt stretches from Heilongjiang in the northeast all the way to parts of Xinjiang in the northwest and Tibet in the southwest (see Figure P.1). Despite its label as the Belt of "Agriculture and Pastoralism," the Belt is in fact home to peoples with multiple livelihoods, including cropping, herding, hunting, foraging, and fishing across the extensive expanse of about 650,000 sq. km. It is about 4.5% of China's total territory, larger than Ukraine's 580,000 sq. km. Two-thirds of this Interwoven Belt, an area of about 430,000 sq. km, is located in today's IM. Within IM, the Belt varies in width. In the arid western and central IM, the Belt measures between 100 and 200 km north to south, while the eastern section of the belt widens to over 300 km, thanks mostly to the relatively higher annual precipitation of around 400 mm. In short, Inner Mongolia, especially East IM, makes up the bulk of China's Interwoven Belt.

The term "interwoven," in my reading, connotes both spatial and temporal dynamics. It is about mixes of peoples and livelihoods across uneven terrains, and the way such mixes shift over time. To find out what an Interwoven Belt looks like and how it works on the ground, I first tried to locate the Interwoven Belt on a map of China. But I got lost almost immediately. Mapping the ephemeral "mixscape" between two presumably unadulterated zones is to grapple with three moving targets: the pastoral, the agricultural, and the mixed zone between the two polar reference zones. Given the variability of rural economies and ecologies, drawing boundaries around "agricultural" and "pastoral" zones is just as baffling as defining a mixed zone that contains both. My struggles to identify a boundary line on the map mainly come from the following complications.

Under the umbrella term, "pastoralism," are practices as diverse as mobile and semi-mobile pastoralism, sedentary, and semi-sedentary pastoralism, and many other modes in-between and beyond, such as sheltered husbandry. Also, herding varies according to the type of livestock kept. In East IM today, livestock includes not just those considered to be "typical" Mongolian ones, like camel, cattle, and sheep, but also pigs and chicken, which are traditionally associated with Han Chinese farms. Grazing patterns of sheep, for example, also vary: pasture grazing on naturally occurring plants, "rangeland" grazing on planted grasses in cleared forests, and a seasonal, alternating mix of open grazing and feeding on dried fodder and feed crops like corn and alfalfa. Similarly, "agriculture" involves widely diverse types from commodity to semi-commodity to subsistence crops, and different combinations thereof. Agriculture also features varying cropping scales and methods from intensive, semi-intensive, to low-impact rotational cropping; from dry to irrigated farming. The list goes on. The picture gets even more complicated when considering the fact that hunting, lumbering, gathering, and fishing during different seasons in different micro environments are also part of the mixed livelihoods in the hills and the lowlands of East IM.[55]

Temporality complicates the matter further still. The many modes of herding and cropping and the multiple ways they mix with one another in any given space also shift and reconfigure with varied frequencies. Their relative significance in land use, labor, and capital input, as well as contribution to household subsistence needs and cash income change seasonally, annually, and over a longer period of time; the mixes are also dictated by market fluctuation as well as variable rainfall, extreme weather, and natural calamities, which is of particular concern in arid, high-altitude land.

North Jerim sits at the heart of the belt of mixes and shifts. To better comprehend these moving pieces on the ground, I zoom in on one of the banners in north Jerim: Horqin Right Front (Horqin RF) Banner.

II.2 Ethnoterritorial Dynamisms of Horqin Right Front Banner

Located in the northern part of north Jerim (see Figure 8.1), today's Hinggan League, Horqin RF's northern half sits at the foot of the Daxing'anling Mountains, while its southern half features lower rolling hills. Less than 3% of the banner's current jurisdiction, at its southeastern corner, is made of alluvial plains. Two west-to-east running rivers curve across the banner: the Tao'er in the north and the Guiliu in the south (see Figure 8.2). Originating from the Daxing'anling Mountains, the rivers are fed by snow melt and summer rainfall. The river systems generate extensive networks of streams, wetlands, and springs, creating fluvial plains in the highlands and lower slopes that support dry farming. But like many dryland rivers, their runoff volume fluctuates radically between different seasons and years, often resulting in

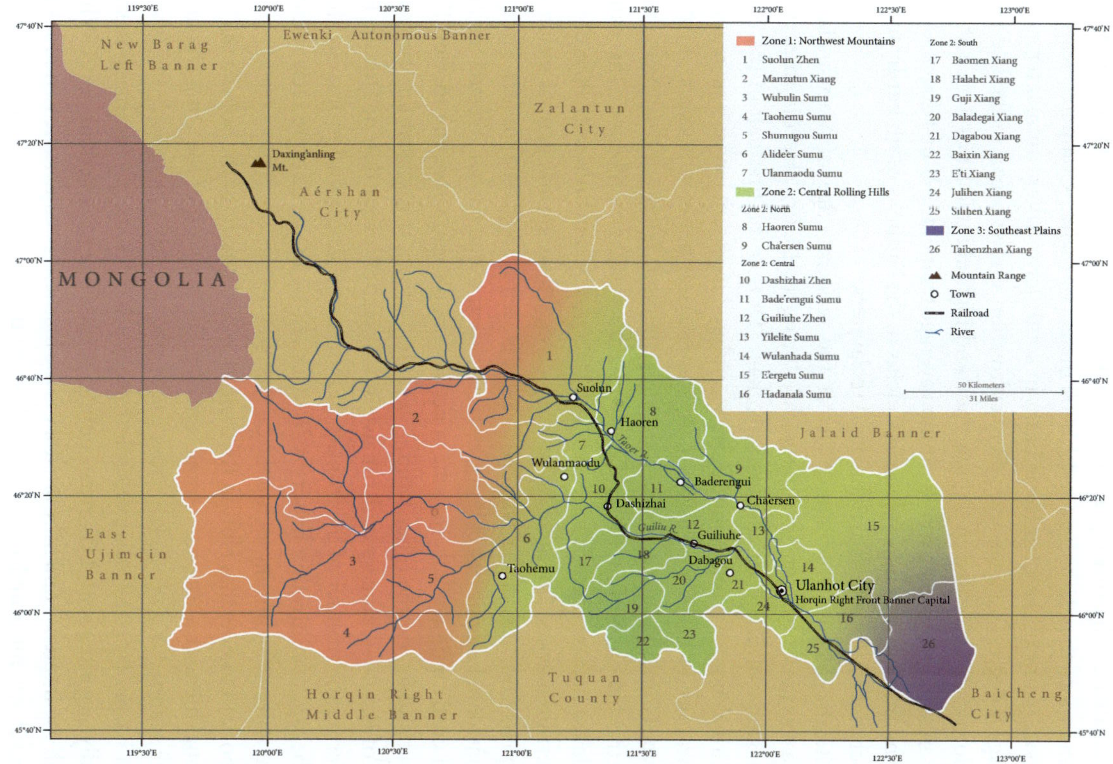

Figure 8.2 Map of contemporary Horqin Right Front Banner and its three ecological zones
Source: Cartographer: Alan Pong.

destructive summer floods and spring and fall droughts. The river basins guide the direction of farming expansion through both their conductive and disruptive powers. But what ultimately shapes the livelihood and ethnoterritorial mixes and shifts in Horqin RF Banner is the tyranny of altitude.

Horqin RF was late to intensive cultivation for a reason. Stretching between N 45°40' and N 47°40' altitude (as a reference, Ontario, Canada and Hokkaido, Japan sit at 45th parallel north), three quarters of its terrain stands at over 500 meters above sea level, and more than half rises up to 1,000 meters or higher. Compared with the broad alluvial plains of the Liao River Basin in south Jerim where annual temperatures average 6 degrees Celcius and where cultivation sprawl began in the late 18th century, Horqin RF is located in high-latitude and high-altitude lands with a short, three-four-month growing season. Its annual average temperatures of 4 degrees Celcius in the banner's south and –3 degrees Celcius in the banner's north hardly made it the first choice for state or individual land reclaimers.[56]

Geopolitically, Horqin RF Banner sits at the western edge of Manchuria. If Manchuria was the "storm center of the world" during the 1930s,[57] Horqin RF served as the repository of Manchuria's storm wreckage. During the first half of the 20th century, China's northeast, including East IM, endured incessant havoc from regime-changing wars and warlords' turf wars to the imperial war between Russia and Japan fighting over China. Refugees of wars, state reclamation, floods, and famines were swarming throughout Horqin RF, and the banner's rugged terrain beyond the state's reach made it a natural hideout for rebels and fugitives. Meanwhile, with 90% of the banner's terrain deemed "inarable" in official books,[58] the state and private reclamation enterprise saw most of the banner as negligible leftovers at best. In fact, Horqin RF was considered a financial liability, as reclamation in the bandit-infested terrain came with costly military bills that the state was unable and unwilling to foot. For Mongol outlanders, on the other hand, it was the last resort reserved for the most desperate of the lot—refugees and runaways. Cultivation expansion of Horqin RF in north Jerim, the frontier of the frontier in the least desirable and profitable hills, in short, began its cultivation history as a place left by thwarted state reclamation attempts at a time of whirling sociopolitical storms.

It is important to note that Horqin RF Banner, albeit ranking at the bottom of IM's jurisdictional hierarchy, was not a small territory. During most of the Qing Dynasty, the banner spanned 40,000 sq. km, close to the size of today's Demark. After it was more than halved by state reclamation in the early 20th century, Horqin RF is still substantially larger than most Chinese counties at the same jurisdictional level. What comes with the immense and hilly territory is the banner's considerable variations in physical environment from its lower to higher terrains. Such internal variation matters greatly in local geopolitical and socio-environmental dynamics and in outlander Mongols' struggles for survival and survival strategies. The way local livelihoods mixed and shifted also varied in Horqin RF's different areas. To gain a closer look at outlanders' survival strategies in different environments of the banner, I drew up an ethnoterritorial map that divides Horqin RF Banner into three sub-banner zones defined by two elements (see Figure 8.2). One is altitude, the other the ethnic mix. Zone 1 features the northwest mountains (600 to 1,500 meters above sea level); the highest-altitude segment of the banner sustains a Mongol majority. Han Chinese are the majority in Zone 3, the lowest segment of the banner in the southeast plains (<200 meters). In between Zones 1 and 3 sits Zone 2, the central rolling hills (200 to 600 meters), which hosts a relatively balanced ethnic ratio between Mongols and Han Chinese. These three ethnoterritorial zones also developed different ethnoterritorial dynamisms.

The balanced ethnic ratio in numerical terms at one specific territorial level, like Zone 2 in this case, does not necessarily mean that Mongols and Han Chinese are intersecting evenly across the entire zone, nor does it automatically lead to a more "integrated" ethnoterritorial structure. To understand how different peoples live and make a living on the ground in a multiethnic place, we need to explore the spatial distribution of peoples and livelihoods at multiple levels along a territorial hierarchy, instead of fixating on just one specific territorial level. Very often, the ratio balance at one territorial level breaks down into multiple ethnic enclaves at the next level below, not unlike the existence of various ethnic neighborhoods in a "multiethnic" city.

These ethnoterritorial dynamisms of mix and segregation (or "de-mixing") along the territorial hierarchy play out throughout China, a country built on 55 minority nationalities and the Han Chinese majority. China-based scholars have characterized China's ethnoterritorial distribution as "mixing at one territorial level, segregating at the next level down" (*dazaoju xiaojuju*). This ethnoterritorial pattern repeats across China's territorial hierarchy, from the national, provincial, and sub-provincial levels all the way down to the sub-village level.[59] As mentioned in Chapter 5, IMAR distinguishes itself from Tibet Autonomous Region (TAR) and Xinjiang Uyghur Autonomous Region (XUAR) in its much more granular ethnic mix at very low jurisdictional levels. Chinese policy thinkers often consider IMAR's ethnoterritorial granularity as a spatial manifestation of China's successful ethnic integration. However, little has been discussed about the other side of the coin, that is, the pattern of segregation, or de-mixing, in IMAR. In short, the ethnoterritorial dynamics, when examined through multiple territorial levels, is structured by not just mixing but also de-mixing; not just integration and assimilation, but also segregation and tension.

Horqin RF Banner's microscopic model of a more balanced ethnic ratio (hence, more mixed) at the banner level and the de-mixing at the sub-banner zone level (e.g., the Chinese-dominant Zone 3 and the Mongol-dominant Zone 1) offers an opportunity to examine such ethnoterritorial tensions between integration and segregation. To explore these tensions further, I scale down and divide Zone 2, which is ethnically more balanced compared with Zones 1 and 2, into three subzones and identify a distinct mode of ethnoterritorial dynamisms in each.

In this section, I examine three sets of such ethnoterritorial tension at three territorial levels: the banner, the sub-banner zone, and the subzone. At the top is the banner. Below it, I divide the banner into three sub-banner zones. Among the three sub-banner zones, I go further into Zone 2 and divide Zone 2 into three subzones. Figure 8.2 depicts Horqin RF's three ethnoterritorial sub-banner zones based on its present-day jurisdictional order.[60]

Generally speaking, throughout the 20th century, the higher up one goes in elevation in Horqin RF Banner, the more Mongols one meets. Yet, the correlation cannot be explained away by cultural ecology, which assumes the choice of habitat and livelihood a matter of cultural preferences; nor is it a matter of historical inevitability.[61] In the drylands, fertile soil with access to water and moderate temperature are good for both herding and farming. The fact that Mongols congregated in the coldest and most rugged hills within Horqin RF, just like their congregation in the hilly north Jerim at large, is the result of a violent history of resource struggles played out in the uneven terrains of East IM. Mongols did not congregate in the northern hills of Jerim or Horqin RF Banner because of their cultural preferences, but rather because they were driven out of the warmer and more fertile lowlands that were suitable for herding, farming, and living. In addition, while there is a strong historical correlation between altitude and ethnicity, the link between ethnicity and livelihoods is less clear. Not all Mongols were perpetually, exclusively, and universally pastoral, nor were all Chinese agricultural. The association between a people and a mode of livelihood is neither purely natural nor essentially cultural.

As the stories of Horqin RF in the following pages will show, the relationship between peoples and livelihoods are developed in the actors' struggles over resource access and their strategies for survival in a specific time and place. These struggles and strategies transpire in mixed and shifting modes of livelihoods at different territorial levels of the region, the banner, the sub-banner zone, and the subzone villages in East IM during the turbulent time of the first half of the 20th century. Such dynamisms continued to evolve under the regimes of collectivism, decollectivization, and conservationism from the second half of the 20th century to the present moment. Through what I call "multi-scalar ethnoterritorial dynamisms," I try to decouple the usual association between peoples and livelihoods by situating them in geographical and historical contexts.

The stories of Horqin RF's ethnoterritorial dynamisms in this section is told via three sub-banner zones and their shifts over two time periods—the 1900s to the 1940s and the 1940s to the 2010s.

Figure 8.3 summarizes these mixes and shifts in the three sub-banner zones. I label these zones as ethnoterritorial zones. They are defined by altitude for its ecological, geopolitical, and social significance, and by their Mongol-Chinese population ratios.[62] These two nexuses, altitude and ethnic structure, help to tell stories about the mix of peoples and livelihoods in a three-way ethnoterritorial relationship among the Mongol outlanders, native Mongols, and Han Chinese settlers.

I will now elaborate on these ethnoterritorial dynamisms of mixes and shifts zone-by-zone. Again, following the itinerary of the outlander Mongols, I begin with their first stop—Zone 3, the southeast plains.

The Southeast Plains

Horqin RF's Zone 3, the southeast plains, lies in the banner's southeast corner. Contributing a mere 3% of the banner's jurisdictional area today, Zone 3 borders the fertile Liao River Plain to its south and east (both of which used to be part of the banner's territory until the early 20th century, as elaborated upon earlier), and is

<table>
<tr><th></th><th>19th–early 20th century</th><th>1900s–1940s</th><th>1940s–2010s</th><th>Mongol-Chinese Ratio by 1988</th></tr>
<tr><td>Zone 1
600–1,500 meters above sea level

Mongol-dominant Northwest Mt.</td><td rowspan="2">*Semi-mobile pastoralism

*Pastoral-style low-impact dry farming (namuγ tariy-a)</td><td>*Influx of outlander Mongols

*Class division btw native Mongol land and herd owners and outlander Mongol tenant farmers and shepherds

*Labor division between outlanders' intensified namuγ tariy-a and natives' semi-sedentary pastoralism</td><td>*Cultivation expansion and continuation of namuγ tariy-a

*Pastural decollectivization and distributional gap

*Well-endowed herders' advantage in capital-intensive agropastoralism

*Expansion of industrial farming and emergence of environmental deterioration and conflicts</td><td>7:3</td></tr>
<tr><td>Zone 2
200–600 masl

Ethnically Mixed Central Rolling Hills</td><td>*Congregation of the outlander Mongols in the higher north subzone, and Han Chinese in the lower south subzone. More balanced ethnic mix in the central subzone</td><td rowspan="2">*Post-reform reclamation fever; intensification and expansion of various forms of livelihoods, including farming, herding, timbering, and foraging, followed by deforestation and soil erosion

*Farmers' aspiration for pasto-agriculture

*Rapid urban growth since the 2000s</td><td>Zone level:
1:1.1

Subzones
North: 9:1
Central: 4:6
South: 1:9</td></tr>
<tr><td>Zone 3
< 200 masl

Chinese-dominant Southeast Plains</td><td>*19thCentury: Reclamation by outlander Mongols

*Early 20th Century: State reclamation and Banners' territorial concession</td><td>*Influx of Chinese and exodus of Mongols

*More established landowning outlander Mongols managed to stay

*Stalled state reclamation and thriving private reclamation

*Frontier style farming undertaken by both the Chinese and outlander Mongol settlers</td><td>2:8</td></tr>
</table>

Figure 8.3 Livelihood and ethnic mixes and shifts of Horqin Right Front Banner's three ecological zones (1900s to 2010s)

endowed with alluvial plains at an elevation below 200 meters. It boasts a warmer and wetter climate, with 140 frost-free days a year—the longest in the banner—and an annual precipitation rate of over 420 mm.[63] This small, but comparatively cultivation-friendly, corner of Horqin RF has long boasted the highest population density in the banner, with Han Chinese accounting for 80% of local residents by the late 1980s.

Like other parts of the southern alluvial plains of north Jerim that I outlined earlier, the southeast plains of Horqin RF also became the first target of state reclamation in the banner in the early 20th century. Again, on the tail of state reclamation, anti-reclamation momentum spread from southern Jerim to the southeast plains of Horqin RF. Insurgent leaders now recruited growing hordes of rebels, fugitives, and reclamation refugees to fuel rampant banditry and new rounds of insurgences in this area. The aforementioned legendary rebel leader, Togtokh, for example, expanded his influence from south Jerim and continued to attack state reclamation in Horqin RF and its neighboring banners.

But the insurgents in Horqin RF's southeast plains did not simply repeat their repertoire of actions in south Jerim, again thanks to geography. Fleeing from Jesoto, the refugees had south Jerim to flee to; when driven out of south Jerim, they had southeast plains of Horqin RF in north Jerim, to hope for. But after that, they were left with the high and cold mountains, which felt so close yet so far. The southeast plains were the last promise in Horqin RF for the uprooted outlanders and dispossessed banner natives alike. With their backs pressed against the mountains and with all-time high stakes, Horqin RF Banner members' battles against state reclamation in the southeast plains escalated.

The scale and scope of the resistance in the southeast plains was unprecedented in 20th century Jerim. As presented earlier, insurgences in south Jerim during the late Qing involved migrants and banner natives who followed cult leaders and low-ranking banner officers to sabotage the reclamation operation and attack Han Chinese settlers. In those cases, jasaghs, the banner heads who cooperated with reclamation officials and profited from state reclamation, often led the crackdown on the rebels. In other words, anti-reclamation insurgences in south Jerim were primarily a local and internal affair. But anti-reclamation insurgences in north Jerim were of a much greater magnitude. Feeling more desperate than their counterparts in the south and eager to take advantage of the opportune moment of regime change from the Imperial to the Republican era, the banner jasaghs themselves led the insurgences in north Jerim. Their goal was not just to drive out state reclamation and repatriate the banner territories. Rather, these jasaghs waged wars of independence from the newly established Republican regime, forged regional alliances across banners, and obtained financial and military support from foreign powers. The matter was of a national and international scope.

One such insurgency was ignited by Horqin RF's legendary jasagh, Udai (1860–1920, Wutai in Chinese), in 1912, the year following the establishment of the Republican government. Jasagh Udai was no stranger to reclamation. Since the late 19th century and before state reclamation came to Horqin RF Banner, Udai had mortgaged large tracts of the banner's fertile southeast plains to land merchants to pay for his lofty debts from politicking in Beijing, a financial maneuver that was common among banner elites at the time (see Chapter 6).

Udai also knew his geopolitical game. During the last decade of the Qing, his banner stood at the frontlines against the lurking foreign powers of Russia and Japan, especially after the Ruso-Japanese War in 1905. The Qing court desperately needed the support of north Jerim's banner chiefs to defend the empire's northeastern front. Meanwhile, the expansion-minded Russians were highly interested in making friends with Mongolian banner leaders, and they provided Udai with generous loans and Russian-made arms.[64]

In 1908, banking on his enhanced bargaining position with the Qing court, Udai negotiated with the Taching Government Bank, the central bank of the Qing court, to bail out his debt to the Russia-controlled Chinese Eastern Railway Company. In exchange, Udai offered his banner's land tracts, railway access and mining concessions to the Bank. But the land tracts that Udai brought to the bargaining table were in the bandit-ridden high hills of the north, and the Bank's negotiator preferred the fertile southeast plains that could be liquidated more easily. The ill-timed negotiations fell apart with the victory of the Republican Revolution in 1911. The new Republican government had little appetite for the old mess from the overthrown regime, and Udai subsequently switched allegiances to the Russia-backed, newly independent (Outer) Mongolian leader, Bogd Khan. Bogd Khan granted Udai a new noble title and outfitted him with thousands of Russian Berdan rifles. An emboldened Udai declared independence and ordered Han Chinese businesses, settlers, and officials to leave Horqin RF. Udai's bold moves created cascading effects, and his neighbors, Horqin Right Rear and Zalaid Banners, also declared independence. Thirty-plus ravaging battles later, Udai seized Zhendong County (today's Baicheng), the administrative center of state reclamation in the banner's southeast. The greatly alarmed northeast warlord affiliated with the Republican regime sent 8,000 soldiers and cavalry to quell Udai. Udai's Russian ally did not formally join the battle, but they did dispatch soldiers to stations along the Chinese Eastern Railway and agitate the warlords' army. Udai held on for a year, but was eventually defeated by the Republican-warlord force. He took the usual fugitive route, fleeing to the banner's northwestern mountains in Suolun before his Russian ally escorted him to Küriye, today's Ulaanbaatar.

In the aftermath of the insurgency, several high-ranking banner elites and Lamaist monks who had joined the rebellion were executed. As many as 156 commanders in Udai's armed forces were on the Republican warlord's most-wanted list. Tens of thousands of Mongols fled the war zone in Horqin RF's southeast to the hills in the banner's north and northwest. Some fled further north across the banner border to Xilingol and Hulunbuir Leagues. The retreat was devastating. In one instance, on their way to Cha'ersen in the northern hill of Horqin RF, many Mongols, who were considered to be Udai's followers and sympathizers, were slaughtered in a gorge by the Tao'er River, where the warlord's cavalry blocked their escape on both ends.[65]

Jasagh Udai's campaign for independence was not an outlier case. The year 1912 witnessed many more armed conflicts across East IM, where banner leaders had long felt threatened by encroaching state reclamation efforts by the late Qing. Seizing the historic opportunity of the Qing's fall and inspired by Outer Mongolia's successful independence campaign, the top banner leaders of Hulunbuir and Xilingol in the northeast as well as those of northern Je'uda and southern Jerim either formally declared independence from the new Republic and/or joined forces to attack county governments and reclamation bureaus.[66]

Threatening the new Republic's territorial integrity and regional warlords' territorial interests, the unprecedented banner independence mobilization was met with brutal military repression. As a result, few banner rebels succeeded in gaining ground in formal politics. Even so, rebel leaders and followers who turned to banditry remained decisive territorial actors in Horqin RF and across north Jerim.

Anti-reclamation insurgencies and bandit endemics sustained one another. Suppressed insurgencies in one place produced future leaders and potential recruits for new insurgencies in neighboring areas and beyond. As state reclamation continued into the Republican-warlord era, more dispossessed and displaced Mongol natives and outlanders filled the ranks of bandit gangs. Armed conflicts created more of an ever-present guerilla warfare than random and occasional skirmishes between sheriffs and robbers. While some rebel bands were larger and better armed than others, the overall decentralized nature of their organization may have weakened their territorial claims. Yet, the decentralized organization was also what made it difficult for the late Qing or the Republican-warlord government to eradicate them completely.

The bandit endemics, in turn, undermined state reclamation programs in north Jerim during the first half of the 20th century. It was banditry, more than Udai's revolt, that created long-lasting impact on Horqin RF's ethnoterritorial dynamisms during the first half of the 20th century.

Even before Udai's independence war, late Qing reclamation officials reported that reclamation survey crews were regularly sabotaged, the reclamation headquarters looted, and tax records burned by reclamation resistors and "barbarian bandits."[67] The assaults were devastating enough to halt land surveys and force project abandonment. Many of the reclamation initiatives were in fact repeated attempts at reviving previously failed projects. Other listed projects were revisits of earlier project areas to rake out parcels left from previous land enclosures. After each round of raking, the listed land tracts for lease sales were of progressively poorer quality, often found in salty marshes, sandy mounds, or steep slopes with diminishing appeal to potential lessees. Reclamation offices would reduce lease fees for the poor-quality parcels to boost sales. Or they would simply grant the unmarketable remnant parcels to displaced native banner households as "subsistence land." Reclamation projects in north Jerim, even in cases in which large land tracts were successfully leased out to speculative capital, did not land the state treasury the expected windfalls. During the late Qing era, no more than one-third of all lease fees were duly paid.[68] In cases in which subdivided tracts were leased to small land brokers and settlers, the Reclamation Bureau never managed to collect tax dues, for the yields were too low. In the end, many projects with ambiguous boundaries and incomplete and conflicting transaction records were transferred from the frustrated Reclamation Bureau to county governments to "tie up loose ends."[69]

In 1913, a deeply concerned Republican reclamation official who had previously served the Qing court, Wang Shiren (1881–1937), reported that most of the leased land tracts in north Jerim's reclamation zone remained uncultivated.[70] In Horqin RF alone, although 70% of the banner's land was reported to have been leased and enclosed for reclamation, only 5% of the leased land tracts were actually cultivated, most of which did not generate the anticipated tax and fee revenues.[71]

State reclamation's dismal performance in the north stood in striking contrast with that of the warmer and more marketable land of south Jerim, where 80% to 100% of leased land was reported to have been duly leased out and cultivated. Wang regretted that "the rich soil (of north Jerim) shall remain fields of rock."

In short, the late Qing state's reclamation efforts in the northern hills generated tremendous upheaval and endemic banditry, yet the state treasury gained little from the reclamation programs.

The Qing state's thwarted projects were taken up by the warlords after China's imperial era ended in 1911. Under the new Republican regime, reclamation in Horqin RF was enforced by one of Republican China's most formidable warlords, Zhang Zuolin (or Chang Tso-lin, 1875–1928). Marshal Zhang held supreme power in China's northeast in the 1910s and 1920s. Commanding the 180,000 strong Northeastern Army, Zhang appropriated large tracts of land from banners in East IM and leased them out to merchant capital and/or established opium plantations to finance his military operations. In 1928, as the Japanese offense in China's northeast escalated, Marshal Zhang was assassinated by the Japanese army in a train bombing. His son, Zhang Xueliang (or Chang Hsueh-liang, 1901–2001), inherited the Northeastern Army at the age of 27. One month after his father's demise, the Young Marshal, as Zhang Xueliang was often called, announced an ambitious reclamation plan in Jerim League. He reorganized his artillery battalions into Reclamation Corps (*tunkenjun*) and proceeded to build military-farming colonies in Jerim.

In Horqin RF, the Young Marshal's Reclamation Corps began its operations by clearing the main obstacle to reclamation: bandits and reclamation insurgents. In the process of eradicating the bandits, military personnel of all ranks, from the marshal himself and his top commanders to officers and soldiers, came to be the new landlords in the banner's most desirable southeast plains. In the same fashion as the late Qing's reclamation, the Young Marshal sold land tracts of various sizes through networks of merchant capital and land brokers. The main difference was that the warlord's operation was of greater ferocity.[72] While the late Qing emperors sent dozens of armed soldiers to escort reclamation crews to Horqin RF, Marshal Zhang's reclamation corps consisted mainly of soldiers equipped with firearms and were organized into ranked battalions, treating reclamation zones as occupied territory. While the late Qing's reclamation chief followed old-fashioned, diplomatic etiquette and negotiated with banner leaders, Marshal Zhang's reclamation was a matter of martial order. Regiments of armed and mounted soldiers showed up unannounced, and thuggish soldiers, many of whom were former bandits, robbed and drafted local Mongols. In one recorded incident, when 800 elderly bannermen petitioned for the Reclamation Corps' commander to spare native bannermen's homes and subsistence land allotments, the petitioners' villages were raided and the petition leader, a banner noble, was imprisoned on the charge of sheltering bandits and illegally planting opium.[73]

The brutality of the bandit-like soldiers drove away many native and outlander Mongols alike from the southeast of Horqin RF. But how effective were Marshal Zhang's soldiers in farming and farm management? One case reported by a reclamation manager offers a glimpse into the challenges. In 1928, 193 demobilized officers and soldiers of Zhang's Northeastern Army were said to have volunteered to join reclamation in Horqin RF. The army's commander promised these veterans a total of 20,000 mu of land, but the local office of the Reclamation Corps in Horqin RF only managed to find 9,000 mu of "secondary-grade" land parcels. A year later, only 1,000 out of the originally planned 20,000 mu were allocated to the veterans and cultivated.[74] Again, it was a 95% implementation gap, a striking parallel with the case reported by Wang Shiren in 1913.[75]

But the implementation gaps in state reclamation projects did not mean the land in question just sat there in limbo. Where state and military reclamation stalled, private reclamation thrived. Notwithstanding Wang Shiren's lament that the "fertile soil remained fields of rocks" in north Jerim, the "uncultivated" land on the official books did not stay uncultivated for long, if at all. It was just that on the ground, these tracts were controlled by a vast array of landholders from military generals, officers, and land merchants to local bosses and land brokers. Where the state failed emerged active land markets and a land-based class pyramid. At the top of this pyramid were landholding officials and military men; in the middle were land merchants and brokers, money lenders, commodity traders, and small landowners who were usually owner-cultivators; while tenants, landless traveling petty traders, craftsmen, farmhands, sharecroppers, and day laborers trudged at the bottom.

The organization, or lack thereof, of cultivation in southeast Horqin RF stood in contrast to that of Hetao in West IM illustrated in Chapter 7. Horqin RF had its fair share of land merchants like Hetao. But few land merchants in Horqin RF managed to consolidate land tracts and build hydro turfdoms as their counterparts did in Hetao of West IM. Compared with the Hetao Plain, large and congruous land tracts were found far and few between in the hilly terrain of Horqin RF. Even in its relatively flat southeast, the better-quality tracts intersected with poor soils and were scattered across nooks and crannies of valleys and on recesses of slopes, or along narrow stream banks hemmed in by steep gorges. The fragmentary fields and landholdings made it difficult to build waterworks. On the other hand, Horqin RF's southeast enjoyed a longer stretch of 120 to 140 frost-free days a year, an annual precipitation rate of 400 to 420 mm, and extensive networks of streams and springs, all of which made it possible to practice rainfed farming without extensive investment in irrigation. To make up for the low yields, settlers cleared land in chance locations. Rampant private land clearance, a decentralized landholding structure, and scattered crop fields together created a fragmented social and spatial organization of cultivation in Horqin RF's southeast.

Within the cold and dangerous north Jerim, the relatively arable southeast plains of Horqin RF also attracted Han Chinese settlers from south of the Great Wall and south Jerim. The fact that the southeast was closer to the Chinese administrative center and military base in the counties of Tuquan and Baicheng (which were carved out of the Horqin RF Banner's jurisdiction) also provided a much-needed, however contingent, sense of safety for Han Chinese settlers to brave the bandit-infested frontier of the frontier.

Han Chinese settlements in Horqin RF's southeast usually started with a group of land reclaimers. A relatively well-off head settler would first recruit a dozen or so men and bring tools, draft animals, grain, and firearms to clear the raw land leased from native Mongols or local authorities. The lead settler would become the landlord with social and economic authority, and the men he recruited would work as sharecroppers, tenants, and laborers who cooked, tended to the horses, dug wells, and safeguarded the compounds.[76] To defend against banditry, the settlers' houses were built close to one another, and their homes, granaries, horse and cattle barns, as well as vegetable gardens were closed in by rammed-earth walls reinforced with batteries. Rich landlords, the prime targets of bandit pillage, were better armed and their fortifications more elaborate.[77] In these fortifications, landlords and their tenants formed an integrated unit of production and defense against bandits who frequented the populous southeast, especially during droughts and floods, to "borrow grains."

Many southeast settlements of Horqin RF that started out with a Mongol majority eventually became Han Chinese dominant ones. As banner natives recruited Chinese migrants to farm their land, Chinese tenants expanded their families, brought in their relatives, and cleared more land of their own, similar to what they did in south Jerim. Han Chinese settlers became owner-cultivators, and the village evolved from a Mongolian to an ethnically mixed settlement. Over time, Chinese settlers, who usually had larger households than Mongols, outnumbered their Mongol neighbors. The presence of the warlords' soldiers, who were mostly Han Chinese, further emboldened the Chinese settlers. The increasing presence and influence of Han Chinese drove the remaining Mongols away. Within a few decades, these settlements shifted from a Mongolian majority to a relatively balanced ethnic mix, then to a Chinese majority. By the 1930s and 40s, Han Chinese had become the majority in most of the southeast settlements.[78]

In East IM, settlements were called *nutuys*.[79] In southeast Horqin RF, there were native *nutuys* as well as mixed *nutuys* consisting of outlander Mongols and Chinese. Most of the outlander Mongols who managed to stay in the southeast were those who had arrived in the early 19th century. They had called the area home for over a century before the influx of Chinese migrants in the early 20th century. The way the outlanders established farming settlements had been similar to that of the Chinese: a better-endowed or trusted leader would recruit a group of men to lease a tract of raw land from the natives and convert it into cropping fields. This leader would clear more land whenever and wherever possible. Since outlanders were despised by banner natives, many of the outlanders' settlements were built close to Chinese ones and, hence, created ethnically mixed *nutuys*. Although mixed, the boundary between Chinese and outlander clusters in a *nutuy* was still clearly demarcated.[80] As mentioned earlier, ethnic mix at one territorial level often pushes the demix to the next level below.

Like with Han Chinese settlers, landownership statuses of outlander Mongols varied. In the 19th century, when land competition was less tense in north Jerim, a hardy and hard-working outlander tenant family could become small owner-cultivators through tireless reclamation over several generations.[81] The successful outlander Mongol landowners, especially those who were multilingual, entrepreneurial, and politically connected, would become land merchants and brokers. But in the banner as a whole, small Chinese owner-cultivators greatly outnumbered their Mongolian counterparts at a ratio of about 4:1.[82]

As mentioned earlier, variations abound under the umbrella term of "agriculture." In the southeast plains of Horqin RF, what kind of "agriculture" was practiced by either Han Chinese or Mongol outlanders? Most scholars have suggested that outlander Mongols in East IM engaged in "Chinese-style" cropping characterized by "Chinese" crops like sorghum, soy, corn, potato, and vegetables, and employed "Chinese" cropping methods that featured greater labor input in sowing, ploughing, fertilizing, and weeding.[83] But how "Chinese" were the farming methods practiced in Horqin RF's southeast plains?

It turns out it was not very "Chinese" at all. Han Chinese settlers' dry farming in Horqin RF (and its neighboring banners in north Jerim) in the 19th and the first half of the 20th centuries was not identical to dry farming in the North China Plain on several counts. The first distinction concerns the size of the farms. A family that held 100 mu of land would be considered rich in the North China Plain. But in north Jerim, an economically sustainable family farm usually ranged between 500 and 1,500 mu.[84] As a result of extensive land clearance to compensate for the low yields, the large-sized family farms were made of multiple plots in different locations. Dispersed plots also allowed north Jerim farmers to practice rotational farrow to preserve the thin topsoil, apply minimal amounts of fertilizer, and spread out the risk of drought, flood, frost, and locust infestations. This style of "wide cultivation, thin harvest" (*guangzhong boshou*) is also found in north China. But the scale was much larger in north Jerim, made possible by under-regulated private land clearance and made necessary by the cold climate and poor soil in the high lands of north Jerim.

With expanded cultivation and scattered fields came the new role and ownership of stock animals. Camels had been long gone in the banner's southeast. Horses were common in the area. But, since pastures had greatly shrunk due to cultivation expansion, some native Mongol pastoralists would rather sell their horses than put their beloved animals to the abasing duty of plowing. Most of the natives' horses were sold to Chinese settlers who could afford them. Given that their fields were scattered across an uneven terrain in multiple sites with fallowing patches in between, Chinese settlers needed a more efficient mode of transportation than their own legs or a mule-pulled cart. The horses were employed as mounts, and, to the dismay of their former native owners, as draft animals. Meanwhile, outlander Mongols, who had less hang-ups about horses, were mostly tenant-workers and were simply too poor to afford horses. Instead, outlanders would keep donkeys as draft animals. They also raised a few sheep for dairy, something that Chinese villagers rarely did in the early 20th century.[85]

Another change concerned pigs and chickens, the domesticated animals characteristic of Chinese farming villages that were now widely found in north Jerim. By the 1930s, native Jerim landowners had developed a taste for pork, and their outlander Mongol tenants would raise pigs to pay their annual rent in kind at a flat rate of one pig and 100 liters of Mongol millet.[86] As most outlanders could not afford cattle or sheep for meat, chicken was their alternative source of animal protein.

To sum up, the cultivation history of Horqin RF's southeast plains during the first half of the 20th century featured stymied state reclamation, escalated Mongol rebellion, and fragmented cultivation expansion. Meanwhile, the influx of Han Chinese settlers and the massive exodus of Mongols led to a Chinese majority in the southeast. Chinese settlers and the remaining Mongols, depending on their capacities, kept different animals for different purposes: Chinese tasked horses with transportation and farming, and outlander Mongols raised pigs to pay their land rents in kind. These practices were neither generically "Chinese" nor "Mongolian," but rather the result of ethnoterritorial mixes and shifts in the agricultural frontier of East IM.

What about the majority of native and outlander Mongols who had been driven out of the southeast by the late Qing's state reclamation, or those who had tried to flee from Jasagh Udai's failed insurgency and the warlords' thuggish reclamation soldiers? Most of Horqin RF's southeast native pastoralists trekked up to Zone 1, the northwest mountains. The farming outlanders' destinations were split between the northwestern mountains of Zone 1 and the central rolling hills of Zone 2.[87] I will first follow the outlanders to the northwest mountains.

The Northwest Mountains

Horqin RF's northwest mountains in the first half of the 20th century featured class divisions between native Mongol land- and herd-owners and outlander Mongol tenants and shepherds, their labor division in herding and cropping, and the transformation of both pastoral-style cropping and highland-style semi-mobile pastoralism.

When outlander Mongols first arrived in the northwestern mountains, they would tenant farm, sharecrop, and clear land for landowning native pastoralists in areas far enough to avoid interfering with the main grazing routes and grounds. The pastoralist migrants from south Jerim would shepherd for native herd owners. They were paid in livestock, and some became small herd owners after several years.

Under this class and labor divide, outlander farmers would pay annual land rents at a flat rate of 100 liters of Mongolian millet and a pig, just as they did in the southeast. Native landowners of the highlands, who now also developed a taste for pork but kept a distaste for farming, continued with semi-mobile pastoralism (that is, mobile grazing in the late spring-summer and sedentary grazing in their home base during the winter and early spring) and relied on livestock for cash income.

The crops and cropping methods that outlanders adopted in the northwest highlands were different from those in Horqin RF's southeast plains. If farming in the southeast, as mentioned earlier, was the north Jerim brand of "wide cultivation, thin harvest," here in the highland, outlanders' farming was closer to the pastoral-style of dry farming, called *namuγ tariy-a* in Mongolian.

Namuγ tariy-a is a form of pastoral cropping common in arid and semi-arid Central Asia.[88] In East IM, *namuγ tariy-a* has been widely practiced by pastoralists since before the Mongol empire. Its primary adversity-resistant native grain varieties—Mongolian millet and buckwheat—were an essential part of the steppe diet.[89]

Most Chinese literature on the agrarian transformation of the northern steppe did not acknowledge the existence of *namuγ tariy-a*. In the few that did, *namuγ tariy-a* was called *mansazi*, a Chinese transliteration that translates to "randomly casting seeds," implying a primitive cropping method with minimal plowing, seedbed sowing, and weeding. In the eyes of Han Chinese who farmed with intensive labor input and exhaustive soil use, *namuγ tariy-a* was proof of Mongols' primitivity and laziness and a cause for Mongolia's underdevelopment in general.[90]

Based on archival and field research, the Japan-based historian Junichi Yoshida (2016a) and his Mongolian student Altanγaraγ (2012) offered an alternative view. They suggested that the logic of *namuγ tariy-a* is to supplement, not substitute, pastoralism. It accommodates, but does not interrupt, pastoralists' calendars nor their carefully calculated plans of labor and land allocation.

In the late spring after a good rain, pastoralists who practiced *namuγ tariy-a* sowed the seeds in the spring and winter pastures, which were warmer than the higher-altitude summer pasture. Late spring was also the time when pastoralists were busy preparing for their move to the summer pasture. To save time and labor, minimal plowing and weeding was performed before sowing. Neither seedbeds nor field ridges were built, nor was fertilizer applied. After the seeds were cast, horses were led to stomp across the fields to press down on the seeds. Altanγaraγ (2012) explained that, in addition to saving time and labor, this method also served to retain soil moisture in an area with an annual precipitation rate of 400 mm, but an evaporation rate of as high as 2,000 mm. The minimal amending of the soil helped protect its thin crust and prevent moisture loss in the dry spring. For the same reason of preserving soil moisture at the root zone, weeds were allowed to grow to 3 to 4 inches tall before seeds were sown.

Namuγ tariy-a fields rotated every one or two years. In dry years, crops were planted in the moist lower valley; in wet years, crops were planted on higher, better-drained slopes. The shape of the fields could be round, half-moon, or square. They were scattered at the peripheries of the main pastures and were rarely expanded into large, congruent fields. Unlike Chinese farmers who measured their wealth by the size of their farmland, pastoralists paid far greater attention to the size of their herds and showed little interest in expanding the size of their *namuγ tariy-a* fields.

After sowing, pastoralists departed with their herds for the summer pasture. They did not return to their winter-spring pasture to harvest the crops until right before the first frost. Between sowing and harvesting, no mid-term plowing or weeding was performed, since the pastoralists were busy tending to their herds in the summer pasture. When harvesting, only the plant spikes were cut, while stems and roots were left intact to preserve soil moisture.

Furthermore, the *namuγ tariy-a* crops were more diverse than what was usually reported. Junichi Yoshida (2016) noted that there were at least three main varieties of *namuγ tariy-a* millet, named by their respective growing periods: the 60-day, 70-day, and 90-day millet. The variety planted in any given year was chosen according to the date of the first spring rain. The 90-day millet was chosen if the rain came early that year. The crop variety also corresponded with the moisture level of the field in which it was planted. For instance, the 70-day millet was planted in the "70-day millet field." Similarly, there were three major varieties of native buckwheat and three corresponding types of buckwheat fields. In terms of consumption, Altanγaraγ (2012) reported that pastoralists prepared their beloved millet in a variety of ways. Millet could be boiled by itself or added to lamb soup to make congee; it could be soaked to expand then dried before roasting; or it could be roasted raw on heated sand. Roasted millet would be mixed with milk tea, yogurt, milk, or stirred into raw fat.

In short, the pastoralists cared about their millet too much to simply toss the seeds randomly and hope for the best. The Chinese transliteration *mansazi* has missed the complexity of the pastoral mode of cropping in highland East IM. Pastoral Mongols' attachment to millet even earned them the nickname "roasted millet bags" (*qaγuruγsan budaγan-u aγuta*).[91] This derogatory term was what the resentful rent-paying outlander Mongol farmers used for their pastoralist landlords. Ridicule aside, the pastoralists' love for millet was not just about dietary preference, but also food security. The cold and drought-resistant *namuγ tariy-a* crops, which were mainly for subsistence, were indispensable in an environment prone to recurrent droughts, severe snow and ice storms, and contagious diseases that could lead to massive livestock losses.

With the arrival of outlander Mongols in the mountains in the early 20th century, *namuγ tariy-a* began to change. Outlanders provided welcome labor for grain production and introduced semi-intensive cropping that involved lightly plowing the land before sowing, using sowing tools for a more even seed casting, covering the sown seeds with a layer of soil, and performing mid-term weeding. Outlanders also diversified the crops and planted corn, potato, and sorghum. But the semi-intensive cropping and new crops did not replace *namuγ tariy-a*. With erratic rainfall and low yields in the highlands, variants of *namuγ tariy-a* crops and cropping method continued to play a significant role in highland farming throughout most of the 20th century.

Meanwhile in the 1930s, the northwest mountains' semi-mobile pastoralism began to change. The change was not precipitated directly by warlord's reclamation, but by its by-product: bandit endemics.

Semi-mobile pastoralism, which was practiced only by rich pastoralists with large enough livestock herds and pasture access, had been a frequent target for the proliferating "horse thefts" in the northwest mountains since the early 20th century. As a result, those who owned hundreds of horses and cattle and thousands of sheep shifted to more sedentary pastoralism. They built permanent houses secured by rammed-earth walls. Horses that could not be locked up were closely monitored by hired watchmen. Cattle and sheep now grazed in nearby pastures during the day and spent the night in fenced paddocks. Hunters armed with shotguns were hired to take day and night shifts to guard herds and homes. With the reduction in grazing radius, even the die-hard pastoralists recruited more outlander farmers to convert their far-off and less frequented pastures to cropping fields that mixed *namuγ tariy-a* grains with new crops. They also did away with large livestock like camels that require large pastures extending too far from the settlements, and instead focused on smaller-sized livestock like sheep and goats. To supplement their reduced income from livestock, and with the help of outlander labor, cash crops like soy were brought in and their cropping method was further intensified.

The ethnoterritorial mix of pastoral-dominant northwest mountains during the first half of the 20th century, in short, featured a division of labor and class between two types of Mongols: native land- and herd-owners and outlander farming tenants. As this mode of mix took shape, it also began to change. The 1930s and 1940s saw the rise in semi-intensive cropping that diversified the traditional *namuγ tariy-a* crops. Native pastoralists concomitantly turned from semi-mobile to semi-sedentary pastoralism.

Under the Communist regime since the 1950s, the mixes in northwest mountains continued to shift through collectivization (starting in 1956), the Great Leap Forward (1958–60), and the racialized Cultural Revolution (1966–76) that shamed herders for allegedly "relying on farmers for grain supplies."[92] The goal of these highly moralized and demoralizing political campaigns was to discourage the "backward" *namuγ tariy-a* and to promote modern and intensive farming. Massive swathes of pasture were cleared and converted to farmland. But overall production of officially promoted crops, like corn and wheat, remained low in the stubbornly cold and dry mountains. So, the good old *namuγ tariy-a* persisted.

The Horqin RF Banner Gazetteer recorded that in 1946, on the eve of the Communist takeover of IM, Mongolian millet and buckwheat in the *namuγ tariy-a* tradition made up 58% of the banner's total planted land, exceeding the combined acreage of corn, rice, wheat, soy, potato, and sunflower fields. By 1979, on the eve of market reform and decollectivization and after decades of state promotion of intensive modern farming techniques and cash crops, Mongolian millet and buckwheat still occupied no less than 30% of the total planted area in Horqin RF Banner.[93] By 1988, a decade since market reform started, the percentage of *namuγ tariy-a* fields dropped to 16%. As commodity and industrial farming expanded throughout IMAR in the post-reform era, the decline of subsistence *namuγ tariy-a* became increasingly notable. However, the decline was far from an inevitable, linear process.

Between 2001 and 2004, Yoshida and Altanγaraγ made three research trips to East IM's agricultural centers of Jesoto, Je'uda, and Jerim Leagues. There they found multiple sites still practicing *namuγ tariy-a*, especially in north Jesoto as well as in both south and north Jerim. Yoshida (2016a) and a local researcher I talked to explained that it was not necessarily a continuation of the tradition, but *namuγ tariy-a*'s comeback brought on by multiyear droughts in the early 2000s. In fact, depending on how one defines *namuγ tariy-a*, most eastern Mongol farmers continued to mix commodity with *namuγ tariy-a* crops in various ways for a number of reasons. In addition to providing basic food security during dry years, *namuγ tariy-a* millet and buckwheat were planted to maximize land use in the residual lots that were too uneven or irregularly shaped for planting and harvesting machines, now commonly used in many areas in East IM. Or they were used as pioneer crops on newly cleared "raw" land for the first couple of years before commodity crops, like mung beans and corn, could be planted.[94] The mixed livelihoods of the mountains continued to evolve through the 21st century. Under the policy of industrial farming and ranching, conservation tensions in the hills have escalated. I will turn to contemporary conservation tensions in the northwest mountains in the last section of this chapter. For now, I will move with the outlander Mongols to the central rolling hills, Zone 2 of Horqin RF Banner.

The Central Rolling Hills

Sitting between the northwest mountains and the southeast plains, the central rolling hills of Zone 2 have the most balanced mix of Mongols and Chinese at a ratio of 1.0 to 1.1.

However, as mentioned earlier, a balanced ethnic ratio at one territorial level could be skewed at the next level down. Along the gradual slope of the rolling hills of Zone 2, there are three subzones of different altitudes, from the higher north to the lower south, each with its own ethnic blend. Again, Mongols were the overwhelming majority in the northern subzone, while Han Chinese held the majority in the southern subzone. In the central subzone, the ethnic ratio was more balanced. More importantly, regardless of the ethnic makeup, villagers of all three subzones of the central rolling hills engaged in mixed livelihoods, albeit in varying configurations of ethnic mixing. In the highest northern subzone, where the elevation averages 500 meters above sea level, officially classified "farming-herding mixed households" (*bannong banmuhu* in Chinese, which literally means "half-agricultural, half-pastoral" households) made up 77% to 90% of the total population, while the rest were "pure" farming or pastoral households. In the central and southern subzones, where elevation averages 300 meters above sea level (about 100 to 300 meters lower than the northern subzone), farming had been in place along the riverbanks and sloping valleys since the 1930s. Still, 30% to 75% of village households in the central and southern subzones were registered as mixed households.[95]

Beyond the official figures and classification, however, more questions arise: what are the ways in which farming and herding mix within and across villages? How do such mixes evolve over time in varying dryland environments? How do we understand the livelihood mixes as a dynamic process of diversification? In the following section, I follow a farming family and a herding family in Zone 2 and trace their attempts to diversify their livelihoods. Instead of adopting the generalizing term "agropastoralism," I make the distinction between two directions of diversification: one is agropastoral, the other pastoagricultural. The herding family in this study has followed the "agropastoral" path, and the farming family has followed the "pastoagricultural" one. Here, the "agropastoral" path refers to the process of livelihood diversification from pastoralism to a mix of herding and cropping. The "pastoagricultural" path refers to diversification from farming to a mix of farming and herding. The distinction between these two paths begins with their starting points, one from herding the other farming; and in two places within Zone 2, one in a herding-predominant area, the other a farming-predominant area. The starting points and places condition the two families' access to resources and their capacities to diversify, leading to divergent results in their ventures and misadventures.

III Agropastoral and Pastoagricultural Ventures

I start with a village in the northern subzone of Zone 2 in Horqin RF, called Fresh Springs,[96] where I conducted fieldwork and collected oral histories in 2017 and 2019, followed by online interviews between 2020 and 2022.

Focusing on Fresh Springs Village as my research site was the result of anything but rigorous sampling. In 2016 I met a Mongolian graduate student, Wave, when I gave a talk at a university in China. Up till then, my fieldwork had been focused on the western, pastoral-dominant Alxa League in IMAR (Chapters 1 and 2) and the farming villages in Hexi Corridor of Gansu Province (Chapters 3 and 4). In that talk, I compared Mongol herders' and Chinese farmers' strategies of surviving China's conservation policies in the new millennium. After the talk, Wave approached me and suggested that I had missed an important actor and place (she was too kind to raise the question publicly during the talk): the Mongol farmers of East IM. The next summer, I followed Wave to her home village, Fresh Springs, in Horqin RF Banner, to learn how much I had missed. I cannot thank Wave enough for opening my eyes to the worlds of Mongol farmers and the agropastoral and pastoagricultural entanglements of East IM, the heart of IM's "half-agricultural, half-pastoral" belt. I will reflect on telling place-driven stories and the connections between ethnography and theorization in the concluding chapter. For now, I trace Wave's family histories along her paternal and maternal lines. On her paternal side, it was mainly a history; on her maternal side, it was mainly a herstory.

III.1 Reclamation and Revolution

History of the Bo Family

I call Wave's paternal lineage the Bos. Wave's paternal great-great grandfather was among the Mongol refugees from Jesoto, and likely among the refugees of the aforementioned Jindandao Massacre. Like hundreds of thousands of other Jesoto refugees, he found his way to south Jerim in the early 20th century. For the new arrivals, the populous south Jerim served as a first stop to rest their feet. There, the landless refugees labored in exchange for food. They worked as sharecroppers or tenants, and some lucky ones became small owner-cultivators. But to expand the family, they needed to venture further to the hilly north Jerim where the state's presence was negligible and rent minimal, as outlined earlier.

That was what Wave's great grandfather Leopard (born in 1925) did. In the mid-1940s, Leopard set off north with his two older brothers, Boyi and Darem. The three Bo brothers first labored and tenanted in the relatively populous Baderengui (see Figure 8.2), located in the middle reaches of the Tao'er River. Baderengui, which means "prosperity" in Mongolian, was blessed with extensive stream networks. Irrigated rice fields had been established by Manchu settlers no later than 1940, during the Manchukuo era. While tenanting in Baderengui in the late 1940s, the Bo brothers

Figure 8.4 Farming on a hill slope in Horqin Right Front Banner
Source: Photo credit: Author.

teamed up with another family, the Has, to clear land in the upper-middle reaches of the Tao'er River, in Fresh Springs Village in the northern hills.

The Bos and the Has were the first settler families to clear and cultivate the land in Fresh Springs. They were later joined by two other families: the five Lan brothers and the three Ding brothers. All were outlander Mongols with farming backgrounds.

Fresh Springs, with its 700-meters-high elevation, spring droughts, summer floods, and winter snowstorms—on top of the rocky terrain—were far from cropping-friendly. But its low barrier of entry was what drew the young settlers looking for land with minimal rents. In addition, sitting at the foothills of the Daxing'anling Mountains, Fresh Springs' high elevation was made up for by the relatively high humidity by IM standards—an annual precipitation of 400 mm, with a workable period of 100 to 110 frost-free days. The site was also blessed with networks of streams and springs that made it possible to practice rain-fed farming of cold-resistant crops. Crop yields in the hilly Fresh Springs were no comparison to those of the warmer south Jerim plains. But for those who were able and willing to work hard, the low rents and good prospects of claiming land ownership were appealing. The woods, streams, and pastures offered a variety of food sources and subsistence supplies. For the Bo family, one additional advantage of Fresh Springs was that it was only 50 km away from their home base in Baderengui, or a two day's journey on ox cart. Although traveling was possible only during the winter and early spring when the river was frozen over, the relative proximity between the reclamation site and the home base made it manageable to obtain supplies from their base in Baderengui during the first couple of years when the newly cleared and planted fields yielded little. The reclaimers could also winter in Baderengui before they were able to build homes in the new reclamation sites of Fresh Springs.

Another early settler family of Fresh Springs was the three Ding brothers. They were flood refugees from Taonan, southeast of Horqin RF,[97] in today's Jilin Province. The Ding family had four brothers but only three came to Fresh Springs. The youngest brother, following Mongolian custom, stayed behind in Taonan with his parents and inherited the parents' land while his older brothers left to clear land of their own. The Ding brothers first stopped in Tuquan, another populous and farming-dominant southern county like Taonan, before they made it to Fresh Springs in the late 1940s. Upon arrival, they tended cattle for local herd owners before they began to clear land for cropping.

The land that the early settler families in Fresh Springs cleared sat on the more accessible and more humid northern part of the village. As the village population grew, latecomers and younger generations expanded cultivation towards the rockier and drier areas in the southern part of Fresh Springs. Each clan tended to congregate, creating small clusters of settlements in Fresh Springs. Along the banks of the Tao'er River, there were other settlements like Fresh Springs that comprised of small clan clusters. Most of these settlers were also outlander Mongols.

During the era of collectivism, Fresh Springs was organized into two production teams. By the late 1950s, there were a total of 40 households amongst the two teams. The production team leaders, who were often one and the same as lineage heads, organized their teams to continue with land clearance to expand cultivation for the growing village.

Fresh Springs did not grow just out of natural population increase. During the early years of the communist era, self-initiated and government-sent settlers continued to arrive in Fresh Springs, many of whom were flood or drought refugees from south of the Great Wall. When the newcomers arrived, production team leaders would grant them residency permits (*luohuzheng*). That aside, the process was much like in the pre-communist days: the new arrivals stayed with and worked for their relatives in the village. At a time when population density was low and labor supply was short, locals generally did not mind having extra hands around to help with the backbreaking job of turning rocky land into crop fields. During my fieldwork, one long-retired village accountant recalled an incident in which a group of 20-plus flood refugee families from Liaoning Province in northeast China came to Fresh Springs in the mid-1960s. The village head quickly accepted and settled them. But these migrants were "brought back" only two years later by the head of their home village where farm labor was also badly needed.

While Fresh Springs might have been a beacon of hope for the outlander refugee settlers, it did not shield them from the devastating Cultural Revolution that swept China from 1966 to 1976.

The Cultural Revolution in IM, similar to that in Tibet, was heavily racialized and more violent than in most other places in China.[98] In 1966, Ulanhu (1907–1988), the prominent Mongol Communist Party leader and the founding chairman of IMAR in 1947 (see Chapter 5), was purged.[99] Ulanhu's fall was followed by a witch hunt called "*wasu*," which means "expose and eradicate" in Chinese. Wasu was an abbreviation of "exposing Ulanhu's underground gang and eradicating Ulanhu's poisonous influence." Under the iron-fisted command of the Peoples' Liberation Army (PLA), General Teng Haiqing, who was dispatched from the Beijing Military Region to IMAR, the Cultural Revolution turned into massive ethnic persecution and wasu terror in IMAR. The official report cited that more than 346,000 ethnic Mongol party cadres, military officers and soldiers, government officials, workers, intellectuals, religious leaders, and villagers were persecuted for their alleged connections with the Inner Mongolian People's Revolution Party (*neirendang*). Neirendang was active in the 1920s during the heyday of modern Mongol nationalism, but the party had lost its steam by the 1930s. During the Cultural Revolution, the name neirendang was reactivated to label the alleged Mongol separatists and to justify their political purge.

The violent witch hunt of "wasu" criminalized Mongol ethnicity and led to atrocious tortures, injuries, decapitations, and fatalities. The official record showed 16,222 wasu fatalities, and another 87,188 amputations by armed fights and torture. Bahe, an exiled Mongol writer estimated a much higher toll—50,000 fatalities and 500,000 amputations—all at a time when the Mongol population in IMAR was about 1.4 million.[100] The terror and fear that General Teng created in IMAR during the wasu era was so deeply entrenched that, according to the Japan-based Mongolian writer Yang, Haiying (2013),[101] parents would silence crying children by whispering "General Teng is coming!".

If the real numbers of wasu fatalities, decapitations, and victims of persecution sit somewhere between the official figures and Bahe's estimates, the magnitude of wasu violence is comparable to the aforementioned, horrendous Jindandao Massacre of Mongols in the late 19th century, which registered a Mongolian death toll of 80,000 to 160,000 and resulted in refugees on the order of 300,000 to 400,000.[102]

According to Yang's (2014) calculations, which were based on interviews, official archives, and personal memoirs, Horqin RF Banner was among the worst-hit banners in IMAR during wasu, with at least 500 fatalities in the banner.[103] In 2017, when I asked Wave's grandmother May about her experience of the Cultural Revolution in Fresh Springs, May remembered it only by its local name, "wasu" instead of "Cultural Revolution."[104] Like political campaigns elsewhere in rural China during the Cultural Revolution, political and personal frictions fed off one another within the politics of resource competition. Yang (2014) wrote about Chinese farmers' violent attacks on Mongol farmers during wasu in Horqin RF. But resource violence is not always structured by inter-ethnic conflicts. May's recollections were of vicious fights among her Mongol neighbors in Fresh Springs, where Mongols are the predominant majority. In 1968, at the height of *wasu*, Fresh Springs was split between two rival factions. Darem, one of the three Bo brothers, formed a coalition with the Lan brothers against the other faction in the village. The Lans, though they arrived later than the Bo brothers, had grown more powerful in the village, thanks to their big family of five brothers and their sons, all of whom lived in Fresh Springs at that time. But Darem's two brothers and their families were still based in Baderengui, and Darem was the only patriarch in his generation who settled in Fresh Springs. As the Lan brothers became increasingly aggressive and dominant in the village's wasu campaigns, Darem sought to break off. The Lan brothers saw it as treachery. The Bo-Lan coalition turned into an infight, and the Lan brothers attacked Darem, who had already been blacklisted as being a part of the exploitative landlord class in the previous "Four Cleanups" political campaign. The Lan brothers put Darem in the center of a struggle meeting to publicly humiliate him. They lashed Darem with a nail-studded whip at the public meeting before tossing him on an oxen cart. The cart was driven on a bumpy road while a man sat on Darem's skull until he bled to death.

Darem died childless. But he did not die alone. When he first settled in Fresh Springs Village, Darem adopted one of his brother Leopard's five sons, Square (born in 1950), and brought Square to Fresh Springs. Square's biological father, Leopard, his four brothers, and his uncle, Boyi, stayed in the clan base of Baderengui.

In Fresh Springs, Darem also adopted two daughters from fellow settler families—one from the Ha family, and the other, May (born in 1949), from the Ding Family. May moved into Darem's home at the age of 11, as a child bride for Darem's adopted son, Square. In 1968, the 19-year-old May married the 18-year-old Square. Thus, in the last days of Derem's life in 1968, his family in Fresh Springs comprised of Darem and his wife, his adopted son Square, his adopted daughter-turned-daughter-in-law (and Square's wife) May, and the adopted daughter from the Ha family.

As wasu raged in Fresh Springs Village, May was expecting her first child, Victory. To keep safe, May was sent to the village in Baderengui, where her husband's biological father and brothers, uncle and nephews all lived. On the very same day that Darem was tortured to death in Fresh Springs, May and Square's first son, Victory, was born in Baderengui.

After Darem's tortured death, his land was taken away and divided up by three Fresh Springs families: the formidable Lans, the Has, and the Jins. Now fatherless, powerless, and landless in Fresh Springs, Darem's adopted son, Square, moved back to Baderengui to join his biological family that was big enough to have a strong hold in Baderengui.

The dual-based reclamation efforts of the Bo brothers, as it turned out, represented a dilemma for the settlers. The dual base proved to be useful in places of scarcity and during times of turmoil. In the low-yielding cold and dry hills, reclamation in two locations helped to sustain the clan and to expand their landholdings. After the horrific wasu and Darem's tragic death in Fresh Springs, the Bo family in Baderengui also offered refuge for the vilified Square and his young family.

The solidarity of the dual-based Bo clan was maintained mainly via two kinds of adoption. One was same-generation adoption, like in the case of Darem adopting his brother Leopard's son, Square. The other was a customary Mongolian practice, in which the first child of the young couple is raised by the paternal grandparents.

Following this tradition, Square's first son, Victory, grew up in Baderngui in the home of his paternal grandmother[105] until he turned 13. Victory therefore had two places he called home, although he had only one inheritance entitlement from his grandparents. The practice of cross-generational adoption in this case contributed to maintaining the connection between the branches of the Bo clan across the two settlements.

Despite its advantages, a clan spread across two bases also risked losing power in both, especially for small clans. In Fresh Springs Village, Darem, the sole patriarch of the Bo family, did his best to build cross-family coalitions within the village via community endogamy and adoption. Even so, a large clan that stuck together in the same village proved to be more effective in gaining political influence, since physical violence was never far away from the struggle to survive. The Lan clan, with their five brothers, each with several sons, all of whom settled in Fresh Springs Village, were able to act in unity and often with a brutality that made other fellow villagers think twice before rubbing the Lan brothers the wrong way. Darem's demise during wasu is a case in point. After the violent wasu, the Lans became the largest landholding family in the village.

In the aftermath of wasu, the Lans stayed in power and headed the production team, locally called "*gachada*" for over a decade. Villagers referred to village leaders by their family names, as power was associated with the family rather than the individual. The Lans shared power with the Dings, May's maiden family. May had two brothers. One of the Ding brothers, as one of the only two literate men of his generation in the village, served as the production team accountant, an influential position second only to the production team leader. The other Ding brother was selected to be trained as a "barefoot doctor," an innovation in the rural health care system during the Mao era. May herself was trained as a barefoot midwife. Barefoot doctors and midwives still needed to work to earn work points (which were then converted into annual income), but theirs was relatively lightweight labor and their position more prestigious. They could attend training sessions in other larger villages from time to time, and they received some literacy education. Their medical expertise in villages that had no alternative health services also earned them respect and gifts of gratitude, like meat, butter, eggs, and canned foods (canned oatmeal, for instance), which were considered luxury items in even as late as the 1990s in the poor village. After the barefoot doctor system was formally abolished in the mid-1990s, May and her brother continued to provide affordable healthcare for poor villagers and perform abortions for unwed women.

In 1983, rural decollectivization came to Fresh Springs Village and production teams were dismantled. Collective cropland was redistributed among village members, generating at least three sets of bookkeeping for villagers' landholdings. According to the state tax record, each village member received eight mu (0.53 hectares) of "contracted land." In the village head's books, every villager received 15 mu. In reality, each villager received 20 mu. Out of the 20 mu that each village member obtained from land redistribution, 15 mu was subject to village surcharges; out of the 15 mu, 8 mu was also subject to state taxes. The remaining 5 mu was exempt from both state tax and village surcharges. This formula therefore integrated three levels of formality. The state tax-obligated land sat at the top, but it accounted for less than half of what villagers actually owned. Following rural decollectivization was market liberalization and grain price hikes. The new development fueled a land reclamation fever in Fresh Springs Village. Most families expanded their holdings far beyond the original allocation of 20 mu per person. These newly reclaimed parcels of land would be free from both state taxes and village dues.

Land reclamation was rarely a solo feat. While a few mu here and there could be cleared and planted by individual hard-working families who had sufficient labor force, large-scale reclamation on the rocky terrain required multifamily, collective efforts. Earthmovers were unavailable in the 1980s in Fresh Springs Village and, even if they were, would be too costly for most villagers even today. Throughout the reclamation rush of the 1980s and 1990s, it took dozens of men and women laboring together for months to clear the land, level the rocky and uneven terrain, replace the topsoil, plant wind shelter trees, drain the marshland, and provide logistical support, among other drudgeries. Village leaders, be they the "production team leader" of the collective era or the "party secretary" of the decollectivization era, were expected to take the lead in planning and organizing collective reclamation. Village politics centered largely on the expansion and distribution of collectively reclaimed land. As villages in China started holding elections in the early 1990s,[106] those who were competent reclamation leaders and fair land distributors would win the villagers' votes. The collectively reclaimed land that was allocated to individual participating families would be subject to village surcharges.

During the reclamation rush in the 1980s and 1990s, the total area of cropland in Fresh Springs Village increased by 30% to 40%. Cultivation expanded beyond the usual farming area in the slow sloped north and climbed up the steeper slopes in the village's western and eastern hills, which were formerly used only for grazing, lumbering, and foraging.

With the dust from wasu settled and decollectivization starting, Square and his wife, May, returned to Fresh Springs Village from Baderengui to claim their share of the redistributed land. Under new village leadership, Square took over the position of village accountant from Ding Li, May's brother. Square and May joined the collective land clearance enterprise while also working hard to clear a few more mu on their own.

But Victory, Square's eldest son and Wave's father, was less committed to the back-breaking labor of farming. Growing up with his pampering grandparents in Baderengui, Victory was able to complete primary and middle school in the 1970s and early 1980s. In Fresh Springs, Victory's schooling made him the best educated man of his generation. The schools he attended offered Mandarin and Mongolian-track classes for Mongol students.[107] Victory's grandparents chose the Mandarin track for him—which was considered the language of the future. After middle school, Victory worked as a traveling pesticide salesman in the neighboring Jalaid

Banner. In 1988, at the age of 20, he married Orchid, whom he met in primary school.

Herstory of the Lu Family

Victory's marriage to Orchid marks the beginning of a new chapter of the Bo family's migration history in two ways. Spatially, unlike Victory's forefathers' moves from reclamation frontier to reclamation frontier, Victory and Orchid had their sights set on the city as market reform spread in East IM. And, in terms of the initiator of their migration, unlike Victory's forefathers' moves that were led by men, Victory and Orchid's move develops as a "her-story" that revolves around women in Orchid's maiden family, especially Orchid's older sister who later became a Red Guard during the Cultural Revolution. This herstory also includes the paths of Orchid herself and Orchid's three daughters, River, Ocean, and Wave.

The herstory of the Bo family's attempts to move to the city starts with Orchid, Wave's mother, followed by the three daughters. But to contextualize that herstory, a brief review of Orchid's paternal family in Blessing Village[108] in Horqin RF will help:

Orchid was born in 1964 in Blessing Village. Like Fresh Springs, Blessing is located in the northern subzone of Zone 2 in Horqin RF (see Figure 8.2). The arrival story of Orchid's family in Blessing Village started out similar to that of Victory's family in Fresh Springs Village—propelled by racialized resource struggles and violence, natural calamities, and political turmoil.

Orchid's father had a Chinese name, Lu, Yongli (b. 1919). Like many borderland peoples, Yongli had mixed cultural affiliations. Yongli's mother, Knot, was born to an outlander Mongol family from Tumd and his father was born in Fenghuangcheng, the Manchu heartland in what is today's Dandong, Liaoning Province. Growing up in the heartland of Manchuria and being bilingual in Mongolian and Mandarin, Yongli also had a Mongolian name used only by his immediate family members and close acquaintances. In public, he went by his official name in Chinese. In 1947, to escape a destructive flood in Liaoning, Yongli ventured north with his two younger brothers and one sister. They made their first stop in Gegenmiao, the populous Lamaist center in the southern corner of Horqin RF. In Gegenmiao, Yongli, the eldest of the four siblings, assumed the paternal role and married off his younger sister to a local family. Then the three Lu brothers trekked on, and ended up in Suolun Township in the northwest mountains (Zone 1) of Horqin RF.

In Suolun, Yongli worked as a farmhand for an outlander Mongol landowner, and eventually married his boss' only daughter, Knot, who was 12 years his junior. Yongli became a son-in-law through a matrilocal marriage (*shangmen nüxu*), which was common among landless refugee men. Wang, Tongchun, the Dragon King of Hetao presented in Chapter 7, also started out as a *shangmen nüxu*. Yongli later worked at the Suolun railroad station as a construction worker. A few years later, wasu came to Suolun Town. Knot had a stepbrother who, like many Mongols at the time, tried to flee to the Mongolian People's Republic (today's Mongolia) to escape the racial violence of wasu. He and 11 other Mongol men planned to cross the border into

Mongolia from mountainous A'ershan, north of Suolun Township, but was arrested and jailed for 15 years. Their familial connection with a "traitor" in the eyes of the authorities made life in Suolun miserable for Yongli and Knot. In the late 1960s, when Yongli was in his late 40s, he and Knot left Suolun with their three sons, two daughters, and Yongli's two younger brothers. They found their way first to Debaisi (in Zone 2 of Horqin RF Banner), where Yongli worked in a railroad station for a year, before arriving in Blessing Village to start clearing land. As a *shangmen nüxu*, Yongli received a share of Knot's parents' wealth when they left Suolun, and the funds supported the family's reclamation efforts in Blessing Village.

In Blessing, Yongli and his family joined a production team, while Yongli's younger brother joined another team nearby. Each of the two Lu brothers had 10 children; Yongli and Knot had three more sons and two more daughters after arriving in Blessing Village. Their family of six sons and four daughters made for a formidable presence in the village, and Yongli became the production team leader for a few years before passing the job to his eldest son. Yongli's second eldest son held another important position in Blessing Village as the "grain distributor" in charge of measuring and distributing millet harvest to production team members. As mentioned earlier, millet was a native, resilient *namuy tariy-a* crop that continued to be a staple grain in Blessing Village during the collectivist era.

Up to this point, as with the Bo family, the Lu's family history still revolved around the family forefathers' land reclamation ventures. Moreover, the Lus' men had a much larger and more powerful presence in Blessing.

The game changer for the Lu family was Yongli and Knot's first child, a daughter named Ling. Born in 1950, Ling did not move with her parents from Suolun Township to Blessing Village. Again, following the Mongolian tradition, Ling stayed with her grandparents—Knot's parents in Suolun, because Knot and Yongli's marriage was matrilocal. At that time, Suolun Township was the headquarters of border defense, the timber industry, and the hub of rail transportation in the Daxing'anling Mountains. It was a place where government agencies and good schools were concentrated. Growing up pampered by her well-connected grandparents in Suolun, Ling received a much better education than did any of her other nine siblings who grew up with Yongli and Knot in the countryside. Her luck was even better than Victory's who also grew up with the grandparents, considering that Victory received his education in rural schools. Ling, on the other hand, received a proper primary education in the administrative center of Suolun Township where government officials and their families were concentrated. Ling then went on to attend a Mongolian middle school in an even larger city, Ulanhot, the capital city of Hinggan League (what used to be north Jerim League). During the last year of middle school, at the height of the Cultural Revolution, Ling joined the Red Guard in Ulanhot. Along with millions of other Red Guards from all over China, Ling traveled to Beijing in 1966 to pledge loyalty to Chairman Mao in Tiananmen Square.

With her political credentials, Ling became a CCP member, a career move that set her further apart and above the rest of the Lu family. Under the CCP policy that encouraged interethnic marriage among party members, Ling married Wen, a Han

Chinese. Like Ling, Wen had also grown up in Suolun Township. He, too, was a Red Guard and had been received by Mao in Tiananmen in 1966. As the political turmoil of the Cultural Revolution receded in the early 1980s, Wen was appointed as director of the State Tax Bureau in Dashizhai Township (see Figure 8.2), and Ling found a state-sector job in a supply and distribution station in Dashizhai as well. Dashizhai, the largest town in Horqin RF Banner in the 1980s with a population of 30,000, is located in the central subzone of Zone 2. The strategically located township held the state granary and was the administrative and commercial center of Horqin RF. As the young couple settled in Dashizhai Township, Ling tried to help her younger sister Orchid move to Dashizhai from Blessing Village. Orchid was 19 then, with three years of primary school education. But during her three years of schooling, Orchid spent most of her time caring for her many brothers' many children and often had to miss school. Ling, a revolutionary and the eldest of the 10 siblings of the Lu family, decided to help her baby sister, who was 14 years her junior, escape the trap of young women's life in the village.

For villagers in the central rolling hills of Horqin RF, moving to Dashizhai Township was a pivotal step up from the impoverished countryside. But rural-urban mobility in the 1980s, even to a rural township, required an urban residency permit. The permit was an administrative tool for regulating urban population growth. Although it was not circulated freely in the market and its volume was subject to local authority's control in Dashizhai in the 1980s, the substantial permit fees made it feel like a commodity. So in Orchid's own words, Ling "purchased" the Dashizhai urban residency for her and found her a temporary job at a leather tannery in town.

In 1988, after living with Ling's family and working various odd jobs for five years in Dashizhai Township, Orchid married Victory. Orchid and Victory first met back in Blessing Village, where they had attended school. Victory was good-looking, had fine skin and was well-educated compared to most men in Orchid's circle. Orchid fell deeply in love, and, against her older sister Ling's and her brother-in-law Wen's caution, Orchid did not mind the fact that Victory was more into the arts than physical labor. After they got married, Victory moved to Dashizhai to join Orchid. The new couple subsequently had three daughters between 1989 and 1992 while in Dashizhai: River, Ocean, and Wave. While in Dashizhai, Victory floated from temporary job to temporary job, never managing to get an urban residency permit.

In 1994, Victory lost his job once more after an argument with his supervisor. This was also the year when his home village Fresh Springs began to update its village membership registry in parallel with a cadastral survey of the village land. The survey was to prepare for the upcoming second round of household contracted land redistribution. Household contracted land was the term used for collectively owned land that was distributed to individual village households in the reform era, as mentioned in Chapter 4. The first round started in 1983 and lasted for 15 years. The second round of distribution was meant to adjust land allocation among village households based on household membership changes from death, birth, and/or marriage. Now that Victory had a wife and three children, the couple wanted to seize the historic opportunity to gain access to land. Against her sister Ling's advice, Orchid transferred her and her daughters' precious urban residency status back to the village in order to be eligible for land redistribution. The family of five moved back to Fresh Springs Village. Their move back to the village marked the end of the Bo family's first, but not last, stint in urban migration.

The Bo family went back to Fresh Springs Village to farm. But their aspiration went beyond farming. Theirs was a vision of "pastoagriculture," that is, while anchored in farming, they strove to build livestock on the side to increase financial stability. As a farming household trying to diversify their income source by venturing into herding, the Bos' pastoagricultural path is different from "agropastoralism," which takes the opposite direction, diversifying from herding into farming. The difference is critical in dissecting the "mixes" in the rural livelihoods of East IM. It shows that the "mixed," or the officially termed "half-agricultural, half-pastoral" livelihood—is not a static state with a fixed relationship between herding and farming, but dynamic processes of livelihood diversification that come with different hurdles and possibilities. The two directions of diversification are undertaken by two types of families in two types of places. The former is represented by small and poor farming families, like the Bo family, in a farming-dominant area like Fresh Springs Village in the rolling hills of Zone 2 of Horqin RF Banner. The latter is represented by the better-endowed herding families in a herding-dominant area of the northwestern mountains of Zone 1 of Horqin RF, who were better equipped to take advantage of agropastoralism in IMAR's new rural economy. I will elaborate on the significance of such a distinction in environmental conservation in the last section of this chapter. For now, I will proceed with stories about the two types of families in two places, starting with the Bo family's pastoagricultural aspirations.

III.2 Farmers' Pastoagricultural Aspirations

Upon the Bo family's return from Dashizhai Township to Fresh Springs Village in 1994, Victory took over his father, Square's, job as the village accountant. The Bos' were also ready to receive their allotted land from the village collective.

The year 1997 started the second round of readjustments of household contracted land nationwide. According to the book, this policy required updating land allocations based on the life cycle changes of village households. As mentioned in the Jin family's history in Chapter 4, families were expected to return land allotments of the deceased and of married-off daughters to the village collectives to be redistributed to families who had new members from marriage and/or birth. Across rural China, however, this second round of land redistribution was implemented with wide-ranging local variations and created countless conflicts and grievances. As introduced in Chapter 4 on agrarian Minqin, Jin Three's sons, who were born after the initial round of land redistribution, for example, never received the land to which they were entitled because their village never implemented the second round of land redistribution. Most villagers viewed land allocation from the first round of land redistribution in 1983 as permanent and inheritable assets, regardless of its legalistic term "contracted land." Many had also invested in improving their parcels for over a decade, and/or had circulated their holdings in the informal land market. On the ground, the landholding arrangements in the post-Mao contractual land rights system, despite China's constitutionally enshrined state and collective land ownership, were almost as entangled as the private land market in many small peasant economies. In a peripheral farming region like Horqin RF, where land reclamation was common and local officials' regulatory capacity was limited, the landholding structure was only more labyrinthian.

In Fresh Springs, between 1983 when village land was first decollectivized and when the second round of land redistribution took place in 1997, the village's overall cultivation had greatly expanded through both individual and collective land reclamation. The newly cleared land created a three-way dilemma for the village leader: first, the expansion had not escaped the attention of the state tax bureau, which was now equipped with technologies of aerial photography and remote sensing. The village leaders needed to compile a convincing enough set of figures of taxable cropland to reflect the expansion. Second, on the other hand, the village head could not afford the political cost of enraging his fellow villagers by reporting the true figures. Because social stability maintenance, as mentioned in the Introduction, is a key policy mandate that can make or break a political career. Third, the village head needed the villagers to pay their village dues, which were calculated on the basis of landholdings, to fund the self-financed village governance.

The political dilemma called for creative accounting. In Fresh Springs, few families returned their deceased family members' plots to the communal pot despite the official second round of land readjustment policies in 1997, as mentioned previously. In addition, as a result of collective reclamation over the previous decade, every village member now formally received 10 mu of land subject to state tax. And each had 15 mu subject to village surcharges.

Orchid and Victory had three daughters, so the family of five, upon their return, was allotted 75 mu of land in the village books, or 50 mu according to state tax records. In 2000, Victory's father, Square, died at the age of 50 from a stroke.[109] So, in addition to the 75 mu of land allocated to his family, Victory inherited 8 mu of land from his father. The land was located in the flatter area north of the village, and Victory, or, rather, Orchid, labored to clear another 5 mu adjoining Victory's inherited lot. This 13 mu of land was not accounted for in state tax records. Almost every family in the village had reclaimed land passed down within the family for which they were not prepared to pay state taxes. Also, many cleared much larger tracts of land than the Bo family did, because, according to his mother May, Victory was "too lazy."

To preempt a potentially explosive issue over land registration and taxation, the village leader performed some creative accounting. Their creative accounting started with putting the individually reclaimed parcels back in the village book first, recording them as "collective grazing land." A few months later, these parcels would be "redistributed" back to individual families, following the guidelines of the second round of land readjustment that included redistribution of collective grazing land. This way, the state policy of redistribution (or, in official terms, "readjustment") would appear to have been implemented and the village leader duly updated the records of the villagers' landholdings. Privately reclaimed and inherited land stayed with their rightful owners and potential conflict in the village was averted.

Out of the Bo family's extra 13 mu of land, only those inherited from Victory's father, 8 mu in total, appeared in the state's and the village's books while the remaining 5 mu remained completely off the book. In addition, the Bos had another 25 mu in their holdings. This 25 mu was salary payment in kind. Victory served as the village accountant between 1994 and 2004, a position that was funded by the village's own means and at the village's discretion. Victory was paid not with cash but with a well-located parcel—of the substantial size of 25 mu—that was on the village's own books but off the state tax record.

In sum, the Bos' landholding now looked like this: the family had 113 mu of land in total, scattered between the hilly south and flatter north sides of the village. In the village leader's books, the Bo family had 108 mu. The state tax record showed half of the family's actual holdings, at 58 mu.

But even when the Bos managed to hide half of their land holdings from the state and state agricultural tax was abolished after 2004, farming in an increasingly capital-intensive rural economy does not guarantee financial stability. Nor does farming prepare the family for social mobility through children's education, similar to what the Jin family in Chapter 4 had attempted. Planting cash crops at high densities and on poorer soil comes with mounting production costs in genetically modified high-yielding seeds, chemical fertilizer, herbicides, and pesticides.[110] This increased investment ran an even higher risk due to market fluctuations in commodity soy, adzuki beans, and mung beans, three of the most popular crops in Fresh Springs Village in the 2010s. The spring droughts, summer floods, and early frosts that had always dogged the hilly north were becoming more destructive and more frequent since the 2000s, posing yet another risk to villagers' investments in cash cropping.

As a result, the Bos' 113 mu of land, an impressive size by Chinese standards, were hardly enough to keep the family of five afloat. The family struggled with chronic and cyclical debts to pay for seeds and fertilizer, all while raising three school-aged children.

Most of the Bos' fellow villagers in Fresh Springs faced a similar financial predicament. The Ming family, however, was an exception, thanks to their visionary decision made from early on. Farmland, important as it is, was not the only asset of the village collective that was redistributed among village households. Upon the onset of decollectivization in 1983, every village household also received seven to eight sheep or goats in addition to the contracted land. But for individual families, small herds were hard to keep as they did not warrant a designated shepherd. Short on cash and labor, many farming families sold their redistributed herds in the early 1980s. The three Ming brothers, however, went against the trend. They borrowed money and bought up their neighbors' shares of livestock at a low price in the buyer's market, and managed to reach the requisite economy of scale and became a pastoral family in a farming-dominant village. With access to collective grazing land, the Ming brothers continuously expanded their herds. By the end of the 1990s, they owned about 1,000 heads of sheep.

Once the economy of scale was reached, herding gave the Mings an edge in the new rural economy, as the capital threshold of keeping livestock was also on the rise. In Fresh Springs Village, the population more than tripled over the second half of the 20th century from 40 to 130 households (about 700 registered residents). With population growth came cultivation expansion. Former grazing lands, woodlands, and wetlands were cleared, drained and turned into cropping fields. Consequently, villagers' access to open grazing shrank significantly, leading to their increasing dependence on cash-bought fodder, which further raised the barrier of entry for small farmers hoping to keep a herd on the side (see Chapter 2).

The visionary Ming brothers became the envy of their village neighbors who relied heavily on farming. Unlike the latter who depended solely on their fall harvests for cash income, the Mings enjoyed a steady stream of income year-round by selling wool and lamb in different seasons. Livestock also makes for a high-yielding financial asset through reproduction, especially when compared to the meager interest incurred from a bank account. A healthy and well-fed herd of 100 ewes at reproductive age could be expected to grow to a herd of 170–190 in a good year. Most rams were sold at age two or three, whereas ewes were kept to expand the herd.[111]

In the 2000s, under the environmental conservation policies, Fresh Springs Village was placed under the programs of "retiring cultivation and recovering grassland," similar to the cultivation reduction programs that Minqin went through (see Chapter 3 and Chapter 4). Farming households were greatly affected by the new policy because they needed to retire some of their cropland. But the Ming family benefitted from the program: their herds could now graze on the retired cropland that their neighbors were forced to forfeit.

The Ming brothers were also able to maintain a sizable farm through renting cropland from their neighbors who had left farming and the village. Their stable cash flow enabled a virtuous cycle that could sustain capital-intensive farming and herding and allowed the Ming brothers to take advantage of cross-nurturing between herding and farming. They could graze sheep in harvested fields and feed sheep with cornstalks, an ideal condition often cited by advocates of agropastoralism in the policy world. Money makes money. In Fresh Springs, the Mings became the moneylender for their poor farming neighbors. Cash also enables future projects. The Ming children were able to go to better schools in larger and much more costly cities.

Other Fresh Springs farmers took note of the difference that raising livestock made for the Ming family. To start a herd from scratch, farmers needed surplus from cropping. To generate enough surplus from the low-yielding soil, farmers again turned to clearing more land. The two golden decades of unbridled land clearance helped some farming families, especially those who had enough relatives in the village to form a team to clear land for farming. With the extra income from the expanded farm, they were able to build a herd of a few dozen sheep and become pastoagricultural households.[112]

The Bo family also followed suit in trying to make more money to start building a herd of sheep. Victory, as the village accountant and an amateur photographer and guitar player, was uninterested in breaking his back to clear more land like his neighbors. The family relied on Orchid to take up most of the farm work while keeping a couple of pigs and a hundred chickens on the side. The chickens produced eggs and meat for family consumption and produce-swapping, but little cash. Not unlike her ancestral outlander Mongols in the early 20th century, Orchid could only afford a donkey, but not a horse, as a draft animal.

And the Bos had little luck with money. In 1997, for instance, the family enjoyed a bumper crop and harvested 2,000 kg of soy. According to Orchid's recount, a dealer came to the village and bought the soy at 5,700 yuan. But the dealer claimed that he did not have enough cash with him. He took the soy and left Victory an IOU guaranteed by a neighbor. Later the dealer delivered the cash to the neighbor guarantor. But the neighbor kept the money and spent it on a milling machine and started a soy-processing business. The Bos took the neighbor to court, where the judge ordered the neighbor to sell the soybean mill and pay back the Bos. The neighbor did not comply with the court order and died of cancer a year later. The money dispute died with him unresolved.

Once more Orchid's motherly sister, Ling, stepped in. To help the Bos earn cash, Ling bought fashionable clothes from the city for Orchid to retail in the village. But village neighbors and relatives would stop by and pick up the clothes as freebies. It was hard for Orchid, and even harder for Victory, to ask their neighbors and relatives, who were often one and of the same, to pay. The clothing business folded. Ling then gave Orchid and Victory a loan to start a wholesale business in medicinal herbs and wild mushrooms, which grew in abundance in the hills surrounding Fresh Springs. But village foragers sold the Bos herbs that were covered with dirt and mushrooms that were presoaked in water to boost the weight. Victory was reluctant to confront the relatives, especially the elderly who made up the majority of local foragers. The herb business, too, never got off the ground. Tired of fighting with their relatives and with Victory over his timid business style, Orchid gave up on the business after they exhausted the loan a year later.

Earning cash to start a herd proved to be harder than expected. So, Victory and Orchid tried to start a herd without cash. The couple let neighbors' herds graze in their post-harvest corn and soy stubble fields, accepting a goat or a sheep as payment. After several rounds of such exchanges, the Bo family managed to assemble a herd of 10 goats, including a crippled one, and one sheep. Sheep were worth more than goats at the time, and the Bos earned their sole sheep from letting a neighbor's sheep graze their crop residue for a week. The 11-head flock made for a modestly encouraging start to the Bos' pastoagricultural aspirations. But the Bos, like other small herd owners, did not have spare labor to shepherd the small herd. They paid to join a large herding family that had designated shepherds to take a flock of several hundred sheep for open grazing on the hills during the summer and fall. In the winter, the shepherd would bring the herds back to their owners.

On a fateful day in November 2004, right after their herd had been returned to their own corral, Orchid was away visiting her daughters, River and Ocean, at their school in Cha'ersen Township. Victory was entrusted with the herd in Orchid's absence. That night, Victory attended a wedding banquet in the village, got drunk, and forgot to lock the corral gate. The goats wandered out and started walking towards the large herds they grazed with over the summer. A neighbor caught the goats on the way, split them with his two brothers, each blending the Bos' goats with their own to make them difficult to identify. Soon after, the three brothers sold the stolen goats to outside dealers to completely remove any trace of theft.

When Orchid returned to Fresh Springs the next day after the goats wandered off, Victory was still hungover, and neighbors gave conflicting accounts of where they last saw the goats. Orchid sought help from her own brothers in Blessing Village. One of her brother's sons came to Fresh Springs and took Orchid in his truck to look for the lost goats from farm to farm. As an unexperienced herd owner, and because their goats had been cared for by others for most of the year, Orchid was unable to identify her own goats that were now blended in large flocks. The ownership marks on the goats' ears, made when they were young, had grown unrecognizable by then. Orchid went to two shamans for help, only to receive more conflicting messages about the goats' whereabouts. The loss was devastating. The fact that no one in Fresh Springs would help her recover the lost goats was disheartening. Coming from a big family with six brothers in Blessing Village, Orchid was keenly aware of the vulnerability of her position in Fresh Springs. Her husband was the only Bo patriarch of his generation in the village, and they did not have any sons. Their family was in a similar predicament to that of Victory's grandfather, Darem, who was the sole Bo patriarch in the village during the 1960s. When Darem was labeled as being a part of the politically despised "landlord" class and tortured to death by the Lan brothers during the violent wasu struggles, not even Darem's in-laws were of much help. As for the lost goats of the Bo family in 2004, it was not until 2019, when the incident hardly mattered anymore, that a distant cousin in Fresh Springs told Orchid what had happened to her goats 15 years prior. In any event, the irreversible loss at the time was the last straw that broke Orchid's hope of building a herd and stabilizing the family's finances via pastoagriculture. Exhausted and disillusioned, Orchid accepted her older sister, Ling's, help once again and moved her family to the city. This time, the Bos bypassed small towns like Dashizhai and went straight for Ulanhot, the capital city of Hinggan League.

So, the Bo family of Fresh Springs of the central rolling hills (Zone 2) failed to materialize their pastoagricultural aspirations. But their in-laws in the pastoral Zone 1, the northwest mountains of Horqin RF (see Figure 8.2) had a different experience with their attempts to diversify from herding to an agropastoral venture.

III.3 Herders' Agropastoral Advantages

In 2012, the Bos' eldest daughter, River, married her high school sweetheart. Two years later, their second eldest daughter, Ocean, got married, also to her high school sweetheart. Both sons-in-law are from Mongol families in the northwestern mountains of Horqin RF Banner. After getting married, both young couples lived in their own apartments in Dabagou, a township adjacent to the city of Ulanhot and a boom town since it became the seat of Horqin RF Banner in 2016.

When River and Ocean, both college educated, attractive, bright, and perfectly bilingual in Mongolian and Mandarin, decided to marry Mongol men with only high school education and from the pastoral mountains, Victory and Orchid expressed some reservations. Growing up in the 1970s when agricultural modernity was considered the future for IM and schooled in Mandarin, a language that promised a step closer to mainstream society, both Victory and Orchid went by their Chinese names and felt distant from, if not disdainful of the backward pastoral world in the mountains. They worried that their daughters were "marrying down" to less educated men of inferior pastoral backgrounds, despite the young men's kind personalities, good looks, and unwavering devotion to their daughters. But their concerns dissipated quickly as they came to see the competitive edge of a pastoral family with a solid financial footing in the new rural economy of East IM.

Dalai, Ocean's husband, was born in Union, a *gacha* (Mongolian village) in Zone 1, the northwestern mountains. The pastoralism-dominant zone went through decollectivization in the 1980s and 1990s, like Zone 2. The collectively owned livestock and rangelands were redistributed to pastoral families, which subsequently fueled expansion of both livestock and farms and the rapid growth of commercial agropastoralism in the area.

As mentioned earlier, the year-round stream of income and more effective accumulation of wealth through livestock reproduction made pastoral families, like the Mings in Fresh Springs Village of Zone 2, the envy of their farming neighbors. Compared with pastoral families in the farming-dominant area of Zone 2, many pastoralists in the pastoral-dominant Zone 1 enjoyed an even greater advantage in expanding into agropastoralism in East IM's new rural economy. To begin with, they had access to much larger rangelands and they started off with larger herds. The benign cycle of a year-round income stream and faster capital accumulation for expansion found among the pastoral families of Zone 2 repeats in Zone 1, too, on an even grander scale and broader scope. Here in Union gacha, where the Bo family's in-laws lived, the land- and cash-endowed pastoralists were able to hire labor to clear land for feed cropping, install costly irrigation systems, purchase and/or hire farming machines for planting, harvesting, and processing, build durable storage facilities and safer animal shelters, and earn additional rental income from leasing out part of their land for others to plant and graze. Thanks to a warmer climate since the 2000s, feed and food crops could now grow in the higher altitude in the northwestern mountains of Horqin RF. The pastoral families also fared better despite grazing restrictions. Their large pasture helped bring their herd-to-land ratios below the grazing restriction threshold, as described in Chapter 2. They could rent out a stretch of their pasture to others, convert more pasture to plant feed crops like corn for sheltered husbandry, and even sell feed crops to others.

But not all herders in the mountains of Zone 1 were able to take advantage of agropastoralism in the new economy. Similar to the widening gap between small farmers and pastoralists in the farming area of Zone 2, the gap between large and small pastoralists in Zone 1 also grew after pastoral decollectivization. Like in the farmland redistribution system, rangeland redistribution was calculated by family size. Also, a family's political connections and position critically shaped what they received. Large and influential families, often those of village and township cadres, came out much better off than other villagers. On the other end of the spectrum were small pastoral families whose landholdings were too small to survive the compounded impact of droughts and grazing restrictions, as they could ill afford to rent pasture or purchase pricy fodder. Many resorted to reducing their flock size and leasing their land to industrial farm investors. Their reduced herds triggered a vicious cycle of quickly diminishing cash income and increasing debt, bringing small herders below the poverty line. This situation is similar to that of small herding families in central and western IMAR under decollectivization and destocking policies, as outlined in Chapter 2.

The family of Dalai, the Bos' in-laws, stood between these two polar ends. Understanding the ecological and economic benefits of large rangeland that enabled rotational grazing and flexible land use allocation and diversification, Dalai's father and two uncles combined their contracted rangeland and formed a unit of production smaller than a village collective but larger than an individualized family ranch. The three families together had access to a congruous piece of rangeland across "three hilltops" that were "too vast to count in mu," Dalai told me. Together, the three brother's families owned about 2,000 sheep and over a hundred cattle at one point and were able to jointly invest in mechanization, private service roads, and irrigation system for agropastoral diversification and expansion.

Unlike the Bo sisters, Dalai grew up with few money worries. His parents were able to afford Dalai's schooling in the city throughout the 2000s from primary through high school. Dalai attempted the college entrance exam for three consecutive years. Even though he failed each time, he faced little pressure to make his costly education pay off. His family's financial stability seemed to have made him much less anxious about the future than did the Bo sisters. (In Chapter 9 I will talk about the future aspirations and anxiety of Mongol students in the national college and job races.) Dalai was a big fan of the Golden State Warriors, the Nation Basketball Association (NBA) basketball team, and would not miss a game with its point guard Stephen Curry for the world. After Dalai and Ocean were married, Dalai's parents purchased, with cash, a new apartment for the new couple in Dabagou, the aforementioned boomtown adjacent to Hinggan League's capital city, Ulanhot. During my visit to Horqin RF, whenever and wherever we ate out, Dalai was always put in charge of ordering food, because he was considered more familiar with the good life than the Bo sisters.

The Bo family's unfulfilled pastoagricultural aspirations and Dalai's family's ability to take advantage of agropastoralism tell much about the divergent experiences of herding and farming families in their efforts to diversify livelihoods in decollectivized rural East IM. The relationship between herding and cropping in a mixed rural economy is not a new question in rangeland studies. As a type of land use and biome, rangeland is generally defined as native grasslands, shrublands, savannas, and marshes that are inhabited mostly by pastoralists and grazed by wildlife and livestock. Rangeland with more managed vegetation for grazing is usually called grazing land. Rangeland environments are harsh and population thin, albeit with variations between colder/higher and warmer/lower, and between wetter and dryer types of rangeland.[113] Robin Reid et. al. (2008) have listed cropping expansion for feed and for food, in addition to other activities like mining, infrastructure building, and settlements, as a major cause of rangeland transformation and shrinkage over the last few millennia.[114] Researchers on cropping expansion in Africa and Central Asia's rangelands have also expressed concerns over resource competition between herding and cropping that have brought social and environmental conflicts to rangelands.[115] My studies presented in Chapter 2 on the pastoral transformation in IMAR largely support this conclusion. I will elaborate further on the conservation tensions in East IM's "Interwoven Belt of Agriculture and Pastoralism" in the last section of this chapter.

Policy thinkers, on the other hand, have been more optimistic about the livelihood compatibility, as opposed to resource competition, between cropping and herding in rangelands. A report produced by the United Nations Convention to Combat Desertification (UNCCD) in 2017, for example, defines agropastoralism as "pastoralists' practices of grazing or feeding on crop residue and grazing fallow land" that permit the "maintenance of sustainable equilibrium among pastures, livestock, and people."[116]

My stories about post-reform Horqin RF, however, suggest that such compatibility is not a given. Herding-cropping compatibility is possible at the grassroots level when agropastoralists have sufficient access to land, livestock, and cash, as illustrated in the case of the Ming family in Fresh Springs Village in the central rolling hills of Zone 2 and Dalai's family in the banner's northwestern mountains of Zone 1 in Horqin RF Banner. However, for cash-poor farmers like the Bos, their attempts to diversify from farming to pastoagriculture proved to be an uphill battle.

The uneven results of Horqin RF villagers' attempts to diversify their livelihoods are made clear through emphasizing the spatial and temporal dynamics of the stories. Most of the contemporary research on livelihood mixes in rangelands have focused on the trends of diversification, intensification, and fragmentation of land use and ecological services in rangelands.[117] In these cases, the term "agropastoralism" refers to a state and a process of diversification from herding to the mix of herding and farming. In this framing, pastoralism analytically anchors the changes and serves as the starting place and time of the unidirectional transformation from pastoral to agropastoral livelihoods. Here, "agro" is an add-on component. This framework seems to fit various rangelands in Central Asia and Africa that have seen sizable cropping and settlement expansion into former grazing areas in recent decades. But what about rangelands and grazing lands that have turned into various intersecting modes of grazing, cropping, settlements, among other uses over the course of centuries? Over this long haul, the modes of the mixes have shifted multiple rounds and have engendered multiple starting places and directions of diversification. How do we grapple with the fluid histories of the mixes and shifts with many starting and ending points in a place like East IM's "Interwoven Belt of Agriculture and Pastoralism"? More specifically, in Horqin RF Banner, what could have been considered a type of rangeland and used mostly for grazing by pastoralists centuries ago, has since evolved into different modes of mixed livelihoods, under different land use categories, and undertaken by various land users and owners in its variegated terrains. The fact that the livelihood strategies of these peoples have largely defied the ethnicity-livelihood pairing of Mongolian as herders and Han Chinese as farmers—as presented by Mongol farmers—only complicates the story even further. Where does one begin to tell a story of so many moving pieces?

So far in this chapter, I have told the story by following its lead actors, the itinerant outlander Mongol farmers. In Section I, I traced their migration from Jesoto and Je'uda Leagues of Central-East IM to Jerim League of East IM, followed by their subsequent, multi-stopped moves within Jerim and within Horqin RF that eventually shaped the ethnoterritorial mixes and shifts in the three sub-banner zones of Horqin RF, as presented in Section II. I also followed the ways in which the Mongol outlanders interacted with other actors—native Mongol land- and livestock-owners and Han Chinese settlers alike—as they moved from the lower to higher terrains in Jerim League and within Horqin RF. The places out of which they tried to make a new home are not historically predetermined by what they are considered most suitable for—herding, farming, or otherwise. The semi-arid and hilly lands of Horqin RF, what would be clearly classified as a rangeland for non-intensive open grazing, was far from ideal for farming. But it was the only hope of survival for the desperate landless and stockless Mongol outlander refugees after they fled the massacre in their home banners. With few resources at their disposal in an environment of great uncertainty, they eked out a minimum living by clearing the hilly slopes and praying for rain, instead of tax collectors, to come. Meanwhile, they made the best out of the place as homes, grazing lands, croplands, and grounds for fishing, hunting, logging, and gathering. As the population continued to grow and the economy transformed, production activities on all fronts expanded and intensified. The transformation created and was created by fierce resource competition, uprooted lives, ruptures in livelihoods, and an endless search for sites of survival and hope. Horqin RF's ethnoterritorial dynamisms, in short, cannot be summarized with linear logic about land use or biome changes. Instead, it concerns the territorial processes that involve interwoven geopolitical, ethnoterritorial, and environmental dynamisms of the place.

Treating the livelihood mixes and shifts as territorial processes of geopolitical, ethnoterritorial, and environmental dynamisms helps identify the divergent modes of mix and multiple directions of shift. In the pastoral-dominant northwestern mountains (Zone 1) of the banner, or the mixed area of the central rolling hills (Zone 2), pastoral households with the capacity to diversify, such as that of Dalai's family or the Ming family, were able to take advantage of what an agropastoral livelihood could offer. Dry farmers like the Bo family in the farming areas of Zone 2 with low productivity, on the other hand, had limited surplus to invest in diversifying from dry farming to pasto-agriculture. For them, a more secure pastoagricultural livelihood remained an aspiration. In that sense, the two directions of livelihood diversification in East IM—agropastoralism and pastoagriculturalism in the era of market reforms—have followed divergent trajectories and produced highly uneven social and environmental results. Such divergence in the process of livelihood diversification makes the case for plural agropastoralisms. More importantly, by introducing the spatial conditions of the variations, these cases bring in a perspective that does not simply endorse or criticize the idealized model of agropastoralism.

Ocean's marriage to Dalai, in the end, was not a downward union. Nor did it follow the pattern of rural women "marrying up" to urban men for social mobility.[118] Instead, it was a marriage within rural Horqin RF between a farming family that had failed in pastoagricultural diversification and an agropastoral family that had been successful in taking advantage of post-decollectivization livelihood diversification.

The distinction between the two families in two ethnoterritorial zones also showcases the social geography of the marriage market in Horqin RF. In post-decollectivization Horqin RF, people are keenly aware of the gap between herding and farming. Families of the pastoral-dominant area endowed with access to large areas of land, like Dalai's family, have enjoyed greater financial stability than those in agriculture-dominant areas like the Bo family. Wealth in turn boosts the well-to-do herding family's desirability in China's increasingly competitive marriage market, especially for rural men (see Chapter 1). In rural Horqin RF, the geography of marriage partnerships follows the banner's two major river basins: the Tao'er that winds along the north and northwest, its banks and valleys populated mostly by struggling small farmers like the Bo family; and the Guiliu in the higher-altitude west and southwest, dominated by pastoral families like Dalai's. Given China's highly skewed sex ratio of 136 men to 100 single women among those aged 35 to 45 as of 2014, women are almost always the choosers.[119] For women from the poorer, farming Tao'er Basin, the most desirable marriage partners in Horqin RF were men from the better-off, pastoral Guiliu Basin. Men from the farming-dominant Tao'er Basin were the least desirable suitors on the market, thus representing the other end of the spectrum. Like many of the Bo family's male relatives in Fresh Springs Village, they had little chance of finding a wife without having to pay the bride's family an exorbitant bride price and buying an apartment in the town center, a price which often sent the groom's family into insurmountable debt. In one case of a family in Fresh Springs, the parents of a groom had to flee the village after the wedding to dodge debt collectors.

In any event, for Ocean the farm girl from the Tao'er Basin and Dalai the pastoral boy from the Guiliu Basin, the future was to be built neither on the farm nor the pasture, but in the city. And it was Dalai's well-off agropastoral family from the mountains that enabled the young couple's move to the city. In fact, all three of the Bo sisters, Ocean, River, and Wave, had moved to the city by the early 2010s.

But cities are inseparable from the country, and urban aspirations are often intertwined with rural despair. Before following the Bo sisters' move to the city in Chapter 9, I look at what they left behind in the countryside, focusing on the environmental tensions in their home village. It turns out that a mixed rural livelihood, be it the pastoagricultural Zone 2 or the agropastoral Zone 1, does not guarantee environmental sustainability.

IV Mixed Livelihoods and Mounting Conservation Tensions

I will start with Fresh Springs Village in the central rolling hills.

In the central rolling hills of Zone 2, especially the extensively cultivated middle reaches of the Tao'er River,[120] the soil had severely deteriorated by the mid-1980s. According to Horqin RF Banner's *Gazetteer*, these towns and sumus suffered from "overgrazing, excessive foraging of medicinal herbs, timber and fuel wood overharvesting, illegal reclamation, and pest and rat infestation," especially in the areas in close proximity to the villages.[121] Environmental deterioration climbed up as upward expansion of production continued. Located at 700 meters above sea level at the mid-upper reaches of the Tao'er, Fresh Springs' population more than tripled from 40 households in the 1950s to 130 in the 2000s. Fresh Springs villagers were also among the most ardent land reclaimers. During the land clearing fever of the 1980s and 1990s, encouraged by rising food prices in the liberalized market and a warming climate, the previously unreachable hills in the east and west of the village were converted to cropland. By the early 2000s, Fresh Springs' soil was showing clear signs of exhaustion.

But it was not just cropping on the steep slopes that accelerated soil erosion. The expanded cropping was accompanied by progressively intensified land use and resource extraction across sectors, most notably in herding. Many of the villagers in Fresh Springs, like the Bos, had failed in their pastoagricultural pursuits and left the village. The farmland they left behind was leased out to other villagers to expand their family farms and ranches. In the nearby Blessing Village, where Orchid's maiden family live, one of Orchid's brothers, Xing, managed to raise nine cows by 2015. Having married a Han Chinese woman, Xing also tended a farm of soy and corn while working as an electrician for the township government. His cows open-grazed in the village's remaining pastures, retired cropland, and fed on corn and bean stalks from his own farm as well as on purchased feed. Xing's family herd was sizable by local standards and the most successful pastoagricultural attempt out of both the Bo and the Lu families. Wave recalled that when Xing acquired his first two cows in 2012, he was so overjoyed that it brought tears to his eyes. Keeping sheep and cows and expanding the herd was an aspiration for most farmers, but only few managed to reach far enough. In addition to individual endeavors to diversify into stocking, like what Xing achieved, government programs also brought more livestock to the village. Government-sponsored productive conservation-cum-poverty alleviation programs were launched in the hilly villages of central Horqin RF Banner, similar to those in pastoral Alxa (Chapters 1 and 2) and agricultural Minqin (Chapters 3 and 4). These government programs materialized most notably via sheltered husbandry financed by private capital and policy loans.

It was a memorable moment in the summer of 2017 when I went with Xing to visit a local cattle ranch, a poverty alleviation project boasting more than 60 cattle. Upon entering the ranch, the 46-year-old Xing beamed with child-like excitement. He bustled about to check out everything in the ranch: the cattle, the hay-cutting and feed-mixing machines, the water pumping and filtering system, the forklift truck, the lofty shelter, and the warehouse. He stepped on the railings of the pens to get a closer look at the cattle and talk to the ranch workers, undisturbed by the agitated watchdogs growling at him relentlessly. On our way out, Xing, the son of an outlander Mongol farming family, told me he hoped to expand his livestock one day and build a modern ranch just like the one we had visited.

Xing might still be far from his dream ranch, and it was uncertain if or when he would get there. But his drive and aspirations certainly represented the race to expand livestocking in the pastoagricultural villages in East IM of the new millennium. Ranches of varied scales—small ones like Xing's and large, modern, policy-loan funded ones like the one Xing and I visited, and even larger ones—brought much increased livestock population that grazed upon shrinking and overgrazed pastures in the mixed villages. In the frontier of the frontier, more forest land was cleared and wetlands drained for grazing, ranching, as well as food and feed cropping. In addition to livestock expansion, commercialization of medicinal herbs also accelerated the loss of ground cover and other products of the remaining forests. By the 2000s, fuel wood supply of the hills around the village was visibly diminishing. Forests that were once home to wild boars and wolves and that had sent wandering deer to village homes as recently as the mid-1990s were now balding. Deforestation fueled the cycle of soil erosion and increasingly destructive summer floods, drowning crops and livestock alike. The grass of village rangeland that used to be tall and thick enough to obscure a child up till the late 1990s had shrunk down and thinned out in the 2000s. The increasingly warmer winters brought droughty springs, which delayed planting and shortened the growing season. What used to be occasional "drought-fighting" (*kanghan*) measures, like extracting and/or buying expensive groundwater to irrigate the fields after sowing and during crop development, now became routine practice. Winter temperatures rose and became too high to kill microbes in the soil, making pesticides yet another unavoidable and pricey investment in farming.

Meanwhile, reclamation continued under the programs of productive conservation and poverty alleviation, similar to the course in the herding- and farming-dominant regions reviewed in Chapters 1 to 4. In Horqin RF, to fight the droughts, the regional government has built dams on the higher reaches of the Tao'er River, diverting runoff to irrigation canals. The party secretary of a neighboring village of Fresh Springs told me that he had planned to take advantage of the new canals and hoped to attract a "boss from outside" (*waidi laoban*) who could bring capital to turn the drained riverbeds into cropland and upgrade villagers' rain-fed corn and adzuki bean fields into more profitable wet rice paddies. Horqin RF residents read these new initiatives, however they were branded, as government-led reclamation and followed suit on their own on the dried-up riverbeds. So the contradiction between government-sponsored reclamation in the name of productive conservation and poverty alleviation on one side and the ban on private reclamation in the name of environmental conservation on the other, as outlined in the Introduction and Chapters 1–4, has found its local expression in the pastoagricultural area of central Horqin RF. In this case, the mixes of livelihoods have intensified various land uses and exacerbated soil deterioration in multiple directions.

On top of the environmental deterioration from intensified farming, herding and foraging, the first decade of the 2000s also brought conservation restrictions to Horqin RF. Within the banner, the heavily cultivated and grazed land of the central rolling hills of Zone 2, where Fresh Springs Village is located, was considered by the government to be among the most severely degraded land. The mixed livelihoods of Zone 2, therefore, bore the double brunt of grazing bans and cultivation reduction. Also, as a part of the productive conservation program, retired soy farms were converted into grazing land or feed-crop farms. But prolonged droughts and overall soil deterioration had contributed to the spread of unpalatable or poisonous plants that led to livestock death grazing in the "recovered" or "recovering" grazing land. The same principle of "carrying capacity" that justifies grazing bans and destocking, as outlined in Chapter 2, was also applied in Horqin RF, creating a similar set of social and environmental contradictions. Because grazing bans were calculated based on the herd-to-pasture ratio, well-off pastoagricultural families rented pastures outside of the restricted zone to maintain economies of scale in herding, and they were able to grow or purchase fodder crops to keep the herds. The less endowed families, with limited access to grazing land but with the need to maintain an economy of scale, risked confiscation and penalty for exceeding the stocking ratio assigned by regulators. So, they grazed their livestock at night or crossed over the fences of enclosed grazing land. Droughts and grazing restrictions brought the price of fodder to a record high. Fines for illegal grazing that were often arbitrarily issued by pasture and forest patrols became another big-ticket expense. Meanwhile, poor quality grasses with lower nutritional value significantly lowered livestock fertility rates. Between droughts, floods, grazing and cultivation restrictions and associated fines, villagers struggled at both fronts of environmental deterioration and conservation restrictions. Many were at the end of their tethers. Social tensions mounted. It was hardly an accident that in the early 2010s, when two villagers in Fresh Springs faced yet another fine issued by a local pasture patrol for illegal grazing, the enraged villagers hopped on their trucks to chase the pasture patrol, and their trucks crashed into the patrol's four-wheel drive, causing injuries on both sides. A few years later on another occasion, villagers themselves fought over four government-granted "poverty alleviation" sheep. As a result of villagers' fist fights by the delivery truck, the sheep was taken back by the township government.

The increasing income gap and rising social tensions in rural China under productive conservation, again, is not new. I have presented the conservation contradictions and conflicts in pastoral western and central IMAR in Part I and agricultural Minqin of Gansu Province in Part II. In the mixed rural economy in East IMAR, the contradictions have come from both farming and herding, creating compounded environmental stress and multistranded conservation conflicts. The stress and conflicts have come together to create even more inflammatory social tension.

The social-environmental tensions in the pastoagricultural villages of the Interwoven Belt of Agriculture and Pastoralism in East IM did not go unnoticed. For China's policymakers, the issue at hand was one of environmental degradation-induced rural poverty hence social instability. The official narrative emphasized the overlapping geographies of poverty, environmental degradation, and minority populations. Relocation and productive conservation were again identified as the solutions to this "environment- and culture-induced" poverty, as presented in the Introduction of this book. Since 1986, at the inauguration of China's Poverty Alleviation programs, Horqin RF has been listed as a "National-level Poor Banner," along with over 800 other state-recognized poor counties and banners in China.[122] In 2011, the central government stepped up its effort to address poverty and drew a map of 14 "Concentrated and Contiguous Regions of Extreme Poverty" across China, mostly in the interior mountainous regions wherein minorities are concentrated. Horqin RF was again included in one such region drawn around the southern foothills of the Da'xinganling Mountains.[123] On this map, the Southern Foothills of the Da'xinganling Mountains Region, which included jurisdictions of northeastern IMAR and its neighboring Heilongjiang and Jilin Provinces, measured 145,000 sq. km. Two-thirds of the 8.3 million people of this "Region of Extreme Poverty" lived in rural areas; 1.1 million were ethnic minorities (mostly Mongols). The policy document indicated that 14.1% of the region's total area was sandified; 19.1% of its 450,000 hectares of farmland was salinized. Soil erosion and pollution also plagued the region. Meanwhile, only 30% of the cropland in the region was irrigated and close to 40% of its population did not have access to clean water.[124]

Being part of a region of "extreme poverty," Fresh Springs and its neighboring villages were targeted by various kinds of poverty alleviation programs. When I visited Fresh Springs in 2017, various such programs—groundwater pumping stations, roads, and bridges, subsidized high-yielding seeds, subsidized industrial farms, and the aforementioned subsidized ranches, as well as direct cash subsidies to officially identified poor households—had been in place for several years. Some poor families were moved into government-built "poverty alleviation housing." And those who were not eligible for poverty alleviation housing were pressed by local officials to build new homes under the programs of "Ten Comprehensive Rural Development Programs," mostly out of their own pockets.

The "Ten Comprehensives" program was meant to improve the look of the village. These new homes, covered under the standard bright red or sky-blue colored steel-sheet rooftops (see Figure 8.4), cost about 50,000 yuan each to build in 2016. The government promised to reimburse 6,000 yuan for each new home. Many used family savings and took out loans to build the "Ten Comprehensive" homes. Yet, out of the four families I talked to in one village, two told me that they had not received the funds after construction had been completed. One said they received only 4,000 yuan. The under- and undelivered poverty alleviation cash subsidies were another complaint. A more thorough survey is needed before any conclusion about the delivery of the program can be drawn. Most of the families in Fresh Springs and Blessing Villages, other than a few aforementioned successful pastoagricultural families, relied on remittances from family members working in the coal mines in Shaanxi, shepherding for livestock owners in other regions, driving trucks, or serving in restaurants in Ulanhot and other northeastern cities.[125]

What the Bo sisters left behind was one of the poorest villages of one of the poorest banners/counties in one of the officially identified 14 poorest regions in all of China. Not to mention, the village was one with exhausted soil in the heavily cultivated and grazed hilly and chilly land of Zone 2 of Horqin RF.

What about the Bos' in-laws, Dalai and his family in the pastoral northwestern mountains of Zone 1?

In Horqin RF, which was labeled as the as "National-Level Poor Banner," the highlands of Zone 1 represented a beacon of hope. In a warming climate,[126] the high mountains of Zone 1 have become Horqin RF's new cultivation frontier and the site of modern agro-pastoralism. Here cultivation expansion on the slower slopes at high altitudes was not limited to planting feed crops to support pastoralism. As the central government continued to promote capital intensive agriculture since the 1990s and the state planners designated IM as a "Base of Commodity Grain Production," (see Introduction) industrial farms have been climbing up Horqin RF's northwestern mountains despite repeated reclamation bans since 1998. In October 2019, China's state news agency, Xinhua, reported a case of illegal reclamation in Manzutun, a pastoral township in the northwestern mountains of Horqin RF. According to the report, five "outside bosses" reached an agreement with the local leader in 1998 to drain the highland marshes to build large wheat and rape farms. Over the ensuing two decades, the five investors cleared about 60,000 mu (4,000 hectares) of land. This large-scale reclamation followed the frontier mode of continuous expansion and rotational cultivation. It also came with new millennium characteristics. In the new era, reclamation in the now warmer highlands was greatly fortified by large capital and modern equipment. Earthmovers were deployed to dig several kilometers-long ditches to drain the marshes; tractors to plough the rich, albeit thin, topsoil of the land that had not been cultivated before; combine harvesters, which work best in expansive and monoculture fields have found homes in the slow and vast slopes of the highland. Chemical fertilizers, pesticides, and drought- and cold-tolerant crop varieties were also part of capital-intensive industrial farming in the highlands. The only limit to this upward march seemed to be the local state's capacity to build the supporting infrastructure in the mountains. In 2015, to facilitate the investors' projects (which were, in turn, framed by the central government's initiative of "commodity grain production expansion," as outlined in Introduction), the leader of Manzutun built four spray-irrigation systems fed by groundwater. But the irrigation systems and the deep wells have idled since their completion due to insufficient power supplies.[127]

What the Xinhua report, as presented above, did not cover was Manzutun herders' protests against the local government-sponsored land grabs for industrial farming. According to a report by Radio Free Asia (RFA) in 2016, 30 herders in Manzutun were detained by local police for protesting against the local government that had appropriated their rangelands and leased them to industrial farm investors. It was unclear whether the two reports focused on the same villages in Manzutun's vast territory of 2,800 sq. km, but the sources of conflict were similar. In the latter case reported by RFA, the upstream industrial farms that had drained the wetlands and applied chemical fertilizer also polluted the soil and water in the protesting herders' pastures. As springs and streams were drained and polluted, herders told RFA that they had to resort to digging deeper wells of 20 to 60 meters for clean water.[128]

South from Manzutun, Dalai's well-to-do family in a neighboring township expanded the size of their sheep stock and corn fields on their sizable rangeland from 100 to 300 mu between 2014 and 2017. Dalai's family ranch-farm was no comparison to the large industrial farm up in Manzutun, but theirs was not a lone case in Zone 1 either. Highland agropastoralists of varied scales have converged in their efforts to expand Horqin RF's new production frontiers in both herding and cropping.

The environmental outlook of Horqin RF's new production frontiers in the highlands can be better understood in the broader geographical context of East IM as a whole and from a longer historical view dating back to the pre-reform era.

As mentioned in Section I of this chapter, the history of cultivation expansion in South Je'uda (today's Chifeng Municipality), where many of Jerim's outlander Mongols came from, and that of south Jerim (today's Tongliao Municipality and a portion of Jilin and Liaoning Provinces), which was the first stopover of the outlander Mongol farming migrants and massacre refugees, can be traced back to the 18th century. Sitting on the broad alluvial plains of the West Liao River, south Je'uda and south Jerim constituted the core of what was called Horqin Pasture. Horqin Pasture attracted both state and individual land reclaimers from early on.[129]

What I did not mention in Section I, though, is the fact that the plains of the West Liao River basin are circumscribed by fixed and semifixed sand dunes to its north, west, and south. Up until the 1950s, reclamation in south Jerim took place mainly in the plains confined by the surrounding fixed sand dunes stabilized by well-established vegetation. But during the campaigns to expand grain production in the 1950s, cultivation moved outwards into the dune fields in the spirit of "moving the mountains and filling the seas." The 1950s also saw East IM's temperature rising steadily and its precipitation dropping, as mentioned earlier. IM-based geographer Wulantuya (1999) pointed out that by the early 1960s, the historic peak of cultivation expansion in south Jerim, the fixed and semifixed sand dunes started to erode, becoming mobile and semi-mobile dunes. In the spring, the strong southwest winds would carry a massive volume of loosened sand and deposit it in farming and grazing fields surrounded by the sand dunes.[130] The loss of farmland and rangeland buried under the sand in south Je'usa and south Jerim led to the renaming of the area from Horqin Pasture to Horqin Sandy Land, which also erased the drastic environmental transformation that had taken place over the second half of the 20th century.[131]

Also in the 1950s and 1960s, the North China Plain experienced a similar process of cultivation expansion and soil deterioration, followed by famines. Famines in the North China Plain, compounded by sandification of former farmland in south Jerim, sent throngs of refugees to north Jerim. The northbound march of cultivation, in other words, was trailed and pushed by cultivation ruins in its south. It was a simultaneous movement of cultivation advance and retreat.

In the 1950s and 60s, Horqin RF of north Jerim (today's Hinggan League) once again served as a depository of disaster refugees joined by political exiles, civil war prisoners, and fugitives, similar to the early 20th century. Within Horqin RF, as the lower lands of Zone 3 and southern segments of Zone 2 grew crowded and soil exhausted, the new arrivals went progressively higher. As mentioned earlier, between the 1950s and the 1980s, Horqin RF's population grew threefold, mostly due to in-migration. The greatest population growth took place in the banner's northwestern mountains (Zone 1) and in the northern subzone of central rolling hills (Zone 2).[132] The upward cultivation expansion in the banner, while creating varied and shifting modes of mixed livelihoods along the way, was trailed and precipitated by cultivation ruins emerging in the banner's south, as was the broader trend in Jerim League as a whole. During the reclamation rush of the 1980s and 1990s, almost all of the newly cleared land in Jerim League was concentrated in hilly north Jerim, and almost all newly cleared land in Horqin RF of north Jerim was concentrated in the banner's northern highlands of Zones 2 and 3.[133] In short, at both territorial levels of Jerim League and Horqin RF Banner, agricultural advance has been accompanied by agricultural retreat. The landscape of the agricultural frontier is characterized by the juxtaposition between new frontiers in the north and the ruins of former frontiers in the south.

From these geographical and historical perspectives of the simultaneous process of cultivation advance and retreat and of cultivating new frontiers as the old ones exhaust, the most recent reclamation projects of Manzutun of Horqin RF Banner's northwestern hills can be seen as being a part of the continued northbound hike in production expansion. It is just that the recent activity in Manzutun was armed with greater capital and technological might to cope with the increasingly challenging growing conditions. In the new millennium, the limits of the physical environment and the limitless impulse of production expansion—in both directions of agropastoral and pastoagricultural—have grown increasingly entangled. What is the future of such entanglements?

In China's policy circle, as mentioned earlier, jurisdictions of mixed livelihoods are called "half-agricultural, half-pastoral" banners or counties. The underlying assumption is that these jurisdictions are "suitable and have the potential to go either agricultural or pastoral" (*yinong yimu*). Just like the fact that current cultivation expansion takes place in former rangelands and transforms the area from pastoral to a "half-and-half" area, the current "half-and-half" area bears policy makers' expectations to "de-mix" and become an agriculture-dominant region in the future. The half-and-half area, as it turns out, propels future agricultural possibilities like a launching pad. In the second half of the 20th century, the half-and-half jurisdictions of Zone 2 in Horqin RF went through this exact process. By the late 1990s, cultivation of both feed and food had reached the Banner's highlands of Zone 1, turning the pastoral-dominant zone into a new "half-and-half" area, featuring a new mode of agropastoralism that included both capital intensive industrial farming and intensified pastoralism. These simultaneous processes of production diversification, intensification and expansion subsequently marginalized both small farming and herding families. Compared with the areas that are predominantly pastoral or agricultural, the half-and-half areas have been afflicted by the worst of both worlds and fraught with just as much, if not more, socioeconomic and environmental tensions. Would the "either-or" fluidity in the heartland of mixed economies dissolve into a "neither-nor" outlook in the future? For the three Bo sisters who have now settled in the city, the answer is an emphatic yes.

In Chapter 9 I will tell the story about Wave, considered the most successful among the three Bo sisters, who made it to a metropolitan center via the exceedingly competitive college and job races in present-day China. Chapter 9 also brings us from the politics of nature to that of culture in Part IV, "Sociocultural Aspirations across the Great Wall."

Notes

1. The histories of Han Chinese migration to northeastern IM have been well documented. See, for example, Zhang, Shizun. 2003. "Qingdaidongbei yimin [The northeastern-bound migration during the Qing era]." Doctoral dissertation in History. Northeast Normal University; and Ma, Pingan. 2009. *Jindaidongbeiyiminyanjiu [Studies of Migration in Modern Northeastern China]*. Jinan: Qilu Press. Stories about Han Chinese settlers who ventured out to the great northeastern wilderness beyond the Great Wall, commonly known as "*chuangguandong*," have made into contemporary Chinese novels, films, and TV dramas. But little scholarly or popular attention has been paid to Mongol farmers' migration, which was even more dramatic and traumatic, as it involved not just famine and wars, but also ethnic massacre in the late 19th century that drove close to half a million Mongols from their home banners to East IM. For this rarely told story about the farming Mongols' intra-regional migration, I consulted Mongolian scholars' works in Chinese published between early 2000s and mid-2010s. These authors and their works warrant a special note, starting from their family and education backgrounds. Most of the Mongolian students in China and IMAR's graduate programs in the humanities and social sciences come from East IM. Students from agriculture-dominant East IM are generally considered more sinicized compared to their counterparts from pastoral western and central-northern IMAR. The former tends to have a better grasp of Mandarin Chinese; the latter, Mongolian. East IM students are also perceived to be more competitive

in China's national college and graduate school entrance exams, a topic to which I will turn in Chapter 9. These Mongolian scholars with East IM backgrounds, especially those with multilingual proficiency in the fields of history, geography, ethnology, linguistics, and literary studies, and some in professional schools like education and public policy, have greatly enriched the Chinese literature on East IM's cultivation expansion between the 18th and 21st centuries with a ground-up perspective. Most of these scholars collected oral histories in their home villages or banners in East IMAR for case studies. They used both Chinese and Mongolian archival materials, and some can also use Japanese, Russian, and/or Manchurian sources. Some of these authors explicitly stated that their intention for using Mongolian and other non-Chinese sources was to provide an alternative perspective. I will discuss this source in the Conclusion.

2. Source of map: base on Reardon-Anderson, James. 2005. *Reluctant Pioneers: China's Expansion Northward, 1644-1937.* p.44. Redwood City, CA: Stanford University Press.
3. Bai, Meirong. 2016. "Qingdai zhelimumeng waiqimengguren lishi ruoganwenti yanjiu-yi kalaqin tumoteren weizhongxin [Certain Issues in the History of Outlander Mongols in Qing's Jerim League: With a Focus on Migrants from Harqin and Tumed]." PhD dissertation in Ethnology. Inner Mongolia University, p. 10.
4. These intra-regional Mongol migrants included those from Jesoto League's Harqin and Tumd Banners as well as southern Je'uda League's Naiman and Aohan Banners.
5. Burensain Borjigin. 2007. *Jinxiandaimengguren nonggeng cunluoshehuidexingcheng [Formation of the Mongolian Farming Villages and Society in Modern History]*, p. 1. Hohhot: Inner Mongolia University Press. Translated from Japanese to Chinese by Narangerel.
6. Shuangxi. 2011. "*Jindandao shijianyudongnan menggurendebeiqian [The Jindandao Incident and the* Northbound Move *of Southeastern Mongols]*." Doctoral dissertation in Minority History. Inner Mongolia University, pp. 20–22 and 41–52. The case is drawn from Bai, Meirong. 2016. Ibid. pp. 47–48.
7. Tayama, Shigeru. 1987 [1954]. *Qingdaimenggushehuizhidu [Social System of Qing's Mongolia]*, pp. 215–220. Beijing: Shangwu Publisher. Translated from Japanese to Chinese by Pan, Shixian.
8. Atwood, Christopher. 2012. "Banner, *Otog*, Thousand: Appanage community as the basic unit of traditional Mongolian society." *Mongolian Studies* 34: 1–76.
9. Bai, Yushuang. 2011. "Qingdaikalaqinmengurende beiqianjiqiyingxiang [The impact of Harqin Mongols' northbound migration during the Qing]." *Journal of Inner Mongolia Normal University (Philosophy And Social Science edition)* 40 (1): 74–77.
10. Bai, Meirong. 2016. Ibid. p. 127.
11. Bai, Meirong. 2016. Ibid. p. 30.
12. Bailadugeqi, Jinhai, and Saihang. 2002. *Mengguminzutongshi [The General History of the Mongol People]*, Vol. 5, p. 85. Hohhot: Inner Mongolia University Press.
13. Shuangxi. 2011. Ibid. p. 33.
14. Huc, Evariste Régis. 1991 [1850]. *Souvenirs d'un Voyage dans la Tartarie, le Thibet, et la Chine pendant les Années 1844, 1845, et 1846*, pp. 21–22. Beijing: China Tibetan Studies Publisher. Translated from French to Chinese by Geng, Sheng. *Dadanxizang lüxingji [Remembrances of a Journey in Tartary and Tibet].* This travelog covers today's IM, Ningxia, Gansu, Qinghai, and Tibet.
15. For an analysis of deforestation and an acute shortage of fuel in northern China, see Kenneth Pomeranz. 1993. *The Making of a Hinterland: State, Society and Economy in Inland North China, 1853–193*, pp. 120–126. Oakland, CA: University of California Press.

16. For an analysis of the politics of resource access, see Ribot, Jesse and Nancy Lee Peluso. 2003. "A theory of access." *Rural Sociology* 68 (2): 153–181.
17. Shuangxi. 2011. Ibid. p. 22.
18. Sun, Qingzhang and Tiezheng Zhou. 1930. "Chaoyang Xianzhi." *Chaoyang County Gazetteer* 33, p. 19. Published by Chaoyang County.
19. Bai, Meirong. 2016. Ibid. p. 64.
20. Shuangxi. 2011. Ibid. p. 34.
21. Interview with an elderly woman in East IM, who retold the story in which her Han Chinese grandfather told her about his own grandfather's experience in the late 19th century. July 2017.
22. For the estimated total death toll of "over 100,000" of both Mongols and Chinese, see Sun, Qingzhang and Tiezheng Zhou. 1930. Ibid. p. 23. That figure included only two counties of Chaoyang and Jianchang. These two counties were carved out of Harqin banners' territories during the Qing and were at the center of the massacre. Given the fact that the massacre had spread to other neighboring counties and banners, the death toll could easily be double. See the editors' note in Wang, Guojun. 2006 [1918]. *Menggujiwen [Chronicles of Mongolia]*, p. 44. Hohhot: Inner Mongolia People's Press. For the estimate of the Chinese death toll, see Shuangxi. 2011. Ibid. p. 122.
23. Wang, Guojun. 2006 [1918]. *Menggujiwen [Chronicles of Mongolia]*, p. 14. Hohhot: Inner Mongolia People's Press.
24. Shuangxi. 2011. Ibid. p. 107; Bailadugeqi, Jinhai and Saihang. 2002. Ibid. p. 75.
25. Shuangxi. 2011. Ibid. p. 31.
26. Wang, Guojun. 2006 [1918]. Ibid. p. 19; Shuangxi. 2011. Ibid. pp. 134–137.
27. See, for example, Gu, Kuixiang. 1980. "Qingmo Jindanjiaoqiyichutan [A preliminary study of the Jindanjiao uprising]." *Journal of Liaoning University* 2: 45–50; Yang, Xi. 1995. "Jindandaojiaoqiyiyuanyinchutan [A preliminary study of the cause of the Jindanjiao uprising]." *Journal Of Jinzhou Normal College (Social Science edition)* 4: 107–109; Yao, Haishan. 2006. "Lunchaoyangjindandaoqiyide fandiqingxiang [The anti-imperialism in Chaoyang County's Jindandao uprising]." *Journal Of Liaoning Normal University (Philosophy & Social Science edition)* 29 (2): 126–128.
28. Burensain Borjigin. 2004. "The complex structure of ethnic conflict in the frontier: Through the debates around the 'Jindandao Incident' in 1891." *Inner Asia* 6 (1): 41–60.
29. The figure of 400,000 refugees between 1891 and the 1930s comes from Shuangxi. 2011. Ibid. p. 125. The figure of "more than 300,000" refugees is drawn from Bailadugeqi, Jinhai, and Saihang. 2002. Ibid. p. 78. Shaungxi (2011: 124) reported that over 6,000 households fled Harqin Right Banner. Assuming the average household size was four, there were 24,000 refugees in one of the eight Banners who were hit the hardest during the massacre. In Tumd Left Banner, local officials reported that two-thirds of the banner territory was seized, and all the homes, temples, and granaries were burned down. In Naiman Banner, "nine out of ten homes were empty" after the massacre (Bailadugeqi et al. 2002. Ibid. p. 77).
30. The emotional trauma left by the massacre lasted long after the incident. In 1988, during China's short-lived post-Mao political opening, the Committee of Political Consultative Conference of today's Aohan Banner and Chifeng Municipality, where the massacre started almost a century ago, launched a project to collect oral histories of the massacre. In his dissertation, Shuangxi (2011) quoted some of these oral histories. What is striking in these revelations, to say nothing of the bone-chilling details of the slaughter, was

that few Mongols, once captured by the Chinese cult rioters, seemed to have tried to fight back even when they outnumbered the rioters. According to the interviewed elders, it was because Mongols were made to believe that the Han Chinese cult rioters who wore red bandanas (and hence were called "Red Hats") possessed the supernatural power of riding on clouds and resistant to deadly weapons. The Mongols, once under siege and horror-struck by the Red Hats' presumably inescapable power, felt it was futile to resist. Riding on Mongols' fear, the Han Chinese rioters were able to butcher an outsized number of Mongols. On one occasion, two Red Hats were said to have commanded over a hundred Mongols to line up and kneel down. Then the two Red Hats executed the hostages one by one from both ends of the line (Shuangxi. 2011. Ibid. p. 108). Shuangxi's reference was "hongmaozishijian xuanbian, neibuban. [Information about the Red Hat Incident, Internal edition]," dated 1989. Publisher unidentified. The accuracy of these tales, retold over three generations, is hard to verify. What the tales do reveal is the trauma of genocide that lived much longer than the massacre itself. Many Mongols today preferred avoiding the topic, and the massacre was generally unknown to those born after 1990. Two of my hosts in East IM—both were schooled in the post-1990s era and majored in social sciences in college and grad school during the 2010s—heard about the Jindandao Massacre for the first time only when I asked them about it. It is important to note that the Jindandao Massacre was not the last time Mongols went through such a pogrom. In Section III of this chapter on the history of two Mongol settler families in Horqin Right Front Banner of north Jerim, I will touch on the racialized Cultural Revolution in IM and how it transpired in the villages.

31. Burensain Borjigin. 2004. Ibid.
32. Bai, Meirong. 2016. Ibid. pp. 34–38.
33. The average size of a banner during the Qing era was about 1,500 households, albeit with regional variations. See Atwood, Christopher. 2012. Ibid. p. 9.
34. Bai, Meirong. 2016. Ibid. p. 57.
35. Bai, Meirong. 2016. Ibid. p. 100.
36. Bai, Meirong. 2016. Ibid. p. 120.
37. Shuangxi. 2011. Ibid. pp. 74–75.
38. Shuangxi. 2011. Ibid. pp. 134–135.
39. Bai, Meirong. 2016. Ibid. pp. 120–121.
40. Bailadugeqi, Jinhai, and Saihang. 2002. Ibid. Wang, Yuhai. 2000. *Fazhanyubiange: qingdai neimenggudongbu youmuxiangnongdezhuanxing [The Shift from Pastoralism to Agriculture in Qing's East Inner Mongolia]*, pp. 117–118. Hohhot: Inner Mongolia University Press.
41. Unless noted otherwise, I use Nicolas Poppe's transliterations for Mongolian persons' names in this chapter.
42. Wang, Yuhai. 2000. Ibid. pp. 113–117.
43. Burensain Borjigin. 2004. Ibid. p. 46.
44. Prince Demčugdongrub was seen by the Chinese Nationalist Party (KMT) as *Hanjian*, a traitor to the Chinese nationhood. The term "Hanjian", a moral concept condemning Chinese who collaborate with enemies of China was applied to not just Han Chinese "traitors", but also to the Mongol, Hui Muslim, and Manchu peoples in China. See Bulag, Uradin. 2010. *Collaborative Nationalism: The Politics of Friendship on China's Mongolian Frontier*. p. 103. Lanham, MD: Rowman & Littlefield.

45. For elaboration on the fluid ethnic identities in East IM see Lattimore, Owen. 1932. *Manchuria: Cradle of Conflict*. pp. 39–58. New York: MacMillan Company. Lattimore saw the relationships between Han Chinese and other border peoples in what he called the "reservoir" region to be more social than racial. These peoples included Mongolianized Han Chinese and those of mixed blood who were socioculturally Mongolian, and those sinicized, agricultural Mongols of Jesoto and Je'uda Leagues (the outlanders discussed in this chapter). Lattimore also noted identity shifts, that is, Han Chinese migrants who had "turned Mongolian," then "turned Chinese" at different geopolitical moments since the 18th century. This mixed group functioned alternatively as a "rearguard of the Mongols and advanced guard of the Chinese." Such a function, Lattimore argued, is different from the frontiersmen of American colonization who were prevailingly conscious of being at the front of the advances, and seldom went completely native. The difference is due to the fact that there was no such ethnoterritorial "reservoir" in American history and no alternation of political ascendancy.
46. Due to the lack of historical climate data for north Jerim, I use contemporary data published by the Hinggan League government in 2015 as a proxy. Xinganmengxingzhenggongshu [Hinggan League Administrative Office]. 2015. "Ziran dili [Physical Geography]." http://www.xam.gov.cn/xam/_300485/_300834/index.html. Accessed July 21, 2023. See note #126 for East IMAR's climate changes from 1961 to 2007. My interviews with elderlies in Hinggan League invariably suggested a much colder, but wetter, climate in the 1960s and 1970s.
47. In north Jerim, banner members were banned from learning Chinese. Those who spoke Chinese were excluded from banner officialdom. See Borjigid Altanγaraγ [Alatenggariga in Chinese]. 2012. *Jinxiandai neimenggu youmubianqianyanjiu, yizhalaiteqiweili [Transformation of Pastoralism in Modern Inner Mongolia: A Case Study of Jalaid Banner]*, p. 69. Shenyang: Liaoning Ethnicity Press.
48. Bai, Meirong. 2016. Ibid. p 127.
49. A record of Horqin Right Front Banner showed that the merchants had paid only one-third of the conveyance fees. See Xi, Lianhua. 2015. "Ershishijichuqitao'erheliuyu mengqitudikaikenyanjiu [A Study of Land Reclamation in Mongolian Banners in the Early 20th Century Tao'er River Basin]." Doctoral dissertation in Mongolian History. Inner Mongolia University, pp. 56–57.
50. Hobsbawn, Eric. 2000. *Bandits*. New York: The New Press.
51. Burensain Borjigin. 2004. Ibid.
52. Xi, Lianhua. 2015. Ibid. p. 41; Bai, Meirong. 2016. Ibid. p. 73.
53. See Chapter 5 for a comparison of the ethnoterritorial structure among IMAR, XUAR, and TAR.
54. Zhao, Halin et al. 2002. "Beifangnongmujiaocuodaidedilijieding jiqishengtaiwenti [The geographical boundary of northern Interwoven Belt of Agriculture and Pastoralism and its ecological questions]." *Progress in Earth Science* 17 (5): 739–747; Huang, Jianying. 2009. *Beifangnongmujiaocuodai bianqian duimengguzujingjiwenhualeixingdeyingxiang [The Impact of the Changing Northern Interwoven Belt of Agriculture and Pastoralism on Mongolian Economic and Cultural Typologies]*. Beijing: China Minzu University Press.
55. For studies of mixed livelihoods in East IM that include hunting, gathering, and fishing, see Borjigid Altanγaraγ (Alatenggariga in Chinese). 2012. Ibid. pp. 48–53; and Yoshida,

Junichi. 2016. "Jinxiandaineimenggu dongbudiqumenggurende jingjijiegou [The economic structure of Mongols in modern eastern Inner Mongolia]." *Studies in Mongolian History* Vol. 12, pp.36–45. Translated from Japanese to Chinese by Wulan. In this chapter, I focus mainly on the relationship between herding and cropping.

56. This is the reading of the 1980s. See Feng, Xuezhong et al. eds. 1991. *Horqin Right Front Banner Gazetteer*. pp. 98–109. Hohhot: Inner Mongolia People's Press.
57. Lattimore, Owen. 1932. Ibid. p. 4.
58. Chagemandula, 2012. "Jindaixing'anmengdiqutudiwenti yanjiu [Land Issues of Modern Hing'an Region]." PhD dissertation in Mongolian History. Inner Mongolia University, p. 110.
59. The term "*dazaju, xiaojuju*" was underdefined in most of these works. In my reading, it mainly refers to the spatial distribution of minorities at the national and subnational levels. That is, China as a whole has multiple nationalities (*dazaju*), and most minority nationalities concentrate in the officially designated autonomous regions, like IMAR and Tibet Autonomous Region (TAR) (*xiaojuju*) and some subregional autonomous jurisdictions, as mentioned in Chapter 5. This pattern of "*dazaoju, xiaojuju*" applies to two-thirds of China's minority population, but few works have been done on the multi-scale distributional pattern of the minorities in these regions. The other third belong to a different category called "mixed and scattered" (*zasanju*) peoples. They reside in nonautonomous jurisdictions across rural and urban areas in China, mixing with the Han majority and/or other minorities in a much more decentralized and granular way. Most of China-based scholars' works focused on the sociocultural assimilation among these "*zasanju*" minorities in China's southwest, especially in the urban areas. See, for example, Wei, Xinchun. 2013. "Chengshihuajinchengzhong shaoshuminzujuzhugejujiminzuguanxi detiaoshi—yichengdushiweili [The residential pattern of minorities and adjustment of ethnic relationship in the process of urbanization: The case of Chengdu]." *Journal of Southwest Ethnicity University (Humanity & Social Science edition)* 5: 28–31; and Ma, Xiaoxia. 2011. "Zasanjuduominzuhunhexuexiaozhong minzu wenhuachuanchengdefansi—jiyuduiyunnanwenshan, dalidekaocha [Reflections on ethnic cultural heritage in a multi-nationality school in a zasanju area: Case studies of Wenshan and Dali of Yunnan Province]." *Jiaoyujiaoxue yanjiu [Research on Education and Pedagogy]* 7 (9): 77–79. The zasanju areas, which have risen rapidly in the cities since the 1990s, are generally perceived as the path towards and the sign of harmonious ethnic relations.
60. Topographically, Horqin RF Banner and A'ershan City share different sections of the Da'xinganling mountains. The resource rich and strategically positioned A'ershan, from where the two major river systems of Horqin RF, the Tao'er and the Guiliu originate, was part of Horqin RF's jurisdiction during the Qing and most of the 20th century. In 1992, A'ershan's 7,000 sq. km expanse was parceled out from Horqin RF Banner's jurisdiction and placed under the authority of the A'ershan Economic Development Zone, which subsequently became A'ershan city in 1996. The partition of the immense mountain area from Horqin RF Banner in 1992 was not the first time Horqin RF Banner lost a substantial portion of its territory. Under different regimes from the late imperial era to the present, the Banner's jurisdiction has continued to shrink. Its forests were enclosed as state forests, its pastures as state horse farms and ranches. Most of all, in the early 20th century, its fertile land in the southeastern half was enclosed for state reclamation and subsequently placed under the authority of neighboring county and provincial governments.

61. See the critique of cultural ecology in Watts, Michael. 1983. "On the poverty of theory: Natural hazards research in context." In *Interpretations of Calamity from the Viewpoint of Human Ecology*, edited by Hewitt, K., pp. 231–62. Boston: Allen & Unwin Inc. In the case of nomadism, historical anthropologist Wang, Min-ke argued that nomadism entails heterogenous forms of livelihood strategy in a highly variable environment. Nomadism is not an inevitable historical given, but a deliberate geopolitical choice. See Wang, Min-ke. 2009. *Yumuzhedejueze: mianduihandi guodebeiyayoumubuzu [The Nomad's Choice: The First Encounter between Northern Nomads and Imperial China]*. Taipei: Lianjing Press.
62. I use demographic data at the township level as the base of my calculation of the ethnic ratios in this table. But only the 1988 data was available. Feng, Xuezhong et al. (1991) suggested that the ethnic ratio remained relatively stable between the 1930s and the 1980s. See Feng, Xuezhong et al. 1991. Ibid. pp. 208–210.
63. In places where surface runoff or groundwater was more easily accessible, Korean migrants from Manchuria had been planting wet rice since the late 1920s. In 2017, I visited a village in the southeast belt of the Banner where wet rice paddies were widely planted. But their yields were uneven from year to year and place to place, and many returned to dry farming because of recurrent droughts. See also Feng, Xuezhong et al. 1991. Ibid. p. 295.
64. Local officials reported that Russians had shipped modern firearms to East IM from as early as 1904 and 1905, and that Udai had exchanged horses for bullets and distributed the rifles and bullets to his banner members to fight the bandits. See Tian, Zhihe and Xuezhong Feng. 1991. *Minguochuniandongbu mengqi dulishijianyanjiu [A Study of the Independence Incident in Eastern Banners of Inner Mongolia during the Early Republican Era]*, pp. 74–75. Hohhot: Inner Mongolia People's Press. Most Chinese sources depict Udai as a traitor to the Chinese nationhood. More research and reviews of non-Chinese and non-English materials, which I regrettably am unable to do, are needed for a more comprehensive understanding of Udai's geopolitical strategies.
65. Feng, Xuezhong et al. eds. 1991. Ibid. pp. 732–737; Wang, Wang-sheng. eds. 2008. *Ke'erqin youyiqianqi 370 nian [The 370 Years of Horqin Right Front Banner]*, pp. 53–55. Hohhot: Inner Mongolia Education Press.
66. Tian, Zhihe and Xuezhong Feng. 1991. Ibid. pp. 76–78.
67. Chaogemandula, 2012. Ibid. p. 50.
68. Xi, Lianhua. 2015. Ibid. p. 57.
69. Zhusa. 2009. *Shibadaoershishijichu dongbuneimenggu nonggengcunluohuayanjiu [Formation of Farming Villages in East IM during the 18th–20th Centuries]*, pp. 95–97. Hohhot: Inner Mongolia People's Press.
70. Wang, Shiren (1881–1937), a low-ranking Chinese official, moved to Jerim from Shandong Province of north China when he was a child. His father was an official in a county carved out from Jerim League. Growing up in a Chinese official's family in Inner Mongolia, Wang himself worked in the reclamation office in Jerim during the late Qing Dynasty, followed by a brief career in the Republican army to pacify Udai's insurgence before taking up administrative duties in economic affairs in north Jerim. Unlike Wang Guojun, the aforementioned trilingual Mongolianized Chinese who served in the banner government in Jesoto and reported the horrendous Jindandao Massacre of Mongols in 1891, Wang Shiren was a mainstream modernist who vowed to cure the "illness" of Mongolia. In 1913, at the age of 32, Wang wrote a book entitled "*Zhemengshiji*." See Wang, Shiren. 1913. *Zhemengshiji [A Practical Medicine (Policy Solution) for Jerim League]*. Reprint collected

in Dong, Guanghe and Qi Xi eds., 2011. *Zhongguoxijian difangshiliaojicheng* [*Collection of China's Rare Historical Materials*]. Vol 2, Nos. 75 and 76. Beijing: Xueyuan Publisher. *Zhemengshiji* was a 12-year development plan to build a modern Jerim that would feature modern banking, railroads, a hydraulic system, and mining. The key ingredient in Wang's medicine for Jerim's future was land reclamation. Before prescribing the cure, Wang offered a quick diagnosis of the ailment.

71. Wang's calculation is corroborated by the official records of Zhendong County (the area south of today's Horqin RF Banner). According to Shandan (2006), in the state sanctioned reclamation zone, only 3% of the earmarked reclamation land had been cultivated by 1915. Shandan. 2006. "Ke'erqing youyihouqilishi ruoganwentiyanjiu [Studies of some questions in the history of Horqin Right Rear Banner]." Master's thesis. Inner Mongolia Normal University, p. 20.
72. Xi, Lianhua. 2015. Ibid. p. 115.
73. Chaogemandula, 2012. Ibid. p. 67.
74. Xi, Lianhua. 2015. Ibid. p. 121.
75. In the Suolun mountains, where Marshal Zhang recruited famine refugees to clear the land, 99.9% of the Corps' reclamation zone was uncultivated. See Wulantuya. 1999. "300nianlai ke'erqindetudigenzhiyu shazhihuangmohua [Land Reclamation and Sandification in the Last Three Hundred Years in Horqin]." PhD dissertation in Physical Geography. University of Chinese Academy of Sciences, p. 55.
76. Banditry in the southeast continued into the late 1940s. Official reports of bandit raids came from the hills of Suolun, Wulanmaodu, and Manzutun, Cha'ersen, and Er'egetu, and also from the lower lands of Guji and Balagedai. See Feng, Xuezhong et al. eds. 1991. Ibid. pp. 742–748; and Wang, Wang-sheng. eds. 2008. Ibid. pp. 310–311.
77. Menggen. 2006. "Ershishijichu Zalaiteqide menggucun [Mongolian villages of Jalaid Banner in early 20th century]." *Journal of Inner Mongolia University (Humanity and Social Science edition)* 38 (2): 31–34, p. 32.
78. Zhusa. 2009. Ibid. pp. 266–270.
79. *Nutuγ* is a term for a cluster of settlements. Originally, it was defined by banner members' grazing grounds. Under Japanese colonial rule, it was institutionalized as a sub-banner jurisdictional unit. By 1939, there were seven *nutuγs* in Horqin Right Front Banner. As Han Chinese grew to dominance in rural East IM, some of the Chinese-dominant *nutuγs* came to serve as the launching pad for the Chinese Communist Party's radical, and often violent, land redistribution struggles (Chaogemandula. 2012. Ibid. p. 156). During the 1950s, most *nutuγs* were turned into *sumus* (where Mongols' presence was stronger) or *xiangs* (towns, where Han Chinese were in the majority), but some administrative *nutuγs* that oversaw several *sumus* in the pastoral area stayed till the 1980s.
80. Menggen. 2006. Ibid.
81. Chaogemandula. 2012. Ibid. pp. 74–75.
82. Chaogemandula. 2012. Ibid. p. 110; Zhusa. 2009. Ibid. pp. 316–323.
83. See, for example, Hao, Yaming and Zhiming Bao. 2010. *Tizhizhengceyumengguzu xiangcunshehuibianqian [State Policy and Changes in Mongolian Rural Society]*, p. 58. Beijing: Central Ethnicity University Press.
84. Borjigid Altanγaraγ (*Alatenggariga* in Chinese). 2012. Ibid. p. 97. This is an informative and detailed case study of Jalaid Banner, Horqin RF's eastern neighbor. Jalaid and Horqin RF Banners share similar mixed livelihoods, ethnoterritorial structure, topography, as

well as geopolitical and environmental histories. The author, who grew up in Jalaid, references these similarities between the two banners throughout the book. Due to the lack of micro-level studies of Horqin RF's southeast during the first half of the 20th century, I used this study as a proxy. For outlanders' reclamation in Horqin RF during the second half of the 20th century, to which I will turn in the next section, I use oral histories that I collected during my fieldwork.

85. Borjigid Altanγaraγ. 2012. Ibid. pp. 80–81. Altanγaraγ suggested that by the 1930s, Han Chinese owned more horses than did Mongols in Jalaid Banner.
86. It was 10 *dou*, a Chinese volume unit. 1 dou equals 10 liters.
87. Feng, Xuezhong et al. eds. 1991. Ibid. pp. 25–26. Xi, Lianhua (2015. Ibid. pp. 131–133) also noted that one decisive moment of the Mongols' exodus was during warlord Marshal Zhang's reclamation campaign in the late 1920s. Within a year of the arrival of Marshal Zhang's Reclamation Corps in 1928, the Mongol population in Horqin RF declined by 27,000, about 60% of its starting point at 45,000.
88. Kerven, C., B. Steimann, L. Ashley, C. Dear, and I. Rahim. 2011. "Pastoralism and Farming in Central Asia's Mountains: A Research Review." MSRC Background Paper No. 1. Published September. Originally published at Bishkek, University of Central Asia. Posted at Zurich Open Repository and Archive. https://www.zora.uzh.ch/id/eprint/52730/1/pastoralism_and_farming_in_central_asia_mountains.pdf. Accessed August 1, 2021.
89. Unless otherwise noted, the information on the scope of *namuγ tariy-a* and its transformation in this section mainly comes from Yoshida, Junichi. 2016a. "Neimenggudongbudiqude chuantongnonggengyijihanshi nonggengderongru [Traditional farming and the incorporation of Han-style farming in eastern IM]." *Journal of Inner Mongolia University (Social Science edition)* 42 (4): 36–43. Translated to Chinese by Bao, Huijuan and Alatenggarige; and Borjigid Altanγaraγ. 2012. Ibid. pp. 56–59.
90. See, for example, Wang, Jiange. 2000. "Dingjuyujindai mengguzunongyedebianqian [Sedentarization and transformation of modern Mongolian agriculture]." In *Zhongguolishidililuncong [Collection of studies in China's Historical Geography]* 2: pp. 25–42, p. 26; Seyin. 1998. *Mengguyoumushehuidebianqian [Transformation of Mongolian Pastoral Society]*, p. 114. Hohhot: Inner Mongolia People's Press. The two authors shared the view that Chinese-style farming is more intensive and also more advanced, compared to the "backward" *namuγ tariy-a.*
91. Borjigid Altanγaraγ. 2012. Ibid. p. 24.
92. The popular, moralistic slogan of the time was "Herders should not shamelessly rely on farmers for grain supplies," "*muminbuchi kuixinliang*."
93. Feng, Xuezhong et al. eds. 1991. Ibid. pp. 308–311.
94. Yoshida, 2016a. Ibid. p. 42. Interview in Hohhot, 2017. Also see Bao, Yongmei. 2013. "Bannongbanmuqumengguzu nongmumin shouzhiwentidiaochayanjiu—yi wulijimuren sumuweili [Survey of Household Income and Expenditure of Mongolian Farmer-Herders in the Half-Agricultural/Half-Pastoral Areas: A Case Study of Wulijimuren Sumu (of Jarud Banner)]." Master's thesis in Ethnology. Inner Mongolia Normal University, p. 20.
95. Author's calculation based on data from Feng, Xuezhong et al. eds. 1991. Ibid. pp. 70–89 and pp. 207–210.
96. All village names and personal names in this chapter are fictional.
97. Taonan was a part of Horqin RF Banner during most of the Qing era until 1904, when it was carved out of Horqin RF and became a separate county.

98. For the history of Cultural Revolution and *wasu* in IMAR, see, for example, Qi, Zhi. 2010. Neimengwengeshilu: minzufenlie yu wasu yundong [Records of the Cultural Revolution in Inner Mongolia: Ethnic Separatism and Wasu Campaigns]. Hong Kong: Tianxingjian Press, p. 23, note 12; Brown, Kerry. 2007. "The Cultural Revolution in Inner Mongolia 1967–1969: The purge of the "heirs of Genghis Khan." *Asian Affairs* 38 (2): 173–187; Sneath, David. 1994. "The Impact of the Cultural Revolution in China on the Mongolians of Inner Mongolia." *Modern Asian Studies* 28 (2): 409–430; Heaton, William. 1971. "Inner Mongolia: 'Local nationalism' and the Cultural Revolution." *The Mongolia Society Bulletin* 10 (2): 2–34; and Renqin. 2015. "Shilunneimenggu siqing yundong [The Four Cleansing Movement in Inner Mongolia]. *Wengeyu dangdaishi yanjiu [Studies of Cultural Revolution and Contemporary History]*." Published online, June 26. https://www.difangwenge.org/forum.php?mod=viewthread&tid=11368. Accessed November 13, 2023. For the history of Cultural Revolution in Tibet, see, for example, Goldstein, Melvyn et al. 2004. *A Tibetan Revolutionary: The Political Life and Times of Bapa Püntsok Wangyel.* Oakland, CA: University of California Press.
99. For a review of the split between the "western" and "eastern" factions of Mongolian revolutionaries and the profound impact of intra-regional power competition on elite politics of IMAR under the CCP regime, including the rise of Ulanhu who represented the western faction, see Atwood, Christopher. 1992. "The East Mongolian Revolution and Chinese Communism." *Mongolian Studies* 15, The Nicholas Poppe Memorial Issue: 7–83. For the geopolitical and historical contexts and more detailed accounts, see Liu Xiaoyuan, 2004, *Frontier Passages: Ethnopolitics and the Rise of Chinese Communism, 1921–1945.* Redwood City, CA and Washington, DC: Stanford University Press and Woodrow Wilson Center Press; and Liu, Xiaoyuan. 2006. *Reins of Liberation: An Entangled History of Mongolian Independence, Chinese Territoriality, and Great Power Hegemony, 1911–1950.* Redwood City, CA and Washington, DC: Stanford University Press and Woodrow Wilson Center Press.
100. For the discrepancy in death toll estimates, see Qi, Zhi. 2010. Ibid. p. 23, note 12; and Cheng, Tijie. 2009. "Sishiyunianhuishoukan neimengwenge [Looking back at Cultural Revolution in Inner Mongolia forty-plus years later]." *Wengeyu dangdaishi yanjiu [Studies of Cultural Revolution and Contemporary History].* Published online, November 8. https://www.difangwenge.org/forum.php?mod=viewthread&tid=252&extra=page%3D6. Accessed November 13, 2023. For IMAR's population in 1965, Qi, Zhi referenced an "internal document" that registered it at 1.44 million. An online IMAR Gazetter published in 2007 recorded the Mongolian population in IMAR at 133 million in 1964. http://116.113.96.251:8080/Search/SearchContent.aspx?RootId=20130808145243089&BookId=20170709115013354. Accessed October 4, 2021. The link was broken by November 13, 2023.
101. Yang, Haiying. 2013. "Ulanhu, a nationalist persecuted by the Chinese Communists." *Comparative Studies of Humanities and Social Sciences. Graduate School of Letters* 32. Japan: Nagoya University.
102. Yang Haiying called *wasu* a Mongolian genocide. See Yang, Haiying. 2017. *The Truth about the Mongolian Genocide during the Chinese Cultural Revolution.* Center for Research on Asia. Faculty of Humanities and Social Sciences. Japan: Shizuoka University.
103. Yang, Haiying. 2014. *Meiyoumubeide caoyuan: mongguren yu wenge datusha [A Pasture without Tomb Stones: Massacres of Mongols during the Culture Revolution].* Taipei: Baqi Wenhua Press. Translated from Japanese by Liu, Yingbo and Yanzi Liu.

104. Tellingly, *wasu* was news to Wave, who grew up in the 1990s. No one in the family had ever mentioned it to her and *wasu* was absent from her history textbooks. She heard about the term for the first time from her grandmother in 2017 during my interviews.
105. By the time Victory was born, his grandfather, Leopard, had died of a stroke at the age of 45.
106. In 1987, the National Peoples' Congress passed the Experimental Organic Law of Village Elections, which came into effect in June 1988. In 1998 the law achieved permanent status, thus signaling the party's acceptance of this new system of rural governance. By 2006, every village in China had organized at least one competitive election for the village committee chair and members, each for a three-year term. For the politics of village elections, See O'Brien, Kevin. 2010. "Understanding China's grassroots election." In *Grassroots Election in China*, edited by O'Brien, Kevin and Shuisheng Zhao, pp. xi–xvi. Milton Park: Routledge.
107. For Mongol students' bilingual education and identification politics in present-day IMAR, see Chapter 9.
108. Fictional name.
109. Strokes afflicted many locals, mostly (but not exclusively) men, a circumstance that people in IM often attributed to heavy drinking.
110. For studies on the increased application of chemical fertilizer and pesticides in Horqin RF in the 2010s, see Bao, Zeming. 2016. "Xiandaihuabeijingxiabannongbanmuqu mengguzu cunluohuanjingwenti jiqiyingduo: yineimenggu ke'erqinyouyiqianqi manghagachaweili [The Environmental Problem of Mongolian Villages in the Half-Agricultural and Half-Pastoral Region under Modernization: A Case Study of Mangha Village in Horqin RF Banner]." Master's thesis in Environmental Sociology. Inner Mongolia University, pp. 7–13.
111. Interviews with herding families and families of mixed livelihoods in Xilingol (2011 and 2012) Bayannur (2011), Ejina (2012 and 2013), and Horqin RF (2017). These figures varied across times and places and were conditioned by many factors. On average, the ratio between ewes and rams in a herd was kept at about 100:4 for breeding purposes.
112. In his 2007 survey of Horqin Right Center Banner, Horqin RF Banner's western neighbor, Wang, Xiaoyi also found a similar transformation. See Wang, Xiaoyi. 2009. *Huangjingyalixiade caoyuanshequ [Pastoral Communities under Environmental Pressure]*, pp. 144–145. Beijing: Social Science Academic Press.
113. I thank Nathan Sayre of UC Berkeley Geography for guiding me through rangeland studies. For the definition of rangelands and an overall review of rangeland development at a global scale, see Reid, Robin S., Maria E. Fernandez-Gimenez, and Kathleen A. Galvin. 2014. "Dynamics and resilience of rangelands and pastoral peoples around the globe." *Annual Review of Environment and Resources* 39: 217–242.
114. Reid, Robin S. et al. 2008. "Global significance of extensive grazing lands and pastoral societies: An introduction." In *Fragmentation in Semi-Arid and Arid Landscapes: Consequences for Human and Natural Systems*, edited by Galvin, Kathleen, Robin Reid, Roy Behnke, and Thompson Hobbs, pp. 1–24, p. 9. Dordrecht: Springer.
115. See, for example, Neupert, Ricardo F. 1999. "Population, nomadic pastoralism and the environment in the Mongolian Plateau." *Population and Environment* 20: 413–441; Little, Peter D. 2003. *Somalia: Economy without a State.* Bloomington, IN: University Press; Geist, Helmut J. and Eric F. Lambin. 2004. "Dynamic causal patterns of desertification." *BioScience* 54: 817–829. For an earlier critique of cropping expansion in pastoral areas,

see, Hjort, Anders. 1981, "Herds, trade and grain: Pastoralism in a regional perspective." In *The Future of Pastoral Peoples*, edited by John G. Galaty, Dan Aronson, and Philip C. Salzman, pp. 135–143, p. 140. Ottawa: International Development Research Center.

116. Sanz, Maria J. et al. 2017. "Sustainable Land management contribution to successful land-based climate change adaptation and mitigation. A report of the society-policy interface," p. 73. Bonn: United Nations Convention to Combat Desertification. For an earlier policy report, see Williams, T. O., Tarawali, S., Hiernaux, P., and Fernandez-Rivera, S. 2004. "Sustainable crop-livestock production for improved livelihoods and resource management in West Africa." Proceedings of an International Conference held at the International Institute of Tropical Agriculture. Ibadan, Nigeria, November 19–22, 2001. Published by International Livestock Research Institute in Nairobi, Kenya. The question of ecological equilibrium and disequilibrium has been central to environmental studies, but it is beyond the scope of this book. See Behnke, Roy, Ian Scoones, and Carol Kerven. 1993. *Range Ecology at Disequilibrium. New Models of Natural Variability and Pastoral Adaptation in Africa Savannas.* London: Overseas Development Institute.
117. For elaboration on rangeland diversification, see Kerven, C., B. Steimann, L. Ashley, C. Dear, and I. Rahim. 2011. Ibid. For elaboration on rangeland fragmentation, see Galvin, Kathleen, Robin Reid, Roy Behnke, and Thompson Hobbs. 2008. *Fragmentation in Semi-Arid and Arid Landscapes: Consequences for Human and Natural Systems.* Dordrecht: Springer.
118. Intermarriage between rural women and urban men has long been considered the path for social mobility for rural women in China. In reality, that path is often blocked by urban families' prejudice against women from the countryside. See Beynon, Louise. 2004. "Dilemma of the heart: Rural working women and their hope for the future." In *On the move: Women and Rural-to-Urban Migration in Contemporary China*, edited by Arianne Gaetano and Tamara Jacka. New York: Columbia University Press.
119. See Chapter 1 on the correlation between one's credit rating (assessed by Ant Financial) and marriage market standing, mostly for men.
120. Such as the townships of Cha'ersen, Dabagou, Balagedai, Halahei, E-ti, and E'rgetu in the middle and southern segments of the zone (see Figure 8.2).
121. Feng, Xuezhong et al. eds. 1991. Ibid. p. 145.
122. Liu, Jian. 2006. *Xinjieduanfupinkaifade chengjiuy tiaozhan [Achievements and Challenges of the New Phase of Poverty Alleviation-Oriented Development]*, pp. 489–504. Beijing: China Finance and Economics Press.
123. The 14 "Concentrated and Contiguous Regions of Extreme Poverty" (*jizhonglian-piantekundiqu*) that cover a total of 680 cities, counties, and banners, was presented by China's State Council as the "toughest battlefield of China's war against poverty." This map of poverty directed central transfers for development projects like irrigation, roads, and tourism. All of these 14 Regions of Extreme Poverty are located in China's northwestern, western, and southwestern interior and mostly in the border regions of mountain ranges. These are also where China's minority population is concentrated. The term "concentrated and contiguous region" emphasizes the overlapping physical and cultural geography of poverty within each region, suggesting a causal connection among nature, ethnicity, and "extreme poverty."
124. Poverty Alleviation and Development Leading Group, National Development and Reform Committee, State Council of PRC. 2012. "Daxing'anling nanlupianqu quyufazhan yufupingongjianguihua, 2011–2020 (Regional Development and Poverty

Alleviation Plan for the Contiguous Region of Daxing'anling Mountains' Southern Foothills)." Within Hinggan League, six contiguous jurisdictions were included in this region, those are: Horqin RF, Horqin Right Center, and Jalaid Banners, as well as Tuquan County, A'ershan City, and Ulanhot Municipality. The document attributed the low level of local residents' non-farming income, at 19% (about half of the national average), to their "weak sense of the market" and "poor education." Low non-farming income has led to low overall income. With an average income per capita that is 34% lower than the national average, 12% of the region's population fell under the national poverty line, defined as 1,274 yuan (approximately US$200) in annual income.

125. In 2020, the IMAR government announced that all 31 officially identified "poor banners and counties" in IMAR have been alleviated from poverty. 2020. "Neimenggu pinkunqixianquanbuzhaimao [All poor banners and counties of IMAR have been alleviated from poverty]." *Xinhuanet.* Published online, April 19. http://www.xinhuanet.com/politics/2020-04/19/c_1125876732.htm. Accessed November 18, 2023.
126. Gao, Tao et al. 2009. "Jinnian (1961–2007) neimenggudiqujiangshuiheqiwende shikongbianhuatezheng [The change in precipitation and temperature in Inner Mongolia in recent years between 1961 and 2007]." *Climatology of Inner Mongolia* 1: 3–8. The authors pointed out that Inner Mongolia had been turning warmer and dryer between 1961 and 2007, especially northeast IM, where average winter temperatures had risen by over 1.83 C° over the last 40 years. East IM also experienced the most radical decline in precipitation over the same period. In the seven years from 2001 to 2007, the annual precipitation in northeast IM dropped by 86.3 mm, and by 60.4 mm in southeast IM.
127. Ren, Junchuan et al. 2019. "Caoyuanshise: sandaojinlingweihenanzhi keyouqianqisikailanken [The Pasture in tatters: What can explain the continued illegal and rampant land clearance despite three reclamation bans]." Xinhua News Agency. Published October 28. http://www.xinhuanet.com/politics/2019-10/28/c_1125159996.htm. Accessed November 16, 2023.
128. Long, Qiao. 2016. "Neimenggu Keerqinyouyiqianqi muminqingyuan sanshirenbeizhua [Thirty pastoralist petitioners of Horqin Right Front Banner arrested]." Radio Free Asia. Published April 29. https://www.rfa.org/mandarin/yataibaodao/shaoshuminzu/ql3-04292016101728.html. Accessed November 16, 2023.
129. For a general review of East IM's environmental and livelihood transformation during the 20th century, see Yoshida, Junichi. 2016b. Translated from Japanese to Chinese by Wulan, "Jinxiandaineimenggudongbudiqu mengurendejingjijiegou' [Economic structure of modern Mongols in East Inner Mongolia]." *Menggushiyanjiu [Studies of Mongolian History].* 0: 36–45.
130. The cultivated area of Jerim League grew from 470,000 to 540,000 mu from the late 1980s to the late 1990s, of which 99.3% occurred in the hilly northern Jerim. Between 1949 and 1995, as cropland in south Jerim was reduced by a third, the cultivation frontline advanced 0.26°W (from 121.97 to 121.71°W), and 0.27°N (from 43.57 to 43.84). In the longer trajectory of the three centuries between the 18th and the 20th centuries, the agricultural frontier in East IM advanced between 250 and 390 km north across almost 5 degrees of latitude, and reached beyond 45°N. Wulantuya. 1999. Ibid. pp. 63–69.
131. Interview with a local researcher, 2017.
132. The population of the banner as a whole grew from 112,000 in 1949 to 250,000 in 1964, to 382,000 in 1982, and 400,000 in 1988. Feng, Xuezhong et al. eds. 1991. Ibid. pp. 208–210.
133. Wulantuya. 1999. Ibid.

INTRODUCTION to Part IV:
SOCIOCULTURAL ASPIRATIONS ACROSS THE GREAT WALL

Part IV turns from the politics of conserving nature to that of conserving culture in China's multiethnic northern frontier. Culture and nature are co-productive and inseparable. For sure, the stories from the previous three parts on conserving nature entail plenty of cultural dynamics as well. The politics of conserving culture and nature are both entangled in the territorial struggles of drawing boundaries over issues like what should and should not be included in the conservation plans and zones. Conserving culture and nature also share the temporal aspiration to integrate the past, present, and future: conservationists in both fields often reference the past to reverse the presumed deterioration of the present with the goal of improving future prospects. But for clarity, I separate the stories about nature and culture into different parts with different analytical lens: Parts I to III on conserving nature concern mainly the territorial struggles to access resources like land and water. Part IV on conserving culture is framed by the territorial processes and contradictions in the production of identities and meanings. In the next two chapters, I examine intangible culture like language and tangible culture like historical monuments in China's multiethnic northern frontier.

In Chapter 9, "Moving Up and Out: Mongol Students in China's College and Job Races," I look at Mongol youths' linguistic and sociocultural strategies when participating in China's nationwide, cutthroat competition for college admission and urban jobs.

Inner Mongolia Autonomous Region (IMAR)'s bilingual education in Mandarin and Mongolian is a key element in China's minority policies. But bilingualism has been shrinking since the 1990s, causing critics' concern over Mongol youths' linguistic sinicization. Based on fieldworks, this chapter follows a Mongol farm girl's navigation of IMAR's bilingual education system and China's competitive college and job races. Her identity is built on the promise of upward social mobility as much as on Mongolian language and culture. As the number of college graduates and youth unemployment in IMAR and China has been skyrocketing since the 2010s, the college race has spilt over into competition for white-collar urban jobs. English proficiency has become a prerequisite in both college and job competitions. The double-fronted and trilingual race has boosted an anxiety economy of a hundred billion-dollar tutoring industry. It also necessitated the state's intervention in managing the frustration of those who lost out in the races. Mongol youths' linguistic sinicization is inseparable from a nationwide cultural milieu of hyper competition for a metropolitan future.

In Chapter 10, "Popularizing the Monument: The Wild Great Walls," I focus on China's recent reinforcement of monumentalizing the Great Wall and examine the tension between the past and future in Great Wall Revivalism today. I explore the territorial dilemma arising from making the monument popular. Commonly perceived as a timeless partition between the pastoral and agrarian civilizations, and politically established as the emblem of China's nationhood in the current moment, the Great Wall is in fact a galaxy of under-defined border fortification remnants scattered across an area comparable to the size of today's Denmark. A diverse array of non-state actors has participated in the state's project of monumentalizing the Great Wall in the new millennium. From the south side of the Wall, Han Chinese popular historian-cum-photographers visualize the concept and nationalize the wall-scapes through image production and reenactment. Entrepreneurial peasants living by the Wall ruins near Beijing run mass Great Wall tourism ventures, which also contributed to the patriotic education campaigns. Peasants of the walled villages in remote northern mountains were recruited by heritage preservation agencies of the local governments to guard the remnants. To the north, the IMAR government mobilizes Mongolian "Heritage Patrol on Camelback" to try to reconcile the contradiction between the historically divisive Great Wall and the contemporary drive towards national unity across the Wall. Different participants create vastly divergent meanings and practices in conserving the Great Wall, and consequently, give life to many "wild great walls." The Great Wall and the many wild walls show the territorial dynamisms generated by the ways in which monumentalizing and popularizing the Great Wall enable and derail one another.

9

Moving Up and Out: Mongol Students in China's College and Job Races

The previous chapter ended on the note about the Bo sisters' urban aspiration. Unlike their parents and grandparents, the sisters and their husbands have envisioned a future beyond farming or herding in rural Inner Mongolia Autonomous Region (IMAR). By the early 2010s, all three sisters had settled in the city, albeit in vastly different types of cities via disparate routes.

Wave, the youngest of the three, completed her college and master's degrees at an A-list national university in a metropolitan center south of IMAR. Upon graduation, she applied to a PhD program in the prestigious Peking University but did not receive admission. So she went on to a PhD program at her alma mater for another four years and graduated in 2020. A few weeks before her 30th birthday, Wave was appointed assistant professor at a reputable university in a large city. As I write, Wave has just moved into a brand new, subsidized faculty housing over which she maintains ownership rights. To cope with the Covid isolation, she recruited a roommate—a pet cat named Lucky. Wave's recently widowed mother plans to spend six months a year at Wave's new apartment in the big city.

Wave's two older sisters, Ocean and River, received college degrees from less prestigious B-list universities and married their high school sweethearts, both of whom were from the pastoral region in Horqin Right Front (Horqin RF) Banner.[1] Since the late 2010s, thanks to their in-laws' financial support, both Ocean and River have been living in newly built, modern apartments with their husbands and young children in

Conserving China's Northwest Frontier. You-tien Hsing, Oxford University Press. © You-tien Hsing (2025).
DOI: 10.1093/9780191903908.003.0010

Dabagou, now renamed Horqin Township. Horqin Township, which had a population of 22,000 in the late 2010s,[2] is the seat of Horqin RF and is adjacent to Ulanhot. Ulanhot, which means "Red City," is the capital of Hinggan League in East IMAR. Ulanhot boasted half-a-million residents in the 2010s, and is a medium-sized city by Chinese standards. Thanks to its proximity to Ulanhot and its own reputation as a "town for Mongols," Horqin Township's property market has been booming since the early 2010s. Ocean, a Chinese language and literature major, took advantage of the boom and became a real estate broker in Horqin Township. Ocean's trilingual proficiency in Putonghua, standard and Horqin Mongolian, plus her extensive social networks through her husband's pastoral family secured her clients from the pastoral areas. Compared to the farming families in Horqing RF, pastoral families are much better-endowed home buyers. The oldest sister, River, majored in husbandry in college, worked as an inspector for a meat processing company, then a private kindergarten teacher in Horqin Township before quitting her job after the birth of her second son.

Among the three sisters, Wave has moved the furthest from home. She found her footing outside of IMAR in a major metropolitan center that was about one hundred times larger in population than her sisters' home base, Horqin Township, which few outsiders have heard of. In the eyes of her family, relatives, former classmates, and fellow villagers, Wave is among the most successful in materializing farming Mongols' urban aspiration.

How did Wave get there?

This chapter traces Wave's academic advancement from a rural primary school to an A-list university in a major metropolitan center. Every step along the way from the mid-1990s to the early 2020s, Wave, a bright and high-achieving Mongolian female student from a poor farming family of an impoverished farming area of East IM, navigated China's institutions of social mobility and China's culture of hyper competitiveness.

Wave leads the first two sections of this chapter. On her K-12 schooling in Section I, I follow Wave's path in the Mongolian language-track schools under China's dual-track minority education system, her placement in a high-ranking high school and in the "Pinnacle Class" at the school, and her trilingual schooling in Han Chinese, Mongolian, and English. The school tracks, ranks, and languages have shaped Wave's identification, gearing her up towards the race in China's national college entrance exam, or *gaokao* in Chinese.

In Section II, I detail Wave's gaokao exam and her nerve-racking experience with the college admissions rush. Although gaokao is a "nationally unified" exam, the college admissions process is localized, creating an even more intense and decisive contest than gaokao. But the admissions rush is rarely covered in the literature on China's gaokao and minority education. The school tracks, class ranks, languages, and the college race are critical links to the ways Wave, and other aspiring Mongolian students of IMAR, position themselves for social mobility through China's education system today.

Wave's navigation of the bilingual education system is a story about Mongols *of* China, rather than a static state of Mongols *in* China. While the latter assumes minority's innate and timeless cultural distinctions, the former concerns the fluid ethnic boundaries and dynamic interethnic relations. While few ethnic minorities in China today can be said to have dodged sinicization, it is important to note that the processes and results of sinicization vary greatly across different minority nationalities in different places. Seeing Mongols as being *of* China, not just *in* China, helps us see such variations. In IMAR, this process can be called sinicization with Mongolian characteristics.

Furthermore, Wave's navigation and success also reveal the heterogeneity among the officially-defined ethnic Mongols in term of class, gender, and place of origin. To unpack such internal variations, I use Brubaker and Copper's (2000)[3] relational concept of *identification* instead of the essentialist concept of identity. And I focus on Mongol students' schooling strategies to tell the stories about identification politics in present-day IM.

Branching out from identity to identification via the lens of schooling helps broaden the temporality of ethnic relationships. While identity as an analytical tool often engages politics of the past, identification through the lens of schooling brings in the question of future aspirations, prospects, and expectations of Mongol students and their families of varied class and geographical origins. Lodged in such future-oriented dynamics, Mongol students' identification politics concern not just who they were and who they are, but who and where they *will be*.

Section III takes Mongol students' aspirations further to their job race after college, especially the students who are less successful than Wave. I look at the tensions generated from these college graduates' unfilled expectations, the state's attempts to absorb the educated youths and manage their frustrations, and the private investors' attempts to profit from their anxiety. Here I introduce Art, another Mongol female student who also grew up in Horqin RF Banner like Wave. Art belongs to a group that I term the "local top 17%." They are not in the top 3% of IMAR's gaokao-takers like Wave who are admitted to the national A-list universities. Rather, they are the 30,000 plus close seconds who account for the next 17% of IMAR's gaokao takers admitted to top provincial universities within IMAR. Unlike the top 3% of students who seek futures in the nation's metropolitan centers outside of IMAR, most of the local top 17% will fill the ranks of IMAR's local governments and schools. IMAR's local top 17%, in other words, are future local elites. Whether and how their expectations to land a white-collar job in urban centers within IMAR are fulfilled have even more significant geopolitical implications than what is usually recognized in the literature on China's higher education.

In his study of East Asia's histories of meritocracy, Alexander Woodside (2006)[4] argued that while educated elites could assist their rulers, their failures to enter the ranks of the ruling class could make them feel politically deprived and alienated. Under the right conditions, frustrated local elites would mobilize and rebel, as history has repeatedly shown. In China today, that "right condition" is far from being at the point of transpiring. However, preventing the educated class from deviating from state interests underlies the Chinese government's agenda of expectation and frustration management. China has continued to expand its higher education since the 1990s. By 2021, the number of China's college graduates grew from 2 million in the 1980s to over 10 million a year. The post-financial crisis era also saw China's economy having started to slow down and the job market tightening for college graduates. To absorb the exploding number of college graduates in a slowing economy, the national government has tried to expand graduate school enrollment and public sector employment. IMAR has shared the nation's dilemma of higher education expansion not matching the growth of urban white-collar jobs. IMAR's college graduates (and their heavily vested, and often indebted, families), especially the top 17%, have acutely faced the ever-widening gap between their expectations and job market retrenchment. The policy solution of expanding graduate school enrollment and public sector employment, designed to temper the gap, has only created new contractions in China and IMAR.

Meanwhile, the intensifying competition and widespread anxiety to secure an urban, white-collar future has fueled a test-prep tutoring industry in China with a market size estimated at between US$180 to 300 billion at its peak in the late 2010s.[5] Following the stories about IMAR's top 17% and the state's various attempts to absorb the local elites, I conclude this chapter with stories about China's tutoring industry and anxiety economy which are driven by the nationwide college and job races. As a minority *of* China, IMAR's students and their parents, job seekers, and small entrepreneurs are deeply entrenched in the nation's anxiety economy and socio-culture milieu of hyper competition.

I Multilingual Identification

Wave's navigation during her pre-gaokao years can be examined along three nexuses. The first nexus concerns Wave's choice in IMAR's dual-track schooling system defined by Mongolian and Chinese language as the primary medium of instruction. Wave followed the Mongolian track. Once the choice was made, the dual-track system creates path dependency and is almost irreversible. The second nexus is Wave's placement in the top class of a high-ranking Mongolian-track high school. School and class rankings, corresponding with urban and territorial hierarchy, decidedly differentiates Mongol students of disparate socioeconomic and spatial backgrounds. The third nexus concerns Mongols' multiple modes of multilingualism around English, Chinese, Mongolian, and different dialects at school, at home, and on the street. It turns out, different types of Mongols practice different types of multilingualism across space and time in East IMAR.

For Mongol students like Wave, the dual-track schooling system, the flagship of China's ethnicity policy, builds the foundation of her multilayered identification.

I.1 You Are Your Track

Wave started first grade in 1998 in her home village, Fresh Springs in Horqin RF of East IMAR. (See Chapter 8 for the ethnoterritorial and environmental histories of

Fresh Springs). Her school was a Mongolian-track school, in which Mongolian was the primary language of instruction for all subjects except for Chinese lessons, which, at the time, would begin in third grade.[6]

China's bilingual education system for minority nationalities is an integral part of its multinational statehood. It also entails a unidirectional obligation for minority students to learn Putonghua Chinese, the dominant and official language of China. This one-way bilingualism is intended to bring minorities into the orbit of Putonghua, but not the other way around. Under a dual-track system based on different languages of instruction, Han Chinese students in autonomous regions and minority students who choose to attend Chinese-track schools need not learn the local minority language.

On the other hand, this one-way bilingualism is seen by state leaders as a privilege granted to ethnic minorities, as it allows them to preserve their own linguistic identities. Yet, as presented in Chapter 5, the Chinese Communist Party (CCP) state has not treated all minority nationalities equally. Only the largest and geopolitically important nationalities like Tibetans, Uyghurs, and Mongols, and a few others, are granted the choice between Chinese schools and local ethnicity schools. Among these strategically important minority nationalities, the treatment is uneven. Dual-track education in Tibet Autonomous Region (TAR), for example, is much less accommodating than that in IMAR. Between 1988 and 1998, most Tibetan-track primary schools in rural TAR used Tibetan as the primary language of instruction. Since 1998, most of these Tibetan-track primary schools have shifted to Chinese language instruction. For those that still offer bilingual curricula, Chinese language classes would start from the first grade, not from the third grade, as it had in IMAR since the early 2000s. More importantly, dual-track secondary schooling was much less available in TAR. Since the 1980s, only a few middle schools and high schools in TAR have used Tibetan as the medium of instruction for all subjects. By the early 2000s, no less than 75 percent of the Tibetan-track primary school graduates had to face the choice between spending one more year in a preparatory class to retool themselves in Chinese before entering a Chinese middle school, or just quit formal schooling. The disconnect between primary and secondary schooling in the Tibetan-track deterred Tibetan parents from sending their children to Tibetan primary schools if they could afford it.[7] In addition, under a Tibetan- and Uyghur-targeted policy, the highest-achieving Tibetan and Uyghur students are sent to special Tibetan and Uyghur middle and high school in cities outside of TAR and Xinjiang Uyghur Autonomous Region (XUAR), with an all-Chinese curriculum, except for a few hours of Tibetan or Uyghur language instruction per week. For rural Tibetan and Uyghur students, these fully subsidized schools in cities far from home represent their best chance of getting into an A-list University in China. To get into these highly competitive schools, a superior command of Chinese language is a prerequisite; it also makes another argument for parents to start their children's Chinese schooling as early as possible.

In comparison and until the late 2000s, Mongolian-track schools in IMAR—albeit with declining enrollment and a shrinking numbers of schools since the 1980s[8]—were much more comprehensive. Mongolian-track schools allowed for the consistent use of Mongolian textbooks and Mongolian language instruction in primary and secondary Mongolian-track schools, as well as for certain majors in IMAR-based universities. At the same time, there were no special middle schools or high schools designated for Mongol students outside of IMAR. However, the national drive to align Chinese citizenship with a singular national identity and to promote the unifying label of a *zhonghua minzu* ("Chinese nation" or "Chinese people") started to intensify in the late 2000s,[9] and the comparatively more accommodating approach to Mongolian-speaking students started to shift gradually to that of assimilation.

The policy shift from accommodation to assimilation culminated in 2020, when the IMAR government announced the switch from Mongolian language to Chinese language textbooks and instruction for politics, history, and Chinese classes in all Mongolian-track primary and middle schools. In addition, Mongolian-speaking students were to start Chinese lessons in the first grade, as opposed to the second or third grade. The new policy provoked a round of scholarly debates, school dropouts, social protests, and detention.[10] The debates and discontent focused on the dominance of Putonghua and the consequential decline of Mongolian cultural-linguistic autonomy. The issue of "cultural genocide" implied by the policy shift has captured much of the western media's attention. To assess the impact of this critical policy shift in 2020, it would help to first look at the actual practices in bilingual education on the ground that began long before the widely publicized shift in bilingual policy in 2020.

China's rural education has gone through significant changes over the past half a century. Prior to the mid-1980s, China's national education policy mandated local governments to build primary schools in every village, with the maximum distance between the school and the settlement it served being 2.5 km. Rural villages were expected to meet this policy mandate despite limited provincial financial support. As a result, in Fresh Springs, Wave's home village at the rural periphery where Mongols were in the majority, the one and only village school was a Mongolian-track school staffed by Mongolian-speaking teachers. For most families in Fresh Springs, it was not a matter of choosing between two linguistic tracks, but the lack of a choice. There were Chinese-track primary schools in some large and ethnically mixed villages and towns (see Chapter 8), but that option required extra expenses—tuition, dorm fees, meal plans, and transportation—that few families in Fresh Springs could afford.

The physical condition and pedagogical quality in these mostly village-funded schools left much to be desired. Wave recalled the crumbling mud-brick walls of her school building and the freezing classrooms for the 40 to 50 students. Few teachers, especially the effective and qualified ones, stayed for long. Teachers who left the school were often replaced by village residents with poor qualifications. As most teachers were locals, some teachers had their own children in the school and even in their own classrooms. And, according to Wave, nepotism was common. One teacher regularly made his students help with farm chores, like shucking corn and sunflower seeds during school hours. This teacher also made his students pay extra fees for English tutoring at his home, offered by his middle school daughter who was just three years older than the students. Another teacher was remembered for her ill temper and cruel punishment towards students, even crippling a boy as a result of a particularly harsh beating with a sharp-edged table leg.

When Wave was in the second grade, a charity group called Kind Heart from Shenzhen—a prosperous southern city that has grown from a fishing village to a metropolitan center thanks to its special economic zone established in the 1980s—donated funds to build six new classrooms. The school was subsequently renamed Kind Heart Primary School. During the two years-long construction of the new school, classes were held in villagers' yards and barns scattered across different parts of the village. The new school was completed in 2002 when Wave was in the fourth grade. But the future of the school did not brighten. In 2006 Kind Heart Primary School was closed down for good.[11]

Why was Kind Heart Primary School closed down only four years after its new classrooms were completed? It turns out that Kind Heart Primary School was one of the 370,000 primary schools (over 70% of the national total) in China that were closed down between 1997 and 2010 under a national policy of school consolidation, which entailed school closures and mergers. Though the Ministry of Education has cited declining birthrates as the rationale behind the massive school closures, the actual decline of enrollment in primary schools over the same period was only about 25%. More importantly, 81% of all the closed schools, or 300,000 in total number, were in poor rural areas.[12]

There is another puzzle: why was the school consolidation policy carried out at such a colossal scale and with such speed and efficiency, despite numerous parents' protests? What mobilized the local officials to implement such an unpopular policy?[13]

One of the key answers lies in land-based local finances. The closure of village schools compelled families to send their children to schools in town centers and county seats. It also forced many families to rent (or purchase if they could afford it, like Jin Three of Minqin in Chapter 4) housing in towns to stay with their young schoolers. The consolidation policy fueled a construction boom of new classrooms and dormitories of the expanded schools in county seats that were now accommodating thousands of students each. School consolidation also drove real estate development around the schools in county seats. As You-tien Hsing (2010)[14] has illustrated, property-led urban expansion in rural county seats has been the key to local finances and local state-building. After the initial post-reform experiment with fiscal decentralization that left central coffers with only 20% of the nation's total revenue, the CCP state recentralized its revenue sharing scheme in 1994, and the central government now took over 55% of the national revenue. Local revenue bases were also radically weakened. In 2004, agricultural tax, the lifeline of local revenue in rural areas, was abolished. Meanwhile, the central government delegated more responsibilities, including social welfare programs, schools, and infrastructure investment, to local governments. To resolve this fiscal conundrum, deeply indebted local governments resorted to land sales and real estate development. To boost property value, they needed to create urban centers first. To create urban centers, they tried to draw villagers into town and convert farmland for residential and commercial projects.

Rural school closures, along with other more forceful programs like ecological relocation and poverty alleviation relocation (see Introduction and Chapters 1, 2, 4, and 8), were widely adopted across China for local officials to induce population concentration, create urban centers, and build property-based local finances. Together these programs have fueled China's highly decentralized urban explosion far beyond Beijing and Shanghai since the 1990s. Not all urban expansion projects are successful, for sure. But local government leaders' attempts at various levels to adopt this formula have spread wide and lingered long. More importantly, successful or not, such attempts have created long-lasting social and territorial impacts on rural education.

For villagers in Fresh Springs, as schools were consolidated and parents needed to send young children to schools in town centers and county seats, it was getting increasingly expensive to be poor.[15]

In considering her experience at Kind Heart Primary School, Wave felt she was lucky on two counts. First, despite a high turnover rate of teachers (who were often underqualified to begin with, as mentioned earlier), Wave's first and fourth grade teachers were devoted and qualified teachers who had built a solid foundation for her academic advancement. Second, Kind Heart Primary School was shut down only after she graduated, so Wave was able to complete her primary school education in her home village.

For middle school, Wave had to leave home. In 2003, 12-year-old Wave started middle school in a township some 30 km away from Fresh Springs, close to where her mother, Orchid's, maiden family lived.

Away from home, Wave stayed in the poorly maintained school dorms. The students' daily routine included collecting fuelwood to heat the dorms for the long winter's long nights. Wave often woke up freezing in the middle of the night, as the fires died down much too quickly. During the coldest months, students were sent home to lower school energy bills. What's more, after paying the dorm fees, Wave's parents had little cash left for her meal plan. Wave had two meals a day, starting with a bag of instant noodles for breakfast. For dinner, she walked 30 minutes to the village where her uncles lived and rotated among her four uncles' kitchens. This system did not always work out for Wave. Her uncles were themselves struggling to feed their own children, and some were less than generous toward a growing teenager like Wave who appeared to have a bottomless appetite. Wave recalled her frustration with a particularly parsimonious aunt who would lock her front door as if no one were home whenever she knew Wave would be coming for dinner. That year, Wave recalled, she was "thinking about food all day long."

Wave's middle school offered both Mongolian and Chinese-track classes. Wave and her parents made the strategic decision to stick to the Mongolian-track to be eligible for a partial tuition waiver. Of equal importance, Wave had followed the Mongolian curriculum for core subjects, like math and history, since primary school, and the low-quality Chinese-language lessons at Kind Heart Primary School did not prepare her for the middle school level Chinese curriculum. Switching to the Chinese-track could hurt her grades and disqualify her from the scholarship. At this point, sticking with the Mongolian-track schooling had become a path-dependent decision for Wave and her parents. It was also a road of no return, which I will elaborate upon later.

In 2004, right before the beginning of her second year of middle school, Wave's parents lost their goats and their hope in village life, as presented in Chapter 8. With the help of Orchid's caring sister, Ling, and Ling's Han-Chinese husband Wen, Orchid and Victory moved to Ulanhot, the capital city of Hinggan League. The couple first worked in a small dairy farm in Ulanhada, a *sumu* across the Tao'er River from the urban core of Ulanhot (see Figure 8.2). Like most Chinese cities in the 1990s, Ulanhot started out with a small urban core surrounded by large rural hinterlands under the municipal jurisdiction. These hinterlands, although incorporated into the municipality, remained mostly rural in terms of population density, infrastructure, service availability, and nonfarm activities.

The dairy farm that Orchid and Victor worked for belonged to a colleague of Wen's. Wen was then the vice director of the tax bureau of Ulanhot. Wen's colleague from the tax bureau, like many local officials with access to land and a stable and higher income compared with most rural folks, owned a small enterprise: a small dairy farm on the rural fringes of Ulanhot. Through Wen's introduction, the tax bureau official hired Orchid and Victory to feed, clean, and milk his 30 dairy cows. The job paid 500 yuan a month, close to what the couple would make in a good year back in the village. What was attractive about the job was that it offered a stable source of cash income all year round, and it also came with a brick-walled home for the family. Their new home was a part of the farm facility and sat between the cows' shelter and hay storage. The space was furnished with a traditional firewood-heated bed (*kang*), a must for the long and freezing winters of the northeast. The condition of the new home was better than that of their mud-brick house in Fresh Springs Village, where the windows were covered with plastic sheets. Most of all, the job made it possible for Wave to attend an urban school.

As the Bo family settled in the fringes of Ulanhot, Wave's aunt, Ling, took her to visit the vice principal of Red City Middle, the best middle school in Ulanhot. The school housed two Mongolian-track and seven Chinese-track classes, with 30 to 40 students each. The majority in the Mongolian-track classes, like Wave, were Mongols.[16] In the Chinese-track classes, 60% to 70% of the students were Han Chinese, while the rest were Mongols and other minority nationalities.

The principal of Red City Middle was Han Chinese, while the Mongolian-track was managed by the vice principal, who was Mongol. The vice principal admitted Wave and promised to waive her tuition if she maintained a top-ten standing in class.

For the 13-year-old Wave, the best part of moving to the city was that her parents' income was stable enough to pay for her meal plan at school. With a full stomach, Wave excelled in her Mongolian-track class at Red City Middle and continued to earn the tuition waiver. In comparison, many of Wave's classmates from Kind Heart Primary School did not advance to middle school. In addition, an overwhelming majority of students from Red City Middle either dropped out within their first two years or did not advance to high school after graduation.[17]

As Wave soldiered on at Red City Middle, Orchid and Victory cycled through various jobs in the city. After their first stint at the dairy farm, they worked in an ice cream factory that required working long hours in subzero temperatures, but their joint salary doubled. After that, Orchid clerked a china shop, a grocery store, and then a confectionery specializing in wedding parties. Victory found a job as a night guard in a township government's branch office in Ulanhot. But he spent his days drinking, much to Orchid's dismay. So Victory kept looking until he landed a job drilling core samples for a geological prospecting team. The job paid well: 1,100 yuan a month. At the end of his first year, Victory received a bonus of 10,000 yuan. Ever the education-minded father, Victory used the money to buy Wave her first personal computer.

At Red City Middle, Wave's adherence to the Mongolian track evolved further from a course of path dependency to an irreversible institution. That institution was the high school entrance exam. As an extension of dual-track schooling for Mongol students, the high school entrance exam in IMAR was divided into two strands: one was called *minkaomin* (MKM from here on), referring to the entrance exam written in Mongolian, except for the subject of Chinese language. The other was *minkaohan* (MKH), referring to Chinese-language entrance exam for Mongol students. Mongol students from the Mongolian-track class would take the MKM exam, while Mongol students from the Chinese-track class would take the MKH exam.

The duality of MKM and MKH and the internal differentiation among Mongol students produce one another, and together they shape the process of students' identification. In IMAR, most of the MKM students grew up in Mongol-majority farming and agropastoral villages in East IM or from areas that remained predominantly pastoral in western or central-northern IMAR. While students from farming regions tended to be proficiently bilingual in Mongolian and Mandarin Chinese, like Wave, students from pastoral areas generally had a limited grasp of Mandarin. The MKH students, on the other hand, were ethnic Mongol students who grew up in Han Chinese majority areas and spoke little Mongolian. Some were from areas with a long history of farming (see Chapter 8); others were from families with intermarriage between Mongol and Han Chinese, with local official and school teacher parents, and/or with an urban upbringing.

The distinction between the two trajectories of high school exams persisted into the college entrance exam. To keep up in the college race, it was almost impossible to switch tracks between high school and college entrance exams. As a result, MKM and MKH have become the fundamental identification markers of two types of Mongol students.

Identification markers are about how people see themselves and how they see each other. MKM students were generally considered by MKH students to be less competitive academically and in future prospects. Meanwhile, in the eyes of MKM students, MKH students were irrevocably sinicized Mongolians whose futures were outside of IMAR, and were "fakes" and "sellouts."

In a school that had both MKM and MKH students, such relational identifications drew a boundary between the two groups and regularly fueled fistfights. The MKM group was often led by a male student from the pastoral areas. Dalai, Wave's brother-in-law, for example, was the informal leader of MKM students at his high school in Horqin RF Banner. In Horqin RF, a Chinese-track high school (where Han Chinese and MKH students attend) and a Mongolian-track high school (for MKM students) neighbored one another. The two schools shared student dormitory bathrooms and dining halls, and student fights flared up on almost a daily basis. Fights would break out between Han Chinese and Mongol students, between MKM and MKH students (both are Mongol), or between Han Chinese and MKH students from the Chinese-track school on one side and MKM students on the other. Dalai suspected that the fights were one primary reason for the eventual relocation of the Mongolian-track school to a new campus on the opposite side of the Banner seat, far from the Chinese-track school.

The MKM and MKH tracks institutionalize Mongol students' identification. However, such identification, decisive and divisive as it was, was far from the only nexus of Mongol students' identification politics. Within each of the MKM and MKH tracks, distinctions became more nuanced and even more consequential to the students' future prospects. What mattered just as much, if not more than the MKM and MKH dichotomy, was the ranking of school and class within each of the two tracks.

I.2 You Are Your Rank

In the summer of 2006, Wave took the high school entrance exam and was admitted to Solidarity High in Ulanhot.[18] Her outstanding test scores qualified her for a three-year tuition waiver. More importantly, Solidarity High ranked top among Mongolian-track high schools in Hinggan League. On a larger territorial scale, Wave told me, Solidarity High ranked second out of the 18 Mongolian-track high schools in the region of East IM, and third out of 39 Mongolian-track high schools across the entire IMAR.[19]

School rankings project students' futures. During the toilsome gaokao race, students' future possibilities are assessed at every step, starting from middle school or even primary school. Each student's test score-based performance is duly ranked and reflected in their class and school placements. While the dual-track system of Mongolian and Chinese schools funnels Mongol students into two schooling tracks, school rankings within each track and class rankings within each school make for a more precise sorting mechanism that projects the students' academic and career futures. School and class rankings create the second nexus of Mongol students' identification.

Allow me to start with school ranking.

Synchronized Territorial and School Ranking

In IMAR, like the rest of China, the ranking of high schools, be they in the MKM or MKH track, is determined mainly by the track record of their graduates in college admissions. A similar logic applies to primary and middle schools—their rankings are determined by their ability to send students to high-ranking schools at the next academic level.

Where are the high-ranking schools located, and how do they earn and maintain their high ranks?

Like schools elsewhere, high schools in China compete with one another to attract top students using fellowships and tuition waivers. Money matters for schools, for it allows them to lure the most competitive runners in the college race. Power matters even more. Most high-ranking schools, especially those in poor regions, are public schools,[20] and are an integral part of the state bureaucracy, subject to jurisdictional order and defined by the ranking of their supervising government. The jurisdictional ranking of the school determines the school's access to budgetary resources and, therefore, local reputation. For example, provincial-level high schools are generally better funded, hence more desirable than prefecture-level high schools, which in turn are held in higher regard than county- or banner-level high schools.[21]

The performance of public schools and that of their supervising government are tightly connected. The college admissions results of high schools under the jurisdiction of any given local government are important criteria in local government leaders' performance evaluations. Financially, high performing schools also decisively impact property values in the city, especially in the districts where the schools are located. School performance, in other words, is directly linked to local leaders' career prospects and real estate-based local finances, as mentioned in the previous section. To ensure schools' high performance, local governments routinely intervene in the school admission process to recruit high performing students. Provincial-level governments would assert their supervisory authority to bring the top students from municipal- or county-level jurisdictions to provincial-level under their direct charge. The same logic applies to sub-provincial levels in the local government hierarchy. The result of this territorially filtered and local government-led cherry picking is a synchronization between school ranking and territorial ranking.

The synchronized territorial and school rankings can be found across IMAR. IMAR's top high schools, administrated by the regional government and located in the capital city of Hohhot, get to pick the very top scorers on the high school entrance exam from across the entire IMAR, leaving the second-highest scorers to the top league- and municipality-level high schools. The "picking" order moves further down, where the third-best batch are left for top high schools at the banner and county levels. The case of one student from Horqin RF Banner in 2015, according to a school teacher I talked to in 2017, helps illustrate how the synchronized mechanism of pairing top performing students and top ranking schools lead to their co-production at different jurisdictional levels. Ting, a high performing student from a middle school in Horqin RF had planned to attend the high school of Hinggan League, which was her testing jurisdiction and her home league. Ting did exceptionally well on the exam, which placed her on the top-12 list of all exam takers in the entire IMAR that year. As a result, the top IMAR-level high school in Hohhot, the capital city of IMAR admitted her, bypassing the Hinggan League level school.

This unexpected turn of events was welcomed by Ting and her parents. It is impossible to say no to such an opportunity, as admission came with a substantial scholarship. For 15-year-old Ting, attending the top high school in IMAR's capital city Hohhot meant living 1,200 km away from home. But it was also a giant step closer to gaining a spot at a national-level elite university in a metropolitan center outside of IMAR. IMAR-level schools in Hohhot, especially the top high-ranking ones, receive far better government funding than league-level schools that she had been prepared to attend. The resources and locational advantages of schools in Hohhot also attract the best teachers. Many parents believe that even second or third-ranking schools in IMAR's capital Hohhot are still better than the top schools at the league or municipal level. Furthermore, parents also believe in a benign circle, that is, the top schools in high-level jurisdictions are able to draw exceptionally competitive students, which brings much-needed challenge for otherwise easily distracted teenagers. With sufficient financial resources, top schools adopt a "military-like" or "enclosed" (*fengbishi*) disciplinary style that involves housing all students in dormitories on campus and in-house afterschool tutoring so as to keep students away from the internet cafes that often mushroom right outside the campuses.

The synchronized rankings of schools and jurisdictions roll into a mutually reinforcing territorial order. The aforementioned policy of abolishing rural schools and expanding urban schools since the late 1990s also contribute to this synchronized territorial order. While rural parents struggle to send their children to higher-ranking urban schools in the higher-ranking cities, property values in these cities, especially in the areas around the most prestigious schools, continue to rise, while the real estate market in small-sized, lower-ranking cities have stagnated.[22] The increasing concentration of education resources in the high-ranking cities, in turn, institutionalizes a rural-to-urban, small town-to-large city, and periphery-to-center brain drain. The aspirations of those in the periphery, consequently, are spatialized: the more competitive a student is, the further away from home they should attend school and seek employment. These aspirations are also temporalized: to get a head start and move as far away as possible from the periphery, the student should leave home as early as possible. By the 2010s, IMAR parents with means would send their primary school- or even kindergarten-aged children to large cities, bypassing schools in small rural townships and low-ranking cities that were much closer to their village homes. The wave of village primary school closures in the 1990s and 2000s was followed by dwindling enrollment in many middle and high schools in lower-ranking, small cities and rural townships, sending these schools on a downward spiral.[23]

Within each of the ranked schools, class rankings mattered even more.

Class Rank as Social Status

At Solidarity High, Wave was placed in a "*Pinnacle*" class (*jianziban*) based on her high school entrance exam scores and the results on her placement test. The Pinnacle class had two parallel tracks: one was for science track students (named "the No. 1

Class" in school), while the other was for humanity track students ("the No. 2 Class"), with 30 students each. Female students accounted for half in the science track and 87% (26) in the humanity class. The rest of her cohort was placed in seven classes referred to as "Ordinary" (*putongban*).[24]

Between the Pinnacle and the Ordinary classes, there is a third placement that I call the "Probation" class, officially named "the No. 3 Class." The No. 3 Class students' high school entrance exam scores are those that do not meet the Pinnacle class cutoff by a few points but still stand above the Ordinary class students. They are considered the most promising among the Ordinary. The top three students in the No. 3 class are given the chance to be promoted to the Pinnacle class. Placed in this probational category, the hopeful students compete furiously with one another to prove and improve themselves to gain one of the three spots in the Pinnacle class.

During Wave's time at Solidarity High, the distinction between Pinnacle and Ordinary class students was reinforced further by their social and physical segregation on campus.

The Pinnacle students' classrooms, dorms, and dining halls were housed in an exclusive building separate from the Ordinary students. Pinnacle class students were exempt from participating in schoolwide sporting events. Wave's Pinnacle homeroom teacher went even further, discouraging his students from socializing with Ordinary class students. He worried that the Ordinary students were "low-achieving" and "less virtuous", and could lead the Pinnacle students astray. If a Pinnacle class student and an Ordinary class student ever got into a fight in school, Wave recalled, it was almost always the Ordinary student who got the blame. Romance was strictly forbidden in the Pinnacle class for its perceived threat of distraction. But sparks are part of growing up for the 15- to 17-year-old boys and girls who spend all their time with one another on an enclosed campus. During Wave's second year at Solidarity High, a boy from the Probation class was promoted to Wave's Pinnacle class. The Pinnacle class teacher often reminded him, in front of other Pinnacle students, of his inferior origin from the Probation class. When the teacher found out that a girl in the Pinnacle class had fallen in love with the boy, the teacher threatened to send the boy back down to the Ordinary class if they did not break up. To the teacher's surprise, the boy and the girl decided to transfer down together to the Ordinary class, where no one seemed to be bothered by their relationship.

While the young couple made a splash on campus that year, it is important to note that the two met only after the boy was moved to the girl's Pinnacle class in an extremely segregated campus. Wave told me that in her three years at Solidarity High, she did not make any friends from outside of the Pinnacle class. The institutional, physical, and social segregation turned class placements at school into social status, sharpening the distinctions among Mongol students at the Mongolian-track school.[25]

I.3 You Are Your Speech

Access to English language training draws another dividing line between Pinnacle and Ordinary class Mongol students in MKM track schools like Solidarity High.

Since the early 2010s, as part of China's globalization aspirations, the Ministry of Education has elevated the role of English education for all citizens. English is now part of the core curriculum from primary school to university across the country. English language training and test preparation has boomed (see Section III of this chapter) and English test scores alone can make or break school admissions and employment opportunities.

The elevation of English means the emergence of two types of multilingualism in IMAR's two schooling tracks. Mongol students in the MKH track, which accounted for no less than 70% of all Mongol K-12 students in IMAR in the 2010s,[26] receive a bilingual education and take tests in Chinese and English, like all Han Chinese students, regardless of their class placement. The MKM students, on the other hand, are schooled and tested in three languages (English, Chinese, and Mongolian). In other words, among Mongol students, the MKH students are bilingually trained in Chinese and English, while the MKM students are schooled and tested in three languages. In this section, I focus on MKM students' trilingual schooling and show how such trilingual programs serve to funnel IMAR's Mongol students further into disparate futures.

While all MKM students take classes in three languages, the Pinnacle and Ordinary class students are differentiated by the weight that English carries in their regular curricula. English has a dominant presence in the Pinnacle class while it is marginal in the Ordinary class. Such a distinction is largely shaped by the gaokao grading scheme.

For a humanities-track Pinnacle student in the MKM track like Wave, English has become the most decisive subject in the gaokao race. Wave's gaokao scores were calculated in three segments. The first segment on mathematics accounts for 150 points out of the total of 750; the second segment on humanity subjects accounts for another 300 points that are evenly divided among history, geography, and politics. The remaining 300 points are allocated to three languages: Mongolian, Chinese, and English. For each language test, the full score is 150 points, but only the English test is fully counted at 100%, whereas Mongolian and Chinese are counted at 50% each. The final score of the language segment follows this formula: (1 x English test score) + (0.5 x Chinese test score) + (0.5 x Mongolian test score). In other words, every point Wave earned on her English test carried twice the weight of her Mongolian and Chinese test scores. Because of the weight given to English, and because English is the most challenging subject for most Mongol students, English becomes the decisive subject in the gaokao race for Pinnacle humanities-track students.

Humanities-track students in the Ordinary MKM classes are graded according to the same scheme for mathematics and humanities. The difference lies in the language segment. Up until 2009, out of the total of 300 points allocated to the three languages, Mongolian was fully weighted at 100%. Chinese was weighted at 70%, and English at 30%. In this scheme, the final score of the language segment was calculated with the following formula: (1 x Mongolian test scores) + (0.7 x Chinese test scores) + (0.3 x English test scores). Since 2009, under the shifting ethnicity policy from accommodation towards assimilation, the formula has changed so that Chinese test scores are weighted at 100%, while Mongolian test scores have been lowered to 70%. The new grading scheme for the language segment for humanities-track Ordinary class students is thus: (1 x Chinese test scores) + (0.7 x Mongolian test scores) + (0.3 x English test scores).

Under the CCP state's push for a unified Chinese nationality, the Chinese-language test score weighed more heavily than the Mongolian language test score even for MKM students. What remains unchanged is the light weight of English in Ordinary class students' total gaokao scores. This formula stands in complete contrast to the Pinnacle students' test, in which English test scores are fully counted.

The two gaokao weighing schemes for Pinnacle and Ordinary students in the MKM track are seamlessly converted into two disparate curricula in Solidarity High. In the Pinnacle class, out of a total of 40 regular class hours per week, 10 are scheduled for English, 10 for math, five for Mongolian, and five for Chinese. The remaining 10 hours are divided evenly among history, geography and politics.

In addition to the regular class hours, Pinnacle class students spend another 30 to 35 hours a week with their English teacher during tutoring sessions. On a typical weekday, students get up at 5 a.m. and start the day with running and breakfast, followed by a morning tutoring session from 6 a.m.—8 a.m. The regular classes run from 8:30 a.m. to 5 p.m., with a 30-minute lunch break. Students return to their classroom again from 7 p.m.—10 p.m. for the evening tutoring session. In total, Pinnacle class students spent 13 hours a day in the classroom, half of which would be devoted to English lessons. And that is just on weekdays. Over the weekend, Pinnacle students often stay on campus for additional English tutoring sessions for another 5 to 10 hours. For Ordinary class students, due to the heavier weight of Chinese and Mongolian test scores in their gaokao grading scheme, much less class time is allocated to English, and they receive little English tutoring.

In addition to class time allocation, the way English was taught also differed.

The Pinnacle class's English teachers are often ethnic Han Chinese and are considered by students to be more qualified and effective than their Mongol counterparts who teach English to the Ordinary class. Beyond stereotyping, such perceptions have an institutional root. In Mongolian-track schools, the medium of instruction for English lessons is Chinese, not Mongolian. English textbooks and tests are written in Chinese, and classroom communication is conducted in Putonghua Chinese and English. In the triangular relationship among Putonghua Chinese, English and Mongolian, the link between English and Mongolian is missing. Mongolian-track students needed to be proficient in Chinese reading and Putonghua listening and speaking to learn English effectively and do well on English tests. Ethnic Mongolian English teachers also needed to be proficient in both Chinese Putonghua and English, a qualification hard to come by among the teachers with Mongolian-track school backgrounds and inadequate English training themselves. As a result, the few effective English teachers are those who were schooled in the Chinese-track, with bilingual instruction in Chinese and English. Such teachers, a precious resource in the peripheral Hinggan League of IMAR, are invariably reserved for the most promising Pinnacle class students. At the other end of the divide, Ordinary class English teachers were mostly ethnic Mongolian teachers who went through the Mongolian-track schools themselves for their English lessons and were generally considered ineffective.

During Wave's final year in Solidarity High, parents of Ordinary class students protested the discriminatory labeling of "Pinnacle" and "Ordinary." The Pinnacle class was subsequently rebranded to "Trilingual" class. But this supposedly neutral naming was just as telling. While both Pinnacle class and Ordinary class students in a Mongolian-track school had trilingual lessons, only students in the prestigious Pinnacle class had the access to solid English training. An Ordinary class graduate told me that the minimal English training she received could hardly qualify her education as a truly "trilingual" one.

The Mongolian language lessons were a mirror case of the English lessons, also shaped by gaokao. Pinnacle class students have Mongolian lessons for only five hours a week, with easier textbooks. Because their future is expected to sit outside of IMAR, most Pinnacle class students in the Mongolian-track school feel that they have little use for the Mongolian language. The Ordinary class students, on the other hand, received more serious Mongolian training because Mongolian language test scores weigh more heavily in their gaokao. Further, the Ordinary class students are more likely to stay in IMAR and use Mongolian for their future careers. Consequently, while both groups of students' Chinese proficiency are consistent with their overall academic performance, Ordinary class students generally have superior Mongolian language proficiency and Pinnacle class students perform much better on English tests.

The divergent language curricula and access to English language training between Pinnacle class and Ordinary class students further entrench the divide between the two classes. Once a student settles in one curriculum, it is nearly impossible to switch to the other. Pinnacle class students are rarely demoted, and Ordinary class students, except for the top few of the aforementioned Probation Class, stand little chance of moving up to the Pinnacle class. Mobility between the two trajectories is rare. The two classes are defined by students' testing performance and reinforced by their disparate, gaokao-dictated curricula, which, in turn, define their social status and future prospects.

As Pinnacle class students toil to improve their English test scores and hence their competitive edge in the gaokao, English comes to project their future promise more than either Chinese or Mongolian does. This English-conditioned future projection, in turn, frames their identification as students beyond the bilingual system of Chinese and Mongolian: Pinnacle class students are those who have a superior grasp of English. The Ordinary class students who receive much less support in English training are identified by their English skills as well, except in the negative. As students with poor outcomes on English tests, they are deemed less compatible with the globalizing China, and less competitive in the college and employment races.

As for the Ordinary class students' Mongolian language proficiency, it is considered useful only for a future confined to a shrinking Mongolian domain within IMAR, and only if the students manage to earn a college degree and find a teaching or government job that requires bilingual capabilities in Chinese and Mongolian. For Ordinary class students from lower ranking schools who have dim prospects of attending competitive colleges, it has been more advisable for them to go for Chinese schooling in the MKH-track instead of the MKM-track—their futures as migrant workers lie in large IMAR cities or outside of IMAR, where Putonghua Chinese dominates.

In this process of differentiation among Mongol students, ethnolinguistic politics go beyond the dichotomy between Chinese and Mongolian speeches. Even for MKM students, most of whom grow up speaking Mongolian and are considered the most "authentic" among Mongol students, their ethnolinguistic identifications are complicated by gaokao-dictated class placements and uneven access to Mongolian and English lessons under the overall dominance of Chinese language as the medium of instruction.

In short, in China's education system, Mongol students' identifications diverge and evolve along the sorting mechanisms of school tracks, class ranks, and speeches.

What about the everyday linguistic practices at home and on the street?

Two surveys conducted in the mid-2000s indicated that 75% to 90% of IMAR residents were bilingual in Chinese and Mongolian.[27] The IMAR-based linguist Bao Xiaohua (2015)[28] found that in East IM's "half-agricultural and half-pastoral" regions (see Chapter 8), where ethnic Mongols concentrate, bilingualism has been practiced in various ways. In the pastoral-leaning area of the interwoven region, Mongolian was spoken more frequently than Chinese; in the city and farming-dominant parts of the interwoven region, like Wave's home village Fresh Springs in Horqin RF, Mongolian and Chinese were used at almost equal frequency. There, Mongolian was for the home and family, Chinese for the public domain. Wave's mother, Orchid (see Chapter 8), for example, is one such bilingual speaker. The question is: what kind of Mongolian and what kind of Chinese does Orchid speak?

The Mongolian that Orchid speaks differs substantially from the Mongolian that Wave learned in school, in terms of pronunciation, vocabulary, and grammar.

At school, Wave learned Chakhar Mongolian, which was officially designated as standard Mongolian in 1956. Chakhar Mongolian is one of several central Mongolian dialects, out of the four regional tongues of central, western, northern, and eastern Mongolian.[29]

At home, Wave speaks to Orchid in Horqin Mongolian, an eastern Mongolian dialect that more than 50% of Mongolian speakers in IMAR use. Horqin Mongolian is the dialect of farming refugees and immigrants, the rootless "short" Mongols (see Chapter 8). It is therefore the most versatile among all the regional dialects, mixing central-eastern Mongolian with Manchurian, Russian, and Chinese dialects.[30]

The fluidity makes Horqin Mongolian the least authentic version of Mongolian in the eyes of other Mongolian speakers, especially those who speak the standardized dialect, Chakhar Mongolian. The perceived linguistic "impurity" of Horqin Mongolian and its speakers' low sociocultural status as landless farming refugees and drifters reinforce one another. These "short" Mongols are also considered "half" Mongols. The general belief that the land of Horqin tribes was never graced by Chinggis Khan's warring itinerary only serves to further marginalize Horqin Mongols and Horqin Mongolian speakers. In modern times, a person with a Horqin accent, even if speaking standard Mongolian, will not be selected to host Mongolian TV programs or anchor TV news. But the Horqin accent is popular in comedy shows as the subject of mockery.[31]

In terms of language attainment in East IM, the official (Chakhar) Mongolian can only be learned systematically at school. The official Mongolian also comes with an official writing system that is aligned with the traditional Mongolian writing system. The codified script reinforces the status of Chakar Mongolian as the standard and "authentic" Mongolian. On the other hand, Horqin Mongolian is seen as "pidgin" Mongolian that is used at home and in Mongolian villages in which most residents do not read or write in any language. Never schooled in official Mongolian, Orchid does not speak, understand, read or write it.

What about Orchid's Chinese, which she deploys fluently when shopping at stores, working in retail in the city of Ulanhot, and chatting with me. It is not exactly official Putonghua Chinese either. Rather, it is a strand of northeastern Chinese dialect. In IMAR, two umbrella categories of Chinese dialect are used. One is found in West IMAR, the other in East IMAR. The two Chinese dialects in IMAR correspond to the two Chinese migration routes from northwestern Chinese provinces, like Shaanxi and Shanxi to West IMAR, and from northeastern provinces like Shandong to East IMAR. Like peoples, languages mingle and localize as they travel. Both the northwestern and the northeastern Chinese dialects were localized in western and eastern IM, and their influences went both ways: Chinese influenced Mongolian and vice versa. The northeastern Chinese dialect that Orchid spoke in Horqin RF had been Mongolianized in its phonetics, tones, vocabulary, and grammar.[32] For instance, the commonly used northeastern Chinese word "*bansheng*," which refers to "small settlements," is rooted in Mongolian. In terms of grammar, when a native Mongolian speaker speaks Chinese, they tended to put the verb last in a sentence, as per Mongolian sentence structure, rather than putting the verb right after the subject like in Chinese.[33] Another example is that the Chinese preposition words, like "in," "to," or "at," are often omitted in the Mongolianized Chinese speech.[34]

Orchid would watch quite a bit of TV after work. In Ulanhot, she had access to two Mongolian and over two hundred Chinese channels via her cable TV subscription. The Chinese programs invariably used Putonghua, and the Mongolian channels used official Mongolian. The substantial differences between official Mongolian and Horqin Mongolian made it hard for Orchid to comprehend the Mongolian TV programs. But the prevalence of Putonghua in her everyday life in the city, and the relatively close connection between northeastern Chinese dialect and Putonghua made it easier for Orchid to enjoy Chinese TV. The 200-strong Chinese TV channels also offered a much wider choice in content than the two Mongolian channels. Over time, Orchid acquired more Putonghua vocabulary, while making little progress in official Mongolian.[35]

What Orchid missed from TV was broadcasting from Mongolia (formerly Mongolian People's Republic), IMAR's northern neighbor. The official language of Mongolia is Khalkha Mongolian, which is close to Chakhar Mongolian, the official Mongolian in China. During the 2000s and early 2010s when satellite communication control in China was relatively relaxed, TV programs from Mongolia were easily accessible and hugely popular in IMAR. But only those who could understand the official Mongolian, mainly those who were schooled in the MKM track, were able to advantage of it. Orchid was not one of them.

Having grown up in the village of northern Horqin RF, Wave speaks Horqin Mongolian fluently and some northeastern Chinese dialect that she had learned from village neighbors and her relatives through their intermarriage. All in all, Wave's multilingualism includes at least five tongues. In and out of classrooms at school, she spoke Chinese Putonghua, official Mongolian, and English. She can also read, write, and test in the three languages well enough to excel at school. At home, she speaks Horqin Mongolian mixed with northeastern Chinese dialect.

Orchid's everyday multilingualism is comprised of three strands: Horqin Mongolian, Mongolianized northeastern Chinese dialect, and Putonghua with a northeastern accent. The boundaries among the three tongues are slippery, and Orchid rarely sticks to only one in her speech. Depending on the occasion, the content, and her interlocutors, she code switches between them in varied ways. With the family, she usually uses Horqin Mongolian mixed with Putonghua; with a store customer, she uses northeastern Chinese mixed with Putonghua. In her social realm, almost everyone is multilingual, albeit with vastly different levels of familiarity with each tongue. The mixes and shifts come to define Orchid's multilingualism, not unlike the ethnoterritorial and livelihood mixes and shifts in East IMAR's "Interwoven Belt of Agriculture and Pastoralism" presented in Chapter 8.

While language lessons in the classroom and language tests for competitive ranking standardize the languages, everyday speech "encompasses a plurality of diverse cultures, languages, and ethnicities."[36] In Horqin RF, a socially and culturally fluid place, labels such as Chinese, Mongolian, or bilingual speakers are not bounded categories. The evolving linguistic practices of Mongols of different generations and social backgrounds warrant a much deeper analysis than what this book can cover. For now, I follow Wave to her race for college admission.

II College Race

II.1 Unified National Exam

China's college entrance exam is popularly known as gaokao in Chinese. Its official name is the Nationwide Unified Examination for Admissions to Universities and

Colleges. The name means what it says: it is a *unified national* exam. Using standardized tests held every year on the same days across the country, gaokao is, in fact, more than just an exam. It is one of the most important sociocultural institutions in present day China. As a key route of social mobility, gaokao has become a milieu that permeates contemporary Chinese economic, social, and cultural life across geographical locations and ethnicities.

Gaokao operates at an unparalleled scale. Since the current format of gaokao began in 1977 in the aftermath of the Cultural Revolution, the number of gaokao participants has grown fivefold. In 2021, 10.78 million students participated in the gaokao that took place in 466,000 testing rooms at 7,200 testing sites across 31 provincial-level jurisdictions in China,[37] supported by 1.4 million test staff, including 950,000 proctors, all in the same two or three days in early June.[38] Two years later in 2023, 2 million more enrolled in gaokao, pushing the total to 12.78 million.[39]

The astounding growth of gaokao participation has been accompanied by China's similarly high-speed expansion of higher education since the late 1990s. The number of higher education institutions (HEIs) in China grew from 715 in 1982 to 3,012 in 2021, of which 2,248, or 75%, were state institutions, and 1,270 were academic colleges, 1,486 were two- or three-year polytechnic colleges. The size of the existing HEIs also increased substantially during the same period.[40] As a result, the total college enrollment numbers grew from 300,000 in 1982 to over 35 million in 2021. The HEIs for adult education and online education added another 17 million to the total number of undergrad enrollment. In the meantime, the number of graduate students in both master's and doctoral programs exploded from 15,000 in 1982 to 3.3 million in 2021.[41] As a result of the dramatic growth in college seats, college admission rates have increased from 17% in 1982 to 90% in 2021.[42]

Despite the massification of college admissions, however, the intake of the top-ranking 100 universities, all of which are public with tuition capped at RMB 5,000 yuan a year, remains stable at around 5%. As for Tsinghua and Peking Universities, the apex pair in China's higher education and popularized as the portmanteau, TsingPe, the combined admission rate was 0.06%, or six out of ten thousand contenders, in 2021.[43] The vastly expanded HEIs and the consistently low admission rates of the elite universities have led to credential inflation of non-elite universities. In the job market and in widely held social perception, the value of a non-elite university degree has diminished as the overall college admission rates have risen. Consequently, competition to get into the elite universities, which have retained their brand name values, has continued to escalate despite and because of higher education expansion.

The massified HEIs and the intensified competition to enter elite universities has made gaokao a milieu that spreads through multiple domains of life in China today. Institutionally, it reinforces standardized elite training; socially and spatially, it regulates the routes of upward and outward mobility; economically, it breeds a US$180-300 billion test-prep industry; culturally, it measures success and failure and gives a sense of purpose to teachers, students, and their families; and affectively, it anchors hopefulness and anxiety, and it invokes life-long pride and regret. TsingPe alums, for example, sometimes put their alma mater on their business cards decades after graduating. Below TsingPe, the degree of pride diminishes with the ranking of one's alma mater.

In popular perception, China's universities can be ranked on an A- to C-list and sublists as follows, based on the level of the national government's investment and sponsorship.[44]

A-List Universities

The A-List includes a total of 137 top universities established mostly by the national government. They are generally considered the nation's best as a result of their official status as the select few in the nation's key programs for higher education advancement.

Over the past two decades, although China's HEIs have expanded rapidly, the admission rates of A-List universities have remained relatively stable. In 2021, the admission rate of A-list universities was 6.2% of the 10.87 million gaokao takers that year. In popular perception, A-list universities are further ranked into the following four leagues:

A-a *Tsinghua and Peking Universities* (TsingPe). Together, this crown pair admitted less than 7,000 students in 2021, a 0.06% admission rate.

A-b *Project 985 Universities.* On May 4, 1998, on the 100th anniversary of Peking University, China's then-President Jiang Zeming announced an ambitious investment plan to build world-class universities for the 21st century. Thirty-nine universities, including Tsingpe, were hand-picked by the national government. They are called Project 985 universities because the date on which President Jiang made the announcement was May 1998, or 98/5 according to Chinese dating format. The 39 universities admitted around 183,000 students in 2021, or about a 1.67% admission rate.

A-c *Project 211 Universities.* Project 211 is another similar, but more inclusive, higher education promotion project initiated by China's Ministry of Education in 1995. It includes 112 universities (including the Project 985 universities). The name "211" comes from the abbreviation of the 21st century and approximately 100 universities. Some of the best provincial-level universities are included in Project 211. Nationwide, 520,000 students were admitted to Project 211 universities in 2021 at an admission rate of 4.8%.

A-d *Double-Best (shuangyiliu) Universities.* This is yet another official designation. There are 137 universities (including Project 985 and 211 universities) in this category. In 2021, all Double-Bests admitted around 670,000 students nationwide, or an admission rate of 6.2%.[45]

What is important to note is that although Chinese education authorities never formally rank the universities this way, its highly selective and specifically targeted funding allocation schemes like Project 985 or Project 211 are read by the public as the ultimate marker of prestige and quality. The fierce competition to gain admission to these nationally recognized and well-funded universities raise these universities' cutoff scores, especially those on the very top. The high thresholds and university reputation reinforce one another, effectively solidifying the universities' ranking even further.

B-List Universities

The B-List includes regular four-year universities established mostly by provincial-level governments. Nationwide, there are approximately 300 or so universities on the B-List.[46] The ranking of the B-List universities is less stable than that of the A-listers, and the criteria vary across provinces. B-List universities can be further ranked into two sub-categories, which reinforce and are reinforced by their gaokao score thresholds.

B-a universities are the top-tier, provincially managed universities. These universities also recruit nationally like A-listers, but the main source of admitted students are from within the province.

B-b listers are the second-tier provincial universities with a lower cutoff gaokao score than that of the B-a listers. These universities have usually been established more recently or have few popular major programs.

In 2021, the B-List universities admitted about 3.2 to 3.8 million, about 30% to 35% of China's gaokao takers.[47]

C-List Universities

The C-List includes 1,500 or so HEIs, most of which had been established since the early 2000s. It contains the lowest-ranking public and private academic HEIs as well as most of the vocational colleges. In 2021, when China's college admission rates reached 90%, more than half of these college admissions were offered by C-List colleges. The high admission rates of the C-List universities have been accompanied by the lowest enrollment rates, as many admits and their families do not consider these low-ranking, for-profit schools worth the expensive tuition, which could be five times higher than A- or B-list universities. To improve enrollment, some better-positioned C-list universities promise students future transfers to B-list universities.[48]

The permeating gaokao milieu and the hyper-awareness of university rankings reinforce one another across place, ethnicity, and class in China today. As such, Wave's gaokao story tells the tale of a high-achieving Mongol student's navigation and aspiration embedded in China's gaokao milieu and university ranking order.

II.2 Localized Admissions Competition

In June 2009, Wave took the gaokao exam. The regular gaokao exam takes two days. But for a MKM student like Wave, it is a grueling three-day examination: in addition to the regular two-day test, Wave had to take the Mongolian language test on the third day. She scored 521 out of a total possible score of 750, and gained admission to University D.[49] University D is one of the Project 985 universities, an A-b Lister. It is located in a metropolitan center that is about a 50-hours train ride from Wave's home in Horqin RF. Granted, University D, sitting near the bottom of the Project 985 universities, was far below the apex twins of TsingPe. It was nevertheless an extraordinary triumph for Wave.

Rationed University Seats

Wave's college admission to a Project 985 university was extraordinary not just because she was a minority woman. It was also because she grew up in a poor farming village in China's periphery unconnected to the power grid until 1998, more than two decades behind the countryside in China's coastal regions. With competition for admittance into elite universities escalating since the 2000s, the class and rural-urban gap in college admissions has increased significantly. Fewer and fewer rural students from poor regions have found their way to TsingPe or other Project 985 universities. Yet, while the rural poor are among those who have the slimmest chances to gain entry to a prestigious university, they are also among the most determined to escape rural poverty via higher education. Wave was one of such students, and one of the very few successful ones.

This is not to say that China does not practice affirmative action in college admissions or other policy areas. Quite the contrary, China has one of the oldest and largest programs of state-sponsored preferential policies for ethnic minorities, originally pioneered in the Soviet Union.[50] Preferential treatment towards minority nationalities include investment in physical infrastructure, public health, and education, among other areas, in minority jurisdictions. Preferential treatment has also extended to individuals in policy areas like family planning (e.g., exemptions from the minimum marriage age and the One-Child policy that was implemented between 1980 and 2016), employment (e.g., favorable consideration in cadre hiring and promotion), business development (e.g., special loans, grants, and tax exemptions), and preferential college admissions. One well-publicized element of preferential college admissions is the addition of points to minority students' gaokao scores to boost their competitive edge. Under the national policy principle, the scale and scope of this bonus point scheme has varied greatly across nationalities and jurisdictions in terms of eligibility and scale of bonus points. Tibetan students in TAR and Uyghur students in XUAR, for example, have been known to enjoy the most generous number of bonus points compared to other minorities in other jurisdictions. The scheme also continues to evolve under a changing political discourse and the particular geopolitical position of the minority jurisdiction in question.

The preferential bonus point scheme for minority gaokao-takers has been in place since the 1950s. A key measure of cultural assimilation and minority elite recruitment for the CCP state, it was seldom questioned for decades. But since the mid-2000s, popular and scholarly debates on the legitimacy of the bonus point scheme have emerged. For its supporters, the bonus point scheme is a matter of justice that lends minority students much deserved assistance to improve their otherwise disadvantaged access to higher education.[51] For its critics, it is a question of fairness. They argue that the bonus point scheme encourages forged ethnic identity, and it also creates reverse discrimination and compromises the quality of higher education.[52]

In the new millennium, the fairness argument has been noticeably louder than the justice argument that is now considered to be too Maoist. This new discourse on fair competition for all nationalities, including the majority Han Chinese, has taken shape at a time when *both* the national drive for ethnic unity over cultural plurality and the college admissions competition have reached new heights. Over the decade between the mid-2000s and mid-2010s, many provinces reduced the scale of bonus points and narrowed the scope of its applicability. Other provinces abolished or have planned to abolish the scheme altogether.[53] Even in XUAR, where its 11 minorities, including the majority minority Uyghurs, enjoyed the most generous bonus of 50 points at the peak of the bonus point policy, the bonus had later been reduced to 15 points. In 2015, the director of the Ethnicity Education Bureau, an agency under the Ministry of Education in the national government, announced that a complete abolishment of the bonus point scheme for all minority students in China was only a matter of time.[54] What remains unchallenged are the bonus points granted to those who represent Chinese nationalist values, such as bonus points allotted to students whose parents have sacrificed their lives for the country or who have served in Tibet, a hardship post that is central to national unity and border security. Every year of a parent's service in Tibet adds one point to the student's gaokao score, regardless of ethnic nationality. Children of decorated military personnel are also granted 10 to 20 additional points. Bonus points that cannot be bought with money make them even more valuable as political currency.

Following the national trend, the IMAR government also planned to abolish preferential treatment for the five eligible minorities in its jurisdiction, including its major minority, Mongols. In 2021, the IMAR Bureau of Education announced that starting from 2024, bonus points for IMAR minority gaokao takers would be halved from 10 to 5 points. By 2026, only students of IMAR's 36 banners in which minorities are concentrated will continue to receive the five bonus points, while students whose residency are registered in the 67 other IMAR counties and districts will have graduated from the program.[55]

Despite heated debates and rapid changes, however, the bonus point scheme is only half the story about minority students' college race even when the scheme was in full swing. The second and more important, yet much less told half of the story, concerns the actual university admissions process that turns the nationally unified exam into localized competition among and within individual provinces and among minority students themselves.[56]

In the college race, the scores of the national gaokao test serve as the baseline for students' qualification. Elite universities set much higher cutoff lines than the rest. But there are always far more qualified students than seats available at elite universities. At the time of massified higher education and credential dilution, a seat in value-retaining elite universities have come to be the object of the ever-intensifying admissions competition. To manage the increasing gap between supply and demand, these prestigious universities allocate a certain number of seats to individual provinces through the quota system.

The quota system is a common tool of territorial governance in China. It channels nationally controlled resources and policy tasks, often in quantitative terms, such as the acreage of land to be afforested with the suosuo (see Chapter 1), the number of native Mongolian cattle to be castrated (see Chapter 2), or the number of greenhouses to be built (see Chapter 4) along the jurisdictional hierarchy from the central to the provincial, and all the way down to the villages.

In the case of allocating university seats, because quotas are conferred to individual provinces, students within a province compete with one another for a limited number of elite university seats. Students' registered residencies decide where they can take the gaokao and join the admissions competition. The quota system effectively localizes the national college competition and subsumed the ethnicity-framed bonus point scheme even before its decline in popularity and use.

In IMAR, Shandong University, for example, a Project 985 university that recruits its students nationwide, set its entrance threshold at 550 points but rationed only five seats to IMAR students in 2018. These five seats were open for competition among all registered IMAR gaokao takers who scored above 550 points on their gaokao. Out of the 180,000 gaokao takers in IMAR that year, about 2,500 in the humanities track and 10,000 in the science track passed that bar. So IMAR's 12,500 high performers, including non-Mongol and Mongols of both MKM and MKH tracks, competed with one another for the five seats at Shandong University. Overall, the number of seats that all Project 985 university allocated to IMAR fluctuated year by year, averaging about 100 to 120 a year in the late 2010s.[57]

Under the quota system, the bonus point scheme for minority students has been further weakened by some elite universities' recruitment policies that do not honor minority bonus points. And even when elite universities do honor the points, they limit their application to only a small number of majors, often the least popular ones. Most of all, the distribution of elite university seats across provincial-level jurisdictions is highly uneven.

All Project 985 universities, though they are administered directly by the national government and recruit nationally, allocate far more seats to their host provinces; most of these universities are located in metropolitan centers of China's prosperous eastern half. Among them, Beijing and Shanghai host a third of China's 39 Project 985 universities, including the highly regarded universities like TsingPe as well as A-b listers like Renmin, Fudan, and Tongji universities. Beijing and Shanghai, the two provincial-level municipalities, together yield an average of about 120,000 gaokao takers a year, a paltry number compared to that of populous provinces like Henan. Henan Province of northern China, which does not have a home-based Project 985 university, had over 1 million gaokao takers in 2020. In 2017, Beijing and Shanghai students' admission rates to Project 985 universities reached 5%, but Henan students' admission rate to Project 985 universities stagnated at 1.1%. The highly uneven inter-provincial allocation of elite university seats, in turn, has created the most hellish competition in populous provinces like Henan. Henan's competitive environment produces a large number of high-scoring students, which has brought the cutoff score in Henan for the same elite university much higher than it is in Beijing—a gap that is as many as 30–50 points or more, depending on the major.[58] Henan students also face another challenge. The higher their gaokao score, the harder their test questions get. To manage the vast territorial discrepancy in quota allocation and admission rates, the national gaokao exam has been split into four regional and several provincial test sets with varying levels of difficulty. While Henan's exam is among the hardest, Beijing students, who face the least competitive admissions race, get the easiest tests and are therefore the subject of envy, if not resentment, by the rest of the gaokao takers and their families in China. The localized operation of the national exam, in other words, inevitably creates and is created by territorial unevenness and contradictions of the presumably unified national institution.

The uneven territorial allocation of elite university seats is notable also at the regional level between China's prosperous eastern regions and its eight minority provinces and autonomous regions (MPARs from here on) in the country's western half.[59] Based on a survey in 2008, Liu Eerduntu (2010)[60] found that TsingPe together admitted 766 students from Beijing alone and 463 students from all of the eight MPARs combined. East coast-located Zhejiang University, one of the top 10 of the Project 985 universities, admitted 2,044 students from its host province of Zhejiang, but only granted 157 seats to students from the eight MPARs combined. Similarly, Nanjing University, another university located on the east coast and also a top 10 university, admitted 1,180 students from its host province of Jiangsu, but only 195 from the eight MPARs.

IM is one of China's eight MPARs. Like Henan and all other MPARs, IM does not host any Project 985 universities. Although IMAR has fewer gaokao takers—averaging 180,000 a year from 2018 to 2021, or about a fifth of Henan's—and its gaokao test is considered less difficult than Henan's, IMAR still receives disproportionately fewer elite university seats than most eastern provinces. Some years, some Project 985 universities do not grant any seats to IM gaokao takers. As a result, IMAR students' admission rate to Project 985 universities has been even lower than Henan's, which was at about 0.1% in 2021.[61]

The competition for elite university seats is further elevated by the competition for popular majors at these universities, which is again subject to quota allocation. Within the same university, the most desirable majors, like English, law, finance, or business management in the humanities track and electrical engineering, computer science, chemistry, or biology in the science track, set the cutoff scores much higher. The admission rates to popular majors are significantly lower than to other majors at the same university. As a result, for most IMAR students who have gained admission to a Project 985 university, they have often found themselves in the "cold" majors, such as physics in the science track or archaeology in the humanities track.

To sum up, the administrative allocation of elite university seats to provinces localizes and territorializes the national college competition. In doing so, it also exacerbates territorial inequality across regions and provinces.

The skewed quota allocation across provinces is just the contradiction found on the supply side. On the demand side and within each province, students' gaokao competitiveness varies greatly between the city and the countryside. As the admissions competition has intensified since the early 2000s, the percentage of rural students admitted to elite universities has declined significantly. Most writers have attributed the growing rural-urban gap in elite university admissions to the urban bias in educational resource distribution, as attested by Wave's primary and secondary schooling presented earlier in this chapter.

But not all rural areas are the same. Rural students' disadvantages in the college race vary by province and region. The rural-urban disparity within each province is compounded by inter-rural disparities between rich and poor provinces and regions.

Based on research on rural students' admission to the prestigious Peking University, sociologists Liu, Yunshan et al. (2009)[62] suggested that in China's richer coastal provinces such as Shandong and Zhejiang, quality high schools are found in many rural counties. By contrast, in western peripheries like IM, Tibet, and Qinghai, the rural-urban disparity in education infrastructure is significantly larger, with the most competitive high schools disproportionately concentrated in their capital cities. As a result, while the prosperous coastal provinces have managed to send more of their rural students from quality county-based high schools to Peking University, almost all the students from the western peripheries who have made it to Peking University were schooled in the capital cities of their respective provinces and autonomous regions. In short, the rural-urban gap in college admissions is much larger in the peripheries, due to the inter-rural disparity in education infrastructure. While the inter-provincial allocation of college seats has created the supply side of territorial disparity, the rural-urban and inter-rural gap in pre-gaokao schooling has created a territorial disparity on the demand side.

Social class disparities further amplify territorial disparities. Liu, Yunshan et al.'s (2009)[63] research shows that, by the late 1990s, close to 70% of Peking University's annual admits came from the families of "cadres" (defined as state-sector employees, military personnel, and teachers), an increase from 50% in the early 1990s. Meanwhile, 20% of the incoming class came from families of "workers" (defined as manual labor and service workers, as well as small private entrepreneurs and clerks)—a percentage that remained relatively stable throughout the 1990s. As for students from rural farming families, their admission rate declined from 30% to 12% over the same period. A more recent study shows that the downward trend of students admitted to elite universities from rural farming families continued into the late 2010s.[64]

Consistent with the aforementioned inter-rural gap, peripheral provinces like IM, Tibet, Qinghai, Ningxia, Guizhou, and Yunnan have manifested a stronger class gap between urban-based cadre families and rural farming families, compared to the coastal region.

Given the fact that these peripheral provinces are also where minority nationalities are concentrated, the territorial disparity in elite college admissions is also an ethnoterritorial one. In most of the peripheral regions, there has been an ethnoterritorial divide between Han Chinese in cities and minorities in the countryside, such as in the case of XUAR and TAR (see Chapter 5). Even in IMAR where Han Chinese are widespread in both cities and the countryside, residents of Hohhot and

Baotou—IMAR's political and economic centers where IMAR's best high schools and universities are concentrated—are predominantly Han Chinese.[65]

On the gender front, the national admission rate of female students to universities has improved from 23% in 1980 to 50% in 2012.[66] Yet, gender distribution is also spatialized. Female students in the universities, especially the elite universities, have predominantly hailed from urban areas. Daughters of rural farming families from poor peripheral provinces, most of which overlap with minority-concentrated jurisdictions, have been the least represented at elite universities.[67]

The ethnoterritorial, class, and gender disparities in China's college admissions rendered Wave a true outlier. As a daughter of a poor farming family in the peripheral countryside of IM, Wave's admission to a Project 985 university was more of an exception than a norm. An exceptional story affords the opportunity to look into what it takes for the least competitive socioterritorial actors to succeed in China's college competition, and the limits of such exceptional success.

Wave in the Admissions Rush

In Wave's view, her exceptional success in getting into a Project 985 university started the day she was admitted to an urban middle school in Ulanhot. Her prospects were further enhanced when she was placed in a Pinnacle class at a top high school in Ulanhot. Having the best schooling that her home region could offer, on top of her own intelligence and diligence, is what got her the 521 points (out of 750) on the national college entrance exam. That hard-earned score qualified her for joining the competition for A-list universities, but it did not guarantee any results. As mentioned earlier, for every seat at a popular major of an elite university, there were tens of thousands of other qualified contenders from one's home province.

The admissions competition to these much sought-after college seats is often described as "*tens of thousands of mounted soldiers competing to cross a single-plank bridge*." To manage this crammed rush to cross the single-plank bridge, IMAR's Bureau of Education, like its counterparts in other provinces, ranks IMAR's college aspirants into three tiers based on their gaokao scores. Those whose gaokao scores reached the first-tier cutoff line, say, 500 points, are awarded the priority to choose their preferred majors and universities on the first day of open enrollment.[68] Students who scored between 400 and 500 points get to enter the admissions race on the second day of open enrollment; those who scored between 300 and 400 points have to wait until the third day to choose from the majors and universities that still have open seats. This enrollment priority is popularly called Tier One (*yiben*), Tier Two (*erben*), and Tier Three (*sanben*), working like three bridges to hopefully relieve the traffic jam. Most of the high-threshold majors at Project 985 universities are open for enrollment on day one for the Tier One students, while the B-list universities and the less desired majors at some A-list universities are available on day two for the Tier Two students.[69] The low-scoring Tier Three students often are left to choose from thousands of low-ranking majors and universities, many of which are private two- or three-year polytechnic C-list colleges.

The tri-tier structure of enrollment, in other words, sorts applicants through a hierarchy. And in each tier, applicants compete with those with a similar level of competitiveness. As such, gaokao scores determine applicants' enrollment priority, but they do not guarantee admission results. Since the gap between available seats in the popular majors of elite universities and the number of Tier One applicants is often the greatest, the day-one bridge is the narrowest, with the most furious competition.

Wave's gaokao score in 2009 landed her in Tier One, so she got to enter open enrollment on the first day. At that time, the platform for open enrollment in IMAR had already been moved online for three years, operating in a real-time interactive system that was praised for its transparency, but also known as a grueling exercise for students.[70]

Wave remembers in vivid detail the drama from the day of the real-time online enrollment period that "determined her future."

At 8 a.m. sharp, Solidarity High's students who had made it to Tier One, about 30 of them, Wave included, entered the computer lab at school. They each grabbed a computer and started scrolling to check the availability of seats in the hundreds of universities and majors open that day. At any given moment, one could only enroll in one university and in a maximum of six majors at that university. To maximize their chances, students monitored the ones in which they enrolled while exploring better options. If there were 1,000 students with the same gaokao score competing for three available seats to a given major in a university, the seats went to the three firstcomers. If a fourth student came in later with a higher score than the first three, the last student of the first three was automatically de-enrolled. On the other hand, if a high-threshold university or major unexpectedly lowered its bar or rationed more seats than normal that year, those who cast a wide net could strike a lucky catch that others with the same score would miss. In a different scenario, a taken seat might suddenly re-open because its previous occupant found a better seat somewhere else. Constant patrolling of the frontlines was critical, and one's pick was not fully secured until the cutoff time of that first day. These conditions meant that speed mattered, and there was little time for deliberation. Information mattered even more, as students needed to know the cutoff scores for their target majors and universities to grab the best spots in their score range before they were taken. Only the few students who scored over 650 points or higher could relax; they had their pick of the best universities even if they came in late. According to Wave, those high-scoring students could game the system for their friends with less competitive scores. They would enroll in a high threshold spot for their friends, hold the spot, fending off other contenders until a few minutes before the cutoff time—a time when most high-scoring students would already be locked in to other majors and universities. Then they would release the seats and select their own major and university at ease with their unbeatably high scores, while their friends would immediately take over the spots they released.

But for most Project 985 university aspirants and their families, the stakes in open enrollment were too high to leave to fate or games. Not unlike in the U.S. where the college admissions frenzy for elite universities has bred a thriving industry of college admissions consultancies,[71] college admissions coaching services have flourished in China, especially since the late 2000s, to help students devise action plans for open enrollment. Because the cutoff lines of the majors and universities in any given year are not available until a couple days before open enrollment starts, the admissions plan involves methodical projections. Coaches amass admissions data from previous years and project the current year's threshold scores for the most desirable humanities and science majors at elite universities. On top of current-year projections, they chart historical trends and matrix them with their client student's estimated gaokao score (based on the average of multiple mock gaokao exams) to tailor a personalized strategic plan for enrollment. The coach sorts the student's options into primary targets ("click on those first so that you can be placed at the top of the roll"), slightly far-fetched catches ("venture there at regular intervals if the primary target looks secure enough, but act quickly"), and lower-threshold backups (in case the student is placed at the bottom of their primary target and could easily be rejected upon the arrival of a higher-scorer). The goal, according to a high school teacher I talked to, is to make one's gaokao score stretch as far as possible while ensuring a safe landing.

In addition to using admissions consultancies, many parents are heavily involved in their children's college admissions process.[72] On one of the numerous gaokao consultancy websites, a college admissions coach likened the college admissions process to a relay: the student runs the first leg by taking the exam and the parents run the next leg by navigating the admissions maze. Urban students rely on their educated parents (usually mothers)[73] to join gaokao parents' chat groups, gather information on- and off-line, and work with an admissions coach to create an action plan before open enrollment starts. It takes a village to send a youngster to a Project 985 university.

But Wave did not have any such support. Wave's parents could not afford the admissions coaching service, nor could they run the second leg of the relay for her.

Without help from coaches or her parents, Wave relied on her head teacher for basic information on the day of enrollment. At Solidarity High, every class had a designated head teacher, and the head teachers of the graduating classes were given a thick Yellow Pages-like college admissions reference book the day before open enrollment. The reference book listed the current-year majors and universities available for IMAR students of different gaokao scoring tiers, as well as the threshold scores, enrollment requirements, and enrollment codes of each major and university. Armed with the reference book, the head teachers were expected to provide their students with basic information and to help them navigate enrollment at the computer lab during open enrollment.

When Wave walked into the computer lab at 8 a.m. on the first day of open enrollment, however, her classroom's head teacher was not there. Rumor had it that the teacher was vacationing on Hainan Island, the tropical paradise off China's southern coast, and his reference book was locked in a drawer that no one had access to. Wave suspected that the teacher had already received his monetary award for some of his students' success on the gaokao exam. Since he would not be further rewarded for his students' admissions results, he saw no point in sticking around. But the head teacher of the science track Pinnacle class was on site with his big reference book. Even so, he was busy helping his own students and had little time for Wave and the humanities track students. Ever so resourceful, Wave elicited help from a boy one year ahead of her, someone who was also a MKM student on the humanities track at Solidarity High. The boy had a similar gaokao score and had successfully gained admission to a Project 985 university. As university enrollment codes remained constant, he shared with Wave the two Project 985 university enrollment codes that he had used the year before. Wave used the tried-and-true codes. She did not succeed with the first one, so she immediately moved to the next, University D. She snatched one of the top three seats offered by University D, and locked in her placement by the 5 p.m. cutoff time. Without knowing the enrollment codes for other universities, Wave could not play the game and try to strike a lucky catch at even more prestigious universities, and she had little idea of what better options her score might have qualified her for.

The admissions stress that Wave experienced in 2009 reached an even higher level for gaokao takers a decade later. In 2022, China had close to 3,000 private consulting firms specializing in college admissions coaching. In IM, the number of admissions coaching services leaped from a couple of dozens in the late 2000s to 231 in 2022. The admissions race has bred a seasonal admissions industry that involves consulting firms leasing internet cafes during the three-day admissions rush, one-on-one on-site admissions coaches, as well as hiring professional "keyboard operators" who type fast. Hiring keyboard operators is crucial because each student makes about, on average, a hundred attempts within the 90-minute enrollment period. Each attempt at enrolling in a major requires keying in the long passcodes for the major and the university. Under pressure, many students are too nervous to type in the codes quickly and accurately; many have confessed that their hands were sweating and shaking during the rush to snag an opening. It is therefore safer to delegate the vital task to calm, dexterous keyboard operators who have gone through the online enrollment themselves before.

According to a journalist reporting from an internet café in Hohhot in 2022, during open enrollment, the café was jam packed with students, teachers, parents, admissions coaches, and keyboard operators hovering over a hundred computer stations with their eyes fixed to the screens. Every family would be armed with a thick reference book that listed all the majors and universities open for enrollment in IMAR as well as with the tailored enrollment strategy print-outs (complete with enrollment codes of more than 100 prioritized majors and universities) that the enrollment coach prepared at 2,000 to 3,000 yuan per client. Yet, despite the meticulous preparations, students could lose their catch to a higher-scoring competitor right before the screen froze at the cutoff time. Or they might find out only after the enrollment period ended that they had missed a higher-ranking major or school they could have gotten into because they had been overly cautious. At the end of each cutoff time, cheers and curses, laughter and tears sprung from different stations. The suspenseful air in the internet cafes has earned them the nickname, "the Inner Mongolia Branch of the New York Stock Exchange."[74]

A Hidden Hurdle: Preparatory Programs

For Wave, back in 2009, there was one more catch after her admission to University D. That enrollment code—the one that Wave's friend gave to her—was for the preparatory program of University D, which is different from the University's regular four-year program. The preparatory program is another preferential admissions policy for minority students from both MKM and MKH tracks. Under this policy, eligible minority students are given the option of entering Project 985 or Project 211 universities with below-the-bar scores by attending a preparatory program for one year (if one is Mongol) or two years (if one is Tibetan or Uyghur) before being formally admitted to the regular four-year program.

Compared with the bonus point scheme that was widely criticized for giving "free" points to minority students, the preparatory program comes with a steep price tag. The preparatory programs at each university have a small cohort, often under a hundred students each. To achieve the economies of scale, many elite universities contract out their programs to private colleges specializing in preparatory programs. The private preparatory programs charge much higher fees than regular public university fees, ranging from 10,000 to 50,000 yuan a year in the mid-2000s, compared to 5,000 yuan a year in a regular public university program.[75] While the "free" bonus points cannot be purchased with money, preparatory programs are available to minority students who were willing and able to pay the cash and invest the extra year in college education. More importantly, as the scale and scope of the bonus point scheme contracted, the preparatory programs have expanded rapidly since the 2000s.[76] Although the preparatory programs are, in theory, optional, the ever-escalating college admissions competition has made the preparatory programs an inevitable path for aspiring minority students to get into a Project 985 or Project 211 university.

This path is not risk-free, however. The preparatory programs serve as another gatekeeper to elite universities. At the end of the preparatory program, MKH students would be tested in three subjects, Chinese, English and math, while MKM students would be tested in two subjects, Chinese and math. If a student failed any one of the subject tests, their admittance offer would be rescinded. There were other tradeoffs. Most preparatory programs do not include the option of declaring a major. So preparatory program graduates face another round of competition over major declaration before starting the regular four-year program and often have limited majors to choose from.

Given the enrollment frenzy, and given the fact that preparatory programs had been normalized as a built-in path for minority students to get into an elite university, Wave did not think twice when she clicked on University D's preparatory program and locked in her spot at a Project 985 university. University D assigned Wave to a private college that hosted the preparatory program admits for more than a dozen elite universities. Located in Zhengzhou, the capital city of Henan Province in northern China, the one-year program charged 10,000 yuan in tuition, room, and board, equivalent to five months of Wave's parents' combined income at the time.

To pay for Wave's preparatory program, Wave's parents hosted a banquet. It was a customary practice in Horqin RF to invite neighbors and relatives to attend an "education advancement banquet" (*shengxueyan*). The banquet is meant to celebrate a child's successful admission to high school or college. It also served as a fundraiser. Han Chinese farmers in Minqin (Chapters 3 and 4) maintain a similar custom. In Minqin, given education's centrality to a farming family's future aspirations, the education advancement banquet would often be more elaborate than a wedding banquet, as evinced by the fact that a whole roasted lamb is usually served at the former but not the latter. Invited guests were expected to bring cash gifts in red envelopes to the banquet. Like gift exchanges in the moral economy, the banquet hosts could expect to be invited to other families' banquets for school advancement, weddings, elderly folks' birthdays, or new births—and to bring a cash gift to repay the "debt of interpersonal feelings" (*renqingzhai*). But the interpersonal and the financial are often intertwined. The pressure to pay back such debts could be high enough to force some families to borrow funds to stuff the red envelope. At the time when Wave needed money for her preparatory program, her parents had accumulated enough credits of interpersonal feelings, and her education advancement banquet netted her family 5,000 yuan.

Wave spent the fall of 2009 and spring of 2010 in the preparatory program far away from home and away from her destined university, University D. In the program, Wave re-learned high school-level mathematics, history, geography, and political studies in Putonghua by using Chinese textbooks. Armed with her Mongolian high school textbooks and two-way dictionaries, she worked hard to retool herself in the Chinese-only curriculum. The curriculum also initiated her into classical Chinese, which she found challenging and likened it to "a foreign language." But the resilient Wave pressed on in the intensive sinicization curriculum. It was another high-stakes year of anxiety, as failure in the preparatory program meant a waste of money, one year of her life, and most of all, her hard-earned place at University D. Wave failed her math test in the first round. She was then given a second, final chance and passed. A year after her gaokao race and admissions rush, Wave finally received a formal letter of admission from University D.

It is important to note that Wave did not benefit from the bonus point scheme. University D, like most other Project 985 universities, does not recognize the 10 bonus points granted to Mongol students.[77] But Wave did get into University D via the preparatory program. The question is: if Wave's success was highly exceptional for a poor farm girl from the periphery of the peripheral IMAR, did the preferential preparatory program help make her case less exceptional among minority students? How much did the preferential preparatory program compensate for the uneven ethnoterritorial distribution of elite college admissions?

The short answer to the question is: not much. Like the regular college race, preparatory programs for elite universities also adopt quota systems in allocating seats to individual provinces. Similar to the situation in regular college admissions, the expansion of preparatory programs across all universities and the increasing number of minority students and their families who strive to pay for the program to gain access to an elite university creates credential inflation of the preparation programs at large. The credential inflation in turn intensifies the competition among minority students to win one of the few preparatory program seats that elite universities allocate to their jurisdictions.

Also, the admissions gap of the minority-preferential preparatory programs bears a strikingly similar structure to that of the regular four-year programs outlined previously, except that it is even more pronounced.

Several surveys conducted in the 2010s of minority students in Project 985 and 211 universities' preparatory programs showed a consistent trend: an increasing percentage of admits have hailed from urban cadre families with parents who hold higher education degrees and are of higher income levels and attended urban primary and middle schools. The higher ranking the university, the higher the percentage of admits are from urban cadre families. What is more, the skyrocketing competition among minority students has led to a continuous rise in the bar for admission to preparatory programs. Originally designed to recruit more minority students to elite universities, the cutoff scores, according to national policy, could be up to 80 points below the standard cutoff line. But a survey of minority students from three autonomous regions in 2016 to 2018 showed that 85% of minority admits got into preparatory programs at an average of 33 points *above* the bar for the preparatory programs, while only 15% of admits got in with scores below the bar—but only at an average of 11 points below the bar, still far higher than the officially set 80 points below the bar. Because the competition has raised the bar beyond the official cutoff line for minority students, the actual advantage for minority students are the few extra seats reserved for them, not the lowered thresholds. Again, the higher the major or the university is ranked, the higher the actual admission threshold is above the official cutoff line. In the 2010s, programs that recruited students at below-the-bar scores were mostly expensive private colleges that charged as much as 30,000 to 80,000 yuan a year.[78] Many low-scoring minority students from poor rural families might be able to gain admission to these programs, but few could afford to attend. Researchers have also found illicit practices at the preparatory programs that are mostly run by profit-driven and under-regulated private colleges. For example, at some programs, many of the new admits are Han Chinese students with forged minority identities.[79]

In short, China's preferential admissions policy for minority students in the past decade has undergone two simultaneous shifts. One is a diminishing bonus point scheme, an administrative approach to manage college competition. The other is the expansion of preparatory programs, a market-oriented mechanism for competition management. Meanwhile, the intensified race to gain admission to elite universities via preparatory programs has seeded close-quarter competition among minority students within each province and autonomous region.

The replication of the national structure of competition in minority jurisdictions and the minority students' navigation of schools and of the college race showcases what I referred to in the opening of this chapter as minorities *of* China, not just *in* China. Minority students' social mobility is tightly intertwined with the national gaokao system, and preferential admission is designed to absorb the most competitive of the minority students into the national system of elite recruitment, not to set them on a separate path. Meanwhile, as an increasing number of minority students compete with one another to get into the national system, the door narrows and the disparity among minority students becomes more pronounced. The national culture of college competition and the state-sanctioned path of social mobility have created the general condition of sinicization of China's minorities. Meanwhile, under the nationally unified college entrance exam, the admissions race is localized, and the conditions of competition vary greatly from region to region, province to province, as presented earlier. Under such regional variations, what minority students in IMAR, as a minority *of* China have gone through is "sinicization with Mongolian characteristics," to paraphrase the popular description of Chinese reform as "marketization with Chinese characteristics."

Being a farm girl from China's periphery and a minority student going through a preparatory program, Wave's admission to University D was exceptional at every level. In 2009, eight out of 80 Pinnacle class students from Solidarity High, from both humanity and science tracks, managed to get into mid- to low-ranking Project 985 universities via preparatory programs. Out of the eight students, Wave was the only one with a farming family background and parents without a college education.

At the preparatory college in Zhengzhou, Wave was also the minority of minorities: she was one of the only two MKM students in her cohort of over 70 students. The rest were MKH students, that is, minority students who attended Chinese-track primary and secondary schools and took the gaokao exam in Chinese. Moreover, most of them were from autonomous regions like TAR and XUAR, both of which are geopolitically less stable than IMAR in the eyes of CCP state leaders, hence in greater need of preferential treatment. Only three, including Wave, came from IMAR.

III Job Race

In 2009, Wave's standing in the top 1.2% of IMAR's 240,630 gaokao-takers and her admission to University D, a Project 985 university, made her an outlier by all standards. Her story illustrates the staggeringly narrow odds that a farm girl from China's periphery faced to get into an elite university.

Wave's admission to University D also shows the limits of minority students' social mobility. University D sits near the bottom of the 39 Project 985 universities, and at a vast distance of more than 150 points below TsingPe's gaokao score threshold. Solidarity High, reputedly the top Mongolian-track high school in Hinggan League and the second best in all of East IM, had never sent a single student to TsingPe to Wave's knowledge, not even through the preparatory programs. Students like Wave, according to Beijing-based sociologist Liu, Yunshan et al. (2009), have a near-zero chance to get into TsingPe. With a keen sense of geography, Liu et al. wrote empathetically: "these students of the peripheral regions could only wish they were born in a different place."[80]

Rural students' competitive disadvantage is undeniably acute. It is nevertheless hard to imagine that these disadvantaged students would cling on to a self-defeating dream for the unreachable crest of TsingPe.

Wave, for one, had never set her eyes on TsingPe. Knowing her possibilities and impossibilities, she adjusted her expectations. Her reference point of success and failure was not whether she got into TsingPe right out of high school. Instead, she envisioned her way up as a step-by-step and stop-by-stop process, which I will elaborate on later. For sure, University D is no TsingPe; it is located in China's downtrodden interior. Nonetheless, University D is located in a provincial capital, and its brand name as a Project 985 university means that it is much better positioned than any universities located within IMAR. Having secured a seat at University D via a preparatory program, Wave felt that she had optimized her chances, at least for a 19-year-old.

What about IMAR's other gaokao aspirants who had worked just as hard and had invested just as much as Wave, but did not make it to A-list universities? The matter of college race is significant for it carries hefty implications for the students' competitiveness in their future race for a job.

III.1 Local Top 17%

In the literature on rural students' failures in China's national college competition, the significance of non-A list universities, or any universities besides TsingPe, has been largely overlooked.[81]

Many writers take TsingPe as an absolute yardstick of success and failure: that is, TsingPe marks the successful turn in rural students' upward mobility. In these scholarly accounts, those who do not make it to TsingPe, or those who do not make it to any A-list university for that matter, are relegated to the "failure" bin. But the Beijing-centered measure of success and failure risks succumbing to analytical elitism. And the non-A-list bin is too voluminous and heterogeneous to skip further examination. Who are these non-A-listers? As the students and their families expect social mobility via the gaokao race, how have they tried to fulfill their expectations via non-A list universities? For those with unfulfilled expectations in the college and job races, where do they channel their frustrations? And how has the state attempted to manage such frustrations?

In IMAR, 185,000 students took the gaokao in 2021. Among them, 5,000, or 3% of the total, were admitted to one of China's 137 A-list universities.[82] Another 17.5%, about 33,000 students, made it to B-a List universities, including the top eight provincial-level universities in IMAR. To simplify, I call this cohort the Local Top 17%.

For the IMAR government, the Local Top 17%, the close seconds in the gaokao race, carry more territorial significance than the top 3% of gaokao takers for two interconnected reasons.

First of all, unlike the top 3% whose future aspirations usually lie beyond IMAR, 70 to 80% of IMAR's top eight universities' graduates stay in IMAR. Because most graduates prefer state sector over private sector employment for prestige and stability, they compete with one another to fill the ranks of government units and schools in

IMAR. The Local Top 17% are the best educated in IMAR and make up the bulk of future local elites. Secondly, the Local Top 17% often feel frustrated compared to the top 3% who enjoy the competitive advantages bestowed upon them by their brand-name universities in the national job market. Frustration comes from high expectations. Compared to those who score below them, the Local Top 17% are also more vested, because they have invested more and thus have higher expectations of what their college degree can and should do for them. As the tension between higher education expansion and white-collar job market contraction has risen since the 2000s in IMAR, like elsewhere in China, the rising frustrations of the deeply vested Local Top 17% is a political concern for local state leaders.

In his studies of East Asian bureaucracies, historian Alexander Woodside (2006)[83] considers educated elites' agitation the first and foremost hazard of modern meritocracies. He defines meritocracies as a replacement of the aristocracy, with elites who are not necessarily landowners or capitalists but knowledge-commanding professional officials. These officials' rankings are determined by exam-based public competition (which started as early as the 7th century CE in China)—such as in the case of today's gaokao—as much as by social class.

In Woodside's account, while educated elites could assist rulers, their failed attempts to enter the rank of the ruling class could make them feel politically alienated and deprived. Examples frustrated exam takers who became a political threat to the ruler abound in East Asian histories. Under the right conditions, they mobilize and rebel against the rulers. The water that carries the boat can also sink it. The Local Top 17% embodies the source of such political tensions and, to use Woodside's term, the "insecurities of textual politics" that are devoid of a sense of moral obligation, in modern bureaucracy.[84]

In this section I tell the stories of three IMAR students who belong to IMAR's Local Top 17%. I start with their expectations and frustrations as they struggled to move up, followed by the state's policy tools to keep a lid on the tensions created by the growing gap between their expectations and experiences. Finally, I show how investors cashed in on families' escalating anxieties created by such tensions. As a case in my thesis on the minority *of* China instead of the minority *in* China, this tale of expectation and frustration management in IMAR is intimately intertwined with the soaring number of college graduates amid intense competition for urban white-collar jobs across China.

The tale of IMAR's Local Top 17% starts with Art,[85] a female Mongolian college graduate like Wave, born in 1988 in a farming village of Horqin RF Banner. Also like Wave, Art was a MKM student. But unlike Wave, Art did not have an aunt who could help her family move to the city so that she could attend an urban middle school. Instead, Art attended a rural middle school in Horqin RF.

Art's parents, like Wave's, ran a family farm with pastoral aspirations (see Chapter 8), treading a thin financial buffer. In the late 1990s, Art's parents had a herd of 12 cattle, and later lost the entire herd during a severe sandstorm in 2002. Under the shield of the sand-darkened sky, a thief ushered Art's family's unguarded cattle—including five pregnant cows—through a fence that had been broken by the storm.

It was a cataclysmic blow to the family, like what Orchid had gone through when she lost her herd (see Chapter 8). Art's father looked for the lost cattle in nearby villages and grazing grounds for a month to no avail. So, he left home to work as a construction worker in Tianjin, a city neighboring Beijing. He started as an entry-level worker, carrying heavy loads and digging, and then he was moved up to cooking and guarding the construction sites at night.

When her family was devastated by their loss of the cattle, Art was in her second year of middle school. That year, Art told me, she "grew up instantly." She became a driven student and ranked at the top of her rural middle school. Her older sister and brother had dropped out of the same middle school a few years prior: her sister did so after the family had a poor harvest one fall, and her brother after he was blamed for a fistfight at school. His teacher had reprimanded him in front of the class, saying "why don't you just go home if you are not interested in studying?" The teenager felt deeply humiliated and never showed his face at school again.

Art was the sole hope to, in her words, "change her family's fate". After the high school entrance exam, she got into Solidarity High, the same high school that Wave attended. But Art's rural middle school had only prepared her to be admitted to an Ordinary class, not a Pinnacle class, at Solidarity High. Supported by her father's "money earned with blood and sweat" (*xuehanqian*), Art devoted all her energy and time to studying. She recalled one time when she studied for hours on end without taking any breaks, her vision weakened. When Art asked for a pair of eyeglasses, her mother, cash stripped, suggested that she look at the stars in the night sky as a remedy. Thankfully, Art's vision improved after she followed her mother's advice. In 2006, with a gaokao score of 499 points, 13 points lower than Wave's in 2009, Art got into Inner Mongolia Normal University (IMNU), a B-a-List university that ranked third among IMAR's top eight provincial-level universities.

Art told me she was not surprised by the result; her placement in an Ordinary class and poor training in English, among other factors, had set her on a path towards a B-List university. She was not disappointed either, as IMNU offered three distinct benefits. First, due to its mandate as the training center for K-12 teachers in Mongolian-track schools, IMNU offered a broad range of humanity-track majors that were taught in Mongolian language to match the subjects taught at K-12 Mongolian-track schools. This was a decisive advantage for MKM students because the wider selection of majors that could match their academic interests was not available to them beyond IMAR. Second, most humanities students in Mongolian-taught majors were exempt from spending an extra year (and the extra expense) in a preparatory program. Last but not least, IMNU is located in Hohhot, IMAR's capital city. It was a big move for Art, and it would give her a head start for a future in the city.

Though Art was neither surprised nor disappointed with the results of her college race, that did not mean that the stakes were low. Quite the contrary, expectations rise alongside the increasing financial and emotional investment at every step along the winding path towards the urban future.

When Art started college in 2006, her tuition—as a minority student—was 2,800 yuan per year (regular tuition was 3,600 yuan per year). With room and board, the total annual expenses added up to about 10,000 yuan. Art's parents were still recovering from the devastating loss of their cattle in 2002, four years prior. To pay for her first year of college, Art's parents borrowed 5,000 yuan from her aunt. In subsequent years, as the family slowly built back their herd, Art's parents would borrow more money, while also selling a couple cows every September when tuition was due, regardless of whether the cattle were at the optimal age for sale. It greatly slowed down the family's herd-size growth for reaching an economy of scale. Art's college expense laid not only the largest claim upon the income of her family of five, but also mortgaged her family's financial future.

In 2010 Art graduated from IMNU, alongside 6.31 million fellow college graduates nationwide, not counting the two- and three-year polytechnic college graduates. In IMAR, the year 2010 recorded 95,000 college graduates, a 20% jump from the previous year.[86] Universities that specialized in presumably more marketable fields produced even more graduates. At Inner Mongolia University of Finance and Economics, for example, the number of graduates increased from 691 in 2001 to 3,875 in 2010, a 5.6-fold growth over one decade. By 2012, the number jumped to 5,176 graduates.[87]

As a graduate of a leading university in IMAR, Art expected to land a stable government job in Hohhot, or in another large city in IMAR such as Ordos or Baotou (see Figure 5.2). Her expectation was shared by no less than 75% of the graduates of IMAR's leading universities, according to a survey conducted between 2009 and 2013. But this expectation materialized only for 6% of the surveyed graduates.[88] The immense gap between college graduates' expectations and their realities on the job market was particularly salient for female MKM graduates like Art.

Consistent with the national trend, female graduates accounted for over 60% of total college graduates throughout the 2000s and 2010s in IMAR. Female graduates' employment rates, however, are around 60% compared to male graduates' 70% across all sectors.[89] Job opportunities also disproportionately favored MKH- over MKM-track graduates; the latter reported 15% to 50% lower employment rates than their MKH counterparts.[90]

Anticipating stiff competition in the job market, Art decided to improve her chances by pursuing a master's degree at IMNU before leaving school. By the time she completed her master's degree in 2013, however, she found that "the boat rises with the water level." Job competition in IMAR had intensified since she enrolled in graduate school. In addition to a 15% annual increase in the number of college graduates, IMAR's job market was now further congested by swarms of master's degree holders like herself. Furthermore, as the job market contracted nationwide, IMAR's top 3% students who had attended national elite universities and hoped to settle in highly competitive metropolitan centers, were now returning to IMAR because of their comparative advantage in IMAR's job market. They compete for local top jobs and take jobs like the one Art had long dreamed of: teaching at a Mongolian-track high school in Hohhot, the capital.

So, Art took another step to improve herself and her chances. She applied for a PhD program at the prestigious Chinese Academy of Science in Lanzhou, the capital city of Gansu Province. She also took a civil service exam written in Mongolian for positions that require bilingual proficiency in Chinese and Mongolian. She did not gain admission to the PhD program, but passed the civil service exam and was given two posting options. One was at the Bureau of Environmental Protection in New Barag Left Banner of Hulunbuir League; the other was at the same bureau in Jalaid Banner of Hinggan League. Both banners are even more hilly and further away from Hohhot, the goal of her career move, than her home town in Horqin RF Banner.

Art figured that she did not spend four years in college and three years in graduate school only to return to the countryside—and in her eyes, to a place that was even more peripheral and backward than where she came from. She declined the offers and worked as a temporary English tutor at a private test-prep school in Hohhot (I will elaborate on the tutoring industry in Section III.3 of this chapter). Art also married her college classmate from IMNU the year after finishing graduate school.

Art's husband, Treasure, is Mongol and grew up in a farming village in today's Tongliao area, or what used to be south Jerim (see Chapter 8 and Figure P.III.1 and Figure P.III.2). It is a flatter, warmer and more productive farming region than Art's home village in the hilly north of Horqin RF. Art told me that Treasure's family was a couple notches better off than hers, as evinced by his family's modern silage production facilities and planting and harvesting machines.[91]

Treasure was a promising young professional himself. With marketable skills in Geographic Information Systems (GIS), Treasure started work at an IMAR-level government agency in Hohhot right after graduating from IMNU in 2010. His appointment was contract-based rather than a formal post (*bianzhinei*), and it did not offer the prospect of promotion. But the job came with partially subsidized housing in Hohhot and the "five insurances and one fund," (*wuxianyijin*). The five types of insurance being pension, medical, unemployment, work-related injury, and maternity, and the one housing fund being that to which the employer and the employee contribute. The "five insurances and one fund" is mandatory for all employers as stipulated in China's social insurance law. On the ground, however, few private employers in IMAR follow this law. Even in the public sector, benefits coverage varies from unit to unit, and is subject to negotiation. Treasure's work unit was a revenue-generating arm of a government unit.[92] Thanks to its contractual work for private companies and other government units, Treasure's unit was well-funded. As a result, skilled workers like Treasure received good benefits and a handsome bonus that greatly outweighed his regular salary of 3,600 yuan per month. In addition, as a contract employee with neither the hope of, nor the anxiety toward, promotion within the formal bureaucracy, Treasure was free from bureaucratic scrutiny. He applied his skills to freelance projects, and even co-founded a startup on the side with two college friends.

Meanwhile, Art kept trying. From 2014 to 2016, she applied to PhD programs each year yet failed all three attempts. In 2016, she also took a teacher recruitment exam written in Chinese to maximize her chances as there were many more

Chinese-track schools than Mongolian-track ones. She passed the exam and was assigned to a Chinese-track middle school in Togtoh County. Compared with the previously assigned civil service postings in the remote countryside, Togtoh is much closer to Hohhot. The teaching position was a formal post covered by the essential "five insurances and one fund." Yet, though its address is within the Hohhot Municipality, Togtoh is actually located in the hilly rural hinterland of Hohhot—and it was not possible to commute there on a daily basis. For one year, Art commuted weekly between her teachers' dorm in Togtoh and her home in Hohhot using "black shuttles," unlicensed ride-share taxis. In September 2016, a year after she started teaching at Togtoh's middle school, she gave birth to her first child and took a six-month maternity leave followed by a two-month sick leave. Thus, for most of her second year at Togtoh's middle school, Art stayed home taking care of her newborn child while preparing for more exams that she hoped would bring her closer to Hohhot.

In May 2016, Art took yet another teacher recruitment exam for schools in the Hui people's district of Hohhot. The Hui District is located in the core of the city. It is an old, deteriorated, less desirable area of Hohhot, and hence the competition over teaching positions there was less fierce. In her third attempt over the three years since completing her master's degree, Art finally landed a formal teaching position conducive to a daily commute in Hohhot, albeit to an undesirable district in the city. A year later, that middle school was demolished to make room for a new expressway. Art was assigned to another middle school in the same district. In 2017, Art and Treasure moved into a new 80-sq.m apartment that they bought with their savings and their parents' savings, to be paid off in installments over four years. In 2019, their second child was born.

For her part in their shared big-city aspirations, Art has held onto her stable job at the middle school in the Hui district, with a monthly take home of 4,300 yuan. Treasure has continued to work on projects in both the public and private sectors and travels for work often, sometimes for as long as a few months at a time for one project. With Treasure being away frequently, Art would be the primary caretaker of their two young children, but received help from her in-laws who moved in with them.

Settling in Hohhot, the young couple built a safety net across both city and countryside. Treasure retained his residency status back in his birth village to secure his entitlement to the decollectivized village land, at 12 mu per villager. Art moved her residency from her birth village to Hohhot. Her joint ownership of the new apartment in Hohhot qualified her for urban residency status. In turn, Art's urban residency has qualified their children to attend K-12 schools in Hohhot, a privilege that neither Art nor Treasure enjoyed when growing up.

In 2022, twelve years since college, Art, now 34, has a family as well as a job and a home in Hohhot. She felt she had done far better than her brother, two years her senior, who did not finish middle school. He was still single and tended a small herd of cattle in their home village back in Horqin RF. Art's sister, who also only completed part of middle school, married into a Han Chinese farming family in their home banner and continues to farm.

But happily-ever-after proves to be elusive. Six years into her job at the middle school in Hohhot, Art became listless for a host of reasons. The first concerns her school. Located in a poor Hui neighborhood with a dwindling population, the school's enrollment was shrinking and thus it could be shut down at any moment. Under Art's assessment, her students were mostly unmotivated and troublemakers, many of whom demonstrated serious "physical and mental health challenges." On top of that, as a low-ranking transfer teacher, Art has been assigned to teach "Political Ethics and the Rule of Law," no one's favorite subject. Of even greater significance, Art saw little prospects of for promotion. Art's school, which stood at a low rank and suffered declining enrollment, received little governmental support and a limited quota for staff promotions.[93] Since she joined the school in 2016, only a small quota for promotions had been allotted to her school. They were granted to colleagues who were better connected and/or those who were willing to take on heavy teaching loads, which entailed staying on campus for 12 hours a day. Such an arrangement was impossible for Art, the mother and primary caretaker of two young children. As a result, Art was stuck at the lowest rank of teachers, with a monthly salary that has remained the same since her first year of teaching at the school in 2016.

Art felt compelled to give it one more try, "so I will not have any regrets in my old age." In May 2022, Art took yet another civil service exam. This time she had her eyes on an entry-level opening at the Bureau of Environmental Protection in Hohhot's municipal government. Because of her low teacher rank, she was not eligible for higher-ranking positions in the government bureaucracy. Even so, this was a job that spoke to her interests more than teaching Political Ethics and the Rule of Law to disengaged middle schoolers. She also hoped that the prospects for promotion in a government bureaucracy would be brighter than at a declining middle school facing imminent closure.

For the position that Art was targeting, there were 182 contenders. The success rate of 0.55% was close to TsingPe's admission rates. Art told me that in some popular government units like the Bureau of Food and Drug Safety, it was not unusual for one entry-level opening to attract thousands of applications. At the end of June, Art found out that she did not pass the written part of the civil service exam, and thus was ineligible for the follow-up interview. Her double burden as a mother and a full-time schoolteacher made it difficult to find time to study, much less to enroll in test-prep classes like many other exam takers do.

Twelve years since college graduation, Art has taken one exam for a master's program, four exams for PhD programs, two civil service exams, and two teacher recruitment exams. After failing her most recent civil service exam, Art planned to try again, and apply—for the fifth time—to a PhD program. In a household covered by "five insurances and one fund," a joint income of more than 10,000 yuan a month, and an apartment in Hohhot, Art could afford the uncertainty of searching for something better. She has remained hopeful despite the delays and detours.

That hopefulness, however, is dissipating quickly among those who have graduated from college after Art. As the 2010s rolled on, the number of college graduates in IMAR has skyrocketed, and competition in the job market has escalated, creating much longer delays and more setbacks in college graduates' job searches.

The story of Tree, another Mongolian female college student who grew up in Jungar Banner, a jurisdiction under today's Ordos Municipality in IMAR's Central-West (see Figure 5.2), shows the growing frustration among IMAR's Local Top 17%. Tree graduated in 2014, four years after Art. That year, China's colleges produced 7 million graduates, and IMAR alone recorded 160,000—nearly double the number since 2010.[94] Tree's story was told by Huang Ruisheng (2018) in his master's thesis on the employment conditions of college graduates from Jungar Banner.[95]

Tree earned a bachelor's degree in accounting from Inner Mongolia University of Finance and Economics, one of the top eight in IMAR. Accounting was, a fast-growing major popular among female students. In 2017, when Huang interviewed her, Tree had been unemployed for three years since graduation.

Right after college, Tree was offered a job as a bookkeeper for a private real estate company in Jungar Banner, her home banner. Her mother thought that a local private firm did not deserve Tree's college degree. She told Tree that she did not sweat out blood and pinch pennies to send her to college only to see her working for the same company where the neighbor's "uneducated" son also worked. If Tree did not get a government job, how could she show her face in public? To save face for her mother, Tree declined the offer from the real estate firm and started studying subjects like Fundamental Knowledge in Public Affairs and learning how to write policy essays for the civil service exams. However, to date, Tree has failed every national and provincial-level civil service exam. Tree lamented that "there are just too many accounting majors out there, all of whom are women, competing for the same few jobs." In IMAR, accounting has been popular among female college students in the "non-science" track who sought training in a marketable skill that also promised more flexible work hours for the future mothers.[96] To express her frustration, Tree quoted the title of a popular song: "*Why Do Women Have to Make Other Women's Lives Hard?*" Furthermore, she lamented, "the cutoff score rises every year because the number of competitors increases every year, and every year there are more top students from top universities joining the race. I can only eat the dust behind these champion runners." Among the many civil service exams that Tree took was the state bank recruitment exam. Tree did pass the preliminary screening. But she could not afford the highly desirable job even if it were offered to her. To be considered for a formal position at the local branch of the state bank, it took more than passing the written exam and interviews. Tree would have to park 1 million yuan in a savings account at the bank for a minimum of three years. Tree told Huang that she started "losing faith in life." It was then that she stopped attending high school and college reunions.

Bridge, a male Mongolian graduate from Jungar Banner, was another college graduate portrayed in Huang's (2018) thesis.[97] Bridge's tale is of entrepreneurship gone astray. Bridge was a class of 2011 graduate from the B-list Inner Mongolia Agricultural University and majored in finance, another promising field that had attracted many of the Local Top 17%. Bridge's college expenses were higher than usual—he took the gaokao twice and attended a year-long private cram school before his second attempt. His younger brother started college the same year he did, thus doubling his parents' financial burden. In 2007, when Bridge started college, his top priority was helping his family's finances. As it happened, there was plenty of money to be made at that time. Bridge's home banner, Jungar is located within the metropolitan region of Ordos. Ordos was China's coal mining center and a major boomtown. According to geographer Max Woodworth (2022),[98] between 2006 and 2011, Ordos, with capital diverted from coal mining and compensation cash distributed to no less than 57,000 households whose land had been appropriated for mining and urban development, became a hub for informal high-interest lending. The creditors were not just big players. Rather, there were the many cash-rich and landless local residents with compensation cash looking for venues to make money with money. In 2010, the volume of non-bank credit in Ordos was estimated by the People's Bank to be 200 billion yuan (about US$30 billion), accounting for 83% of the local GDP that year. By a preliminary calculation, more than 63% of local residents in the Ordos metropolitan region took part in this massive, illicit lending scheme.

Bridge dived into the informal lending network as soon as he started college. His family did not receive compensation cash, but his friends' families did. He brokered loans during his college years and made more than he needed to pay for his tuition. He got himself a nice car and "enjoyed a life with lots of entertainment" for a few years. He did not think he needed a nine-to-five job in the government. But "to save his parents' face," he used his connections to land a temporary, non-payroll job in a unit in Jungar Banner government after graduation. Several months into the job, his boss started to consider paying for his "five insurances" as a reward for Bridge's willingness to take on extra assignments and his skills in fixing office computers. Getting the five-insurance coverage was a step towards becoming a "semi-formal" employee. Just when things were going well for him, the financial bubble in Ordos burst in 2011 after the central government's crackdown. Credit chains broke and loans went bad. One of Bridge's business partners was arrested by Public Security, and Bridge then bore more debt than he could handle. A vengeful creditor called Bridge's boss, and Bridge's illicit money dealings were now a problem in an unfavorable political climate. Bridge was let go, and his father sold the family home to help him pay back the debt. Hoping to make a face-saving comeback, Bridge tried his luck with the high-stakes online lottery, which only dragged him deeper into debt. Finally, after becoming a father, Bridge settled for running a humble mom-and-pop grocery store with his wife. In 2017, Bridge told Huang that his biggest regret in life was that he did not take the civil service exam.

III.2 Frustration Management

Tree's frustration and Bridge's regret, not to mention their parents' profound disappointment, were shared by many of the local Top 17% in IMAR. The ever-narrowing college graduate employment bottleneck has been a major concern of social stability for national and IMAR leaders. Social stability maintenance is a political mandate for central and local government leaders across China (see Introduction). In IMAR, a minority-concentrated border region, social stability maintenance is a particularly high-order geopolitical agenda. Meanwhile, IMAR reported the second highest college graduate unemployment rate of China's 31 provinces in 2016.[99]

China's central leadership has implemented two policy devices to try to put a lid on the escalating problem of college graduate unemployment issues. IMAR leaders are tasked to deploy them locally. One method was to expand graduate schools; the other was to expand public sector employment. Neither device is novel, and both create new contradictions.

Graduate school is a common stopgap solution, especially during economic downturns. Following the global financial crisis in 2008–09, China started expanding graduate school programs—and in particular, master's programs. College graduates, whose number grew more than tenfold in two decades, from 1 million in 2000 to 10.76 million in 2022, responded eagerly to this expansion.[100] Like gaokao, admission to graduate schools requires taking a national standard entrance exam called the Postgraduation Admission Test (PAT). Between 2001 and 2010, the number of people who took the PAT jumped from less than 500,000 to 1.4 million, a period during which the admission rate averaged around 30%. In the ensuing decade from 2010–2022, and particularly since 2020 (and the Covid pandemic), the number of graduate school exam takers exploded: from 1.4 million to 4.57 million (see Figure 9.1).[101] The increase of graduate school hopefuls outpaced graduate school expansion, and the admission rate has dropped, on average, to 24% since 2019. The 6% drop in the admission rate translates to a whopping 3.5 million college graduates who have tried, but failed, to get into graduate schools.

	2010	2016	2020	2022	2010–2022 Growth Rate
National Total	1.4 million	1.77 million	3.41 million	4.57 million	326 %
IMAR	23,376	39,091	75,366	97,563	417%

Figure 9.1 Growth in graduate school exam takers in China and IMAR, 2010 to 2022

Exploding numbers of exam takers and declining admission rates have created a vicious cycle, in which more multi-time veteran applicants join the swelling crowds of fresh college graduates in taking the PAT. In 2022, more than half of the 4.57 million PAT takers had taken the Test at least once before. As the demand surged, the supply shrunk. Many of the graduate school aspirants are alumni of B-list universities and are hoping to get a second chance at attending A-list universities through graduate programs. To maintain their own competitive edge, A-list universities now reserve 30% to 50% of their master's seats for their own graduates, lowering their admission rates to 2–3%.[102]

As the graduate school admissions race intensified, a graduate degree has also become almost mandatory to secure an urban white-collar job. It has been estimated that over 70% of the most desirable jobs at national-level bureaucracies, powerful state-owned enterprises, or large private corporations like Alibaba, Tencent, and Huawei, require at least a master's degree. As spatial mobility is an integral part of social mobility, a master's degree is also required for obtaining residency status in highly desirable cities like Shanghai.[103] In the 2020s, the PAT has been popularly perceived as China's "new gaokao," only that the new gaokao is even more grueling than the gaokao, and with an even lower success rate.

For those who have managed to get into graduate school through China's new gaokao, the challenge is not just the additional expense—they are also running against time. The market value of a master's degree is diminishing rapidly, given the rapid expansion of graduate schools at a time of job market contraction. After spending two or three years in a master's program, students' graduate degrees are even less of a guarantee of ideal employment than it was when they first enrolled, as Art has found out. Graduate school expansion, a policy aimed at frustration management, has therefore aggravated the frustration of what sociologist Wu, Xiaogang calls China's "over-educated youth" and their heavily vested, and often indebted, families.[104] Citing this labor market mismatch, Wu is not optimistic about the capacity for a slowing Chinese economy to produce enough positions for the swelling pools of accountants, environmental engineers, and aerospace technicians.

Contradictions found across the nation are often starker when viewed from IMAR. While China's national figure of graduate school contenders tripled from 2010 to 2022, IMAR saw its figure more than quadruple during the same period (see Figure 9.1).

Tree, the frustrated job seeker from Jungar Banner, had hoped to pass the PAT after her repeated failed job searches, picturing herself finding a future husband in graduate school. Back in 2017 when she talked to Huang, she acknowledged that that path was perilous. That path is looking even more so in the 2020s.

The second device deployed by the state to manage the frustration generated by the widening gap between expectation and reality is to expand state-sector jobs. This solution has again created new contradictions. For one, expanding public sector jobs contradicts the government's repeated efforts to trim state bureaucracy.[105] In order to comply with the national policy of bureaucratic slimming while carrying out the mandate of absorbing college graduates, local government agencies have created new positions in "extra-bureaucracies" (*shiyebian*) that are subsidiary to the elite administrative system and not always fully funded by the state budget. One level down, there are also non-staff positions that are completely off the formal payroll and are mostly short-term contract-based jobs in local government offices. It was what Bridge had for a brief period, as presented previously. Occupying the lower strata of the public sector, many of the extra-bureaucracy and non-staff jobs are created by project grants and are subject to the hiring units' financial capacity and have highly tailored and negotiable terms. Under the central state's ordinance of bureaucracy downsizing, an increasing portion of public sector jobs, especially those at the county and sub-county levels, have become informalized at varying degrees. It has been estimated that by the mid-2010s, no less than 80% of China's 50 million public sector jobs were found in extra-bureaucracy or non-staff positions.[106] The informalization of public sector employment has thus created tensions between college graduates' search for stability in the public sector and the growing instability and precarity of public sector employment.

Since the global financial crisis in 2008–09, the IMAR government has tried to do its part to uphold a politically sustainable employment rate in the region. By 2020, as Covid hit, youth unemployment rates surged in China. That year in IMAR, the first-time employment rates of college graduates dropped from 83% to 68%.[107] IMAR leaders stepped up by expanding the number of government positions, from 1,471 in 2019 to 7,270 in 2020. The 400% increase was the largest among China's 31 provincial-level jurisdictions that year.[108] But even with the 400% increase, the 7,000 plus posts were an insufficient response to the expectations of over 140,000 college graduates in IMAR that year.[109]

To absorb more graduates from the current and previous years, the government encourages college graduates to join the military or go to the countryside. Tens of thousands of short-term contract jobs were created at the grassroots level in village administrations, rural development programs, rural health care, and "Go West" projects.[110] Also, special teaching posts and paid "volunteers" in broadly defined "livelihood-improvement" projects (*minsheng gongcheng*) were created. A banner cadre I met in 2012 in Xilingol League told me that one of his priority tasks was managing student scholarships, interest-free student loans, as well as college graduates' employment; the college graduate employment program was now tied to poverty alleviation schemes. Many of these programs either lowered the threshold for minority graduates or held a reserved quota for bilingual minority candidates. But the official also admitted that most of these jobs were either extra-bureaucracy or non-staff appointments. It was the only way his banner could keep down the size of the formal state payroll and expand public sector employment.[111]

The expansion and informalization of public sector employment go hand in hand, creating an elastic state bureaucracy and precarious public sector employment. During my fieldwork in IMAR throughout the 2010s and my phone interviews in the early 2020s since the onset of the Covid pandemic, the term "turning formal" (*zhuanzheng*) came up frequently. Since most of the new employment opportunities in the public sector were informal and insecure, those who were lucky enough to get a public sector appointment had to go through the wearing process to hopefully move up to a more formal position. As Bridge's experiences have shown, the distinction between formal and informal employment is not binary. Instead, it is a spectrum. Bridge, as a contracted, non-staff employee, was hoping for the "five insurances" coverage that signaled one step up towards a more formal and secure position, and hopefully to be included on the payroll and be "turned fully formal" one day.

In IMAR, a township kindergarten teacher, a contracted employee of the township government, told me "I gave a red envelope with 50,000 yuan to a friend's friend who had connections to get me this contract job. My director promised that I could turn formal in three years." A crew member in the grassland patrol unit of a banner government's bureau of agriculture and pastoralism, worried that "this year seven non-staff employees in my unit are expecting to turn formal but there is only one spot according to my chief. And last Monday I heard a rumor that there might be none at all this year." Like the regular rank-and-file promotion politics that Art experienced at her middle school, "turning formal" is the object of fierce competition, and subject to the tyranny of quotas and the preference of the personnel decision-makers. The competition to "turn formal" could be even more fierce and less transparent than regular promotions. Meanwhile, the quest for employment opportunities and job security turns into the source of prolonged anxiety for many college graduates.

In short, to manage the daunting challenge of rising college graduate unemployment, state policies have created new contradictions at a time of economic slowdown. Expanding graduate schools has intensified job market competition for both college and graduate degree holders. Expanding public sector employment has accelerated the informalization of public sector jobs, thus reducing the job security that was an expected benefit of working in the public sector.

In any event, the elasticity of the state bureaucracy in their public sector job creation, especially the low-level offices in peripheral areas that are often deeply in debt, could only be stretched so thin. A third policy tool to manage college graduates' frustrations would be found in the market. This tool kit includes imposing hiring quotas on local private and semi-private enterprises. It also involves encouraging entrepreneurship among college graduates. The former tool has allegedly produced little more than paper agreements between graduates and private firms.[112] The latter tool is best exemplified by a serial entrepreneur, Blue. Blue is a male Mongol college graduate who grew up in Jungar Banner, whom Huang interviewed in 2017.[113]

Blue graduated in 2012 with a degree in urban planning from a Project 211 university in Xi'an, the largest city in China's northwest. Blue was uninterested in pursuing a nine-to-five government job and instead envisioned creating a business that would amount to a "perfect marriage between high tech and everyday needs." That vision materialized in the form of an automatic car wash service in his home banner of Jungar, under Ordos Municipality. Blue's startup funds came from the cash compensation that his family received in the late 2000s after their land was appropriated by the Ordos municipal government. As mentioned in the previous story about Bridge's loan brokerage, Ordos went through a coal mining and urban boom in the 2000s. To minimize resistance and expedite land rights transfers, the Ordos government paid high-sum compensation of several million yuan each and subsidized new housing to the displaced families.[114] While many of Blue's neighbors invested their compensation cash in underground loan schemes, Blue used part of the cash to install automatic car wash equipment in a retail space his family received, which was also a part of the compensation package, in the town center near his home village. Six months and 110,000 yuan later, Blue closed the shop. He blamed it on the difficulty of running a business in his hometown where he could not act "business-like" with relatives-turned-staff; nor could he argue with neighbors-turned-customers who expected free services. On top of that, he felt that local folks were simply not ready for the modern innovation because "they think machines do not clean cars as well as hands do."

After the car wash service, Blue tried again with a cold drink and dessert shop in which he co-invested with a friend. The shop had a promising location by the entrance of a movie theater in a newly opened modern shopping mall in a larger township of Jungar Banner. But few town folk were drawn in to the expensive-looking shopping mall, so Blue's dessert shop flopped.

In the following year, Blue decided to aim high. He invested one million yuan in a restaurant featuring his home Yekejuu cuisine[115] in a posh, high-rent location of Hohhot, the capital city of IMAR, running a monthly overhead of 100,000 yuan. When Huang interviewed Blue in 2017, Blue's few months-old restaurant was in deep red. Blue hoped business would pick up soon once the restaurant started to draw regulars. He told Huang: "if I lose money again this time, I will not be able to show my face back home."

III.3 Anxiety Economy

While the government attempted to manage the frustration of college graduates and their families by increasing graduate school seats and public sector jobs—and paradoxically creating fiercer competition and even more acute anxiety—the market saw an opportunity for immense profit in an anxiety economy. Over the first two decades of the new millennium, China's test-prep tutoring schools grew into a US$180-300 billion industry, sending the industry's leaders to stock markets in Shenzhen, Hong Kong, and New York and creating billionaires out of tutoring company founders. At a time when the road to elite universities and ideal jobs became tortuous and expectation fulfillment became elusive, providing roadside services to the anxious contestants in the college and job races seemed to promise a more tangible future for the investors.

The institutional foundation of the tutoring market is anchored in the system of competitive ranking. What Wave, Art and other Mongol college graduates have in common, regardless of their school standings and college race results, is their entrenchment in the competitive, test-based ranking system that starts from their first days of school up through their job searches.

IMAR, or China for that matter, is not alone in adopting the competitive ranking system based on standardized, comparable, and commensurable tests, which anthropologist Marilyn Strathern (1996, 2000)[116] calls "audit culture." Audit culture refers to the global trend of applying the logic of financial auditing to multiple other social domains—notably in education—in the pursuit of economic efficiency and regulatory accountability. As a culture, it involves a "new morality of attainment," epitomized by open-ended self-improvement and self-scrutiny through tests. Art's repeated attempts to take various tests to prove and improve herself attests to such morality of attainment. Moreover, in the case of Wave, Art, and others mentioned previously, the morality of attainment concerns more than the self. The drive for improvement is also about the students' sense of obligation and indebtedness to their families that have supported and sacrificed for them. The students live with the expectation to give back by improving the family's socioeconomic status with their academic and career advancement. The family's expectation and the students' sense of indebtedness created a moral imperative for the students to excel for themselves and for their families.

Feeding upon the widespread moral imperative of improving the self and family as well as the anxiety over losing at a time when college and job competition has intensified, the test-prep tutoring industry has grown rapidly in the new millennium. By 2021, there were more than one hundred Chinese education firms listed in the stock markets of New York (NYSE), Hong Kong (HKSE), and Shenzhen (SZSE). Among them, two companies stand out. One is "Good Future" (*Haoweilai*),[117] a K-12 tutoring empire which, at its peak, had an enrollment of 40 million students. The other is "China Public" (*Zhonggong*),[118] which specializes in civil service exam preparation tutoring.

Good Future was established by Zhang Bangxin (1980–), a Peking University grad school dropout who had supported his own college education in the 2000s by tutoring math online and offline for K-5 students. In the ensuing decade as he pursued his PhD degree in biology, he felt that tutoring K-5 students offered a brighter future for him than pursuing a PhD degree. The decade of 2010s saw escalating college and job competition in China in the aftermath of the 2008–09 financial crisis, and parents of future gaokao runners were getting anxious. By focusing on K-5 students, and by adding an advanced Mathematics Olympiad curriculum to regular classes, Zhang's Good Future met parents' belief that the race to the future is determined at the starting point, namely, during primary school, and even kindergarten.

Getting, and staying, ahead builds upon a consequential chain of benchmarks. Placement in a high-ranking class at a high-ranking primary school offers greater assurance for admission to a high-ranking middle school; students of a high-ranking class in a high-ranking middle school have a much better chance to test into a high-ranking high school, and then onto an elite university, whose brand name gives its graduates a leg up in the job race. Given the fact that no less than half of China's middle schoolers do not pass the high school entrance exam and will be destined to go to vocational schools or simply leave schools and join the working class, it is imperative to optimize a child's chances of getting into a high-ranking class and a high-ranking school and stay on top as early as possible. Under this shared belief in an early start, 60% of online and offline enrollment in K-12 tutoring lessons is comprised of primary schoolers, 30% by middle schoolers, and only 10% by high schoolers.[119] For those who manage to get into elite high schools, they participate in inhouse tutoring provided by the school and do not have to seek private tutoring. For those at low-ranking high schools, the hope is too dim to warrant such heavy investment in private tutoring. The primary market for the tutoring industry, in other words, is made up of the most hopeful, that is, parents who have the youngest schoolers whose futures are still wide open.

Targeting students' hopeful and anxious parents, especially those with K-5 graders, Good Future pioneered the practice of allowing parents to sit in at the back of the classroom during lessons. Good Future prides itself on reducing its class size to half of the industrial standard of over 40 students to 20 per class, so that the instructors can pay more attention to their young students. Meanwhile, half of the classroom is taken up by students' parents sitting in the back. Before opening a new school in a new location, Good Future routinely surveys the market by reviewing local parents' online chat groups to see how involved and active local parents are, before finalizing the decision to open a new school.[120]

Fueled by parental anxiety, the industry also fuels parental anxiety. K-12 tutoring is characterized by a low profit margin of between 8% and 11% for most establishments, thanks to its high overhead in personnel and rent for centrally located schools. The low profit margins need to be compensated for by a large sales volume. Emboldened by capital raised in the market and under pressure from shareholders and investors who expect high and quick returns, billions are spent on advertising to increase enrollment. In 2020, Good Future spent 11 billion yuan (US$1.64 billion), or 58% of its total operating costs, on marketing.[121] Good Future was not alone. China's most watched CCTV program, the New Year's Gala (*chunwan*) of 2020 had a lineup of China's top seven tutoring firms buying the most expensive segment of airtime on Chinese TV, at 150 million yuan (about US$22 million) per 30 seconds.[122] The cost was over ten times that of the Oscars (US$2.15 million per 30 seconds)[123] and quadruple the cost of Super Bowl ads (US$5.6 million per 30 seconds)[124] that year. Even parents who have misgivings about subjecting their pre-teens to the stress of long hours of afterschool lessons eventually give in after being bombarded by tutoring companies' advertising campaigns on television, websites, elevators, bus stops, and metro trains, which remind them that "If you join our tutoring class, we will train you; if you do not join us, we will train your competitors."[125]

If the ubiquitous advertisements failed to convince, parents' online chat groups and peer pressure often would. A mother reflected: "I was shielding my 7-year-old against tutoring classes until her best friend's mother told me she had enrolled her daughter in three afterschool classes. I feel I owe the opportunity to my daughter."[126]

Once the students are enrolled, it is the tutors' job to keep them for as many terms as possible. As tutors' pay scales would be directly tied to students' renewal rates, tutors turned into sales people. Parents routinely received thinly disguised marketing spiels from them: "Your daughter is already in the fourth grade. The coming year will be most critical if you want her to get into a key middle school. If you stop now, all your earlier investment will go to waste!"[127]

What did not seem to have gone to waste was Good Future's marketing efforts. In early 2018, eight years after going public, Good Future boasted 4 million enrollments in its in-person classes in 36 cities across China, plus 35 million in its online courses.[128] By the third quarter of 2018, another million students enrolled in its offline classrooms in 648 schools across 43 cities.[129] Good Future started trading on the NYSE in Oct 2010 with a US$1.1 billion market capitalization. By December 2019, its market capitalization reached US$27 billion, and peaked at US$54.1 billion on February 19, 2021.[130]

Good Future's doubled stock market value between the end of 2019 and early 2021 has a lot to do with the Covid pandemic. The Covid shutdown in spring 2020 led to a surge of capital flight from other sectors to tutoring schools, as online tutoring was believed to be the immediate future. In 2020 alone, the industry raised 54 billion yuan (US$8.5 billion), boasting a 267% year-over-year growth.[131] That year, Zhang Bangxin was ranked the 42nd richest person in China, with a net worth fortune of 95 billion yuan (US$14.2 billion), a huge jump from his 2019 net worth of 44 billion yuan. For reference, in 2020 China's richest individual was Jack Ma of Alibaba, with a net worth of 400 billion yuan (US$60 billion).[132]

As market boosters spread the gospel of K-12 tutoring's "inelastic demand" akin to market demand for gasoline, prescription drugs, and utilities, parents struggled to pay the skyrocketing tutoring fees despite China's public education system. In 2019, a Beijing-based professional couple, with an annual household income of 250,000 yuan, paid about 90,000 yuan a year on their second grader's tutoring lessons. These lessons were not just on academic subjects like math and English, but also extracurricular activities in arts and sports like piano, swimming, and Chinese painting that are also evaluated in the applications to elite middle schools. The steep tutoring expenses, which counted for 36% of the couple's total income, plus the mortgage (another 35%) for their apartment in an elite school district, not to mention the personal debts to both sets of grandparents for the down payment, has greatly constrained their household finances. The mother, a mid-career university professor in her mid-40s told me that her situation was not uncommon among her colleagues and friends.[133]

The financial burden was not only on urban parents. In rural areas, parents felt the pressure to enroll their children in the less costly online classes, which still cost at least 100 yuan for a 30-minute session. For families whose major source of income comes from farming (the national average being 1,500 yuan per month), or migrant work (averaging 4,000 yuan per month), two English and two math sessions a week plus textbooks would cost no less than 1,800 yuan a month, about one-third of the household income.[134]

On July 24, 2021, taking the market prophets by surprise, the central government dropped the bomb of "Double Reduction" (*shuangjian*), a regulatory crackdown on the tutoring industry. Double Reduction refers to reducing both the homework load and private tutoring lessons for K-12 students.[135] Under Double Reduction, all K-12 tutoring firms are to be converted into nonprofit organizations and are expelled from the capital market.[136] This was not the first time that the government had attempted to control the overblown industry. But this time investors knew it was for real, not least because the ordinance was issued by China's highest authority: the Communist Party's Central Committee and the State Council.

Share prices of K-12 tutoring firms plummeted overnight. Good Future's capital marketization dropped to less than US$3 billion, losing more than 95% of the market value from its peak.[137] Good Future had to scramble for its own future. Tens of thousands of tutoring schools were shut down. The draconian crackdown brought massive layoffs of tutors of these schools.[138] These tutors were no other than the young college graduates that the government has been trying to find jobs for, as outlined previously. In fact, the K-12 tutoring industry had been a major employer of college graduates during the 2010s: it is estimated to have provided as many as 10 million jobs in 700,000 plus establishments across hundreds of cities in China.[139] The employers were not just the leading national chains like Good Future, but also dozens of regional operators and no less than half a million local establishments, many of which were organized by public school teachers. As jobs seemed to disappear elsewhere, university and local government leaders had welcomed the tutoring schools because they helped improve college graduates' employment rates. Art (of Section III.1 on "Local Top 17%"), for one, taught at a small, local English tutoring school in Hohhot for a year before she found her job at a public middle school in 2014. Big Jin of the three Jin brothers (Chapter 4), who had showed more academic promise than his two younger siblings, also settled on tutoring middle school students in rural Gansu after several failed attempts at other career paths. As mentioned earlier, Zhang, the founder of Good Future himself held no less than seven math tutoring jobs to support his college and graduate school education at Peking University.

Admittedly, tutoring young kids for private employers was far from ideal for most college graduates. But for first-time job seekers of the late 2010s it was among their best options. A 2019 survey of teaching staff from the tutoring schools reported that 41% of the teaching staff were between the ages of 25 and 30 and 21% were between the ages of 30–35; 60% of the teachers had college degrees, and 33%, like Art, held master's degrees.[140] Meanwhile, the pressure on the tutors to double up as sales and even afterschool caregivers of the seven and eight-year-olds led to high turnover rates, which necessitated frequent recruitment campaigns. In the 2010s, tutoring companies were the most active recruiters at campus job fairs in Beijing and beyond, including at IMAR's top universities where fresh graduates were abundantly available.

The crackdown on the K-12 tutoring industry slashed millions of such jobs. Many of the laid-off tutors took the civil service exams, as Art and Tree have tried to do.

This is where the second tutoring king, Li Yongxin (1976–), comes in. Li's tutoring schools specialize in civil service exam preparation. Established in 2001 with his factory worker mother's savings of 30,000 yuan, Li's company went public on the Shenzhen Stock Exchange in 2011 under a shell company, with a market capitalization of 2.6 billion yuan (US$0.39 billion). By 2019, the company was renamed *Zhonggong* ("China Public"), known as Offcn, with a market capitalization of US$15.78 billion.[141]

Like Good Future, Offcn leads the anxiety economy in post-financial crisis China. While Good Future feeds on parental anxiety for their children's gaokao performance, Offcn feeds on college graduates' anxious search for job security—a security that is anchored in the state sector. In China's deeply entrenched statist culture, the state is the ultimate answer, and is perceived as where both obstacles and opportunities are found. In IMAR, like Tree's and other Mongol students' parents proclaimed, working in the state-sector earns face and pride for the family.

In a tightening job market reinforced by the statist culture, even contract jobs in the public sector feel more secure than what is offered by most private firms.

Meanwhile, as an increasing portion of state-sector jobs are informalized, the competition to get into the most secure and stable, elite segments of the state heated up, especially after the Covid slowdown. In 2022, 2.12 million (an increase from 540,000 in 2021) hopefuls took the civil service exam for national government positions, the most desirable public sector jobs. The average success rate was 1% across different government units.[142] That same year, 9 to 10 million more took other civil service exams for provincial and sub-provincial positions. In IMAR in 2020, as the provincial government quadrupled its recruitment plan from the previous year to over 7,200 posts, the civil service exam drew more than 137,000 contenders, resulting in an average success rate of 5.3%. By 2022, there were 120,000 hopefuls competing for 4,100 positions, with an average success rate that had dropped to 3.4%.[143]

Another popular employment outlet is public schools. Like government jobs, these teaching jobs are also increasingly informalized yet still considered to be more secure than working for a private establishment. To be a K-12 school teacher, college graduates would have to take two exams. One is the teaching certificate exam, the other is the teacher recruitment exam. In the teaching certificate exam in 2021, out of the 11 million exam takers, 323,000 (2.9% of the total) were ultimately successful in passing both exams. Among them were fresh college graduates, laid-off tutors from the 2021 crackdown, millions of failed exam takers from the previous years, and those who had already landed a job but hoped to move to a better one, such as in the case of Art who made repeated attempts to improve her standing and move from a rural to an urban school in Hohhot. For every move that Art has attempted, there were multiple tests that she had to go through.

The moral imperative of self-improvement and the anxiety for job security is well captured by a popular saying: "There are three kinds of unfilial piety, those are, not taking the graduate school exam, not taking the civil service exam, and not taking the teacher recruitment exam."[144] The saying is a satirical twist on the Confucian teaching that defines three kinds of unfilial piety as "disobeying the parents, abandoning aged parents, and not having offspring to continue the family line." Art, one of those that make up IMAR's Local Top 17%, has cited a group chat post that she felt best captured the mood of her and the later generations: "at the end of the universe, there lies the civil service exam."

Positioning itself at the "end of the universe," Offcn provides over one hundred types of online and offline tutorials that seamlessly match the vast number of public sector job categories and corresponding tests across China's 31 provinces. It takes multiple tests to land a job, if at all. Many of the tests are for certification, which qualifies successful test-takers for job-specific tests. Job-specific tests are divided into two stages: the written test and the interviews. Only those who are in the top few in written tests can move on to the interviews. As Chinese leaders strive to standardize its recruitment and promotion across China's various government and party organizations that require a great variety of expertise, the list of certification and recruitment tests grows. In addition to the tests for national and provincial core bureaucracy and extra bureaucracy, there are tests designed specifically for state-owned enterprises, cadre promotion, teaching certification and recruitment, law enforcement and judicial units, community work, township and village government, rural development and poverty alleviation programs, village cadre programs, the Go-West program that sends college graduates to western interior rural areas to teach at county and township schools, rural credit cooperatives, local government programs, firefighting units, veterans serving local government programs, banking personnel, medical personnel—the list goes on. Offcn offers not just tutorials for the hundreds of written tests, it also coaches students for job interviews.

Offcn's growth followed the rising anxiety of the exploding numbers of college graduates seeking public sector jobs. A former Offcn employee explained the logic of the anxiety economy: as civil service job competition intensified, the tests grew harder, and test takers' anxiety escalated. The elevated anxiety enabled Offcn to raise its tuition fees. Between 2011 and 2019, Offcn's revenue increased from US$0.55 to 1.32 billion, and peaked at US$1.65 billion in 2020, thanks to its large online services unaffected by the Covid lockdown.[145]

Investors were paying close attention. The Offcn share price started to rise rapidly. Its market capitalization doubled from US$15.79 billion at the end of 2019 to 33.22 billion a year later.[146] In 2019, with a personal net worth of close to US$10 billion, Li took over Good Future's CEO Zhang Bangxin's standing as the richest person in China's education industry and became the 40th richest person in China. A year later, his net worth doubled to US$20 billion, moving him up to become the 19th richest person in China.[147] Emboldened, Li went on an expansion spree: the number of Offcn's local learning centers increased from 701 in 2018 to 1,300 in 2020, spreading over 319 prefecture-level cities out of China's total 333 across 31 provinces. Its teaching staff increased from 9,424 in 2018 to 20,000 in 2020, with more than 45,000 on its payroll.[148] In IMAR alone, Offcn has established 47 learning centers across the autonomous region.[149]

The breakneck pace of expansion and the exponential sales growth of Offcn was built on a pair of financial schemes that Li pioneered.

The first is a counter-intuitive refund policy, which defied the industry norm. If a student did not pass the test or did not get their targeted job, Offcn promised to fully or partially refund them. In its IMAR operations, for example, for 10 days of interview coaching for the exam of "college graduates serving local government programs," the cost was 42,800 yuan in 2018. It was a grave financial commitment, considering China's average disposable income per capita that year was slightly more than 28,000 yuan and about 15,000 yuan in the rural area.[150] To persuade its reluctant customers, Offcn promised to reduce their financial risk by refunding the tuition in the event that they fail the interview. Offcn also offered a variety of packages for customers of different means. For just this one type of exam, Offcn's IMAR branch offered eight different kinds of classes of varying length, intensity, fees, and refund schemes. High-fee classes offer full refunds, and lower-fee ones offer partial refunds.[151] Thanks to the refund policy, Offcn was able to push up their sales volume, creating steady cash flow. The cash flow allowed him to invest in other sectors like real estate and the stock market, which in turn contributed to the company's high profits and share values.

Accounting for 80% of Offcn's sales, the refund scheme has a problem, however. The high exam failure rates had motivated the anxious civil service aspirants to enroll in refundable classes to minimize their potential losses. But the rising failure rates in civil service exams in the late 2010s led to a surge of refund requests: from 44% of sales in 2019 to 66% by the third quarter of 2021. In that quarter alone, the refund rate was close to 80%.[152] In other words, the refund scheme draws students into Offcn's classrooms, but the high number of failures and refund requests also weakened the capital chain.

In 2020, disputes over Offcn breaching its refund agreements proliferated. On Black Cat, an online consumer protection platform, Offcn was the target of more than 2,600 consumer complaints over seriously delayed or undelivered refunds. As is the way of the market, the large volume of complaints subsequently created a growing market for refund-collection legal services. Offcn's reputation began to plummet.

Parallelled with the refund scheme, Offcn used another financial tool to boost sales. This tool was the provision of loans to those who were reluctant or unable to pay the large tuition sum upfront. Offcn would broker a loan agreement between the student and a third-party lender in order to enroll the student. The agreement stipulated that if the student passed the exam, they would pay back the loan; if they failed, Offcn would take on their debt. The loan program pushed up enrollment numbers even faster than the refund scheme, to the extent that many small tutoring schools were forced to fold.

But again, the loan program was undermined by high exam failure rates after its initial success. To defend the program, Offcn openly blamed the students in the program. In Offcn's reasoning, these students did not have to pay anything upfront to take the tutoring classes and therefore were not motivated to study hard for the exam. As a result, their failure rates came out to be higher than usual. As a result of high failure rates, between 2019 and 2021, Offcn accumulated 5.2 billion yuan (US$740 million) in debt and has paid 420 million yuan in interest on this scheme alone.[153]

The unsustainable loan program hurt Offcn's reputation even more than the refund scheme. According to a news report, Offcn's sales representatives would tell prospective students that they would receive a "scholarship," in order to steer unsuspecting students towards signing the loan agreement. And Offcn had a poor record of honoring the agreement and taking over the debt after students failed the exams. Those who signed onto the program and failed the exam found themselves under debts of 20,000 to 30,000 yuan or more, with a 6.6% annual interest rate to boot. Others reported that some of the students have been pursued by debt collecting agencies.[154]

In March 2021, amid these controversies, Li donated 1 billion yuan to his alma mater, Peking University. It was said to be the largest gift from any individual that Peking University, the crown-jewel of China's higher education, has ever received from private donors. At the well-publicized donation ceremony hosted by the chancellor of the university, Li announced that he planned to donate 10 billion yuan more in the future.

A month later, the central government's high voltage "Double Reduction" crackdown on K-12 tutoring industry struck. Offcn was not a main player in the K-12 tutoring market, but the Double Reduction also included a ban on financial operations of all tutoring establishments, which affected Offcn directly. In its third quarter report of 2021, Offcn showed a 70% drop in year-over-year sales and a negative net profit.[155] Between March and December 2021, Offcn's share price plummeted by 80%. About US$20 billion of its market value had evaporated, more than 80,000 employees were laid off, and many more were furloughed. When it rains, it pours. In October 2021, China Securities Regulatory Commission and the Shenzhen Stock Exchange started to investigate Offcn's headlong fall in sales and profits as well as its irregular practices in information disclosure and loan schemes.[156] As of September 30, 2022, Offcn's market capitalization hit the floor at US$3.56 billion or 9% of its peak valuation of US$39.48 billion in November 2020.[157]

There is no shortage of boom-and-bust stories in the history of capital. While those stories share the basic ingredients of mass hype as well as wild surges and violent crashes in price, these bubbles are formed over particular boom and bust instances situated in a specific time and place—be it the Dutch tulip mania of the 17th century or the American dot-com fever of the early 2000s. The story of China's two tutoring kings' rise was complicated by the contradiction between the massification of education that exacerbated, rather than alleviated the mass competition, and the societal anxiety predicated on hyper competition. As the contradictions took on a life of their own and became the object of financial exploits, the Chinese state resorted to drastic measures to rein in the key actors. New contradictions inevitably arose. In the aftermath of the regulatory crackdown on the tutoring industry, the college and job races have not shown any sign of being quelled. And many tutoring classes have gone underground to the point where only the rich can afford the expensive one-on-one, at-home tutoring services under the disguise of "nannies" to avoid government scrutiny. Meanwhile, the crackdown has closed an important, yet under-recognized, employment outlet for millions of college graduates.[158]

Mongol students and their families share the nationwide anxiety over college admissions and job market contraction, as Wave, Art, Tree, Blue, and Bridge's struggles have revealed. IMAR is an integral part of the nation's competitive culture and anxiety economy. The tutoring industry's expansion fed on the rising anxieties of Mongol K-12 students' parents and college graduates in IMAR as much as it did in many other regions in China. K-12 tutoring provided jobs to Mongol college graduates just as it did in other provinces. The regulatory crackdown on the K-12 tutoring industry imposed a similar effect of massive job loss. As for civil service exam prep schools, Offcn had 47 learning centers and hundreds of tutoring programs in IMAR. Another national leading company in civil service exam preparation, Huatu, had a presence in all twelve of IMAR's municipalities and leagues. And Fenbi, yet another national chain that ran offline classes and a large online program, also held a significant share of the IMAR market.

Mongol students were not just an important consumer or source of labor for the nationally organized tutoring industry, some of them were also inspired by the promise of the tutoring business. Sun, a male Mongol college graduate, was one such aspiring entrepreneur.

Sun graduated in 2016 from the B-list Inner Mongolia Agricultural University, with a degree in chemical engineering. Like Tree, Blue and Bridge, Sun is a Jungar

Banner resident whom Huang (2018) interviewed for his master's thesis. During his college years in Hohhot, Sun supported himself by tutoring primary schoolers. It was the boom time of K-12 tutoring in China and in IMAR. Even Inner Mongolia Normal University, like many normal universities in other provinces, took advantage of its local reputation and offered tutoring classes at high fees.[159]

Sun saw its business potential and decided to start a tutoring school in Hohhot after college. Sun's parents were pessimistic about his plan, as they felt their family did not have sufficient savings or connections in the big city to ensure business success. Against his parents' wishes for him to secure a government job, Sun applied for a subsidized office space in the "Business Park for College Graduates" that the Hohhot municipal government had established under the central government's call for incubating college graduates' entrepreneurship. The prerequisite for getting a space in the business park was to take a business training course (the tuition for which the participants needed to pay themselves) organized by the municipal government. But the training course was repeatedly postponed due to low enrollment. The endless wait exhausted Sun and his parent's patience, and Sun aborted his business plan.

All in all, this story about Mongol students in China's college and job races may sound surprisingly similar to the tales from the rest of China, especially China's rural peripheries. That is precisely the point. Rural Mongol students have shared similar aspirations and struggles for upward social mobility like rural Han Chinese students elsewhere, attested by the stories about the three Jin brothers and Jin Three's two sons in Chapter 4. The stories about Wave's K-12 schooling are consistent with the education inequality between rural and urban areas and between rich and poor rural areas in China at large. Wave, Art and other Mongol MKM students' experiences are also deeply entrenched in China's competitive culture for social and spatial mobility via gaokao and urban employment, as well as the anxiety economy brewed by such a sociocultural milieu of hyper competition. For many critics, the similar experience and competitive culture shared by Han Chinese and Mongol students in the gaokao race led have them to the conclusion that Mongols have been sinicized.

For sure these stories could be read as a process of sinicization that has conditioned the minority experiences under the predominant Han Chinese institutions and values of social mobility. But ethnically labeled cultural assimilation captures only a partial picture of the politics of hope and hurdles for Mongol students in IMAR today. What matters just as much is the fact that Mongol students' experiences in the college and job races have diverged significantly, and the competition takes place in both inter- and intra-ethnic realms. Mongol students' heterogeneous experiences in China's college and job races, require an analytical tool beyond the term "sinicization." Once absorbed into the national education system, Mongol students of different gender, class and place backgrounds navigate the dual-track system, compete within and across ethnic nationalities, and strategize and mobilize resources under ever-narrowing minority preferential policies in college admissions. The question at hand goes beyond whether they are sinicized, but under what conditions and in what ways they align with the dominant Han socioculture and how variations occur under the unifying label of Mongol.

In this conceptualization, Mongol students' identification is shaped by their relationships with one another, with other minority nationalities, and with Han Chinese students. Their identification is also conditioned by the territorial dynamisms that create inter- and intra-ethnic competition. Such dynamisms mean that sinicization is not a switch from one finite ethnic orientation to another, but an evolving, relational process of navigation, positioning and adjustment. Unlike identity, which is often entangled with the past, identification mostly resides in the future. For Mongol students, different tracks and ranks hold vastly divergent projections of their future. The school tracks and ranks are about what kind of university they are most likely to get into, what kind of jobs they can realistically hope to find, and what kind of city in which they may be able to settle. Such future-oriented identification in the form of aspiration, expectation, and projection in the sociocultural milieu of hyper competition, in turn, has intensified the state's intervention in frustration management. It has also produced an economy of anxiety.[160] Mongol students' struggles for social mobility to move up and out of the peripheral region are deeply entrenched in the national institution and culture of aspiration, competition, and anxiety. Their sociocultural identifications define how sinicization works and what sinicization means for them. It is sinicization with Mongolian characteristics in IMAR today.

Notes

1. See Chapter 8 on the agropastoral and pastoagricultural dynamics of Horqin RF Banner in East IMAR.
2. China Office for National Statistics. 2020. Guojia tongji ju nongcun shehui jingji diaocha si [China Office for National Statistics, Bureau of Rural Social and Economic Survey]. China County Year Book, the Township Section. Beijing: China Statistics Press.
3. Brubaker, Rogers and Frederick Cooper. 2000. "Beyond 'Identity.'" *Theory and Society* 29 (1): 1–47.
4. Woodside, Alexander. 2006. *Lost Modernities: China, Vietnam, Korea and the Hazard of World History*. Cambridge, MA: Harvard University Press.
5. The estimate of the size of the tutoring industry varied in different sources, and it also fluctuated at different times. The figures of US$180–300 billion come from the following sources: Zhou, Zhongyu, 2019, "Jiaoyushichangbinghuoliang zhongtian sandajiaopeijutou shizhijunpoqianyi [Ice and fire in education market, market value of the top three exceeds RMB 100 billion each]," *Nanfang Daily*, 25 October, 2019. http://news.china.com.cn/live/2019-10/25/content_582419.htm. Accessed April 28, 2024. The author cited a consulting firm's report on the average market value of China's 55 listed education companies at RMB 14.5 billion, which totaled US$117 billion at the exchange rate of US$1:6.8 yuan. But this figure did not take into account the numerous medium- and small-sized tutoring schools and unregistered programs, which would contribute another US$80–100 billion, according to a finance journalist I talked to in 2018. According to China Institute of Managerial Science, the size of the tutoring market reached 2.24 trillion yuan in 2017, or US$344 billion, but dropped to US$187 billion in 2018. See China Institute of Managerial Science. 2019. "2019 zhongguojiaoyupeixunhangye shichangguimofenxi jihangyefazhanfenxi (2019 analysis of the market size and future development of China's

tutoring industry)." China Institute of Managerial Science, 10 April, 2019. http://www.zgypxw.cn/portal.php?mod=view&aid=31. Accessed May 20, 2024. Link broken by June 30, 2024. After the government's crackdown on the tutoring industry in July 2021, however, the size of the market shrank radically to US$4.8 billion, as illustrated later in this chapter. See 2022 jiaopeihangye yanjiubaogao (Report on Tutoring Industry), published on *21st Century Economic Report* website. https://www.21jingji.com/article/20220128/herald/25cc678f7e81fc352f816eb544488f9c.html. Accessed July 4, 2024.

6. Since 2020, Chinese-language lessons started in the first grade at Mongolian-track schools, and Mandarin replaced Mongolian language in several subjects. The radical move triggered protests and a wave of Mongolian parents transferring their students from Mongolian to Chinese-track schools and further shrank the number of Mongolian-track classes and schools. While the change in 2020 was radical, it was not unprecedented. For an overview of the changing bilingual education policies and practices in IM from the prerevolution era to the early 2000s, see Wulantuke. 2011. "Neinenggu muqu minzujiayu bianqian [Transformation of ethnic minority education in the pastoral region of Inner Mongolia]." In *Neimenggu muqu shehuibianqian yanjiu [Studies of Social Transformation in Pastoral Regions of Inner Mongolia]*, edited by Nashunbayier et al., pp. 98–163. Hohhot: Inner Mongolia University Press. The author, like several other IMAR-base scholars, noted that the decline in the number of Mongolian-track K-12 schools and in number of students had begun in the 1990s. What happened in the much-publicized event in 2020 was an ongoing trend accelerated by a radical policy shift. For the sociocultural impacts of the shifting language education policy in IMAR, see Rong, Yan. 2014. "Chengzhenhua jinchengzhongde muqujiaoyuxianzhuang yuchengyin: yineimenggu zizhiqu mengshi, qixian weili [Current problems and causes of school education in the urbanization process of pastoral regions: A case study in Inner Mongolia]." In *Huanjing zainan yu shehuisunshi [Environmental Disaster and Social Costs]*, report by Nandu Foundation, pp. 194–214. http://www.nandufoundation.org/Uploads/file/20141024/5449d2febb5eb.pdf. Accessed November 13, 2020. For reports on the language protests in IMAR in 2020, see Davidson, Helen. 2020. "Inner Mongolia protests at Chinas plans to bring in Mandarin only lessons." *The Guardian*, September 1. https://www.theguardian.com/world/2020/sep/01/inner-mongolia-protests-china-mandarin-schools-language. Accessed November 3, 2021; and Shepherd, Christian and Emma Zhou. 2020. "Authorities quash Inner Mongolia protests." *Financial Times*, September 9. https://www.ft.com/content/c035c3d7-0f96-4e23-b892-2666bc110e20. Accessed November 3, 2021; and a first-person account, in Su, Alice. 2022. "Why was this ethnic Mongolian school teacher branded an enemy of China?." *1843 Magazine*, November 22. https://www.economist.com/1843/2022/11/22/why-was-this-ethnic-mongolian-school-teacher-branded-an-enemy-of-china. Accessed December 1, 2022.
7. Zhang, Tingfang. 2007. *Xizang shaoshu minzu hanyu jiaoxue gaikuang yu yanjiu [Research on the Situation for Chinese Teaching and Study for the Tibetan Ethnic Minority]*. Beijing: Zhongguo Zangxue Chubanshe [Chinese Tibetna Studies Press], pp. 40–44; Ma, Rong. 2011. "Xizang shehuifazhan yu shuangyujiaoyu [Social development and bilingual education in Tibet]." *Zhongguo Zangxue [China Tibetan Studies]* 96: 108–139, p. 118.
8. According to Wulantuke (1997), between 1980 and 1995, Mongolian-track primary schools dropped by 32%, from 4,387 to 2,978; secondary schools dropped by 28% from

501 to 359. The percentage of Mongol students enrolled in Mongolian-track primary schools dropped from 73% in 1980 to 50% in 1995. In secondary schools, the percentage dropped from 67% to 47% during the same period. Meanwhile, overall Mongol students' school enrollment had increased by 30%. Much of the increased enrollment was in Chinese-track schools. Wulantuke. 1997. "Congneimenggu minzujiaoyu zuituchude wenti qi chanshengyuanyi ji duice [Minority education in IMAR: the most distinctive problems and their solutions]." *Studies of Minority Education* 2: 12–15. This trend continued into the 2000s according to several regionally focused studies. See for example, Bao, Yuzhu. 2008. "A study of language contact and shift in Harqin of Ningcheng County, Inner Mongolia." *Chinese Education and Society* 41 (6): 71–93.

9. Elliott, Mark. 2015. "The Case of the Missing Indigene: Debate Over a "Second-Generation" Ethnic Policy." *The China Journal* 73: 186–213.
10. Shepherd, Christian and Emma Zhou. 2020. Ibid.
11. After the closure, the school building was turned into a kindergarten for a year, then it was subsequently taken over by two village families. One of them was the school cook to whom the village owed salary payments. Like Wave's father who was granted 25 mu of land as payment in kind for his work as a village accountant of Fresh Springs (see Chapter 8), the school cook was given three of the six vacated classrooms as salary payment. The other three classrooms were sold to another villager.
12. "Quanguonongcun xiaoxueshiernian jianyiban, chedianbingxiao yinfaxiliewenti [Rural schools halved during the last 12 years, school closures and mergers create a series of problems]." 2011. *China Youth Daily*, December 24. https://www.chinanews.com.cn/edu/2011/12-24/3556162.shtml. Accessed May 4, 2023; Chen, Wei. 2012. "Chedianbingxiao shiniankao: xiangcunjiaoyu cheng chengjixiang ruocunkong [Ten years of rural school closures and mergers: Urban schools squeeze out rural schools, vacating weak villages]." *China News*, March 1. https://www.chinanews.com.cn/edu/2012/03-01/3711906_2.shtml. Accessed May 4, 2023.
13. Political scientists Kevin O'Brien and Liangjiang Li (1999) have argued that Chinese local officials have practiced "selective policy implementation," that is, they would weigh the political cost and benefit to decide which policies to implement, in what way(s) and to what extent. O'Brien, Kevin and Lianjiang Li. 1999. "Selective policy implementation in rural China." *Critical Comparative Politics* 31 (2): 167–186.
14. Hsing, You-tien. 2010. *The Great Urban Transformation: Politics of Land and Property in China*. Oxford: Oxford University Press.
15. Su, De (2005) and Fengjiao Hou (2020) reported similar challenges in today's Tongliao Municipality, what used to be south Jerim presented in Chapter 8. Hou's survey showed a similar situation persisting in rural schools that struggled to stay open in 2018 and 2019. Meanwhile, new problems emerged in the expanded schools in town centers or county seats. They were overcrowded and schooling costs increased greatly for parents, despite free tuition. The new costs include dorm fees, meal plans, and the living and housing expenses for one adult in the family to stay in town to take care of the young students who could be as young as six or seven. School bus-related accidents also rose: the commute between villages and schools far away from the village is often operated by unregulated bus companies hiring unlicensed drivers driving on rugged mountain dirt roads. While some parents sunk into debt to pay for the expenses, others had to let their children stop attending school. See Su, De. 2005. "Duoweishiye xiade shuangyujiaoxuefazhanguan-neimenggudiqu mengguzu zhongxiaoxue gean [Bilingual Education Development: Case

Studies of Mongolian Track Primary and junior Middle Schools in IMAR]." Doctoral dissertation. Minzu University of China; Hou, Fengjiao. 2020. "Kulunqi bannongbanmudiqu menghanshuangyujiaoyu mainlined kunjingji duice: yinemenggutongliaoshi kulunqi liangsuoxuexiaoweli [Impediments of Mongolian-Chinese Bilingual Education in Agropastoral Regions in Inner Mongolia: A Case Study of Two Schools in Kulun Banner of Tongliao Municipality]." Master's thesis. Zhejiang Normal University.

16. At Wave's school, there were also students of other minority nationalities, like Manchus, Evenks and Oroqens who grew up in Mongolianized communities and often had a better grasp of Mongolian than ethnic Mongolian students from eastern IMAR's farming areas.
17. As rural school closures made schooling prohibitively expensive, it also made the remaining schools, especially the dorms, overcrowded and unsafe. In their studies of the Mongolian primary and middle schools in rural Tongliao, De, Su (2005) reported that dropout rates increased significantly after the consolidation policy was implemented. See Su, De. 2005. Ibid. p. 152
18. Fictional name.
19. The school rankings came from Wave. The number of Mongolian-track high schools in IMAR comes from: "Neimenggu youduoshao Mengguzuzhongxue [How many Mongolian ethnic secondary schools does IMAR have?]." 2017. *Mengququan [Mongolia Circle]*, August 15. https://www.sohu.com/a/164829830_645084. Accessed May 7. 2023. This figure includes both Mongolian and Mongolian-Chinese mixed high schools.
20. In 2003, China adopted a policy that allowed nongovernmental actors and investments in K-12 schools. Private K-12 schools with diverse quality and tuition scales have proliferated since. But, with the exception of some private international schools, most of China's private schools are considered inferior to the "key" public schools established by local governments.
21. For a recent study on the increasing disparity between rural and urban high schools and the disadvantages of rural students in *gaokao* competition, see Lin, Xiaoying. 2023. *Xianzhongde haizi: zhongguoxianyu jiaoyushengtai [Students of County-Level High Schools: Education in Chinese counties]*. Shanghai: Shanghai People's Press.
22. Yu, Yang. 2021. "Chaojizhongxue shenhuapomie [The quashed myth of super high school]." *China News Weekly*, December 29. https://www.163.com/dy/article/GSDFUH460514BE2Q.html?f=post2020_dy_recommends. Accessed May 7, 2023.
23. Narentana (2013) found that among the Mongolian-track schools, "key schools" or "experimental schools" in the large cities had no problem attracting students, but the rural Mongolian schools at the county (sumu) level have been struggling to stay open. Narentana. 2013. "Neimenggu shuangyujiaoyu wentiyanjiu-yi keerqinzuoyihouqi weili [Bilingual Education in IMAR: A Case Study of Horqin Left Rear Banner in Tongliao Municipality]." Master's thesis. Northwest Minzu University.
24. In many areas, especially in areas where parents are more involved in school affairs, many schools have long abandoned the discriminatory labels like "Pinnacle" and "Ordinary" classes to avoid hurting the feelings of Ordinary class students and their parents. However, the practice of class ranking and test score-based placement of students has continued.
25. IMAR is far from being alone in channeling students into ranked classes. According to a Beijing-based researcher to whom I talked in 2016, in top-ranking high schools in many Chinese cities, especially the large ones with 5 to 10 thousand enrollments, students are sorted into a pyramid of ranks, branded from bottom to top as "Ordinary," "Rocket," and "TsingPe" classes. Under the "Rocket" category, classes are further ranked into "Small

Rocket" and "Big Rocket." "TsingPe" is the portmanteau of Tsinghua and Peking Universities, China's two most prestigious universities. Students in the TsingPe class are expected to get into TsingPe Universities with projected gaokao scores of at least 680 out of the total of 750. They are also decorated with various prizes won at extracurricular activities in arts and sports as well as at academic competitions like the Mathematics Olympiad.

26. Interview with a university professor in Hohhot 2016.
27. Referencing the China Language Usage Survey published in 2006 by the PRC State Council Language Commission, Enze Han (2011) suggested that 75.5% of residents in IMAR could speak Chinese and Mongolian. Han, Enze. 2011. "The dog that hasn't barked: Assimilation and resistance in Inner Mongolia, China." *Asian Ethnicity* 12 (1): 55–75. Another survey in 2004 showed that 90% of Mongolians in IMAR agropastoral regions were bilingual, and 84% of urban Mongolians were bilingual. See Zhaorigetu (G. Jorigt). 2005. "Neimenggu mengguyu shiyong xiangzhuangdiaochade chubu jieguo [Preliminary results of a Mongolian language usage survey in Inner Mongolia]." Paper presented at China's inaugural International Conference on Ethnolinguistics. https://www.sinoss.net/uploadfile/2010/1130/5011.pdf. Accessed May 9, 2023.
28. Bao, Xiaohua. 2015. "Neineggu tongliaodiqu menghanyuyan jiechuwenti zongshu [Language contact between Mongolian and Chinese in Tongliao area of IMAR]." *Journal of Inner Mongolia University for Nationalities (Social Sciences edition)* 41 (5): 98–101.
29. The process of establishing Chakhar Mongolian as the official Mongolian was contentious. The disagreement among different regional interests did not settle until 1979. See Changbao. 2017. "Congbianyuan daozhongxin: keerqinminge ji keerqin quyuwenhuarentong dechonggu [From the periphery to the center: Transformation of Horqin folk songs and regional cultural identity]."*Journal of Inner Mongolia Normal University (Philosophy & Social Science edition)* 46 (6): 101–106. Also, while the pronunciation of Chakhar Mongolian is close to the Khalkha Mongolian used in Mongolia, the official Mongolian in China maintains its traditional Mongolian writing system. Across the border, the writing system of Khalkha Mongolian in today's Mongolia has been streamlined by adopting the Cyrillic script. As a result, even if Chinese Mongols could communicate orally with their northern Mongol neighbors, Mongols of the two countries are unable to communicate textually. Interview with a scholar in Hohhot, 2014. See Zhou, Minglang. 2003. *Multilingualism in China: The Politics of Writing Reforms for Minority Languages 1949–2002*. New York: Mouton de Gruyter.
30. For example, by the early 2000s, out of the 4,600 commonly used Horqin Mongolian words, 606 of them (13% of total) originate from Chinese verbs, nouns, or adjectives. See Jiang, Genxiong. 2007. "Congyuyanjiechukan mengguyukeerqin tuyudeyanbianfazhan [Evolution of Horqin dialect from the perspective of language contact]." *Journal of Neimenggu Minzu University (Social Science edition)* 6: 48–51, p. 48.
31. Changbao. 2017. Ibid. p. 103; and interview in Ulanhot. 2017.
32. For the studies of interlanguages of East IMAR, see, for example, Hong, Lian. 2013. "Renkouqianyiliudongdui mengguyukeerqinfangyande yingxiang [The impact of migration on Horqin Mongolian dialect]." *Journal of Inner Mongolia Minzu University (Social Science edition)* 1: pp. 40–42; Guo, Xiaoyan. 2014. "Tongliaoshi fangyanyu putonghua tongxingci bijiaofenxi [Comparison of shared vocabularies in Tongliao's (Mongolian) dialect and Putonghua]." *Journal of Languages* 1: 21–22; Zhang, Wanyou. 1997. "Neimenggu hanyufangyan cihuitedian chutan [Vocabularies in Han Chinese dialects in Inner Mongolia]."

Journal of Inner Mongolia Social Sciences 1: 91–94; and Zhang, Huan. 2018. "Menghan shuangyudiqu hanyutongyongyu bianyi [Variations of Han Chinese in Mongolian-Chinese Bilingual Areas]." Doctoral dissertation. Jilin University. pp. 92–96; and Bao, Xiaohua. 2015. Ibid.

33. For example, "我明天去北京" is Mongolianized as "我明天北京去."
34. For example, "孩子在家里种地" is Mongolianized as "孩子家里种地"; and "他被老师批评了" is Mongolianized as "他老师批评了."
35. For example, in Putonghua, cellphone is *shouji* (lit. "hand-held machine"), in standard Mongolian, it is *gar utes* (lit. "line in-hand"). In Putonghua, sneaker is *yundongxie*, in standard Mongolian, it is *gutel* or *shahai*. Orchid would say shouji for "cellphone" and "yundongxie" for sneakers.
36. Mullaney, Thomas. 2012. "Introduction." In *Critical Han Studies: The History, Representation, and Identity of China's Majority*, edited by Thomas Mullaney, James Leibold and Stéphane Gros, pp. 1–20. Oakland, CA: University of California Press.
37. China's provincial-level jurisdictions include provinces, autonomous regions, and the four provincial-level municipalities of Beijing, Shanghai, Tianjin, and Chongqing.
38. Ma, Shuaisha. 2021. "Shishangcanjiarenshu zuiduode gaokao [The largest number of gaokao participants in history]." *China News Network*. June 7. http://www.stdaily.com/cehua/June7th/2021-06/07/content_1151936.shtml. Accessed May 10, 2023; and "Erlingeryinian quanguogaokao baomingrenshu yilongqibawan biqunian zengjiaqiwan [Gaokao enrollment reached 10.78 million in 2021, a 70,000 jump from last year]." 2021. *Sina Education*, June 2. https://edu.sina.com.cn/gaokao/2021-06-02/doc-ikqcfnaz8692202.shtml. Accessed May 10, 2023. The scale of China's gaokao significantly dwarfs the combined size of the Standard Assessment Task (SAT) and the American College Test (ACT), the standard tests required by U.S. universities for admission, which were taken by fewer than 3.5 million students in 2014—a number that has continued to decline since then. See Larmer, Brook. 2014. "Inside a Chinese Test-Prep Factory." *New York Times Magazine*, December 31; and Nietzel, Michael. 2021. "The number of students taking the ACT dropped 22% this year." *Forbes*, October 13. https://www.forbes.com/sites/michaeltnietzel/2021/10/13/the-number-of-students-taking-the-act-dropped-22-this-year/?sh=6a639de5c60a. Accessed January 13, 2022.
39. "Ersanniangaokao baomingrenshu yierqibawanren [Gaokao enrollment of 2023 reached 12.78 million]." 2023. *Sohu News*, March 17. https://www.sohu.com/a/655320472_121387824#. Accessed May 2, 2023.
40. See Hsing, You-tien. 2010. Ibid. Chapter 4, for the connection between new university campuses built on the metropolitan fringe and the growth of the urban real estate market.
41. The rest were adult higher educational institutions (HEIs) and other types of HEIs. See Ministry of Education of the People's Republic of China. 2021. "Gejigelei xuexiao xiaoshu, jiao zhigong, zhuanren jiaoshi qingkuang [Number of Schools, Educational Personnel and Full-time Teachers by Type and Level]." http://www.moe.gov.cn/jyb_sjzl/moe_560/2021/quanguo/202301/t20230104_1038068.html; Ministry of Education of the People's Republic of China. 2021. "Gejigelei minban xuexiao xiaoshu, jiao zhigong, zhuanren jiaoshi qingkuang [Number of Non-government Schools, Educational Personnel and Full-time Teachers by Type and Level]." http://www.moe.gov.cn/jyb_sjzl/moe_560/2021/quanguo/202301/t20230104_1038065.html; "Gaodeng jiaoyu xuesheng shu [Number of Students in Higher Education Institutions]". 2021. http://www.moe.gov.cn/jyb_sjzl/moe_560/2021/quanguo/202301/t20230104_1038055.html. Accessed on May

13, 2023; and Zhao, Ziyang (former Premier of the PRC). 1983. "Rijiubasannian guowuyuan zhengfugongzuo baogao [1983 State Council report on government work]." First session of the Sixth National People's Congress. June 6. http://www.gov.cn/test/2006-02/16/content_200823.htm. Accessed May 11, 2023.

42. "Erlingeryinian gaokaoluqulü jiangchaoguo baifenzhijiushi [College admission rates will exceed 90% in 2021]." *Sohu News*, February 24. https://www.sohu.com/a/452443800_120160470. Accessed May 10, 2023; "Zhongguo gaokaoluqulü bianhua [Changes in China's college admission rates from 1950 to 2022]." *Xixiwang*, August 8. http://m.news.xixik.com/content/4135b07c0b82afff/. Accessed May 10, 2023.
43. Before a more systematic comparison between TsingPe and Harvard admission rates is found, a couple of preliminary figures can help put them in perspective. Harvard University's admission rate in 2021 was 5.2%, based on the applications made to Harvard. See Bishai, Graham and Dianne Lee. 2021. "Meet the class of 2021." *The Harvard Crimson*. https://features.thecrimson.com/2017/freshman-survey/makeup-narrative/. Accessed May 11, 2023; the total number of applications received at Harvard in 2021 amount to about 0.6% of total number of applications made to 900+ U.S. universities through one of the most popular application portals, the Common App. See Rickard, Jenny. 2021. "Common App Application and applicant trends." Common App, March 9. https://mailchi.mp/f3ddd6c16b4a/application-trends-through-march-1. Accessed May 11, 2023.
44. The ranking, conducted mostly by various tutoring and consulting services, has been consistent with the A-list universities, but much less so with the B-listers. Also, the ranking of the majors and universities does not always align. A No. 10 university might have a No. 2 computer science department in the national ranking, for example. But given the sociocultural significance of university brand names, especially for rural students, getting into a higher-ranking and better-known university often matters more than getting into a higher-ranking major at a lower-ranking university.
45. It is telling that 25% of the 670,000 admits to A-List universities in 2021, totaling 167,000, were second- or third-time returning *gaokao* takers who might be admitted to a B-list university in their first attempt, but felt that they could do better. So, instead of attending a B-list university that is worth much less than an A-lister, these students went through a one-year cram school to prepare for the second, or even third try, with *gaokao*. The experienced and vested veteran *gaokao* takers have created an even fiercer college competition.
46. The figure is an estimate based on 10-12 B-list universities per provincial-level jurisdiction. Admittedly, the number and the definition of B-List universities vary greatly across provinces and official data was unavailable.
47. 30–35% is an estimate based on B-list admission rates across provinces, which vary from less than 20% to over 40%.
48. For a report on China's "unloved and half-forgotten" vocational colleges that have trained 40% of China's college students, see 2022. "China's slowdown is hurting the young: The woes of vocational-college graduates are revealing." *The Economist*. November 24. https://www.economist.com/china/2022/11/24/chinas-slowdown-is-hurting-the-young.
49. Fictional name.
50. Sautman, Barry. 1999. "Expanding access to higher education for China's national minorities: Policies of preferential admissions." In *China's National Minority Education: Culture, Schooling, and Development*, edited by Gerard Postiglione, pp. 173–210, p. 173. New York: Falmer.

51. See, for example, Jin, Donghai et al. 2007. "Guanyuwoguo shaoshuminzuxuesheng gaokaoyouhuizhaoshengzhengce ruoganwentide sikao [Reflections on China's minority gaokao bonus point policies]." *Journal of Northwest Normal University (Social Sciences)* 44 (1): 84–88; Du, Shehui. 2014. "Pingquanshiyuxia shaoshuminzuyouhuizhengce [The minority bonus point system from the lens of equal rights]." *Hubei Social Sciences* 11: 23–29.
52. See, for example, Qi, Zhiwei et al. 2013. "Shaoshu minzu kaosheng jiafenzhengce jiqishehuixintai yingxiangyanjiu [Impact of bonus point policies on minority students' mentality]." *Heilongjiang Ethnicity Bimonthly* 4: 13–21.
53. Chen, Bateer et al. 2019. "Cong buchangxinggongping dao duoyangxingchangdao [From compensational fairness to promotion of diversity]." *Jiangsu Higher Education* 10: 28–34.
54. Li, Huanyu. 2021. "Duodishoujin shaoshuminzugaokaojiafen: shaojinshangtianhua, duoxuezhongsongtan [Minority's Gaokao bonus points reduced in many places: (We should) refrain from adding flowers to a garden, (instead we should) send coal to snowy lands]." *Observer Net*, March 31. https://new.qq.com/omn/20210331/20210331A0EFDY00.html. Accessed May 19, 2023.
55. Inner Mongolia Bureau of Education. 2021. "Neimengguchutai shenhuagaokaojiafen gaigegongzuo fangan [Inner Mongolia announces plan to deepen the reform of the gaokao bonus point system]." 2021. Accessed September 15. https://gaokao.chsi.com.cn/gkxx/zc/ss/202109/20210915/2108556667.html. Accessed May 19, 2023. What these 67 counties have in common is that Han Chinese are the dominant local majority, and most of the minority students in these counites are monolingual Chinese speakers, the MKH students in Chinese-track schools.
56. Provincial-level jurisdictions include provinces, autonomous regions, and provincial-level municipalities like Beijing and Shanghai. To streamline the text, I will use "province" to include all three for the rest of this chapter.
57. Shiguanlüyou. 2021. "Gaokao 985 211 zaineimengluqufenzhuxian paiming yuxiangxiangzhong chajuhenda [Surprising cutoff scores of 985 and 211 universities in Inner Mongolia]." August 27. https://www.163.com/dy/article/GICLHLOV054483AE.html. Accessed March 18, 2022. The number of IMAR gaokao takers who scored above 550 in science and humanity tracks in 2018 were found at: http://www.creditsailing.com/school/yfyd/15/2018/2/2691251.html and http://www.creditsailing.com/school/yfyd/15/2018/1/2691210.html. Accessed June 14, 2023.
58. 2019. "Zaizhongguo tongguo gaokao jinru dingjiandaxue youduonan? [How difficult is it to get into top universities via China's gaokao?]." *Fuhuazixun*, June 7. http://zh.innovationkm.com/?p=888. Accessed May 19, 2023.
59. The eight minority jurisdictions include IM, Ningxia Hui, Xinjiang Uyghur, Tibet, and Guangxi Zhuang Autonomous Regions as well as Guizhou, Yunnan, and Qinghai Provinces.
60. Liu, Eerduntu. 2010. "Xinzhongguogaokao minzuqingxiezhengcede huiguyufansi [Review and reflection on minority preferential policies in new China]." *Heilongjiang Ethnicity Bimonthly* 114: 177–180.
61. 2022. "Neimenggugaokao ruoganfen keyishang 985 daxue? [What gaokao score does an Inner Mongolian student need to get into a 985 university?]." *Jushawang*, January 30. http://www.jvsha.com/20860.html. Accessed May 19, 2023; and Yang Laoshi. 2020.

"985 daxuezaineimenggu luqufenshuxianpaiming 2020 [Cutoff scores of 985 universities in Inner Mongolia in 2020]." *Gaokao 100*, November 26. https://www.gk100.com/read_10760.html. Accessed May 19, 2023.

62. Liu, Yunshan et al. 2009. "Jingyingdexuanba:shenfen diyu yuzibendeshijiao [Elite selection from the lens of status, locale, and capital]." *Tsinghua Journal of Education* 30 (5): 42–59.
63. Liu, Yunshan et al. 2009. Ibid. pp. 50–51.
64. In 2020, Tsinghua University celebrated its successful recruitment of rural students who counted for 20% of its incoming cohort that year, after three decades of low rural admittances at 10% to 18%. The progress was brought about by the government-mandated rural student preferential admissions program called "Dream Building" (zhumeng). But Peking University continued to stay at 10% despite the program. See Li, Xiao. 2020. "Qinghuanongcunxuesheng chongxinchaoliangcheng, hanmenchuguizi gengrongyilema? [20% of Tsinghua university's incoming cohort are from rural areas this year—is it easier for poor students to move up now?]." *US China Press*, September 17. https://www.uschinapress.com/static/content/SH/2020-09-17/756227995521523712.html. Accessed May 19, 2023. For the selected rural few who made it to top universities, however, many have encountered sociocultural exclusion in school and on the job market, according to my interviews in 2007, 2010, and 2013 with six professors at three A-list universities in Beijing. Some minority college students have also faced similar challenges. See Pang, Zhihua. 2013. "Gaoxiaoshaoshuminzuxueshengde tedianji jiaoyutujing [Minority college students' special needs in education]." *Journal of Inner Mongolia Agricultural University (Social Science edition)* 15 (1): 106–108.
65. As of 2020, 85.4% of Hohhot's 3.45 million residents were Han Chinese, and 11.6% were Mongol. See Hohhot Bureau of Statistics. 2021. "The 7th population census of Hohhot" May 17, 2021. http://tjj.huhhot.gov.cn/tjyw/tjsj/tjgb/202105/t20210527_943455.html. Accessed August 16, 2023. In the same year in Baotou, IMAR's industrial-mining center, 94% of its 2.83 million residents were Han Chinese, 3% were Mongol. See Baotoushi diqici quanguorenkou puchagongbao jiedu (Interpreting Baotou's 7th population census), *Baotou News*, 7 July, 2021. https://www.baotounews.com.cn/p/748474.html. Accessed Aug 16, 2023. The Han-Mongol ratio in both cities was more skewed than IMAR's average, which stood at 79% Han Chinese and 17% Mongol. See IMAR Bureau of Statistics. 2021. "The 7th population census of IMAR." May 20, 2021. http://www.nmg.gov.cn/tjsj/sjjdfx/202105/t20210526_1596820.html. Accessed August 16, 2023.
66. Guo, C., M. C. Tsang, and X. Ding. 2010. "Gender disparities in science and engineering in Chinese universities." *Economics of Education Review* 29 (2): 225–235, p. 225; Tatlow, Didi Kirsten. 2012. "The female factor: Women in China Face Rising University Entry Barriers." *New York Times*, October 7. https://www.nytimes.com/2012/10/08/world/asia/08iht-educlede08.html.
67. Liu, Yunshan et al. 2009. Ibid. pp. 47–48.
68. The cutoff lines for science- and humanity-track students are different.
69. All provinces follow this three-tiered scheme but with different cutoff lines for each tier, which fluctuate from year to year and are conditioned by the quota the province is allotted and the number of the province's *gaokao* takers in a given year.
70. This online enrollment system is supported by a high-speed network of servers installed specifically for college enrollment in IMAR. This system is praised for its information

transparency, real-time updates of available seats in thousands of majors and universities, and timely confirmation of enrollment results. But since its inauguration in 2006, IMAR has been the only province in China that has adopted the real-time online enrollment system. One explanation of IMAR's unique enrollment system is the combination of its small number of *gaokao* takers, of less than 200,000 a year throughout the 2010s, and the availability of internet infrastructure available in its major cities. It is almost impossible to implement this system in most provinces that have two to six times more *gaokao* takers a year and require much greater investment in telecommunication infrastructure to make it work. Even within IMAR, many rural students have had to travel long distances to cities to take the *gaokao* and to partake in online enrollment because of the weak internet capacity in rural schools and towns. Zhu, Jiabei. 2022. "Neimenggugaokao zhiyuantianbao: yichang guanhu gongpingdeshiyan [College enrollment in Inner Mongolia: An experiment with fairness]." *Xinjing Daily*, July 24. https://news.sina.com.cn/s/2022-07-24/doc-imizmscv3283157.shtml. Accessed May 20, 2023.

71. See, for example, Golden, Daniel et al. 2023. "The Newest College Admissions Ploy: Paying to Make Your Teen a 'Peer-Reviewed' Author." ProPublica. May 18. https://www.propublica.org/article/college-high-school-research-peer-review-publications?utm_source=sailthru&utm_medium=email&utm_campaign=majorinvestigations&utm_content=feature Accessed May 18, 2023.
72. For a US parallel, see for example, Weis, Lois and Kristin Cipollone. 2013. "'Class work': producing privilege and social mobility in elite US secondary schools." *British Journal of Sociology of Education* 34 (5/6): 701–722.
73. Yang, Ke. 2018. "Muzhide jingjirenhua: jiaoyushichanghua beijingxiade muzhibianqian [Motherhood as educational agent: Changes in motherhood under marketized education]." *Journal of Chinese Women Studies* 146: 79–90.
74. Zhu, Jiabei. 2022. Ibid.; Cai, Qing. 2022. "Jiaonitiangaokaozhiyuande kenengshiyijia jianzhugongsi [You might be getting college enrollment advice from an architecture firm]." *Shidai zhoubao [Times Weekly]*, June 14. http://finance.ce.cn/stock/gsgdbd/202206/14/t20220614_37755523.shtml. Accessed May 21, 2023.
75. Teng, Xing and Xiaoyi Ma. 2005. "Zhongguogaodengjiaoyude shaoshuminzuyouhuizhengceyu jiaoyupingdeng [Minority preferential policies in higher education and educational equity in China]." *Ethnic Studies* 5: 10–18.
76. Yang, Lichang and Yueming Yang. 2020. "Wuoguoshaoshuminzu yukejiaoyuzhaoshengzhengcede xianshikunjingyu fazhanlujing [Development and impediments of minority preparatory programs in China]." *Guizhou Ethnic Studies* 41 (4): 149–154.
77. Wave's experience is consistent with the finding from a 2019 survey of over a hundred minority students in a Project 985 University. See Fang, Chenchen and Congbin Guo. 2021. "Jingyingdaxuezhong shaoshuminzu gaokaoyouhuizhengce huodedeyingxiangyinsu [Factors that affect minority students' ability to benefit from gaokao preferential policies]." *Journal of Hebei University (Philosophy and Social Science edition)* 46 (6): 89–96. The authors also found that 83% of the minority students at the surveyed university were from urban areas
78. Yang, Lichang and Yueming Yang. 2020. Ibid. Similar findings are reported in Zheng, Xuesong. 2011. "Shaoshuminzu yukejiaoyuyanjiu—yi zhongyangminzudaxue yukejiaoyu weigean [The Preparatory Programs for Minority Students: A Case Study of Minzu University of China]." Doctoral dissertation. Beijing: Minzu University of China; and Li,

Chunkai and Wei Wu. 2017. "Minzushenfen, chengxiangfengeyu gaodengjiaoyubupingdeng [Ethnicity status, rural-urban divide, and inequality in higher education]." *Beijing Social Sciences* 9: 42–49. Li and Wu, like several other authors, have found that the rural-urban gap in the minority region was greater than that in Han areas.

79. Feng, Jianxin and Jing Zhang. 2016. "Minzuyukejiaoyu huikaomoshi gaigeyanjiu [A study of reforming the minority preparatory program's entrance exam]." *Research on on Higher Education of Nationalities Studies* 4 (1): 7–11.
80. Liu, Yunshan et al. 2009. Ibid. p. 53.
81. Deng, Huang, a Guangdong-based B-list college teacher and nonfiction writer, published a book in 2020 entitled, *wodeerben xuesheng" (My Second Tier students).* Beijing: People's Literature Press. Huang suggested that most of the Second Tier college students, who accounted for no less than 84% of China's college students, are from working-class or peasant families, growing up in rural and peripheral areas with poorly educated parents. These Second Tier students and their families have invested the largest portion of family funds in education, yet faced much greater limits in upward social mobility, compared to high-ranking A-list university students who often grew up in metropolitan centers with well-educated and well-positioned parents. Huang's work is among the first to bring public attention to the great territorial divide among China's college-educated youths in the new millennium.
82. 2021. "Erlingeryinian neimenggugemengshi 985 gaoxiaoluqulü [Admission rates to Project 985 universities of IMAR's leagues and municipalities]." *Houbosji xueyeguihua*, November 17. https://baijiahao.baidu.com/s?id=1716687162540812821&wfr=spider&for=pc&searchword=%E5%86%85%E8%92%99%E5%8F%A4%E9%AB%98%E8%80%83985%E5%BD%95%E5%8F%96%E7%8E%87. Accessed on May 22, 2023.
83. Woodside, Alexander. 2006. Ibid. p. 18.
84. Woodside, Alexander. 2006. Ibid. p. 40. China-based commentators often call *gaokao* the modern day *keju*, the imperial civil service exam. Although *gaokao* and the civil service exam are two separate institutions in present-day China, scholars and officials are often thought to be inseparable: being a scholar is the first step into officialdom.
85. All personal names in this chapter are fictional.
86. Inner Mongolia Normal University. 2010. "Neimengguzizhiqu erlingyilingnian gaoxiaobiyesheng jiuyezhengcexuanchuan [IMAR college graduates employment policies]." June 30. https://wdy.imnu.edu.cn/info/1040/1135.htm. Accessed May 23, 202.
87. Alitangaridi. 2011. "Neimenggudaxuesheng jiuyewentitantao—yineimenggu caijingxueyuanweili [A Study of College Graduates' Employment in Inner Mongolia]." Master's thesis. Inner Mongolia University of Finance and Economics.
88. Bai, Yang. 2015. "Neimengguzizhiqu mengyushouke daxuebiyesheng jiuyewentiyanjiu [A study of Mongolian-track college graduates' employment in IMAR]." Master's thesis. Inner Mongolia University of Finance and Economics, p. 25. By 2020, 73% of IMAR's college graduates, reaching 134,000 that year, still chose to look for jobs within IMAR. See "2020 Neimenggu putonggaoxiao biyeshengjiuyezhiliang niandubaogao [2020 annual report on IMAR's college graduates' employment conditions]." *The Paper*. https://www.thepaper.cn/newsDetail_forward_11402473. Accessed May 24, 2023.
89. A survey of graduates from the top three IMAR universities from 2014 to 2017 shows that the number of jobs explicitly earmarked for male applicants were about 50% higher than those for female. See Wu, Tong. 2018. "Neimenggu gaoxiao nüdaxuesheng

jiuyexianzhuangfenxi ji chengyinyanjiu [Studies of the state of female college graduates' employment]." Master's thesis. Inner Mongolia Normal University, p. 21.

90. Eredun and Hai Ming. 2010. "Mengyushoukeban biyeshengjiuyekunnan yuanyinfenxiji duiceyanjiu." *Journal of Inner Mongolia Agricultural University (Social Science edition)* 50: 185–186 and 207; Bai, Yang. 2015. Ibid. p. 36. In 2020, college graduates of Mongolian (MKM) track in IMAR recorded a 54% employment rate, much lower than IMAR's average of 68%. See Wei, Laihong et al. 2021. "Yiqingduineimenggudaxueshengjiuyede yingxiangyuduiceyanjiu [The impact of COVID on college graduate employment in IMAR and its solution]," *Yangshan Academic Journal*, 34 (4): 109–112, p. 110.
91. Silage is a fermented, preserved, and more nutritious green fodder than untreated fodder, made with corn in China's northwest.
92. See Hsing, You-tien. 2010. Ibid. for details on entrepreneurial bureaucrats in post-reform China.
93. According to a survey published in 2014, for a public employee at the bottom of China's 28-tiered public employee ranking, moving from the bottom to level 18 took 25 years, and only 4% made it. Only 1% of those at level 18 were promoted to level 13. Overall, 90% of China's public employees stayed at level 22 or below for their entire career. See Hu, Ying and Yelan Lian. 2014. "Dashujujiedu zhenshijicenggongwuyuan [Reading through the big data: The reality of low ranking public servants]." *Juece tansuo [Policy Exploration]* 10: 29.
94. Li, Yunping. 2014. "Neimenggu jinnianjiangshixian gaoxiaobiyishengjiuye dashisanwanyishang [More than 130,000 IMAR's college graduates will find jobs this year]." *Xinhua News*, February 4. http://edu.takungpao.com/ksjy/gk/q/2014/0205/2257887.html. Accessed May 24 2023; and Bai, Yang. 2015. Ibid.
95. Huang, Ruisheng. 2018. "Neimengguzhungeerqi daxuesheng jiuyewentiyanjiu [A Study of College Graduates' Employment Conditions]." Master's thesis. Inner Mongolia Agricultural University, pp. 15–16.
96. Interview in Hohhot, July 2014.
97. Huang, Ruisheng, 2018. Ibid. p. 17.
98. Woodworth, Max. 2022. "Urbanization as mass speculative event: Informal finance and city-making in Ordos, Inner Mongolia." In *The Speculative City: Emergent Norms and Forms of the Built Environment*, edited by Chu, Cecilia and Shenjing He, pp. 134–154. Toronto: University of Toronto Press; Woodworth, Max and Michael Ulfstjerne. 2016. "Taking part: The social experience of informal finance in Ordos, Inner Mongolia." *The Journal of Asian Studies* 75 (3): 649–672.
99. "Neimenggudaxueshengjiuyelü quanguodaoshudier [IMAR ranked second to last in college employment rates]." *Meiri Toutiao*, March 14, 2016. https://kknews.cc/zh-sg/education/k3j4abb.html. Accessed April 28, 2024.
100. By 2024, the number of graduates of HEIs rose to nearly 12 million. See "Why so many Chinese graduates cannot find work." April 20, 2024, *The Economist*. https://www.economist.com/china/2024/04/18/why-so-many-chinese-graduates-cannot-find-work. Accessed April 28, 2024.
101. Sources of information from Figure 9.1: Tian, Juanjuan. 2010. "Neimengguliangwanduo tianzhijiaozi bizhankaochang [More than 20,000 attended the grad school entrance exam in Inner Mongolia]." *Inner Mongolia Daily*, January 10. http://commend.nmgnews.

com.cn/system/2010/01/10/010364478.shtml. Accessed on May 25, 2023; Inner Mongolia Center for Education and Examinations. 2021. "2022 nian neimengguyanjiusheng zhaoshengkaoshibaominrenshuwei 97,563 ren [97,563 people registered for the Inner Mongolia graduate school exam in 2022]." Inner Mongolia Center for Education and Examinations, posted on Chinakaoyan, November 26. http://www.chinakaoyan.com/info/article/id/421439.shtml. Accessed June 12, 2022; Chinakaoyan. 2018. "2010–2018 nian kaoyanrenshuyu luqutongji [2010–2018 statistics for grad school exam takers and admission rate from 2010 to 2018]." *Chinakaoyan*, November 15. http://www.chinakaoyan.com/info/article/id/259301.shtml. Accessed May 25, 2023; Zhongguo Jiaoyuzaixian. 2020. "Quanguo geshengshi liniankaoyan baokaorenshu fenxibaogao [Numbers of grad school exam takers by province, 2016–2020]." Zhongguo Jiaoyuzaixian, June 19. https://zhuanlan.zhihu.com/p/149445041. Accessed May 25, 2023.

102. "Koyanpowanjuan sibaiwankaoyanren jishangdumuqiao [Four million graduate school exam takers jostle to cross the single plank bridge]." 2022. *Liseqi Zhiku*, February 14. http://www.idmresearch.com/news/html/?3893.html. Accessed May 25, 2023.
103. "Jinnian 457 wan kaoyandajunli 70% deren jiangwuyuanshangan [70% of the 4.57 million graduate school exam takers will fail]." 2022. Yingliuxue yanjiushengzixun, posted on Sohu, January 6. https://www.sohu.com/a/514681129_121124010. Accessed May 25, 2023. It is important to note that a master's degree from one-year programs of foreign universities, an easier route than going through China's PAT for students who can afford it, no longer qualifies one for residency status in Shanghai, according to this report.
104. Wu, Xiaogang. 2022. "Think gaokao is hard? Try this year's grad school exam." *Sixth Tone*, April 11. https://www.sixthtone.com/news/1010074/think-the-gaokao-is-hard-try-this-years-grad-school-exam. Accessed May 25, 2023.
105. For analyses of China's post-Mao party and state bureaucracies and their downsizing, see Brødsgaard, Kjeld Erik. 2002. "Institutional reform and the bianzhi system in China." *The China Quarterly* 170: 361–386; and Ang, Yuen Yuen. 2012. "Counting cadres: a comparative view of the size of China's public employment." *The China Quarterly* 211: 676–696.
106. In May 30, 2016, China's Ministry of Human Resources and Social Safety announced that China had 7.167 million civil servants by the end of 2015. See "2015 nianduo renliziyuan he shehuibaozhang shiyefazhan tongji gongbao [2015 Statistical Bulletin on the Development of Human Resources and Social Security]." 2016. Ministry of Human Resources and Social Safety of the People's Republic of China. May 30. http://www.mohrss.gov.cn/SYrlzyhshbzb/zwgk/szrs/tjgb/201805/W020220325393602506892.pdf. Accessed May 26, 2023. The announcement triggered heated debates among researchers on the gap between the official figure and the actual size of China's public sector employees that were fully or partially, formally or informally on the state payroll across all levels and sectors. The researchers suggested that if one counted all three categories of public sector employees (the core administrative, the extra-bureaucracy and the non-staff personnel), the number would be at 50 million to over 70 million. See Liu, Sunan. 2016. "Zhongguo gongwuyuanzongshu 716.7wanren zhuanjiacheng caizhenggongyangrenyuan yue 5000 wanren [China has 7.167 million public servants, experts said the 'state dependents' are at about 50 million]." *Jiemian*, June 20. https://www.jiemian.com/article/706182.html. Accessed May 26, 2023.
107. Wei, Laihong et. al. 2021, Ibid. p. 109.

108. Han, Feng. 2020. "Duoshengfen kuozhaogongwuyuan, qizhongneimenggu zengjia 400% [Many provinces expand public sector employment; among them, IMAR expanded by 400%]." *China News Net*, June 12. https://origin-view.inews.qq.com/a/20200612A007SW00. Accessed May 25 2023.
109. A quarter of the 7,000 new jobs in IMAR were said to be in the Public Security units, and most of them were earmarked for male applicants only, according to an online post on 2020-07-23 by Asirnaiba Lidasheng. See posts in reply to "2020 nian duo shengfen kuozhao gongwuyuan, qizhongneimenggu zengjia 400%, jinnianshi baokao gongwuyuan de zuijia shijima?" [In 2020, many provinces will expand their public sector jobs, and Inner Mongolia will increase by 400%. Is this the best time to apply for public sector jobs?]." 2020. Zhihu. https://www.zhihu.com/question/400913686. Accessed May 27, 2023.
110. The policy is called "Three Supports and One Facilitation" (sanzhi yifu). The "Three Supports" refers to supporting education, agricultural (including pastoral, forestry, and hydraulic) projects, and health care in rural areas; the "One Facilitation" refers to facilitating rural revitalization.
111. Interview in Xilingol, 2012.
112. Many colleges and majors were said to report highly inflated employment rates in order to retain their eligibility to recruit new students. See Dai, Zhixin. 2019. "Daxuejiuyelüzaojia haishi qiutukunjingredehuo [Forged college graduate employment rates: Blame the 'prisoner's dilemma']." *Pongpai*, May 14. https://news.sina.com.cn/c/2019-05-14/doc-ihvhiews1714406.shtml. Accessed May 27, 2023. The author is a researcher at the Institute of Finance and Tax Research at Renmin University in Beijing. As early as 2006, CCTV, China's main state TV station, reported that a private college inflated its graduates' employment rate from 20% to 96%. See "Ruci 'jiuye' [Behind the employment rate]." 2006. Jiaodian Fangtan, posted on CCTV. August 5. http://news.cctv.com/society/20060805/101922.shtml. Accessed May 27, 2023. The report says that the college forced the graduating students to sign forged "employment agreements" before receiving their diplomas. These students who signed the forged agreements not only did not really get a job but also lost their preferential status in civil service exam, which was granted only to unemployed fresh college graduates. In 2006, such fraud was rampant enough for the Ministry of Education to set up a hotline for reporting such cases. See "Jiaoyubuyisheli jubaodianhua fangzhigaoxiao jiuyelüzaojia [Ministry of Education set up a hotline for reporting forged college employment rates]." 2006. CCTV, August 4. http://news.cctv.com/education/20060804/101454.shtml. Accessed May 27, 2023. The government has made repeated attempts to curb the fraudulent practice. In 2020, the Ministry of Education launched a nationwide survey of college graduate employment status to establish a database independent from the universities' self-reported figures. But a report posted on a Chinese American scholar's website in 2022 stated that many Chinese universities continued to inflate the employment figures by no less than 50%. Graduates could even mail order a fake "certificate of employment" at 99 yuan a piece, and submit it to the university in exchange for their diploma. See Zaker. 2002. "96% jiuyelu shiwei 20% daxiejinnian haiganzaojiama? [20% employment blown up to 96%, dare universities forge the employment rates this year?]." *Scholars Update*, June 19. http://scholarsupdate.hi2net.com/news.asp?NewsID=32690. Accessed May 27, 2023.
113. Huang, Ruisheng. 2018. Ibid.
114. Woodworth, Max and Michael Ulfstjerne. 2016. Ibid.

115. Yekejuu League is called Ordos Municipality today.
116. Strathern, Marilyn. 1996. "From improvement to enhancement: An anthropological comment on audit culture." *The Cambridge Journal of Anthropology* 19 (3): 1–21, p. 3; Strathern, Marilyn. 2000. *Audit cultures: Anthropological Studies in Accountability, Ethics and the Academy.* London: Routledge.
117. New York Stock Exchange (NYSE): TAL Education.
118. Shenzhen Stock Exchange (SZSE): Offcn.
119. Li, Ziming and Wei Du. 2021. "Yanlizhengzhi jiaopeichanye nengfouxiaochu jiaoyuneijuan? [Would cracking down on the tutoring industry stop educational involution?]." *China Daily*, September 2. https://caijing.chinadaily.com.cn/a/202109/02/WS61303045a3101e7ce97618d9.html. Accessed May 28, 2023.
120. Huang, Yanhua. 2020. "Cong yumihong, zhangbangxin, Li Yongxin kanjiaoyushoufujinjiezhinan [The advancement of the tutoring industry's richest: Yu Minhong, Zhang Bangxin and Li Yongxin's business trajectories]." *Jiemian*, November 28. https://www.jiemian.com/article/5332450.html. Accessed May 28 2023.
121. He, Jun. 2022. "Jiaopeisanjutou chenchuanqiusheng [Three tycoons of the tutoring industry struggling to survive on a sinking boat]." *Jiemian*, June 13. https://www.jiemian.com/article/7585536.html. Accessed May 28, 2023.
122. Zhen, Xiangqing. 2020. "Yimiaoguanggao 520wanyuan, zanzhuyichangchunwan daodixuyaoduoshaoqian? [5.2 million yuan for one second of ad time, how much does it cost to sponsor a New Year's Gala?].". *Touzhongwang*,. January 19. https://www.sohu.com/a/367821243_323328. Accessed May 28, 2023. The link was broken by June 13, 2023.
123. Graham, Megan. 2021. "Oscars sells out ad inventory despite awards show ratings declines." CNBC. April 23. https://www.cnbc.com/2021/04/22/oscars-sells-out-ad-inventory-despite-awards-show-ratings-declines.html. Accessed May 28, 2023.
124. Majidi, Michele. 2023. 'Average cost of a 30-second Super Bowl TV commercial in the United States from 2002 to 2023'. Statistica. February 10. https://www.statista.com/statistics/217134/total-advertisement-revenue-of-super-bowls/. Accessed May 28, 2023.
125. An advertisement posted in a rapid transit station in Beijing, summer of 2018.
126. Interviews in Beijing, 2019. I heard similar comments in IMAR and Gansu in 2014, 2016, and 2017.
127. Interview in Lanzhou, 2016.
128. Song, Qinghui. 2018. "Xueersizhangbangxin chengxinjinbalinghoushoufu honglishifounengchixu? [Zhang Bangxin became (China's) richest under 40, will his fortune sustain?]." *Yidu*, March 18. https://read01.com/Q3Lg6R6.html. Accessed May 28, 2023.
129. "Congxindongfang haoweilaideng jiaoyujutou dongxi 2019 nian K12 peixunfazhanqushi" Gain insight into the development trend of K12 training in 2019 from education giants such as New Oriental and Good Future, and gain opportunities in the storm of reform." 2019. iEDU Touzirenjulebu, posted on Xuebangjishu. January 10. http://www.xuebangsoft.com/newsAction/getNews/769.do?from=app. Accessed May 28, 2023.
130. "TAL Education Group (TAL): TAL Education Group Market Cap." 2023. *YCharts*. Updated May 26. https://ycharts.com/companies/TAL/market_cap. Accessed May 29, 2023.
131. He, Jun. 2022. Ibid.; Zhu, Ling. 2021. "Pengyouquan yibanrendou shiyele wokandao jiaopeidesiwanghe xinsheng [Half of my social circle lost their jobs: Death and rejuvenation of the tutoring industry]." *Chuangyebang*, August 17. https://posts.careerengine.us/p/611ba9ac4ee8df60a722a10e. Accessed May 28, 2023.

132. See "Qianqiu dujiaoshou bang [Global Unicorn List]." Hurun report. www.hurun.net. Accessed July 18, 2022.
133. Interview in Beijing, July 2019. This case echoes a 2011 survey of 5,000 households in eight large Chinese cities. The survey showed that children's education counted for 35% of household expenditure and 30% of household income. See Hu, Yongmei et al. 2015. "Yingzijiaoyu shifoukuoda jiaoyubujundeng [Does shadow education widen educational disparity?]." *Peking University Education Review* 13 (3): 29–46, p. 30. A more recent nationwide survey of 40,000 households shows that the private tutoring expense was on the rise for households across income levels in both urban and rural areas. While absolute spending on children's private tutoring rose the fastest in the case of urban households with high-income and college-educated parents (especially mothers), which reached over 25% of total household income, the percentage of household expenditures on children's private tutoring was higher in rural and migrant-worker households in the city. See Wei, Yi. 2021. "2017–2019 woguo yiwujiaoyujieduanxuesheng jiatingjiaoyuzhichuqingkuangbianhua [The change in education expenditures of households with K-12 students from 2017 to 2019]." *Zhongguojiaoyucaizheng [Chinese Educational Finance]* No. 5. http://ciefr.pku.edu.cn/images/cbw/kyjb/2021/06/22/16D99F9D00F7BAFDC70CB3EE08ED6301.pdf. Accessed May 29, 2023. The Beijing-based economist, Ren Zeping, cited the prohibitively high education costs to explain China's rapidly declining birth rates, despite the shift from the One-Child policy to a total lift of the restriction in 2016. In 2018, China's birth rate dropped to below 1.5%, which is even lower than the advanced economies' average of 1.67%. See Ren, Zeping et al. 2019. "2019 nian zhongguoshengyubaogao [2019 Report on China's Birth Rate]." Hengda (Evergrande) Research Institute. January 2. http://pdf.dfcfw.com/pdf/H3_AP201901041282086287_1.pdf. Accessed May 29, 2023.
134. Bureau of Statistics. 2021. "2020nian quanguojumin renjunkezhipaishouru [Chinese residents' Disposable income per capita in 2020]". 2021. Bureau of Statistics, posted by CCTV. February 28. http://m.news.cctv.com/2021/02/28/ARTIWxGLQ7ebOKmtXNclr8xP210228.shtml. Accessed May 30, 2023. Poor rural families spent a higher percentage of household income even in public schools, because of the extra expenses in commuting and boarding. And private tutoring accounted for over 70% of the total education expenditures. See Qian, Xiaoye et al. 2015. "Yiwujiaoyujieduan chengzhenjiaoting jiaoyuzhichude gouchengjibupingdeng [Inequality in household K-12 education expenditure]." *Education and Economy* 6: 25–33.
135. While the "Double Reduction" was meant to reduce the burden of students and their parents, it has driven private tutoring underground, and moved the format from group classes to the much more costly one-on-one sessions. As a result, the gap in the competitive edge between rich and poor families' school children widened even further. See Liu, Yunshan. 2023. "jiaoyuweihelunwei liyijituan boyide lesechang? (Why did education become the wasteland for business gambling?)" *Beijing Cultural Review (Wenhua zongheng)*, August 14, 2023. https://mp.weixin.qq.com/s/t9Nm7nUaURaI7aCyXG7gjA. Accessed Aug 15, 2023.
136. General Office of the State Council and General office of the CCP Central Committee. 2021. "Guanyujinyibujianqing yiwujiaoyujieduan xueshengzuoyefudanhe xiaowaipeixunfudande yijian [Opinion on reducing homework load and supplementary tutoring burdens of K-12 students]." July 24. http://www.moe.gov.cn/jyb_xxgk/moe_1777/moe_1778/202107/t20210724_546576.html. Accessed May 30, 2023.

137. 2022. "TAL Education Group (TAL): TAL Education Group Market Cap." *YCharts*, Updated August 2. https://ycharts.com/companies/TAL/market_cap. Accessed August 2, 2022.
138. Zhou, Cissy. 2022. "60,000 staff cut as China's New Oriental Education pivots business." *Nikkei Asia*, January 10. https://asia.nikkei.com/Business/Education/60-000-staff-cut-as-China-s-New-Oriental-Education-pivots-business. Accessed May 30, 2023; He, Jun. 2022. Ibid.
139. Liu, Yujie and Yutong Wang. 2021. "Zijiejiaoyudacaiyuan qianwanjiaopeirencai hequhecong? [Where could the tutoring industrys' ten million laidoff staff go?]." Posted on Yubaibaiwang, August 5. https://hryhy.com/article/5639493.html. Accessed May 30, 2023.
140. Liepin, a Chinese online job board, reported these figures in its "2019 jiaoyupeixunhangye jiaoshicongyezhe dashujubaogao [The big data on private tutor employment conditions in 2019]." 2019. *Sohu*, September 11. https://www.sohu.com/a/340247992_100206836. Accessed May 30, 2023.
141. 2023. "Market capitalization of Offcn Education (002607.SZ)." Companies Market Cap. Updated May 30. https://companiesmarketcap.com/offcn-education/marketcap/. Accessed May 31, 2023. This webpage shows Offcn's financial data starting from 2011, when Offcn was first listed on SZSE.
142. Ren, Jing. 2021. "2022 guokao jinkaikao [The 2022 national civil service exam starts today]." *China News*, November 28. https://www.chinanews.com.cn/sh/2021/11-28/9617624.shtml. Accessed May 30, 2023. The success rate of the national civil service exam in 2022 was 68:1. In 2023, another half a million more joined the race. The 2.6 million civil exam takers brought the success rate down to 70:1, or 1.4%. See 2023. "An ever-growing cohort of public servants in China." *China Scope*. April 25. http://chinascope.org/archives/31761. Accessed May 30, 2023.
143. Figures are from the following webpages of Huatu, a national chain of civil service exam preparation. See "2022 nian neimenggu shengkao baomingrenshu tongji [Statistics on the number of applicants for the 2022 Inner Mongolia Provincial Examination]." 2022. *Huatu*, April 25. http://www.huatu.com/2022/0425/2504759.html. Accessed May 30, 2023; "2020 nian neimenggu gongwuyuan kaoshi baomingrenshu tongji [Statistics on the number of applicants for the 2020 Inner Mongolia Civil Service Examination]." 2020. *Huatu*, June 21. http://www.huatu.com/2020/0621/1957001.html. Accessed May 30, 2023.
144. "Buxiaoyousan: bukaogong, bukaoyan, bukaojiao" in Chinese.
145. "Market capitalization of Offcn Education (002607.SZ)." 2023. Companies Market Cap. Updated May 30. https://companiesmarketcap.com/offcn-education/marketcap/. Accessed May 31, 2023.
146. "Market capitalization of Offcn Education (002607.SZ)." 2023. Ibid.
147. "Qianqiu dujiaoshou bang [Global Unicorn List]". Hurun report. www.hurun.net. Accessed May 30, 2023.
148. Huang, Yanhua. 2020. Ibid.
149. Information drawn from the webpage of Offcn's IMAR regional center. https://www.51gouke.com/nmghhht/3-25-gk5884.html. Accessed June 17, 2022. This page no longer existed by May 31, 2023.
150. Bureau of Statistics. 2019. "2018 nian jumin shouru he xiaofei zhichu qingkuang [Residential Income and Consumption Expenditure in 2018]." Gov.cn. January 21. https://www.gov.cn/xinwen/2019-01/21/content_5359647.htm. Accessed May 31 2023.

151. Huang, Yanhua. 2020. Ibid.
152. Zhai, Yuanyuan. 2022. "Caiyuan jiangxin tuifeinan kaogongrenanjie zhonggonghu-atukunjing [Layoffs, paycuts, refund delays: Zhonggong and Huatu (company)'s financial distress not resolved by civil service exam fever]." *Tech Xingqiu*, June 16. https://www.sohu.com/a/557747176_120073179. Accessed May 31, 2023.
153. Yang, Guang and Zi Rui. 2022. "Conghaojuanbeidadao beijianguanlian zhonggong jiaoyu yunluozhimi [From a RMB 1 billion donation to Beida to the fraud investigation: the mystery of Offcn's demise]". Baobian. January 4. https://wallstreetcn.com/articles/3648887. Accessed May 31, 2023.
154. "Gongwuyuankaoshihuobao cuishengqianyijifuhao zhonggongjiaoyuliyongxin geimuxiaobeidajuan shiyi [Explosive civil service exam bred the super rich, Offcn's Li Yongxin donated 1 billion yuan to alma mater Peking University]." 2021. *Daily Economic News*, March 4. https://finance.sina.com.cn/stock/s/2021-03-04/doc-ikftpnnz1787936.shtml. Accessed May 31, 2023.
155. Zhai, Yuanyuan. 2022. Ibid.
156. Yang, Guang and Zi Rui. 2022. Ibid.
157. "Market capitalization of Offcn Education (002607.SZ)." 2023. Companies Market Cap. Updated May 30. https://companiesmarketcap.com/offcn-education/marketcap/. Accessed May 31, 2023.
158. By June 2023, China's youth (ages 16–24) unemployment rate in cities reached a record high of 21.3%. The government has stopped publishing the data since then. *The Economist* estimated that the unemployment rate for the cohort with a university education could be as high as 25.2% in 2020, the last year for which census data are available. Given the slowdown of the Chinese economy and other trends, the journal estimated that over a third of young college graduates might be unemployed by 2024. See *The Economist*, April 20, 2024. Ibid.
159. Interview with a university professor in Hohhot, summer 2012.
160. Since 2021, the term "*tang-ping*" ("lying flat" in Chinese, or "quiet quitting") has grown popular in China. Generally perceived as a backlash against the culture of hyper competition, "lying flat" refers to the rising trend of young people rejecting the mounting social pressure to succeed in the rat race for college admission, white-collar urban employment, home ownership and child rearing. The trend was popular enough to receive government sanctions. See Davidovic, Ivana. 2022. "'Lying flat': Why some Chinese are putting work second." BBC News, February 15, 2022. https://www.bbc.com/news/business-60353916. Further research is needed to assess the prevalence and regional, gender, and class variations of the phenomenon: who under what circumstances are trying to lie flat, and in what ways. Wave, for one, dismissed "lying flat" as an option only for those who could afford it.

10
Popularizing the Monument: The Wild Great Walls

During my visits to Ejina and Minqin (Chapters 1 through 4), among other places in the northwest, I often came across ruins of border fortification structures of various forms. These remnants in the drylands looked bewilderingly different from the manicured Badaling section of the Great Wall near Beijing that I have visited before. Some of them were stand-alone structures, such as beacon towers, others were sections of walls of varied lengths and heights, made of rammed earth or even dried suosuo wood (see Chapter 1). Still others are trenches below ground level. My guides referred to them as remnants of the Great Wall, the emblematic monument of present-day China's national identity. Some local villagers I met saw the battered ruins as dirt mounds that could be recycled into fertilizer, or brick piles that could be reused to mend animal pens. In other locations, villagers saw themselves as the guardians of national heritage and patrolled the ruins regularly. When asked about the Great Wall that had historically divided the rivalrous Mongol and Han Chinese territories, Wave, the successful Mongol student who leads Chapter 9 on China's college and job races, responded: "I really don't care. I have crossed the Wall and settled on its southside anyway." But many others, especially Han Chinese I met, seemed to care a great deal about the Great Wall, albeit in many different ways. So, what is the Great Wall and what does it mean to different peoples in the northern frontier?[1]

In China, the new millennium marks a critical moment for monumentalizing the Great Wall. In the early 2000s, two decades into China's post-Mao market reform, the monumental Wall was triple-tasked with sustaining economic growth in the aftermath of a global financial crisis, mobilizing sociocultural consensus in the midst of

Conserving China's Northwest Frontier. You-tien Hsing, Oxford University Press. © You-tien Hsing (2025).
DOI: 10.1093/9780191903908.003.0011

rising ethnoterritorial tensions, and reinforcing the global standing of China's soft power. Monumentalizing the Great Wall, in that sense, is not unlike the ecological programs of combating desertification reviewed in the Introduction and Chapter 1 of this book

Unlike what a common misconception says, the Great Wall is not visible from the moon.[2] Still, traversing China's immense northern borderlands, the Great Wall, or the "Long Wall" (*changcheng*), is crowned as the world's largest heritage structure.[3] As an iconic national monument, the Great Wall is central to China's cultural politics today. The Great Wall-centered cultural politics evolve around a set of intertwining historical and territorial tensions that come to the fore under what I term Great Wall Revivalism. Great Wall Revivalism at the current moment refers to efforts that began in the late 1980s, which have boomed since the 2000s, of constructing the Great Wall as a national monument and the attempts to reconcile the historical and territorial tensions rising from monumentalizing the Great Wall. While monumentalizing the Great Wall has been initiated mainly by state actors, Great Wall Revivalism goes beyond the realm of the state. Many state and non-state actors have participated in Great Wall Revivalism. While the state actors are mostly the usual suspects like the State Administration of Cultural Heritage (SACH) and its local agencies, the non-state actors come from popular historians, photographers, heritage enthusiasts, and peasants who live near the widely spread Wall ruins across the mountains and deserts of the northern frontier. Great Wall Revivalism has gained traction among many people in China, generated divergent conservation practices, and created disparate meanings for its participants with different inspirations in different locations where the very "Long" Wall reaches. Their diverse practices in conserving the Great Wall have given life to many "wild great walls," a direct translation from the Chinese "*yechangcheng*," which I use in the title for this chapter.

The moniker, "wild," denotes several meanings. First of all, administratively, the moniker refers to wall ruins that are not listed in official heritage protection programs or ruins that are listed but not authorized for tourism development. However, the utility of this definition dissipates as I look into the diverse conservation practices on the ground that involve walls of ambiguous official status. The second denotation of "wild" walls, mostly in popular discourse, concerns their spatial character, that is, the wall ruins are "wild" for their disparate locations across China's immense northern border regions. Many of them are also physically dilapidated—a stark contrast to the well-located and -groomed Great Wall sections near Beijing that are prominently featured on China's stamps and state leaders' official portraits. Thirdly, in my use of the term, the wild walls are associated with a wide range of non-state actors who hold divergent visions and follow different courses of action in their participation in Great Wall Revivalism. The wildness, in this sense, concerns the dynamics between the participants and the ruins with which they are associated. In their diverse forms of engagement with the wild walls, the non-state actors converge in popularizing the monumental Great Wall. In the meantime, they also create new meanings that do not always align with the official discourse. As Great Wall Revivalism continues to inspire diverse practices and generate new meanings, Great Wall monumentalization also requires perpetual maintenance by the state.

Built on my fieldwork in Inner Mongolia Autonomous Region (IMAR) and Hebei Province, this chapter traces the multiple actors' engagement in turning the monumental Great Wall popular. In these processes, the Great Wall and the wild great walls get progressively more entangled as we move from one actor to the next. For clarity, I use "the Great Wall" when it comes to the official discourse and the non-state actors' adherence to the monumental Wall. I use the lower-case "wild great walls" when discussing the relationship between the grassroots actors and the ruins, regardless of the official status of the ruin in question.[4]

I start the chapter with a brief review of the historical and territorial tensions derived from the state's attempts to monumentalize the Great Wall. This review is followed by stories about four non-state participants in Great Wall Revivalism. The first participant is the urban-based popular historian-cum-photographers who contribute to nationalizing the wall-framed landscape and visualizing national memories and nostalgia through photography of the wallscape, rephotography of historic wall-framed images produced by photographers of the early 20th century, and reenactment of Sino-Japanese battle scenes on the Great Wall. The second group of participants is the entrepreneurial peasants who live near the wall ruins and run mass tourism at the under-regulated sections of the wild walls in the outskirts of metropolitan Beijing. The third group of participants is the villagers living in remote wall ruin sites in the mountainous eastern Hebei, far from the casual tourist routes. These peasants see themselves as descendants of the wall's builder-defenders and take pride in serving as one of the 5,000 officially appointed grassroots guardians of the Great Wall.

These three participants of Great Wall Revivalism—the photographers, the mass tourism operators, and the peasant-turned guardians of the Great Wall hold widely divergent visions and practices. But they share a pan-Han Chinese and south-of-the-Great-Wall identity. The fourth grassroots participants live on the opposite side of the Wall. These are Mongolian "Camelback Heritage Patrols" in Inner Mongolia Autonomous Region (IMAR). As mentioned in Chapter 5, IMAR, with 17% to 18% of its population registered as Mongol, is where China's Mongol nationals concentrate. Meanwhile, more than one-third of China's Great Wall and wild wall ruins are located in IMAR, thanks to the long history of warfare among Han Chinese and various steppe powers in today's IMAR. The story about the officially named "Camelback Heritage Patrols" tells the ways in which IMAR's local government has tried to reconcile the inconvenient history of the divisive Great Wall with its contemporary reincarnation as the emblem of national unity across both sides of the Wall.

One of the debates in critical heritage studies focuses on gaps and contradictions between local memories and the "authorized heritage discourse."[5] But the intertwined dynamics between the Great Wall and the wild great walls are less of a clear-cut contradiction between two opposing stances. Rather, I treat Great Wall Revivalism as a process in which society's participation shapes, enables, and also distracts and disrupts the processes of monumentalizing the Great Wall.[6] Such processes of societal participation in monument-making are not fully programmable, nor are the results always intentional. Like the conservation mobilization of planting suosuo in the desert (see Chapter 1), heritage mobilization around the Great Wall national icon draws a wide array of participants. While these actors participate in Great Wall Revivalism, they derail as much as they affirm the conceptual integrity of the Great Wall. The analytical tension, therefore, arises not just between authorized and popular discourses. Rather, the tension is lodged in the multiple nexuses of interactions among varied state and non-state actors who are dealing with the physical ruins on the ground under the sublime concept of the Great Wall.

I Monumental Tensions

If the monument is defined as a nation-builders' attempt to create a unified vision of the past, around which to forge the ideal of continuity and to naturalize a singular national identity, it is almost inevitable that such a monument would embody as many contradictory memories and competing meanings as it does shared ones. Often, the more radically the society transforms and the more heterogeneous a society becomes, the stronger the need for nation-building to unify the disparate memories via monument building.[7] Such contradictions are embedded in the monuments, despite the illusion of coherence and permanence—especially in those built with stone and concrete. Therefore, the challenge for the state is not just to build a monument, but more importantly, to make the monument popular and its intended message heard. But the ways to make a monument popular vary, and their success not guaranteed. Therefore, the politics of monument is better understood as contingent processes of monumentalization.

Like the ecological conservation programs that generated social and territorial tensions, the state's attempts to monumentalize the Great Wall have generated historical and territorial tensions.

The historical tension in monumentalizing the Great Wall transpires between the state-sanctioned concept of historical continuity of the Wall and the knotty histories of discontinuity of northern border fortifications. In the official historiography, endorsed by the United Nations Educational, Scientific, and Cultural Organization (UNESCO) World Heritage Committee, the timeless Great Wall is the product of two thousand years of persistent endeavors by successive dynasties between the 3rd century BCE and the 17th century CE.[8] The Wall as an accumulative project symbolizes the continuity of the Han Chinese-centered polity that has commanded over what is known as China today. Such a vision about continuity matters as much for the future of the nation as its past. But it does not align with the disjointed histories of disparate border walls and other structures built by a variety of territorial contenders in China's vast northern borderlands at different times under oscillating geopolitical orders.[9]

The historical discontinuity of the border walls is produced by several processes. For starters, not every ruler of imperial China was interested in building walls. In fact, none of China's major unified regimes between the fall of the Han in 220 CE and the Late Ming of the mid-16th century demonstrated much interest in border walls, with the exception of the short-lived Sui Dynasty (581 to 618 CE). The Tang

Dynasty (618 to 907 CE), for instance, had strong ethnic and cultural roots in the northern steppe and is considered the most cosmopolitan era in Chinese history. Several ambitious early Tang emperors sought to expand their influence in Central Asia, but they were confident enough to do so through diplomacy, royal marriages, subsidies, and trade, instead of building fortifications. The late Tang, however, saw the rise of northern powers, which, among other factors, brought an end to the Great Tang. The Tang's successor, the Song (960 to 1279 CE), took note and built a fortification section on the foundations of the Qin Wall that was originally built to fend against the Western Xia (or Tangut) Empire (1038 to 1227 CE). But the Song court eventually conceded the entire northern territory to the Jurchens.[10]

Furthermore, Han Chinese were not the only wall builders. The northern steppe, since the fall of the Tang, was under constant warfare and was controlled by the Khitans that established the Liao Dynasty (907 to 1125) and Jurchens of the Jin Dynasty (1115 to 1234). The Jin avidly built extensive walls and trenches to fend off the rising power of the Mongols. And because of the locations of the warring rivals, the Jin walls were located significantly further up north than the border fortifications built during other historical periods.[11]

Mongols, who established the Yuan Dynasty (1271 to 1368) and already controlled Central Asia and beyond, saw little need for walls built during previous eras that did not reflect the Mongol empire's borders. After the Yuan, the Ming Dynasty (1368 to 1644) was generally known as the most devoted wall builder of the late imperial era. The last empire, the Qing (1644 to 1911), established by the Manchus of the northeast, did not need to fortify the walls because its continental empire had greatly expanded beyond the fortification walls to the north and the west.[12] In short, the Great Wall was not built by consistently devoted rulers throughout Chinese history. It was, instead, a series of border fortifications built by various territorial contenders of various ethnic origins in present-day China's vast northern borderlands and beyond. Despite the encompassing term "the Great Wall," the fortification structures with disjointed pasts are remnants of the ever-shifting geopolitical orders of the region.

Also contrary to popular perception, the Great Wall is not a single structure but rather a series of fragmented border fortifications built by different rulers. Among the various walls, the best-known ones are those built during the early imperial Qin-Han Periods (221 BCE to 220 CE) and those built during the late imperial era by the Ming Dynasty (1368 to 1644 CE). Most of the Qin-Han walls are located further north of the Ming walls, with their greatest distance at over 800 km apart.[13]

Multiple walls were built not just across different dynasties, but also during the same dynasty by the same or different emperors. The wall-building emperors of the Han Period had built multiple walls with a distance of more than 100 km apart between the southmost to the northmost one.[14] Similarly, the Ming built several walls and did not hold a consistent policy towards wall-building during its 276-year reign. Ming emperors went from an earlier phase of expansionism, during which they did not build a protective and constraining wall, to a later phase of wall construction with durable and expensive brick and masonry after an ambitious Ming emperor was captured and held hostage by Mongols during a military expedition.

Meanwhile, the geographical focus of fortification gradually shifted from the northwest to the northeast, closer to the capital city of Beijing, in order to protect the Ming emperors.

What the multitude of walls reveal is the fluctuating territorial reach of China's imperial powers. Historian I-tien Hsing (2022)[15] suggested that depending on the geopolitical balance of the time, the walls were built as military offense just as much as they were for defense. The shifting walled frontlines represent both the empires' territorial conquests and concessions.

At the height of imperial military might, such as under the ambitious Emperor Wu of the Han Dynasty, the Emperor pushed the walls further north into the steppe beyond the previous borders to declare triumphant military conquests and demarcate his new territorial gains. At other times, like during the mid-to-late Ming when the court was too weak to hold onto territory gained from previous reigns, the emperors conceded their territory and moved the walled frontline south, with reluctance and regret. The retreat was for self-preservation. Such military defeat and territorial concession were often depicted in literary expressions of shame and remorse over the imperial "loss," as well as yearning for militaristic vengeance and territorial "recovery." Emotions aside, military exploits are rarely cheap. Building the walls for either defense or offense was financially ruinous, and the projects contributed to socioeconomic and political crises for Han and Ming wall-building emperors alike.[16]

In addition to the multiple walls built by the unified empires of Han and Ming, there were other wall-building powers. During the pre-unified Warring States Period in the 5th century BCE, for example, border walls were built to mark territorial advances and retreats by the warring states of mixed and varied ethnoterritorial roots. The geopolitical relationships among them were far more fluid than what is commonly perceived of the Wall as an absolute civilizational demarcation between two rivalries: the agrarian Han Chinese in the south and the pastoral steppe nomads in the north. Even under the unified empires, Han Chinese-identifying warlords and local turf builders at the edge of the empire would declare their territorial autonomy and guard their sovereignty with wall fortifications. In fact, the emperors would launch much harsher military actions against these Han Chinese "traitors" at the periphery of the empire than they would with the "barbarians" in the north. [17] These warlords at the empire's edge needed the fortification just as much as the northern "barbarians." Also, as mentioned earlier, from the 10th to the 13th centuries, the most devoted wall builders were not Han Chinese but the Jurchen Jin regime that competed with Mongols in the north. In other words, for a good part of the 2,000-year-long history in the immense northern plains and steppes, there existed not two opposing civilizations and polities, each holding large expanses of contiguous territory on each side of the resolute Great Wall. Instead, there were many fortified pockets of powers of varying scales held by various turf builders of varied and mixed ethnoterritorial backgrounds. The geopolitical structure of the northern territory was much more fragmentary than what the commonly perceived bipolar model suggests.[18] The history of the walls hardly presupposes continuous, dynasty-after-dynasty additions to a single structure that separates a permanent pair of rivals. The wall-building endeavors led by various territorial contenders fluctuated throughout history, with extended periods of inaction juxtaposed with active wall building.

The disjointed geopolitical histories left abundant physical traces. Many fortification ruins of varied forms and conditions spread across the lands and waters of China's northern terrains today. Underneath the blanket term of "Great Wall" lies a galaxy of border demarcations, fortifications (such as wall stretches, trenches, crenellations, passes, and fortresses, watch and beacon towers), as well as military logistic support facilities like administrative and living quarters, warehouses, and brick-making sites. Some of these structures were built on top of or as an extension to earlier structures, others have been found in locations far apart from one another. Some are strung together into a linear formation, others much less so. For the linear sections of wall ruins, the surviving foundations follow multiple orientations. The walls do not only travel in the east-west direction as what is popularly perceived, but also north-south, or northeast-southwest, and northwest-southeast, depending on the geomorphology and the geopolitical dynamics of the place and time. This indefinite assortment of structures covers a diverse array of landscapes—deserts, mountains, and water, and were built in different styles with different materials. For example, the earlier walls built in the Qin and Han periods were constructed with rammed earth, clay, and bundled twigs (including dried suosuo, the "miracle desert shrub" that leads the story in Chapter 1)—materials that made for faster constructions, yet were more prone to erosion.[19] Fortifications built in the late Ming period in the mid-16th century, including the sections featured on postcards and stamps today, were constructed with brick and masonry, which were more durable and more labor-intensive.[20]

The variable fortification structures that spread over the expansive northern terrain prove to be a daunting challenge for anyone who aspires to institute the Great Wall as one definitive monument of national continuity and integration. The challenge is compounded by the fact that the Great Wall as an object of heritage-making is far from timeless. The historical discontinuity of wall-building means that the history of wall decay is almost as long as that of wall construction. In the meantime, as fragments of the national monument have started to erode and disappear at an accelerated pace in recent decades, ruins that were repaired, renovated, and reinvented under the regime of heritage conservation have been added to this constellation of fragments of the Great Wall. This raises the question of authenticity and complicates the task of building a coherent national monument.

The historical, territorial, and physical fragmentation of the border wall remnants create a pair of intertwined tasks for monumentalizing the Great Wall. One is heritagization, that is, turning the elusive concept of the Great Wall into an integrated piece of heritage "property," as the UNESCO World Heritage Committee (WHC) terms it. The other is turning an otherwise nebulous task, including taking stock of the physical remnants and making them legible for the state, drawing up protection plans and rules, and assigning responsibilities for plan implementation and rule enforcement to local state agencies. A process that could be termed "projectization." If successfully executed, the two interconnected tasks, one of heritagization and the other projectization, can reinforce one another. Projectization, as a time-honored bureaucratic approach of turning irresolvable puzzles into governable objects, could help in incorporating the physical fragments into a conceptually unified landmark of heritage property. Heritagization, on the other hand, naturalizes the Great Wall as the epic symbol of the nation and legitimizes the state's investment and mobilizational efforts to projectize the task of monumentalizing the Wall.

For Great Wall conservationists, 2006 marks a watershed year. That year, the Regulation on the Protection of the Great Wall was adopted. Meanwhile, the SACH launched an unprecedented Great Wall Resource Survey and Identification (GW Survey from here on) initiative. The national GW Survey was assigned to individual provinces, down to municipalities and counties, following China's usual task delegation system along the bureaucratic hierarchy. Data collected at each level were compiled and reported to the next level up. The survey ended in 2010. In 2012, the SACH publicized a summary of the survey results. Demonstrating the Great Wall's aggregate immensity, the summary focused on the numerical magnitude of the national monument: a total of 16 provinces, 445 counties, and a total area of more than 40,000 sq. km were surveyed. The GW Survey involved 1,295 professionals from 361 government agencies of cultural heritage, surveying, mapping, and geoinformation. The result of the survey was a vast amount of data that included 46,111 registration forms, 196,588 sets of photos, 20,606 drawings, 31,070 video clips, and 596 rubbings and copies of stone carvings. Advanced technologies were adopted in the Survey, including remote sensing, three-dimensional scanning, and digital image measurement. These data informed the production of high-resolution digital line graphics, digital orthophoto maps, and a digital elevation model of the Great Wall. Based on these data, the SACH now had an official inventory for the Great Wall ruins: 10,051 segments that compose the Wall, 1,764 counts of border moats and trenches, 29,510 free-standing buildings, 2,211 fortresses and passes, and 185 instances of other types of ruins. Most importantly, after centuries of speculation on the length of the Great Wall, we now have an authoritative and science-backed figure of 21,196.18 km for the total length of the Wall. Accompanying the inventory is a list of 404 counties in 15 northern provinces (and provincial-level autonomous regions and municipalities) where the Wall ruins are found and duly registered. These local governments are responsible for protecting the Wall ruins, and have the authority to "cultivate Great Wall resources" (*liyong changchengziyuan*) located in their jurisdictions.[21] The exact ways to "cultivate Great Wall resources" are unspecified in the official documents. But this term is usually understood as turning heritage sites into economic resources, such as developing Wall-themed heritage tourism.

The bureaucratic, quantitative approach to conservation, however, is controversial. Jing Ai, a prominent Beijing-based archeologist, for instance, published an article at the inauguration of the GW Survey in 2006 and listed the potential pitfalls of such surveys. He pointed out the inconsistent terminologies for and definitions of the different architectural components, building materials, styles, and construction methods that vary from place to place and period to period that are included in the

Survey as part of the Great Wall. The problem of inconsistency was compounded by the fact that local gazetteer authors and scholars who participated in the Survey on the ground often employed highly localized nomenclatures without a shared denominator. Jing further questioned the quality of data collected by the thousands of project-based and inadequately trained grassroots surveyors, which only added to the problem of inconsistency found in the projectization of the Great Wall. Inconsistencies would result in arbitrary and unaccountable inclusion and exclusion of ruins in local calculations of Great Wall resources.[22] It was a case of bureaucratic-style simplification, Jing lamented.

That year, Jing also published his monograph, *A History of China's Great Wall*,[23] the first of such an ambitious scope in modern China by an academic. In the book, Jing devoted an entire chapter to the lasting inquiry into the length of the Great Wall. Though many of Jing's other writings were based on archaeological field findings, his analysis of the Wall's total length was drawn primarily from historical texts. Jing tabulated textual records from different historical periods, adjusting for the various measurement units, and eliminated duplicate tallies, and arrived at the figure of 21,147.93 km. This figure is very close to the official GW Survey figure of 21,196.18 km. Does the negligible difference, reached through two vastly divergent measuring methods, lend credibility to the conclusion that the length of the Great Wall is in the neighborhood of 21,000 km? An archaeologist who participated in the survey, however, told me that "the closeness of the two figures is a sheer coincidence." He explained that there were quite a few fundamental disagreements between Jing and the Survey team over what counts as being a part of the Great Wall. For example, the official figure included 2,000 km of "natural barriers" such as high mountain chains and waterways that were not manmade but played a significant role in border fortification. Jing, however, insisted that natural barriers should not be counted as part of the Great Wall.[24]

But the question of the actual length of the Great Wall is beyond methodological debates. Scientific precision and bureaucratic prowess can only go so far in the pursuit of accuracy. Field surveyors examining heritage objects dispersed over an area of 40,000 sq. km, about the size of today's Denmark, faced the impossible mission of standardizing terminology and criteria for qualifying heritage objects across local geographies and histories. Historic texts on the matter, which Jing consulted, are also known to be "rough approximations at best."[25]

Moreover, as is with the millennia-old politics of calculating taxable harvest and draftable men, the hierarchically ordered reporting system in the national GW Survey was afflicted by local governments' balancing acts. The increasing political importance of protecting the Great Wall was a double-edged sword for local governments. The longer the list of cultural heritage remnants that local officials submit to the supervising government, the greater the financial and organizational responsibility they would have to shoulder for repairing and protecting the listed heritage structures in their jurisdictions. Worse, if heritage property is found damaged or looted, the blame could be placed on the officials themselves.[26] On the other hand, the growing emphasis on heritage conservation presented an opportunity for local officials to gain attention from their supervisors and boost their performance records for career advancement. This dilemma is particularly evident in the poor, peripheral jurisdictions, where many of the Wall ruins are located, and where local officials have few other economic resources and growth projects to show for. Reports produced at each level of the data-collection hierarchy and compiled at the next level up are therefore subject to such political calculations. Hiding or inflating the "harvest" could occur under different circumstances, hence tarnishing the validity of the data of local "Great Wall Resources."

The gap is but one aspect of the challenges facing the monumentalization of the Great Wall.

The mega-scaled GW Survey was a bureaucratic approach to create a quantifiable object of governance out of the immeasurable and rapidly disappearing galaxy of ruins. But monumentalizing the Great Wall goes beyond running an inventory check. It also concerns forging momentum around the monument. That is, making the national monument popular. The energy needed to build and sustain such momentum does not derive solely from the state. Monumentalizing a national symbol of unity and identity is an ever-evolving process that requires "perpetual management by the state and continued participation by the people."[27] Who are these people, and how do they participate in monumentalizing the Great Wall?

Among the most obvious non-state participants of the state project are the academics who serve as policy researchers. But in the case of monumentalizing the Great Wall, it is different during the first two decades of the new millennium. Despite the Great Wall's iconic status, academic research on the Great Wall by career archaeologists, except for the early imperial Qin-Han structures, has been curiously scant.[28] The national GW Survey, high-profile as it is, was not accompanied by systematic archaeological excavations. Several professional archeologists I met in the 2010s attributed such research gaps to the national policy of restricting archaeological excavations of the most valuable sites to prevent damage to ancient remnants inflicted by the excavation work itself.

A Beijing-based archaeologist offered a few additional explanations. For one, in the text-privileging tradition of historical studies, written archives often supersede archaeological finds. Since the bulk of the extant physical remains of the Wall were built as recently as the late 16th century during the Ming period from which textual records are abundantly available, the archeological artifacts are considered less important. In addition, the cultural layers and the scale and scope of artifacts found in the Wall ruins have been too scattered and fragmentary to build a cultural type that is often built on better-defined archaeological sites, like that of the famous Yangshao Culture. Building a cultural type could make a name for the archaeologist. The unpromising research yields in border wall archaeology does not help with archaeologists' career building. Nor do the limited academic yields justify the high costs of Great Wall excavation projects that involve searching for evasive ruins across expansive terrains, exhausting negotiations with local officials from the multiple jurisdictions where the dig would take place, the strenuous hikes and months of harsh living conditions at the remote Wall sites, where even water supplies are not guaranteed.[29] From the perspective of professional historians, on the other hand, written histories are known for their omissions and inconsistencies. Without systematic archaeological findings for cross-referencing, especially for the study of the early imperial era from which few textual archives are available, it is difficult to resolve the inconsistencies, making the Great Wall as a research subject even more challenging.[30] Furthermore, the discipline of History is customarily bounded by dynasty-based periodization. But historical investigations of the Great Wall often entail multi-dynastic studies, which do not easily fall into the chronologically structured field of History. Cross-dynastic research becomes further entangled given the fact that historical documentation of the Great Wall is imbued with "gaps, myths, and continued reinventions."[31] In short, for professional archaeologists and historians, the Great Wall as a research topic does not pay off for the most part.

The lacunae left by professional archaeologists and historians in Great Wall studies have been duly taken up by popular historians.

II Popular Historians and Wall Photographers

II.1 A Comprehensive History of the Great Wall

Popular historians of the Great Wall are history enthusiasts with various professional backgrounds, such as engineers, school teachers, writers, and local officials. Compared to the cautious academics, their attitude towards the Great Wall has been much more audacious. While most professional historians have shied away from offering conclusive answers or big picture accounts, popular historians have taken pride in authoring what they believe to be a comprehensive history of the Wall. While it takes years for professional archaeologists to publish excavation reports on specific segments of ancient fortifications in obscure sites, popular historians have published, in a timely fashion, compendia and encyclopedias that claim to cover the "entire Wall."

In 1984, the Sino-British Joint Declaration concerning the return of Hong Kong to China was signed in Beijing. That year, several major news agencies organized a high-profile event to raise funds for repairing the badly deteriorated structures of the Ming-era Great Wall near Beijing, the most visited and visualized section of the Wall. To endorse this event, China's then-leader, Deng Xiaoping, gifted the organizing committee a couplet that reads: "Love our China, repair our Great Wall" (aiwozhonghua, xiuwochangcheng). This couplet has been quoted widely by advocates of Great Wall conservation since then. It was not the first time in recent memory in which the Great Wall has been mobilized as a symbol of China's national unity and territorial integrity. A similar evocation of associating China's nationhood with the Great Wall can be found during the Second Sino-Japanese War, as I will elaborate on later in this chapter. The term "Great Wall" is also included in the lyrics of China's national anthem. Deng's endorsement of the Great Wall in the meaningful year of

1984 was followed by concrete acts of institutionalizing the monument. Four years later, three young engineers between the ages of 25 and 30 published a co-authored, 386-page compendium, entitled "*Investigation of the Great Wall of the Ming Dynasty*," based on their 16 months and 10,000 miles of trekking from the eastern to the western end of the Great Wall.[32] The three men have often been regarded as the Chinese pioneers who traveled the entire length of the Wall, and their 1988 *Investigation* as the first to provide a comprehensive review of the Wall built during the Ming Dynasty (1368 to 1644). The compendium follows China's territorial order and is organized by the nation's jurisdictional hierarchy from provinces and municipalities to counties to convey the comprehensiveness of the book that covers the entirety of the Wall and of the nation's territory.

Following their epic journey, the three young authors were joined by several prominent political and cultural figures to found the Great Wall Society, which was inaugurated in the Great Hall of the People, China's most esteemed state building, itself a monument, in Beijing in 1987. Registered as a civic association, the Great Wall Society is nonetheless widely perceived as a para-governmental organization, chaired by former top government and military leaders.[33] The aim of the Great Wall Society is to "proclaim the glorious spirit of the Chinese People, and to study, conserve, and promote the Great Wall."[34] To that end, some members of the Society advocated to establish Great Wall Studies as an independent academic discipline. In 1994, the Society published a 1,278-page-long *Encyclopedia of the Great Wall*.[35] In 2016, funded by Phoenix Media Publishing Group, a publicly listed company with a state-sector background and one of the largest media groups in China, the Great Wall Society published a 10-volume, 12,500-page *Chronicles of the Great Wall of China*.[36] This monumental publication had two chief editors: the senior editor is the CEO of Phoenix Media Group that funded the project. The junior editor is Dong Yaohui, one of the three co-authors of the 1988 "*Investigation*" and the Vice Chair of the Great Wall Society. Intended to be the ultimate source of information and knowledge on the Great Wall, the *Chronicles* took 10 years to complete by an army of more than 200 authors and volume editors recruited from universities, research institutes, government agencies, and gazetteer editorial committees from the different jurisdictions where the Great Wall ruins are located. To elevate its visibility, the publication of the *Chronicles* was accompanied by the release of a China Central Television (CCTV) production of a 12-episode TV series entitled "*The Great Wall: Stories of China*."[37]

For popular historians, the connection between the Great Wall and national identity seems self-evident. Their writings expressed the way the physicality of the Wall itself—especially the most awesome stretches of it—manifests supreme authority. The gigantic Wall remnants traversing mountain ridges, often likened to a majestic dragon, have the effect of transporting visitors "above and beyond" their imaginary of space.[38] The sublime structures built on steep slopes and high ridges of the mountains, when attributed to the "Chinese people's wisdom and perseverance," were meant to demonstrate the superiority of the Chinese people and inspire a great sense of national pride.[39] The Wall's alleged 2,000 years of history adds temporal endlessness to its spatial boundlessness. The spatial, temporal, cultural, and technological greatness of the Wall together build a grand vision of China's past, while projecting its present and future as a unified nation.

A vision it is. But what kind? Cultural Study scholar Carlos Rojas (2010) chose "sublime" to describe the Wall as an "aesthetic category ... beyond human understanding," and explains that the Wall's contemporary appeal lies in the fact that "it appears so eminently comprehensible ... as an accessible fragment of the infinite—an easily intelligible symbol." [40] In other words, what makes the Great Wall popular is not just its sublime quality, but also the accessibility to and intelligibility of such sublimity. From Rojas' observation comes the next question: who has been accessing the Wall and contributing to its intelligibility?

II.2 Visualizing the Vision

Since the 2000s, hiking and photographing the Great Wall ruins have been among the most popular ways of approaching the Wall's sublimity. History enthusiasts hike to visit the watch towers that crown the Wall, enjoy magnificent views from atop, and take shots of the ruins and the Wall-framed landscape, sometimes with themselves in the frame and sharing the compositions on social media with captions of melancholic invocations. For many, taking photographs of the Wall on a hike feels like a productive way of connecting with history. Some lucky visitors would find fragments of old china or stoneware on the hikes. Websites devoted to Great Wall enthusiasts, hikers, and photographers have grown rapidly since the early 2000s. Photographers of varied skill levels post their Wall shots to these websites. Many of the photos feature the dual aesthetics of nostalgia and monumentality:[41] a decayed earthen wall remnant paired with the arid frontier landscape or a stretch of solemn, snow-capped brick wall meandering across the frame against the backdrop of layered mountain ranges and clouds, all drenched in dramatic lighting. The various ways the ruins and landscapes shape one another have inspired endless works of artistic expression. The photos are often accompanied by lyrical paeans, denoting the photographers' sentiments that meld the wallscape of the nation's grandeur and beauty. Other photos are accompanied by historical tales of the Wall. The Wall, which aggrandizes and is aggrandized by nature, signifies the nation's timeless and expansive territorial possession.[42]

Photographs dominate the popular representation of the Wall. Hiking and photographing the Great Wall is both an affective and aesthetic experience. Compared with textual representations, visual images enjoy greater aesthetic appeal. Compared with other forms of visual representation, photographs command a persuasive power drawn from their ability to instantly capture the details of a scene through "realist technology."[43] As Roland Barthes (2000) wrote, photographs have a twofold role as referents and proofs of the past.[44] The popular historians' narratives about the Wall and the photographed wallscape together reinforce a more concrete national identity expressed by the grandiose Wall and wallscape. The well-circulated photographs also render heritage portable, reaching audiences far and near.[45] For those who have not seen the sight with their own eyes, the photos help inspire a once-in-a-life-time visit to the Great Wall.

The ability of photographs to capture the "real likeness" and to prove the existence of an object is particularly relevant in Great Wall-themed landscape photography. It is because only about 300 km out of the 21,196 km of the Wall are built of durable brick and stone, and only a small fraction of the Great Wall's immeasurable length is as great as it used to be. These stretches, especially the famous Badaling section north of Beijing that has been visited by millions, including the likes of Prime Minister Fidel Castro, Queen Elizabeth II, and President Obama, are the most photogenic segments of the Wall. Through the reproduction and wide circulation of the image of the Badaling section, this one magnificent and manicured brick-and-mason section of the Wall has come to visually represent the 21,000 km-long Wall. This image has appeared on China's stamps, serves as the logo of the Beijing Olympics, and can be found on the wall of President Xi Jinping's office, embellishing his official portrait. On the other hand, most of the rest of the Wall—no less than two-thirds of it—has deteriorated beyond recognition and is visually underwhelming or is simply invisible above ground. They are unsuitable visual references of the Great Wall. The photographic images of the Badaling segment are used to represent the Great Wall. As a whole, the brick-and-mason wall also serves as a model in many Great Wall restoration projects in other areas, including the northwest where the border walls were originally made of rammed earth in a very different style and scale.

As the small sections of the Ming-style brick wall became the standard image of the Great Wall, the Great Wall photographers who preferred artistic originality and diversity started to look elsewhere to expand their repertoire. They set out to photograph less-visited segments of the Wall in distant mountains, and some vowed to trek the "entire Wall," like the three pioneers who co-authored the 1988 *Investigation*, in order to capture stunning and previously unseen images in distant lands far from Beijing. But how *entire* is the entirety, and *whose* entirety is more entire? As presented earlier, border fortifications are multilayered and overlapping, located across immense lands and varied landscapes with different levels of accessibility in different seasons. As a result, most trekkers who claimed to have traveled the entire Wall ended up following divergent routes and fashioning the "entirety" in their own ways.

Many turned the ambitious project of capturing the entirety of a boundless giant into collective endeavors. Wall photographers and popular historians, often one and the same, are networked through various associations and websites devoted to the Great Wall, especially Great Wall photography. They go on photography trips together, organize Great Wall photography competitions, post pictures of the Walls on websites, and publish print photo albums. The images of various ruins are compiled under the unifying label of the Great Wall. And like the Wall compendia, the photo albums are organized jurisdictionally by province and by county, which imbue a sense of geographical congruence to the impromptu sightings and disconnected sites. As such, scattered ruin fragments find their place in the nation's territorial order.

While the collectivized project might or might not bring consensus on the Wall's entirety, what matters just as much is the photographers' commitment to the pursuit of the ideal of an entirety. The ideal, in turn, further validates the visionary integrity of the national monument.

Adventurism is also part of the draw of Great Wall photography. The most committed Wall photographers, many of whom are males born in the 1960s and 70s, are determined to endure hardship across rugged terrain and weather the unpredictable mountain climate for the promise of spectacular and original shots. Their pursuits are traceable actions, and the photographs are tangible products of their physical strength and spiritual commitment to the Great Wall. Through the products of their tremendous efforts—photos, research essays, and travelogues—Wall enthusiasts have contributed to filling in the blanks, connecting the dots, and visualizing the puzzle pieces for a grand, unitary vision of the Great Wall.

II.3 Rephotography and Reenactment

Among the popular historian-cum-photographers, the most committed ones also engage in rephotography and reenactment.

In 2012, a Beijing-based veteran Great Wall photographer, Zhang Baotian, published a photo album entitled *Remembrance of the Great Wall*.[46] His album is a rephotographic project that contains over 500 Great Wall photos taken between the mid-19th and mid-20th centuries by 21 European, American, Japanese, and Chinese traveler-photographers. These original shots are paired with reproductions taken by Zhang and his fellow rephotographers between 2000 and 2010. The originals and replicas are placed side-by-side in the book, accompanied by Zhang's captions and short essays.

Some of Zhang's essays concern the histories of specific Wall sites and structures, while others tell vivid stories about Zhang's own search for the perfect reproduction of earlier Great Wall images. Trained as an electrical engineer at the prestigious Tsinghua University with a specialization in program decoding, Zhang methodically explained the process of "decoding" the under-provenanced Great Wall photos taken decades, or even a century, earlier. His work of "decoding" the old photos started from locating the original scenes and vantage points: where were these photos taken and from what exact spots and angles? He would first examine the architectural style and materials of the wall remnants and the landscape shown in the original and consult archival materials. He then followed leads from his preliminary research with safari hunt-like field surveys in the probable area. The hunt for the exact location where past images were produced involved strenuous bush-whacking through rough country terrain on unbeaten paths. To reproduce the image as faithfully as possible, the replica would be shot at the same time of the day in the same season for similar lighting conditions and foliage. Zhang also tried to use the same aperture and shutter speed, correcting for the changes in photographic technologies over time.

In Zhang's album, the paired photos are organized by province, in accordance with the nations' territorial hierarchy like the aforementioned *Great Wall Encyclopedia*. But there is deviation from this spatial order. In Zhang's album, the Second Sino-Japanese War, which took place between 1937 and 1945 during the Second World War, enjoys a special section of its own. Under this spotlight, this section features rephotography of the images taken by wartime photojournalists in the battlefields.

The Great Wall across China's northern mountain ranges formed the frontline between the invading Japanese troops from Manchuria in China's northeast and the Communist military base in the northwest. The Second Sino-Japanese War holds a prominent place in official Chinese Communist Party (CCP) history. The trauma of the war and the glory of the hard-earned victory are rejuvenated regularly to this day. War stories and heroes continue to dominate contemporary curricula of patriotic education in classrooms and in designated Patriotic Education Bases throughout China, especially in the northwest where the CCP was based in the 1930s. Numerous feature films, documentaries, and TV series have been produced to pay homage to the heroic CCP Eighth Route Army who fought against the Japanese aggressors. These commemorations transcend the generational gaps between those who experienced the war and those who have only been taught about it.

During the Sino-Japanese War, the battlefield photos of the Great Wall, published in wartime pictorials, were popularized together with a patriotic song that called for defending the motherland with the spirit of a "new Great Wall" that would be "built with our flesh and blood," which later became the national anthem of the PRC. The fusion of the Wall and the War brings distant memories of the Great Wall closer to contemporary Chinese national sentiment.

Born in 1947 in northern China where memories of Japanese soldiers' brutality run deep, Zhang was particularly partial to wartime photos of the Wall. He and his fellow photographers vowed to follow in the footsteps of wartime photojournalists and revisit all the battlefronts on which the Eighth Route Army fought and from where wartime journalists reported. They sought to reproduce the same scenes from the same vantage points.

In 2007, Zhang rephotographed a well-known 1937 image made by a wartime photojournalist, Fang Dazeng (nicknamed Xiao Fang), of a Badaling Wall section. Accompanying the paired photos was a recount of Xiao Fang's tragically short life and his disappearance during an assignment to the battlefront. Zhang also spent half of the essay recounting the successful hunt for the location where Xiao Fang captured the legendary photo image. Zhang proudly called the reproduction a "successful meeting with Xiao Fang across time with locational precision on the Great Wall."[47]

Rephotographers also reenact some of the battlefront scenes. A good example is a photo originally shot by another legendary wartime photojournalist, Sha Fei, in the autumn of 1937 in Shanxi Province.[48] The original photo (Figure 10.1) entitled "Command Site of the Eighth Route Army at Chajian Ridge," features six soldiers behind an earthen barricade. Five of them are positioned adjacent to the barricade, fixing their gaze on a mountain ridge capped by four watch towers of the Great Wall, which had been occupied by Japanese troops. The man who appears to be a commander stands with one leg perched upon the uneven ground to steady his balance. His comrade, standing abreast leans forward, propping up his chest on his left elbow to support the weight of his body.

Figure 10.1 Command site of the Eighth Route Army on Chajian Ridge, photographed by Sha Fei, fall 1937

Source: Image scanned from the original photo in the Harvard Yenching Library collection.

Two soldiers lie prone on either side of the standing men, aiming their rifles at the enemy. The viewer cannot see any of the men's faces, but we can clearly discern the energy in their tense and purposeful stillness. Their unfaltering vigilance could erupt in shooting and artillery shelling at any moment. While the unmistakable Great Wall and the watch towers that outline the contours of the ridge accentuate the figures in the frame, this photo represents Sha Fei's signature wartime photojournalist style: the figures and their positions are narratively arranged and visually dominant. The perspective of the lens is oriented to align the viewer's eye level with the subjects' line of sight, a compositional device that transports the viewer to the scene of action.[49] In Zhang's book, the recreation of this legendary wartime image was reenacted by three photographers (Figure 10.2). The photograph was taken by Li Ju, another veteran Great Wall photographer, in 2008. Two photographer-cum-reenactors, including Zhang himself (in the orange-color jacket), posed as the commanders, while the third took on the role of the solider who lies prone with his head up, all assuming the same body language of intent concentration.

Zhang and his fellow reenactors are in good company. Reenactment is also popular with history enthusiasts of the American Civil War. American Civil War reenactors are often preoccupied with the nuanced details of battle scenes and insist on period-appropriate uniforms and prop weaponry in order to accurately "connect with history."[50] By contrast, the three reenactors in this photo seem less concerned with the props. The figures in the reenactment image wear brightly colored outdoor jackets instead of the northern Chinese soldiers' cotton-padded suits, betraying the recreational nature of the activity. The warm, tawny lighting of early autumn in the retake has much softened the austerity of the black-and-white wartime image. Upon closer inspection of the 2008 shot, the rifle that the "soldier" is holding is in fact a tripod.

Figure 10.2 Photographer Li Ju's reenacted photo in 2008 of original photo taken by Sha Fei in 1937
Source: Photo credit: Li, Ju.

There are other inconsistencies in the reproduced image as well. The visually prominent watch towers—the emblematic structures of the Great Wall that punctuate the linear Wall in Sha Fei's original version—have completely disappeared in the retake. Zhang explained in his note that because the watch towers were occupied by Japanese troops during the war, so the "anti-Japanese soldiers and people destroyed the towers."[51] To fill the void left by the missing towers, the three reenactors take up more space in the new frame, while the Great Wall sans watch towers has become much less distinct in the distance. The visual focus of the new format is on the three reenactors themselves, especially the central figure in the bright orange jacket. The photographers' replica wartime image is, after all, a product of their own place in history: a time of peace and prosperity and of nostalgia.[52]

In Zhang's own reflection, he shares that his relentless chase for images of yesteryear goes beyond his own emotional gratification. Rephotography and reenactment is his and his fellow history-minded photographers' way of paying homage to grassroots heroes. It was also a reminder to his fellow citizens of frontline soldiers' selfless devotion in defending their nation against imperialists' invasion. To carry out this mission, Zhang went on to collect oral histories of veteran soldiers and their families and visited the soldiers' burial sites after the publication of *Remembrance*.[53]

Zhang also considers rephotography a contribution to conserving the rapidly disappearing Great Wall. To demonstrate the immediate utility of rephotography to heritage conservation, Zhang tells two stories in his book about the ways photographers' retakes of deteriorated Great Wall ruins have helped persuade the local government initiate restoration projects. In both cases, the vintage photos were used as references for restoration.[54] Zhang states that the comparisons of then-and-now images apprise the viewer of the fragility of the Great Wall, enhancing the sense of urgency, hence drawing greater public attention to the national monument.

Zhang's intention went further than helping with restoring the past. In many cases, Wall structures in the original image had been completely destroyed or severely deteriorated long before the replica image had been taken. As a result, the new image can only show the original site, but not the original sight, and this void proves to be a pedagogic moment. The image that features Wall ruins and the image that does not, when placed side-by-side, amount to a visual argument foregrounding the imperative of protecting the Great Wall. Accompanied by textual captions and notes, the paired images become viewing guides. Viewers are educated about what they could have seen if the Wall had remained intact, or what will be seen if the Wall is restored. The chronologically arranged images of the same site do not just convey quiescent bygones, but tangible future possibilities. The nostalgic desire to restore the past, after all, is a project of modernity aimed at the future, as presented in the Preface of this book.[55] It is not by coincidence, therefore, to find that many of the enthusiastic popular historian-cum-photographers of the Wall, not unlike environmental activists, are also active organizers and lecturers of Great Wall workshops, field trips, and camps for adults and school children through which to expound upon the iconic national monument and the urgency of protecting it for present and future generations.[56]

Rephotography hence creates a sense of historical continuity that connects the past with the future, an effect that is compatible with the project of monumentalizing the Great Wall. But there is more to the rephotographers' project. For the popular historian-cum-photographers, the issue of historical continuity is not just about the Great Wall itself, but also about the lineage of images, image-making, and image-makers of the Wall. It turns out that Zhang and his fellow photographers belong to a long tradition of Great Wall photography and rephotography that has included both Chinese and Western photographers since the mid-19th century.

As Zhang and his fellow photographers were rephotographing the Wall ruins, a Beijing-based British writer-photographer from Manchester, William Lindesay, published his rephotographic album "*The Great Wall Revisited*" in 2007, five years prior to the publication of Zhang's *Remembrance*. A former long-distance runner, Lindesay ran and walked the "whole length" of the Wall in 1987 and published a travelog in 1989.[57] He subsequently founded an association called the International Friends of the Great Wall in Beijing. His 2007 book, *Revisited*, contains 72 pairs of meticulously replicated images placed next to the original photos shot by earlier photographers. Lindesay's referent images were the works of foreign "pioneer explorers" at the turn of the century. But he made an exception for the Chinese legendary wartime photojournalist, Sha Fei, whose photo Li Ju rephotographed in 2008, as shown in (Figure 10.2).

In 2005, Lindesay rephotographed Sha Fei's 1937 scene but without the reenactors who were included in Li Ju's retake. Lindesay recognized Sha Fei's wartime contribution in his notes, but he was captivated mostly by the background in Sha Fei's frame: the wall structure itself. In Lindsay's photo, he moved the wall from the background to the foreground and removed human figures from the photo. In addition, Lindesay pointed out that Sha Fei was not the first photographer to capture the legendary view of the historicized site.

The first photographer who shot from this vantage point, Lindesay emphasized, was William Geil (1865–1925) (Figure 10.3), an American missionary who traveled extensively in China and wrote several popular travelogs. Allegedly the first traveler to ever hike "the entire length" of the Great Wall, Geil and his team traversed the

Figure 10.3 Chajian Ridge, by William Geil, 1908

Source: Geil, William, 1909, p. 140.

Wall from east to west in 1908 and published the classic "*The Great Wall of China*" in 1909.[58]

William Lindesay dedicated his 2007 *Revisited* to William Geil, crowning Geil as the "first explorer of the Great Wall of China." The preface of *Revisited* was entitled "*The Wall of two Williams*." That title was also used for a 10-episode miniseries hosted by Lindesay and produced by China Network TV in 2007[59] as well as for another book Lindesay published in China in 2012.

In the opening episode of the TV series "*The Wall of Two Williams*," Lindesay points out that the "two Williams had met on the Great Wall eighty years apart." He adds that "although Geil has passed away, I felt Geil and I were together as a team." Similar to what Zhang did in his photo album, much of the text in Lindesay's *Revisited* and the TV series focuses on the technicalities and physical challenges of pursuing the locations from the original scenes, the aesthetics of the vintage images, and the exhilaration of finally locating the original photographers' viewing spots.

In the album Lindesay also dedicates sizable space to the biographies of pioneer explorer-photographers. The process of scouring the terrain for the original scene is a tradition of adventurous pilgrimage to the origin of a lineage of images. The original sight thus becomes a revered site for generations of photographers to commemorate. Lindesay mused "... maybe I am the reincarnation of William Geil."[60]

Not to be outdone, Zhang went further in his efforts to connect with legendary image-makers. He brought the daughter of Sha Fei, the wartime photojournalist and creator of Figure 10.1, to the location where Sha Fei had shot the iconic image, "Eighth Route Army fighting on the Great Wall." In Zhang's photograph, Sha Fei's daughter holds a copy of the iconic photo while standing in the exact spot where Sha Fei had taken the original photo.[61] In this new photo, Sha Fei's original frame is no longer the primary concern. What seems to matter just as much is the spot where the masterpiece had been created. On this spot arises a new sight for commemoration: Zhang's triumph in decoding the puzzle and building the lineage with image-makers at the very location where the image was born. With the daughter of the master photographer in the new frame, such a photographic lineage is further reinforced by blood lineage.

As photographers channel their artistic energy and cultural inspiration into reproducing legendary images, the site of visual memories becomes that of visual creativity. The history of the Wall intertwines with the history of image-making of the Wall. As photographers identify with their cultural heroes by hunting down the original locations to "bask in the aura of artistic glory,"[62] the image-making of the Wall is further historicized by a lineage of image-makers.

The tales of image-making and image-makers of the Wall show the generative energy of Great Wall Revivalism.

With rephotography, photographers cite their motivation as "connecting with history" when trying to hold an idolized image of a frozen moment as a point of reference for history. Yet, in their practice, that very attempt of image reproduction diverges. Remnants deform, sites transform, memories flee, and referents shift. To materialize the aspiration of connecting with the nation's history, the image makers inevitably go through historical processes of selective remembering and visual rendering framed by their own references and preferences. Lindesay and Zhang held the same image-making hero in mind, and they shared the same reference image when rephotographing the same site at Chajian Ridge. Yet, the two rephotographers ultimately produced vastly different images. Despite the shared vision of historical continuity and connection, multiple creators' rephotography yields distinct sights.

Two more examples help to further illustrate the endless possibilities derived from a shared fascination with the Great Wall. One concerns a nationalistic gulf within the lineage of image reproduction, and the other, China's changing discourse on heritage preservation.

In August 1908, the aforementioned American travel writer William Geil took a picture of himself with an American flag that he had brought with him on the trip traversing the Great Wall (see Figure 10.4). The photo was taken in front of a travel

"The Last Brick." Dr. Geil at the end of the Great Wall

Figure 10.4 William Geil in Jiayu Fortress with the U.S. national flag

Source: Geil, William, 1909, p. 382.

lodge at Jiayu Fortress, where he stayed, at the western end of the Great Wall. Geil posed next to the U.S. flag, beaming with pride at the conclusion of his historic journey across the "entire" Great Wall. Shortly afterwards, he was treated by the fortress official to a 19-course banquet that included sea cucumber, a luxurious Chinese delicacy for the most noble guests.[63] A century later, in August 2008, Zhang Baotian, the author of the aforementioned *Remembrance*, also took a picture of himself in front of a segment of earthen wall that looks similar to the background of Geil's self-portrait, with the same photographic composition (Figure 10.5). But Zhang displays the five-star Red Flag of the People's Republic of China. Unlike Geil's somewhat reserved gesture, Zhang's two arms extend out to hold the corners of the flag with radiant avidity. The two pictures were set side-by-side in Zhang's book (see Figures 10.4 and 10.5).[64]

While Geil's photo is in black-and-white, Zhang's colored photo is dominated by the bright red of the PRC national flag in the center of the frame. The message must

Figure 10.5 Zhang Baotian in Jiayu Fortress with the Chinese national flag
Source: Photo credit: Li, Ju.

have seemed obvious enough that Zhang did not add a caption to the pairing. With multiple creators and shifting referents, the history with which photographers wish to connect remains an elusive and unstable object.[65]

Such instability also complicates the pedagogical role of rephotography in heritage conservation.

With multiple moments of image reproduction, rephotography has come to serve as a visual biography of Wall ruins. A good example is found in four chronologically arranged images of Yanmen Fortress in Zhang's album.[66] The first image of the fortress, taken by French archaeologist Édouard Shavannes (1865–1918) in 1907, depicts the four-centuries old structure in reasonably good shape. The fortress originally had a tall base made of brick and masonry, topped by a stately wooden pavilion and surrounded by supporting buildings. In 1984, seven years after the end of the Cultural Revolution that left many historical structures in China destroyed, the three aforementioned authors of *Investigation* visited the fortress site. They took a picture of the ruins of the fortress. By then all the wooden structures, including the landmark pavilion, had completely vanished. Zhang noted that the structures were intentionally destroyed by the Japanese army during the Sino-Japanese War. The third image, shot in 2008 by Zheng Yan, another veteran Wall photographer, shows a rebuilt pavilion atop the base, but in a more elaborate style than what the 1907 photo had shown. By 2011, when Zhang himself visited the fortress at the height of Great Wall Revivalism, the surrounding structures were also rebuilt, but the scale of the structures were significantly larger and taller than the original ones.

In this visual biography, the fortress has gone through several transformations—from a neglected ruin into a celebrated national heritage site. Rephotographer Zhang might have intended to use these four chronologically ordered images across a century to present the historical continuity of a monument. But what this archaeology of images brings to view is precisely the unstable nature of the monument. It also visualizes the tension between the monumental instability and the effort to restabilize it, as presented in the taller, larger new structure that transforms both the sight and the site under rising Great Wall Revivalism.

To recap, popular historian-photographers have participated in Great Wall Revivalism with their spectacular wallscape images that contribute to visualizing a national identity with the Great Wall and popularizing the national icon. Wrapped in patriotic sentiment, their participation also went off on a tangent by reproducing images and building artistic lineages with iconic image-makers. These Wall-inspired photographic ventures forestall a binary explanatory model that treats the photographers' projects as either a form of resistance against, or an affirmation of, the discourse on the continuity, coherence, and permanence of monuments. Their most impactful contribution to Great Wall Revivalism, after all, is their very act of participation that builds up the momentum and propels the Great Wall as a generative monument.

Popular historian-photographers, most of whom are urban professionals, did not go unaccompanied when they embarked on strenuous expeditions hunting for lost images in the unfamiliar terrain. On these trips, they sought help from villagers living in the mountainous walled areas. In Zhang's and Lindesay's albums of rephotography, "village elders" or "peasant friends" were duly recognized for their roles as informants and hiking guides. Itinerant rephotographers would show their peasant friends the vintage images and ask them to help identify and lead the way to the locations where they could see the same view.

In a different context, however, peasants who live near the ruins have been accused by conservationists and officials of plundering wall bricks to fix their own homes or animal pens and selling masonry slabs with historic engravings to tourists, as noted in the opening of this chapter. Peasants were also said to have crushed the walls and use the crumbles as fertilizer, planted crops right next to the foot of the walls, carved away at the walls' foundation to expand cultivation, cracked the wall structure to hunt for medicinal insects, and grazed and sheltered their sheep in the Wall ruins. The Wall's accelerated decay, according to conservationists and officials, have the peasants' ignorance to blame.[67] Some of the Great Wall enthusiasts' educational camps have been held in poor, mountainous wall-side villages for schoolchildren, in hopes of bringing heritage awareness to peasants through educating their children.

In all these accounts, peasants are portrayed as passive informants, active thieves, or ignorant destroyers of the national monument. In the age of heritage conservation under China's rapidly unraveling rural economy, however, peasants' ways of participating in Great Wall Revivalism and the types of walls they engage with have diverged. In what follows, I will illustrate two types of peasants who actively participated in Great Wall Revivalism with different ways in two different places. One is the entrepreneurial peasants who run mass tourism businesses by the wild great walls on the fringes of Beijing's metropolitan area. The other is the peasant guardians of the wild great walls in the remote mountain villages far from the nation's capital.

III Wild Wall Tourism

Beijing was the capital of the Ming Dynasty (1368 to 1644), which built the bulk of extant wall fortifications. To protect emperors in the capital, extensive brick and stone walls were built along the northern mountain ridges on the fringes of Beijing. Today, with its concentration of white-collar workers, Beijing has seen a rapid rise in Great Wall tourism in the midst of China's overall growth in rural tourism since the 2000s. Much improved road systems and increased private car ownership rates in metropolitan Beijing have also contributed to the swathes of weekenders pouring in from the city to trek the wall ruins in the scenic countryside.

There are five well-groomed and -visited Great Wall sections, such as Badaling and Mutianyu, north of Beijing. There are many more under-restored and unsanctioned segments of the wild great walls scattered along Beijing's northern mountainous fringe, estimated to span 600 km in aggregate length. Taking advantage of their proximity to the official Great Wall sections and other tourist attractions in metropolitan

Beijing, entrepreneurial villagers have built guesthouses on their orchards and crop fields near the wall ruins.

Huanghuacheng (Yellow Flower Citadel, HHC from here on) is one such thriving destination of wild great wall tourism. Located 75 km north of Beijing city proper, HHC features a Ming-era wall ruin that spans 12.4 km and, during its historical peak, was crowned with 49 watch towers of varied sizes. A section of the HHC has been submerged by a lake-turned-reservoir. The reservoir was built in 1971 on the former site of a destroyed wall pass. The reservoir also submerged part of the HHC wall, creating what locals call a "Water Great Wall." The Water Great Wall has become the main attraction of HHC, where Yellow Flower villagers live and farm on its premises.

HHC is well located between two of the most visited segments of the officially sanctioned Great Wall: the Mutianyu section to the east, and the Juyong Pass to the west, each about 20 km away in opposite directions. HHC was little known to outsiders until the early 1990s when art school students in Beijing started going there for plein-air painting. By the mid-2000s, HHC became one of the most popular wild great wall hiking destinations in the Beijing metropolitan region.

Being a wild great wall and not recognized as a national-level heritage site until 2013, HHC did not undergo restoration in the 1990s and 2000s, and, therefore, has retained the authentic feel of a ruin. On the other hand, unlike many other segments of the wild great walls that are too steep and dangerous to climb, HHC is more tourist-friendly. Most visitors find it fairly easy to hike up to the Ming-era watchtower on the hilltop, where they can get a bird's-eye view of the scenic area. Thanks to its reputation as a pristine, yet accessible, wall and its convenient location, HHC has become well-known among domestic and foreign tourists alike, boasting an annual volume of over half a million visitors by the early 2020s.[68] These tourists found lodging in various kinds of accommodations. Along the major expressways from Beijing to HHC, there was one large hotel with hundreds of rooms and ten medium-sized resorts built by private and state-sector investors from Beijing. In the area near Yellow Flower Village and adjacent to the HHC site on the hilly slopes, local villagers have established more than two hundred farmhouse-turned lodges. Some of the lodges were built by investors who leased the chestnut or apricot orchards from the villagers. The lease fee for a piece of choice orchard land large enough to build a guesthouse with 10 to 15 rooms, a parking lot, a restaurant, and a pick-your-own-fruit orchard could fetch an annual sum of RMB 170,000 yuan (about US$25,000) in the late 1990s. The lease fee was three to four times more than the profit one could gain from growing fruits.

Orchards at higher elevations are too steep to build tourist facilities but are the closest to the wild wall structures. Owners of these orchards have cleared a portion of their land to build rudimentary trails that lead to the wall. They installed steel ladders that lean against the wall to access the last mile before reaching the top of the wall. For access to this last mile, which would take you to the top of the wall, Yellow Flower villagers charged tourists a fee for "orchard maintenance." To reach the most accessible and popular watch tower of the HHC, tourists needed to pass through multiple orchards with different owners. As a result, tourists would pay orchard maintenance fees at multiple stops on their way up. If they chose to walk along the top of the wall and take another trail down to see different views, they would pay additional fees upon their return. From the villagers' perspective, the fees, although deemed illegal by the Beijing municipal government, were justified as compensation for the damage inflicted upon their fruit trees and the garbage left behind by tourists who passed through the orchards to reach the wall.

The village and township governments welcome the spillover of tourism from Beijing to the wild great walls in their jurisdiction. The wild wall makes a name for the otherwise unknown village and help attract investors to the poor foothill villages in the periphery of metropolitan Beijing.[69] Local leaders felt that wild wall tourism, although deemed illegal by their supervising governments, could be justified by the national policy of "setting the stage with culture and running the show with economic principles."[70]

By the late 1990s, dozens of such hiking trails were developed along the hillside orchards in Yellow Flower Village. Village households were said to have been bringing home an annual income of 30,000 to 40,000 yuan from the tolls. In the meantime, tensions among villagers mounted. Villagers of influential clans competed with one another to set up toll booths and monopolize lucrative tourism businesses, such as charging fees for parking and recreational fishing in the reservoir on village premises. Verbal conflicts have led to armed fights and jail terms for some of those involved.[71]

The wild wall tourism-induced conflicts alarmed the Beijing municipal government. The Municipal Cultural Heritage Administration subsequently took action to ban villagers' wild wall businesses on the grounds that heavy foot traffic from tourism would damage the fragile wall structures. Officials erected signs that made explicit the illegality of climbing the HHC ruin, and local regulators would confiscate villagers' steel ladders. But new ladders would reappear, and recalcitrant villagers continued to host and charge tourists after the inspectors left.

In the early 2000s, the frustrated municipal authority tried a different approach to tame the villagers. A Beijing municipal government-sponsored development company started a project to build the HHC Water Great Wall Park (HHC Park from here on) in Yellow Flower Village, citing the policy of "heritage conservation through development." The plan was to convert village orchards into an enclosed recreational complex, to restore a section of the crumbling HHC ruins inside the fenced-in park, and to streamline the scenic routes and consolidate tourism development. The villagers would be compensated for the orchards incorporated into the park project. But Yellow Flower villagers, after living "under the feet of the emperor" for generations, are neither pushovers nor strangers to the art of negotiating with the state. They insisted on receiving compensation for their orchards commensurate with the loss from toll fees and other tourism income rather than the earnings from orchard harvests on which they depended prior to the tourism boom. The prohibitively high cost of such demands for compensation slowed down the government's plan to reign in the wild wall and to profit from tourism income. Unable to gain access to the land adjacent to the main section of HHC wall, the local government-sponsored developer built the HHC Park by the aforementioned reservoir adjacent to the village, but far from the main wild wall's scenery and hiking routes. The land around the reservoir had already been in the hands of the government since as early as the 1970s, when appropriation of village land for public projects was much easier for local governments. As a result of the municipal government's inability to incorporate village land for the Park, most of the HHC wild walls stayed outside of the official HHC Park and remained as wild as before, controlled by villagers who have now consolidated dozens of hiking trails into four routes, with two toll booths each way. The toll increased from 5 to 10 yuan per stop, still cheaper than the entrance fee for the officially sanctioned HHC Park at 45 yuan per head.

As a result of the Beijing municipal government's attempt to consolidate the HHC wild great wall, the wall site now exists half-wild, half-tamed, caught in an uneasy compromise between villager-operated wild great wall tourism and municipal government-sponsored HHC Park tourism. The power relationship is far from a balanced one. Villagers' wild wall businesses have been considerably affected by the officially sponsored, gated, and fee-charging HHC Park since 2004. All the road signs on the expressway from Beijing to the HHC site steer visitors directly towards the entrance of the HHC Park, bypassing the smaller, less noticeable entrances of the roads that lead to the HHC wild wall. Only those in the know and who consult social media postings and backpackers' blogs ("Don't be misled by the official road signs!") are able to find the Yellow Flower villagers' wild great wall. Villagers' income from tourism dwindled. A villager lamented that the annual lease fee for his orchard with tourist facilities went down to 80,000 yuan (from 170,000 yuan at its peak before the establishment of the HHC Park) in a mere two years. Some villagers pressed on by running parking lots, boat rentals, fishing tours, lodgings, and dining facilities. Others folded their businesses.

In 2013, HHC was elevated to become a national-level key heritage site and government scrutiny on illegal tourism operations intensified. Yet by 2020, before Covid hit, the illicit, wild side of the Great Wall has continued to draw in tourists despite the government's signs that prohibit hiking the wild walls. Visitors could trek and camp on the wall overnight before they reach the authorized Juyong Pass or Mutianyu section of the Great Wall in either direction of HHC.

So far, this story about the Great Wall in the Beijing metropolitan region has included three types of walls. The first type is the iconic Great Wall sections like Juyong Pass, Badaling, and Mutianyu. They rank at the highest, national level in China's heritage conservation hierarchy and are put under the direct supervision of the national government. The second type is the local government-sponsored Great Wall tourist destinations, like the HHC Park. The third type is the villagers' wild great walls. The national and local state-sponsored Wall and entrepreneurial villagers' wall, despite the discrepancy in their modes of governance, are all integral parts of Great Wall Revivalism and contribute to the increased volume of Great Wall tourism in the region.[72] Together the Wall and the wild walls attract visitors and bolster the Great Wall as a brand name. Meanwhile, each type of Great Wall occupies a niche market of Great Wall tourism. The manicured and best-known Badaling Great Wall fits the interests of tourists who seek famous social media-worthy vistas and received over 10 million visits in 2023.[73] The raw, unmediated, and sometimes dangerous wild great walls attracted those with a taste for adventure and ruin aesthetics. A three-generation family from Sichuan Province may insist on visiting Badaling for a family photo, whereas a young, Beijing-based female architect who visited both the HHC Park in 2016 and the HHC wild wall in 2017 told me that the wild wall was "much more fun." Scaling the unpaved trails and weaving through orchards brings one closer to nature, and the grandeur of the views from the summit of the wild wall conjures more powerful sensations of sublimity. She was disappointed by the sterilized HHC Park because of its neatly built concrete steps leading to the recently rebuilt and manicured wall structure. She likened the experience to "walking upstairs to a Beijing flat," only to reach a restricted view of the mountains thanks to the Park's distance from the primary HHC wall site, as mentioned earlier. The safe and enclosed HHC Park that the municipal developer built, she complained, was over-crowded and teeming with noisy kids.

One can always question the efficacy of mass tourism—in either the tamed or wild walls—in forging a national identity. Long gone are the days, if they ever existed, when the masses could be mobilized by party discipline or socialist ideals alone. In the post-Mao era, the CCP tried to maintain its mobilizational capacity by keeping the Communist Revolution alive. To keep the Revolution alive in the age of commercialism, it is helpful to make revolutionary history fun and profitable.

Great Wall mass tourism, therefore, is better understood in the context of Red Tourism, an initiative launched by the CCP to promote patriotic education. In 1991, two years after the Tiananmen Massacre, the CCP state carried out a patriotic education campaign "in a much more practical and sophisticated way,"[74] compared to the political mobilization programs under Mao. The patriotic education campaign explicitly targeted the younger, post-revolution generation, and focused on entertainment.[75] In addition to traditional channels like school curricula and textbooks, the patriotic education programs employed pop culture (films and TV series), traditional and national holidays (from the Lunar New Year's festival to the Army Day celebration), and heritage tourism as vehicles through which to advance patriotic education, for which Red Tourism holds a critical front. Between 2004 and 2007, more than 400 million people visited over 150 designated Red Tourism destinations that commemorate the trauma and glory of the CCP, the People's Liberation Army, and the Communist Revolution. Also, linking patriotic education with tourism for rural development is also a policy goal. Most Red Tourism sites are located in the poor interior regions where the Red Army occupied and fought against the Nationalists or the Japanese in the 1930s and 1940s. Today, Red Tourism in these areas is double-tasked with patriotic education and poverty alleviation. Red Tourism is also a form of Green Tourism.[76] Largely untouched by post-Mao market reforms, the northern and northwestern hilly villages have retained much of their natural scenery and folk culture. Their slow-paced development, a sore spot for post-Mao reformers, turned out to be an asset for rural tourism and the nostalgia economy of the new millennium.

The Great Wall, with its formidable physical presence stretching atop mountain ranges as both natural and historical landscapes, makes for an ideal site for combining the leisure economy with patriotic education. Three of the popular, authorized Great Wall sections (Badaling, Xifengkou, and the Shanhai Pass) are on the official list of "Patriotic Education Bases." But these sections do not monopolize patriotic education. Tourism of the wild great walls also contributes to it—and makes revolutionary history even more fun.

Compared to visiting the manicured Great Wall section like Badaling with well-paved steps and big crowds, it is cooler to visit the wild walls, like the HCC. Wild great wall visitors, many of whom are young and able-bodied, often post photos on social media of themselves hiking the steep slopes or standing in front of the dilapidated ruins, accompanied by comments about their bravado and sentiments about connecting with the nation's history. One of the most widely cited quotes in these captions is "You are not a real man if you have not been to the Great Wall," which Chairman Mao wrote during the Long March in 1935 when he passed through the walled mountains in the northwest. Less can be more. Braving the "wild" great walls and scaling the unpaved trails and unrestored ruins attest to one's manhood. Unmediated by modern intervention, the experience feels authentic. To use a popular expression, the wild great walls have kept "their own juice and original flavor" (*yuanzhi yuanwei*), unlike the Badaling Great Wall, which is deemed to be mainly for seniors and visitors from rural areas. As a young engineer from Beijing put it: "Because there is little governmental planning and few propaganda messages around the wild walls, I feel closer to the real history of China and to the roots of my motherland."[77] For him, the affective connection among the self, the nation, and history meld "more naturally" in the absence of omnipresent, blatant guidance from the state. It is also worth noting that, unlike many other officially designated Red Tourism destinations in the remote countryside, wild great wall tourism does not require state subsidies either directly through infrastructure investment or indirectly through organized Red Tourism trips paid for by various governmental sponsors. Despite the regulatory fissure it represents, wild wall tourism helps with cultural mobilization with little state investment.

It would be naïve, of course, to assume that visitors are passively indoctrinated by patriotic messages when visiting the walls, wild or tamed. Touring the Great Wall or the wild great walls does not automatically strengthen one's identification with the nation. Such visits can be a process of creating new memories of the visit itself, instead of remembering the nation's past. The visit could produce a collective social identity with the hundreds of millions of other visitors to the most well-recognized Great Wall sections (sections such as Badaling that "one must visit at least once in a lifetime"). For those who scale the challenging wild walls, the hike also proves them to be a brave soul like the many others who have done it before and posted their feats on social media. Still, the authorized Great Wall sections and the many wild walls that derive their cultural significance from the Great Wall together serve as referents of social identity-building for the visitors, adding yet another venue for popularizing the Great Wall as a national monument.

IV Grassroots Heritage Guardians

To strengthen citizens' attachment to the Great Wall, it would seem helpful to encourage them to engage with the various kinds of walls through hiking and enjoying the tactile qualities of the ruins. Yet, many devoted Great Wall conservationists and popular historian-photographers are critical of wild wall mass tourism. They worry that careless tourists trekking up the battered walls could accelerate the fragile ruins' process of decay. They also disapprove of the hyper-commercialization of wild wall tourism and the peasants whom they consider to be exploiting this national treasure. As such, the photographers have looked further beyond the popular wild walls in metropolitan Beijing for something less "contaminated." In poor mountainous villages in Hebei Province, four to five hours car ride away from Beijing via the expressways and winding local roads, where few casual urban tourists would reach, they found pristine wall ruins. There they also found more "authentic" peasants who are not like the opportunistic mass tourism operators near Beijing, but rather committed guardians of the priceless heritage of the nation. The conservationists and photographers see these peasant guardians of the Great Wall as grassroots heroes who share the same cultural and historical mission as themselves.

IV.1 Peasant-turned Great Wall Guardians

Lao Zhang (meaning "Old Zhang")[78] is one such peasant-turned guardian of the Great Wall. Lao Zhang's home village, Chengziyu, sits on the foothills of a stretch of Ming-era Wall in eastern Hebei Province. The portion of the Wall in his home village stands at an average of 500 to 600 meters in altitude and is located about 240 km east of Beijing. Geographic proximity to the nation's capital has made Hebei one of the poorest provinces in China. The analogy that "the area directly under the lantern does not receive light" is often invoked to describe the stark economic contrasts between Beijing and its poor neighbor, Hebei. The mountain villages in eastern Hebei are among the most impoverished in the poor province and have been home to an outflow of emigrants since the 1980s.

The eastern Hebei mountains are also home to a better-preserved, 142 km-long stretch of Ming-era Wall made of brick and masonry, connected by watch towers. The Chengziyu section is well-known among Wall enthusiasts not just for its impressive structure, but also for Lao Zhang, the first peasant member of the aforementioned prestigious Beijing-based Great Wall Society.

According to newspapers and TV coverage, Lao Zhang started voluntary patrolling the wall segment near his village home in as early as 1978, when he realized the ruins were rapidly deteriorating.[79] He trekked the 10 km-long wall ruins that included 32 watch towers and eight beacon towers almost daily even in the freezing winter and roasting summer. During his patrols, he would reinsert loose wall bricks, blot out tourists' graffiti, pick up trash, and prevent fellow villagers from grazing sheep, hunting scorpions, or collecting herbs on the wall ruins. Although his self-appointed role as guardian of the Great Wall did not win him popularity in the village, as the news stories went, he never yielded. These reports were invariably accompanied by photos of Lao Zhang himself. In one, he is shown carrying "a small sickle to cut through trails and a handful of roasted peanuts and a small bottle of barley liquor for lunch." Another photo shows him surrounded by foreign and Chinese visitors on the wall while gesturing at the ruins and telling stories. Yet another shows him putting bricks that had fallen out back into the ancient structure, against a background of wall ruins.

Lao Zhang's fame has grown with the rise of Great Wall Revivalism since the mid-2000s. There have been many reports about his volunteer work in protecting the nation's treasure. Being an avid writer himself, he published his collection of Chengziyu folktales in print and his historical research about the Chengziyu wall online. He would post his photos with captions to his WeChat account on a daily basis. His posts reported on the visits of government officials, foreign guests, and journalists whom he guided to see the wall in his village. In addition, as an avid photographer himself, Lao Zhang shared shots of spring blossoms of Chengziyu village and the fall harvests of his home farms, wallscapes with big skies and changes in seasonal vegetation, and snow-capped brick ruins and himself braving the cold. Old Zhang is also a prolific poet. He would frequently post poems in colloquial language about his wall patrols, the visits he received from dignitaries, the seasonal changes, his wife's country cooking and his joyous drinking, as well as his wholesome life in the mountains. Following a Chinese literary tradition, he sometimes would compose the first half of a poem and invite his followers on WeChat to write the second half to complete a four-verse poem. He would also re-post journalists' stories about him as well as his portraits taken by famous photographers.

In 2012, Lao Zhang was appointed as a representative of the Committee of Political Consultative Conference of his county of Funing in Hebei Province, an honor that is not often extended to peasants.[80] Selected as one of the "Most Beautiful People of Funing County," the photo of Lao Zhang, a man in his late-50s then with dark skin, was posted all over the streets in the county seat. In 2016, Lao Zhang was named the Model Guardian of the Great Wall by the SACH. Central, provincial, and municipal TV stations featured him in various Great Wall conservation programs. Lao Zhang has also been appointed as a Special Chair Lecturer on heritage tourism at the University of Tianjin's School of Business. That same year, the SACH launched a Great Wall Guardian Program nationally, which recruited villagers living near the Great Wall ruins to regularly patrol the heritage sites so as to protect the ruins. Lao Zhang was appointed by the local Cultural Heritage Bureau to be one of the 4,650 Great Wall guardians in China.

I visited Lao Zhang in Chengziyu village in July 2017. Compared to the conveniently located HHC wall that took only an hour to reach by car from Beijing, Chengziyu sits four hours away from Beijing, first by train then by car.

Lao Zhang's home in the village was not hard to find. Amongst the flat village homes, his house stood out: it was a new, three-story concrete building that sat on a terraced lot. Seven characters written in bright red—"*changchengbaohu gongzuozhan*" (Work Station of Great Wall Protection)—with each character standing at over 4 feet in height, was erected on top of the flat roof. The large, red characters and official sounding name of the building faced the road that connects Chengziyu Village to the city, with their backs facing the village center. At the bottom of the terraced lot, tomato, corn, and eggplant grew in the vegetable garden surrounded by chestnut trees and a parking lot that could accommodate eight 50-seat tour buses.

At the top of the terraced land, the three-story building was fenced off by a six-foot tall brick wall. The wall was covered by a 25-foot long, brightly colored, well-made poster. The left half of the horizontal poster featured a slogan that read: "Taste the ancient Wall, study Great Wall culture; photograph Great Wall scenery, explore Great Wall folklore. Natural green foods, nutrition, health and exercise." At the bottom of the slogan was Lao Zhang's name and title, "Director of Great Wall Work Station," followed by his two cellphone numbers. Plastered across the right half of the poster was a life-sized photo of none other than Lao Zhang himself against a backdrop of a watch tower ruin. In the photo Lao Zhang wore the army-green uniform of the Great Wall guardians, standing straight, raising his right arm to greet the viewer.

Lao Zhang's three-story house contained five guest rooms, a large conference room, and an unusually large kitchen on the ground floor. It was a family operation: Zhang's wife and daughter-in-law were in charge of cooking and cleaning the guesthouse, while Lao Zhang took visitors to hike the wall ruins. Lao Zhang took pride in offering fresh produce from their home garden and in his wife's rustic cooking. The menu did not offer the usual white rice, but rather a multigrain bowl and heaps of vegetables for health-conscious Great Wall lovers from the city and abroad.

One weekday in July 2017, Lao Zhang hosted sixteen visitors in four groups to hike the wall: a tourist family of three from Australia (Lao Zhang customarily called them "honorable foreign guests," or *wai-bin*), a Beijing-based photographer carrying heavy photography equipment, a group of officials from the Baoding municipal government's Science Development Committee who were themselves hosting visitors from another province to show them Hebei's heritage treasures and its patriotic peasant. I also joined the group after having lunch at Zhang's family diner. Full of contagious energy, the swarthy 62-year-old peasant guardian led the way on our hike to the prized wall. He wore his army-green Great Wall guardian uniform shirt, unbuttoned given the hot day. On the hike, he told vivid stories about various segments of the wall in his village and the watch towers, especially the "Zhang Family's Watch Tower." One of the visiting officials in the group said to me: "Lao Zhang is a real celebrity! What he does is truly beyond what one would expect of a peasant." Others in the group took turns having their pictures taken with Lao Zhang, who was always placed in the center of the photo, wearing a pair of sunglasses and a broad, confident smile.

Lao Zhang can be seen as a social entrepreneur with a strong sense of mission. His in-depth tour was no mass tourism show like the kind at the HHC wild wall presented in the previous section. What motivated him to voluntarily patrol the wall for almost four decades? To that frequently asked question, his repeated answer was "my ancestors were Great Wall builder-soldiers. I am only carrying on the duty passed down to me."

Lao Zhang's reference to his lineage of the Great Wall builders and border defenders was derived from the history of border conflicts during the Ming Dynasty. The establishment of the Ming in 1368 CE forced the Mongol rulers, who reigned during the preceding Yuan Dynasty (1279 to 1368 CE), to retreat to the northern steppe. But the Mongol forces continued to cross the border and raided the farming colonies in the south. One of the Ming generals, the legendary Qi Jiguang (1528–1588) was dispatched by the emperor to secure the northern frontier. General Qi oversaw the project of building a total of 1,290 km of border fortifications on mountain ridges in Hebei in order to protect the emperors in Beijing.[81]

The best of General Qi's soldiers, who were also part of the labor force for constructing the fortifications, were said to have been recruited from Yiwu of Zhejiang Province on China's southeast coast. Under General Qi's leadership, Yiwu soldiers were highly regarded as the most rigorously trained and disciplined military force at the time. Their affiliation with the highly acclaimed General Qi and their professionalism made the "Yiwu Troops" (sometimes they were simply called the "Qi-Lineage Troop" (*qijiajun*)) an epithet that has come to denote prestige and honor. Many of the Yiwu soldiers were said to have settled in and established families in the walled villages of the Hebei mountains. Today, many local villagers see themselves as descendants of the Yiwu Troops. Gazetteer writers and journalists have written about the honorable blood connection between Chengziyu villagers in the eastern mountains of Hebei and migrant Great Wall builder-defenders from coastal Yiwu.[82] That lineage, connecting Chengziyu of the inland region with Yiwu of the coastal region, was what Lao Zhang was referring to.

However, Mingyu,[83] another guesthouse owner-villager I met in Chengziyu Village, had a different story to tell. Mingyu told me he was among the first entrepreneurs in the village. He became rich by running a small and illicit coal mine in the 1990s. The mine was shut down after a few years during a government crackdown. In 1999, Mingyu leased 30 mu of village collective land by the foothills and built a four-unit, single-story house to accommodate artists and photographers from Beijing who came to Chengziyu for the authentic wall ruins and vernacular architecture in the pristine mountain village. At that time, Chengziyu was a hidden gem known only to the Beijing artists' circle. Mingyu befriended visiting writers, painters, and photographers, and his business steadily expanded by word of mouth in the 2000s. But his remained a quotidian operation. Visitors hiked and walked around the village taking photos during the day and came back to the guesthouse at night to drink and play mahjong. He and his wife did little more than cooking and cleaning. Unlike his fellow villager Lao Zhang, Mingyu did not have the charisma of a tour guide nor a flair for storytelling, poetry, or social media content creation. The attention that Lao Zhang received from city visitors, government officials, and foreigners apparently aroused envy in the village. Mingyu was critical of Lao Zhang's practices in running a lodging business from his new and conspicuous three-story house, and snarked, "Back in 1999, Lao Zhang was working for me as a day laborer to build my guesthouse."[84]

When asked about the legendary Yiwu Troops and their descendants in the village, Mingyu dismissed it briskly: "... there are no records to prove any of it. Lao Zhang was plenty bold to name the best-preserved watch tower in Chengziyu after his own surname, Zhang Lineage Tower, and tell people that his ancestors built it. I am a Zhang too, but I do not tell stories like that."

Both Lao Zhang and Mingyu had their points. There were records, albeit fragmentary, from tomb epitaphs that commemorated eastern Hebei villagers' ancestry hailing from various places in Zhejiang Province, if not specifically Yiwu.[85] But Mingyu's suspicions were also valid. Very few textual records are available to prove direct lineage between villagers today and General Qi's troops from the 16th century.

There are a few other empirical discrepancies as well. To begin with, the number of soldier-laborers recruited from Zhejiang was said to be 3,000,[86] whereas the total number of workers involved in building the 1,290 km-long fortifications was estimated at over 300,000.[87] In other words, the Yiwu soldiers made only a small fraction of the total recruits, if present at all. Legendary heroism aside, wall builders and soldiers experienced hardship and danger in building and guarding fortifications on the high mountain ridges in the remote frontier land. Arthur Waldron (1990) quoted an account of the soldier-builders' living conditions at the construction site: "diet was poor, officers cruel, lonely hours manning watch towers in the snows of winter frequently led to frostbite or worse."[88] Based on the Ming records of supply inventories, Yang, Wenhe (2006) estimated that the soldiers who built the watch tower were fed little more than a bowl of watery rice soup a day.[89] It was hardly a top career choice for most. Scholars have suggested that most of the wall soldier-builders were in fact landless peasants, exiles, criminals-turned-corvée laborers, and famine refugees from south of the wall.[90] Cao Shu-ji, a leading scholar on China's migration history, found that while many villagers in eastern Hebei claimed to have ancestral roots in "the south," archival records from the 14th century and later show that migrants were mostly from Shandong Province. Shandong is "south" of Hebei, but it is not as far south as Zhejiang in China's southeast, where Yiwu is located.[91]

The frontier was a destination for the destitute. Migrants moved to the frontier not necessarily to defend it, but to survive via farming, gathering, petty trade, and manual labor (see Chapters 6 to 8). And traders, refugees, and exiles were highly mobile. During the Ming-Qing transition period in the mid-17th century, the northeast-based Manchus fought and marched across the Shanhai Pass (Mountain Sea Pass), the "First Pass Under Heaven" near the eastern end of the Ming-era wall and took Beijing. Chengziyu Village in eastern Hebei sat at the center of the inter-dynastic warfare. With its tumultuous geopolitical histories, it is hard to imagine that borderland settlements like Chengziyu remained stable nor would family lines be traceable,[92] especially when considering the fact that most penurious peasants and laborers were illiterate and unable to keep written lineage records. Even when written lineage records were available, the records vary in their definitions of blood ties, and they were often compiled by elite families citing honorable ancestral origins to claim social status and/or property control.[93]

But such quibbles over credibility should not distract us from the poetry of lineage building or the role that local legends play in forging connections between personal and national histories. The legendary quality of the claims and the reverence with which Lao Zhang held his pedigree are meaningful in their own right. Although Lao Zhang was among the most eloquent, he was not the sole representative, in augmenting peasants' links with the legendary Great Wall builder-soldiers. In the summer of 2017, I visited another peasant Great Wall guardian, Xiao Liang (meaning "Young Liang"),[94] in a different stretch of wall ruins in eastern Hebei, called Yumuling. Born in 1987, Xiao Liang was hailed as being among the youngest Great Wall guardians. He was not nearly as articulate as Lao Zhang. But like Lao Zhang, Xiao Liang was a member of the prestigious Great Wall Society and was equally passionate about protecting the Great Wall. When I met him in 2017, Xiao Liang cited the same motivation for his voluntary patrol of the wall ruins for the past 12 years: he is an heir to the Great Wall builder-soldiers. He felt obligated to protect what his ancestors had built.

Anthropologists and historians have pointed out the importance of place-based affinity in Chinese lineage building.[95] It is the kinship-territorial nexus, rather than a narrowly defined blood connection that generates varied practices of lineage building. Moreover, lineage is not a fixed structure, but a process of devising, revising, and historicizing connections with people and places. Lao Zhang and Xiao Liang's connection with wall builder-soldiers, therefore, can be seen as an act of "lineaging," mediated by the wall ruins. Their ancestors were among those who built and guarded the Great Wall, and as the descendants, Lao Zhang and Xiao Liang carry on the honorable duty. Hereditary professions and occupations were a part of the imperial system, a practice that continued into socialist China. But the peasant Great Wall guardians today are tasked with a revised job description. Their ancestors from five centuries ago were heroic protectors of the frontier territory against invading enemies, whereas now they are protecting the wall ruins from fellow citizens' abuse.

Taking on the job of Great Wall guardian is not about direct material gain. Starting out as volunteers, Lao Zhang and Xiao Liang were paid about 200 yuan (about US$30) a month by the local branch of Administration of Cultural Heritage when the Great Wall guardian program first started. They both cited the extremely low pay as the reason that compelled them to find other income sources. Lao Zhang ran his Great Wall Protection Station as a country B&B, while Xiao Liang moved back and forth between his village home and his work on construction sites in the city of Tianjin.[96] However, they both also took pride in this work and reveled in their fame as a peasant guardian of the national treasure. Xiao Liang, being unusually young for a Great Wall guardian, has also attracted quite a bit of media attention like Lao Zhang. With a grandfather who had served in the Red Army as a foot soldier, Xiao Liang appeared particularly dignified in his army-green guardian uniform with the official badge pinned to his chest. He suggested that I take a picture of him in his uniform and the matching cap, saluting the camera in military fashion. He turned out to be a great selfie photographer himself, posting many of his own images in front of the watch tower on his WeChat page, accompanied by succinct, zealous captions about his unwavering devotion to the Wall. On our hike, Xiao Liang asked me to teach him some English expressions so that he could better communicate with foreign visitors at the Yumuling wall. We started with basic greetings, but soon after that he wanted to move to longer and more specific sentences about the history of the Yumuling wall. It seemed to me that it was the wall in his village, rather than the distant Great Wall in Beijing, that had anchored his connection to the national monument.

In fact, in my conversation with Xiao Liang during the visit, he often omitted the word, "builders" and repeatedly affirmed that he was a "heir of the Yumuling great wall." The local wall makes the national Great Wall relatable. The Yumuling wall is therefore both a wild wall and a part of the Great Wall. Such relationship between the local wall and the national Wall is built through presumed lineage affiliations and the physical presence of the ruin, which carries national significance under Great Wall Revivalism. The lineage and the nation as identity referents were meaningful in different ways for Xiao Liang. He took pride in his position as an officially appointed peasant guardian under a national program, a role that he felt had elevated him above his fellow peasants. But it was the Yumuling wall in the village that has mediated such associations and brought him the attention of the state. When we were back in his village home, Xiao Liang showed me pictures of him and his six-year-old daughter hiking together as they patrolled the Yumuling wall, explaining his intention to pass on the duty of protecting the wall to her.

Regardless of the veracity of the legend, an ancestral link with local wall ruins is how peasant guardians of the Great Wall connect their local and personal histories to the nation's history. This popular discourse has inspired local government leaders in both Hebei and Zhejiang Provinces. The coastal region of Zhejiang, from where some of the wall-builders were said to have originated, is one of the wealthiest areas in China in the post-reform era. The mountainous eastern Hebei, where the wall builders' descendants now live, is among the poorest. Great Wall Revivalism has given local governments in both Zhejiang and Hebei a stage on which to forge a mutually beneficial connection with the national monument.

Zhejiang is known for its successful rural industrialization in the first phase of China's market reforms. Its GDP consistently ranks among the top three of all provinces in China. In the 1980s, Yiwu stood out in Zhejiang for its manufacturing of consumer goods. By the mid-1990s, Yiwu had grown to host China's largest wholesale center for small merchandise such as toys, household items, and fashion accessories. But coastal Yiwu's newly established wealth has been tainted by its reputation as the home to pirates in imperial times and low-end manufacturers and petty traders in the contemporary market economy. Yiwu's nouveau riche were in need of culture—not just any culture, but a culture that aligns with the nation's political trends today in order to gain media attention and to improve its public image. In addition, as an early industrializer that struggled to upgrade since the global financial crisis hit in the late 1990s, Yiwu government leaders have been looking for new development projects. In the age of Great Wall Revivalism, the ancestral linkage with northern villagers near the Great Wall could rebrand Yiwu and elevate it onto the more respectable cultural-political map of the nation.

The Yiwu City Gazetteer Office, a municipal government unit in charge of writing the official history of Yiwu, was quick to act.[97] The Gazetteer editors took pilot trips to sites in Hebei and neighboring northern provinces where Yiwu Troops had been posted centuries ago. They collected tombstone epitaphs and interviewed elderly villagers who remembered what their grandfathers had told them about their ancestral origins. Then the Yiwu government invited journalists, photographers, writers, and officials on a tour to visit these sites in Hebei. Following this, they invited several descendants of the Yiwu Troops from Hebei to their ancestral hall in Yiwu.

To reciprocate Yiwu leaders' efforts, the governor of Funing County in Hebei, which was a hub for Yiwu descendants, led a delegation to Yiwu City, citing the importance of strengthening the blood connection between the two places. The county governor's visit also initiated negotiations to establish a Yiwu merchandise trade center in the Funing county seat.

The highly publicized Great Wall-mediated reconnections between Yiwu and Funing subsequently piqued the interests of Qinhuangdao municipal government, which ranks one level higher than Funing County. Not to be surpassed by the county leader under him, the Qinhuangdao municipal leader launched a publicity campaign, starting with a blanket survey of all villages within the entire municipality—not just Funing County—to take stock of ancestral connections between Qinhuangdao residents and those of Yiwu. After the survey, a 600-strong Qinhuangdao delegation booked all the cars of a special train and travelled to Yiwu together. The Qinhuangdao delegation collaborated with the Yiwu government to orchestrate a publicity campaign to bring attention to this momentous reunion, which culminated in a "Qinhuangdao-Yiwu Week" in Yiwu city. To commemorate the historic event, the Qinhuangdao delegation gifted the Yiwu Museum stone arrow heads and pottery found on and around the wall ruins in eastern Hebei. The cultural exchange brough both tangible and intangible results: a 70,000 sq. meter-large Qinhuangdao-Yiwu Small Merchandise Trade Center, bigger than the one in Funing, was built in the newly established Qinghuangdao Development Zone. The Trade Center was subsequently listed as a Hebei provincial-level Key Investment Project, and Yiwu Troop descendants were to be given special discounted rates if they leased a shop space in the center. Meanwhile, Yiwu, the coastal home of pirates and petty merchants was rebranded as the origin of the Great Wall's builder-defenders.

Mediated by legendary wall builders and initiated by entrepreneurial local leaders, the two places located 1,500 kilometers and five centuries apart, have thus built a lineage that references the Great Wall. Extending from the presumed bloodline and place of origin, this lineage triangulates the connection among Hebei's local walls, Zhejiang's claims of being the ancestral home of wall builder-defenders, and the nation's Great Wall. Such blood and place connection with the Great Wall also contributes to naturalizing the association of the Great Wall with the biological origin of the Chinese people. Just like the Yellow River is revered as China's Mother River, the Great Wall is epitomized as China's Father Wall. The earnest wild wall guardian Xiao Liang called himself an "heir of the Great Wall." Zhang Baotian, the devoted wall rephotographer and author of the photo album *Remembrance of the Great Wall* from the previous section, purposefully addresses the Great Wall in masculine terms ("he" instead of "she") in his texts in order to express his "respect for the Great Wall as for my own father."[98]

But all these connections between blood and place and the associations among the personal, the local and the national are built within a Han Chinese-centered socio-cultural discourse. The three non-state participants in Great Wall Revivalism whom I have presented so far—the popular historian-cum-photographers, the peasant operators of wild wall mass tourism, and the peasant guardians of the wall ruins on the mountain ridges—are all Han Chinese with a south-of-the-Wall identity. The last but not least non-state participants in Great Wall Revivalism live on the opposite side of the Great Wall, in today's Inner Mongolia Autonomous Region (IMAR). To reconcile the historical rivalries between the two sides of the Wall with the current project of forging national unity across the Wall can be a thorny task for IMAR's local governments. In the next section I look at how IMAR's local officials steered the Great Wall monumentalization project on the ground, with a focus on the local initiative called "Camelback Heritage Patrols."

IV.2 Mongolian Camelback Heritage Patrols

For Han Chinese, who make up a 91% majority, the Great Wall could be the symbol of a unified nation under the unifying "Chinese nationality" (*zhonghua minzu*) that encompasses all of the fifty-six officially classified ethnic nationalities in China today. But how do Mongols, who were the Han Chineses' territorial rivals not too long ago, but have since been unified under sino-centric nationalism, see the divisive Wall? For the purpose of this chapter, a more focused question would be, how do IMAR's local officials navigate this political and discursive minefield that could disrupt the otherwise "harmonious ethnic relationship" while carrying out the job of monumentalizing the Great Wall? This political dilemma calls for extraordinary care for another reason: today, IMAR hosts the largest inventory of wall ruins among the 15 walled provinces and autonomous regions in China. Thanks to the long history of the Han Chinese-Mongol rivalries and the territorial conflicts among various northern powers of various ethnoterritorial identities, as reviewed in the first section of this chapter, more than 7,500 km of the wall ruins, about one-third of the national total, are located in IMAR. These ruins have been said to have "accumulated over the course of eleven historical periods from the Warring States (475 to 221 BCE) to the Ming (1368 to 1644 CE)."[99] The large quantity of remnants presents a cultural resource that could potentially build local officials' career and hopefully local economies, if leveraged tactfully with imagination and without triggering disharmonious ethnic relationships.

One common strategy of monumentalization is selective remembering. In the official narratives about the Great Wall, certain segments and time periods of the wall, such as the aforementioned segments of the Ming Wall that served as the front-line during the Second Sino-Japanese War, have received more mentions, and in much greater detail, than others. In IMAR, the walls that divided the territories of non-Han Chinese nomadic powers were talked about more frequently than the walls that divided the territories between Han Chinese and Mongols (and their ancestors with other names). One prominent example of the former is the Jin's border trenches. During the 10th and 13th centuries, two enthusiastic wall builders on the steppe, the Khitans of the Liao Dynasty and the Jurchens of the Jin Dynasty built long walls and trenches against another non-Han power, the Mongols. Today, some of the Jin trenches in central and eastern IMAR are in relatively good condition for that time period, and much of IMAR's heritage conservation efforts have been built around them. For local officials, it seemed safer to focus on military infrastructure built by two warring non-Han Chinese peoples and, thus, left the Han Chinese out of it.

Selective remembering begets selective forgetting. Wall ruins in western IMAR from the early imperial period, as mentioned earlier, were built by ambitious Qin-Han emperors who launched devastating wars against the Xiongnu, who are perceived as being closely related to the Mongols. In the official narrative, this part of the history is drenched in language of cultural assimilation and ethnic integration, as elaborated by Tong, Guoqing, the Director and Party Secretary of IMAR's Bureau of Cultural Affairs. In a public speech, Director Tong spelled out the rationale behind protecting the Great Wall in IMAR. First, the Great Wall represents cross-cultural exchange and the integration of many peoples and cultures in China today. Second, the formidable ancient structures represent the wisdom and perseverance of a shared ancestry among all the peoples of China who built them. Third, the Great Wall was the site where the brave peoples in China fought their common enemy—the Japanese invaders during the Sino Japanese War. And lastly, the Wall in IMAR is a valuable local resource for tourism development.[100]

Director Tong's policy directive, consistent with the party line with a touch of his own rhetorical creativity, was the easy part of the job. A greater challenge would come from implementation. How do local officials set out to conserve the wall ruins without provoking "ethnicity sentiments" (*minzu qingxu*) of Mongols? Treading this tightrope, they tried to bypass historical entanglements and focus on the physical and technical-managerial ends of the task. Whatever physical remnants are left in IMAR are neutralized as "shared cultural heritage of all peoples in today's IMAR" and the remnants are to be indiscriminately protected and utilized as cultural resources for heritage tourism development and patriotic education.

The "Camelback Heritage Patrol" program is one such local inventions inaugurated in 2011. It is called "Camelback Heritage Patrol" in places such as Alxa League in western IMAR, where there are more camels, and "Horseback Heritage Patrol" in places such as Xilingol League in central IMAR, where camels have been hard to come by since pastoral decollectivization (see Chapter 2). Sure enough, IMAR's first heritage patrol program was established in Xilingol League, where the bulk of the aforementioned Jin-era border trench remnants are located.[101]

The Horse/Camelback Heritage Patrol program is an IMAR adaptation of the Peasant Guardian of the Great Wall program that was inaugurated in Hebei Province, where Lao Zhang and Xiao Liang live (see the previous section), and set the precedent for creating a national model. But IMAR differs from other walled provinces in that, as the second-largest provincial-level jurisdiction in China, IMAR has much lower population density. Few people live near the ruins across IMAR's immense territory. Severe desertification in recent decades and ecological relocation, as presented in the Introduction and Chapters 1 and 2, have driven local residents even further away from the ruin sites located mostly in the remote and sandy rural areas. The Camelback/Horseback Heritage Patrol program was expected to resolve the challenge of safeguarding distant and scattered ruins across the immense terrain and in often inaccessible sites. Initial success came not long after the program had launched. In the snowy winter of 2013, the patrols of Xilingol League made it onto national news when they caught a group of tomb raiders in action and retrieved over 100 precious cultural artifacts, including gold, bronze, silver, and glass wares, silk textiles, and leather goods. The tomb turned out to be a part of a burial site that had hosted multiple tombs. Archaeologists conducted rescue excavation of three tombs that year and two more the following year. They suggested that the tombs had belonged to a Northern Wei (386 to 543 CE) aristocratic clan of the 4–5th century CE. The Northern Wei was established by Xianbei. Xianbei was one of the largest confederations of tribes residing in the steppes and mountains of today's Mongolia, IMAR, and northeastern China since the East Han Period (25 to 220 CE). It was a multilingual, multiethnic, and multi-livelihood confederation of tribes that included pre- and proto-Mongol and Turkic speakers. Among all Xianbei tribes, the most successful, Tuoba, founded the Northern Wei Empire (386 to 534 CE).[102] It was the first time that tombs of Northern Wei aristocrats had been identified and excavated in IMAR. The spectacular, high-value cultural artifacts found in the tombs, such as the intricate gold wares, make for captivating museum displays, and the successful retrieval of the treasures made for a sensational media story. The discovery was subsequently selected as one of China's "Ten Major Archaeological Discoveries" of 2014, for it manifests the "long history of thriving economic and cultural exchanges between the east and the west along the Silk Road."[103] According to the official statement, the tombs, Han or non-Han, are heritage shared by all "Chinese people."

In 2017, I asked a scholar in Beijing about this historic discovery. The scholar confirmed its archaeological significance. He also added that the fact that the burial grounds belonged to non-Han Chinese elites might have made it easier for the local government to publicize the case of catching the looters to earn political credit, because it circumvented the potentially embarrassing situation in which a Mongol heritage patrol contributes to the protection of Han Chinese-associated heritage.[104] I was not able to verify the scholar's comment, as several other scholars I talked to preferred not to comment on it. There are other intriguing dynamics that also beg further inquiry: while members of the Peasant Guardians of the Great Wall in Hebei Province, such as Lao Zhang and Xiao Liang, proudly wore the military green uniforms that brandished the characters "Great Wall" on the back and chest, the official name of Xilingol's heritage patrol program is "Horseback Cultural Heritage (Great Wall) Patrol," with the term "Great Wall" only in parentheses. In the press release of the heritage patrols' triumphant rescue of the national treasures, the words "Great Wall" were omitted. To build universal heritage over competing histories, it seemed inevitable that the nation's Great Wall needed to accommodate local sensibilities—at least up to a certain point. Since 2013, as China's ethnicity politics continued to unravel, and ethnicity plurality has been significantly overshadowed by the promotion of a unitary Chinese nationality that focuses on integration. Great Wall heritage conservation in IMAR followed the shifting national trend. By 2023, when the celebrated archaeological discovery of Northern Wei aristocrats' tombs in 2013 found its way back to the national headline again under a renewed campaign of Great Wall conservation, the words "Great Wall" were spelled out loud and clear in the subject line.[105] Over the decade between 2013 and 2023, the need for subtlety seems to have dissipated.

As news-worthy as the Camelback Heritage Patrols might be, the daunting task of protecting IMAR's ancient ruins is beyond what the few patrols—160 members on the most-publicized Xilingol crew on horseback, and a few dozen on camelback in Alxa—could possibly handle. The terrain is too expansive and jagged, and the icy, snowy, and stormy winter, which is when tomb raiders are most active, is too long for the few brave patrols to keep an eye on the heritage structures. A horseback patrol in Xilingol reported that to make a day trip to the ruin site under his charge 70 km from home, he needed to truck his horse to the site, prepare the horse, then ride on horseback for at least another 30 km. And this is possible only when weather and road conditions permit and if his own beat-up, light-weight truck cooperates.[106] Compared to Lao Zhang and Xiao Liang's daily hikes to the wall ruins in eastern Hebei, as demanding as they are, heritage patrolling in IMAR is a much more strenuous undertaking that cannot be performed frequently nor regularly.

In the meantime, ruins continue to degenerate. Environmental deterioration accelerates the ruins' decay. Many ancient ruins in IMAR are located in areas that suffer soil erosion, mud slides, and dust storms that often bury or corrode the ruins. A case in point is my trip in 2013 to visit a well-known archeological site in western IMAR, where the famous wooden slips used by border troops of the Han Dynasty were found. The site of this important archaeological find is in an area where long stretches of Han-era border fortifications like beacon towers are located. After a bumpy four-hour ride through the sand dunes and gravel gobi on a roasting afternoon in July, my host, a local official of the bureau of cultural affairs and keen conservationist, was unable to find the site. The official suspected that the site might have been buried by the mobile sand dunes and that the tall posts that had been erected to mark the site had been blown away by the dust storms earlier that spring. At another heritage site of the ancient walled city, Heicheng, in Ejina, now a popular tourist attraction (see Chapter 2), the heritage site manager would haul away hundreds of truckloads of sand that accumulate and bury half of the walled city in order to prepare for the tourist season that commences in the fall.

Ruins of structures and settlements indicate environmental and social-political changes. Settlements are abandoned because of warfare, climate change, river course shifts, or intensive land use that lead to oases drying out and lakes turning into sandy fields. Both nature and culture cause heritage deterioration, but growth projects that have been in place since the mid-late 20th century have been particularly destructive in IMAR. Road construction and mining, among other factors that have contributed to environmental deterioration, have wrecked historical remnants dated from the pre- and early imperial to the late imperial periods.[107] It was estimated that over 20% of IMAR's Ming walls had disappeared by the late-2000s.[108]

Of all human-inflicted damages to the ruins, tomb robbery has been the most severe. The discovery of the Northern Wei tombs in Xilingol in 2013, as presented earlier, started with tomb robbery and was followed by hurried rescue archaeology. Five years later, in 2018, news broke out again about two robbers who were arrested in a county called Guyang under Baotou Municipality in central-western IMAR for illegal possession of ancient artifacts. According to the report published by the *Procuration Daily*, the two men heard that Guyang locals would often find fragments of ancient artifacts around the beacon tower ruins that date back to the Qin Era (221 to 206 BCE) and decided to try their luck. They purchased a metal detector (standard equipment for tomb robbing) online, studied archival materials to locate the sites, and dug around several beacon tower ruins and found a load of ancient coins and spearheads. As they dug, they also irreversibly damaged the tower structures.[109]

Tomb robbing is an old profession. IM's tomb robbers have plenty of company in world histories. Tomb robbery in contemporary China has escalated since the 1980s, and unreported robberies and unaccounted for artifacts were said to greatly outnumber those that have been retrieved.[110] Tomb robbery does not just concern policy makers, scholars, and conservationists. Its adventurous vein and the potential for overnight wealth has also inspired TV thrillers and popular literature.[111]

One common regret of the archaeologists I talked to was that they often arrived too late to the ancient burial site. By the time they arrive on the scene, the robbers have already plundered the most valuable artifacts. Archaeologists could only "pick up the crumbs" left by the looters. More importantly, the remaining artifacts from the looted and disturbed sites lose their provenance and much of their research value because they have been decontextualized.[112] Archaeologists also work against local villagers' deep suspicions. A senior archaeologist told me that in some rural areas, local villagers believe that the treasures buried under their crop fields do not belong to the state nor the archaeologists who work for the state. Rather, the treasures are gifts from the villagers' ancestors, especially those valuable objects made of gold, silver, or jade. Entitled villagers would steal the archaeological finds and violent conflicts would erupt. The tension around the excavation site could be so acute that local police would be positioned around the sites to protect the archaeologists and the artifacts.[113]

As ancient ruins disappear, new ones emerge. A 2007 survey conducted by IMAR's Center for Great Wall Research of over 10,000 local residents concluded that over 90% of IMAR's residents did not know that IMAR hosts Great Wall heritage. The journalist, who referenced the survey, thereby suggested that the Great Wall in IMAR was destroyed mainly due to ignorance.[114] I was struck by the survey result: how could the 7,500 km-long wall structures in IMAR be invisible to the locals? In 2013, at the first chance I had, I asked a Mongol college student if she knew about IMAR's Great Wall. She told me there is no Great Wall in IMAR. I showed her the photo of the ruins of a Han-era beacon tower made with rammed earth and clay found in western

IMAR—one of the most celebrated wall remnants by historians and archaeologists. But she was not convinced: "that is not the Great Wall. It looks nothing like the Great Wall that I have seen on TV. What's there to see in this big mound of mud?"[115] Her question was answered by some local governments that had leveled the unimpressive mud walls and mounds and replaced them with a replica of the most recognizable and more majestic Badaling section of the Ming Wall built with bricks and masonry, as an effort to develop heritage tourism.[116] Such "fake Great Walls" have received criticism from China's conservationists and UNESCO's WHC alike.[117] The SACH subsequently issued bans on arbitrary and destructive restoration of the wall ruins. Since then, in well-located sites that have the potential to develop heritage tourism, a popular local approach entailed building grand and elaborate photo-worthy entrance gates to the heritage park. Inside the park, the untouchable and often visually unimpressive remnants were surrounded by eye-catching statues, sculptures, enlarged replicas of historical structures, and heritage objects for social media posting.[118]

As demonstrated above, monumentalization requires societal participation. The state project of monumentalizing the Great Wall, an elusive concept with entangled histories and indefinite contents, is an open-ended process that shapes and is shaped by a diverse array of participants under Great Wall Revivalism in the 21st century. Urban-based popular historian-cum-photographers visualize the concept and nationalize the wallscapes through image production and reproduction. Entrepreneurial peasants living by the wild great walls at the fringe of metropolitan Beijing run mass tourism and play an important role in patriotic education campaigns in post-Revolution China. The poorly compensated peasant-turned guardians of the wall ruins in mountain villages find local and personal connections with the national Great Wall and garner media attention as they patrol the wild great walls near their village homes. The Mongolian Camel/Horseback Heritage Patrols, on the north side of the Great Wall, show IMAR government's inventive attempts to reconciliate the contradiction between a historically divisive border fortification and the contemporary drive towards reinforcing the meaning of the Great Wall as a symbol of national unity. At the confluence of Great Wall Revivalism, various non-state actors participate with diverse motivations and practices—a process not unlike antidesertification mobilization around the miracle shrub of suosuo presented in Chapter 1.

Popular participation in Great Wall Revivalism has also brought divergent results. In their patriotic act, the photographers devote much of their artistic energy towards creating iconic images and connecting with legendary image-makers beyond a nationalistic program. Peasant entrepreneurs of wild wall tourism help make patriotic education fun. But fierce business competition also breeds escalating tensions among villagers, local governments, and private investors, while expanding wall tourism often leads to heritage dilapidation. Peasant guardians of the Great Wall, while pledging to a national cause, identify themselves mostly through a personalized and localized linkage with the local walls near and dear to them. The Mongolian heritage patrols, some of whom are now equipped with drones to monitor the ruin sites,[119] seemed to have reached a plateau by the early 2020s. Charged with the daunting mission of safeguarding the widespread ruins across an immense terrain, it has been hard to beat the good news of the aforementioned heritage patrol who successfully protected ancient tombs of the Northern Wei aristocrats in 2013. By 2023, the very story from a decade ago was still being highlighted the media coverage on IMAR government's achievements in Great Wall heritage protection.[120]

Nationwide, Great Wall Revivalism draws in fresh cohorts of participants. Tencent, China's technology giant and the formidable competitor of Alibaba that spearheaded the campaign for planting virtual and real suosuo shrubs in the desert (see Chapter 1), established a cultural heritage fund to restore two sections of the Great Wall near Beijing and to build a digital platform devoted to heritage education and protection, including offering a virtual reality game for users to experience the Great Wall on their computer screens in a season of their choice.[121] Meanwhile, in 2017, the WHC expressed concerns about "inappropriate tourism facilities that threaten the authenticity of the Great Wall," and the construction of a high-speed railway near Beijing that serves as a "prime example of potentially damaging new construction projects that threaten the wall structure and increase visitor numbers without implementing appropriate measures to mitigate the impacts of mass tourism."[122] The problem was subsequently resolved in 2021, as the WHC was satisfied with the Chinese government's measures to address the problems.[123] More recently, in 2023 and 2024, long after the Regulation on the Protection of the Great Wall was adopted in 2006, more cases about Great Wall ruins being destroyed by mining and construction were reported,[124] and more stringent policy guidelines on cultural heritage protection were issued.[125] Monumentalizing and popularizing the Wall continue to enable and derail one another. Together, The Great Wall and the many wild walls attached to and generated from the Wall tell a story too wild to be tamed by a tidy plot or a single monument.

Notes

1. Due to the fact that place selects me in my fieldwork, as I will elaborate in the concluding chapter, my interviews for this chapter expanded from Inner Mongolia to Beijing metropolitan region and Hebei Province of northern China, not the strictly defined northwest.
2. Roberts, Claire and Geremie R. Barmé eds. 2006. *The Great Wall of China*, p. 291. Sydney: The Powerhuose Museum Publishing.
3. Roberts, Claire and Geremie R. Barmé eds. 2006. Ibid. p. 10.
4. It is difficult to determine the level of "wildness" of a wall ruin. Part of the ambiguity comes from the challenge of governing the ungovernable, which is elaborated in the first section of this chapter. In the official Great Wall conservation programs, heritage sites are organized hierarchically, from the highest, national level down to provincial, municipal, and county levels. The ranking reflects the relative value of the heritage site or object, it also obligates the corresponding local governments to protect it. But only a handful of the most iconic sections of the Great Wall are well-groomed and closely watched by designated agencies under the national or provincial governments. Many of the Great Wall ruins are located across China's expansive north and northwest regions

with vastly diverse physical conditions and levels of accessibility. Such fragmentation makes it exceedingly challenging for heritage conservation bureaucracies to rank, classify, and manage the Wall sites. In addition, these sites at different jurisdictional ranks are placed under local governments with vastly different financial and organizational capacities. Not all officially listed Great Wall heritage sites enjoy budgetary priority at the local level when it comes to protection and conservation expenses, especially in the case of sites that show little potential for tourism development. As a result, local governments sometimes avoid listing Wall ruins in their jurisdiction in order to avoid the responsibility of protecting the sites. My visits to local ruin sites in Shanxi, Gansu, Hebei, Ningxia, and IMAR between 2010 and 2017 have led me to wonder which list is longer: the official list of the Great Wall heritage sites compiled by the national heritage agency, or that of the ruins that are omitted by local officials. To streamline the story of this chapter, I chose to define the wild great walls by their relationship with grassroots actors, instead of their official status in the national or provincial heritage protection programs.

5. Smith, Laurajane. 2006. *Uses of Heritage*. New York: Routledge. For a general critique of heritage, see Lowenthal, David. 1985. *The Past is a Foreign Country*. Cambridge: Cambridge University Press.
6. Komar, Vitaly and Alexander Melamid. 1994. "We remember, or so it seems." In Ashton, Dore ed. *Monumental Propaganda*, pp. 43–55. New York: Independent Curator Incorporated. Also reprinted in Komar, Vitaly and Alexander Melamid. 1996. "We remember, or so it seems." *ANY*: *Architecture New York* 15: 22–26.
7. Young, James. 2003. "Memory/monument." In Nelson, Robert and Richard Shiff eds. *Critical Terms for Art History*, 2nd edition, pp. 234–247. Chicago: The University of Chicago Press.
8. UNESCO World Heritage Website. "The Great Wall." *UNESCO World Heritage Website.* http://whc.unesco.org/en/list/438. Accessed January 5, 2024.
9. Hsing, I-itien. 2022. *Google diqiuyuqinhan changcheng [Google Earth and the Great Wall of the Qin and Han Dynasties].* Taipei: Sanmin Publisher.
10. Tackett, Nicolas. 2017. *The Origin of the Chinese Nation: Song China and the Forging of an East Asian World Order*. Cambridge: Cambridge University Press. 2022. Hsing, I-tien. Ibid. p. 214. For a detailed discussion of the border walls of the Song Period, see Tackett, Nicolas. 2008. "The Great Wall and conceptualizations of the border under the northern Song." *Journal of Song-Yuan Studies* 38: 99–138.
11. See Li, Xiaocong and Chen Jun. 2016. *Zhongguochangchengzhi tuzhi [Chronicles of the Great Wall of China: The Wall in Maps and Pictures].* Nanjing: Jiangsu Fenghuangkexuejishu Press; and Waldron, Arthur. 1990. *The Great Wall of China: From History to Myth*, p. 97. Cambridge: Cambridge University Press.
12. The purpose of the Qing's Willow Palisade between Manchuria and China was mainly for migration control rather than for military purposes.
13. The figure 800 km is the author's estimate based on Li, Xiaocong's (2016) map of the Great Wall. Li, Xiaocong et al. 2016. Ibid. The closest distance between the Han and Ming walls is 10 meters, located in Shandan County of Zhangyi Municipality in the Hexi Corridor of Gansu Province, according to a local scholar I talked to in Gansu in 2013.
14. Combing through Google Earth images, Hsing, I-tien (2022. Ibid. pp. 195–211, pp. 218–224) found ruin traces in linear formations that are about 50 km north of what is usually considered the northernmost wall built during the Han Dynasty. Hsing also suggested that this newly found wall makes three, instead of the commonly assumed two,

Han walls. Hsing also emphasized that this finding needs to be verified by archaeological excavations. The territorial implications of the shifting Han walls are significant. Before the Han, the Qin emperor built the wall along the northern side of the Yin mountains (in today's Central IM), a long-held natural and cognitive barrier between the agrarian and pastoral worlds, to fend off the steppe powers. But at the onset of the Han Period, the first Han reign was weak and had to retreat and moved the wall to the south side of the Yin. Later during the Han, under the ambitious Emperor Wu ("Emperor Marshal"), the Han's military might prevailed over the steppe forces, and the location of the wall was pushed north not once but likely twice, reaching a new frontline more than 100 km north of the first Han wall. The two Han emperors, in other words, built three walls: the first one signified a southward retreat from the earlier frontline of the Qin wall; the later two marked Emporer Wu's retaking of the northern steppe and expansion further beyond the Qin and early Han walls. The north-advancing walls, argued Hsing, tell much about the territorial aggression of the Han Emperor Wu. The territorial aggression was legitimized by the imperial world order of "all under heaven is King's land" (*putianzhixia mofeiwangtu*) and "all under heaven as one family" (*tianxiayijia*), with the Han Chinese emperor as the patriarch.

15. Hsing, I-tien. 2022. Ibid.
16. Nicolas Tackett (2008. Ibid.) suggested that improving tax revenue in the border region was another important reason for constructing border fortifications during the Song period.
17. Hsing, I-tien. 2011. *Tianxiayijia: Huangdiguanliaoyushehui [All under Heaven as One Family: Emperors, Bureaucracy, and Society]*, pp. 84–135. Beijing: Zhonghua Publisher.
18. Tackett, Nicolas. 2008. Ibid. p. 121.
19. However, Hsing, I-tien pointed out that, thanks to aridity and soil salinization in western IMAR and the technique of mixing plant twigs with earth, fortification structures made with rammed earth during the early imperial periods are much more durable than might have been expected. Hsing has visited many of the rammed earth beacon tower ruins and found them "hard like rocks." Personal conversation in Taipei, 2019.
20. It took approximately 100 men to construct the same length of wall using stones that a single man could build using the rammed earth method. See Rojas, Carlos. 2010. *The Great Wall: A Cultural History*, p. 105. Cambridge, MA: Harvard University Press.
21. The State Administration of Cultural Heritage. 2016. "*Changchengziyuandiaocha yurending [Survey and Classification of Great Wall Resources]*." The Great Wall Heritage of China, November 9. http://www.greatwallheritage.cn/CCMCMS/html/1/54/index.html. Accessed January 5, 2024.
22. Jing, Ai. 2006. "Guanyuchangchengdiaochade guifanhua biaozhunhuawenti [Regularization and standardization issues in Great Wall survey]." October 17. posted on Changchengxiaozhan Website. http://www.thegreatwall.com.cn/public/gwwx.php?action=view&id=702&mode=view. Accessed January 5, 2024.
23. Jing, Ai. 2006. *Zhongguo changchengshi [A History of the Great Wall of China]*. Shanghai: People's Press.
24. Interview in Beijing, 2017.
25. Carlos Rojas (2010) cautioned against using this figure and suggested that trying to get close to the walls' actual length is an attempt to "use quantitative measures to address a problem that is inherently conceptual." Rojas, Carols. 2010. Ibid. pp. 17–18.
26. Interview with a conservationist in Beijing, 2017.

27. Mullaney, Thomas. 2010. *Coming to Terms with the Nation: Ethnic Classification in Modern China*, p. 135. Oakland, CA: University of California Press.
28. For an introduction on archaeological findings of the Great Wall built during the pre- and early imperial eras, see Xu, Pingfang. 2006. "Archaeology of the Walls." In Roberts, Claire et al. Ibid. pp. 52–56. The archaeological studies of the Ming Wall pick up in the 2000s. Still, it was not until the end of 2023 when the first archaeological report on the Ming Wall in Beijing metropolitan region, entitled "Beijing changchengkaogu" (*Beijing Great Wall Archaeology*, Vol. 1, Beijing: Science Publisher), was published by academic archaeologists at the Beijing Institute of Archaeology. Xu, Jing. 2023. "Zhongguokaokuxuejie shoubumingchangchengkaogu fajue zhuantibaogaofabu [China's first archaeological report on the Ming Great Wall was published]." *China News*, December 22. https://www.chinanews.com.cn/cul/2023/12-22/10133476.shtml. Accessed January 6, 2024.
29. Interview July 2017, Beijing.
30. Interview June 2012, Beijing.
31. See the opening chapter of Rojas, Carols. 2010, Ibid., entitled "A Unity of Gaps;" and the subtitle of Waldron, Arthur. 1990. Ibid., "*From History to Myth*."
32. Huaxiazi. 1988. *Ming Changchengkaoshi [Investigation of the Great Wall of Ming Dynasty]*. Beijing: Dangan Press. Huaxiazi is the collective pen name of the three young trekker-authors: Dong, Yaohui, who worked in the Bureau of Electricity of Qinhuangdao City; Wu, Deyu, who worked in the Industrial Technology Glass factory of Qinhuangdao City, and Zhang, Yuanhua, who worked in the Northeastern Optics Equipment factory of Changchun City. Huaxiazi translates to "sons of the Huaxia people." In popular discourse, "Huaxia" is often used interchangeably with Han Chinese. The authors explained that they chose this pen name because "the descendants of the Huaxia people should be the first to travel the entire length of the Great Wall."
33. Top government leaders habitually chair the Great Wall Society. In 1987, Xi Zhongxun, a legendary CCP official and the father of China's current leader Xi Jinping, for example, was the inaugural Honorary Chair of the Great Wall Society. Huang Hua, the former Foreign Minister and Vice Premier, was the Inaugural Chair. See the official website of The Great Wall Society. 2022. https://www.thegreatwall.cn/#/articleDetail?id=3246. June 25. Accessed January 6, 2024.
34. From website of The Great Wall Society. http://www.thegreatwall.cn/xuehui/. Accessed July 3 2017. Link was broken by January 5, 2024.
35. The Great Wall Society. 1994. *Changchengbaikequanshu [Encyclopedia of the Great Wall]*. Changchun: Jilin People's Press.
36. Chen, Haiyan and Yaohui Dong eds. 2016. *Zhongguochangchengzhi [Chronicles of the Great Wall of China]*. Nanjing: Pheonix Science and Technology Publisher.
37. See CCTV website. https://tv.cctv.com/2015/10/16/VIDA1444978093386899.shtml. Accessed January 7, 2023.
38. See Stewart, Susan. 1992. *On Longing: Narratives of the Miniature, the Gigantic, the Souvenir, the Collection*, p. 90. Durham, NC: Duke University Press. The quote comes from this context:

> The very fact that you can climb inside and to the top of the Eiffel Tower, the Statue of Liberty, or the statue of William Penn on the tower of Philadelphia's City Hall, simultaneously speaks to an abstract transcendence above and beyond the viewer and the possibility that the viewer can unveil the giant, can find the machinery hidden in the god and approach a transcendent view of the city himself or herself.

39. Luo, Zhewen. 1988. "Investigation of the Great Wall of Ming Dynasty." "Preface" to Huanxiazi. Ibid.
40. Rojas, Carols. 2010. Ibid. p. 14.
41. Susan Sontag (1973) put it well: "photographs actively promote nostalgia ... all photographs testify to time's relentless melt." Sontag, Susan. 1973. *On Photography*, p. 15. NY: Picador.
42. The relationship between national identity and landscape has been elaborated in, for example, Daniels, Stephen. 1993. *Fields of Vision: Landscape Imagery and National Identity in England and the United States.* Cambridge: Polity; and Helsinger, Elizabeth. 1996. *Rural Scenes and the Representation of Britain, 1815–1850.* Princeton, NJ: Princeton University Press.
43. McCalman, Iain and Paul Pickering. 2010. "From realism to affective turn: An agenda." In *Historical Reenactment: From Realism to the Affective Turn*, McCalman, Iain and Paul Pickering eds., pp. 1–17. NY: Palgrave MacMillan.
44. Barthes, Roland. 2000. *Camera Lucida: Reflections on Photography*, trans. Richard Howard. pp. 76–77. London: Random House.
45. Jones, Andrew. 2010. "Portable monuments: Architectural photography and the 'forms' of empire in modern China." *Positions* 18 (3): 599–631.
46. Zhang, Baotian. 2012. *Zhuixunyuanqude changcheng [Remembrance of the Great Wall].* Hangzhou: Zhejiang Science and Technology Publishing. The title of his album in Chinese is slightly different from its official English title. A literal word-for-word translation is "Pursuit of the Distant and Disappearing Great Wall." Zhang is among the most active Great Wall historian-photographers, and a board member of the Great Wall Society.
47. Zhang, Baotian. 2012. Ibid. p. 410.
48. Like Xiao Fang, Sha Fei also died young, but from a known cause. Sha Fei was executed in 1950, at the age 38, after the Second Sino-Japanese War was over, for killing his Japanese doctor when he was under treatment for tuberculosis in a hospital in Shijiazhuang of Hebei Province, where many of the medical staff were Japanese who stayed in China after the war. It was speculated that the tragedy was caused by Sha Fei's post-traumatic distress from the war. But to make peace with the greatly unnerved Japanese medical staff whom the newly established communist regime badly needed, the court martial of People's Liberation Army (PLA), of which Sha Fei was a member, decided to execute Sha Fei. See Sha Fei's daughter's memoire: Wang, Yan. 2005. *Tiesejianzheng: wodefuqin shafei [Witness of Iron Color: My Father Sha Fei].* Beijing: Social Science Academic Press. The book has an English title, *My Father H. Szeto.*
49. See an analysis of Sha Fei's works in Brown, Shana. 2012. "Sha Fei, the Jin-Cha-ji Pictorial, and the documentary style of Chinese wartime photojournalism]." In Henriot, Christian and Wen-hsin Yeh eds., *History in Image: Pictures and Public Space in Modern China.* China Research Monograph #66, Center for Chinese Studies, Institute of East Asian Studies, University of California at Berkeley, pp. 55–80. pp. 77–80.
50. In the U.S. and Britain since the 1980s, historical enactment has gained popularity in theatrical performance, museum exhibits, historical tourism, film, and photography. Scholars of popular culture suggest that reenactment is about actively interpreting the past rather than passively witnessing it. The simulation of historical scenes evokes reenactors' strong emotional satisfaction and gratification through the feeling of "connecting with history." One of the most popular themes of historical reenactment in the U.S. and Britain is war, especially the military rather than the civilian aspects of the American Civil War and the Second World War. See Nichols, Bill. 2008. "Documentary

reenactment and the fantasmatic subject." *Critical Inquiry* 35: 72–89; McCalman, Iain and Paul Pickering, eds., 2010. *Historical Reenactment: From Realism to the Affective Turn.* Basingstoke: Palgrave MacMillan; Agnew, Vanessa. 2004. "Introduction: What is reenactment?" *Criticism* 46 (3): 327–339; Baraniecka-Olszewska, Kamila. 2017. "Historical reenactment in photography: Familiarizing with the otherness of the past." In Demski, Dagnoslaw et al. eds., *The Multi-Mediatized Other: The Construction of Reality in East and Central Europe 1945–1980.* Budapest: Institute of Archaeology and Ethnology, Polish Academy of Sciences.

51. Zhang, Baotian. 2012. Ibid. p. 426.
52. There were several other retakes of Sha Fei's wartime photos in Zhang's book that had the reenactors carrying tripods like machine guns over their shoulders, mimicking the soldiers in the originals guarding a gate of the Great Wall or triumphantly marching through a gate (Zhang, Baotian. 2012. Ibid. pp. 426, 456, 458). As David Lowenthal (1985) put it, "... the past as we know it is partly a product of the present; we continually reshape memory, rewrite history, refashion relics." Lowenthal, David. 1985. Ibid. p. 26.
53. Bolian Society, 2013, Interview with Zhang Baotian, May 2. http://photo.artron.net/20130502/n444184_1.html. Accessed May 9, 2017. Link was broken by January 7, 2024.
54. Zhang, Baotian. 2012. Ibid. pp. 520–523.
55. Also see Boym, Svetlana. 2002. *The Future of Nostalgia.* New York: Basic Books.
56. A prime example of Great Wall activism in China is a website called *ChangchengXiaozhan [A Small Site on the Great Wall].* http://www.thegreatwall.com.cn/. See interview of the webmaster Zhang Jun in Roberts, Claire et al. Ibid. pp. 33–35.
57. Lindesay, William. 2007. The Great Wall Revisited: From the Jade Gate to Old Dragon's Head. Beijing: China Intercontinental Press; Lindesay, William. 1989. *Alone on the Great Wall.* Wheat Ridge, CO: Fulcrum Publishing.
58. Geil, William Edgar. 1909. *The Great Wall of China.* New York: Sturgis & Walton Company.
59. Shijijilupian: Lianggeweiliandechangcheng [Ten documentary series: "Two Williams' Great Wall]." http://livechina.ipanda.com/lm/lgwldcc/index.shtml. Accessed January 8, 2024.
60. In a similar tone, Zhang Baotian commemorated another wartime photojournalist, Fang Dazeng (nicknamed Xiao Fang). Zhang's 2012 essay, entitled, "I was standing on where Xiao Fang stood on the Great Wall." (Zhang, Baotian. Ibid. p. 410), focused on the successful hunt for the location of a 1937 photo of the Great Wall by Xiao Fang in the Badaling section. Zhang proudly called the event "a successful and (precisely located) meeting with Xiao Fang on the Great Wall."
61. Zhang, Baotian. 2012. Ibid. pp. 432–433.
62. Photographers' identification with a heroic photographer and their visual memories is akin to literary memories. This quote is from Denton, Kirk. 2014. *Exhibiting the Past: Historical Memory and the Politics of Museums in Post Socialist China*, p. 217. Honolulu: University of Hawaii Press. Denton referenced Strassberg, Richard. 1994. *Inscribed Landscapes: Travel Writing from Imperial China.* Oakland, CA: University of California Press. Strassberg maintained that in the Chinese literary tradition, a place becomes famous for being the site of a major literary work, such as the Orchid Pavilion (p. 63). In Strassberg's original words: "The Cave of the Three Travelers ... is a prime example of the literary shrine, a scenic spot immortalized by a writer which is then inscribed on the literary map. Such a place subsequently becomes part of the cultural itinerary and a place of pilgrimage for later writers" (p. 137).

63. Geil, William. 1909. Ibid. pp. 382–383.
64. Zhang, Baotian. 2012. Ibid. p. 385.
65. I thank Dan O'Neill of UC Berkeley East Asian Languages and Cultures for this insightful observation.
66. Zhang, Baotian. 2012. Ibid. p. 306.
67. Lu, Ming. 2015. "Yechangchengxianzhuang sanchengchengqiangxiaoshi renweichaizhuan gaifang [Current state of wild great walls: 30% of the walls have disappeared due to intentional destruction, people build houses with wall bricks]." *Xinmin Evening News*, July 19. http://www.xinhuanet.com//politics/2015-07/19/c_128035226.htm. Accessed January 9, 2024.
68. The tourist figure is taken from the company website of Beijing Huanghuacheng Tourism Development company, which is a subsidiary of Beijing Capital Highway Development Group. https://www.bchd.com.cn/Organization/Co-show-Detail.html?DetailId=59. Accessed March 22, 2024.
69. The Chinese municipal jurisdiction includes the urban core and immense rural hinterland, all within the boundary of the municipality, and under the authority of the municipal government. See Hsing, You-tien. 2010. *The Great Urban Transformation: Politics of Land and Property in China*, pp. 94–97. Oxford: Oxford University Press.
70. Popular in the 1990s and 2000s, this slogan in Chinese is "*wenhuadatai, jingjichangxi*." Since the late 2010s, critics of the hyper commercialization of culture have advocated for the opposite, that is "build the stage with economic principles; run the show with culture." See, for example, Chen, Pingyuan. 2018. "Bufangjingjidatai wenhuachangxi [Why not build the stage with economy, and let culture run the show]." *Beijing Daily*, November 5. http://theory.people.com.cn/BIG5/n1/2018/1105/c40531-30381637.html. Accessed January 9, 2024.
71. The review of the Huanghuacheng tourism controversy is based on the following sources: Wu, Jingjing. 2006. "Reyechangchengchengchumen remenxuanze, qibaohuxianzhuangburongleguan [Wild great walls become popular tourist destinations; their physical conditions do not warrant optimism]." *Xinhua Net*, May 10. http://www.gov.cn/jrzg/2006-05/10/content_277459.htm. Accessed January 9, 2024; Liu, Binglu. 2005. "Beijinghuairouyechangcheng xianzhuangkanyou Huanghuacheng liyiluanju [Worrisome conditions of Beijing's wild great walls: Entangled economic interests in Huanghuacheng." *New Beijing Daily*, May 20. http://news.sohu.com/20050520/n225635493.shtml. Accessed January 9, 2024; Unknown author. 2005. "Huairouyechangchengbaohukanyou, cunminwuliqiangziyuan [Worrisome state of Huairou's wild great walls, villagers' armed fights over [tourism] resources]." May 21. http://www.bicon.com/3g/id/5340903/. Accessed May 4, 2017. Link broken January 9, 2024; Wang, Jian. 2004. "Wubainianhuanghuachengchangcheng shoucidaxiu jiangjianshengtailüyoufengjingqu [Thee five hundred-years old Huanghuagcheng section of the Great Wall under renovation to build an ecotourism park]." *Beijing Entertainment News*, March 21. https://news.sina.cn/sa/2004-03-21/detail-ikkntiak9721485.d.html. Accessed January 9, 2024.
72. Meanwhile the much-increased tourist volume in the HHC area, connected by waterways and reservoirs, has brought pollution to Huairou Reservoir, one of Beijing's major sources of water supply for household use. Feng, Songling. 2020. "ankaishoufeizhandao zhoubianshuikuwuranyanzhong yemanlüyou zhengzaishanghai yechangcheng [Illegal trails led to reservoir pollution; barbaric tourism is damaging the

wild great wall]." Banyuetan 15. August 19. http://www.xinhuanet.com/politics/2020-08/19/c_1126388001.htm. Accessed March 22, 2024

73. In 2023, Badaling Great Wall received over 10 million visitors. Li, Yao. 2023. "badalingchangcheng jingqu nianyoukejiedailiang shoupoqianwanrenci [Visitors to Badaling Great Wall exceeded 10 million for the first time]." *Beijing Daily*, December 19, 2023. http://changcheng.ctnews.com.cn/2023-12/19/content_154345.html. Accessed March 22, 2024.
74. Zhao, Suisheng. 1998. "A State-led Nationalism: The Patriotic Education Campaign in Post Tiananmen China." *Communist and Post-Communist Studies* 31 (3): 287–302, p. 298.
75. Wang, Zheng. 2008. Ibid.
76. Denton, Kirk. 2014. Ibid. pp. 219–220.
77. Interview, 2017, Beijing.
78. Lao Zhang is among the best-known peasant-turned guardians of the Great Wall in China, who has given numerous newspaper interviews and has made countless local and national TV appearances. Instead of fictionalizing his name, which seems unnecessary, I use his last name Zhang in this chapter. For an interesting parallel about local residents who work as monument patrols, see the study of Maya heritage sites in Yucatán, Mexico in Breglia, Lisa. 2006. *Monumental Ambivalence: The Politics of Heritage*. Austin, TX: University of Texas Press.
79. See, for example, Xiao, Guangming et al. 2017. "Nongminshouhu yuanzhiyuanweichangcheng sanshijiuzai pannianqingrenjieban [Peasant safeguarded the authentic Great Wall for 39 years, hoping to see younger generations take over]." *China News*, June 22. http://www.chinanews.com/sh/2017/06-22/8258640.shtml. Accessed January 10, 2024; Hao, Ye. 2023. "Hebeichangchenglouzhang zhangheshan: Changchengshiwo shengmingdeyibufen [Zhang Heshan, the commander of the Great Wall watch tower (said), 'The Great Wall is a part of my life']." *China News*, May 3. https://www.chinanews.com.cn/sh/2023/05-03/10000981.shtml. Accessed January 10, 2024. For a recent CCTV documentary (on Society and Law Channel) entitled "Changchengshouwangzhe hebeinongmin zhangheshan weizunfumingshouchangcheng 43nian [Hebei's peasant Great Wall guardian Zhang Heshan realizes his father's wish and safeguards the Great Wall for 43 years]." https://www.youtube.com/watch?v=pTcBzQFU_wo. December 19. Accessed January 10, 2024.
80. The Committee of Political Consultative Conference and the People's Congress are the two primary channels that organize China's political participation built on the territorial hierarchy from the central, provincial, and municipal down to county levels.
81. For the records of Qi Jiguang and the history of wall construction under his supervision, see Liu, Ruzhong. 2006. "Manning the Wall: Qi Jiguang." In Roberts, Claire et al. 2006, Ibid. pp. 182–188. But Liu does not make any suggestions about whether villagers in eastern Hebei are descendants of the wall builder-defenders.
82. Wu, Chaohai. 2012. "Caihongfeijiananbeiwenhuagoutongliangdi-Changchengyiwuwen hua duijieceji [The flying rainbow bridge that connects Yiwu with the Great Wall]." *Journal of Chinese Gazetteer* 9: 57–62; Jiang, Shouyang. 2017. "Sishigurenzai: changchengxiade yiwubing jianzhengzhe [The past is still with us: it is witnessed by the Great Wall Yiwu Troop]." *Zhejiang News*. June 21. https://news.zgyww.cn/system/2017/06/21/010105573.shtml. Accessed January 13, 2024; CCTV documentary series *Yuanfangdejia [Home Afar]*. 2015. "Changchengxiadeshouwang [Guardians by the Great Wall]."

Episode 14, October 15. https://tv.cctv.com/2015/10/15/VIDE1444906929028416.shtml. Accessed January 13, 2024.

83. Fictional name.
84. Interview, 2017, Hebei.
85. Li, Qiang. 2017. "Yiwubinghouyi: changchenglianjieqisobainianxuemaiqinqing [Descendants of Yiwu troops: The Great Wall connects lineage affinity across 400 years]." September 8. https://www.sohu.com/a/190537774_800604. Accessed January 11, 2024.
86. Liu, Ruzhong. 2006. Ibid. p. 182.
87. Luo, Zhewen. 2006. "The Great Wall of China." In Roberts, Claire et al. 2006, Ibid. pp. 42–51, p. 48. Lu, Zhewen (1924–2012) was an architectural historian who studied under the renowned architectural historian Liang, Sicheng. Widely considered as modern China's pioneer in Great Wall conservation, Luo wrote *Changchengshihua [History of the Great Wall]* as early as 1963 (Beijing: Zhonghua Publisher; revised and republished in 2018 by Beijing Press) and was instrumental in the inscription of several Chinese heritage properties onto the UNESCO World Heritage list.
88. Waldron, Arthur. 1990. Ibid. p. 150.
89. Yang, Wenhe. 2006. "The Wall at work." In Roberts, Claire et al. 2006, Ibid. pp. 174–181, p. 178.
90. Waldron, Arthur. 1990. Ibid. p. 150. Historian Li, Sanmo has also suggested that many landless peasants were recruited to the frontier to farm, not to fight. Merchants were equally active in these border areas trading salt and military supplies. See Li, Sanmo. 1994. "Mingdaibianfangyu bianken [Defense and farming colonies in Ming's frontier]." *Chinese Studies of Frontier Geography and History* (4): 20–26; and Li, Sanmo. 2005. *Mingdaishiyanmaoyiyu bianfangbianken [Salt Trade, Frontier Defense and Farming Colonies during the Ming Period].* Studies of Salt Culture Series, Vol. 1, pp. 169–174. Chengdu, Sichuan: Bashu Publisher.
91. Cao, Shuji. 1997. *Zhongguo Yimingshi [History of Migration in China]*, Vol. 5. Ming Period. p.342. Fuzhou: Fujian People's Press.
92. See Duara, Prasenjit. 1988. *Culture, Power and the State: Rural North China 1900–1942.* Redwood City, CA: Stanford University Press. Duara suggested that the rise and decline of rural settlements in northern and northwestern China was closely linked to the fate of the imperial state, especially given the environmental fragility of the region.
93. I thank Wen-hsin Yeh of Berkeley History and I-tien Hsing of the Institute of History and Philology at Academia Sinica for their insights during our personal conversations on lineage in Chinese history. Also see Duara, Prasenjit. 1988. Ibid.; and Ebrey, Patricia. 1985. "Family and kinship in Chinese history." *Trends in History* 3 (3-4): 151–162.
94. Xiao Liang is a nickname. Like Lao Zhang, Xiao Liang (which means "young Liang") appeared in quite a few newspaper reports and made a CCTV appearance for his being "the youngest peasant-turned guardian of the Great Wall." For reports about Xiao Liang, see, for example, Chen, Chong'er. 2017. "Changchengbaohuyuan meiyue 120 yuanbuzhurengjianshou [Guardian of the Great Wall perseveres at the low monthly pay of 120 yuan]." *Tencent Dayan Net*, July 17. http://bj.jjj.qq.com/a/20170717/050443.htm#p=1. Accessed January 11, 2024. For stories about other grassroots Great Wall guardians, see the "Small Site on the Great Wall [Changcheng xiaozhan]." www.thegreatwall.com.cn. *WeChatID: ILOVEGREATWALL.*

95. See, for example, Cohen, Myron. 2005. *Kinship, Contracts, Community and State: Anthropological Perspectives on China*. Redwood City, CA: Stanford University Press; Ebrey, Patricia and James Watson eds. 1987. *Kinship Organization in Late Imperial China, 1000–1940*. Oakland, CA: University of California Press.
96. In 2020, Xiao Liang was badly injured in a motorcycle accident. His conservationist friends posted a fundraising call on the website of "Small Site on the Great Wall." The call was accompanied by Xiao Liang's own narration of his work as a Great Wall guardian and his family's dire financial situation. See 2020. "Womenzenmorenxinrangta duziyirenkang—Yumulingchangchengbaohuyuan xiaolingshuaishang jixujiuzhu [How could we leave him by himself to shoulder the heavy burden—Yumuling Great Wall guardian Xiaoliang is injured and in urgent need of support]." www.thegreatwall.com.cn, March 20. https://www.sohu.com/a/381784169_658345. Accessed January 11, 2024.
97. The following was reported by Wu, Chaohai. 2012. Ibid.
98. Zhang, Baotian. 2012. Ibid. "Preface."
99. "Baohuchangcheng neimengguzaixingdong [Inner Mongolia taking action to protect the Great Wall]." 2016. *Beifang Xinbao*, November 1. https://weibo.com/ttarticle/p/show?id=2309351001304037648095266350. Accessed January 11, 2024.
100. IMAR Bureau of Cultural Affairs. 2016. "Jiadachangchengbaohulidu, chuanchengwenhuagenmai, ningjuminzujingshen [Reinforce Great Wall protection, build cultural roots, and integrate minzu spirit]." March 11. http://www.nmgwh.gov.cn/xx/tt/201603/t20160311_131845.html. Accessed May 10, 2017. The link was broken by November 30, 2023.
101. Han, Xueying and Bao Yin. 2023. "Xuetianxilingeledacaoyuan mumarenweihe feichi changchengbian [Why do the pastoralists ride along the Great Wall in the snowy Xilingol pasture?]." CCTV News, April 7. http://changcheng.ctnews.com.cn/2023-04/07/content_140041.html. Accessed January 9, 2024.
102. Golden, Peter. 2013. "Some notes on the Avars and Rouran." In Curta, Florin and Bogdan-Petru Maleon eds., *The Steppe Lands and the World Beyond*, pp. 43–66. Iași: Editura Universității Alexandru Ioan Cuza. p. 47; Wei, Jian. 2004. *Neimenggudiqu xianbeimuzangdefaxianyuyianjiu, [Archaeology of the Xianbei Burial Grounds in Inner Mongolia]*. Beijing: Science Publisher; Zhu, Hong. 1994. "Renzhongxueshangde xiongnu xianbeiyuchidan [Xiongnu, Xianbei and Khitan: A physical anthropological analysis]." *Beifanwenwu (Northern Cultural Heritage)* 38: 7–13.
103. 2015. "2014 nianduquanguoshida kaoguxinfaxian [China's ten major archaeological new discoveries from 2014]." *China Cultural Heritage News*, April 20. http://www.kaogu.cn/zixun/2014shida/2015/0420/49975.html. Accessed January 12, 2024; for news coverage of the discovery, see Wurihan. 2014. "Neimenggumabeiwenwubaohudui zhuihuibaijianguojiajiwenwu [Inner Mongolia's Horseback Heritage Patrols retrieved a hundred pieces of national-level cultural artifacts]." *Xinhua Net*, August 20. http://art.people.com.cn/n/2014/0820/c206244-25500519.html. Accessed January 4, 2024; Li, Yubo. 2015." Caoyuanshang mabeiwenwubaohu qibing: yewaiwenbaoxinshengliliang [Horseback Heritage Patrols: Pastural cavalry, a new force to protect open-air cultural heritage]." *Workers' Daily*, November 30. https://ah.ifeng.com/travel/detail_2015_11/30/4608059_0.shtml. Accessed January 11, 2024.
104. Interview, 2017 Beijing.

105. See, for example, Halina. 2023. "Mabeiwenwu (changcheng) baohudui: cemayangbian shouhuchangcheng [Heritage (Great Wall) Patrol on Horseback: Riding the horse to protect the Great Wall]." Xinhua News. December 6. http://www.news.cn/politics/2023-12/06/c_1130012032.htm. Accessed January 6, 2024.
106. Halina. 2023. Ibid.
107. Yang, Xin. 2007. "Neimengmingchangcheng youzaoheifacaikuangzhe wajue pohuaiy uqianpingmi [IMAR's Ming Great Wall were destroyed again by illegal mining activities, over a thousand square meters of the Wall was eradicated]." *People's Daily*, November 23. http://cn.chinagate.cn/culture/2007-11/23/content_9282481.htm. Accessed January 12, 2023; Peng, Hu. 2006. "Neimengyiduanzhaochangcheng zaodaxingwajuejiwa 98mi [98-meter-long Zhao era Great Wall was destroyed by an excavator]." *Xinhua News*, November 27. http://scitech.people.com.cn/GB/5093176.html. Accessed April 12, 2016. Link broken January 12, 2024; 2009. "Neimengzuilaoqinhanchangcheng zaoyaozhan [The oldest Great Wall in IMAR from the Qin-Han periods was cut in halves]." *Epoch Times*, October 31. http://www.epochtimes.com/gb/9/10/31/n2707308.htm. Accessed January 12, 2024.
108. He, Yong. 2009. "Neimengjingneiyu 1/5 mingchangchengyixiaoshi zhuyaoshirenweiyinsusuozhi [Over one-fifth of IMAR's Ming Great Wall have disappeared, mainly caused by human factors]." *People's News Net*, February 10. http://www.china.com.cn/culture/txt/2009-02/10/content_17254179.htm. Accessed March 17, 2016. Link broken January 12, 2023.
109. Zhang, Xiaokai. 2018. "Wanggoutanceyi daojuewenwu pohuaiqinchangchengzhongbeibu [Robbers arrested for destroying Qin-era Great Wall and cultural heritage with detectors bought online]." *Jiancha ribao [Procuration Daily]*, May 27. http://collection.sina.com.cn/jczs/2018-05-27/doc-ihcaqueu8172077.shtml. Accessed January 12, 2024; Lin, Man. 2017. "Kuangyezhonggududechangcheng beiyuchundedaomuzhe pohuai [Lonely Great Wall in desolate fields destroyed by vacuous tomb raiders]." https://www.sohu.com/a/132212482_658345. Accessed January 13, 2024.
110. For investigatory journalism on China's antique supply and circulation networks, see Wu, Shu. 2009. *Sheizaishoucongzhongguo [Who Is Collecting China]*. Taipei: Dayan Press; and Wu, Shu. 2010. *Sheizaipaimaizhongguo [Who Is Auctioning out China]*. Taiyuan: Shanxi People's Press.
111. See Tim Mitchell (2002) for a similar situation present in Egypt, where TV thrillers about tomb robbing in the Valley of Kings were popular in the 1970s. In those stories, villagers were often depicted as tomb robbers. Mitchell, Tim. 2002. *Rule of Experts: Egypt, Techno-Politics, Modernity* Oakland, CA: University of California Press.
112. Interviews in Sichuan (2009), Ningxia (2011), Hunan, Beijing, Hebei, and IM (2012).
113. Interview 2012, Beijing.
114. Li, Yubo. 2008. "Jinjiuchengneimenguren buzhineimengguyouchangcheng changcheng pinzaopohuai [close to 90% of IMAR's residents do not know that the Great Wall exists in IMAR [which has led to] rampant destruction of the Great Wall]." *China Youth Daily*, November 11. https://news.ifeng.com/mainland/200811/1111_17_871979.shtml. Accessed January 12, 2024.
115. Interview 2013, Hohhot.
116. Yan, Xiangling et al. 2015. "Wanlichangcheng pinweizhishang—xinhuashejizheguchan gcheng baohuxianzhuang diaocha [The trauma of the ancient Great Wall—Xinhua agency journalists' investigatory report]." *XinhuaNet*, October 13. http://big5.xinhuanet.

com/gate/big5/news.xinhuanet.com/culture/2015-10/14/c_128315864.htm. Accessed March 12, 2016. Link broken January 12, 2024.

117. Liu, Weitao. 2012. "Shouwangchangcheng, shouhulishi: quanguozhengxiefu ningxia, neimenggudiaoyan changchengbaohuzhuangkuang [Guard the Great Wall, protect the history: National People's Political Consultative Committee members visiting Ningxia and Inner Mongolia to investigate the current state of Great Wall protection]." *People's Daily*, May 30. http://www.qstheory.cn/wh/whjs/201205/t20120530_161074.htm. Accessed April 14, 2016. The link was broken by January 12, 2024; World Heritage Committee. 2017. "The Great Wall: Analysis and Conclusion by World Heritage Centre and the Advisory Bodies." https://whc.unesco.org/en/soc/3642. Accessed January 6, 2024.

118. Although it is beyond the scope of this chapter, the stories presented here could be contextualized in the ongoing debates on heritage conservation and restoration in China and beyond. Under 19th century European modernism, the heritage conservation debates were framed by two opposing camps. The "*restoration*" camp, led by Eugene Viollet-le-Duc (1814–1879) promoted the idea that restoration is not to preserve, repair, or rebuild it; it is to return it to a condition of completeness which could have never existed at any given time. See Viollet-le-Duc, Eugène-Emmanuel. 2018. *On Restoration*. New York: Franklin Classics Trade Press. The publication is an English translation of Viollet-le-Duc's original text in *Dictionnaire raisonné de l'architecture française du XIe au XVIe siècle* (1854–1868) published in 1875. Restorationists believed the necessity of intervention, aiming at turning ancient, deteriorated buildings aesthetically more pleasing, even if there is insufficient historical documentation (construction drawings or old photos) or a lack of original building materials, tools, or craftsmanship. Purist preservationists like John Ruskin (1819–1900), on the other hand, chose the concept of "*conservation*" over "restoration" as a way to remain "honest" to history. He suggested that we should allow ruins to remain in a state of ruin to visually expose the passage of time with minimal intervention, if at all. The great value of any building is in its age. In *The Seven Lamps of Architecture* (1849) Ruskin wrote: "[I]t is impossible, as impossible as to raise the dead, to restore anything that has ever been great or beautiful in architecture." Ruskin, John. 1885. *The Seven Lamps of Architecture*, p. 184. New York: John B. Alden. In the 20th century, the dualistically framed debate, spread from Europe to the U.S. and then to Asia. While new generations of preservationists found various creative ways to preserve heritage and tried to strike a balance between restoration and conservation, the debate remained entrapped in the temporal tension of "how to bring life to the past," as Jorge Otero-Pailos put it. See Otero-Pailos, Jorge. 2007. "Preservation's Anonymous Lament." *Future Anterior* 4 (2) winter: ii–vii, p. iii. Similar debates among scholars and policy thinkers continued into the 21st century. Under a global heritage boom, creativity is considered necessary, by an increasing number of heritage practitioners, when dealing with temporal tensions between the past, the present, and the future. Yet the controversies over authenticity continued: is the structure really old or does it just look old? And how old is old? How do we evaluate the authenticity of a 16th century building repaired with stones cut in the 18th century? If a shrine in Nara was completely rebuilt recently, but with construction techniques of the 8th century and timber of traditional tree species planted specifically for the purpose of restoration, is this shrine authentic enough? In the attempts to attain the unattainable past, how much creativity is allowed before the structure loses its authenticity, hence the authority derived from authenticity? In China, in

the 1930s, the University of Pennsylvania and Harvard University-trained architectural historian Liang Sicheng (1901–72) brought back to China European ideals and practices in heritage preservation. Liang tried to establish China's architectural history. Against the traditional Chinese practices of regular renovation, reuse, and recycling of buildings and building materials, he promoted heritage preservation that uses as little new additions as possible. See Liang, Sicheng. 1981 (1945). *Zhongguojianzhushi [History of Chinese Architecture].* Taipei: Mingwen Publisher. While Liang's ideal is now widely accepted by conservationists in China, the actual practices continue to vary.

119. State Commission of Cultural Heritage. 2020. "Mabeituofengwurenji, neimenggumizhiwenwu baohuwang [Horseback, camelback, and drones: Inner Mongolia weaves a tight net for cultural heritage protection]." *China Grassland*, October 29. http://grassland.china.com.cn/2020-10/29/content_41341098.html. Accessed January 13, 2024.
120. Halina. 2023. Ibid.
121. 2023. "Tengxun SSV fuzongcai geyan: Tengxunyongjishuweiwenbaolingyu tigongyuan yuanbuduan deziyuan [Vice CEO of Tencent SSV Ge, Yan (says): Tencent deploys technology to provide resources for cultural heritage protection]." Tencent News/SSV, November 16. https://new.qq.com/rain/a/20231116A09DFO00. Accessed January 13, 2024.
122. World Heritage Committee. 2017. "The Great Wall: Analysis and Conclusion by World Heritage Centre and the Advisory Bodies." https://whc.unesco.org/en/soc/3642. Accessed January 6, 2024.
123. World Heritage Committee. 2021. "The Great Wall: 2021, Decisions adopted by the Committee in 2021." https://whc.unesco.org/en/soc/4191. Accessed January 6, 2024.
124. Da, Mo. 2023. "Changchengyizhipinzaopohuaisheizhiguo [Who is to blame for the frequent destruction of the Great Wall]." *Southern Daily*, December 12. https://opinion.southcn.com/node_a7b2ba4370/15bfe1d18c.shtml. Accessed January13, 2024; China Environment News. 2023. "Weiguiwakuang zhedizhangguozhaochangchengyizhizaopohuai jinsheng 855 mi [Illegal mining destroyed the Great Wall of the Zhao Kingdom of the Warring States (plural) Period; only 855 meters of the structure remain]." *China Environment Public Account*, December 11. https://wap.peopleapp.com/article/7283143/7121836. Accessed January 13, 2024. A Small Site on the Great Wall. 2024. "Shanxi Hequ: sheishi luoquanbaochangchengbeihuide muhoutuishou? [Who is behind the demolition of Luoquanbao Great Wall in Hequ, Shanxi Province?]." *Fayanzhaojinshenghuo*, January 11. https://mp.weixin.qq.com/s/TJkPxCZrIaZSt6lpTEy4QA. Accessed January 13, 2024.
125. State Commission of Cultural Heritage. 2023. "Guanyujinyibujiaqiangchangcheng baohudetongzhi [Notification on strengthening protection of the Great Wall]." Policy no: wenyubaofa [2023] #38, December 8. https://www.gov.cn/zhengce/zhengceku/202312/content_6919551.htm. Accessed January 13, 2024.

Conclusion

Telling Place-Driven Stories: Methods, Analyses, and Theorization

Place tells and drives stories. Stories give meaning to place. This book tells place-driven stories with the goal of exploring the meanings of places in China's northwest.

As noted in the Preface, I see *place* as the interconnection of three analytical layers: the physical location and environment, the socio-organizational locale, and the discursively constructed sense of place. These three layers are interwoven processes that converge in place and actively shape, instead of passively contain, social transformation. As a process, place is as much about time as it is about space. Territory, as politicized place, drives power processes in places, forges interconnections, builds territorial dynamisms, and enables territorialized social analyses.

As also noted in the Preface, I use territorial dynamism as a conceptual tool to tell stories about complex places and times across multiple territorial scales: the global, national, regional, local, and anywhere in between. With the intention of telling the multi-scalar place stories arose the question of execution: *where* to begin? Among all the possible scales from which to launch a place story, I find the grassroots story to be the most fertile and least predictable. From the bottom up, grassroots stories generate multilayered meanings of place. Yet, grassroots stories, crowded with diverse local actors in divergent physical, social, and discursive transformations, are inevitably noisy and untamable by a tidy narrative or a grand theory. In many ways, telling place-driven stories from the grassroots level is not unlike trying to herd a clowder of cats. To preserve the stories and keep the cats kicking, I chose to nurture them in a garden that seeds surprises and preserves complexity instead of squeezing them into a bag that confines the cats and sterilizes the stories.

Telling a place-driven story from the ground up, while trying to make untamable stories legible and meaningful is a matter of experimentation. This experiment affords several interconnected methodological, analytical, and theoretical implications. In this concluding chapter, I reflect on my experiment with these interconnections that have shaped the place-driven stories in this book.

Conserving China's Northwest Frontier. You-tien Hsing, Oxford University Press. © You-tien Hsing (2025).
DOI: 10.1093/9780191903908.C03.0012

I. Ethnography in Selective Places

I tell multivocal place stories mainly through ethnography. Ethnography, like life, defies planning. The places where I try to carry out ethnographical work select and deselect me. The fact that place defines me as an outsider during my fieldwork offers little reassurance. As an outsider, I have little say in choosing an *ideal* research site that fits *my* research plans.

At the onset of this project, I had a general research direction in a geographical area, that is, the politics of conserving culture and nature in China's arid northwest, far away from my previous research sites on China's eastern seaboard. But I had little idea where in the immense expanse of the northwest I should or could focus on. Through direct and indirect contacts and chance encounters, I conducted pilot studies over the course of three long summers in various places in Gansu, Ningxia, Shaanxi, and Inner Mongolia (IM). Missteps there were quite a few. While preparing for my first visit to IM, for example, I expected to meet Mongol nomads but arrived in the steppe only to find immense corn and wheat fields in the Yellow River Loop Plain in Hetao of West IM. I felt disappointed and disoriented. Determined to see the "authentic" Mongolian steppe with grazing animals, I ventured out to the pastoral areas in Central IM, where I was met with herders without herds and herds without pastures. Meanwhile, chance encounters led me on a detour to the farming county of Minqin in Gansu, the showcase site of China's desertification crisis management. In public and policy discourse, Minqin was presented as a hopeless farming area that would soon be swallowed up by the encroaching sand dunes. Yet, in Minqin, I met farmers who were actively searching for farmland within and beyond the officially sanctioned crisis zone, strategizing to survive not just desertification but more immediately, the water restrictions imposed by conservation policies. These farmers' active strategization for survival, albeit with varying degrees of success, contradicted with what I had read about the immobilized ecological victims. As I grappled with my confusion and tried to learn, unlearn, and relearn at each stop, this book found its shape.

During my sojourns, some places turned out to be more accessible than others, and some contacts lasted longer than others. At times, unpleasant meetings drove me away from places: one involved an aggressive local boss, and another concerned two extorting local thugs. At other times, the rejections were more subtle. When de-selected by place, whatever burning questions I had hoped to pursue in that place became impractical. By incidental encounters and sheer luck, three places—Ejina and Horqin Right Front (Horqin RF) Banners of Inner Mongolia Autonomous Region (IMAR), and Minqin County of Gansu Province—eventually selected me: they allowed me to stay and revisit.

Take my fieldwork in Fresh Springs Village[1] in Horqin RF Banner of East IMAR (Chapter 8) for example. In 2016, I met a Mongol graduate student, Wave, when I gave a talk at a university in China. Up till then, my fieldwork had focused on the western, pastoral-dominant Alxa League in IMAR (Chapters 1 and 2) and the farming villages in Hexi Corridor of Gansu Province (Chapters 3 and 4). In that talk, I compared the

Mongol herders' and Han Chinese farmers' strategies of surviving China's conservation policies since the 2000s. After the talk, Wave approached me and hinted that I had missed an important actor and place: the Mongol farmers of East IM, where she grew up. The next summer, I followed Wave to her home village, Fresh Springs in Horqin RF, to learn how much I had missed. I cannot thank Wave enough for opening my eyes to the worlds of Mongol farmers and the agropastoral and pastoagricultural entanglements of East IM, the heart of IM's "half-agricultural, half-pastoral" belt, as presented in Chapter 8. Through Wave's generous family, neighbors, and relatives, I was selected by Horqin RF, where I was able to visit several villages and towns, conduct repeated and lengthy interviews and collect oral histories across generations.

These incidental encounters are not necessarily accidental ethnography. Once a place and people accept me, I reciprocate their generosity and trust. I respond to their curiosities about me and open up about my job, my research, my home, my family, and my hopes and worries. Without demanding answers to *my* research questions, I try to understand my hosts' concerns through their words and silences, action and inaction, presence and absence, and join in on their activities and travels when invited. And I try to help (such as teaching their children English) without getting in the way as much as I could. With the understanding that any interview and participatory observation during fieldwork is affected by my presence and colored by the power dynamics of the occasion, I do my best to make ethnography an exchange of life experiences instead of one-way Question-and-Answer sessions. The narratives derived from such exchanges is a process of co-production: my presence, perception, expectation, reaction, and emotions like excitement, empathy, bewilderment, anxiety, and frustration are all part of the interactions between me and my hosts in specific places, moments, and circumstances.[2]

Place that selects and deselects me is a *selective place*. Selective place is also pedagogical. Place poses new questions, and place broadens and deepens my original direction of inquiry. As Wave took me to visit her relatives in Fresh Springs Village, one of the many things I learned was how different Wave was from her kin.

Before the visit, I saw Wave as a farm girl from a poor, hilly East IMAR village who had made it (see Chapter 9). Trudging through numerous competitive exams and breaking the class, gender, and ethnoterritorial barriers, Wave triumphed in getting into a prestigious university in a metropolitan center with a promising urban future beyond the peripheral, rural IMAR. I identified her with her rural origin more than with her achievements in the city. In the villages, Wave's kin saw her differently: Wave was an enviable inspiration and a role model for their children. Her identity was associated with her achievements, not her origins. During our village visits together, our hosts were kind enough to heed *my* inquiries about agropastoral transformation in the village. But they were eager to steer the conversation towards their children and grand children's schooling. Wave's cousins, aunts, uncles, grand uncles, and grand aunts seized the opportunity of Wave's visit to solicit her advice on strategies in choosing school tracks—what are the advantages and disadvantages of attending Mongolian versus Mandarin-track schools? How should they prepare their children or grandchildren for the upcoming high school or college entrance exams? How should they project their children's future, based on their current grades and rankings at school? Is it too late to invest in the costly tutoring classes? As I watched Wave fielding the questions, I was impressed with Wave's rich knowledge on the subject. Admittedly, I could understand only about half of the conversations, given that they switched between Mongolian and Putonghua. Wave filled me in afterwards about her experience in the convoluted bilingual education system in IMAR. In our many follow-up conversations, Wave recounted in vivid detail about her arduous preparations for the college entrance exam and the nerve-wracking, real-time online enrollment battle for college admission. As the conversation went further, she shared with me her setbacks and lucky encounters as she maneuvered the winding paths from a peripheral Mongolian farming village to one of the top universities in China. Wave's recount of her experiences eight years after the exams (such as her scores on every subject in the mock and formal college entrance exams) with extraordinary detail reveals just how much the competition meant to her. I realized that the college race is just as relevant as agropastoralism in Mongolian farming families' aspirations for the future.

I had previously noted the importance of children's schooling in upward mobility in my studies of the Han Chinese farmers in Minqin (Chapter 4). At the onset of this study, I had presumed a fundamental distinction between the Mongol and Han Chinese students (and their families), in the same way I was looking for the "authentic" Mongol herders and their "alternative modernity." In Wave's home village, I was therefore surprised to find that rural Mongolian and Han Chinese families shared a similar set of aspirations and followed a similar path for upward mobility. I then consulted the literature on Mongols' cultural assimilation in China today. These writings helpfully illustrated the predicaments of the bilingual education policy and the drastic decline of younger generation Mongols' Mongolian proficiency and their assimilation into the dominant Han Chinese culture and language, Putonghua Mandarin. But Wave's recounts of her bilingual schooling in which English mattered more than either Putonghua or Mongolian went beyond the question of linguistic assimilation and accommodation. Her stories also opened my eyes to Mongol students' deep entrenchment not just in the linguistic orbit of Putonghua, but in China's nationwide sociocultural milieu of hyper competition, crystalized in college and job races and ballooning in the post-financial crisis era. Mongols students of IMAR are an integral part of such sociocultural milieu.

The ethnoterritorial dynamism in this case is structured by Mongol students' navigation of IMAR's bilingual school system under China's national education institutions that are parallel to the territorial hierarchy across the national, regional, and subregional levels. The story is less about an alternative modernity or a disparate future for the minority in IMAR's rural peripheries. Rather, it shows the intertwined modernities that are entrenched in highly uneven paths towards a shared aspiration of the future. Wave and other Mongol students, as their navigation and struggle in China's college and job races have shown, are not in isolation. Their experiences are intimately intertwined with and actively shape the national politics of social mobility. The story, in other words, is about Mongols *of* China, not just Mongols *in* China.[3]

I elaborate on the stories about Mongols *of* China further by looking at the variations under the encompassing label of China's "minority nationalities." China's minority nationalities are placed in hierarchical order based on their population size and geopolitical significance in the eyes of the state and are treated accordingly. Education policies for Mongol students in IMAR are different from Tibetans in Tibet Autonomous Region, for example. Moreover, under the umbrella label of "Mongol" as a nationality, Mongol students are far from a homogeneous entity. Mongol students of diverse social and spatial backgrounds have embarked on divergent trajectories within IMAR's minority education system. Seeing the variations not as an inconvenient disruption but a caution against simplified stories, I tell the stories about IMAR's "Local Top 17%." The Local Top 17% of IMAR's college exam takers are those who are highly vested in the exam but score just below the "Top 3%" and gain admission to not the nation's, but IMAR's, top universities. These Local Top 17%, who fill the ranks of IMAR's governments and schools, have played a more critical role than the Top 3% in the ethnoterritorial politics of IMAR. Yet unlike the Top 3%, the Local Top 17%, in IMAR or in China's other minority and nonminority regions, are rarely touched upon in the literature on China's educational inequality and social mobility.

In this experiment with telling place-driven stories of Horqin RF, what started out as a distraction from my original questions turned into a bridge that connected the stories of conserving nature with that of conserving culture in this book via the lens of minority language education and its sociocultural dynamics. This story subsequently built half of Chapter 9, "Moving Up and Out: Mongol Students in China's College and Job Races" in Part IV, "Sociocultural Aspirations across the Great Wall." The story about the Local Top 17% then incubated the story about the state's management of frustration in IMAR and China's anxiety economy at a time of rising youth unemployment, in the last section of Chapter 9.

My ethnography is composed of chance encounters, detours, and reroutings. Place selects and deselects me. Place raises and evades questions. Place steers and curbs my inquiries. Yet, being reactively selected by place does not preclude proactive analysis and theorization thanks to the generative power of place.

II. Analyzing Generative Place

Selective place is analytically generative. Horqin RF, for example, as a place that selects me and poses new questions, also expands the scope of my research which, in turn, helps enrich my understanding of the meaning of the place in question.

As noted earlier, the Mongol farmers, agropastoralists, and pastoagriculturalists in Horqin RF whom Wave took me to visit prompted me to look beyond the dichotomy between pastoral Mongols in Ejina and agrarian Han Chinese in Minqin. That visit also opened a Pandora's box and expanded this study in other unplanned directions.

In order to contextualize the ethnoterritorial and livelihood mixes and shifts I saw in Wave's home village in East IMAR, I felt the need to extend my research to the higher territorial scales of IMAR as a whole region, including West, Central, and East IMAR. In order to trace the histories of agrarian transformation of IMAR that have shaped present-day conservation politics, I also extended the temporal scope of this study to include the geopolitical, ethnoterritorial and environmental histories in the three subregions of IMAR at the most critical moments of their transformations since the late imperial time, from the mid-18th century to the early 2020s. My fieldwork notes revealed more stories when they were connected with historical materials.[4]

The geographical extension of this story means that place stories are not just anchored on the ground, they also engender stories *from* the ground up. The extension to the entire IMAR helps contextualize Horqin RF. It also works the other way around: the upward extension shows that a particular locality is more than a parochial interest or an isolated "case" or "site." The place in question is a definitive part that contributes to an indefinite whole.[5] In fact, place extends along many directions: upwards, downwards, and sideways. My Horqin RF-engendered stories extend upwards to several territorial scales: to Hing'an League, East IMAR, IMAR, and China. The Banner stories also extend downwards to sub-banner zones, subzones, individual villages and families. They also extend sideways to neighboring banners and villages. At different territorial scales, the extension also moves inwards (be it the banner or the village), and it travels outwards to connect with other areas far and near. Each direction of the extensions identifies differences and similarities, deepens observations, advances the analyses, and adds meaningful layers to the place stories that are anchored in Horqin RF. As geographer Doreen Massey (1994)[6] pointed out, place is unbounded. Place is the interconnection of nodal points. I find the multidirectional and multi-scalar extensions a productive way of identifying and analyzing such interconnections.

The multidirectional and multi-scalar extension of place stories raises new questions and generates richer analyses. Generative place also brings in key actors who are otherwise muted by resolute theories or trimmed by monotonous narratives. Many such key actors return to the stories via temporal extensions. The three sub-regions of IM between the 18th century and the present, for instance, introduce key non-state territorial actors who led the agrarian transformation in each of the subregions. These actors, who defy conventional labelling, range from land-water barons, Belgium Catholic missionaries, multiethnic bandits, regional and local warlords, and Mongol massacre refugee-turned farmers. In official historiographies of IMAR's agricultural transformation, these actors are either invisible or sidelined. By bringing these under-represented territorial actors back in, this temporally broadened story promises a fresh look at a bigger picture.

Unbounded and multilayered place also orients actors' identification and shapes their territorial relationships with one another. Such territorial identification stretches beyond the static framework of identity politics defined by a fixed territorial unit. The Mongol farming refugees who fled the massacre from Central-East to East IM at the dawn of the 20th century, as depicted in Chapter 8, for example, were seen as outlanders by native East IM banner members. These Mongolian refugees then formed an unlikely territorial alliance with their fellow outsiders—the Han Chinese settlers—in tax revolts in East IM. Converging in place and territory, these actors led the untold stories about the fluid ethnoterritorial alignment in which cross-ethnic coalitions are formed just as often as ethnic rivalries surface in the tumultuous environmental and geopolitical transformation of IM.

As the usual and not-so-usual actors tell complex and layered place stories of "kaleidoscopic quality," to borrow historian Nicola Di Cosmo's words,[7] these stories defy "hard and fast systemic theories," and they fit poorly within a point-by-point comparison. For sure, comparison is key to contextualizing place stories empirically and theoretically. In Chapter 5, for instance, I compare China's three autonomous regions of IM, Tibet, and Xinjiang to show IMAR's distinctively fragmented ethnoterritorial structure before going into the three subregions of IMAR in the ensuing Chapters 6, 7, and 8. In various parts of the book, I have compared territorial dynamisms across time and place for contextualization. I contextualize the challenge of metering groundwater in Minqin by comparing it to similar efforts made in California during the water crisis in the 2000s (Chapter 4) in order to show the magnitude of the challenge in Minqin. On another occasion, I contextualize the hydro turfdom in 19th century Hetao of West IM by comparing it with Wittfogel's hydraulic empire, Geertz' irrigation society, and Chang Chungli's Chinese gentry-led local society (Chapter 7) in my attempt to distinguish the hydro turfdom from other types of water-territorial politics. The discursive politics of resource scarcity in Minqin's water conservancy is compared to that of western India written by Lyla Mehta (Chapter 4). It is a way of contextualizing the globally circulated, neoliberal concept of scarcity that has been implemented beyond China.

However, I do not strive for a seamlessly balanced and structured comparison across time and place. Each place develops its territorial dynamisms, tells its stories and contributes a segment of a shared story about conserving China's northwest. In the case of Part III on agropastoral entanglements, for example, each of the three subregions of IM tells its own segment of the shared story about cultivation expansion in the IM steppe at different times. Stories from all three subregions touch upon the politics of land, water, labor, capital, and social organization—all of which are key elements in agricultural expansion. Yet, the relative weight of and configurations among these elements vary across the three sets of subregion-based stories. The configurations of the politics around these elements are too dynamic to be bogged down by a water-with-water, land-with-land comparison across the places and times. To keep the energy of the place stories, I identify one critical territorial dynamism in one place at one particularly transformative moment in cultivation expansion history in each of the three subregions, data permitting. This experiment results in three sets of territorial dynamisms for the three chapters in Part III: land commodification of the 18th century Tumd Plain in Central IM (Chapter 6); hydro turfdoms of the mid-19th to mid-20th century Yellow River Loop Plain in West IM (Chapter 7); and Mongol refugee farmers of the early 20th to early 21st century who fled the ethnic massacres of Central-East IM to the Daxingan'ling Mountains in East IM (Chapter 8). They are not comparable in a point-by-point fashion, but together they present some of the key mechanisms of agricultural transformation while preserving the agency of actors and the autonomous energy of places across multiple territorial and temporal scales in Inner Mongolia's steppes.

My attempts to marry ethnographic, archival, and secondary materials bring out not just more voices, but also more gaps and inconsistencies across these materials. It is ceaselessly challenging to connect the scattered dots and keep the fragments manageable for a legible story. Yet, the kaleidoscopic forms of information generated by place and converging in place stories also offer the opportunity to unveil unexpected connections and tell important, yet untold, stories—all to further enrich the meaning of place.

For example, as mentioned in the Preface, one key source of materials I used for stories about the history of Mongol farmers (Chapter 8) is doctoral dissertations and monographs on agrarian transformation in East IM. These historical accounts, published in Chinese, are authored by three generations of multilingual Mongolian scholars who use Mongolian, Chinese, Japanese, and Russian materials, and who have collected oral histories to write about their home banners and villages. Most of these authors are from East IMAR, the allegedly most "sinicized" subregion of IMAR. As a result, most of their works focus on East IMAR. This regional bias of knowledge production is far from accidental. A Hohhot-based university professor estimated that more than 80% of Mongolian doctoral students and more than half of Mongolian master's students in IMAR are from East IMAR. While Mongolian academics in IMAR, many of whom are also from East IMAR, try to expand their research westward by recruiting Mongolian-speaking students from the understudied West IMAR, especially pastoral-dominant areas of the west, they find few candidates. The professor attributed this regional gap in higher education attainment, hence knowledge production, to socioeconomic disparity. Rural families of the predominantly poorer, agricultural, and more sinicized East IMAR work hard to support their youngsters' social mobility through education. The most promising students from the east strive for advanced degrees, and the most successful among them become academics and publish their research works, like the authors whose works I referenced. Students from West IMAR, especially rural Alxa, which is usually considered to be the least sinicized part of IMAR, on the other hand, often demonstrate lower proficiency in Putonghua and, just as critical, in English (see Chapter 9), which impedes their academic advancement onto prestigious colleges and graduate programs. The professor also commented that students from West IMAR seem to feel less pressure to move up and out of their home region through the hyper competitive college race, the way Wave did. The difference is particularly salient for those western Inner Mongolia students from families who have managed to keep, and even expand, their herds and grazing land after three decades of pastoral decollectivization and destocking policies, as presented in Chapter 2. Their herds, if successfully retained and expanded, can build a much more solid foundation of family wealth than crops and small farmland do for families in the crowded East IMAR. The younger generations of these successful herding families, according to the professor, need not worry nearly as much about their financial future as their counterparts in East IMAR. Why would they bother jumping through all the hoops to get into a graduate program in Hohhot, or even Beijing, only to find more daunting and demoralizing competition in the job market upon graduation (Chapter 9)? Also, even in the pastoral-dominant area of Horqin RF in East IMAR, as noted in Chapter 8, Dalai, Wave's brother-in-law, who is from a well-to-do pastoral family, did not feel the urgency that Wave did to make his education pay off. In this experiment with telling place-driven stories, the "secondary" sources, such as the dissertations, become primary sources for the question of regionally-biased knowledge production. What started as "background" information about agrarian expansion in East IMAR came to the forefront in leading a new line of inquiry and added another layer of meaning to the generative place-driven story.

When conducting fieldwork in selective place and telling stories of generative place, I rely on the concept of territory to better understand the meaning of place in China's northwest frontier. However, I do not aim to build a theory *of* or *about* territory. Instead, I try to theorize *with* territory.

III. Theorizing with Territory

As noted in the Preface, territory is politicized place. In this book I have used several territory-derived terms, most notably, "territorial dynamism" and "territorialized social analysis" to tell the place-driven stories. Territorial dynamism is a toolkit that includes three analytical and story-framing devices: first, seeing place and territory as processes; second, connecting territorial processes across multiple territorial scales; and third, conducting "territorialized social analysis", which is built on the first two. Territorial dynamism, as a tool kit, frames the stories about the agentive territorial actors and the transformative territorial tensions derived from the autonomous energy of place.

Territorial dynamism, as a set of analytical and framing tools, serves to facilitate my experiment with theorization. Generative place stories are endlessly fertile, and place-driven theoretical explorations are devoid of a conclusive theoretical truth. Instead, I write with the following theoretical aspirations: to denaturalize what is often perceived as a given, connect what appears separate and reconfigure presumed linkages, offer reflexive and novel redescriptions, and render opaque events more intelligible. Because theorization is an experimental process with these aspirations in mind, it seems more productive to focus on developing the analytical tools to facilitate this process instead of striving for a conclusive theoretical affirmation.

Among the three analytical tools I listed above, the third one, *territorialized social analysis*, is the key link between place-driven stories and theorization with territory. This link therefore warrants further elaboration. In what follows I will recount the stories from Ejina of West IMAR, as presented in Chapter 2, to elaborate on this experiment.

I will begin with the distinction between "territorialized social analysis" and "social-spatial analysis."

Many social researchers conduct social-spatial analysis, that is, investigating the spatial manifestations of social dynamics, such as centralized or decentralized urban growth that reflects the centralized or decentralized state and private sector's investments; immigrant enclaves shaped by immigrants' socioeconomic marginalization; or reinforced border demarcations that come with escalating geopolitical tensions between neighboring powers. Such social inquiries involve key spatial dynamics like centralization, decentralization, marginalization, and boundary reinforcement. But in these analyses, the spatial dynamics are reduced to sideshows – they are merely the results of the social, political, and economic drama that is on the main stage.

Relocation is another quintessential social-spatial question. As outlined in the Introduction and Chapters 1 and 2, under the regime of productive conservation, China's policymakers often perceive ecological relocation as the answer to rangeland recovery and poverty alleviation. On the other hand, many social researchers argue that relocation, along with other conservation measures like destocking and grazing bans, has devastated pastoral environments and livelihoods. Yet, despite their contrasting conclusions, mainstream policymakers and critical social researchers have treated space in a similar manner. In their framings, space is a container, playing a supporting role in the show led by social transformation.

Under such shared framings of relocation, both advocates and critics of ecological relocation programs assume that relocation is a matter of moving from a fixed-point A to a fixed-point B. The departing point and the destination of the relocation are assumed to be scrupulously programmed by local officials and closely followed by the relocated "ecological refugees." The ecological refugees in the resettlements are assumed to be, by mainstream policymakers, "improved," or, by critics, "demobilized." Above all, both narratives presume automatic sedentarization of herders, and both end in the physical containment of the resettlements. The resettlement, with happy or miserable relocated herders, is the site where the story opens and concludes.

Such social-spatial inquiries shaped my expectations before my fieldwork: will I meet the content or the despondent herders? Perhaps I would meet some of each? But they did not prepare me to see one empty resettlement after another. I could not find any herders in my first visits to the resettlements in central and western IM. So, in the following trips to Ejina of western IMAR, where I was able to stay and revisit, I tried to look beyond the resettlements, the presumed ending of the story about the relocated herders.

As I looked, I found that herders still moved around. But it was a new mode of mobility. The most puzzling moment in my research turned out to be the most promising.[8] In herders' new modes of mobility, the timing, duration, destinations, and the purposes of their movement were deeply intertwined with a diversifying rural economy in western IMAR. Just as important, the ostensible "sedentarizing" resettlements, especially those located near the town center, could actively enable this new mode of mobility. With a flexible division of labor among the family members, relocated herders in Ejina turned their resettlement housing units into youth hostels for ecotourism in the fall, and the families would winter in the solar-heated resettlement homes. But they spent other seasons in other places. They camped out for months to hunt for the commodity herb, congrong, in the spring pasture; they excavated semiprecious gem stones in the Gobi during the summer. All the while, they kept camels and sheep beyond the grazing ban zones.

Place-based resources that motivate such mobility are unevenly distributed, however. For instance, my research assistant from eastern IMAR was envious of Ejina herders' access to congrong and gemstones, which are not found in her home village in eastern IMAR. A scholar from central IMAR explained that it was the immense and very dry western IMAR, where population density is low and the average size of household contracted rangeland is large (at least five times larger than that in the rest of IMAR) that has enabled Ejina families to gain access to valuable congrong and gemstones in different parts of Ejina Banner. Also, herders who were relocated to remotely-located resettlements were not able to take advantage of ecotourism like the Ejina herders could. Within Ejina, herder families' capacity to take advantage of place-based income-generating opportunities varied just as much. The stories about my host family and their relatives' new mode of mobility, therefore, might be seen as "unrepresentative." A similar question is also found in the story about Wave (see Chapter 9). However, Wave's exceptional case shows what it takes for a female Mongol student from a poor farming village to make it to a top national university. It also reveals the limits of Wave's upward mobility. In the same light, the stories about Ejina herders show some of the favourable outcomes of herders' strategization to survive conservation in the dryland, but also the limits of their efforts. Wave tried, but never made it, to the nation's very top, Peking University. And Wave has found a job in a second-tier metropolitan center in the northwest, but not the most desirable Beijing, Shanghai, or Shenzhen. Similarly, in Ejina, as my host family developed a new mode of mobility, they also engaged in new challenges, such as rampant congrong gang thefts and big capital's bold moves to take over the ecotourism business in Ejina. But the stories do not stop at these limitations either. In a place-driven story in which interactions between places and actors continue to co-produce possibilities and impossibilities, possibilities and impossibilities also endlessly generate one another.

Such generative interactions and co-productions help me conceptualize Ejina herders' place-driven, *territorialized strategies*. Their territorialized strategies, in turn, inform my *territorialized social analysis*. Through territorialized social analysis, "relocation" turns from a linear and singular move with fixed starting and ending locations to territorial processes. As relocation activates the territory processes and territorializes my analyses, it reveals the territorial dynamisms built upon the tension between policymakers' intentions to sedentarize herders and herders' attempts to dodge, survive, or participate and even take advantage of the policies whenever possible. It is just that the way the herders participate in the state program does not always align with the intention of the policy maker. While the resettlement is built to contain movement, relocated herders mobilize it to facilitate a new mode of mobility.

By definition, the territorial dynamism generated from the tension in territorial processes has a temporal nexus. The possibilities and impossibilities co-produce one another over time as the environment, conservation discourse, and rural economies change from decade to decade and year to year. On a smaller temporal scale, Ejina herders' new modes of mobility played out seasonally. The relocatees would hunt wild congrong in the sandy suosuo fields in the spring, dig for desert rose in the Gobi desert during the summer, and host tourists in their well-located relocation homes in the fall. Some of the income-generating activities would last for two to three months, while others would be concentrated within the span of a couple of weeks. Like pastoralists' movements among seasonal rangelands, herder families rotate among different residential bases during different seasons. With this new mode of mobility under the increasingly diversifying rural economy of western IMAR, such seasonality follows multiple calendars instead of just the pastoral calendar.

Theoretically, this territorialized social analysis foregrounds Ejina herders' agency, dislodges the presumed causation between resettlements and sedentarization, and offers an alternative redescription of state-society relationships. Territorialized social analysis helps me resist three temptations often found in social theories, namely, reductionism, victimization, and cultural essentialism.

The first temptation concerns the dichotomous framing of the authoritarian state versus grassroots resistance. When applying this grand narrative, the empty resettlements I found during my first visits in the summer may have been seen as an act of the herders' concerted resistance against the authoritarian state's imposition of sedentarization. However, my later findings have deviated from this standard storyline. Ejina herders did not reject nor run away from the resettlements, especially those that were well-located and adequately built, and those that came with land allotments. Instead, they incorporated the resettlement that meant to sedentarize them into a new mode of mobility. The mobility and immobility do not preclude one another. Instead, both roll into a seasonalized and territorialized scheme of movement. My host family's resettlement homes would be empty in the spring and most of the summer when hunting for wild congrong and desert rose in the Gobi. Come autumn, they would leverage their conveniently located resettlement homes by converting them into hostels during the tourist season. From November to March, the solar-heated apartments proved to be helpful during the long and freezing Mongolian winter. In this scheme, herders incorporate state-built housing into their multi-sited seasonal mobility. It is *because of* the state, not *despite* the state, that relocatee herders in Ejina reconfigured their mobile livelihood strategies. The key is that herders started utilizing the resettlement units in a way that did not necessarily align with the state's intentions.

Second, seeing resettlement as a territorialized processes of resettling and as a part of herders' survival strategies also prevents double-victimizing relocatee herders. The relocation programs, along with other conservation programs detailed in Chapter 2, have victimized many of the herding families in multiple ways already. However, assigning them the role of victim in the built-in implication of the statist theory risks overlooks herders' agency. Ejina herders have certainly had plenty of struggles, failures, and despair. My host families have lost most of their livestock under destocking campaigns, and destocked herders in the Huyang forests have had to fight hard against the local state-sponsored ecotourism investor who tried to monopolize ecotourism in Ejina. But as mentioned earlier, possibilities and impossibilities continue to generate one another and stories end in neither. Herders in their survival struggles cannot be reduced to paralyzed or immobilized victims.[9] Instead, they actively identified and mobilized resources within their reach with vastly varying degrees of success and failure. While my host family managed to survive relocation and destocking with a new mode of mobility, their new mobility did not liberate them from uncertainties and new types of struggles. Recognizing such adaptation and resilience and understanding their limits avoids double-victimizing the relocatee herders: first by relocation policies, then by a theoretically predestined victimhood.

Lastly, the territorialized social analysis of Ejina herders' new mobility helps denaturalize the usual conceptualization of "nomadism" wrapped in cultural essentialism. Herders' mobility, of the old or new form, is not a cultural given, nor does it necessarily make a case for a romanticized nomadic autonomy. Pastoralism and nomadism in practice rarely follow universal definitions and patterns. Prior to the recent rise of conservationism, Inner Mongolian herders' seasonal grazing across different pastures followed carefully configured routes. The routes were designed in accordance with the changing environments and evolving territorial governing systems. The new modes of mobility under conservation are the result of a spatial configuration of a particular time and place. The pastoralists' mobility, in any event, does not fit the popular imagination in which nomads roam in the open steppe because of their innate yearning for freedom. A largely forgotten history of Ejina illustrates this point further.

As a geopolitical hotspot on the frontier, Ejina was chosen as the site of the East Wind Aerospace Base where China launched its first rocket in 1960. To build the aerospace launching base, the military appropriated one-third of Ejina's rangeland (about 40,000 sq. km) in 1958. According to official records, 1,112 herders and 72 Lamaist monks, about one-third of Ejina's population at the time, were displaced from their home pastures under the military order. Military truck convoys were sent to move their belongings, and the residents moved with their flocks on foot or on camelback. Given the secretive nature of the military action, relocatees were not told why they were moved. Many had guessed that the move was to make space for mining. They were also unsure of where they were being moved to. Without explanation or prewarning, the assigned destinations changed multiple times after they had departed from their home pasture. As a result of repeated rerouting that created confusion and chaos, many lost their precious belongings, including fur pelts and heirloom furniture that were trucked away by the military movers. The places in which they ended up were either too cold in the mountains, too dry in the heart of the Gobi, or amid too hostile of locals. So, they had to keep moving. The long move was an epic of disruption and deprivation. The displaced and dispossessed herders, who called themselves "homeless drifters," crossed the harsh sandy lands, freezing mountain routes, and the Gobi thousands of kilometers away from their home in search of habitable and hospitable pastures. Their traumatizing journeys lasted anywhere from eight to 14 years, or even longer for some families. In their involuntary move, these reluctant "nomads" struggled with the devastating loss of livestock, property, social support, and lives, and received little compensation from the state.[10]

This history of devastating displacement due to a national defense project exposes the limits of an essentialist definition of nomadism as a timeless, cultural, or natural given. Ejina herders do not move around as free-willed nomads. They often move and are made to move by forces beyond the presumed Mongolian nomadic tradition. Like everyone else, they live in place and in history, not in any "-isms."

In sum, the stories about Ejina herders' new mode of mobility help dodge the theoretical pitfalls of the bifurcation of state authoritarianism and societal resistance, the double victimization of the relocated herders stripped of their agency, and naturalization of nomads and essentialization of nomadism. Instead, the dynamics of ecological relocation in Ejina can be better understood as processes of herders' agentive, territorialized strategization. Such agency is materialized through herders' resourceful survival strategies just as, if not more, often than through confrontational resistance against the state.

I have applied territorialized social analysis to other place stories in this book as well. In Chapter 3, "Hope of the Hopeless: Recharging the Dried-up Qingtu Lake in Minqin," for example, I use "dual marginality" to territorialize the interconnection between Minqin's geopolitical and hydrosocial marginality throughout the 20th century, which in turn contextualizes the significance of, and adds meaning to, Minqin's rise to stardom in China's conservationism in the 21st century. In Chapter 4, "Opportunity in Scarcity: Building a National Model of Water Conservancy," also about Minqin, I connect the fierce water competition with the contentious and hierarchical relationship between jurisdictions at the upper and lower reaches of the Shiyang River. Both the water users' physical location within the irrigation system and their jurisdictional rank in the watershed structure the water competition and thereby territorialize the everyday politics of water conservancy. The territorialized politics of water conservancy is found at multiple scales, from the entire watershed down to village households whose fields are located at different sections with different degrees of accessibility to water channeled through the multileveled local irrigation system. The disputes and violence in water struggles across multiple territorial scales, via territorialized social analysis, show the contradictions in Minqin's water conservancy under China's regime of productive conservation.

More examples of territorialized social analysis can be found in Chapter 8 on Mongol farmers. In that story, I territorialize the livelihood mixes and shifts by distinguishing the agropastoral and the pastoagricultural processes. Spawning out of different environments and initiated by different actors—one being herders in the highlands trying to diversify into farming, the other being farmers in the lower-altitude, more crowded rolling hills trying to diversify into raising livestock—these two processes have developed along different directions of livelihood diversification. Such territorial *processes* of diversification, not just the static or even mixture of two distinctive types of livelihoods, produce different social and environmental consequences in the two locations and escalate conservational tensions in the mixed economy of Horqin RF Banner as a whole.

Moreover, the two paths towards livelihood diversification show the disparate territorialized aspirations of the pastoagriculturalists and agropastoralists. The intertwined relationship between the livelihood strategies of the present and aspirations for the future, both territorialized, is an important angle in territorialized social analysis and central to this book on nature, culture, and future. Such intertwined relationships between present strategies and future aspirations are also illustrated in Chapter 4 on Minqin farmers' strategies of surviving conservation. Jin Three, the resilient onion farmer and "ecological refugee" of Minqin, territorializes his strategies of surviving water conservancy by commuting between his home base in the heavily regulated crisis zone and the neighboring town with few restrictions on planting the thirsty, but more profitable, onion crops. As Jin Three's territorialized strategies accelerated soil exhaustion beyond the crisis zone, he placed his territorialized aspiration on his two sons' future success in the college race and in scoring white-collar jobs in a city as far away from Minqin's salty soil as possible.

Chapter 9, "Moving Up and Out: Mongol Students in China's College and Job Races," tells another story about territorialized future aspirations. In this chapter, I review the synchronized territorial authority and school ranking, and the increasing urban-rural disparities in education resources, which, in turn, have accelerated the territorial processes of the rural-to-urban, small town-to-large city, and periphery-to-center brain drain. The aspirations of those in the periphery, consequently, are territorialized: the more academically promising a student is, the further away from home he/she is expected to attend school and seek employment. These aspirations are also temporalized: to get a head start and move as far away as possible from the periphery, the student should leave home as early as possible. By the 2010s, IMAR parents with funds or determination to toil would send their primary school or even kindergarten-aged children to large cities, bypassing schools in neighboring small rural townships and cities. The wave of village primary school closures in the 1990s and 2000s was followed by dwindling enrollment in many middle and high schools in marginalized townships and cities, sending these schools and rural towns on a downward spiral. As more villagers move to large cities for better schools, territorialized aspirations accelerate the vicious cycle of emptying out school-less villages and socioeconomic deterioration of the countryside. Also in Chapter 9, the territorial tension between the national unified college entrance exam and the localized college admissions competition makes for yet another example of territorialized social analysis. Through these territorialized social analyses, what was previously opaque is rendered more explicit and what appeared disparate has found analytical connections, such as the co-production between the state's increasing investment in rural development and education on the one hand, and the decline of rural villages and rural schools on the other. Territorialized social analysis also unveils the contradictions between national college entrance exams that aim to create equal opportunities for all and the territorialized college enrollment competition that has generated as many hurdles as hopes for minority students in the rural peripheries.

This experiment of theorization with territory is inspired by, built on, and contextualized in existing literature across disciplines. Examples of such foundations and inspirations can be found in every chapter of this book.[11] While influenced profoundly by these writers, I also find myself following questions arising from places themselves. I look to the literature to contextualize, compare and expand upon questions from my fieldwork. But I try to avoid looking to the literature for answers to my puzzles and avoid upholding existing theories as the destination for my explorations. As these place-driven stories keep unfolding, the interpretations drawn from the literature are most helpful when they are treated as "interconnected but not interlocked"[12] with stories on the ground.

There are many unruly components in this project. Selective place resists research plans. Generative place expands research scales and scopes unexpectedly. Theorizing with territory brings me to grapple with the possibilities and impossibilities shaped by agentive actors and generative places. What kind of book could such a way of storytelling produce?

As I followed the lead of actors and places instead of a predetermined plan to write place-driven stories, I inevitably produce a book with missing links. One salient example of such missing links in this book is the mining activities in China's northwest. Readers may have expected this book on conserving China's northwest to address this central issue. But it does not. And it was not due to the lack of trying on my part. After several failed attempts in the mining areas of Inner Mongolia and Shaanxi, I decided that I would focus on other places that allowed me to tell their stories with a meaningful level of depth and nuance. Such depth and nuance come from taking fieldwork as exchanges of life experience and building trusting relationships (of varying degrees) when circumstances allow, not from twisting arms and pushing for a comprehensive book project that contains all the predetermined key links.

I consider the missing links in this "following-the-lead" approach a trade-off and a matter of choice. As the expected story eluded me, unexpected stories found their way into this book. I chose to give chance encounters a chance and nurture the unplanned offshoots. One example of such unplanned offshoots is my meeting with Wave, the Mongol student from eastern IMAR. When I went to her home village, I thought I was going to study Mongol farmers. Instead, I ended up writing an additional chapter about Mongol students' struggles as they navigate China's college and job races. Few readers might have expected to find this story in a book on conserving China's northwest. But Wave, Art and their families steered me to some of the most unexpected, yet highly relevant, tales about China's varying and changing minority education policies on the ground in the northwest. These stories are about the politics of conserving culture, and they are not limited by the conventional definition of heritage conservation. Rooted in IMAR, Wave and Arts' stories hold the key to understanding China's development in the decades to come. Mongol students' college and job races are intimately connected with China's sociocultural milieu of hyper competition today. The stories about competition extend to a section on the state's attempts to manage college graduates' (including Mongol students') escalating frustrations as youth unemployment rises. From the state's frustration management came another section on the role of the market, that is, China's hundred billion dollar tutoring industry that feeds on the collective anxiety brought about by the ever-growing gap between jobs and job seekers. These interwoven stories, contingent as they might appear, are meaningful to the actors with whom I interact and they enrich the meaning of the place and time I try to understand.

Plan-defying place does not help me when it comes to writing a comprehensive book. Yet the richness of place-driven stories helps deepen and broaden the big picture beyond usual viewpoints. The interconnected dynamics in each chapter are not confined by the usual topical headings like the state, market, and society. At the center of this book is place that sows the seeds of unbounded gardens with unpredictable blooms.[13] The prolific Tang Dynasty poet, Wang Wei (691–761 CE), captured this generative way of storytelling well: "As the walk along the river comes to an end, I pause to muse at the clouds forming in the sky."[14]

To conclude my reflections on methods, analyses, and theorization, I trade a bag for a garden in my place-driven storytelling. Selective place defies research plans, and generative place spawns unpredictable puzzles. A place like China's northwest—with its immense and uneven terrains crowded with zestful actors and reverberating territorial dynamisms—can hardly be tamed by a unifying narrative or a definitive conclusion. Instead, with the help of territorialized social analysis, I aim to denaturalize the norms, unveil hidden connections and decouple unchecked ones, offer novel redescriptions, and render muddy events more legible. With stories about intertwined relationships among actors' territorialized legacies from the past, their territorialized strategies of the present and their territorialized aspirations for the future, I seek to present the agency of actors and the autonomous energy of places that give meanings to nature, culture, and future in China's northwest frontier.

Notes

1. Village and personal names are fictionalized.
2. For a critique on conducting research as a disembodied spectator, dispassionate observer, or an all-seeing god, see Haraway, Donna. 1991. *Simians, Cyborgs, and Women: The Reinvention of Nature*. London: Routledge.
3. I owe the idea of "the Mongol of China, not just in China" to David Treuer, who has written extensively on Native Americans. See, for example, Treuer, David. 2019. *The Heartbeat of Wounded Kne: Native America from 1890 to the Present*. New York: Riverhead Books. A writer on the social, cultural, and environmental transformation in IMAR, whom I met in Beijing, has likened Mongols of China to Native Americans.
4. One of my regrets is my lack of knowledge in Mongolian language. I am not able to use the primary sources in Mongolian that this project calls for.
5. In his discussion about particularity and generality, Andrew Sayer (1991) suggested that the "part" and the "whole" are interdependent, and that the "*part ... imprints onto or structures the rest of the whole, and the whole is contained in part*." See Sayer, Andrew. 1991. "Behind the locality debate: Deconstructing geography's dualisms." *Environment and Planning A* (23): 283–308, p. 298. I thank Gill Hart of Berkeley Geography for the

discussion of the locality debate. See Hart, Gill. 2016. "Relational Comparison Revisited: Marxist Postcolonial Geographies in Practice." *Progress in Human Geography* 42 (3): 371–394. For a discussion of contextualization, see Burawoy, Michael. 1998. "The extended case method." *Sociological Theory* 16 (1): 4–33.

6. Massey, Doreen. 1994. *Space, Pace and Gender.* Minneapolis, MN: University of Minnesota Press.
7. Di Cosmo, Nicola. 1999. "State formation and periodization in Inner Asia History." *Journal of World History* 10 (1): 1–40, pp. 13–14.
8. Darnton, Robert. 1984. *The Great Cat Massacre and Other Episodes in French Cultural History*. New York: Basic Books. P. 262.
9. Geographer Michael Watts (2000) has commented on the importance of recognizing the "slow violence and the delayed effects" brought by fast capitalism. See Watts, Michael. 2000. "Struggles over Geographies Violence, freedom, and development at the Millennium." Hettner Lecturers 3, p. 8. Heidelberg: University of Heidelberg, Department of Geography. For sure, the cash subsidies that these relocated herder families received varied, and the conditions changed over the years, and their operation of youth hostels during the ecotourism season was greatly affected by the Covid pandemic in the early 2020s. More follow-ups and longer-term studies will help trace that slow violence and the delayed effects. Also, Ron Nixon (2011) has written about the devastating impact on conservation refugees after they are moved out of the domain of their "living knowledge as (their) ... place loses its life sustaining features." See Nixon, Rob. 2011. *Slow Violence and the Environmentalism of the Poor*, p. 19. Cambridge, MA: Harvard University Press. Both scholars insightfully pointed out the temporal dimension in geographies of violence. Based on the cases of atmospheric nuclear tests in the Marshall Islands (p.7) and the "protracted ...casualties inflicted by dichlorodiphenyltrichloroethane (DDT)" (p. 6), Nixon remarked that these "desperate entrapments" inevitably "immobilize" the conservation refugees, and that the refugees are "goners with nowhere to go" (Nixon 2011: 19). My stories focus on the diverse processes and uneven results of relocated herders' struggle in Ejina and IMAR in the 2010s. Instead of assuming inevitable and universal immobility, I explore under what circumstances, in what ways, and to what extent these relocated herders succeeded and failed in their mobility and immobility.
10. "Chaogetu and Culture and History Committee of Political Consultation Committees of Alxa League and Ejina Banner." 2011. In *Lishi dejiyi: Ejinaqi yu Dongfeng hangtianjidi jiansheshiliao [Memory of History: Ejina and the Construction of East Wind Aerospace Base].* Hohhot: Inner Mongolia People's Press. This publication is a Chinese translation of a Mongolian text published in the 1980s. I was told by a local researcher that the Chinese edition that I have is a watered-down and censored version of the Mongolian original. At the Ejina Banner Museum that I visited in 2012, this episode was displayed with photos and captions that emphasized the patriotic Mongol herders' selfless devotion to the national defense cause, while the trauma inflicted by the relocation was completely omitted from view.
11. For example, in the Introduction, "A Productive Crisis: Desertification in China's Northwest," I evoke environmental historian Diana Davis' critique on the confusion between desert and desertification in the colonial and post-colonial histories of the arid lands. In Chapter 2, "Mobility Under Restrictions: Ejina Herders Surviving Rangeland Conservation," I examine the rangeland enclosure and herder relocation programs in IMAR

against the globally-circulating model of "carrying capacity" developed in rangeland studies, on which geographer Nathan Sayre has written a systemic critique. In Chapter 4, "Opportunity in Scarcity: Building a National Model of Water Conservancy," I frame my stories of Minqin's water conservancy by expanding developmental sociologist Lyla Mehta's "constructed scarcity" to "constructed and lived scarcity" as well as "constructed and lived opportunity." In Chapter 7 "Hydro Turfdoms: Barons, Priests and Bandits in West IM in the 19th–20th Centuries," I develop a territorialized analysis by devising the term "hydro turfdom," which is inspired by geographer Gu Jiegang's writings from the 1930s. The hydro turfdom fits neither the Wittfogelian model of hydraulic empire nor the Geertzian model of irrigation society. In Chapter 9, "Moving Up and Out: Mongol Students in China's College and Job Races," I borrow sociologists Roger Brubaker and Frederick Cooper's concept of "identification" instead of "identity" in my analysis of Wave's navigation of China's institutions of social and spatial mobility. In Chapter 10, "Popularizing the Monument: The Wild Great Walls," I build the story around grassroots actors' participation in conserving the Great Wall with the help of works advanced by scholars in history, critical heritage studies, art history, and literary studies. At a more general level, many more scholars have shaped this project. I am deeply influenced by geographers such as John Agnew, Gillian Hart, Doreen Massey, Michael Watts, among others, through their works on geographical thinking, political ecology, and geopolitics. The framing of my stories is also greatly inspired by historians and anthropologists like Christopher Atwood, Burensain Borjigin, Uradyn Bulag, Nicola Di Cosmo, Nianyong Han, I-tien Hsing, Hong Jiang, Wenjun Li, Robert Marks, Thomas Mullaney, Enhe, Peter Perdue, Kenneth Pomeranz, David Sneath, Ming-ke Wang and Alexander Woodside, among others, via their writings on China and Inner Mongolia's environmental and ethnoterritorial histories as well as the geopolitical transformations of China and its Central Asian frontier. These scholars' works are referenced throughout this book.

12. Darnton, Robert. 1984. Ibid. p. 262.
13. I thank Ken Pomeranz for the discussion of the connection between the expected and unexpected topics in this book.
14. "*xingdaoshuiqiongchu, zuokanyunqishi*," in Wang Wei's poem entitled "*Zhongnan bieye*" [Retreat to the Zhongnan Mountain].

List of Chinese Terms

(Names of persons, jurisdictions, rivers, and mountains are not included)
aiwozhonghua, xiuwochangcheng 愛我中華, 修我長城
Alashan qishi 阿拉善奇石
bannong banmuhu 半農半牧戶
bansheng 板升
bantukeshitongxiaer, saiwaihuangshanjinpitian 版圖可識同遐邇,塞外荒山盡闢田
Bazhijian 八支箭
bianzhinei 編制內
bingzai 兵災
buxiaoyousan: bukaogong, bukaoyan, bukaojiao 不孝有三:不考公,不考研,不考教
Caoyuanpai草原派
Changcheng 長城
Changchengbaohu gongzuozhan 長城保護工作站
chaobian 超編
chaozai 超載
chexiang bingzhen 撤鄉併鎮
chuangtian 闖田
chunwan 春晚
congrong蓯蓉
daiditoucheng 帶地投誠
daodahang 倒大行
daomu 盜牧
dashuili 大水利
dazaoju, xiaojuju 大雜居,小聚居
dipazi 地耙子
dishang 地商
dizhutang 地主堂
Dongjuyanhai 東居延海
Dongsanmeng 東三盟
duoyan 躲鹽
duyan 堵鹽
Duyanlong 獨眼龍
erben 二本
fangyan 防鹽
fangyangsannian, geigexianzhang yebudang 放羊三年, 給個縣長也不當
feihuo 匪禍
fengbishi 封閉式
fujiandi 浮鹼地
gaiyan 改鹽
gancao甘草
gaokao 高考
gebitan戈壁灘
gouqi 枸杞
guangzhong boshou廣種薄收

Haoweilai 好未來
Heicheng 黑城
Hetao 河套
Houtao 後套
Huanghuacheng 黃花城
hufei 胡匪
huyang 胡楊
jianguozhu 建國主
Jianziban 尖子班
jiaoan 教案
jiaofei 教匪
jiaoyu lixian教育立縣
jiegao qushui 桔槔取水
Jindandao 金丹道
jingzhai 京債
jiushi guanwai 就食關外
Jizhonglianpian tekundiqu 集中連片特困地區
Juyan hanjian居延漢簡
kanghan 抗旱
kangyan 抗鹽
kantian tian看天田
laojiandi 老鹼地
Laomotou老魔頭
Laotouhui老頭會
liyong changchengziyuan 利用長城資源
luohuzheng 落戶證
mansazi 漫撒子
minkaohan 民考漢
minkaomin 民考民
minsheng gongcheng 民生工程
minzu qingxu 民族情緒
meizi jiaoyou 糜子教友
Mujiale 牧家樂
muminbuchi kuixinliang 牧民不吃虧心糧
naiyan 耐鹽
Neirendang 內人黨
Nongjiale 農家樂
nongmu jiaocuodai 農牧交錯帶
nuoqiongwo, gaiqiongye, huanqiongmao, baqionggen 挪窮窩、改窮業、換窮貌、拔窮根
paiyan 排鹽
peijiaodi 賠教地
Pingwang tangzhu 平王堂主
putianzhixia mofeiwangtu普天之下莫非王土
Putongban 普通班
Qiantao 前套
Qijiajun 戚家軍
qiongshan eshui窮山惡水
Quanfeihuojiaoji 拳匪禍教記
qushen 渠紳
renjin shatui 人進沙退
rensuidizou, disuishuizou 人隨地走,地隨水走

renqingzhai 人情債
roucongrong肉蓯蓉
sanben 三本
sanzhiyifu 三支一扶
shachanye 沙產業
shamohua 沙漠化
shahua 沙化
shajin rentui 沙進人退
shangmen nüxu上門女婿
Shaqi Ejina 沙起額濟纳
shawozi 沙窩子
shenfanwoyan 深翻窩鹽
shengxueyan 升學宴
Shigequanfugai 十個全覆蓋
shiyebian 事業編
shuangjian雙減
Shuangyiliu 雙一流
suosuo 梭梭
suoyang 鎖陽
tangping 躺平
taizhandi 台站地
tianxia yijia 天下一家
tianzhutang 天主堂
Tunkenjun屯墾軍
tunken shubian 屯墾戍邊
waibin 外賓
waidi laoban外地老板
Wasu 挖肅
wenhuadatai, jingjichangxi 文化搭台 經濟唱戲
wuxian yijin 五險一金
xiafang下放
xiajiaozi 下餃子
xiao shuili 小水利
Xiezhenglikao 邪正理考
xingdaoshuiqiongchu, zuokanyunqishi 行到水窮處 坐看雲起時
xiyan 洗鹽
xuehanqian 血汗錢
yangtu 陽土
yechangcheng 野長城
yiben 一本
yifadaiguan 以罰代管
yiminshibian 移民實邊
yinong yimu 宜農宜牧
yintu 陰土
yisha zaotian 移沙造田
yiqiu 移丘
yiyan 抑鹽
yongbuzhangdi 永不丈地
yongdianhu 永佃户
yongdianquan 永佃權
yuguan 淤灌

yuanzhi yuanwei 原汁原味
zasanju 雜散居
zhangzisong 樟子松
Zhemengshiji 哲盟實劑
zhishazaolin 治沙造林
Zhonggong 中公
Zhongnongpai 重農派
zhuanzheng 轉正
zhudingpeng fangzi 住頂棚房子
zhumeng 築夢
Zhonghua minzu 中華民族

Index

For the benefit of digital users, indexed terms that span two pages (e.g., 52–53) may, on occasion, appear on only one of those pages.

Tables, figures, and boxes are indicated by an italic *t*, *f*, or *b*.